# Modern C++: Efficient and Scalable Application Development

Leverage the modern features of C++ to overcome difficulties in various stages of application development

**Richard Grimes**
**Marius Bancila**

BIRMINGHAM - MUMBAI

# Modern C++: Efficient and Scalable Application Development

First Published: November 2018
Production Reference: 1191218

Published by Packt Publishing Ltd.
Livery Place, 35 Livery Street
Birmingham, B3 2PB, U.K.
ISBN 978-1-78995-173-8

www.packtpub.com

mapt.io

Mapt is an online digital library that gives you full access to over 5,000 books and videos, as well as industry-leading tools to help you plan your personal development and advance your career. For more information, please visit our website.

## Why Subscribe?

- Spend less time learning and more time coding with practical eBooks and Videos from over 4,000 industry professionals

- Improve your learning with Skill Plans built especially for you

- Get a free eBook or video every month

- Mapt is fully searchable

- Copy and paste, print, and bookmark content

# Packt.com

Did you know that Packt offers eBook versions of every book published, with PDF and ePub files available? You can upgrade to the eBook version at www.packt.com and as a print book customer, you are entitled to a discount on the eBook copy. Get in touch with us at customercare@packtpub.com for more details.

At www.packt.com, you can also read a collection of free technical articles, sign up for a range of free newsletters, and receive exclusive discounts and offers on Packt books and eBooks.

# Contributors

## About the Authors

**Richard Grimes** has been programming in C++ for 25 years, working on projects as diverse as scientific control and analysis and finance analysis to remote objects for the automotive manufacturing industry. He has spoken at 70 international conferences on Microsoft technologies (including C++ and C#) and has written 8 books, 150 articles for programming journals, and 5 training courses for Microsoft. Richard was awarded Microsoft MVP for 10 years (1998-2007). He has a reputation for his deep understanding of the .NET framework and C++ and the frank way in which he assesses new technology.

**Marius Bancila** is a software engineer with 15 years of experience in developing solutions for the industrial and financial sectors. He is the author of Modern C++ Programming Cookbook and The Modern C++ Challenge. He focuses on Microsoft technologies and mainly develops desktop applications with C++ and C#. He is passionate about sharing his technical expertise with others, and for that reason, he was recognized as a Microsoft MVP for more than a decade. He can be contacted on Twitter at `@mariusbancila`.

# About the Reviewers

**Angel Hernandez** is a highly regarded senior solutions, architect and developer with over 15 years of experience, mainly in the consulting space. He is an 11-time Microsoft (2006-2016) MVP award recipient in Visual Studio and Development Technologies category (formerly, Visual C++), and he is currently a member of the Microsoft MVP Reconnect Program. Angel is also a TOGAF practitioner. He has deep knowledge of Microsoft and open source technologies (*nix Systems), and he's an expert in managed and native languages, C# and C++ being his favorites.

**David V. Corbin** began programming during the heyday of the mini-computer era, starting with the DEC PDP-8. His early career was in the defense industry, progressing from the company's first software technician to being the technical lead of the engineering software department, with much of the work being done in C. He cofounded Dynamic Concepts in 1984 to facilitate the introduction of the PC into business environments (this is the same year the original IBM AT was introduced). By the early 1990s, much of his application development had started migrating to C++. Even after 25 years, C++ remains a valued tool in his development arsenal. In 2005, he began to focus on improving the software development and delivery process via the application of ALM principles. Today, he continues as the President and Chief Architect of Dynamic Concepts and works directly with clients, providing guidance in the rapidly changing ecosystem.

**Aivars Kalvāns** is the lead software architect at Tieto Latvia. He has been working on a Card Suite payment card system for more than 16 years and maintains many of core C++ libraries and programs. He is also responsible for C++ programming guidelines, secure coding training, and code reviews. He organizes and speaks at internal C++ developer meetups.

**Arun Muralidharan** is a software developer with over 8 years of experience as a systems and full-stack developer. Distributed system design, architecture, event systems, scalability, performance, and programming languages are some of the aspects of a product that interest him the most. He is an ardent fan of C++ and its template metaprogramming; he likes how the language keeps his ego in check. So, one would find him working on C++ most of the time.

**Nibedit Dey** is a technopreneur with a multidisciplinary technology background. He has a bachelor's in biomedical engineering and a master's in digital design and embedded systems. Before starting his entrepreneurial journey, he worked for L&T and Tektronix for several years in different R&D roles. He has been using C++ to build complex software-based systems for the last 8 years.

# Packt Is Searching for Authors Like You

If you're interested in becoming an author for Packt, please visit authors.packtpub.com and apply today. We have worked with thousands of developers and tech professionals, just like you, to help them share their insight with the global tech community. You can make a general application, apply for a specific hot topic that we are recruiting an author for, or submit your own idea.

# Table of Contents

# Preface

C++ is one of the most widely used programming languages. It is fast, flexible, and efficient which is used to solve many programming problems.

The objective of this Learning Path is to make you familiar and comfortable with C++. You will become familiar with the constructs of the C++ programming by learning about the language structures, functions, and classes which will help you identify the execution flow through the code. You will explore and understand the importance of the C++ standard library as well as memory allocation for writing better and faster programs.

This Learning Path also deals with understanding the challenges that come with advanced C++ programming. You will learn about advanced topics such as multithreading, networking, concurrency, performance, meta-programming, lambda expressions, regular expressions, testing, and many more in the form of recipes.

By the end of this Learning Path, you will become an expert in C++.

## Who This Book Is For

This Learning Path is designed for developers who want to gain a solid foundation with C++. A computer, an Internet connection, and the desire to learn how to code in C++ are all you need to get started with this Learning Path.

## What This Book Covers

Chapter 1, *Understanding Language Features*, covers C++ statements and expressions, constants, variables, operators, and how to control execution flow in applications.

Chapter 2, *Working with Memory, Arrays, and Pointers*, covers how memory is allocated and used in C++ applications, how to use built-in arrays, the role of C++ references, and how to use C++ pointers to access memory.

Chapter 3, *Using Functions*, explains how to define functions, how to pass parameters-by-reference and by-value using a variable number of parameters, creating and using pointers to functions, and defining template functions and overloaded operators.

`Chapter 4`, *Classes*, describes how to define new types through classes and the various special functions used in a class, how to instantiate a class as an object and how to destroy them, and how to access objects through pointers and how to write template classes.

`Chapter 5`, *Using Standard Library Containers*, covers all the C++ Standard Library container classes and how to use them with iterators and the standard algorithms so that you can manipulate the data in containers.

`Chapter 6`, *Using Strings*, describes the features of the standard C++ string class, converting between numeric data and strings, internationalizing strings, and using regular expressions to search and manipulate strings.

`Chapter 7`, *Diagnostics and Debugging*, explains how to prepare your code to provide diagnostics and to enable it to be debugged, how applications are terminated, abruptly or gracefully, and how to use C++ exceptions.

`Chapter 8`, *Learning Modern Core Language Features*, teaches you about modern core language features including type inference, uniform initialization, scoped enums, range-based for loops, structured bindings, and others.

`Chapter 9`, *Working with Numbers and Strings*, discusses how to convert between numbers and strings, generate pseudo-random numbers, work with regular expressions, and various types of string.

`Chapter 10`, *Exploring Functions*, dives into defaulted and deleted functions, variadic templates, lambda expressions, and higher-order functions.

`Chapter 11`, *Standard Library Containers, Algorithms, and Iterators*, introduces you to several standard containers, many algorithms, and teaches you how to write your own random access iterator.

`Chapter 12`, *Math Problems*, contains a series of math exercises to warm you up for the more challenging problems in the next chapters.

`Chapter 13`, *Language Features*, proposes problems for you to practice operator overloading, move semantics, user-defined literals, and template metaprogramming aspects such as variadic functions, fold expressions, and type traits.

`Chapter 14`, *Strings and Regular Expressions*, has several problems for string manipulation, such as converting between strings and other data types, splitting and joining strings, and also for working with regular expressions.

`Chapter 15`, *Streams and Filesystems*, covers output stream manipulation and working with files and directories using the C++17 `filesystem` library.

Chapter 16, *Date and Time*, prepares you for the upcoming C++20 extensions to the chrono library, with several calendar and time zone problems that you can solve with the date library, on which the new standard additions are based.

Chapter 17, *Algorithms and Data Structures*, is one of the largest chapters and contains a variety of problems where you need to utilize the existing standard algorithms; others are where you need to implement your own general-purpose algorithms or data structures, such as circular buffer and priority queue. The chapter ends with two rather fun problems, Dawkins' Weasel program and Conway's Game of Life program, where you can learn about evolutionary algorithms and cellular automata.

# To Get the Most out of This Book

The readers should be equipped with the following configurations of the environment:

1. C++11 (Intel, IBM, Sun, Apple, and Microsoft, as well as the open source GCC)
2. Visual C++ 2017 Community Edition
3. VC++ 2017 on Windows
4. GCC 7.0 or Clang 5.0 on Linux and Mac

If you don't have the latest version of the compiler, or you want to try another compiler, you can use one that is available online. Although there are various online platforms that you could use, I recommend https://wandbox.org/ for GCC and Clang and http://webcompiler.cloudapp.net/ for VC++.

While working with a compiler with C++17 support, you will need a complete list of required libraries.

# How to generate projects for Visual Studio 2017

Do the following in order to generate Visual Studio 2017 projects to target the x86 platform:

1. Open a command prompt and go to the build directory in the source code root folder.
2. Execute the following CMake command:

```
cmake -G "Visual Studio 15 2017" .. -DCMAKE_USE_WINSSL=ON -
DCURL_WINDOWS_SSPI=ON -DCURL_LIBRARY=libcurl -
DCURL_INCLUDE_DIR=..\libs\curl\include -DBUILD_TESTING=OFF -
DBUILD_CURL_EXE=OFF -DUSE_MANUAL=OFF
```

3. After completion, the Visual Studio solution can be found at `build/cppchallenger.sln`.

If you want to target the x64 platform instead, use the generator called `"Visual Studio 15 2017 Win64"`. Visual Studio 2017 15.4 supports both `filesystem` (as an experimental library) and `std::optional`. If you use a previous version, or just want to use the Boost libraries instead, you can generate the projects using the following command, after you properly install Boost:

```
cmake -G "Visual Studio 15 2017" .. -DCMAKE_USE_WINSSL=ON -
DCURL_WINDOWS_SSPI=ON -DCURL_LIBRARY=libcurl -
DCURL_INCLUDE_DIR=..\libs\curl\include -DBUILD_TESTING=OFF -
DBUILD_CURL_EXE=OFF -DUSE_MANUAL=OFF -DBOOST_FILESYSTEM=ON -
DBOOST_OPTIONAL=ON -DBOOST_INCLUDE_DIR=<path_to_headers> -
DBOOST_LIB_DIR=<path_to_libs>
```

Make sure that the paths to the headers and static library files do not include trailing backslashes (i.e. \).

# Download the Example Code Files

You can download the example code files for this book from your account at `www.packt.com`. If you purchased this book elsewhere, you can visit `www.packt.com/support` and register to have the files emailed directly to you.

You can download the code files by following these steps:

1. Log in or register at `www.packt.com`.
2. Select the **SUPPORT** tab.
3. Click on **Code Downloads & Errata**.
4. Enter the name of the book in the **Search** box and follow the onscreen instructions.

Once the file is downloaded, please make sure that you unzip or extract the folder using the latest version of:

- WinRAR/7-Zip for Windows
- Zipeg/iZip/UnRarX for Mac
- 7-Zip/PeaZip for Linux

The code bundle for the book is also hosted on GitHub at `https://github.com/PacktPublishing/Modern-C-plus-plus-Efficient-and-Scalable-Application-Development`. In case there's an update to the code, it will be updated on the existing GitHub repository.

We also have other code bundles from our rich catalog of books and videos available at `https://github.com/PacktPublishing/`. Check them out!

# Download the color images

We also provide a PDF file that has color images of the screenshots/diagrams used in this book. You can download it here: `https://www.packtpub.com/sites/default/files/downloads/Cplusplus_Efficient_and_Scalable_Application_Development.pdf`

# Conventions Used

Code words in text, database table names, folder names, filenames, file extensions, pathnames, dummy URLs, user input, and Twitter handles are shown as follows: "The writer intended to type `c = a + 8 / b + 1;` and : they pressed comma instead of a `/`."

A block of code is set as follows:

```
inline auto mult(int lhs, int rhs) -> int
    {
        return lhs * rhs;
    }
```

When we wish to draw your attention to a particular part of a code block, the relevant lines or items are set in bold:

```
if (op == ',' || op == '.' || op < '+' || op > '/')
    {
        cout << endl << "operator not recognized" << endl;
        usage();
        return 1;
    }
```

Any command-line input or output is written as follows:

```
C:\Beginning_C++Chapter_02\cl /EHsc calc.cpp
```

**Bold**: New terms and important words are shown in bold. Words that you see on the screen, for example, in menus or dialog boxes, appear in the text like this: "The **calling convention** of the function determines whether the calling function or the called function has the responsibility to do this."

Warnings or important notes appear like this.

Tips and tricks appear like this.

# Get in Touch

Feedback from our readers is always welcome.

**General feedback**: If you have questions about any aspect of this book, mention the book title in the subject of your message and email us at customercare@packtpub.com.

**Errata**: Although we have taken every care to ensure the accuracy of our content, mistakes do happen. If you have found a mistake in this book, we would be grateful if you would report this to us. Please visit www.packt.com/submit-errata, selecting your book, clicking on the Errata Submission Form link, and entering the details.

**Piracy**: If you come across any illegal copies of our works in any form on the Internet, we would be grateful if you would provide us with the location address or website name. Please contact us at copyright@packt.com with a link to the material.

**If you are interested in becoming an author**: If there is a topic that you have expertise in and you are interested in either writing or contributing to a book, please visit authors.packtpub.com.

# Reviews

Please leave a review. Once you have read and used this book, why not leave a review on the site that you purchased it from? Potential readers can then see and use your unbiased opinion to make purchase decisions, we at Packt can understand what you think about our products, and our authors can see your feedback on their book. Thank you!

For more information about Packt, please visit packt.com.

# Understanding Language Features

1

In this chapter, you will be diving into the utmost depths and learn the various language features to control the flow in your code.

## Writing C++

C++ is a very flexible language when it comes to formatting and writing code. It is also a strongly typed language, meaning there are rules about declaring the types of variables, which you can use to your advantage by making the compiler help you write better code. In this section, we will cover how to format C++ code and rules on declaring and scoping variables.

## Using whitespace

Other than string literals, you have free usage of white space (spaces, tabs, newlines), and are able to use as much or as little as you like. C++ statements are delimited by semicolons, so in the following code there are three statements, which will compile and run:

```
int i = 4;
i = i / 2;
std::cout << "The result is" << i << std::endl;
```

The entire code could be written as follows:

```
int i=4;i=i/2; std::cout<<"The result is "<<i<<std::endl;
```

There are some cases where whitespace is needed (for example, when declaring a variable you must have white space between the type and the variable name), but the convention is to be as judicious as possible to make the code readable. And while it is perfectly correct, language-wise, to put all the statements on one line (like JavaScript), it makes the code almost completely unreadable.

If you are interested in some of the more creative ways of making code unreadable, have a look at the entries for the annual International Obfuscated C Code Contest (http://www.ioccc.org/). As the progenitor of C++, many of the lessons in C shown at IOCCC apply to C++ code too.

Bear in mind that, if the code you write is viable, it may be in use for decades, which means you may have to come back to the code years after you have written it, and it means that other people will support your code, too. Making your code readable is not only a courtesy to other developers, but unreadable code is always a likely target for replacement.

# Formatting Code

Inevitably, whoever you are writing code for will dictate how you format code. Sometimes it makes sense, for example, if you use some form of preprocessing to extract code and definitions to create documentation for the code. In many cases, the style that is imposed on you is the personal preference of someone else.

Visual C++ allows you to place XML comments in your code. To do this you use a three--slash comment (///) and then compile the source file with the /doc switch. This creates an intermediate XML file called an xdc file with a <doc> root element and containing all the three--slash comments. The Visual C++ documentation defines standard XML tags (for example, <param>, <returns> to document the parameters and return value of a function). The intermediate file is compiled to the final document XML file with the xdcmake utility.

There are two broad styles in C++: **K&R** and **Allman**.

Kernighan and Ritchie (K&R) wrote the first, and most influential book about C (Dennis Ritchie was the author of the C language). The K&R style is used to describe the formatting style used in that book. In general, K&R places the opening brace of a code block on the same line of the last statement. If your code has nested statements (and typically, it will) then this style can get a bit confusing:

```
if (/* some test */) {
    // the test is true
    if (/* some other test */) {
        // second test is true
    } else {
        // second test is false
    }
} else {
    // the test is false
}
```

This style is typically used in Unix (and Unix-like) code.

The Allman style (named after the developer Eric Allman) places the opening brace on a new line, so the nested example looks as follows:

```
if (/* some test */)
{
    // the test is true
    if (/* some other test */)
    {
        // second test is true
    }
    else
    {
        // second test is false
    }
}
else
{
    // the test is false
}
```

The Allman style is typically used by Microsoft.

Remember that your code is unlikely to be presented on paper, so the fact that K&R is more compact will save no trees. If you have the choice, you should choose the style that is the most readable; the decision of this author, for this book, is that Allman is more readable.

If you have multiple nested blocks, the indents can give you an idea of which block the code resides in. However, comments can help. In particular, if a code block has a large amount of code, it is often helpful to comment the reason for the code block. For example, in an `if` statement, it is helpful to put the result of the test in the code block so you know what the variable values are in that block. It is also useful to put a comment on the closing brace of the test:

```
if (x < 0)
{
    // x < 0
    /* lots of code */
}   // if (x < 0)

else
{
    // x >= 0
    /* lots of code */
}   // if (x < 0)
```

If you put the test as a comment on a closing brace, it means that you have a search term that you can use to find the test that resulted in the code block. The preceding lines make this commenting redundant, but when you have code blocks with many tens of lines of code, and with many levels of nesting, comments like this can be very helpful.

# Writing Statements

A statement can be a declaration of a variable, an expression that evaluates to a value, or it can be a definition of a type. A statement may also be a control structure to affect the flow of the execution through your code.

A statement ends with a semicolon. Other than that, there are few rules about how to format statements. You can even use a semicolon on its own, and this is called a null statement. A null statement does nothing, so having too many semicolons is usually benign.

# Working with Expressions

An expression is a sequence of operators and operands (variables or literals) that results in some value. Consider the following:

```
int i;
i = 6 * 7;
```

On the right side 6 * 7 is an expression, and the assignment (from i on the left-hand side to the semicolon on the right) is a statement.

Every expression is either an **lvalue** or an **rvalue**. You are most likely to see these keywords used in error descriptions. In effect, an lvalue is an expression that refers to some memory location. Items on the left-hand side of an assignment must be lvalues. However, an lvalue can appear on the left- or right-hand side of an assignment. All variables are lvalues. An rvalue is a temporary item that does not exist longer than the expression that uses it; it will have a value, but cannot have a value assigned to it, so it can only exist on the right-hand side of an assignment. Literals are rvalues. The following shows a simple example of lvalues and rvalues:

```
int i;
i = 6 * 7;
```

In the second line, i is an lvalue, and the expression 6 * 7 results in an rvalue (42). The following will not compile because there is an rvalue on the left:

```
6 * 7 = i;
```

Broadly speaking, an expression becomes a statement by when you append a semicolon. For example, the following are both statements:

```
42;
std::sqrt(2);
```

The first line is an rvalue of 42, but since it is temporary it has no effect. A C++ compiler will optimize it away. The second line calls the standard library function to calculate the square root of 2. Again, the result is an rvalue and the value is not used, so the compiler will optimize this away. However, it illustrates that a function can be called without using its return value. Although it is not the case with std::sqrt, many functions have a lasting effect other than their return value. Indeed, the whole point of a function is usually to do something, and the return value is often used merely to indicate if the function was successful; often developers assume that a function will succeed and ignore the return value.

# Using the Comma Operator

Operators will be covered later in this chapter; however, it is useful to introduce the comma operator here. You can have a sequence of expressions separated by a comma as a single statement. For example, the following code is legal in C++:

```
int a = 9;
int b = 4;
int c;
c = a + 8, b + 1;
```

The writer intended to type c = a + 8 / b + 1; and : they pressed comma instead of a /. The intention was for c to be assigned to 9 + 2 + 1, or 12. This code will compile and run, and the variable c will be assigned with a value of 17 (a + 8). The reason is that the comma separates the right-hand side of the assignment into two expressions, a + 8 and b + 1, and it uses the value of the first expression to assign c. Later in this chapter, we will look at operator precedence. However, it is worth saying here that the comma has the lowest precedence and + has a higher precedence than =, so the statement is executed in the order of the addition: the assignment and then the comma operator (with the result of b + 1 thrown away).

You can change the precedence using parentheses to group expressions. For example, the mistyped code could have been as follows:

```
c = (a + 8, b + 1);
```

The result of this statement is: variable c is assigned to 5 (or b + 1). The reason is that with the comma operator expressions are executed from left to right so the value of the group of expressions is the tight-most one. There are some cases, for example, in the initialization or loop expression of a for loop, where you will find the comma operator useful, but as you can see here, even used intentionally, the comma operator produces hard-to-read code.

# Using Types and Variables

It is useful to give basic information here. C++ is a strongly typed language, which means that you have to declare the type of the variables that you use. The reason for this is that the compiler needs to know how much memory to allocate for the variable, and it can determine this by the type of the variable. In addition, the compiler needs to know how to initialize a variable, if it has not been explicitly initialized, and to perform this initialization the compiler needs to know the type of the variable.

C++11 provides the `auto` keyword, which relaxes this concept of strong typing. However, the type checking of the compiler is so important that you should use type checking as much as possible.

C++ variables can be declared anywhere in your code as long as they are declared before they are used. *Where* you declare a variable determines *how* you use it (this is called the **scope** of the variable). In general, it is best to declare the variable as close as possible to where you will use it, and within the most restrictive scope. This prevents *name clashes*, where you will have to add additional information to disambiguate two or more variables.

You may, *and should*, give your variables descriptive names. This makes your code much more readable and easier to understand. C++ names must start with an alphabetic character, or an underscore. They can contain alphanumeric characters except spaces, but can contain underscores. So, the following are valid names:

```
numberOfCustomers
NumberOfCustomers
number_of_customers
```

C++ names are case-sensitive, and the first 2,048 characters are significant. You can start a variable name with an underscore, but you cannot use two underscores, nor can you use an underscore followed by a capital letter (these are reserved by C++). C++ also reserves keywords (for example, `while` and `if`), and clearly you cannot use type names as variable names, neither built in type names (`int`, `long`, and so on) nor your own custom types.

You declare a variable in a statement, ending with a semicolon. The basic syntax of declaring a variable is that you specify the type, then the name, and, optionally, any initialization of the variable.

Built-in types must be initialized before you use them:

```
int i;
i++;            // C4700 uninitialized local variable 'i' used
std::cout << i;
```

There are essentially three ways to initialize variables. You can assign a value, you can call the type constructor (constructors for classes will be defined in Chapter 4, *Classes*) or you can initialize a variable using function syntax:

```
int i = 1;
int j = int(2);
int k(3);
```

These three are all legal C++, but stylistically the first is the better because it is more obvious: the variable is an integer, it is called `i`, and it is assigned a value of 1. The third looks confusing; it looks like the declaration of a function when it is actually declaring a variable.

Chapter 4, *Classes* will cover classes, your own custom types. A custom type may be defined to have a default value, which means that you may decide not to initialize a variable of a custom type before using it. However, this will result in poorer performance, because the compiler will initialize the variable with the default value and subsequently your code will assign a value, resulting in an assignment being performed twice.

## Using constants and literals

Each type will have a literal representation. An integer will be a numeric represented without a decimal point and, if it is a signed integer, the literal can also use the plus or minus symbol to indicate the sign. Similarly, a real number can have a literal value that contains a decimal point, and you may even use the scientific (or engineering) format including an exponent. C++ has various rules to use when specifying literals in code. Some examples of literals are shown here:

```
int pos = +1;
int neg = -1;
double micro = 1e-6;
double unit = 1.;
std::string name = "Richard";
```

Note that for the `unit` variable, the compiler knows that the literal is a real number because the value has a decimal point. For integers, you can provide a hexadecimal literal in your code by prefixing the number with `0x`, so `0x100` is `256` in decimal. By default, the output stream will print numeric values in base 10; however, you can insert a **manipulator** into an output stream to tell it to use a different number base. The default behavior is `std::dec`, which means the numbers should be displayed as base 10, `std::oct` means display as octal (base 8), and `std::hex` means display as hexadecimal (base `16`). If you prefer to see the prefix printed, then you use the stream manipulator `std::showbase` (more details will be given in Chapter 5, *Using the Standard Library Containers*).

C++ defines some literals. For `bool`, the logic type, there are `true` and `false` constants, where `false` is zero and `true` is 1. There is also the `nullptr` constant, again, zero, which is used as an invalid value for any pointer type.

# Defining constants

In some cases, you will want to provide constant values that can be used throughout your code. For example, you may decide to declare a constant for π. You should not allow this value to be changed because it will change the underlying logic in your code. This means that you should mark the variable as being constant. When you do this, the compiler will check the use of the variable and if it is used in code that changes the value of the variable the compiler will issue an error:

```
const double pi = 3.1415;
double radius = 5.0;
double circumference = 2 * pi * radius;
```

In this case the symbol `pi` is declared as being constant, so it cannot change. If you subsequently decide to change the constant, the compiler will issue an error:

```
// add more precision, generates error C3892
pi += 0.00009265359;
```

Once you have declared a constant, you can be assured that the compiler will make sure it remains so. You can assign a constant with an expression as follows:

```
#include <cmath>
const double sqrtOf2 = std::sqrt(2);
```

In this code, a global constant called `sqrtOf2` is declared and assigned with a value using the `std::sqrt` function. Since this constant is declared outside a function, it is global to the file and can be used throughout the file.

The problem with this approach is that the preprocessor does a simple replacement. With constants declared with `const`, the C++ compiler will perform type checking to ensure that the constant is being used appropriately.

You can also use `const` to declare a constant that will be used as a **constant expression**. For example, you can declare an array using the square bracket syntax (more details will be given in `Chapter 2`, *Working with Memory, Arrays, and Pointers*):

```
int values[5];
```

This declares an array of five integers on the stack and these items are accessed through the `values` array variable. The 5 here is a constant expression. When you declare an array on the stack, you have to provide the compiler with a constant expression so it knows how much memory to allocate and this means the size of the array must be known at compile time. (You can allocate an array with a size known only at runtime, but this requires dynamic memory allocation, explained in Chapter 2, *Working with Memory, Arrays, and Pointers*.) In C++, you can declare a constant to do the following:

```
const int size = 5;
int values[size];
```

Elsewhere in your code, when you access the `values` array, you can use the `size` constant to make sure that you do not access items past the end of the array. Since the `size` variable is declared in just one place, if you need to change the size of the array at a later stage, you have just one place to make this change. The `const` keyword can also be used on pointers and references (see Chapter 2, *Working with Memory, Arrays, and Pointers*) and on objects (see Chapter 4, *Classes*); often, you'll see it used on parameters to functions (see Chapter 3, *Using Functions*). This is used to get the compiler to help ensure that pointers, references, and objects are used appropriately, as you intended.

## Using Constant Expressions

C++11 introduces a keyword called `constexpr`. This is applied to an expression, and indicates that the expression should be evaluated at compile type rather than at runtime:

```
constexpr double pi = 3.1415;
constexpr double twopi = 2 * pi;
```

This is similar to initializing a constant declared with the `const` keyword. However, the `constexpr` keyword can also be applied to functions that return a value that can be evaluated at compile time, and so this allows the compiler to optimize the code:

```
constexpr int triang(int i)
{
    return (i == 0) ? 0 : triang(i - 1) + i;
}
```

In this example, the function `triang` calculates triangular numbers recursively. The code uses the conditional operator. In the parentheses, the function parameter is tested to see if it is zero, and if so the function returns zero, in effect ending the recursion and returning the function to the original caller. If the parameter is not zero, then the return value is the sum of the parameter and the return value of `triang` called with the parameter is decremented.

This function, when called with a literal in your code, can be evaluated at compile time. The `constexpr` is an indication to the compiler to check the usage of the function to see if it can determine the parameter at compile time. If this is the case, the compiler can evaluate the return value and produce code more efficiently than by calling the function at runtime. If the compiler cannot determine the parameter at compile-time, the function will be called as **normal**. A function marked with the `constexpr` keyword must only have one expression (hence the use of the conditional operator `? :` in the `triang` function).

# Using Enumerations

A final way to provide constants is to use an `enum` variable. In effect, an `enum` is a group of named constants, which means that you can use an `enum` as a parameter to a function. For example:

```
enum suits {clubs, diamonds, hearts, spades};
```

This defines an enumeration called `suits`, with named values for the suits in a deck of cards. An enumeration is an integer type and by default the compiler will assume an `int`, but you can change this by specifying the integer type in the declaration. Since there are just four possible values for card suits, it is a waste of memory to use `int` (usually 4 bytes) and instead, we can use `char` (a single byte):

```
enum suits : char {clubs, diamonds, hearts, spades};
```

When you use an enumerated value, you can use just the name; however, it is usual to scope it with the name of the enumeration, making the code more readable:

```
suits card1 = diamonds;
suits card2 = suits::diamonds;
```

Both forms are allowed, but the latter makes it more explicit that the value is taken from an enumeration. To force developers to specify the scope, you can apply the keyword `class`:

```
enum class suits : char {clubs, diamonds, hearts, spades};
```

With this definition and the preceding code, the line declaring `card2` will compile, but the line declaring `card1` will not. With a scoped `enum`, the compiler treats the enumeration as a new type and has no inbuilt conversion from your new type to an integer variable. For example:

```
suits card = suits::diamonds;
char c = card + 10; // errors C2784 and C2676
```

The enum type is based on char but when you define the suits variable as being scoped (with class) the second line will not compile. If the enumeration is defined as not being scoped (without class) then there is an inbuilt conversion between the enumerated value and char.

By default, the compiler will give the first enumerator a value of 0 and then increment the value for the subsequent enumerators. Thus suits::diamonds will have a value of 1 because it is the second value in suits. You can assign values yourself:

```
enum ports {ftp=21, ssh, telnet, smtp=25, http=80};
```

In this case, ports::ftp has a value of 21, ports::ssh has a value of 22 (21 incremented), ports::telnet is 22, ports::smtp is 25, and ports::http is 80.

Often the point of enumerations is to provide named symbols within your code and their values are unimportant. Does it matter what value is assigned to suits::hearts? The intention is usually to ensure that it is different from the other values. In other cases, the values are important because they are a way to provide values to other functions.

Enumerations are useful in a switch statement (see later) because the named value makes it clearer than using just an integer. You can also use an enumeration as a parameter to a function and hence restrict the values passed via that parameter:

```
void stack(suits card)
{
    // we know that card is only one of four values
}
```

# Declaring Pointers

Since we are covering the use of variables, it is worth explaining the syntax used to define pointers and arrays because there are some potential pitfalls. Chapter 2, *Working with Memory, Arrays, and Pointers*, covers this in more detail, so we will just introduce the syntax so that you are familiar with it.

In C++, you will access memory using a typed pointer. The type indicates the type of the data that is held in the memory that is pointed to. So, if the pointer is an (4 byte) integer pointer, it will point to four bytes that can be used as an integer. If the integer pointer is incremented, then it will point to the next four bytes, which can be used as an integer.

 Don't worry if you find pointers confusing at this point. Chapter 2, *Working with Memory, Arrays, and Pointers,* will explain this in more detail. The purpose of introducing pointers at this time is to make you aware of the syntax.

In C++, pointers are declared using the * symbol and you access a memory address with the & operator:

```
int *p;
int i = 42;
p = &i;
```

The first line declares a variable, p, which will be used to hold the memory address of an integer. The second line declares an integer and assigns it a value. The third line assigns a value to the pointer p to be the address of the integer variable just declared. It is important to stress that the value of p *is not* 42; it will be a memory address where the value of 42 is stored.

Note how the declaration has the * on the variable name. This is common convention. The reason is that if you declare several variables in one statement, the * applies only to the immediate variable. So, for example:

```
int* p1, p2;
```

Initially, this looks like you are declaring two integer pointers. However, this line does not do this; it declares just one pointer to integer called p1. The second variable is an integer called p2. The preceding line is equivalent to the following:

```
int *p1;
int p2;
```

If you wish to declare two integers in one statement, then you should do it as follows:

```
int *p1, *p2;
```

# Using Namespaces

Namespaces give you one mechanism to modularize code. A namespace allows you to label your types, functions, and variables with a unique name so that, using the scope resolution operator, you can give a *fully qualified name*. The advantage is that you know exactly which item will be called. The disadvantage is that using a fully qualified name you are in effect switching off C++'s *argument-dependent lookup* mechanism for overloaded functions where the compiler will choose the function that has the best fit according to the arguments passed to the function.

Defining a namespace is simple: you decorate the types, functions, and global variables with the `namespace` keyword and the name you give to it. In the following example, two functions are defined in the `utilities` namespace:

```cpp
namespace utilities
{
    bool poll_data()
    {
        // code that returns a bool
    }
    int get_data()
    {
        // code that returns an integer
    }
}
```

 Do not use semicolon after the closing bracket.

Now when you use these symbols, you need to qualify the name with the namespace:

```cpp
if (utilities::poll_data())
{
    int i = utilities::get_data();
    // use i here...
}
```

The namespace declaration may just declare the functions, in which case the actual functions would have to be defined elsewhere, and you will need to use a qualified name:

```cpp
namespace utilities
{
    // declare the functions
    bool poll_data();
```

```
    int get_data();
}

//define the functions
bool utilities::poll_data()
{
    // code that returns a bool
}

int utilities::get_data()
{
    // code that returns an integer
}
```

One use of namespaces is to version your code. The first version of your code may have a side-effect that is not in your functional specification and is technically a bug, but some callers will use it and depend on it. When you update your code to fix the bug, you may decide to allow your callers the option to use the old version so that their code does not break. You can do this with a namespace:

```
namespace utilities
{
    bool poll_data();
    int get_data();

    namespace V2
    {
        bool poll_data();
        int get_data();
        int new_feature();
    }
}
```

Now callers who want a specific version can call the fully qualified names, for example, callers could use `utilities::V2::poll_data` to use the newer version and `utilities::poll_data` to use the older version. When an item in a specific namespace calls an item in the same namespace, it does not have to use a qualified name. So, if the `new_feature` function calls `get_data`, it will be `utilities::V2::get_data` that is called. It is important to note that, to declare a nested namespace, you have to do the nesting manually (as shown here); you cannot simply declare a namespace called `utilities::V2`.

The preceding example has been written so that the first version of the code will call it using the namespace `utilities`. C++11 provides a facility called an **inline** namespace that allows you to define a nested namespace, but allows the compiler to treat the items as being in the parent namespace when it performs an argument-dependent lookup:

```
namespace utilities
{
    inline namespace V1
    {
        bool poll_data();
        int get_data();
    }

    namespace V2
    {
        bool poll_data();
        int get_data();
        int new_feature();
    }
}
```

Now to call the first version of `get_data`, you can use `utilities::get_data` or `utilities::V1::get_data`.

Fully qualified names can make the code difficult to read, especially if your code will only use one namespace. To help here you have several options. You can place a `using` statement to indicate that symbols declared in the specified namespace can be used without a fully qualified name:

```
using namespace utilities;
int i = get_data();
int j = V2::get_data();
```

You can still use fully qualified names, but this statement allows you to ease the requirement. Note that a nested namespace is a member of a namespace, so the preceding `using` statement means that you can call the second version of `get_data` with either `utilities::V2::get_data` or `V2::get_data`. If you use the unqualified name, then it means that you will call `utilities::get_data`.

A namespace can contain many items, and you may decide that you only want to relax the use of fully qualified names with just a few of them. To do this, use `using` and give the name of the item:

```
using std::cout;
using std::endl;
cout << "Hello, World!" << endl;
```

This code says that, whenever `cout` is used, it refers to `std::cout`. You can use `using` within a function, or you can put it as file scope and make the intention global to the file.

You do not have to declare a namespace in one place, you can declare it over several files. The following could be in a different file to the previous declaration of `utilities`:

```
namespace utilities
{
    namespace V2
    {
        void print_data();
    }
}
```

The `print_data` function is still part of the `utilities::V2` namespace.

You can also put an `#include` in a namespace, in which case the items declared in the header file will now be part of the namespace. The standard library header files that have a prefix of `c` (for example, `cmath`, `cstdlib`, and `ctime`) give access to the C runtime functions by including the appropriate C header in the `std` namespace.

The great advantage of a namespace is to be able to define your items with names that may be common, but are hidden from other code that does not know the namespace name of. The namespace means that the items are still available to your code via the fully qualified name. However, this only works if you use a unique namespace name, and the likelihood is that, the longer the namespace name, the more unique it is likely to be. Java developers often name their classes using a URI, and you could decide to do the same thing:

```
namespace com_packtpub_richard_grimes
{
    int get_data();
}
```

The problem is that the fully qualified name becomes quite long:

```
int i = com_packtpub_richard_grimes::get_data();
```

You can get around this issue using an alias:

```
namespace packtRG = com_packtpub_richard_grimes;
int i = packtRG::get_data();
```

C++ allows you to define a namespace without a name, an **anonymous** namespace. As mentioned previously, namespaces allow you to prevent name clashes between code defined in several files. If you intend to use such a name in only one file you could define a unique namespace name. However, this could get tedious if you had to do it for several files. A namespace without a name has the special meaning that it has **internal linkage**, that is, the items can only be used in the current translation unit, the current file, and not in any other file.

Code that is not declared in a namespace will be a member of the `global` namespace. You can call the code without a namespace name, but you may want to explicitly indicate that the item is in the `global` namespace using the scope resolution operator without a namespace name:

```
int version = 42;

void print_version()
{
    std::cout << "Version = " << ::version << std::endl;
}
```

# C++ Scoping of Variables

The compiler will compile your source files as individual items called **translation units**. The compiler will determine the objects and variables you declare and the types and functions you define, and once declared you can use any of these in the subsequent code within the scope of the declaration. At its very broadest, you can declare an item at the global scope by declaring it in a header file that will be used by all of the source files in your project. If you do not use a namespace it is often wise when you use such global variables to name them as being part of the global namespace:

```
// in version.h
extern int version;

// in version.cpp
#include "version.h"
version = 17;

// print.cpp
#include "version.h"
void print_version()
{
    std::cout << "Version = " << ::version << std::endl;
}
```

This code has the C++ for two source files (`version.cpp` and `print.cpp`) and a header file (`version.h`) included by both source files. The header file declares the global variable `version`, which can be used by both source files; it declares the variable, but does not define it. The actual variable is defined and initialized in `version.cpp`; it is here that the compiler will allocate memory for the variable. The `extern` keyword used on the declaration in the header indicates to the compiler that `version` has **external linkage**, that is, the name is visible in files other than where the variable is defined. The `version` variable is used in the `print.cpp` source file. In this file, the scope resolution operator (`::`) is used without a namespace name and hence indicates that the variable `version` is in the global namespace.

You can also declare items that will only be used within the current translation unit, by declaring them within the source file before they are used (usually at the top of the file). This produces a level of modularity and allows you to hide implementation details from code in other source files. For example:

```cpp
// in print.h
void usage();

// print.cpp
#include "version.h"
std::string app_name = "My Utility";
void print_version()
{
    std::cout << "Version = " << ::version << std::endl;
}

void usage()
{
    std::cout << app_name << " ";
    print_version();
}
```

The `print.h` header contains the interface for the code in the file `print.cpp`. Only those functions declared in the header will be callable by other source files. The caller does not need to know about the implementation of the `usage` function, and as you can see here it is implemented using a call to a function called `print_version` that is only available to code in `print.cpp`. The variable `app_name` is declared at file scope, so it will only be accessible to code in `print.cpp`.

If another source file declares a variable at file scope, that is called `app_name`, and is also a `std::string` the file will compile, but the linker will complain when it tries to link the object files. The reason is that the linker will see the same variable defined in two places and it will not know which one to use.

A function also defines a scope; variables defined within the function can only be accessed through that name. The parameters of the function are also included as variables within the function, so when you declare other variables, you have to use different names. If a parameter is not marked as `const` then you can alter the value of the parameter in your function.

You can declare variables anywhere within a function as long as you declare them before you use them. Curly braces (`{ }`) are used to define code blocks, and they also define local scope; if you declare a variable within a code block then you can only use it there. This means that you can declare variables with the same name outside the code block and the compiler will use the variable closest to the scope it is accessed.

Before finishing this section, it is important to mention one aspect of the C++ **storage class**. A variable declared in a function means that the compiler will allocate memory for the variable on the stack frame created for the function. When the function finishes, the stack frame is torn down and the memory recycled. This means that, after a function returns, the values in any local variables are lost; when the function is called again, the variable is created anew and initialized again.

C++ provides the `static` keyword to change this behavior. The `static` keyword means that the variable is allocated when the program starts just like variables declared at global scope. Applying `static` to a variable declared in a function means that the variable has internal linkage, that is, the compiler restricts access to that variable to that function:

```
int inc(int i)
{
    static int value;
    value += i;
    return value;
}

int main()
{
    std::cout << inc(10) << std::endl;
    std::cout << inc(5) << std::endl;
}
```

By default, the compiler will initialize a static variable to 0, but you can provide an initialization value, and this will be used when the variable is first allocated. When this program starts, the `value` variable will be initialized to 0 before the `main` function is called. The first time the `inc` function is called, the `value` variable is incremented to 10, which is returned by the function and printed to the console. When the `inc` function returns the `value` variable is retained, so that when the `inc` function is called again, the `value` variable is incremented by 5 to a value of 15.

# Using Operators

Operators are used to compute a value from one or more operands. The following table groups all of the operators with equal *precedence* and lists their *associativity*. The higher in the table, the higher precedence of execution the operator has in an expression. If you have several operators in an expression, the compiler will perform the higher-precedence operators before the lower-precedence operators. If an expression contains operators of equal precedence, then the compiler will use the associativity to decide whether an operand is grouped with the operator to its left or right.

 There are some ambiguities in this table. A pair of parentheses can mean a function call or a cast and in the table these are listed as `function()` and `cast()`; in your code you will simply use `()`. The + and – symbols are either used to indicate sign (unary plus and unary minus, given in the table as +x and –x), or addition and subtraction (given in the table as + and –). The & symbol means either "take the address of" (listed in the table as &x) or bitwise AND (listed in the table as &). Finally, the postfix increment and decrement operators (listed in the table as x++ and x--) have a higher precedence than the prefix equivalents (listed as ++x and --x).

| Precedence and Associativity | Operators |
|---|---|
| 1: No associativity | `: :` |
| 2: Left to right associativity | `. or -> [] function() {} x++ x-- typeid const_cast dynamic_cast reinterpret_cast static_cast` |
| 3: Right to left associativity | `sizeof ++x --x ~ ! -x +x &x * new delete cast()` |
| 4: Left to right associativity | `.* or ->*` |
| 5: Left to right associativity | `* / %` |
| 6: Left to right associativity | `+ -` |
| 7: Left to right associativity | `<< >>` |
| 8: Left to right associativity | `< > <= >=` |
| 9: Left to right associativity | `== !=` |
| 10: Left to right associativity | `&` |
| 11: Left to right associativity | `^` |
| 12: Left to right associativity | `|` |
| 13: Left to right associativity | `&&` |
| 14: Left to right associativity | `||` |
| 15: Right to left associativity | `? :` |

| | |
|---|---|
| **16**: Right to left associativity | `= *= /= %= += -= <<= >>= &= \|= ^=` |
| **17**: Right to left associativity | `throw` |
| **18**: Left to right associativity | `,` |

For example, take a look at the following code:

```
int a = b + c * d;
```

This is interpreted as the multiplication being performed first, and then the addition. A clearer way to write the same code is:

```
int a = b + (c * d);
```

The reason is that * has a higher precedence than + so that the multiplication is carried out first, and then the addition is performed:

```
int a = b + c + d;
```

In this case, the + operators have the same precedence, which is higher than the precedence of assignment. Since + has left to right associativity the statement is interpreted as follows:

```
int a = ((b + c) + d);
```

That is, the first action is the addition of b and c, and the result is added to d and it is this result that is used to assign a. This may not seem important, but bear in mind that the addition could be between function calls (a function call has a higher precedence than +):

```
int a = b() + c() + d();
```

This means that the three functions are called in the order b, c, d, and then their return values are summed according to the left-to-right associativity. This may be important because d may depend on global data altered by the other two functions.

It makes your code more readable and easier to understand if you explicitly specify the precedence by grouping expressions with parentheses. Writing b + (c * d) makes it immediately clear which expression is executed first, whereas b + c * d means you have to know the precedence of each operator.

The built-in operators are overloaded, that is, the same syntax is used regardless of which built-in type is used for the operands. The operands must be the same type; if different types are used, the compiler will perform some default conversions, but in other cases (in particular, when operating on types of different sizes), you will have to perform a cast to indicate explicitly what you mean.

# Exploring the Built-in Operators

C++ comes with a wide range of built-in operators; most are arithmetic or logic operators, which will be covered in this section. The memory operators will be covered in Chapter 2, *Working with Memory, Arrays, and Pointers,* and the object-related operators in Chapter 4, *Classes.*

# Arithmetic Operators

The arithmetic operators +, −, /, *, and % need little explanation other than perhaps the division and modulus operators. All of these operators act upon integer and real numeric types except for %, which can only be used with integer types. If you mix the types (say, add an integer to a floating-point number) then the compiler will perform an automatic conversion. The division operator / behaves as you expect for floating point variables: it produces the result of the division of the two operands. When you perform the division between two integers a / b, the result is the whole number of the divisor (b) in the dividend (a). The remainder of the division is obtained by the modulus %. So, for any integer, b (other than zero), one could say that, an integer a can be expressed as follows:

```
(a / b) * b + (a % b)
```

Note that the modulus operator can only be used with integers. If you want to get the remainder of a floating-point division, use the standard function, std:;remainder.

Be careful when using division with integers, since fractional parts are discarded. If you need the fractional parts, then you may need to explicitly convert the numbers into real numbers. For example:

```
int height = 480;
int width = 640;
float aspect_ratio = width / height;
```

This gives an aspect ratio of 1 when it should be 1.3333 (or 4 : 3). To ensure that floating-point division is performed, rather than integer division, you can cast either (or both) the dividend or divisor to a floating-point number.

## Increment and Decrement Operators

There are two versions of these operators, prefix and postfix. As the name suggests, prefix means that the operator is placed on the left of the operand (for example, ++i), and a postfix operator is placed to the right (i++). The ++ operator will increment the operand and the -- operator will decrement it. The prefix operator means "return the value *after* the operation," and the postfix operator means "return the value *before* the operation." So the following code will increment one variable and use it to assign another:

```
a = ++b;
```

Here, the prefix operator is used so the variable b is incremented and the variable a is assigned to the value after b has been incremented. Another way of expressing this is:

```
a = (b = b + 1);
```

The following code assigns a value using the postfix operator:

```
a = b++;
```

This means that the variable b is incremented, but the variable a is assigned to the value before b has been incremented. Another way of expressing this is:

```
int t;
a = (t = b, b = b + 1, t);
```

 Note that this statement uses the comma operator, so a is assigned to the temporary variable t in the right-most expression.

The increment and decrement operators can be applied to both integer and floating point numbers. The operators can also be applied to pointers, where they have a special meaning. When you increment a pointer variable it means *increment the pointer by the size of the type pointed to by the operator*.

# Bitwise Operators

Integers can be regarded as a series of bits, 0 or 1. Bitwise operators act upon these bits compared to the bit in the same position in the other operand. Signed integers use a bit to indicate the sign, but bitwise operators act on every bit in an integer, so it is usually only sensible to use them on unsigned integers. In the following, all the types are marked as unsigned, so they are treated as not having a sign bit.

The & operator is bitwise AND, which means that each bit in the left-hand operand is compared with the bit in the right-hand operand in the same position. If both are 1, the resultant bit in the same position will be 1; otherwise, the resultant bit is zero:

```
unsigned int a = 0x0a0a; // this is the binary 0000101000001010
unsigned int b = 0x00ff; // this is the binary 0000000000001111
unsigned int c = a & b;  // this is the binary 0000000000001010
std::cout << std::hex << std::showbase << c << std::endl;
```

In this example, using bitwise & with 0x00ff has the same effect as providing a mask that masks out all but the lowest byte.

The bitwise OR operator | will return a value of 1 if either or both bits in the same position are 1, and a value of 0 only if both are 0:

```
unsigned int a = 0x0a0a; // this is the binary 0000101000001010
unsigned int b = 0x00ff; // this is the binary 0000000000001111
unsigned int c = a & b;  // this is the binary 0000101000001111
std::cout << std::hex << std::showbase << c << std::endl;
```

One use of the & operator is to find if a particular bit (or a specific collection of bits) is set:

```
unsigned int flags = 0x0a0a; // 0000101000001010
unsigned int test = 0x00ff;  // 0000000000001111

// 0000101000001111 is (flags & test)
if ((flags & test) == flags)
{
    // code for when all the flags bits are set in test
}
if ((flags & test) != 0)
{
```

```
                // code for when some or all the flag bits are set in test
    }
```

The `flags` variable has the bits we require, and the `test` variable is a value that we are examining. The value (`flags & test`) will have only those bits in the `test` variables that are also set in `flags`. Thus, if the result is non-zero, it means that at least one bit in `test` is also set in `flags`; if the result is exactly the same as the `flags` variable then all the bits in `flags` are set in `test`.

The exclusive OR operator `^` is used to test when the bits are different; the resultant bit is 1 if the bits in the operands are different, and 0 if they are the same. Exclusive OR can be used to flip specific bits:

```
    int value = 0xf1;
    int flags = 0x02;
    int result = value ^ flags; // 0xf3
    std::cout << std::hex << result << std::endl;
```

The final bitwise operator is the bitwise complement `~`. This operator is applied to a single integer operand and returns a value where every bit is the complement of the corresponding bit in the operand; so if the operand bit is 1, the bit in the result is 0, and if the bit in the operand is 0, the bit in the result is 1. Note that all bits are examined, so you need to be aware of the size of the integer.

## Boolean Operators

The `==` operator tests whether two values are exactly the same. If you test two integers then the test is obvious; for example, if x is 2 and y is 3, then x `==` y is obviously `false`. However, two real numbers may not be the same even when you think so:

```
    double x = 1.000001 * 1000000000000;
    double y = 1000001000000;
    if (x == y) std::cout << "numbers are the same";
```

The `double` type is a floating-point type held in 8 bytes, but this is not enough for the precision being used here; the value stored in the x variable is `1000000999999.9999` (to four decimal places).

The != operator tests if two values are not true. The operators > and <, test two values to see if the left-hand operand is greater than, or less than, the right-hand operand, the >= operator tests if the left-hand operand is greater than or equal to the right-hand operand, and the <= operator tests if the left-hand operand is less than or equal to the right-hand operand. These operators can be used in the if statement similar to how == is used in the preceding example. The expressions using the operators return a value of type bool and so you can use them to assign values to Boolean variables:

```
int x = 10;
int y = 11;
bool b = (x > y);
if (b) std::cout << "numbers same";
else    std::cout << "numbers not same";
```

The assignment operator (=) has a higher precedence than the greater than (>=) operator, but we have used the parentheses to make it explicit that the value is tested before being used to assign the variable. You can use the ! operator to negate a logical value. So, using the value of b obtained previously, you can write the following:

```
if (!b) std::cout << "numbers not same";
else    std::cout << "numbers same";
```

You can combine two logical expressions using the && (AND) and || (OR) operators. An expression with the && operator is true only if both operands are true, whereas an expression with the || operator is true if either, or both, operands are true:

```
int x = 10, y = 10, z = 9;
if ((x == y) || (y < z))
    std::cout << "one or both are true";
```

This code involves three tests; the first tests if the x and y variables have the same value, the second tests if the variable y is less than z, and then there is a test to see if either or both of the first two tests are true.

In a || expression such as this, where the first operand (x==y) is true, the total logical expression will be true regardless of the value of the right operand (here, y < z). So there is no point in testing the second expression. Correspondingly, in an && expression, if the first operand is false then the entire expression must be false, and so the right-hand part of the expression need not be tested.

The compiler will provide code to perform this *short-circuiting* for you:

```
if ((x != 0) && (0.5 > 1/x))
{
    // reciprocal is less than 0.5
}
```

This code tests to see if the reciprocal of x is less than 0.5 (or, conversely, that x is greater than 2). If the x variable has value 0 then the test $1/x$ is an error but, in this case, the expression will never be executed because the left operand to && is false.

# Bitwise Shift Operators

Bitwise shift operators shift the bits in the left-hand operand integer the specified number of bits given in the right-hand operand, in the specified direction. A shift by one bit left multiplies the number by two, a shift one bit to the right divides by 2. In the following a 2-byte integer is bit-shifted:

```
unsigned short s1 = 0x0010;
unsigned short s2 = s1 << 8;
std::cout << std::hex << std::showbase;
std::cout << s2 << std::endl;
// 0x1000
s2 = s2 << 3;
std::cout << s2 << std::endl;
// 0x8000
```

In this example, the s1 variable has the fifth bit set (0x0010 or 16). The s2 variable has this value, shifted left by 8 bits, so the single bit is shifted to the 13th bit, and the bottom 8 bits are all set to 0 (0x10000 or 4,096). This means that 0x0010 has been multiplied by $2^8$, or 256, to give 0x1000. Next, the value is shifted left by another 3 bits, and the result is 0x8000; the top bit is set.

The operator discards any bits that overflow, so if you have the top bit set and shift the integer one bit left, that top bit will be discarded:

```
s2 = s2 << 1;
std::cout << s2 << std::endl;
// 0
```

A final shift left by one bit results in a value 0.

It is important to remember that, when used with a stream, the operator << means *insert into the stream*, and when used with integers, it means *bitwise shift*.

## Assignment Operators

The assignment operator = assigns an lvalue (a variable) on the left with the result of the rvalue (a variable or expression) on the right:

```
int x = 10;
x = x + 10;
```

The first line declares an integer and initializes it to 10. The second line alters the variable by adding another 10 to it, so now the variable x has a value of 20. This is the assignment. C++ allows you to change the value of a variable based on the variable's value using an abbreviated syntax. The previous lines can be written as follows:

```
int x = 10;
x += 10;
```

An increment operator such as this (and the decrement operator) can be applied to integers and floating-point types. If the operator is applied to a pointer, then the operand indicates how many whole items addresses the pointer is changed by. For example, if an int is 4 bytes and you add 10 to an int pointer, the actual pointer value is incremented by 40 (10 times 4 bytes).

In addition to the increment (+=) and decrement (−=) assignments, you can have assignments for multiply (*=), divide (/=), and remainder (%=). All of these except for the last one (%=) can be used for both floating-point types and integers. The remainder assignment can only be used on integers.

You can also perform bitwise assignment operations on integers: left shift (<<=), right shift (>>=), bitwise AND (&=), bitwise OR (|=), and bitwise exclusive OR (^=). It usually only makes sense to apply these to unsigned integers. So, multiplying by eight can be carried out by both of these two lines:

```
i *= 8;
i <<= 3;
```

# Controlling Execution Flow

C++ provides many ways to test values and loop through code.

# Using Conditional Statements

The most frequently used conditional statement is `if`. In its simplest form, the `if` statement takes a logical expression in a pair of parentheses and is immediately followed by the statement that is executed if the condition is `true`:

```
int i;
std::cin >> i;
if (i > 10) std::cout << "much too high!" << std::endl;
```

You can also use the `else` statement to catch occasions when the condition is `false`:

```
int i;
std::cin >> i;
if (i > 10) std::cout << "much too high!" << std::endl;
else        std::cout << "within range" << std::endl;
```

If you want to execute several statements, you can use braces (`{ }`) to define a code block.

The condition is a logical expression and C++ will convert from numeric types to a `bool`, where 0 is `false` and anything not 0 is `true`. If you are not careful, this can be a source of an error that is not only difficult to notice, but also can have an unexpected side-effect. Consider the following code, which asks for input from the console and then tests to see if the user enters -1:

```
int i;
std::cin >> i;
if (i == -1) std::cout << "typed -1" << endl;
std::cout << "i = " << i << endl;
```

This is contrived, but you may be asking for values in a loop and then performing actions on those values, except when the user enters -1, at which point the loop finishes. If you mistype, you may end up with the following code:

```
int i;
std::cin >> i;
if (i = -1) std::cout << "typed -1" << endl;
std::cout << "i = " << i << endl;
```

In this case, the assignment operator (=) is used instead of the *equality* operator (==). There is just one character difference, but this code is still correct C++ and the compiler is happy to compile it.

The result is that, regardless of what you type at the console, the variable i is assigned to -1, and since -1 is not zero, the condition in the `if` statement is `true`, hence the true clause of the statement is executed. Since the variable has been assigned to -1, this may alter logic further on in your code. The way to avoid this bug is to take advantage of the requirement that in an assignment the left-hand side must be an lvalue. Perform your test as follows:

```
if (-1 == i) std::cout << "typed -1" << endl;
```

Here, the logical expression is `(-1 == i)`, and since the `==` operator is commutative (the order of the operands does not matter; you get the same result), this is exactly the same as you intended in the preceding test. However, if you mistype the operator, you get the following:

```
if (-1 = i) std::cout << "typed -1" << endl;
```

In this case, the assignment has an rvalue on the left-hand side, and this will cause the compiler to issue an error (in Visual C++ this is `C2106 '=' : left operand must be l-value`).

You are allowed to declare a variable in an `if` statement, and the scope of the variable is in the statement blocks. For example, a function that returns an integer can be called as follows:

```
if (int i = getValue()) {
    // i != 0     // can use i here
} else {
    // i == 0     // can use i here
}
```

While this is perfectly legal C++, there are a few reasons why you would want to do this.

In some cases, the conditional operator `?:` can be used instead of an `if` statement. The operator executes the expression to the left of the `?` operator and, if the conditional expression is `true`, it executes the expression to the right of the `?`. If the conditional expression is `false`, it executes the expression to the right of the `:`. The expression that the operator executes provides the return value of the conditional operator.

For example, the following code determines the maximum of two variables, a and b:

```
int max;
if (a > b) max = a;
else       max = b;
```

This can be expressed with the following single statement:

```
int max = (a > b) ? a : b;
```

The main choice is whichever is most readable in the code. Clearly, if the assignment expressions are large it may well be best to split them over lines in an `if` statement. However, it is useful to use the conditional statement in other statements. For example:

```
int number;
std::cin >> number;
std::cout << "there "
          << ((number == 1) ? "is " : "are ")
          << number << " item"
          << ((number == 1) ? "" : "s")
          << std::endl;
```

This code determines if the variable `number` is 1 and if so it prints on the console `there is 1 item`. This is because in both conditionals, if the value of the `number` variable is 1, the test is `true` and the first expression is used. Note that there is a pair of parentheses around the entire operator. The reason is that the stream `<<` operator is overloaded, and you want the compiler to choose the version that takes a string, which is the type returned by the operator rather than `bool`, which is the type of the expression `(number == 1)`.

If the value returned by the conditional operator is an lvalue then you can use it on the left-hand side of an assignment. This means that you can write the following, rather odd, code:

```
int i = 10, j = 0;
((i < j) ? i : j) = 7;
// i is 10, j is 7

i = 0, j = 10;
((i < j) ? i : j) = 7;
// i is 7, j is 10
```

The conditional operator checks to see if `i` is less than `j` and if so it assigns a value to `i`; otherwise, it assigns `j` with that value. This code is terse, but it lacks readability. It is far better in this case to use an `if` statement.

# Selecting

If you want to test to see if a variable is one of several values, using multiple `if` statements becomes cumbersome. The C++ `switch` statement fulfills this purpose much better. The basic syntax is shown here:

```
int i;
std::cin >> i;
switch(i)
{
```

```
case 1:
    std::cout << "one" << std::endl;
    break;
case 2:
    std::cout << "two" << std::endl;
    break;
default:
    std::cout << "other" << std::endl;
}
```

Each case is essentially a label as to the specific code to be run if the selected variable is the specified value. The default clause is for values where there exists no case. You do not have to have a default clause, which means that you are testing only for specified cases. The default clause could be for the most common case (in which case, the cases filter out the less likely values) or it could be for exceptional values (in which case, the cases handle the most likely values).

A switch statement can only test integer types (which includes enum), and you can only test for constants. The char type is an integer, and this means that you can use characters in the case items, but only individual characters; you cannot use strings:

```
char c;
std::cin >> c;
switch(c)
{
    case 'a':
        std::cout << "character a" << std::endl;
        break;
    case 'z':
        std::cout << "character z" << std::endl;
        break;
    default:
        std::cout << "other character" << std::endl;
}
```

The break statement indicates the end of the statements executed for a case. If you do not specify it, execution will *fall through* and the following case statements will be executed even though they have been specified for a different case:

```
switch(i)
{
    case 1:
        std::cout << "one" << std::endl;
        // fall thru
    case 2:
        std::cout << "less than three" << std::endl;
```

```
        break;
    case 3:
        std::cout << "three" << std::endl;
        break;
    case 4:
        break;
        default:
        std::cout << "other" << std::endl;
    }
```

This code shows the importance of the break statement. A value of 1 will print both one and less than three to the console, because execution *falls through* to the preceding case, even though that case is for another value.

It is usual to have different code for different cases, so you will most often finish a case with break. It is easy to miss out a break by mistake, and this will lead to unusual behavior. It is good practice to document your code when deliberately missing out the break statement so that you know that if a break is missing, it is likely to be a mistake.

You can provide zero or more statements for each case. If there is more than one statement, they are all executed for that specific case. If you provide no statements (as for case 4 in this example) then it means that no statements will be executed, not even those in the default clause.

The break statement means *break out of this code block,* and it behaves like this in the loop statements while and for as well. There are other ways that you can break out of a switch. A case could call return to finish the function where the switch is declared; it can call goto to jump to a label, or it can call throw to throw an exception that will be caught by an exception handler outside the switch, or even outside the function.

So far, the cases are in numeric order. This is not a requirement, but it does make the code more readable, and clearly, if you want to *fall through* the case statements (as in case 1 here), you should pay attention to the order the case items.

If you need to declare a temporary variable in a case handler then you must define a code block using braces, and this will make the scope of the variable localized to just that code block. You can, of course, use any variable declared outside of the switch statement in any of the case handlers.

Since enumerated constants are integers, you can test an `enum` in a `switch` statement:

```
enum suits { clubs, diamonds, hearts, spades };

void print_name(suits card)
{
    switch(card)
    {
        case suits::clubs:
            std::cout << "card is a club";
            break;
        default:
            std::cout << "card is not a club";
    }
}
```

Although the `enum` here is not scoped (it is neither `enum class` nor `enum struct`), it is not required to specify the scope of the value in the `case`, but it makes the code more obvious what the constant refers to.

# Looping

Most programs will need to loop through some code. C++ provides several ways to do this, either by iterating with an indexed value or testing a logical condition.

## Looping with Iteration

There are two versions of the `for` statement, iteration and range-based. The latter was introduced in C++11. The iteration version has the following format:

```
for (init_expression; condition; loop_expression)
    loop_statement;
```

You can provide one or more loop statements, and for more than one statement, you should provide a code block using braces. The purpose of the loop may be served by the loop expression, in which case you may not want a loop statement to be executed; here, you use the null statement, `;` which means *do nothing*.

Within the parentheses are three expressions separated by semicolons. The first expression allows you to declare and initialize a loop variable. This variable is scoped to the `for` statement, so you can only use it in the `for` expressions or in the loop statements that follow. If you want more than one loop variable, you can declare them in this expression using the comma operator.

The `for` statement will loop while the condition expression is `true`; so if you are using a loop variable, you can use this expression to check the value of the loop variable. The third expression is called at the end of the loop, after the loop statement has been called; following this, the condition expression is called to see if the loop should continue. This final expression is often used to update the value of the loop variable. For example:

```
for (int i = 0; i < 10; ++i)
{
    std::cout << i;
}
```

In this code, the loop variable is `i` and it is initialized to zero. Next, the condition is checked, and since `i` will be less than 10, the statement will be executed (printing the value to the console). The next action is the loop expression; `++i`, is called, which increments the loop variable, `i`, and then the condition is checked, and so on. Since the condition is `i < 10`, this means that this loop will run ten times with a value of `i` between 0 and 9 (so you will see **0123456789** on the console).

The loop expression can be any expression you like, but often it increments or decrements a value. You do not have to change the loop variable value by 1; for example, you can use `i -= 5` as the loop expression to decrease the variable by 5 on each loop. The loop variable can be any type you like; it does not have to be integer, it does not even have to be numeric (for example, it could be a pointer, or an **iterator object** described in Chapter 5, *Using the Standard Library Containers*), and the condition and loop expression do not have to use the loop variable. In fact, you do not have to declare a loop variable at all!

If you do not provide a loop condition then the loop will be infinite, unless you provide a check in the loop:

```
for (int i = 0; ; ++i)
{
    std::cout << i << std::endl;
    if (i == 10) break;
}
```

This uses the `break` statement introduced earlier with the `switch` statement. It indicates that execution exits the `for` loop, and you can also use `return`, `goto`, or `throw`. You will rarely see a statement that finishes using `goto`; however, you may see the following:

```
for (;;)
{
    // code
}
```

In this case, there is no loop variable, no loop expression, and no conditional. This is an everlasting loop, and the code within the loop determines when the loop finishes.

The third expression in the `for` statement, the loop expression, can be anything you like; the only property is that it is executed at the end of a loop. You may choose to change another variable in this expression, or you can even provide several expressions separated by the comma operator. For example, if you have two functions, one called `poll_data` that returns `true` if there is more data available and `false` when there is no more data, and a function called `get_data` that returns the next available data item, you could use `for` as follows (bear in mind; this is a contrived example, to make a point):

```
for (int i = -1; poll_data(); i = get_data())
{
    if (i != -1) std::cout << i << std::endl;
}
```

When `poll_data` returns a `false` value, the loop will end. The `if` statement is needed because the first time the loop is called, `get_data` has not yet been called. A better version is as follows:

```
for (; poll_data() ;)
{
    int i = get_data();
    std::cout << i << std::endl;
}
```

Keep this example in mind for the following section.

There is one other keyword that you can use in a `for` loop. In many cases, your `for` loop will have many lines of code and at some point, you may decide that the current loop has completed and you want to start the next loop (or, more specifically, execute the loop expression and then test the condition). To do this, you can call `continue`:

```
for (float divisor = 0.f; divisor < 10.f; ++divisor)
{
    std::cout << divisor;
    if (divisor == 0)
    {
        std::cout << std::endl;
        continue;
    }
    std::cout << " " << (1 / divisor) << std::endl;
}
```

In this code, we print the reciprocal of the numbers 0 to 9 (0.f is a 4-byte floating-point literal). The first line in the for loop prints the loop variable, and the next line checks to see if the variable is zero. If it is, it prints a new line and continues, that is, the last line in the for loop is not executed. The reason is that the last line prints the reciprocal and it would be an error to divide any number by zero.

C++11 introduces another way to use the for loop, which is intended to be used with containers. The C++ standard library contains **templates** for container classes. These classes contain collections of objects, and provide access to those items in a standard way. The standard way is to iterate through collections using an **iterator** object. More details about how to do this will be given in Chapter 5, *Using the Standard Library Containers*; the syntax requires an understanding of pointers and iterators, so we will not cover them here. The range-based for loop gives a simple mechanism to access items in a container without explicitly using iterators.

The syntax is simple:

```
for (for_declaration : expression) loop_statement;
```

The first thing to point out is that there are only two expressions and they are separated by a colon (:). The first expression is used to declare the loop variable, which is of the type of the items in the collection being iterated through. The second expression gives access to the collection.

In C++ terms, the collections that can be used are those that define a begin and end function that gives access to iterators, and also to stack-based arrays (that the compiler knows the size of).

The Standard Library defines a container object called a vector. The vector template is a class that contains items of the type specified in the angle brackets (<>); in the following code, the vector is initialized in a special way that is new to C++11, called **list initialization**. This syntax allows you to specify the initial values of the vector in a list between curly braces. The following code creates and initializes a vector, and then uses an iteration for loop to print out all the values:

```
using namespace std;
vector<string> beatles = { "John", "Paul", "George", "Ringo" };

for (int i = 0; i < beatles.size(); ++i)
{
    cout << beatles.at(i) << endl;
}
```

Here a `using` statement is used so that the classes `vector` and `string` do not have to be used with fully qualified names.

The `vector` class has a member function called `size` (called through the `.` operator, which means "call this function on this object") that returns the number of items in the `vector`. Each item is accessed using the `at` function passing the item's index. The one big problem with this code is that it uses random access, that is, it accesses each item using its index. This is a property of `vector`, but other Standard Library container types do not have random access. The following uses the range-based `for`:

```
vector<string> beatles = { "John", "Paul", "George", "Ringo" };

for (string musician : beatles)
{
    cout << musician << endl;
}
```

This syntax works with any of the standard container types and for arrays allocated on the stack:

```
int birth_years[] = { 1940, 1942, 1943, 1940 };

for (int birth_year : birth_years)
{
    cout << birth_year << endl;
}
```

In this case, the compiler knows the size of the array (because the compiler has allocated the array) and so it can determine the range. The range-based `for` loop will iterate through all the items in the container, but as with the previous version you can leave the `for` loop using `break`, `return`, `throw`, or `goto`, and you can indicate that the next loop should be executed using the `continue` statement.

# Conditional Loops

In the previous section we gave a contrived example, where the condition in the `for` loop polled for data:

```
for (; poll_data() ;)
{
    int i = get_data();
    std::cout << i << std::endl;
}
```

In this example, there is no loop variable used in the condition. This is a candidate for the `while` conditional loop:

```
while (poll_data())
{
    int i = get_data();
    std::cout << i << std::endl;
}
```

The statement will continue to loop until the expression (`poll_data` in this case) has a value of `false`. As with `for`, you can exit the `while` loop with `break`, `return`, `throw`, or `goto`, and you can indicate that the next loop should be executed using the `continue` statement.

The first time the `while` statement is called, the condition is tested before the loop is executed; in some cases you may want the loop executed at least once, and then test the condition (most likely dependent upon the action in the loop) to see if the loop should be repeated. The way to do this is to use the `do-while` loop:

```
int i = 5;
do
{
    std::cout << i-- << std::endl;
} while (i > 0);
```

Note the semicolon after the `while` clause. This is required.

This loop will print 5 to 1 in reverse order. The reason is that the loop starts with `i` initialized to 5. The statement in the loop decrements the variable through a postfix operator, which means the value before the decrement is passed to the stream. At the end of the loop, the `while` clause tests to see if the variable is greater than zero. If this test is `true`, the loop is repeated. When the loop is called with `i` assigned to 1, the value of 1 is printed to the console and the variable decremented to zero, and the `while` clause will test an expression that is `false` and the looping will finish.

The difference between the two types of loop is that the condition is tested before the loop is executed in the `while` loop, and so the loop may not be executed. In a `do-while` loop, the condition is called after the loop, which means that, with a `do-while` loop, the loop statements are always called at least once.

# Jumping

C++ supports jumps, and in most cases, there are better ways to branch code; however, for completeness, we will cover the mechanism here. There are two parts to a jump: a labeled statement to jump to and the `goto` statement. A label has the same naming rules as a variable; it is declared suffixed with a colon, and it must be before a statement. The `goto` statement is called using the label's name:

```cpp
int main()
{
    for (int i = 0; i < 10; ++i)
    {
        std::cout << i << std::endl;
        if (i == 5) goto end;
    }

end:
    std::cout << "end";
}
```

The label must be in the same function as the calling `goto`.

Jumps are rarely used, because they encourage you to write non-structured code. However, if you have a routine with highly nested loops or `if` statements, it may make more sense and be more readable to use a `goto` to jump to clean up code.

# Using C++ language features

Let's now use the features you have learned in this chapter to write an application. This example is a simple command-line calculator; you type an expression such as 6 * 7, and the application parses the input and performs the calculation.

Start Visual C++ and click the **File** menu, and then **New**, and finally, click on the **File...** option to get the **New File** dialog. In the left-hand pane, click on **Visual C++**, and in the middle pane, click on **C++ File (.cpp),** and then click on the **Open** button. Before you do anything else, save this file. Using a Visual C++ console (a command line, which has the Visual C++ environment), navigate to the `Beginning_C++` folder and create a new folder called `Chapter_02`. Now, in Visual C++, on the **File** menu, click **Save Source1.cpp As...** and in the **Save File As** dialog locate the `Chapter_02` folder you just created. In the **File name** box, type **calc.cpp** and click on the **Save** button.

The application will use `std::cout` and `std::string`; so at the top of the file, add the headers that define these and, so that you do not have to use fully qualified names, add a `using` statement:

```
#include <iostream>
#include <string>

using namespace std;
```

You will pass the expression via the command-line, so add a `main` function that takes command line parameters at the bottom of the file:

```
int main(int argc, char *argv[])
{
}
```

The application handles expressions in the form `arg1 op arg2` where `op` is an operator and `arg1` and `arg2` are the arguments. This means that, when the application is called, it must have four parameters; the first is the command used to start the application and the last three are the expression. The first code in the `main` function should ensure that the right number of parameters is provided, so at the top of this function add a condition, as follows:

```
if (argc != 4)
{
    usage();
    return 1;
}
```

If the command is called with more or less than four parameters, a function `usage` is called, and then the `main` function returns, stopping the application.

Add the `usage` function before the `main` function, as follows:

```
void usage()
{
    cout << endl;
    cout << "calc arg1 op arg2" << endl;
    cout << "arg1 and arg2 are the arguments" << endl;
    cout << "op is an operator, one of + - / or *" << endl;
}
```

This simply explains how to use the command and explains the parameters. At this point, you can compile the application. Since you are using the C++ Standard Library, you will need to compile with support for C++ exceptions, so type the following at the command-line:

```
C:\Beginning_C++Chapter_02\cl /EHsc calc.cpp
```

If you typed in the code without any mistakes, the file should compile. If you get any errors from the compiler, check the source file to see if the code is exactly as given in the preceding code. You may get the following error:

```
'cl' is not recognized as an internal or external command,
operable program or batch file.
```

This means that the console is not set up with the Visual C++ environment, so either close it down and start the console via the Windows Start menu, or run the **vcvarsall.bat** batch file.

Once the code has compiled you may run it. Start by running it with the correct number of parameters (for example, `calc 6 * 7`), and then try it with an incorrect number of parameters (for example, `calc 6 * 7 / 3`). Note that the space between the parameters is important:

```
C:\Beginning_C++Chapter_02>calc 6 * 7

C:\Beginning_C++Chapter_02>calc 6 * 7 / 3

calc arg1 op arg2
arg1 and arg2 are the arguments
op is an operator, one of + - / or *
```

In the first case, the application does nothing, so all you see is a blank line. In the second example, the code has determined that there are not enough parameters, and so it prints the usage information to the console.

Next, you need to do some simple parsing of the parameters to check that the user has passed valid values. At the bottom of the `main` function, add the following:

```
string opArg = argv[2];
if (opArg.length() > 1)
{
    cout << endl << "operator should be a single character" << endl;
    usage();
    return 1;
}
```

The first line initializes a C++ `std::string` object with the third command-line parameter, which should be the operator in the expression. This simple example only allows a single character for the operator, so the subsequent lines check to make sure that the operator is a single character. The C++ `std::string` class has a member function called `length` that returns the number of characters in the string.

The `argv[2]` parameter will have a length of at least one character (a parameter with no length will not be treated as a command-line parameter!), so we have to check if the user typed an operator longer than one character.

Next you need to test to ensure that the parameter is one of the restricted set allowed and, if the user types another operator, print an error and stop the processing. At the bottom of the `main` function, add the following:

```
char op = opArg.at(0);
if (op == 44 || op == 46 || op < 42 || op > 47)
{
    cout << endl << "operator not recognized" << endl;
    usage();
    return 1;
}
```

The tests are going to be made on a character, so you need to extract this character from the `string` object. This code uses the `at` function, which is passed the index of the character you need. (`Chapter 5`, *Using the Standard Library Containers*, will give more details about the members of the `std::string` class.) The next line checks to see if the character is not supported. The code relies on the following values for the characters that we support:

| Character | Value |
|-----------|-------|
| +         | 42    |
| *         | 43    |
| -         | 45    |
| /         | 47    |

As you can see, if the character is less than `42` or greater than `47` it will be incorrect, but between `42` and `47` there are two characters that we also want to reject: `,` (`44`) and `.` (`46`). This is why we have the preceding conditional: "if the character is less than **42** or greater than **47**, or it is **44** or **46**, then reject it."

The `char` data type is an integer, which is why the test uses integer literals. You could have used character literals, so the following change is just as valid:

```
if (op == ',' || op == '.' || op < '+' || op > '/')
{
    cout << endl << "operator not recognized" << endl;
    usage();
    return 1;
}
```

You should use whichever you find the most readable. Since it makes less sense to check whether one character is *greater than* another, this book will use the former.

At this point, you can compile the code and test it. First try with an operator that is more than one character (for example, `**`) and confirm that you get the message that the operator should be a single character. Secondly, test with a character that is not a recognized operator; try any character other than +, *, -, or /, but it is also worth trying . and ,.

Bear in mind that the command prompt has special actions for some symbols, such as "&" and "|", and the command prompt may give you an error from it by parsing the command-line before even calling your code.

The next thing to do is to convert the arguments into a form that the code can use. The command-line parameters are passed to the program in an array of strings; however, we are interpreting some of those parameters as floating-point numbers (in fact, double-precision floating-point numbers). The C runtime provides a function called atof, which is available through the C++ Standard Library (in this case, <iostream> includes files that include <cmath>, where atof is declared).

It is a bit counter-intuitive to get access to a math function such as atof through including a file associated with stream input and output. If this makes you uneasy, you can add a line after the include lines to include the <cmath> file. The C++ Standard Library headers have been written to ensure that a header file is only included once, so including <cmath> twice has no ill effect. This was not done in the preceding code, because it was argued that atof is a string function and the code includes the <string> header and, indeed, <cmath> is included via the files the <string> header includes.

Add the following lines to the bottom of the main function. The first two lines convert the second and fourth parameters (remember, C++ arrays are zero-based indexed) to double values. The final line declares a variable to hold the result:

```
double arg1 = atof(argv[1]);
double arg2 = atof(argv[3]);
double result = 0;
```

Now we need to determine which operator was passed and perform the requested action. We will do this with a switch statement. We know that the op variable will be valid, and so we do not have to provide a default clause to catch the values we have not tested for. Add a switch statement to the bottom of the function:

```
double arg1 = atof(argv[1]);
double arg2 = atof(argv[3]);
double result = 0;

switch(op)
{
}
```

The first three cases, +, −, and *, are straightforward:

```
switch (op)
{
    case '+':
        result = arg1 + arg2;
        break;
    case '-':
        result = arg1 - arg2;
        break;
    case '*':
        result = arg1 * arg2;
        break;
}
```

Again, since char is an integer, you can use it in a switch statement, but C++ allows you to check for the character values. In this case, using characters rather than numbers makes the code much more readable.

After the switch, add the final code to print out the result:

```
cout << endl;
cout << arg1 << " " << op << " " << arg2;
cout << " = " << result << endl;
```

You can now compile the code and test it with calculations that involve +, −, and *.

Division is a problem, because it is invalid to divide by zero. To test this out, add the following lines to the bottom of the switch:

```
case '/':
    result = arg1 / arg2;
    break;
```

Compile and run the code, passing zero as the final parameter:

```
C:\Beginning_C++Chapter_02>calc 1 / 0
1 / 0 = inf
```

The code ran successfully, and printed out the expression, but it says that the result is an odd value of inf. What is happening here?

The division by zero assigned `result` to a value of NAN, which is a constant defined in `<math.h>` (included via `<cmath>`), and means "not a number." The `double` overload of the insertion operator for the `cout` object tests to see if the number has a valid value, and if the number has a value of NAN, it prints the string **inf**. In our application, we can test for a zero divisor, and we treat the user action of passing a zero as being an error. Thus, change the code so that it reads as follows:

```
case '/':
if (arg2 == 0) {
    cout << endl << "divide by zero!" << endl;
    return 1;
} else {
    result = arg1 / arg2;
}
break;
```

Now when the user passes zero as a divisor, you will get a `divide by zero!` message.

You can now compile the full example and test it out. The application supports floating-point arithmetic using the +, −, *, and / operators, and will handle the case of dividing by zero.

# Summary

In this chapter, you have learned how to format your code, and how to identify expressions and statements. You have learned how to identify the scope of variables, and how to group collections of functions and variables into namespaces so that you can prevent name clashes. You have also learned the basic plumbing in C++ of looping and branching code, and how the built-in operators work. Finally, you put all of this together in a simple application that allows you to perform simple calculations at the command line.

In the following chapter, you will learn about working with memory, arrays, and pointers.

# Working with Memory, Arrays, and Pointers

# 2

C++ allows you to have direct access to memory through pointers. This gives you a lot of flexibility, and potentially it allows you to improve the performance of your code by eliminating some unnecessary copying of data. However, it also provides an extra source of errors; some can be fatal for your application or worse (yes, worse than fatal!) because poor use of memory buffers can open security holes in your code that can allow malware to take over the machine. Clearly pointers are an important aspect of C++.

In this chapter, you'll see how to declare pointers and initialize them to memory locations, how to allocate memory on the stack and, C++ free store, and how to use C++ arrays.

## Using memory in C++

C++ uses the same syntax as C to declare pointer variables and assign them to memory addresses, and it has C-like pointer arithmetic. Like C, C++ also allows you to allocate memory on the stack, so there is automatic memory cleanup when the stack frame is destroyed, and dynamic allocation (on the C++ free store) where the programmer has the responsibility to release memory. This section will cover these concepts.

# Using C++ pointer syntax

The syntax to access memory in C++ is straightforward. The & operator returns the address of an object. That *object* can be a variable, a built-in type or the instance of a custom type, or even a function (function pointers will be covered in the next chapter). The address is assigned a typed pointer variable or a void* pointer. A void* pointer should be treated as merely storage for the memory address because you cannot access data and you cannot perform pointer arithmetic (that is, manipulate the pointer value using arithmetic operators) on a void* pointer. Pointer variables are usually declared using a type and the * symbol. For example:

```
int i = 42;
int *pi = &i;
```

In this code, the variable i is an integer, and the compiler and linker will determine where this variable will be allocated. Usually, a variable in a function will be on a stack frame, as described in a later section. At runtime, the stack will be created (essentially a chunk of memory will be allocated) and space will be reserved in the stack memory for the variable i. The program then puts a value (42) in that memory. Next, the address of the memory allocated for the variable i is placed in the variable pi. The memory usage of the previous code is illustrated in the following diagram:

The pointer holds a value of 0x007ef8c (notice that the lowest byte is stored in the lowest byte in memory; this is for an x86 machine). The memory location 0x007ef8c has a value of 0x0000002a, that is, a value of 42, the value of the variable i. Since pi is also a variable, it also occupies space in memory, and in this case the compiler has put the pointer *lower* in memory than the data it points to and, in this case, the two variables are not contiguous.

With variables allocated on the stack like this, you should make no assumptions about where in memory the variables are allocated, nor their location in relation to other variables.

This code assumes a 32-bit operating system, and so the pointer `pi` occupies 32 bits and contains a 32-bit address. If the operating system is 64 bits then the pointer will be 64 bits wide (but the integer may still be 32 bits). In this book, we will use 32-bit pointers for the simple convenience that 32-bit addresses take less typing than 64-bit addresses.

The typed pointer is declared with a * symbol and we will refer to this as an `int*` pointer because the pointer points to memory that holds an `int`. When declaring a pointer, the convention is to put the * next to the variable name rather than next to the type. This syntax emphasizes that the *type pointed* to is an `int`. However, it is important to use this syntax if you declare more than one variable in a single statement:

```
int *pi, i;
```

It is clear that the first variable is an `int*` pointer and the second is an `int`. The following is not so clear:

```
int* pi, i;
```

You might interpret this to mean that the type of both variables is `int*`, *but this is not the case*, as this declares a pointer and an `int`. If you want to declare two pointers, then apply * to each variable:

```
int *p1, *p2;
```

It is probably better just to declare the two pointers on separate lines.

When you apply the `sizeof` operator to a pointer, you will get the size of the pointer, not what it points to. Thus, on an x86 machine, `sizeof(int*)` will return 4; and on an x64 machine, it will return 8. This is an important observation, especially when we discuss C++ built-in arrays in a later section.

To access the data pointed to by a pointer, you must **dereference** it using the * operator:

```
int i = 42;
int *pi = &i;
int j = *pi;
```

Used like this on the right-hand side of an assignment, the dereferenced pointer gives access to the value pointed to by the pointer, so `j` is initialized to 42. Compare this to the declaration of a pointer, where the * symbol is also used, but has a different meaning.

The dereference operator does more than give read access to the data at the memory location. As long as the pointer does not restrict it (using the `const` keyword; see later), you can dereference the pointer to write to a memory location too:

```
int i = 42;
cout << i << endl;
int *pi { &i };
*pi = 99;
cout << i << endl;
```

In this code, the pointer `pi` points to the location in memory of the variable `i` (in this case, using the brace syntax). Assigning the dereferenced pointer assigns the value to the location that the pointer points to. The result is that on the last line, the variable `i` will have a value of 99 and not 42.

# Using Null Pointers

A pointer could point to anywhere in the memory installed in your computer, and assignment through a dereferenced pointer means that you could potentially write over sensitive memory used by your operating system, or (through direct memory access) write to memory used by hardware on your machine. However, operating systems will usually give an executable a specific memory range that it can access, and attempts to access memory out of this range will cause an operating system memory access violation.

For this reason, you should almost always obtain pointer values using the `&` operator or from a call to an operating system function. You should not give a pointer an absolute address. The only exception to this is the C++ constant for an invalid memory address, `nullptr`:

```
int *pi = nullptr;
// code
int i = 42;
pi = &i;
// code
if (nullptr != pi) cout << *pi << endl;
```

This code initializes the pointer `pi` to `nullptr`. Later in the code, the pointer is initialized to the address of an integer variable. Still later in the code, the pointer is used, but rather than calling it immediately, the pointer is first checked to ensure that it has been initialized to a non-null value. The compiler will check to see if you are about to use a variable that has not been initialized, but if you are writing library code, the compiler will not know whether the callers of your code will use pointers correctly.

The type of constant `nullptr` is not an integer, it is `std::nullptr_t`. All pointer types can be implicitly converted to this type, so `nullptr` can be used to initialize variables of all pointer types.

# Types of Memory

In general, you can regard memory as being one of four types:

- Static or global
- String pool
- Automatic or stack
- Free store

When you declare a variable at the global level, or if you have a variable declared in a function as `static`, then the compiler will ensure that the variable is allocated from memory that has the same lifetime as the application--the variable is created when the application starts and deleted when the application ends.

When you use a string literal, the data will also, effectively, be a global variable, but stored in a different part of the executable. For a Windows executable, string literals are stored in the `.rdata` PE/COFF section of the executable. The `.rdata` section of the file is for read-only initialized data, and hence you cannot change the data. Visual C++ allows you to go a step further and gives you an option of **string pooling**. Consider this:

```
char *p1 { "hello" };
char *p2 { "hello" };
cout << hex;
cout << reinterpret_cast<int>(p1) << endl;
cout << reinterpret_cast<int>(p2) << endl;
```

In this code, two pointers are initialized with the address of the string literal `hello`. In the following two lines, the address of each pointer is printed on the console. Since the `<<` operator for `char*` treats the variable as a pointer to a string, it will print the string rather than the address of the pointer. To get around this, we call the `reinterpret_cast` operator to convert the pointer to an integer and print the value of the integer.

If you compile the code at the command line using the Visual C++ compiler, you will see two different addresses printed. These two addresses are in the .rdata section and are both read-only. If you compile this code with the /GF switch to enable string pooling (which is default for Visual C++ projects), the compiler will see that the two string literals are the same and will only store one copy in the .rdata section, so the result of this code will be that a single address will be printed on the console twice.

In this code, the two variables p1 and p2 are automatic variables, that is, they are created on the stack created for the current function. When a function is called, a chunk of memory is allocated for the function and this contains space for the parameters passed to the function and the return address of the code that called the function, as well as space for the automatic variables declared in the function. When the function finishes, the stack frame is destroyed.

The **calling convention** of the function determines whether the calling function or the called function has the responsibility to do this. In Visual C++, the default is the __cdecl calling convention, which means the calling function cleans up the stack. The __stdcall calling convention is used by Windows operating system functions and the stack clean up is carried out by the called function. More details will be given in the next chapter.

Automatic variables only last as long as the function and the address of such variables only make any sense within the function. Later in this chapter, you will see how to create arrays of data. Arrays allocated as automatic variables are allocated on the stack to a fixed size determined at compile time. It is possible with large arrays that you could exceed the size of the stack, particularly with functions that are called recursively. On Windows, the default stack size is 1 MB, and on x86 Linux, it is 2 MB. Visual C++ allows you to specify a bigger stack with the /F compiler switch (or the /STACK linker switch). The gcc compiler allows you to change the default stack size with the --stack switch.

The final type of memory is **dynamic memory** created on the **free store** or sometimes known as the **heap**. This is the most flexible way of using memory. As the name suggests, you allocate memory at runtime of a size determined at runtime. The implementation of the free store depends on the C++ implementation but you should regard the free store as having the same lifetime as your application, so memory allocated from the free store should last at least as long as your application.

However, there are potential dangers here, particularly for long-lived applications. All memory allocated from the free store should be returned back to the free store when you have finished with it so that the free store manager can reuse the memory. If you do not return memory appropriately, then potentially the free store manager could run out of memory, which will prompt it to ask the operating system for more memory, and consequently, the memory usage of your application will grow over time, causing performance issues due to memory paging.

# Pointer Arithmetic

A pointer points to memory, and the type of the pointer determines the type of the data that can be accessed through the pointer. So, an int* pointer will point to an integer in memory, and you dereference the pointer (*) to get the integer. If the pointer allows it (it is not marked as const), you can change its value through pointer arithmetic. For example, you can increment or decrement a pointer. What happens to the value of the memory address depends on the type of the pointer. Since a typed pointer points to a type, any pointer arithmetic will change the pointer in units of the *size* of that type.

If you increment an int* pointer, it will point to the *next* integer in memory and the change in the memory address depends on the size of the integer. This is equivalent to array indexing, where an expression such as v[1] means you should start at the memory location of the first item in v and then move one item further in memory and return the item there:

```
int v[] { 1, 2, 3, 4, 5 };
int *pv = v;
*pv = 11;
v[1] = 12;
pv[2] = 13;
*(pv + 3) = 14;
```

The first line allocates an array of five integers on the stack and initializes the values to the numbers 1 to 5. In this example, because an initialization list is used, the compiler will create space for the required number of items, hence the size of the array is not given. If you give the size of the array between the brackets, then the initialization list must not have more items than the array size. If the list has fewer items, then the rest of the items in the array are initialized to the default value (usually zero).

The next line in this code obtains a pointer to the first item in the array. This line is significant: an array name is treated as a pointer to the first item in the array. The following lines alter array items in various ways. The first of these (`*pv`) changes the first item in the array by dereferencing the pointer and assigning it a value. The second (`v[1]`) uses array indexing to assign a value to the second item in the array. The third (`pv[2]`) uses indexing, but this time with a pointer, and assigns a value to the third value in the array. And the final example (`*(pv + 3)`) uses pointer arithmetic to determine the address of the fourth item in the array (remember the first item has an index of 0) and then dereferences the pointer to assign the item a value. After these, the array contains the values { 11, 12, 13, 14, 5 } and the memory layout is illustrated here:

| Before | | | | | After | | | |
|---|---|---|---|---|---|---|---|---|
| pv → | 01 | 00 | 00 | 00 | pv → | 0b | 00 | 00 | 00 |
| | 02 | 00 | 00 | 00 | v[1] → | 0c | 00 | 00 | 00 |
| | 03 | 00 | 00 | 00 | pv[2] → | 0d | 00 | 00 | 00 |
| | 04 | 00 | 00 | 00 | (pv + 3) → | 0e | 00 | 00 | 00 |
| | 05 | 00 | 00 | 00 | | 05 | 00 | 00 | 00 |

If you have a memory buffer containing values (in this example, allocated via an array) and you want to multiply each value by 3, you can do this using pointer arithmetic:

```
int v[] { 1, 2, 3, 4, 5 };
int *pv = v;
for (int i = 0; i < 5; ++i)
{
    *pv++ *= 3;
}
```

The loop statement is complicated, and you will need to refer back to the operator precedence given in Chapter 1, *Understanding Language Features*. The postfix increment operator has the highest precedence, the next highest precedence is the dereference operator (`*`), and finally, the `*=` operator has the lowest of the three operators, so the operators are run in this order: ++, *, *=. The postfix operator returns the value *before* the increment, so although the pointer is incremented to the next item in memory, the expression uses the address before the increment. This address is then dereferenced which is assigned by the assignment operator that replaces the item with the value multiplied by 3. This illustrates an important difference between pointers and array names; you can increment a pointer but you cannot increment an array:

```
pv += 1; // can do this
v += 1; // error
```

You can, of course use indexing (with `[]`) on both array names and pointers.

# Using Arrays

As the name suggests, a C++ built-in array is zero or more items of data of the same type. In C++, square brackets are used to declare arrays and to access array elements:

```
int squares[4];
for (int i = 0; i < 4; ++i)
{
    squares[i] = i * i;
}
```

The `squares` variable is an array of integers. The first line allocates enough memory for *four* integers and then the `for` loop initializes the memory with the first four squares. The memory allocated by the compiler from the stack is contiguous and the items in the array are sequential, so the memory location of `squares[3]` is `sizeof(int)` following on from `squares[2]`. Since the array is created on the stack, the size of the array is an instruction to the compiler; this is not dynamic allocation, so the size has to be a constant.

There is a potential problem here: the size of the array is mentioned twice, once in the declaration and then again in the `for` loop. If you use two different values, then you may initialize too few items, or you could potentially access memory outside the array. The ranged `for` syntax allows you to get access to each item in the array; the compiler can determine the size of the array and will use this in the ranged `for` loop. In the following code, there is a deliberate mistake that shows an issue with array sizes:

```
int squares[5];
for (int i = 0; i < 4; ++i)
{
    squares[i] = i * i;
}
for(int i : squares)
{
    cout << i << endl;
}
```

The size of the array and the range of the first `for` loop do not agree and consequently the last item will not be initialized. The ranged `for` loop, however, will loop through all five items and so will print out some random value for the value of the last value. What if the same code is used but the `squares` array is declared to have three items? It depends on the compiler you are using and whether you are compiling a debug build, but clearly you will be writing to memory *outside* of that allocated to the array.

There are some ways to mitigate these issues. The first one is declaring a constant for the size of the array and use that whenever your code needs to know the array size:

```
constexpr int sq_size = 4;
int squares[sq_size];
for (int i = 0; i < sq_size; ++i)
{
    squares[i] = i * i;
}
```

The array declaration must have a constant for the size, and that is managed by using the `sq_size` constant variable.

You may also want to calculate the size of an already allocated array. The `sizeof` operator, when applied to an array, returns the size in bytes of the *entire* array, so you can determine the size of the array by dividing this value by the size of a single item:

```
int squares[4];
for (int i = 0; i < sizeof(squares)/sizeof(squares[0]); ++i)
{
    squares[i] = i * i;
}
```

This is safer code, but clearly it is verbose. The C runtime library contains a macro called `_countof` that performs this calculation.

# Function parameters

As illustrated, there is an automatic conversion of an array to the appropriate pointer type and this occurs if you pass an array to a function, or return it from a function. This decay to a dumb pointer means that other code can make no assumption about an array size. A pointer could point to memory allocated on the stack where the memory lifetime is determined by the function, or a global variable where the memory lifetime is that of the program, or it could be to memory that is dynamically allocated and the memory is determined by the programmer. There is nothing in a pointer declaration that indicates the type of memory or who is responsible for the deallocation of the memory. Nor is there any information in a dumb pointer of how much memory the pointer points to. When you write code using pointers, you have to be disciplined about how you use them.

A function can have an array parameter, but this means a lot less than it appear to indicate:

```
// there are four tires on each car
bool safe_car(double tire_pressures[4]);
```

This function will check that each member of the array has a value between the minimum and maximum values allowed. There are four tires in use at any one time on a car, so the function *should* be called with an array of four values. The problem is that although it appears that the compiler *should* check that the array passed to the function is the appropriate size, it doesn't. You can call this function like this:

```
double car[4] = get_car_tire_pressures();
if (!safe_car(car)) cout << "take off the road!" << endl;
double truck[8] = get_truck_tire_pressures();
if (!safe_car(truck)) cout << "take off the road!" << endl;
```

Of course, it should have been obvious to the developer that a truck is not a car, and so this developer should not have written this code, but the usual advantage of a compiled language is that the compiler will perform some *sanity checks* for you. In the case of array parameters, it won't.

The reason is that the array is passed as a pointer, so although the parameter appears to be a built-in array, you cannot use facilities you are used to using with arrays like ranged `for`. In fact, if the `safe_car` function calls `sizeof(tire_pressures)`, it will get the size of a double pointer and not 16, the size in bytes of a four `int` array.

This *decay to a pointer* feature of array parameters means that functions will only ever know the size of an array parameter if you explicitly tell it the size. You can use an empty pair of square brackets to indicate that the item should be passed an array, but it really is just the same as a pointer:

```
bool safe_car(double tire_pressures[], int size);
```

Here the function has a parameter that indicates the size of the array. The preceding function is exactly the same as declaring the first parameter to be a pointer. The following is not an overload of the function; it is the *same* function:

```
bool safe_car(double *tire_pressures, int size);
```

The important point is that when you pass an array to a function, the *first dimension* of the array is treated as a pointer. So far arrays have been single dimensional, but they may have more than one dimension.

# Multidimensional Arrays

Arrays can be multidimensional and to add another dimension you add another set of square brackets:

```
int two[2];
int four_by_three[4][3];
```

The first example creates an array of two integers, the second creates a two-dimensional array with 12 integers arranged so that there are four rows of three columns. Of course, *row* and *column* are arbitrary and treat the two-dimensional array like a conventional spreadsheet table, but it helps to visualize how the data is arranged in memory.

Note that there are square brackets around every dimension. C++ is different to other languages in this respect, so a declaration of int x[10,10] will be reported as an error by the C++ compiler.

Initializing multidimensional arrays involves a pair of braces and the data in the order that it will be used to initialize the dimensions:

```
int four_by_three[4][3] { 11,12,13,21,22,23,31,32,33,41,42,43 };
```

In this example, the values having the highest digit reflect the left-most index and the lower digit reflect, the right-most index (in both cases, one more than the actual index). Clearly, you can split this over several lines and use whitespace to group values together to make this more readable. You can also use nested braces. For example:

```
int four_by_three[4][3] = { {11,12,13}, {21,22,23},
                            {31,32,33}, {41,42,43} };
```

If you read the dimensions going left to right, you can read the initialization going into deeper levels of nesting. There are four rows, so within the outer braces, there are four sets of nested braces. There are three columns, and so within the nested braces, there are three initialization values.

Nested braces are not just a convenience for formatting your C++ code, because if you provide an empty pair of braces the compiler will use the default value:

```
int four_by_three[4][3] = { {11,12,13}, {}, {31,32,33}, {41,42,43} };
```

Here, the second-row items are initialized to 0.

When you increase the dimensions, the principle applies: increase the nesting for the right most dimension:

```
int four_by_three_by_two[4][3][2]
    = { { {111,112}, {121,122}, {131,132} },
        { {211,212}, {221,222}, {231,232} },
        { {311,312}, {321,322}, {331,332} },
        { {411,412}, {421,422}, {431,432} }
      };
```

This is four rows of three columns of pairs (as you can see, when the dimensions increase it becomes apparent that the terms **rows** and **columns** are largely arbitrary).

You access items using the same syntax:

```
cout << four_by_three_by_two[3][2][0] << endl; // prints 431
```

In terms of the memory layout, the compiler interprets the syntax in the following way. The first index determines the offset from the beginning of the array in chunks of six integers (3 * 2), the second index indicates the offset within one of these six integer *chunks* itself in chunks of two integers, and the third index is the offset in terms of individual integers. Thus [3][2][0] is *(3 \* 6) + (2 \* 2) + 0 = 22* integers from the beginning, treating the first integer as index zero.

A multidimensional array is treated as arrays of arrays, so the type of each "row" is int[3][2] and we know from the declaration that there are four of them.

# Passing Multidimensional Arrays to Functions

You can pass a multidimensional array to a function:

```
// pass the torque of the wheel nuts of all wheels
bool safe_torques(double nut_torques[4][5]);
```

This compiles and you can access the parameter as a 4x5 array, assuming that this vehicle has four wheels with five nuts on each one.

As stated earlier, when you pass an array, the first dimension will be treated as a pointer, so while you can pass a 4x5 array to this function, you can also pass a 2x5 array and the compiler will not complain. However, if you pass a 4x3 array (that is, the second dimension is not the same as declared in the function), the compiler will issue an error that the array is incompatible. The parameter may be more accurately described as being `double row[][5]`. Since the size of the first dimension is not available, the function should be declared with the size of that dimension:

```
bool safe_torques(double nut_torques[][5], int num_wheels);
```

This says that `nut_torques` is one or more "rows", each of which has five items. Since the array does not provide information about the number of rows it has, you should provide it. Another way to declare this is:

```
bool safe_torques(double (*nut_torques)[5], int num_wheels);
```

The brackets are important here, if you omit them and use `double *nut_torques[5]`, then it means the `*` will refer to the type in the array, that is, the compiler will treat `nut_torques` as a five-element array of `double*` pointers. We have seen an example of such an array before:

```
void main(int argc, char *argv[]);
```

The `argv` parameter is an array of `char*` pointers. You can also declare the `argv` parameter as `char**` which has the same meaning.

In general, if you intend to pass arrays to a function it is best to use custom types, or use the C++ array types.

Using ranged `for` with multidimensional arrays is a bit more complicated than appears on first sight, and requires the use of a reference as explained in the section later in this chapter.

# Using arrays of characters

Strings will be covered in more detail in Chapter 6, *Using Strings*, but it is worth pointing out here that C strings are arrays of characters and are accessed through pointer variables. This means that if you want to manipulate strings, you must manipulate the memory that the pointer points to, and not manipulate the pointer itself.

# Comparing strings

The following allocates two string buffers and it calls the `strcpy_s` function to initialize each with the same string:

```
char p1[6];
strcpy_s(p1, 6, "hello");
char p2[6];
strcpy_s(p2, 6, p1);
bool b = (p1 == p2);
```

The `strcpy_c` function will copy characters from the pointer given in the last parameter (until the terminating `NUL`), into the buffer given in the first parameter, whose maximum size is given in the second parameter. These two pointers are compared in the final line, and this will return a value of `false`. The problem is that the compare function is comparing the values of the pointers, not what the pointers point to. The two buffers have the same string, but the pointers are different, so `b` will be `false`.

The correct way to compare strings is to compare the data character by character to see if they are equal. The C runtime provides `strcmp` that compares two string buffers character by character, and the `std::string` class defines a function called `compare` that will also perform such a comparison; however, be wary of the value returned from these functions:

```
string s1("string");
string s2("string");
int result = s1.compare(s2);
```

The return value is not a `bool` type indicating if the two strings are the same; it is an `int`. These compare functions carry out a lexicographical compare and return a negative value if the parameter (`s2` in this code) is greater than the operand (`s1`) lexicographically, and a positive number if the operand is greater than the parameter. If the two strings are the same, the function returns 0. Remember that a `bool` is `false` for a value of 0 and `true` for non-zero values. The standard library provides an overload for the `==` operator for `std::string`, so it is safe to write code like this:

```
if (s1 == s2)
{
    cout << "strings are the same" << endl;
}
```

The operator will compare the strings contained in the two variables.

# Preventing Buffer Overruns

The C runtime library for manipulating strings is notorious for allowing buffer overruns. For example, the `strcpy` function copies one string to another, and you get access to this through the `<cstring>` header, which is included by the `<iostream>` header. You may be tempted to write something like this:

```
char pHello[5];          // enough space for 5 characters
strcpy(pHello, "hello");
```

The problem is that `strcpy` will copy all the character up to, and including the terminating NULL character and so you will be copying six characters into an array with space for only *five*. You could be taking a string from the user input (say, from a text box on a web page) and think that the array you have allocated is big enough, but a malicious user could provide an excessively long string deliberately bigger than the buffer so that it overwrites other parts of your program. Such *buffer overruns* have caused a lot of programs to be subjected to hackers taking control of servers, so much so that the C string functions have all been replaced by safer versions. Indeed, if you are tempted to type the preceding code, you'll find that `strcpy` is available, but the Visual C++ compiler will issue an error:

```
error C4996: 'strcpy': This function or variable may be unsafe.
Consider using strcpy_s instead. To disable deprecation, use
_CRT_SECURE_NO_WARNINGS. See online help for details.
```

If you have existing code that uses `strcpy`, and you need to make that code compile, you can define the symbol before `<cstring>`:

```
#define _CRT_SECURE_NO_WARNINGS
#include <iostream>
```

An initial attempt to prevent this issue is to call `strncpy`, which will copy a specific number of characters:

```
char pHello[5];              // enough space for 5 characters
strncpy(pHello, "hello", 5);
```

The function will copy up to five characters and then stop. The problem is that the string to copy has five characters and so the result will be no NULL termination. The safer version of this function has a parameter that you can use to say how big the destination buffer is:

```
size_t size = sizeof(pHello)/sizeof(pHello[0]);
strncpy_s(pHello, size, "hello", 5);
```

At runtime this will still cause a problem. You have told the function that the buffer is five characters in size and it will determine that this is not big enough to hold the six characters that you have asked it to copy. Rather than allowing the program to silently continue and the buffer overrun to cause problems, the safer string functions will call a function called the **constraint handler** and the default version will shut down the program on the rationale that a buffer overrun means that the program is compromised.

The C runtime library strings functions were originally written to return the result of the function, the safer versions now return an error value. The `strncpy_s` function can also be told to truncate the copy rather than call the constraint handler:

```
strncpy_s(pHello, size, "hello", _TRUNCATE);
```

The C++ `string` class protects you from such issues.

# Using Pointers in C++

Pointers are clearly very important in C++, but as with any powerful feature, there are issues and dangers, so it is worth pointing out some of the major issues. A pointer points to a single location in memory, and the type of the pointer indicates how the memory location should be interpreted. The very most you can assume is the number of bytes at that position in memory is the size of the type of the pointer. That's it. This means that pointers are inherently unsafe. However, in C++ they are the quickest way to enable code within your process to access large amounts of data.

# Accessing out of Bounds

When you allocate a buffer, whether on the stack or on the free store, and you get a pointer, there is little to stop you from accessing memory you have not allocated--either before or after the position of the buffer. This means that when you use pointer arithmetic, or indexed access on arrays, that you check carefully that you are not going to access data out of bounds. Sometimes the error may not be immediately obvious:

```
int arr[] { 1, 2, 3, 4 };
for (int i = 0; i < 4; ++i)
{
    arr[i] += arr[i + 1]; // oops, what happens when i == 3?
}
```

When you use indexing, you have to keep reminding yourself that arrays are indexed from zero so the highest index is the size of the array minus 1.

# Pointers to Deallocated Memory

This applies to memory allocated on the stack and to memory dynamically allocated. The following is a poorly written function that returns a string allocated on the stack in a function:

```
char *get()
{
    char c[] { "hello" };
    return c;
}
```

The preceding code allocates a buffer of six characters and then initializes it with the five characters of the string literal `hello`, and the `NULL` termination character. The problem is that once the function finishes the stack frame is torn down so that the memory can be re-used, and the pointer will point to memory that could be used by something else. This error is caused by poor programming, but it may not be as obvious as in this example. If the function uses several pointers and performs a pointer assignment, you may not immediately notice that you have returned a pointer to a stack-allocated object. The best course of action is simply not to return raw pointers from functions, but if you do want to use this style of programming, make sure that the memory buffer is passed in through a parameter (so the function does not own the buffer) or is dynamically allocated and you are passing ownership to the caller.

This leads on to another issue. If you call `delete` on a pointer and then later in your code, try to access the pointer, you will be accessing memory that is potentially being used by other variables. To alleviate this problem, you can get into the habit of assigning a pointer to `null_ptr` when you delete it and check for `null_ptr` before using a pointer. Alternatively, you can use a smart pointer object which will do this for you. Smart pointers will be covered in `Chapter 4`, *Classes*.

# Converting Pointers

You can either have typed pointers, or the `void*` pointer. Typed pointers will access the memory as if it is the specified type (this has interesting consequences when you have inheritance with classes, but that will be left for `Chapter 4`, *Classes*. Thus, if you cast a pointer to a different type and dereference it, the memory will be treated as containing the cast type. It rarely makes sense to do this. The `void*` pointer cannot be dereferenced, so you can never access data through a `void*` pointer, to access the data you have to cast the pointer.

The whole reason for the `void*` pointer type is that it can point to anything. In general, `void*` pointers should only be used when the type does not matter to that function. For example, the C `malloc` function returns a `void*` pointer because the function merely allocates memory; it does not care what that memory will be used for.

# Constant Pointers

Pointers can be declared as `const` which, depending on where you apply it, means that the memory the pointer points to is read-only through the pointer, or the value of the pointer is read-only:

```
char c[] { "hello" }; // c can be used as a pointer
*c = 'H';             // OK, can write thru the pointer
const char *ptc {c};  // pointer to constant
cout << ptc << endl;  // OK, can read the memory pointed to
*ptc =  'Y';          // cannot write to the memory
char *const cp {c};   // constant pointer
*cp = 'y';            // can write thru the pointer
cp++;                 // cannot point to anything else
```

Here, `ptc` is a pointer to constant `char`, that is, although you can change what `ptc` points to, and you can read what it points to, you cannot use it to change the memory. On the other hand, `cp` is a constant pointer, which means you can both read and write the memory which the pointer points to, but you cannot change where it points to. It is typical to pass the `const char*` pointers to functions because the functions do not know where the string has been allocated or the size of the buffer (the caller may pass a literal which cannot be changed). Note that there is no `const*` operator so `char const*` is treated as `const char*`, a pointer to a constant buffer.

You can make a pointer constant, change it, or remove it using casts. The following does some fairly pointless changing around of the `const` keyword to prove the point:

```
char c[] { "hello" };
char *const cp1 { c }; // cannot point to any other memory
*cp1 = 'H';            // can change the memory
const char *ptc = const_cast<const char*>(cp1);
ptc++;                 // change where the pointer points to
char *const cp2 = const_cast<char *const>(ptc);
*cp2 = 'a';            // now points to Hallo
```

The pointers cp1 and cp2 can be used to change the memory they point to, but once assigned neither can point to other memory. The first const_cast casts away the const-ness to a pointer that can be changed to point to other memory, but cannot be used to alter that memory, ptc. The second const_cast casts away the const-ness of ptc so that the memory can be changed through the pointer, cp2.

## Changing the Type Pointed To

The static_cast operator is used to convert with a compile-time check, but not a runtime check, so this means that the pointers must be related. The void* pointer can be converted to any pointer, so the following compiles and makes sense:

```
int *pi = static_cast<int*>(malloc(sizeof(int)));
*pi = 42;
cout << *pi << endl;
free(pi);
```

The C malloc function returns a void* pointer so you have to convert it to be able to use the memory. (Of course, the C++ new operator removes the need for such casting.) The built-in types are not "related" enough for static_cast to convert between pointer types, so you cannot use static_cast to convert an int* pointer to a char* pointer, even though int and char are both integer types. For custom types that are related through inheritance, you can cast pointers using static_cast, but there is no runtime check that the cast is correct. To cast with runtime checks you should use dynamic_cast, and more details will be given in Chapters 4, *Classes*.

The reinterpret_cast operator is the most flexible, and dangerous, of the cast operators because it will convert between any pointer types without any type checks. It is inherently unsafe. For example, the following code initializes a wide character array with a literal. The array wc will have six characters, hello followed by NULL. The wcout object interprets a wchar_t* pointer as a pointer to the first character in a wchar_t string, so inserting wc will print the string (every character until the NUL). To get the actual memory location, you have to convert the pointer to an integer:

```
wchar_t wc[] { L"hello" };
wcout << wc << " is stored in memory at ";
wcout << hex;
wcout << reinterpret_cast<int>(wc) << endl;
```

Similarly, if you insert a `wchar_t` into the `wcout` object, it will print the character, not the numeric value. So, to print out the codes for the individual characters, we need to cast the pointer to a suitable integer pointer. This code assumes that a `short` is the same size as a `wchar_t`:

```
wcout << "The characters are:" << endl;
short* ps = reinterpret_cast<short*>(wc);
do
{
    wcout << *ps << endl;
} while (*ps++);
```

# Allocating memory in code

C++ defines two operators, `new` and `delete`, that allocate memory from the free store and release memory back into the free store.

# Allocating individual objects

The `new` operator is used with the type to allocate memory, and it will return a typed pointer to that memory:

```
int *p = new int; // allocate memory for one int
```

The `new` operator will call the *default constructor* for custom types for every object it creates (as explained in `Chapter 4`, *Classes*). Built-in types do not have constructors, so instead a type initialization will occur and this will usually initialize the object to zero (in this example, a zero integer).

In general, you should not use memory allocated for built-in types without explicitly initializing it. In fact, in Visual C++ the debug version of the `new` operator will initialize memory to a value of `0xcd` for every byte, as a visual reminder in the debugger that you have not initialized the memory. For custom types, it is left to the author of the type to initialize allocated memory.

It is important that when you have finished with memory that you return it back to the free store so that the allocator can reuse it. You do this by calling the `delete` operator:

```
delete p;
```

When you delete a pointer, the **destructor** for the object is called. For built-in types, this does nothing. It is good practice to initialize a pointer to `nullptr`, after you have deleted it, and if you use the convention of checking the value of a pointer before using it, this will protect you from using a deleted pointer. The C++ standard says that the `delete` operator will have no effect if you delete a pointer that has a value of `nullptr`.

C++ allows you to initialize a value at the time you call the `new` operator, in two ways:

```
int *p1 = new int (42);
int *p2 = new int {42};
```

For a custom type, the `new` operator will call a constructor on the type; for a built in type, the end result is the same, and is carried out by initializing the item to the value provided. You can also use initialized list syntax, as shown in the second line in the preceding code. It is important to note that the initialization is the memory pointed to, not the pointer variable.

## Allocating Arrays of Objects

You can also create arrays of objects in dynamic memory using the `new` operator. You do this by providing the number of items you want created in a pair of square brackets. The following code allocates memory for two integers:

```
int *p = new int[2];
p[0] = 1;
*(p + 1) = 2;
for (int i = 0; i < 2; ++i) cout << p[i] << endl;
delete [] p;
```

The operator returns a pointer to the type allocated, and you can use pointer arithmetic or array indexing to access the memory. You cannot initialize the memory in the `new` statement; you have to do that after creating the buffer. When you use `new` to create a buffer for more than one object, you must use the appropriate version of the `delete` operator: the `[]` is used to indicate that more than one item is deleted and the destructor for each object will be called. It is important that you always use the right version of `delete` appropriate to the version of `new` used to create the pointer.

Custom types can define their own operator `new` and operator `delete` for individual objects, as well as operator `new[]` and operator `delete[]` for arrays of objects. The custom type author can use these to use custom memory allocation schemes for their objects.

# Handling failed allocations

If the `new` operator cannot allocate the memory for an object, it will throw the `std::bad_alloc` exception and the pointer returned will be `nullptr`. Exceptions are covered in Chapter 7, *Diagnostics and Debugging,* so only a brief outline of the syntax will be given here. It is important that you check for failure to allocate memory in production code. The following code shows how to guard the allocation so that you can catch the `std::bad_alloc` exception and handle it:

```
// VERY_BIG_NUMER is a constant defined elsewhere
int *pi;
try
{
    pi = new int[VERY_BIG_NUMBER];
    // other code
}
catch(const std::bad_alloc& e)
{
    cout << "cannot allocate" << endl;
    return;
}
// use pointer
delete [] pi;
```

If any code in the `try` block throws an exception control it is passed to the `catch` clause, ignoring any other code that has not been executed yet. The `catch` clause checks the type of the exception object and if it is the correct type (in this case an allocation fault), it creates a reference to that object and passes control to the `catch` block, and the scope of the exception reference is this block. In this example, the code merely prints an error, but you would use it to take action to ensure that the memory allocation failure does not affect subsequent code.

# Using Other Versions of the New Operator

Further, a custom type can define a placement operator `new`, which allows you to provide one or more parameters to the custom `new` function. The syntax of the placement `new` is to provide the placement fields through parentheses.

The C++ Standard Library version of the `new` operator provides a version that can take the constant `std::nothrow` as a placement field. This version will not throw an exception if the allocation fails, instead, the failure can only be assessed from the value of the returned pointer:

```
int *pi = new (std::nothrow) int [VERY_BIG_NUMBER];
if (nullptr == pi)
{
    cout << "cannot allocate" << endl;
}
else
{
    // use pointer
    delete [] pi;
}
```

The parentheses before the type are used to pass placement fields. If you use parentheses after the type, these will give a value to initialize the object if the allocation is successful.

## Memory lifetime

The memory allocated by `new` will remain valid until you call `delete`. This means that you may have memory with long lifetimes, and the code may be passed around various functions in your code. Consider this code:

```
int *p1 = new int(42);
int *p2 = do_something(p1);
delete p1;
p1 = nullptr;
// what about p2?
```

This code creates a pointer and initializes the memory it points to and then passes the pointer to a function, which itself returns a pointer. Since the `p1` pointer is no longer needed, it is deleted and assigned to `nullptr` so that it cannot be used again. This code looks fine, but the problem is what do you do with the pointer returned by the function? Imagine that the function simply manipulates the data pointed to by the pointer:

```
int *do_something(int *p)
{
    *p *= 10;
    return p;
}
```

In effect, calling `do_something` creates a copy of a pointer, but not a copy of what it points to. This means that when the `p1` pointer is deleted, the memory it points to is no longer available, and so the pointer `p2` points to the invalid memory.

This problem can be addressed using a mechanism called **Resource Acquisition Is Initialization (RAII)**, which means using the features of C++ objects to manage resources. RAII in C++ needs classes and in particular, copy constructors and destructors. A smart pointer class can be used to manage a pointer so that when it is copied, the memory it points to is also copied. A destructor is a function that is called automatically when the object goes out of scope and so a smart pointer can use this to free memory. Smart pointers and destructors will be covered in `Chapter 4`, *Classes*.

# The Windows SDK and Pointers

Returning a pointer from a function has its inherent dangers: the responsibility for the memory is passed to the caller, and the caller must ensure that the memory is appropriately de-allocated, otherwise this could cause a memory leak with a corresponding loss of performance. In this section, we will look at some ways that the Window's **Software Development Kit (SDK)** provides access to memory buffers and learn some techniques used in C++.

First, it is worth pointing out that any function in the Windows SDK that returns a string, or has a string parameter, will come in two versions. The version suffixed with A indicates that the function uses ANSI strings, and the W version will use wide character strings. For the purpose of this discussion, it is easier to use the ANSI functions.

The `GetCommandLineA` function has the following prototype (taking into account the Windows SDK `typedef`):

```
char * __stdcall GetCommandLine();
```

All Windows functions are defined as using the `__stdcall` calling convention. Usually, you will see the `typedef` of `WINAPI` used for the `__stdcall` calling convention.

The function can be called like this:

```
//#include <windows.h>
cout << GetCommandLineA() << endl;
```

Notice that we are making no effort to do anything about freeing the returned buffer. The reason is that the pointer points to memory that lives the lifetime of your process, so you *should not* release it. Indeed, if you were to release it, how would you do it? You cannot guarantee that the function was written with the same compiler, or the same libraries that you are using, so you cannot use the C++ `delete` operator or the C `free` function.

When a function returns a buffer, it is important to consult the documentation to see who allocated the buffer, and who should release it.

Another example is `GetEnvironmentStringsA`:

```
char * __stdcall GetEnvironmentStrings();
```

This also returns a pointer to a buffer, but this time the documentation is clear that after using the buffer you should release it. The SDK provides a function to do this called `FreeEnvironmentStrings`. The buffer contains one string for each environment variable in the form `name=value` and each string is terminated by a NUL character. The last string in the buffer is simply a NUL character, that is, there are two NUL characters at the end of the buffer. These functions can be used like this:

```
char *pBuf = GetEnvironmentStringsA();
if (nullptr != pBuf)
{
    char *pVar = pBuf;
    while (*pVar)
    {
        cout << pVar << endl;
        pVar += strlen(pVar) + 1;
    }

    FreeEnvironmentStringsA(pBuf);
}
```

The `strlen` function is part of the C runtime library and it returns the length of a string. You do not need to know how the `GetEnvironmentStrings` function allocates the buffer because the `FreeEnvironmentStrings` will call the correct deallocation code.

There are cases when the developer has the responsibility of allocating a buffer. The Windows SDK provides a function called `GetEnvironmentVariable` to return the value of a named environment variable. When you call this function, you do not know if the environment variable is set, or if it is set, or how big its value is, so this means that you will most likely have to allocate some memory. The prototype of the function is:

```
unsigned long __stdcall GetEnvironmentVariableA(const char *lpName,
    char *lpBuffer, unsigned long nSize);
```

There are two parameters that are pointers to C strings. There is a problem here, a char* pointer could be passing *in* a string to the function, or it could be used to pass in a buffer for a string to be returned *out*. How do you know what a char* pointer is intended to be used for?

You are given a clue with the full parameter declaration. The lpName pointer is marked const so the function will not alter the string it points to; this means that it is an *in* parameter. This parameter is used to pass in the name of the environment variable you want to obtain. The other parameter is simply a char* pointer, so it could be used to pass a string *in* to the function or *out*, or indeed, both *in* and *out*. The only way to know how to use this parameter is to read the documentation. In this case, it is an *out* parameter; the function will return the value of the environment variable in lpBuffer if the variable exists, or if the variable does not exist, the function will leave the buffer untouched and return the value 0. It is your responsibility to allocate this buffer in whatever way you see fit, and you pass the size of this buffer in the last parameter, nSize.

The function's return value has two purposes. It is used to indicate that an error has occurred (just one value, 0, which means you have to call the GetLastError function to get the error), and it is also used to give you information about the buffer, lpBuffer. If the function succeeds, then the return value is the number of characters copied into the buffer excluding the NULL terminating character. However, if the function determines that the buffer is too small (it knows the size of the buffer from the nSize parameter) to hold the environment variable value, no copy will happen, and the function will return the required size of the buffer, which is the number of characters in the environment variable including the NULL terminator.

A common way to call this function is to call it twice, first with a zero-sized buffer and then use the return value to allocate a buffer before calling it again:

```
unsigned long size = GetEnvironmentVariableA("PATH", nullptr, 0);
if (0 == size)
{
    cout << "variable does not exist " << endl;
}
else
{
    char *val = new char[size];
    if (GetEnvironmentVariableA("PATH", val, size) != 0)
    {
        cout << "PATH = ";
        cout << val << endl;
    }
    delete [] val;
}
```

In general, as with all libraries, you have to read the documentation to determine how the parameters are used. The Windows documentation will tell you if a pointer parameter is in, out, or in/out. It will also tell you who owns the memory and whether you have the responsibility for allocating and/or freeing the memory.

Whenever you see a pointer parameter for a function, take special care to check the documentation as to what the pointer is used for and how the memory is managed.

# Memory and the C++ Standard Library

The C++ Standard Library provides various classes to allow you to manipulate collections of objects. These classes, called the **Standard Template Library** (**STL**), provide a standard way to insert items into collection objects and ways to access the items and iterate through entire collections (called iterators). The STL defines collection classes that are implemented as queues, stacks, or as vectors with random access. These classes will be covered in depth Chapter 5, *Using the Standard Library Containers*, so in this section we will limit the discussion to just two classes that behave like C++ built in arrays.

# Standard Library arrays

The C+ Standard Library provides two containers that give random access via an indexer to the data. These two containers also allow you to access the underlying memory and since they guarantee to store the items sequentially and contiguous in memory, they can be used when you are required to provide a pointer to a buffer. These two types are both templates, which means that you can use them to hold built-in and custom types. These two collection classes are array and vector.

# Using the stack-based array class

The array class is defined in the <array> header file. The class allows you to create fixed sized arrays on the stack and, as with built-in arrays, they cannot shrink or expand at runtime. Since they are allocated on the stack, they do not require a call to a memory allocator at runtime, but clearly, they should be smaller than the stack frame size. This means that an array is a good choice for small arrays of items. The size of an array must be known at compile time and it is passed as a template parameter:

```
array<int, 4> arr { 1, 2, 3, 4 };
```

In this code, the first template parameter in the angle brackets (<>) is the type of each item in the array, and the second parameter is the number of items. This code initializes the array with an initialize list, but note that you still have to provide the size of the array in the template. This object will work like a built-in array (or indeed, any of the Standard Library containers) with ranged `for`:

```
for (int i : arr) cout << i << endl;
```

The reason is that `array` implements the `begin` and `end` functions that are required for this syntax. You can also use indexing to access items:

```
for (int i = 0; i < arr.size(); ++i) cout << arr[i] << endl;
```

The `size` function will return the size of the array and the square bracket indexer gives random access to members of the array. You can access memory outside of the bounds of the array, so for the previously defined array that has four members, you can access `arr[10]`. This may cause unexpected behavior at runtime, or even some kind of memory fault. To guard against this, the class provides a function, `at`, which will perform a range check and if the index is out of range the class will throw the C++ exception `out_of_range`.

The main advantage of using an `array` object is that you get compile-time checks to see if you are inadvertently passing the object to a function as a dumb pointer. Consider this function:

```
void use_ten_ints(int*);
```

At runtime, the function does not know the size of the buffer passed to it, and in this case the documentation says that you must pass a buffer with 10 `int` type variables, but, as we have seen, C++ allows a built-in array to be used as a pointer:

```
int arr1[] { 1, 2, 3, 4 };
use_ten_ints(arr1); // oops will read past the end of the buffer
```

There is no compiler check, nor any runtime check to catch this error. The `array` class will not allow such an error to happen because there is no automatic conversion into a dumb pointer:

```
array<int, 4> arr2 { 1, 2, 3, 4 };
use_ten_ints(arr2); // will not compile
```

If you really insist in obtaining a dumb pointer, you can do this and be guaranteed to have access to the data as a contiguous block of memory where the items are stored sequentially:

```
use_ten_ints(&arr2[0]);     // compiles, but on your head be it
use_ten_ints(arr2.data()); // ditto
```

The class is not just a wrapper around a built-in array, it also provides some additional functionality. For example:

```
array<int, 4> arr3;
arr3.fill(42);    // put 42 in each item
arr2.swap(arr3); // swap items in arr2 with items in arr3
```

## Using the Dynamically Allocated Vector Class

The Standard Library also provides the `vector` class in the `<vector>` header. Again, this class is a template, so you can use it with built-in and custom types. However, unlike `array`, the memory is dynamically allocated, which means that a `vector` can be expanded or shrunk at runtime. The items are stored contiguously so you can access the underlying buffer by calling the `data` function or accessing the address of the first item (to support resizing the collection, the buffer may change, so such pointers should only be used temporarily). And, of course, as with `array`, there is no automatic conversion to a dumb pointer. The `vector` class provides indexed random access with square bracket syntax and a range check with the `at` function. The class also implements the methods to allow the container to be used with Standard Library functions and with ranged `for`.

The `vector` class has more flexibility than the `array` class because you can insert items, and move items around, but this does come with some overhead. Because instances of the class allocate memory dynamically at runtime there is a cost of using an allocator and there is some extra overhead in initialization and destruction (when the `vector` object goes out of scope). Objects of the `vector` class also take more memory than the data it holds. For this reason, it is not suitable for small numbers of items (when `array` is a better choice).

# References

A reference is an alias to an object. That is, it is another name for the object, and so access to the object is the same through a reference as it is through the object's variable name. A reference is declared using a `&` symbol on the reference name and it is initialized and accessed in exactly the same way as a variable:

```
int i = 42;
```

```
int *pi = &i;    // pointer to an integer
int& ri1 = i;    // reference to a variable
i = 99;          // change the integer thru the variable
*pi = 101;       // change the integer thru the pointer
ri1 = -1;        // change the integer thru the reference
int& ri2 {i};    // another reference to the variable
int j = 1000;
pi = &j;         // point to another integer
```

In this code, a variable is declared and initialized, then a pointer is initialized to point to this data, and a reference is initialized as an alias for the variable. Reference ri1 is initialized with an assignment operator, whereas reference ri2 is initialized using initializer list syntax.

 The pointer and reference have two different meanings. The reference is not initialized to the value of the variable, the variable's data; it is an alias for the variable name.

Wherever the variable is used, the reference can be used; whatever you do to the reference is actually the same as performing the same operation on the variable. A pointer points to data, so you can change the data by dereferencing the pointer, but equally so, you can make the pointer point to any data and change that data by dereferencing the pointer (this is illustrated in the last two lines of the preceding code). You can have several aliases for a variable, and each must be initialized to the variable at the declaration. Once declared, you cannot make a reference refer to a different object.

The following code will not compile:

```
int& r1;              // error, must refer to a variable
int& r2 = nullptr;    // error, must refer to a variable
```

Since a reference is an alias for another variable, it cannot exist without being initialized to a variable. Likewise, you cannot initialize it to anything other than a variable name, so there is no concept of a *null reference*.

Once initialized, a reference is only ever an alias to the one variable. Indeed, when you use a reference as an operand to any operator, the operation is performed on the variable:

```
int x = 1, y = 2;
int& rx = x; // declaration, means rx is an alias for x
rx = y;      // assignment, changes value of x to the value of y
```

In this code, `rx` is an alias to the variable `x`, so the assignment in the last line simply assigns `x` with the value of `y`: the assignment is performed on the aliased variable. Further, if you take the address of a reference, you are returned the address of the variable it references. While you can have a reference to an array, you cannot have an array of references.

# Constant References

The reference used so far allows you to change the variable it is an alias for, therefore it has lvalue semantics. There are also `const` lvalue references, that is, a reference to an object that you can read, but not write to.

As with `const` pointers, you declare a `const` reference using the `const` keyword on a lvalue reference. This essentially makes the reference read-only: you can access the variable's data to read it, but not to change it.

```
int i = 42;
const int& ri = i;
ri = 99;           // error!
```

# Returning References

Sometimes an object will be passed to a function and the semantics of the function is that the object should be returned. An example of this is the `<<` operator used with the stream objects. Calls to this operator are *chained*:

```
cout << "The value is " << 42;
```

This is actually a series of calls to functions called `operator<<`, one that takes a `const char*` pointer, and another that takes an `int` parameter. These functions also have an `ostream` parameter for the stream object that will be used. However, if this is simply an `ostream` parameter then it would mean that a copy of the parameter would be made, and the insertion would be performed on the copy. Stream objects often use buffering, so changes to a copy of a stream object may not have the desired effect. Further, to enable the *chaining* of the insertion operators, the insertion functions will return the stream object passed as a parameter. The intention is to pass the same stream object through multiple function calls. If such a function returned an object then it would be a copy and not only would this means that a series of insertions would involve lots of copies being made, these copies would also be temporary and so any changes to the stream (for example, manipulators such as `std::hex`) would not persist. To address these issues, references are used. A typical prototype of such a function is:

```
ostream& operator<<(ostream& _Ostr, int _val);
```

Clearly you have to be careful about returning a reference since you have to ensure that the object lifetime lasts as long as the reference. This `operator<<` function will return the reference passed in the first parameter, but in the following code a reference is returned to an automatic variable:

```
string& hello()
{
    string str ("hello");
    return str; // don't do this!
}   // str no longer exists at this point
```

In the preceding code, the `string` object only lives as long as the function, so the reference returned by this function will refer to an object that does not exist. Of course, you can return a reference to a `static` variable declared in a function.

Returning a reference from a function is a common idiom, but whenever you consider doing this make sure that the lifetime of the aliased variable is not the scope of the function.

# Temporaries and References

The lvalue references must refer to a variable, but C++ has some odd rules when it comes to `const` references declared on the stack. If the reference is a `const`, the compiler will extend the lifetime of a temporary for the lifetime of the reference. For example, if you use the initialization list syntax, the compiler will create a temporary:

```
const int& cri { 42 };
```

In this code, the compiler will create a temporary `int` and initialize it to a value and then alias it to the `cri` reference (it is important that this reference is `const`). The temporary is available through the reference while it is in scope. This may look a little odd, but consider using a `const` reference in this function:

```
void use_string(const string& csr);
```

You can call this function with a `string` variable, a variable that will explicitly convert to a `string` or with a `string` literal:

```
string str { "hello" };
use_string(str);        // a std::string object
const char *cstr = "hello";
use_string(cstr);       // a C string can be converted to a std::string
use_string("hello");    // a literal can be converted to a std::string
```

In most cases, you'll not want to have a `const` reference to a built-in type, but with custom types where there will be an overhead in making copies there is an advantage and, as you can see here, the compiler will fall back to creating a temporary if required.

# The rvalue References

C++11 defines a new type of reference, rvalue references. Prior to C++11, there was no way that code (like an assignment operator) could tell if the rvalue passed to it was a temporary object or not. If such a function is passed a reference to an object, then the function has to be careful not to change the reference because this would affect the object it refers to. If the reference is to a temporary object, then the function can do what it likes to the temporary object because the object will not live after the function completes. C++11 allows you to write code specifically for temporary objects, so in the case of the assignment, the operator for temporary objects can just *move* the data from the temporary into the object being assigned. In contrast, if the reference is not to a temporary object then the data will have to be *copied*. If the data is large, then this prevents a potentially expensive allocation and copy. This enables so-called *move semantics*.

Consider this rather contrived code:

```
string global{ "global" };

string& get_global()
{
    return global;
}

string& get_static()
{
    static string str { "static" };
    return str;
}

string get_temp()
{
    return "temp";
}
```

The three functions return a `string` object. In the first two cases, the `string` has the lifetime of the program and so a reference can be returned. In the last function, the function returns a string literal, so a temporary `string` object is constructed. All three can be used to provide a `string` value. For example:

```
cout << get_global() << endl;
cout << get_static() << endl;
cout << get_temp() << endl;
```

All three can provide a string that can be used to assign a `string` object. The important point is that the first two functions return along a lived object, but the third function returns a temporary object, but these objects can be used the same.

If these functions returned access to a large object, you would not want to pass the object to another function, so instead, in most cases, you'll want to pass the objects returned by these functions as references. For example:

```
void use_string(string& rs);
```

The reference parameter prevents another copy of the string. However, this is just half of the story. The `use_string` function could manipulate the string. For example, the following function creates a new `string` from the parameter, but replaces the letters a, b, and o with an underscore (indicating the gaps in words without those letters, replicating what life would be like without donations of the blood types A, B, and O). A simple implementation would look like this:

```
void use_string(string& rs)
{
    string s { rs };
    for (size_t i = 0; i < s.length(); ++i)
    {
        if ('a' == s[i] || 'b' == s[i] || 'o' == s[i])
            s[i] = '_';
    }
    cout << s << endl;
}
```

The string object has an index operator (`[]`), so you can treat it like an array of characters, both reading the values of characters and assigning values to character positions. The size of the `string` is obtained through the `length` function, which returns an `unsigned int` (`typedef` to `size_t`). Since the parameter is a reference, it means that any change to the `string` will be reflected in the `string` passed to the function. The intention of this code is to leave other variables intact, so it first makes a copy of the parameter. Then on the copy, the code iterates through all of the characters changing the a, b, and o characters to an underscore before printing out the result.

This code clearly has a copy overhead--creating the `string`, s, from the reference, `rs`; but this is necessary if we want to pass strings like those from `get_global` or `get_static` to this function because otherwise the changes would be made to the actual global and `static` variables.

However, the temporary `string` returned from `get_temp` is another situation. This temporary object only exists until the end of the statement that calls `get_temp`. Thus, it is possible to make changes to the variable knowing that it will affect nothing else. This means that you can use move semantics:

```cpp
void use_string(string&& s)
{
    for (size_t i = 0; i < s.length(); ++i)
    {
        if ('a' == s[i] || 'b' == s[i] || 'o' == s[i]) s[i] = '_';
    }
    cout << s << endl;
}
```

There are just two changes here. The first is that the parameter is identified as an rvalue reference using the `&&` suffix to the type. The other change is that the changes are made on the object that the reference refers to because we know that it is a temporary and the changes will be discarded, so it will affect no other variables. Note that there are now *two* functions, overloads with the same name: one with an lvalue reference, and one with an rvalue reference. When you call this function, the compiler will call the right one according to the parameter passed to it:

```cpp
use_string(get_global()); // string&   version
use_string(get_static()); // string&   version
use_string(get_temp());   // string&& version
use_string("C string");   // string&& version
string str{"C++ string"};
use_string(str);          // string&   version
```

Recall that `get_global` and `get_static` return references to objects that will live the lifetime of the program, and for this reason the compiler chooses the `use_string` version that takes an lvalue reference. The changes are made on a temporary variable within the function, and this has a copy overhead. The `get_temp` returns a temporary object and so the compiler calls the overload of `use_string` that takes an rvalue reference. This function alters the object that the reference refers to, but this does not matter because the object will not last beyond the semicolon at the end of the line. The same can be said for calling `use_string` with a C-like string literal: the compiler will create a temporary `string` object and call the overload that has an rvalue reference parameter. In the final example in this code, a C++ `string` object is created on the stack and passed to `use_string`.

The compiler sees that this object is an lvalue and potentially can be altered, so it calls the overload that takes an lvalue reference that is implemented in a way that only alters a temporary local variable in the function.

This example shows that the C++ compiler will detect when a parameter is a temporary object and will call the overload with an rvalue reference. Typically, this facility is used when writing *copy constructors* (special functions used to create a new custom type from an existing instance) and assignment operators so that these functions can implement the lvalue reference overload to copy the data from the parameter, and the rvalue reference overload to move the data from the temporary to the new object. Other uses are for writing custom types that are *move only*, where they use resources that cannot be copied, for example file handles.

# Ranged for and References

As an example of what you can do with references, it is worth looking at the ranged `for` facility in C++11. The following code is quite straightforward; the array `squares` is initialized with the squares of 0 to 4:

```
constexpr int size = 4;
int squares[size];

for (int i = 0; i < size; ++i)
{
    squares[i] = i * i;
}
```

The compiler knows the size of the array so you can use ranged `for` to print out the values in the array. In the following, on each iteration, the local variable `j` is a copy of the item in the array. As a copy, it means that you can read the value, but any changes made to the variable will not be reflected to the array. So, the following code works as expected; it prints out the contents of the array:

```
for (int j : squares)
{
    cout << J << endl;
}
```

If you want to change the values in the array, then you have to have access to the actual values, and not a copy. The way to do this in a ranged `for` is to use a reference as the loop variable:

```
for (int& k : squares)
{
    k *= 2;
}
```

Now, on every iteration, the k variable is an alias to an actual member in the array, so whatever you do to the k variable is actually performed on the array member. In this example, every member of the `squares` array is multiplied by 2. You cannot use `int *` for the type of k because the compiler sees that the type of the items in the array is `int` and will use this as the loop variable in the ranged `for`. Since a reference is an alias for a variable, the compiler will allow a reference as the loop variable, and moreover, since the reference is an alias, you can use it to change the actual array member.

Ranged `for` becomes interesting for multidimensional arrays. For example, in the following, a two-dimensional array is declared and an attempt is made to use nested loops using `auto` variables:

```
int arr[2][3] { { 2, 3, 4 }, { 5, 6, 7} };
for (auto row : arr)
{
    for (auto col : row) // will not compile
    {
        cout << col << " " << endl;
    }
}
```

Since a two-dimensional array is an array of arrays (each row is a one-dimensional array), the intention is to obtain each row in the outer loop and then in the inner loop access each item in the row. There are several issues with this approach, but the immediate issue is that this code will not compile.

The compiler will complain about the inner loop, saying that it cannot find a `begin` or `end` function for the type `int *`. The reason is that ranged `for` uses iterator objects and for arrays it uses the C++ Standard Library functions, `begin` and `end`, to create these objects. The compiler will see from the `arr` array in the outer ranged for that each item is an `int[3]` array, and so in the outer `for` loop the loop variable will be a *copy* of each element, in this case an `int[3]` array. You cannot copy arrays like this, so the compiler will provide a pointer to the first element, an `int *`, and this is used in the inner `for` loop.

The compiler will attempt to obtain iterators for `int*`, but this is not possible because an `int*` contains no information about how many items it points to. There is a version of `begin` and `end` defined for `int[3]` (and all sizes of arrays) but not for `int*`.

A simple change makes this code compile. Simply turn the `row` variable into a reference:

```
for (auto& row : arr)
{
    for (auto col : row)
    {
        cout << col << " " << endl;
    }
}
```

The reference parameter indicates that an alias is used for the `int[3]` array and, of course, an alias is the same as the element. Using `auto` hides the ugliness of what is actually going on. The inner loop variable is, of course, an `int` since this is the type of the item in the array. The outer loop variable is in fact `int (&)[3]`. That is, it is a reference to an `int[3]` (the parentheses used to indicate that it references an `int[3]` and is not an array of `int&`).

# Using Pointers in Practice

A common requirement is to have a collection that can be an arbitrary size and can grow and shrink at runtime. The C++ Standard Library provides various classes to allow you to do this, as will be described in `Chapter 5`, *Using the Standard Library Containers*. The following example illustrates some of the principles of how these standard collections are implemented. In general, you should use the C++ Standard Library classes rather than implementing your own. Further, the Standard Library classes *encapsulate* code together in a class and since we have not covered classes yet, the following code will use functions that potentially can be called incorrectly. So, you should regard this example as just that, example code. A linked list is a common data structure. These are typically used for queues where the order of items is important. For example, a first-in-first-out queue where tasks are performed in the order that they are inserted in the queue. In this example, each task is represented as a structure that contains the task description and a pointer to the next task to be performed.

If the pointer to the next task is `nullptr` then this means the current task is the last task in the list:

```
struct task
{
    task* pNext;
    string description;
};
```

You can access members of a structure using the dot operator through an instance:

```
task item;
item.descrription = "do something";
```

In this case, the compiler will create a `string` object initialized with the string literal `do something` and assign it to the `description` member of the instance called `item`. You can also create a `task` on the free store using the `new` operator:

```
task* pTask = new task;
// use the object
delete pTask;
```

In this case, the members of the object have to be accessed through a pointer, and C++ provides the `->` operator to give you this access:

```
task* pTask = new task;
pTask->descrription = "do something";
// use the object
delete pTask;
```

Here the `description` member is assigned to the string. Note that since `task` is a structure there are no access restrictions, something that is important with classes and described in `Chapter 4`, *Classes*.

## Creating the Project

Create a new folder under `C:\Beginning_C++` called `Chapter_04`. Start Visual C++ and create a C++ source file and save it to the folder you just created, as `tasks.cpp`. Add a simple `main` function without parameters, and provide support for input and output using C++ streams:

```
#include <iostream>
#include <string>
using namespace std;
```

```
int main()
{
}
```

Above the `main` function, add a definition for the structure that represents a task in the list:

```
using namespace std;
struct task {
    task* pNext;
    string description;
};
```

This has two members. The guts of the object is the `description` item. In our example, executing a task will involve printing the `description` item to the console. In an actual project, you'll most likely have many data items associated with the task, and you may even have member functions to execute the task, but we have not yet covered member functions; that's a topic for `Chapter 4`, *Classes*.

The plumbing of the linked list is the other member, `pNext`. Note that the `task` structure has not been completely defined at the point that the `pNext` member is declared. This is not a problem because `pNext` is a *pointer*. You cannot have a data member of an undefined, or a partially defined type, because the compiler will not know how much memory to allocate for it. You can have a pointer member to a partially defined type because a pointer member is the same size irrespective of what it points to.

If we know the first link in a list, then we can access the whole list and, in our example, this will be a global variable. When constructing the list, the construction functions need to know the end of the list so that they can attach a new link to the list. Again, for convenience, we will make this a global variable. Add the following pointers after the definition of the `task` structure:

```
task* pHead = nullptr;
task* pCurrent = nullptr;
int main()
{
}
```

As it stands, the code does nothing, but it is a good opportunity to compile the file to test that there are no typos:

```
cl /EHsc tasks.cpp
```

# Adding a Task Object to the List

The next thing to do to provide the code is to add a new task to the task list. This needs to create a new `task` object and initialize it appropriately and then add it to the list by altering the last link in the list to point to the new link.

Above the `main` function, add the following function:

```
void queue_task(const string& name)
{
    . . .
}
```

The parameter is a `const` reference because we will not change the parameter and we do not want the overhead of a copy being made. The first thing this function must do is create a new link, so add the following lines:

```
void queue_task(const string& name)
{
    task* pTask = new task;
    pTask->description = name;
    pTask->pNext = nullptr;
}
```

The first line creates a new link on the free store, and the following lines initialize it. This is not necessarily the best way of initializing such an object, and a better mechanism, a constructor, will be covered in Chapter 4, *Classes*. Notice that the pNext item is initialized to `nullptr`; this indicates that the link will be at the end of the list.

The final part of this function adds the link to the list, that is, it makes the link the last in the list. However, if the list is empty, it means that this link is also the *first* link in the list. The code must perform both actions. Add the following code to the end of the function:

```
if (nullptr == pHead)
{
    pHead = pTask;
    pCurrent = pTask;
}
else
{
    pCurrent->pNext = pTask;
    pCurrent = pTask;
}
```

The first line checks to see if the list is empty. If pHead is nullptr, it means that there are no other links and so the current link is the first link, and so both pHead and pCurrent are initialized to the new link pointer. If there are existing links in the list, the link has to be added to the last link, so in the else clause the first line makes the last link point to the new link and the second line initializes pCurrent with the new link pointer, making the new link the last link for any new insertions to the list.

The items are added to the list by calling this function in the main function. In this example, we will queue the tasks to wallpaper a room. This involves removing the old wallpaper, filling any holes in the wall, sizing the wall (painting it with diluted paste to make the wall sticky), and then hanging the pasted wallpaper to the wall. You have to do these tasks in this order, you cannot change the order, so these tasks are ideal for a linked list. In the main function add the following lines:

```
queue_task("remove old wallpaper");
queue_task("fill holes");
queue_task("size walls");
queue_task("hang new wallpaper");
```

After the last line, the list has been created. The pHead variable points to the first item in the list and you can access any other item in the list simply by following the pNext member from one link to the next.

You can compile the code, but there is no output. Worse, as the code stands, there is a memory leak. The program has no code to delete the memory occupied by the task objects created on the free store by the new operator.

# Deleting the task list

Iterating through the list is simple, you follow the pNext pointer from one link to the next. Before doing this, let's first fix the memory leak introduced in the last section. Above the main function, add the following function:

```
bool remove_head()
{
    if (nullptr == pHead) return false;
    task* pTask = pHead;
    pHead = pHead->pNext;
    delete pTask;
    return (pHead != nullptr);
}
```

This function will remove the link at the beginning of the list and make sure that the pHead pointer points to the next link, which will become the new beginning of the list. The function returns a `bool` value indicating if there are any more links in the list. If this function returns `false` then it means the entire list has been deleted.

The first line checks to see if this function has been called with an empty list. Once we are reassured that the list has at least one link, we create a temporary copy of this pointer. The reason is that the intention is to delete the first item and make pHead point to the next item, and to do that we have to do those steps in reverse: make pHead point to the next item and then delete the item that pHead previously pointed to.

To delete the entire list, you need to iterate through the links, and this can be carried out using a `while` loop. Below the `remove_head` function, add the following:

```
void destroy_list()
{
    while (remove_head());
}
```

To delete the entire list, and address the memory leak, add the following line to the bottom of the main function

```
    destroy_list();
}
```

You can now compile the code, and run it. However, you'll see no output because all the code does is create a list and then delete it.

# Iterating the task list

The next step is to iterate the list from the first link following each pNext pointer until we get to the end of the list. For each link accessed, the task should be executed. Start by writing a function that performs the execution by printing out the description of the task and then returning a pointer to the next task. Just above the `main` function, add the following code:

```
task *execute_task(const task* pTask)
{
    if (nullptr == pTask) return nullptr;
    cout << "executing " << pTask->description << endl;
    return pTask->pNext;
}
```

The parameter here is marked as const because we will not change the task object pointed to by the pointer. This indicates to the compiler that if the code does try to change the object there is an issue. The first line checks to make sure that the function is not called with a null pointer. If it was then the following line would dereference an invalid pointer and cause a memory access fault. The last line returns the pointer to the next link (which could be nullptr for the last link in the list), so that the function can be called in a loop. After this function, add the following to iterate the entire list:

```
void execute_all()
{
    task* pTask = pHead;
    while (pTask != nullptr)
    {
        pTask = execute_task(pTask);
    }
}
```

This code starts at the beginning, pHead, and calls execute_task on each link in the list until the function returns a nullptr. Add a call to this function towards the end of the main function:

```
    execute_all();
    destroy_list();
}
```

You can now compile and run the code. The result will be:

```
    executing remove old wallpaper
  executing fill holes
    executing size walls
    executing hang new wallpaper
```

# Inserting Items

One of the advantages of linked lists is that you can insert items into the list by only allocating one new item and changing the appropriate pointers to point to it, and make it point to the next item in the list. Contrast this to allocating an array of task objects; if you want to insert a new item somewhere in the middle, you would have to allocate a new array big enough for the old items and the new one and then copy the old items to the new array, copying in the new item in the right position.

The problem with the wallpaper task list is that the room has some painted wood and, as any decorator knows, it is best to paint the woodwork before hanging the wallpaper, and usually before sizing the walls. We need to insert a new task between filling any holes and sizing the walls. Further, before you do any decorating, you should cover any furniture in the room before doing anything else, so you need to add a new task to the beginning.

The first step is to find the position where we want to put our new task to paint the woodwork. We will look for the task that we want to be before the task we are inserting. Before `main` add the following:

```
task *find_task(const string& name)
{
    task* pTask = pHead;

    while (nullptr != pTask)
    {
        if (name == pTask->description) return pTask;
        pTask = pTask->pNext;
    }
    return nullptr;
}
```

This code searches the entire list for a link with the `description` that matches the parameter. This is carried out through a loop which uses the `string` comparison operator, and if the required link is found, a pointer to that link is returned. If the comparison fails, the loop initializes the loop variable to the address of the next link and if this address is `nullptr` it means that the required task is not in the list.

After the list is created in the main function, add the following code to search for the `fill holes` task:

```
queue_task("hang new wallpaper");

// oops, forgot to paint woodworktask
* pTask = find_task("fill holes");
if (nullptr != pTask) {
    // insert new item after pTask
}
execute_all();
```

If the `find_task` function returns a valid pointer, then we can add an item at this point.

The function to do this will allow you to add a new item after any item in the list that you pass to it and, if you pass `nullptr`, it will add the new item to the beginning. It's called `insert_after`, but clearly, if you pass `nullptr` it also means *insert before the beginning*.

Add the following just above the `main` function:

```
void insert_after(task* pTask, const string& name)
{
    task* pNewTask = new task;
    pNewTask->description = name;
    if (nullptr != pTask)
    {
        pNewTask->pNext = pTask->pNext;
        pTask->pNext = pNewTask;
    }
}
```

The second parameter is a `const` reference because we will not change the `string`, but the first parameter is not a `const` pointer because we will be changing the object that it points to. This function creates a new `task` object and initializes the `description` member to the new task name. It then checks to see if the `task` pointer passed to the function is null. If it is not, then the new item can be inserted *after* the specified link in the list. To do this, the new link `pNext` member is initialized to be the next item in the list, and the `pNext` member of the previous link is initialized to the address of the new link.

What about inserting an item at the beginning, when the function is passed `nullptr` as the item to insert after? Add the following `else` clause.

```
void insert_after(task* pTask, const string& name)
{
    task* pNewTask = new task;
    pNewTask->description = name;
    if (nullptr != pTask)
    {
        pNewTask->pNext = pTask->pNext;
        pTask->pNext = pNewTask;
    }
    else {
        pNewTask->pNext = pHead;
        pHead = pNewTask;
    }
}
```

Here, we make the `pNext` member of the new item to point to the old beginning of the list and then change `pHead` to point to the new item.

Now, in the `main` function, you can add a call to insert a new task to paint the woodwork, and since we also forgot to indicate that it is best to decorate a room after covering all furniture with dustsheets, add a task to do that first in the list:

```
task* pTask = find_task("fill holes");
if (nullptr != pTask)
{
    insert_after(pTask, "paint woodwork");
}
insert_after(nullptr, "cover furniture");
```

You can now compile the code. When you run the code, you should see the tasks performed in the required order:

```
        executing cover furniture
        executing remove old wallpaper
    executing fill holes
    executing paint woodwork
    executing size walls
    executing hang new wallpaper
```

# Summary

It can be argued that one of the main reasons to use C++ is that you have direct access to memory using pointers. This is a feature that programmers of most other languages are prevented from doing. This means that as a C++ programmer, you are a special type of programmer: someone who is trusted with memory. In this chapter, you have seen how to obtain and use pointers and some examples of how inappropriate use of pointers can make your code go horribly wrong.

In the next chapter, we will cover functions which will include the description of another type of pointer: function pointers. If you are trusted with pointers to data and function pointers, you really are a special type of programmer.

# 3
# Using Functions

Functions are the infrastructure of C++; code is contained in functions and to execute that code you have to call a function. C++ is remarkably flexible in the ways that you can define and call functions: you can define functions with a fixed number of parameters or a variable number of parameters; you can write generic code so that the same code can be used with different types; and you can even write generic code with a variable number of types.

## Defining C++ functions

At the most basic level, a function has parameters, has code to manipulate the parameters, and returns a value. C++ gives you several ways to determine these three aspects. In the following section, we will cover those parts of a C++ function from the left to the right of the declaration. Functions can also be **templated**, but this will be left to a later section.

## Declaring and defining functions

A function must be defined exactly once, but through overloading, you can have many functions with the same name that differ by their parameters. Code that uses a function has to have access to the name of the function, and so it needs to have access to either the function definition (for example, the function is defined earlier in the source file) or the declaration of the function (also called the function prototype). The compiler uses the prototype to type-check that the *calling code* is calling the function, using the right types.

Typically, libraries are implemented as separate compiled library files and prototypes of the library functions are provided in header files so that many source files can use the functions by including the headers. However, if you know the function name, parameters, and return type, you can type the prototype yourself in your file.

Whichever you do, you are simply providing the information for the compiler to type-check the expression that calls function. It is up to the linker to locate the function in the library and either copy the code into the executable or set up the infrastructure to use the function from a shared library. Including the header file for a library does not mean that you will be able to use the functions from that library because in standard C++, the header file does not have information about the library that contains a function.

Visual C++ provides a `pragma` called `comment`, which can be used with the `lib` option as a message to the linker to link with a specific library. So `#pragma comment(lib, "mylib")` in a header file will tell the linker to link with `mylib.lib`. In general, it is better to use project management tools, such as **nmake** or **MSBuild**, to ensure that the right libraries are linked in the project.

Most of the C Runtime Library is implemented this way: the function is compiled in a static library or a dynamic link library, and the function prototypes are provided in a header file. You provide the library in the linker command line, and typically you will include the header file for the library so that the function prototypes are available to the compiler. As long as the linker knows about the library, you can type the prototype in your code (and describe it as *external linkage* so the compiler knows the function is defined elsewhere). This can save you from including some large files into your source files, files that will mostly have prototypes of functions that you will not use.

However, much of the C++ Standard Library is implemented in header files, which means that these files can be quite large. You can save compile time by including these header files in a precompiled header.

So far in this book, we have used one source file so all the functions are defined in the same file as where they are used, and we have defined the function before calling it, that is, the function is defined *above* the code that calls it. You do not have to define the function before it is used as long as the function prototype is defined before the function is called:

```
int mult(int, int);

int main()
{
    cout << mult(6, 7) << endl;
    return 0;
}

int mult(int lhs, int rhs)
{
    return lhs * rhs;
}
```

The `mult` function is defined after the `main` function, but this code will compile because the prototype is given before the `main` function. This is called a **forward declaration**. The prototype does not have to have the parameter names. This is because the compiler only needs to know the types of the parameters, not their names. However, since parameter names should be self-documenting, it is usually a good idea to give the parameter names so that you can see the purpose of the function.

# Specifying linkage

In the previous example, the function is defined in the same source file, so there is *internal linkage*. If the function is defined in another file, the prototype will have *external linkage* and so the prototype will have to be defined like this:

```
extern int mult(int, int);          // defined in another file
```

The `extern` keyword is one of many specifiers that you can add to a function declaration. For example, the `static` specifier can be used on a prototype to indicate that the function has internal linkage and the name can only be used in the current source file. In the preceding example, it is appropriate to mark the function as `static` in the prototype.

```
static int mult(int, int);          // defined in this file
```

You can also declare a function as `extern  "C"`, which affects how the name of the function is stored in the object file. This is important for libraries, and will be covered shortly.

# Inlining

If a function calculates a value that can be calculated at compile time, you can mark it on the left of the declaration with `constexpr` to indicate that the compiler can optimize the code by computing the value at compile time. If the function value can be calculated at compile time, it means that the parameters in the function call must be known at compile time and so they must be literals. The function must also be a single line. If these restrictions are not met, then the compiler is free to ignore the specifier.

Related is the `inline` specifier. This can be placed on the left of a function declaration as a suggestion to the compiler that, when other code calls the function, rather than the compiler inserting a jump to the function in memory (and the creation of a stack frame), the compiler should put a copy of the actual code in the calling function. Again, the compiler is free to ignore this specifier.

# Determining the return type

Functions may be written to run a routine and not return a value. If this is the case, you must specify that the function returns `void`. In most cases, a function will return a value, if only to indicate that the function has completed correctly. There is no requirement that the calling function obtains the return value or does anything with it. The calling function can simply ignore the return value.

There are two ways to specify the return type. The first way is to give the type before the function name. This is the method used in most of the examples so far. The second way is called the **trailing return type** and requires that you place `auto` as the return type before the function name and use the `->` syntax to give the actual return type after the parameter list:

```
inline auto mult(int lhs, int rhs) -> int
{
    return lhs * rhs;
}
```

This function is so simple that it is a good candidate to be inlined. The return type on the left is given as `auto`, meaning that the actual return type is specified after the parameter list. The `-> int` means that the return type is `int`. This syntax has the same effect as using `int` on the left. This syntax is useful when a function is templated and the return type may not be noticeable.

In this trivial example, you can omit the return type entirely and just use `auto` on the left of the function name. This syntax means that the compiler will deduce the return type from the actual value returned. Clearly the compiler will only know what the return type is from the function body, so you cannot provide a prototype for such functions.

Finally, if a function does not return at all (for example, if it goes into a never-ending loop to poll some value) you can mark it with the C++11 attribute `[[noreturn]]`. The compiler can use this attribute to write more efficient code because it knows that it does not need to provide code to return a value.

# Naming the function

In general, function names have the same rules for variables: they must begin with a letter or an underscore and cannot contain spaces or other punctuation characters. Following the general principle of self-documenting code, you should name the function according to what it does. There is one exception and these are the special functions used to provide overloads for operators (which are mostly punctuation symbols). These functions have a name in the form of `operatorx`, where x is the operator that you will use in your code. A later section will explain how to implement operators with global functions.

Operators are one example of overloading. You can overload any function, that is, use the same name but provide implementations with different parameter types or different numbers of parameters.

# Function parameters

Functions may have no parameters, in which case the function is defined with a pair of empty parentheses. A function definition must give the type and name of the parameters between the parentheses. In many cases, functions will have a fixed number of parameters, but you can write functions with a variable number of parameters. You can also define functions with default values for some of the parameters, in effect, providing a function that overloads itself on the number of parameters passed to the function. Variable argument lists and default arguments will be covered later.

# Specifying exceptions

Functions can also be marked to indicate whether they will throw an exception. More details about exceptions will be given in `Chapter 7`, *Diagnostics and Debugging*, but there are two syntaxes you need to be aware of.

Earlier versions of C++ allowed you to use the `throw` specifier on a function in three ways: firstly, you can provide a comma separated list of the types of the exceptions that may be thrown by code in the function; secondly, you can provide an ellipsis ( . . . ) which means that the function may throw any exception; and thirdly, you can provide an empty pair of parentheses, which means the function will not throw exceptions. The syntax looks like this:

```
int calculate(int param) throw(overflow_error)
{
    // do something which potentially may overflow
}
```

The `throw` specifier has been deprecated in C++11 largely because the ability to indicate the type of exception was not useful. However, the version of `throw` that indicates that no exception will be thrown was found to be useful because it enables a compiler to optimize code by providing no code infrastructure to handle exceptions. C++11 retains this behavior with the `noexcept` specifier:

```
// C++11 style:
int increment(int param) noexcept
{
    // check the parameter and handle overflow appropriately
}
```

# Function body

After the return type, function name, and parameters have been determined, you then need to define the body of the function. The code for a function must appear between a pair of braces (`{ }`). If the function returns a value, then the function must have at least one line (the last line in the function) with the `return` statement. This must return the appropriate type or a type that can be implicitly converted to the return type of the function. As mentioned before, if the function is declared as returning `auto`, then the compiler will deduce the return type. In this case, all the `return` statements *must* return the same type.

# Using function parameters

When a function is called, the compiler checks all the overloads of the function to find one that matches the parameters in the calling code. If there is no exact match then standard and user-defined type conversions are performed, so the values provided by the calling code may be a different type from the parameters.

By default, parameters are passed by value and a copy is made, which means that the parameters are treated as local variables in the function. The writer of the function can decide to pass a parameter by reference, either through a pointer or a C++ reference. **Pass-by-reference** means that the variable in the calling code can be altered by the function, but this can be controlled by making the parameters `const`, in which case the reason for pass-by-reference is to prevent a (potentially costly) copy being made. Built-in arrays are always passed as a pointer to the first item to the array. The compiler will create temporaries when needed. For example, when a parameter is a `const` reference and the calling code passes a literal, a temporary object is created, and is only available to code in the function:

```
void f(const float&);
```

```
f(1.0);                     // OK, temporary float created
double d = 2.0;
f(d);                       // OK, temporary float created
```

# Passing Initializer lists

You can pass an initializer list as a parameter if that list can be converted to the type of the parameter. For example:

```
struct point { int x; int y; };

void set_point(point pt);

int main()
{
    point p;
    p.x = 1; p.y = 1;
    set_point(p);
    set_point({ 1, 1 });
    return 0;
}
```

This code defines a structure that has two members. In the `main` function, a new instance of `point` is created on the stack and it is initialized by accessing the members directly. The instance is then passed to a function that has a `point` parameter. Since the parameter of `set_point` is pass-by-value, the compiler creates a copy of the structure on the stack of the function. The second call of `set_point` does the same: the compiler will create a temporary `point` object on the stack of the function and initialize it with the values in the initializer list.

# Using default parameters

There are situations when you have one or more parameters that have values that are so frequently used that you want them to be treated as a default value for the parameter, while still having the option of allowing the caller to provide a different value if necessary. To do this, you provide the default value in the parameter list of the definition:

```
void log_message(const string& msg, bool clear_screen = false)
{
    if (clear_screen) clear_the_screen();
    cout << msg << endl;
}
```

In most cases, this function is expected to be used to print a single message, but occasionally the user may want to have the screen cleared first (say, for the first message, or after a pre-determined count of lines). To accommodate this use of the function, the `clear_screen` parameter is given a default value of `false`, but the caller still has the option of passing a value:

```
log_message("first message", true);
log_message("second message");
bool user_decision = ask_user();
log_message("third message", user_decision);
```

Note that the default values occur in the function definition, not in a function prototype, so if the `log_message` function is declared in a header file the prototype should be:

```
extern void log_message(const string& msg, bool clear_screen);
```

The parameters that can have default values are the right-most parameters.

You can treat each parameter with a default value as representing a separate overload of the function, so conceptually the `log_message` function should be treated as two functions:

```
extern void log_message(const string& msg, bool clear_screen);
extern void log_message(const string& msg); // conceptually
```

If you define a `log_message` function that has just a `const string&` parameter, then the compiler will not know whether to call that function or the version where `clear_screen` is given a default value of `false`.

## Variable number of parameters

A function with default parameter values can be regarded as having a variable number of user-provided parameters, where you know at compile time the maximum number of parameters and their values if the caller chooses not to provide values. C++ also allows you to write functions where there is less certainty about the number of parameters, and the values passed to the function.

There are three ways to have a variable number of parameters: initializer lists, C-style variable argument lists, and variadic templated functions. The latter of these three will be addressed later in the chapter once templated functions have been covered.

# Initializer lists

So far in this book, initializer lists have been treated as a kind of C++11 construct, a bit like built-in arrays. In fact, when you use the initializer list syntax using braces, the compiler actually creates an instance of the templated `initialize_list` class. If an initializer list is used to initialize another type (for example, to initialize a `vector`), the compiler creates an `initialize_list` object with the values given between the braces, and the container object is initialized using the `initialize_list` iterators. This ability to create an `initialize_list` object from a braced initializer list can be used by to give a function a variable number of parameters, albeit all of the parameters must be of the same type:

```cpp
#include <initializer_list>

int sum(initializer_list<int> values)
{
    int sum = 0;
    for (int i : values) sum += i;
    return sum;
}

int main()
{
    cout << sum({}) << endl;                        // 0
    cout << sum({-6, -5, -4, -3, -2, -1}) << endl;  // -21
    cout << sum({10, 20, 30}) << endl;              // 60
    return 0;
}
```

The `sum` function has a single parameter of `initializer_list<int>`, which can only be initialized with a list of integers. The `initializer_list` class has very few functions because it only exists to give access to the values in the braced list. Significantly, it implements a `size` function that returns the number of items in the list, and `begin` and `end` functions that return a pointer to the first item in the list, and to the position after the last item. These two functions are needed to give iterator access to the list, and it enables you to use the object with the ranged-`for` syntax.

This is typical in the C++ Standard Library. If a container holds data in a contiguous block of memory, then pointer arithmetic can use the pointer to the first item and a pointer immediately after the last item to determine how many items are in the container. Incrementing the first pointer gives sequential access to every item, and pointer arithmetic allows random access. All containers implement a `begin` and `end` function to give access to the container *iterators*.

In this example, the `main` function calls this function three times, each time with a braced initializer list, and the function will return a sum of the items in the list.

Clearly this technique means that each item in the *variable* parameter list has to be the same type (or a type that can be converted to the specified type). You would have the same result if the parameter had been a `vector`; the difference is that an `initializer_list` parameter requires less initialization.

# Argument lists

C++ inherits from C the idea of argument lists. To do this, you use the ellipses syntax ( . . . ) as the last parameter to indicate that the caller can provide zero or more parameters. The compiler will check how the function is called and will allocate space on the stack for these extra parameters. To access the extra parameters, your code must include the `<cstdarg>` header file, which has macros that you can use to extract the extra parameters off the stack.

This is inherently type-unsafe because the compiler cannot check that the parameters that the function will get off the stack at runtime will be the same type as the parameters put on the stack by the calling code. For example, the following is an implementation of a function that will sum integers:

```
int sum(int first, ...)
{
    int sum = 0;
    va_list args;
    va_start(args, first);
    int i = first;
    while (i != -1)
    {
        sum += i;
        i = va_arg(args, int);
    }
    va_end(args);
    return sum;
}
```

The definition of the function must have at least one parameter so that the macros work; in this case the parameter is called `first`. It is important that your code leaves the stack in a consistent state and this is carried out using a variable of the `va_list` type. This variable is initialized at the beginning of the function by calling the `va_start` macro and the stack is restored to its previous state at the end of the function by calling the `va_end` macro.

The code in this function simply iterates through the argument list, and maintains a sum, and the loop finishes when the parameter has a value of -1. There are no macros to give information about how many parameters there are on the stack, nor are there any macros to give an indication of the type of the parameter on the stack. Your code has to assume the type of the variable and provide the desired type in the va_arg macro. In this example, va_arg is called, assuming that every parameter on the stack is an int.

Once all parameters have been read off the stack, the code calls va_end before returning the sum. The function can be called like this:

```
cout << sum(-1) << endl;                          // 0
cout << sum(-6, -5, -4, -3, -2, -1) << endl;      // -20 !!!
cout << sum(10, 20, 30, -1) << endl;              // 60
```

Since −1 is used to indicate the end of the list, it means that to sum a zero number of parameters, you have to pass at least one parameter, that is −1. In addition, the second line shows that you have a problem if you are passing a list of negative numbers (in this case −1 cannot be a parameter). This problem could be addressed in this implementation by choosing another *marker value*.

Another implementation could eschew the use of a marker for the end of the list, and instead use the first, required, argument to give the count of the parameters that follow:

```
int sum(int count, ...)
{
    int sum = 0;
    va_list args;
    va_start(args, count);
    while(count--)
    {
        int i = va_arg(args, int);
        sum += i;
    }
    va_end(args);
    return sum;
}
```

This time, the first value is the *number of arguments* that follow, and so the routine will extract this exact number of integers off the stack and sum them. The code is called like this:

```
cout << sum(0) << endl;                           // 0
cout << sum(6, -6, -5, -4, -3, -2, -1) << endl;   // -21
cout << sum(3, 10, 20, 30) << endl;               // 60
```

There is no convention for how to handle the issue of determining how many parameters have been passed.

The routine assumes that every item on the stack is an `int`, but there is no information about this in the prototype of the function, so the compiler cannot do type checking on the parameters actually used to call the function. If the caller provides a parameter of a different type, the wrong number of bytes could be read off the stack, making the results of all the other calls to `va_arg` invalid. Consider this:

```
cout << sum(3, 10., 20, 30) << endl;
```

It is easy to press both, the comma and period keys, at the same time, and this has happened after typing the `10` parameter. The period means that the `10` is a `double`, and so the compiler puts a `double` value on the stack. When the function reads values off the stack with the `va_arg` macro, it will read the 8-byte `double` as two 4-byte `int` values and for code produced by Visual C++ this results in a total sum of `1076101140`. This illustrates the type unsafe aspect of argument lists: you cannot get the compiler to do type checks of the parameters passed to the function.

If your function has different types passed to it then you have to implement some mechanism to determine what those parameters are. A good example of argument lists is the C `printf` function:

```
int printf(const char *format, ...);
```

The required parameter of this function is a format string, and importantly this has an ordered list of variable parameters and their types. The format string provides the information that is not available via the `<cstdarg>` macros: the number of variable parameters and the type of each one. The implementation of the `printf` function will iterate through the format string and when it comes across a format specifier for a parameter (a character sequence starting with %) it will read the expected type off the stack with `va_arg`. It should be clear that C-style argument lists are not as flexible as they appear on first sight; moreover, they can be quite dangerous.

# Function features

Functions are modularized pieces of code defined as part of your application, or in a library. If a function is written by another vendor it is important that your code calls the function in the way intended by the vendor. This means understanding the calling convention used and how it affects the stack.

# Call stack

When you call a function, the compiler will create a stack frame for the new function call and it will push items on to the stack. The data put on the stack depends on your compiler and whether the code is compiled for the debug or release build; however, in general there will be information about the parameters passed to the function, the return address (the address after the function call), and the automatic variables allocated in the function.

This means that, when you make a function call at runtime, there will be a memory overhead and performance overhead from creating the stack frame before the function runs, and a performance overhead in cleaning up, after the function completes. If a function is inlined, this overhead does not occur because the function call will use the current stack frame rather than a new one. Clearly, inlined functions should be small, both in terms of code and the memory used on the stack. The compiler can ignore the `inline` specifier and call the function with a separate stack frame.

# Specifying calling conventions

When your code uses your own functions, you do not need to pay any attention to *calling conventions* because the compiler will make sure the appropriate convention is used. However, if you are writing library code that can be used by other C++ compilers, or even by other languages, then the calling convention becomes important. Since this book is not about interoperable code we won't go into much depth, but instead will look at two aspects: function naming and stack maintenance.

# Using C linkage

When you give a C++ function a name, this is the name that you will use to call the function in your C++ code. However, under the covers, the C++ compiler will *decorate* the name with extra symbols for the return type and parameters so that overloaded functions all have different names. To C++ developers, this is also known as **name mangling**.

If you need to export a function through a shared library (in Windows, a **dynamic linked library**), you must use types and names that other languages can use. To do this, you can mark a function with `extern "C"`. This means that the function has C linkage and the compiler will not use C++ name mangling. Clearly, you should use this only on functions that will be used by external code and you should not use it with functions that have return values and parameters that use C++ custom types.

However, if such a function does return a C++ type, the compiler will only issue a warning. The reason is that C is a flexible language and a C programmer will be able to work out how to turn the C++ type into something usable, but it is poor practice to abuse them like this!

 The extern "C" linkage can also be used with global variables, and you can use it on a single item or (using braces) on many items.

## Specifying how the stack Is maintained

Visual C++ supports six calling conventions that you can use on a function. The __clrcall specifier means that the function should be called as a .NET function and allows you to write code that has mixed native code and managed code. C++/CLR (Microsoft's language extensions to C++ to write .NET code) is beyond the scope of this book. The other five are used to indicate how parameters are passed to a function (on the stack or using CPU registers) and whose responsibility it is to maintain the stack. We will cover just three: __cdecl, __stdcall, and __thiscall.

You will rarely explicitly use __thiscall; it is the calling convention used for functions defined as members of custom types, and indicates that the function has a hidden parameter that is a pointer to the object that can be accessed through the this keyword in the function. More details will be given in the next chapter, but it is important to realize that such member functions have a different calling convention, especially when you need to initialize function pointers.

By default, C++ global functions will use the __cdecl calling convention. The stack is maintained by the calling code, so in the calling code each call to a __cdecl function is followed by code to clean up the stack. This makes each function call a little larger, but it is needed for variable argument lists to be used. The __stdcall calling convention is used by most of the Windows SDK functions and it indicates that the called function cleans up the stack so there is no need for such code to be generated in the calling code. Clearly, it is important that the compiler knows that a function uses __stdcall because, otherwise, it will generate code to clean up a stack frame that has already been cleaned up by the function. You will usually see Windows functions marked with WINAPI, which is a typedef for __stdcall.

# Using recursion

In most cases the memory overhead of a call stack is unimportant. However, when you use recursion it is possible to build up a long chain of stack frames. As the name suggests, recursion is when a function calls itself. A simple example is a function that calculates a factorial:

```
int factorial(int n)
{
    if (n > 1) return n * factorial(n - 1);
    return 1;
}
```

If you call this for 4, the following calls are made:

```
factorial(4) returns 4 * factorial(3)
    factorial(3) returns 3 * factorial(2)
        factorial(2) returns 2 * factorial(1)
            factorial(1) returns 1
```

The important point is that in the recursive function there must be at least one way to leave the function without recursion. In this case, it will be when `factorial` is called with a parameter of 1. In practice, a function like this should be marked as `inline` to avoid creating any stack frames at all.

# Overloading functions

You can have several functions with the same name, but where the parameter list is different (the number of parameters and/or the type of the parameters). This is *overloading* the function name. When such a function is called, the compiler will attempt to find the function that best fits the parameters provided. If there is not a suitable function, the compiler will attempt to convert the parameters to see if a function with those types exists. The compiler will start with trivial conversions (for example, an array name to a pointer, a type to a `const` type), and if this fails the compiler will try to promote the type (for example, `bool` to `int`). If that fails, the compiler will try standard conversions (for example, a reference to a type). If such conversions results in more than one possible candidate, then the compiler will issue an error that the function call is ambiguous.

# Functions and scope

The compiler will also take the scope of the function into account when looking for a suitable function. You cannot define a function within a function, but you can provide a function prototype within the scope of a function and the compiler will attempt (if necessary through conversions) to call a function with such a prototype first. Consider this code:

```
void f(int i)    { /*does something*/ }
void f(double d) { /*does something*/ }

int main()
{
    void f(double d);
    f(1);
    return 0;
}
```

In this code, the function `f` is overloaded with one version that takes an `int` and the other with a `double`. Normally, if you call `f(1)` then the compiler will call the first version of the function. However, in `main` there is a prototype for the version that takes a `double`, and an `int` can be converted to a `double` with no loss of information. The prototype is in the same scope as the function call, so in this code the compiler will call the version that takes a `double`. This technique essentially *hides* the version with an `int` parameter.

# Deleted functions

There is a more formal way to hide functions than using the scope. C++ will attempt to explicitly convert built-in types. For example:

```
void f(int i);
```

You can call this with an `int`, or anything that can be converted to an `int`:

```
f(1);
f('c');
f(1.0); // warning of conversion
```

In the second case, a `char` is an integer, so it is promoted to an `int` and the function is called. In the third case, the compiler will issue a warning that the conversion can cause a loss of data, but it is a warning and so the code will compile. If you want to prevent this implicit conversion you can *delete* the functions that you do not want callers to use. To do this, provide a prototype and use the syntax `= delete`:

```
void f(double) = delete;

void g()
{
    f(1);    // compiles
    f(1.0); // C2280: attempting to reference a deleted function
}
```

Now, when the code attempts to call the function with a `char` or a `double` (or `float`, which will be implicitly converted to a `double`), the compiler will issue an error.

# Passing by value and passing by reference

By default, the compiler will pass parameters by value, that is, a copy is made. If you pass a custom type, then its *copy constructor* is called to create a new object. If you pass a pointer to an object of a built-in type or custom type, then the *pointer* will be passed by value, that is, a new pointer is created on the function stack for the parameter and it is initialized with the memory address passed to the function. This means that, in the function, you can change the pointer to point to other memory (this is useful if you want to use pointer arithmetic on that pointer). The data that the pointer points to will be passed by a reference, that is, the data remains where it is, outside of the function, but the function can use the pointer to change the data. Similarly, if you use a reference on a parameter then it means that the object is passed by the reference. Clearly, if you use `const` on a pointer or reference parameter then this will affect whether the function can change the data pointed to or referenced.

In some cases, you may want to return several values from a function, and you may choose to use the return value of the function to indicate if the function executed correctly. One way to do this is to make one of the parameters an *out* parameter, that is, it is either a pointer or a reference to an object or container that the function will alter:

```
// don't allow any more than 100 items
bool get_items(int count, vector<int>& values)
{
    if (count > 100) return false;
    for (int i = 0; i < count; ++i)
    {
```

```
            values.push_back(i);
    }
    return true;
}
```

To call this function, you must create a `vector` object and pass it to the function:

```
vector<int> items {};
get_items(10, items);
for(int i : items) cout << i << ' ';
cout << endl
```

Because the `values` parameter is a reference it means that when `get_values` calls `push_back` to insert a value in the `values` container it is actually inserting that value into the `items` container.

If an out parameter is passed via a pointer it is important to look at the pointer declaration. A single `*` means that the variable is a pointer, two means that it is a pointer to a pointer. The following function returns an `int` through an out parameter:

```
bool get_datum(/*out*/ int *pi);
```

The code is called like this:

```
int value = 0;
if (get_datum(&value)) { cout << "value is " << value << endl; }
else                   { cout << "cannot get the value" << endl;}
```

This pattern of returning a value indicating success is frequently used, particularly with code that accesses data across process or machine boundaries. The function return value can be used to give detailed information about why the call failed (no network access?, invalid security credentials?, and so on), and indicates that the data in the out parameters should be discarded.

If the out parameter has a double `*` then it means the return value is itself a pointer, either to a single value or to an array:

```
bool get_data(/*in/out*/ int *psize, /*out*/ int **pi);
```

In this case, you pass in the size of the buffer you want using the first parameter and on return you receive the actual size of the buffer via this parameter (it is in/out) and a pointer to the buffer in the second parameter:

```
int size = 10;
int *buffer = nullptr;
if (get_data(size, &buffer))
{
```

```
        for (int i = 0; i < size; ++i)
        {
            cout << buffer[i] << endl;
        }
        //delete [] buffer;
    }
```

Any function that returns a memory buffer must document who has the responsibility of deallocating the memory. In most cases, it is usually the caller, as assumed in this example code.

# Designing functions

Often functions will act upon global data, or data passed in by the caller. It is important that when the function completes, it leaves this data in a consistent state. Equally so, it is important that, the function can make assumptions about the data before it accesses it.

# Pre- and post-conditions

A function will typically alter some data: values passed into the function, data returned by the function, or some global data. It is important when designing a function that you determine what data will be accessed and changed and that these rules are documented.

A function will have pre-conditions, assumptions about the data that it will use. For example, if a function is passed a filename, with the intention that the function will extract some data from the file, whose responsibility is it to check that the file exists? You can make it the responsibility of the function, and so the first few lines will check that the name is a valid path to a file and call operating system functions to check that the file exists. However, if you have several functions that will perform actions on the file, you will be replicating this checking code in each function and it may be better to put that responsibility on the calling code. Clearly, such actions can be expensive, so it is important to avoid both the calling code and the function to perform the checks.

Chapter 7, *Diagnostics and Debugging*, will describe how to add debugging code, called **asserts**, that you can place in your functions to check the values of the parameters to make sure that the calling code is following the pre-condition rules you have set. Asserts are defined using conditional compilation and so will only appear in **debug builds** (that is, C++ code compiled with debugging information). **Release builds** (completed code that will be delivered to the end user) will conditionally compile asserts away; this makes the code faster, and if your testing is thorough enough, you can be assured that pre-conditions are met.

You should also document the post-conditions of your function. That is, assumptions about the data returned by the function (through the function return value, out parameters, or parameters passed by a reference). Post-conditions are the assumptions that the calling code will make. For example, you may return a signed integer where the function is meant to return a positive value, but a negative value is used to indicate an error. Often functions that return pointers will return `nullptr` if the function fails. In both cases, the calling code knows that it needs to check the return value and only use it if it is either positive or not `nullptr`.

# Using invariants

You should be careful to document how a function uses data external to the function. If the intention of the function is to change external data, you should document what the function will do. If you don't explicitly document what the function does to external data, then you must ensure that when the function finishes such data is left untouched. The reason is that the calling code will only assume what you have said in the documentation and the side-effects of changing global data may cause problems. Sometimes it is necessary to store the state of global data and return the item back to that state before the function returns.

An example of this, is the `cout` object. The `cout` object is global to your application, and it can be changed through manipulators to make it interpret numeric values in certain ways. If you change it in a function (say, by inserting the `hex` manipulator), then this change will remain when the `cout` object is used outside the function.

Create a function called `read16` that reads 16 bytes from a file and prints the values out to the console both in hexadecimal form and interpreted as an ASCII character:

```
int read16(ifstream& stm)
{
    if (stm.eof()) return -1;

    int flags = cout.flags();
    cout << hex;
    string line;

    // code that changes the line variable

    cout.setf(flags);
    return line.length();
}
```

This code stores the state of the `cout` object in a temporary variable, `flags`. The `read16` function can change the `cout` object in any way necessary, but because we have the stored state it means that the object can be restored to its original state before returning.

# Function pointers

When an application is run, the functions it will call will exist in memory somewhere. This means that you can get the address of a function. C++ allows you to use the function call operator (a pair of parentheses enclosing the parameters `()`) to call a function through a function pointer.

# Remember the parentheses!

First, a simple example of how function pointers can cause difficult to notice bugs in your code. A global function called `get_status` performs various validation actions to determine if the state of the system is valid. The function returns a value of zero to mean that the system state is valid and values over zero are error codes:

```
// values over zero are error codes
int get_status()
{
    int status = 0;
    // code that checks the state of data is valid
    return status;
}
```

The code could be called like this:

```
if (get_status > 0)
{
    cout << "system state is invalid" << endl;
}
```

This is an error because the developer has missed off the `()`, so the compiler does not treat this as a function call. Instead, it treats this as a test of the memory address of the function, and since the function will never be located at a memory address of zero, the comparison will always be `true` and the message will be printed even if the system state is valid.

# Declaring function pointers

The last section highlights how easy it is to get the address of a function: you just use the name of the function without the parentheses:

```
void *pv = get_status;
```

The pointer pv is only of mild interest; you now know where in memory the function is stored, but to print this address you still need to cast it to an integer. To make the pointer useful, you need to be able to declare a pointer through which the function can be called. To look at how to do this, let's go back to the function prototype:

```
int get_status()
```

The function pointer must be able to call the function passing no parameters and expecting a return value of an integer. The function pointer is declared like this:

```
int (*fn)() = get_status;
```

The * indicates that the variable fn is a pointer; however, this binds to the left, so without the parentheses surrounding *fn the compiler would interpret this to mean that the declaration is for an int * pointer. The rest of the declaration indicates how this function pointer is called: taking no parameters and returning an int.

Calling through a function pointer is simple: you give the name of the pointer where you would normally give the name of the function:

```
int error_value = fn();
```

Note again how important the parentheses are; they indicates that the function at the address held in the function pointer, fn, is called.

Function pointers can make code look rather cluttered, especially when you use them to point to templated functions, so often code will define an alias:

```
using pf1 = int(*)();
typedef int(*pf2)();
```

These two lines declare aliases for the type of the function pointer needed to call the `get_status` function. Both are valid, but the `using` version is more readable since it is clear that `pf1` is the alias being defined. To see why, consider this alias:

```
typedef bool(*MyPtr)(MyType*, MyType*);
```

The type alias is called `MyPtr` and it is to a function that returns a `bool` and takes two `MyType` pointers. This is much clearer with `using`:

```
using MyPtr = bool(*)(MyType*, MyType*);
```

The tell-tale sign here is the `(*)`, which indicates that the type is a function pointer because you are using the parenthesis to break the associatively of the `*`. You can then read outwards to see the prototype of the function: to the left to see the return type, and to the right to get the parameter list.

Once you have declared an alias, you can create a pointer to a function and call it:

```
using two_ints = void (*)(int, int);

void do_something(int l, int r){/* some code */}

void caller()
{
    two_ints fn = do_something;
    fn(42, 99);
}
```

Notice that, because the `two_ints` alias is declared as a pointer, you do not use a * when declaring a variable of this type.

# Using function pointers

A function pointer is merely a pointer. This means that you can use it as a variable; you can return it from a function, or pass it as a parameter. For example, you may have some code that performs some lengthy routine and you want to provide some feedback during the routine. To make this flexible, you could define your function to take a **callback pointer** and periodically in the routine call the function to indicate progress:

```
using callback = void(*)(const string&);

void big_routine(int loop_count, const callback progress)
{
    for (int i = 0; i < loop_count; ++i)
    {
```

```
        if (i % 100 == 0)
        {
            string msg("loop ");
            msg += to_string(i);
            progress(msg);
        }
        // routine
    }
}
```

Here `big_routine` has a function pointer parameter called `progress`. The function has a loop that will be called many times and every one hundredth loop it calls the callback function, passing a `string` that gives information about the progress.

 Note that the `string` class defines a `+=` operator that can be used to append a string to the end of the `string` in the variable and the `<string>` header file defines a function called `to_string` that is overloaded for each of the built-in types to return a `string` formatted with the value of the function parameter.

This function declares the function pointer as `const` merely so that the compiler knows that the function pointer should not be changed to a pointer to another function in this function. The code can be called like this:

```
void monitor(const string& msg)
{
    cout << msg << endl;
}

int main()
{
    big_routine(1000, monitor);
    return 0;
}
```

The `monitor` function has the same prototype as described by the `callback` function pointer (if, for example, the function parameter was `string&` and not `const string&`, then the code will not compile). The `big_routine` function is then called, passing a pointer to the `monitor` function as the second parameter.

If you pass callback functions to library code, you must pay attention to the calling convention of the function pointer. For example, if you pass a function pointer to a Windows function, such as `EnumWindows`, it must point to a function declared with the `__stdcall` calling convention.

The C++ standards uses another technique to call functions defined at runtime, which is, functors. It will be covered shortly.

# Templated functions

When you write library code, you often have to write several functions that differ only between the types that are passed to the function; the routine action is the same, it's just the types that have changed. C++ provides *templates* to allow you to write more generic code; you write the routine using a *generic type* and at compile time the compiler will generate a function with the appropriate types. The templated function is marked as such using the template keyword and a list of parameters in angle brackets (<>) that give placeholders for the types that will be used. It is important to understand that these template parameters are types and refer to the types of the parameters (and return a value of the function) that will be replaced with the actual types used by calling the functions. They are not parameters of the function, and you do not (normally) provide them when you call the function.

It is best to explain template functions with an example. A simple maximum function can be written like this:

```
int maximum(int lhs, int rhs)
{
    return (lhs > rhs) ? lhs : rhs;
}
```

You can call this with other integer types, and smaller types (short, char, bool, and so on) will be promoted to an int, and values of larger types (long long) will be truncated. Similarly, variables of unsigned types will be converted to the signed int which could cause problems. Consider this call of the function:

```
unsigned int s1 = 0xffffffff, s2 = 0x7fffffff;
unsigned int result = maximum(s1, s2);
```

What is the value of the result variable: s1 or s2? It is s2. The reason is that both values are converted to signed int and when converted to a signed type s1 will be a value of $-1$ and s2 will be a value of 2147483647.

To handle unsigned types, you need to *overload* the function and write a version for signed and unsigned integers:

```
int maximum(int lhs, int rhs)
{
    return (lhs > rhs) ? lhs : rhs;
}

unsigned maximum(unsigned lhs, unsigned rhs)
{
    return (lhs > rhs) ? lhs : rhs;
}
```

The routine is the same, but the types have changed. There is another issue--what if the caller mixes types? Does the following expression make any sense:

```
int i = maximum(true, 100.99);
```

This code will compile because a `bool` and a `double` can be converted to an `int` and the first overload will be called. Since such a call is nonsense, it would be much better if the compiler caught this error.

# Defining templates

Returning back to the two versions of the `maximum` function, the routine is the same for both; all that has changed is the type. If you had a generic type, let's call it T, where T could be any type that implements an `operator>`, the routine could be described by this pseudocode:

```
T maximum(T lhs, T rhs)
{
    return (lhs > rhs) ? lhs : rhs;
}
```

This will not compile because we have not defined the type T. Templates allow you to tell the compiler that the code uses a type and will be determined from the parameter passed to the function. The following code will compile:

```
template<typename T>
T maximum(T lhs, T rhs)
{
    return (lhs > rhs) ? lhs : rhs;
}
```

The template declaration specifies the type that will be used using the `typename` identifier. The type `T` is a placeholder; you can use any name you like as long as it is not a name used elsewhere at the same scope, and of course, it must be used in the parameter list of the function. You can use `class` instead of `typename`, but the meaning is the same.

You can call this function, passing values of any type, and the compiler will create the code for that type, calling the `operator>` for that type.

It is important to realize that, the first time the compiler comes across a templated function, it will create a version of the function for the specified type. If you call the templated function for several different types, the compiler will create, or instantiate, a *specialized* function for each of these types.

The definition of this template indicates that only one type will be used, so you can only call it with two parameters of the same type:

```
int i = maximum(1, 100);
double d = maximum(1.0, 100.0);
bool b = maximum(true, false);
```

All of these will compile and the first two will give the expected results. The last line will assign b to a value of `true` because `bool` is an integer and `true` has a value of `1+` and `false` has a value of `0`. This may not be what you would want, so we will return to this issue later. Note that, since the template says that both parameters must be the same type, the following will not compile:

```
int i = maximum(true, 100.99);
```

The reason is that the `template` parameter list only gives a single type. If you want to define a function with parameters of different types, then you will have to provide extra parameters to the template:

```
template<typename T, typename U>
T maximum(T lhs, U rhs)
{
    return (lhs > rhs) ? lhs : rhs;
}
```

This is done to illustrate how templates work; it really does not make sense to define a maximum function that takes two different types.

This version is written for two different types, the template declaration mentions two types, and these are used for the two parameters. But notice that the function returns `T`, the type of the first parameter. The function can be called like this:

```
cout << maximum(false, 100.99) << endl; // 1
cout << maximum(100.99, false) << endl; // 100.99
```

The output from the first is 1 (or if you use the `bool alpha` manipulator, `true`) and the result of the second line is `100.99`. The reason is not immediately obvious. In both cases, the comparison will return `100.99` from the function, but because the type of the return value is `T`, the returned value type will be the type of the first parameter. In the first case, `100.99` is first converted to a `bool`, and since `100.99` is not zero, the value returned is `true` (or 1). In the second case, the first parameter is a `double`, so the function returns a `double` and this means that `100.99` is returned. If the template version of `maximum` is changed to return `U` (the type of the second parameter) then the values returned by the preceding code are reversed: the first line returns `100.99` and the second returns `1`.

Note that when you *call* the template function, you do not have to give the types of the template parameters because the compiler will deduce them. It is important to point out that this applies only to the parameters. The return type is not determined by the type of the variable the caller assigns to the function value because the function can be called without using the return value.

Although the compiler will deduce the template parameters from how you call the function, you can explicitly provide the types in the called function to call a specific version of the function and (if necessary) get the compiler to perform implicit conversions:

```
// call template<typename T> maximum(T,T);
int i = maximum<int>(false, 100.99);
```

This code will call the version of `maximum` that has two `int` parameters and returns an `int`, so the return value is `100`, that is, `100.99` converted to an `int`.

## Using template parameter values

The templates defined so far have had types as the parameters of the template, but you can also provide integer values. The following is a rather contrived example to illustrate the point:

```
template<int size, typename T>
T* init(T t)
{
    T* arr = new T[size];
```

```
    for (int i = 0; i < size; ++i) arr[i] = t;
    return arr;
}
```

There are two template parameters. The second parameter provides the name of a type where T is a placeholder used for the type of the parameter of the function. The first parameter looks like a function parameter because it is used in a similar way. The parameter size can be used in the function as a local (read-only) variable. The function parameter is T and so the compiler can deduce the second template parameter from the function call, but it cannot deduce the first parameter, so you *must* provide a value in the call. Here is an example of calling this template function for an int for T and a value of 10 for size:

```
int *i10 = init<10>(42);
for (int i = 0; i < 10; ++i) cout << i10[i] << ' ';
cout << endl;
delete [] i10;
```

The first line calls the function with 10 as the template parameter and 42 as the function parameter. Since 42 is an int, the init function will create an int array with ten members and each one is initialized to a value of 42. The compiler deduced int as the second parameter, but this code could have called the function with init<10, int>(42) to explicitly indicate that you require an int array.

The non-type parameters must be constant at compile time: the value can be integral (including an enumeration), but not a floating point. You can use arrays of integers, but these will be available through the template parameter as a pointer.

Although in most cases the compiler cannot deduce the value parameter, it can if the value is defined as the size of an array. This can be used to make it appear that a function can determine the size of a built-in array, but of course, it can't because the compiler will create a version of the function for each size needed. For example:

```
template<typename T, int N> void print_array(T (&arr)[N])
{
    for (int i = 0; i < N; ++i)
    {
        cout << arr[i] << endl;
    }
}
```

Here, there are two template parameters: one is the type of the array, and the other is the size of the array. The parameter of the function looks a little odd, but it is just a built-in array being passed by a reference. If the parentheses are not used then the parameter is `T&` `arr[N]`, that is, an N-sized built-in array of references to objects of type `T`, which is not what we want. We want an N-sized built-in array objects of type `T`. This function is called like this:

```
int squares[] = { 1, 4, 9, 16, 25 };
print_array(squares);
```

The interesting thing about the preceding code is that the compiler sees that there are five items in the initializer list. The built-in array has five items, thus calls the function like this:

```
print_array<int,5>(squares);
```

As mentioned, the compiler will instantiate this function for every combination of `T` and `N` that your code calls. If the template function has a large amount of code, then this may be an issue. One way around this is to use a helper function:

```
template<typename T> void print_array(T* arr, int size)
{
    for (int i = 0; i < size; ++i)
    {
        cout << arr[i] << endl;
    }
}

template<typename T, int N> inline void print_array(T (&arr)[N])
{
    print_array(arr, N);
}
```

This does two things. First, there is a version of `print_array` that takes a pointer and the number of items that the pointer points to. This means that the `size` parameter is determined at runtime, so versions of this function are only instantiated at compile time for the types of the arrays used, not for both type and array size. The second thing to note is that the function that is templated with the size of the array is declared as `inline` and it calls the first version of the function. Although there will be a version of this for each combination of type and array size, the instantiation will be inline rather than a complete function.

# Specialized templates

In some cases, you may have a routine that works for most types (and a candidate for a templated function), but you may identify that some types need a different routine. To handle this, you can write a specialized template function, that is, a function that will be used for a specific type and the compiler will use this code when a caller uses types that fit this specialization. As an example, here is a fairly pointless function; it returns the size of a type:

```
template <typename T> int number_of_bytes(T t)
{
    return sizeof(T);
}
```

This works for most built-in types, but if you call it with a pointer, you will get the size of the pointer, not what the pointer points to. So, `number_of_bytes("x")` will return 4 (on a 32-bit system) rather than 2 for the size of the `char` array. You may decide that you want a specialization for `char*` pointers that uses the C function, `strlen`, to count the number of characters in the string until the `NUL` character. To do this, you need a similar prototype to the templated function, replacing the template parameter with the actual type, and since the template parameter is not needed you miss this out. Since this function is for a specific type, you need to add the specialized type to the function name:

```
template<> int number_of_bytes<const char *>(const char *str)
{
    return strlen(str) + 1;
}
```

Now when you call `number_of_bytes("x")` the specialization will be called and it will return a value of 2.

Earlier, we defined a templated function to return a maximum of two parameters of the same type:

```
template<typename T>
T maximum(T lhs, T rhs)
{
    return (lhs > rhs) ? lhs : rhs;
}
```

Using specialization, you can write versions for types that are not compared using the > operator. Since it makes no sense to find the maximum of two Booleans, you can delete the specialization for `bool`:

```
template<> bool maximum<bool>(bool lhs, bool rhs) = delete;
```

This now means that, if the code calls `maximum` with `bool` parameters, the compiler will generate an error.

# Variadic templates

A variadic template is when there is a variable number of template parameters. The syntax is similar to variable arguments to a function; you use ellipses, but you use them on the left of the argument in the parameter list, which declares it a *parameter pack*:

```
template<typename T, typename... Arguments>
void func(T t, Arguments... args);
```

The `Arguments` template parameter is zero or more types, which are the types of the corresponding number of arguments, `args`, of the function. In this example, the function has at least one parameter, of type `T`, but you can have any number of fixed parameters, including none at all.

Within the function, you need to unpack the parameter pack to get access to the parameters passed by the caller. You can determine how many items there are in the parameter pack using the special operator, `sizeof...` (note the ellipses are part of the name); unlike the `sizeof` operator, this is the item count and not the size in bytes. To unpack the parameter pack, you need to use the ellipses on the right of the name of the parameter pack (for example, `args...`). The compiler will expand the parameter pack at this point, replacing the symbol with the contents of the parameter pack.

However, you will not know at design time how many parameters there are or what types they are, so there are some strategies to address this. The first uses recursion:

```
template<typename T> void print(T t)
{
    cout << t << endl;
}

template<typename T, typename... Arguments>
void print(T first, Arguments ... next)
{
    print(first);
    print(next...);
}
```

The variadic templated `print` function can be called with one or more parameters of any type that can be handled by the `ostream` class:

```
print(1, 2.0, "hello", bool);
```

When this is called, the parameter list is split into two: the first parameter (1) in the first parameter, `first`, and the other three are put in the parameter pack, `next`. The function body then calls the first version of `print` which, prints the `first` parameter to the console. The next line in the variadic function then expands the parameter pack in a call to `print`, that is, this calls itself recursively. In this call, the `first` parameter will be 2.0, and the rest will be put in the parameter pack. This continues until the parameter pack has been expanded so much that there are no more parameters.

Another way to unpack the parameter pack is to use an initializer list. In this case, the compiler will create an array with each parameter:

```
template<typename... Arguments>
void print(Arguments ... args)
{
    int arr [sizeof...(args)] = { args... };
    for (auto i : arr) cout << i << endl;
}
```

The array, `arr`, is created with the size of the parameter pack and the unpack syntax used with the initializer braces will fill the array with the parameters. Although this will work with any number of parameters, all the parameters have to be the same type of the array, `arr`.

One trick is to use the comma operator:

```
template<typename... Arguments>
void print(Arguments ... args)
{
    int dummy[sizeof...(args)] = { (print(args), 0)... };
}
```

This creates a dummy array called `dummy`. This array is not used, other than in the expansion of the parameter pack. The array is created in the size of the `args` parameter pack and the ellipsis expands the parameter pack using the *expression* between the parentheses. The expression uses the comma operator, which will return the right side of the comma. Since this is an integer, it means that each entry of `dummy` has a value of zero. The interesting part is the left side of the comma operator. Here the version of `print` with a single templated parameter is called with each item in the `args` parameter pack.

# Overloaded operators

Earlier we said that function names should not contain punctuation. That is not strictly true because, if you are writing an operator, you *only* use punctuation in the function name. An operator is used in an expression acting on one or more operands. A unary operator has one operand, a binary operator has two operands, and an operator returns the result of the operation. Clearly this describes a function: a return type, a name, and one or more parameters.

C++ provides the keyword `operator` to indicate that the function is not used with the function call syntax, but instead is called using the syntax associated with the operator (usually, a unary operator the first parameter is on the right of the operator, and for a binary operator the first parameter is on the left and the second is on the right, but there are exceptions to this).

In general, you will provide the operators as part of a custom type (so the operators act upon variables of that type) but in some cases, you can declare operators at a global scope. Both are valid. If you are writing a custom type (classes, as explained in the next chapter), then it makes sense to encapsulate the code for an operator as part of the custom type. In this section, we will concentrate on the other way to define an operator: as a global function.

You can provide your own versions of the following unary operators:

```
!  &  +  -  *  ++  --  ~
```

You can also provide your own versions of the following binary operators:

```
!=  ==  <  <=  >  >=  &&  ||
%  %=  +  +=  -  -=  *  *=  /  /=  &  &=  |  |=  ^  ^=  <<  <<=  =  >>  =>>
->  ->*  ,
```

You can also write versions of the function call operator (), array subscript [], conversion operators, the cast operator (), and `new` and `delete`. You cannot redefine the ., .*, ::, ?:, # or ## operators, nor the "named" operators, `sizeof`, `alignof` or `typeid`.

When defining the operator, you write a function where the function name is operator*x* and *x* is the operator symbol (note that there is no space). For example, if you define a struct that has two members defining a Cartesian point, you may want to compare two points for equality. The struct can be defined like this:

```
struct point
{
    int x;
    int y;
};
```

Comparing two point objects is easy. They are the same if x and y of one object are equal to the corresponding values in the other object. If you define the == operator, then you should also define the != operator using the same logic because != should give the exact opposite result of the == operator. This is how these operators can be defined:

```
bool operator==(const point& lhs, const point& rhs)
{
    return (lhs.x == rhs.x) && (lhs.y == rhs.y);
}

bool operator!=(const point& lhs, const point& rhs)
{
    return !(lhs == rhs);
}
```

The two parameters are the two operands of the operator. The first one is the operand on the left-hand side and the second parameter is the operand on the right-hand side of the operator. These are passed as references so that a copy is not made, and they are marked as const because the operator will not alter the objects. Once defined, you can use the point type like this:

```
point p1{ 1,1 };
point p2{ 1,1 };
cout << boolalpha;
cout << (p1 == p2) << endl; // true
cout << (p1 != p2) << endl; // false
```

You could have defined a pair of functions called equals and not_equals and use these instead:

```
cout << equals(p1,p2) << endl;      // true
cout << not_equals(p1,p2) << endl; // false
```

However, defining operators makes the code more readable because you use the type like the built-in types. Operator overloading is often referred to as *syntactic sugar*, syntax that makes the code easier to read--but this trivializes an important technique. For example, smart pointers are a technique that involves class **destructors** to manage resource lifetime, and are only useful because you can call the objects of such classes as if they are pointers. You can do this because the smart pointer class implements the -> and * operators. Another example is **functors**, or function objects, where the class implements the () operator so that objects can be accessed as if they are functions.

When you write a custom type, you should ask yourself if overloading an operator for your type makes sense. If the type is a numeric type, for example, a complex number or a matrix - then it makes sense to implement arithmetic operators, but would it make sense to implement the logical operators since the type does not have a logical aspect? There is a temptation to redefine the *meaning* of operators to cover your specific operation, but this will make your code less readable.

In general, a unary operator is implemented as a global function that takes a single parameter. The postfix increment and decrement operators are an exception to allow for a different implementation from prefix operators. Prefix operators will have a reference to the object as a parameter (which the operator will increment or decrement) and return a reference to this changed object. The postfix operator, however, has to return the value of the object before the increment or decrement. Thus, the operator function has two parameters: a reference to an object that will be changed and an integer (which will always be a value of 1); it will return a copy of the original object.

A binary operator will have two parameters and return an object or a reference to an object. For example, for the `struct` we defined previously, we could define an insertion operator for `ostream` objects:

```
struct point
{
    int x;
    int y;
};

ostream& operator<<(ostream& os, const point& pt)
{
    os << "(" << pt.x << "," << pt.y << ")";
    return os;
}
```

This means that you can now insert a `point` object to the `cout` object to print it on the console:

```
point pt{1, 1};
cout << "point object is " << pt << endl;
```

# Function objects

A function object, or **functor**, is a custom type that implements the function call operator: (`operator()`). This means that a function operator can be called in a way that looks like it is a function. Since we haven't covered classes yet, in this section we will just explore the function objects types that are provided by the Standard Library and how to use them.

The `<functional>` header file contains various types that can be used as function objects. The following table lists these:

| Purpose | Types |
|---|---|
| Arithmetic | `divides, minus, modulus, multiplies, negate, plus` |
| Bitwise | `bit_and, bit_not, bit_or, bit_xor` |
| Comparison | `equal_to, greater, greater_equal, less, less_equals, not_equal_to` |
| Logical | `logical_and, logical_not, logical_or` |

These are all binary function classes, other than `bit_not`, `logical_not`, and `negate`, which are unary. Binary function objects act on two values and return a result, unary function objects act on a single value and return a result. For example, you could calculate the modulus of two numbers with this code:

```
modulus<int> fn;
cout << fn(10, 2) << endl;
```

This declares a function object called `fn` that will perform modulus. The object is used in the second line, which calls the `operator()` function on the object with two parameters, so the following line is equivalent to the preceding line:

```
cout << fn.operator()(10, 2) << endl;
```

The result is that the value of 0 is printed on the console. The `operator()` function merely performs the modulus on the two parameters, in this case `10 % 2`. This does not look too exciting. The `<algorithm>` header contains functions that work on function objects. Most take predicates, that is, logical function objects, but one, `transform`, takes a function object that performs an action:

```
// #include <algorithm>
// #include <functional>

vector<int> v1 { 1, 2, 3, 4, 5 };
vector<int> v2(v1.size());
fill(v2.begin(), v2.end(), 2);
vector<int> result(v1.size());

transform(v1.begin(), v1.end(), v2.begin(),
    result.begin(), modulus<int>());

for (int i : result)
{
    cout << i << ' ';
}
cout << endl;
```

This code will perform five modulus calculations on the values in the two vectors. Conceptually, it does this:

```
result = v1 % v2;
```

That is, each item in `result` is the modulus of the corresponding item in `v1` and `v2`. In the code, the first line creates a `vector` with the five values. We will calculate the modulus of these values with 2, so the second line declares an empty `vector` but with the same capacity as the first `vector`. This second `vector` is filled by calling the `fill` function. The first parameter is the address of the first item in the `vector` and the end function returns the address after the *last* item in the `vector`. The final item in the function call is the value that will be placed in the `vector` in every item starting with the item pointed to by the first parameter up to, but excluding, the item pointed to by the second parameter.

At this point, the second `vector` will contain five items and each one will be 2. Next, a `vector` is created for the results; and again, it is the same size as the first array. Finally, the calculation is performed by the `transform` function, shown here again:

```
transform(v1.begin(), v1.end(),
    v2.begin(), result.begin(), modulus<int>());
```

The first two parameters give the iterators of the first `vector` and from this the number of items can be calculated. Since all three `vector`s are the same size, you only need the `begin` iterator for v2 and `result`.

The last parameter is the function object. This is a temporary object and only exists during this statement; it has no name. The syntax used here is an explicit call to the constructor of the class; it is templated so you need to give the template parameter. The `transform` function will call the `operator(int,int)` function on this function object for each item in v1 as the first parameter and the corresponding item in v2 as the second parameter and it will store the result in the corresponding position in `result`.

Since `transform` takes any binary function object as the second parameter, you can pass an instance of `plus<int>` to add a value of 2 to every item in v1, or pass an instance of `multiplies<int>` to multiply every item in v1 by 2.

One situation where function objects are useful is when performing multiple comparisons using a predicate. A predicate is a function object that compares values and returns a Boolean. The `<functional>` header contains several classes to allow you to compare items. Let's see how many items in the `result` container are zero. To do this, we use the `count_if` function. This will iterate over a container, apply the predicate to every item, and count how many times the predicate returns a value of `true`. There are several ways to do this. The first defines a predicate function:

```
bool equals_zero(int a)
{
    return (a == 0);
}
```

A pointer to this can then be passed to the `count_if` function:

```
int zeros = count_if(
    result.begin(), result.end(), equals_zero);
```

The first two parameters indicate the range of values to check. The last parameter is a pointer to the function that is used as the predicate. Of course, if you are checking for different values you can make this more generic:

```
template<typename T, T value>
inline bool equals(T a)
{
    return a == value;
}
```

Call it like this:

```
int zeros = count_if(
    result.begin(), result.end(), equals<int, 0>);
```

The problem with this code is that we are defining the operation in a place other than where it is used. The `equals` function could be defined in another file; however, with a predicate it is more readable to have the code that does the checking defined close to the code that needs the predicate.

The `<functional>` header also defines classes that can be used as function objects. For example, `equal_to<int>`, which compares two values. However, the `count_if` function expects a unary function object, to which it will pass a single value (see the `equals_zero` function, described previously). `equal_to<int>` is a binary function object, comparing two values. We need to provide the second operand and to do this we use the helper function called `bind2nd`:

```
int zeros = count_if(
    result.begin(), result.end(), bind2nd(equal_to<int>(), 0));
```

The `bind2nd` will *bind* the parameter 0 to the function object created from `equal_to<int>`. Using a function object like this brings the definition of the predicate closer to the function call that will use it, but the syntax looks rather messy. C++11 provides a mechanism to get the compiler to determine the function objects that are required and bind parameters to them. These are called lambda expressions.

# Introducing lambda expressions

A lambda expression is used to create an anonymous function object at the location where the function object will be used. This makes your code much more readable because you can see what will be executed. On first sight, a lambda expression looks like a function definition in-place as a function parameter:

```
auto less_than_10 = [](int a) {return a < 10; };
bool b = less_than_10(4);
```

So that we don't have the complication of a function that uses a predicate, in this code we have assigned a variable to the lambda expression. This is not normally how you would use it, but it makes the description clearer. The square brackets at the beginning of the lambda expression are called the **capture list**. This expression does not capture variables, so the brackets are empty. You can use variables declared outside of the lambda expression and these have to be *captured*. The capture list indicates whether all such variables will be captured by a reference (use [&]) or by a value (use [=]). You can also name the variables that will be captured (if there are more than one, use a comma-separated list) and if they are captured by a value, you use just their names. If they are captured by a reference, use a & on their names.

You could make the preceding lambda expression more generic by introducing a variable declared outside of the expression called limit:

```
int limit = 99;
auto less_than = [limit](int a) {return a < limit; };
```

If you compare a lambda expression to a global function, the capture list is a bit like identifying the global variables that the global function can access.

After the caption list, you give the parameter list in parentheses. Again, if you compare a lambda to a function, the lambda parameter list is equivalent to the function parameter list. If the lambda expression does not have any parameters, then you can miss out the parentheses altogether.

The body for the lambda is given in a pair of braces. This can contain anything that can be found in a function. The lambda body can declare local variables, and it can even declare static variables, which looks bizarre, but is legal:

```
auto incr = [] { static int i; return ++i; };
incr();
incr();
cout << incr() << endl; // 3
```

The return value of the lambda is deduced from the item that is returned. A lambda expression does not have to return a value, in which case the expression will return void:

```
auto swap = [](int& a, int& b) { int x = a; a = b; b = x; };
int i = 10, j = 20;
cout << i << " " << j << endl;
swap(i, j);
cout << i << " " << j << endl;
```

The power of lambda expressions is that you can use them in cases when a function object or a predicate is needed:

```
vector<int> v { 1, 2, 3, 4, 5 };
int less_than_3 = count_if(
    v.begin(), v.end(),
    [](int a) { return a < 3; });
cout << "There are " << less_than_3 << " items less than 3" << endl;
```

Here we declare a `vector` and initialize it with some values. The `count_if` function is used to count how many items in the container are less than 3. So, the first two parameters are used to give the range of items to check, and the third parameter is a lambda expression that performs the comparison. The `count_if` function will call this expression for every item in the range that is passed in via the a parameter of the lambda. The `count_if` function keeps a running count of how many times the lambda returns `true`.

# Using functions in C++

The example in this chapter uses the techniques you have learned in this chapter to list all the files in a folder, and subfolders, in order of file size, giving a listing of the filenames and their sizes. The example is the equivalent of typing the following at the command line:

**dir /b /s /os /a-d folder**

Here, `folder` is the folder you are listing. The `/s` option recurses, `/a-d` removes folders from the list, and `/os` orders by size. The problem is that without the `/b` option we get information about each folder, but using it removes the file size in the list. We want a list of filenames (and their paths), their size, ordered by the smallest first.

Start by creating a new folder for this chapter (`Chapter_05`) under the `Beginning_C++` folder. In Visual C++ create a new C++ source file and save it as `files.cpp` under this new folder. The example will use basic output and strings. It will take a single command line parameter; if more command-line parameters are passed, we just use the first one. Add the following to `files.cpp`:

```
#include <iostream>
#include <string>
using namespace std;

int main(int argc, char* argv[])
{
    if (argc < 2) return 1;
    return 0;
```

```
    }
```

The example will use the Windows functions, `FindFirstFile` and `FindNextFile`, to get information about files that meet a file specification. These return data in a `WIN32_FIND_DATAA` structure, which has information about the filename, the file size, and file attributes. The functions also return information about folders too, so it means we can test for subfolders and recurse. The `WIN32_FIND_DATAA` structure gives the file size as a 64-bit number in two parts: the upper and lower 32 bits. We will create our own structure to hold this information. At the top of the file, after the C++ include files, add the following:

```
using namespace std;

#include <windows.h>
struct file_size {
    unsigned int high;
    unsigned int low;
};
```

The first line is the Windows SDK header file so that you can access the Windows functions, and the structure is used to hold the information about a file's size. We want to compare files by their sizes. The `WIN32_FIND_DATAA` structure provides the size in two `unsigned long` members (one with the upper 4 bytes and the other with the lower 4 bytes). We could store this as a 64-bit number, but instead, so that we have an excuse to write some operators, we store the size in our `file_size` structure. The example will print out file sizes and will compare file sizes, so we will write an operator to insert a `file_size` object into an output steam; since we want to order the files by size, we need an operator to determine if one `file_size` object is greater than the other.

The code will use Windows functions to get information about the files, in particular their name and size. This information will be stored in a `vector`, so at the top of the file add these two highlighted lines:

```
#include <string>
#include <vector>
#include <tuple>
```

The `tuple` class is needed so that we can store both a `string` (the filename) and a `file_size` object as each item in the `vector`. To make the code more readable add the following alias after the structure definition:

```
using file_info = tuple<string, file_size>;
```

Then just above the `main` function add the skeleton code for the function that will get the file in a folder:

```
void files_in_folder(
    const char *folderPath, vector<file_info>& files)
{
}
```

This function takes a reference to a `vector` and a folder path. The code will go through each item in the specified folder. If it is a file, it will store the details in the `vector`; otherwise, if the item is a folder it will call itself to get the files in that subfolder. Add a call to this function at the bottom of the `main` function:

```
vector<file_info> files;
files_in_folder(argv[1], files);
```

The code has already checked that there is at least one command line argument, and we use this as the folder to examine. The `main` function should print out the file information, so we declare a `vector` on the stack and pass this by reference to the `files_in_folder` function. This code does nothing so far, but you can compile the code to make sure that there are no typos (remember to use the `/EHsc` parameter).

Most of the work is carried out in the `files_in_folder` function. As a start, add the following code to this function:

```
string folder(folderPath);
folder += "*";
WIN32_FIND_DATAA findfiledata {};
void* hFind = FindFirstFileA(folder.c_str(), &findfiledata);

if (hFind != INVALID_HANDLE_VALUE)
{
    do
    {
    } while (FindNextFileA(hFind, &findfiledata));
    FindClose(hFind);
}
```

We will use the ASCII version of the functions (hence the trailing A on the structure and function names). The `FindFirstFileA` function takes a search path, and in this case, we use the name of a folder suffixed with a *, meaning *everything in this folder*. Notice that the Windows function wants a `const char*` parameter, so we use the `c_str` function on the `string` object.

If the function call succeeds and it finds an item that meets this criterion, then the function fills in the `WIN32_FIND_DATAA` structure passed by the reference and it also returns an opaque pointer which will be used to make subsequent calls on this search (you do not need to know what it points to). The code checks to see if the call was successful, and if so, it repeatedly calls `FindNextFileA` to get the next item until this function returns 0, indicating there are no more items. The opaque pointer is passed to `FindNextFileA` so that it knows which search is being checked. When the search is complete, the code calls `FindClose` to release whatever resources Windows allocates for the search.

The search will return both file and folder items; to handle each differently, we can test the `dwFileAttributes` member of the `WIN32_FIND_DATAA` structure. Add the following code in the `do` loop:

```
string findItem(folderPath);
findItem += "";
findItem += findfiledata.cFileName;
if ((findfiledata.dwFileAttributes & FILE_ATTRIBUTE_DIRECTORY) != 0)
{
    // this is a folder so recurse
}
else
{
    // this is a file so store information
}
```

The `WIN32_FIND_DATAA` structure contains just the relative name of the item in the folder, so the first few lines create an absolute path. The following lines test to see if the item is a folder (directory) or a file. If the item is a file, then we simply add it to the vector passed to the function. Add the following to the `else` clause:

```
file_size fs{};
fs.high = findfiledata.nFileSizeHigh;
fs.low = findfiledata.nFileSizeLow;
files.push_back(make_tuple(findItem, fs));
```

The first three lines initialize a `file_size` structure with the size data, and the last line adds a `tuple` with the name of the file and its size to the `vector`. So that you can see the results of a simple call to this function, add the following to the bottom of the `main` function:

```
for (auto file : files)
{
    cout << setw(16) << get<1>(file) << " "
        << get<0>(file) << endl;
}
```

This iterates through the items in the `files` vector. Each item is a `tuple<string, file_size>` object and to get the `string` item, you can use the Standard Library function, `get`, using 0 as the function template parameter, and to get the `file_size` object you call `get` with 1 as the function template parameter. The code calls the `setw` manipulator to make sure that the file sizes are always printed in a column 16 characters wide. To use this, you need to add an include for `<iomanip>` at the top of the file. Notice that `get<1>` will return a `file_size` object and this is inserted into `cout`. As it stands, this code will not compile because there is no operator to do this. We need to write one.

After the definition of the structure, add the following code:

```
ostream& operator<<(ostream& os, const file_size fs)
{
    int flags = os.flags();
    unsigned long long ll = fs.low +
        ((unsigned long long)fs.high << 32);
    os << hex << ll;
    os.setf(flags);
    return os;
}
```

This operator will alter the `ostream` object, so we store the initial state at the beginning of the function and restore the object to this state at the end. Since the file size is a 64-bit number, we convert the constituent parts of the `file_size` object and then print it out as a hexadecimal number.

Now you can compile and run this application. For example:

**files C: \windows**

This will list the names and sizes of the files in the `windows` folder.

There are two more things that need to be done--recurse subfolders and sort the data. Both are straightforward to implement. In the `files_in_folder` function, add the following code to the code block of the `if` statement:

```
// this is a folder so recurse
string folder(findfiledata.cFileName);
// ignore . and .. directories
if (folder != "." && folder != "..")
{
    files_in_folder(findItem.c_str(), files);
}
```

The search will return the . (current) folder and .. (parent) folder, so we need to check for these and ignore them. The next action is to recursively call the `files_in_folder` function to obtain the files in the subfolder. If you wish, you can compile and test the application, but this time it is best to test the code using the `Beginning_C++` folder because recursively listing the Windows folder will produce a lot of files.

The code returns the list of files as they were obtained, but we want to see them in order of file size. To do this we can use the sort function in the `<algorithm>` header, so add an include to this after the include for `<tuple>`. In the `main` function, after the call to `files_in_folder`, add this code:

```
files_in_folder(argv[1], files);

sort(files.begin(), files.end(),
    [](const file_info& lhs, const file_info& rhs) {
        return get<1>(rhs) > get<1>(lhs);
} );
```

The first two parameters of the `sort` function indicate the range of items to check. The third item is a predicate, and the function will pass two items from the `vector` to the predicate. You have to return a value of `true` if the two parameters are in order (the first is smaller than the second).

The predicate is provided by a lambda expression. There are no captured variables so the expression starts with `[]` and this is followed by the parameter list of the items being compared by the `sort` algorithm (passed by `const` reference, because they will not be changed). The actual comparison is carried out between the braces. Since we want to list the files in ascending order, we have to ensure that the second of the two is bigger than the first. In this code, we use the `>` operator on the two `file_size` objects. So that this code will compile, we need to define this operator. After the insertion operator add the following:

```
bool operator>(const file_size& lhs, const file_size& rhs)
{
    if (lhs.high > rhs.high) return true;
    if (lhs.high == rhs.high) {
        if (lhs.low > rhs.low) return true;
    }
    return false;
}
```

You can now compile the example and run it. You should find that the files in the specified folder and subfolders are listed in order of the size of the files.

# Summary

Functions allow you to segment your code into logical routines, which makes your code more readable, and gives the flexibility of being able to reuse code. C++ provides a wealth of options to define functions, including variable argument lists, templates, function pointers, and lambda expressions. However, there is one main issue with global functions: the data is separate from the function. This means that the function has to access the data via global data items, or data has to be passed to a function via a parameter every time the function is called. In both cases, the data exists outside the function and could be used by other functions unrelated to the data. The next chapter will give a solution to this: classes. A `class` allows you to encapsulate data in a custom type, and you can define functions on that type so that only these functions will be able to access the data.

# 4
# Classes

C++ allows you to create your own types. These custom types can have operators and can be converted to other types; indeed, they can be used like built-in types with the behavior that you define. This facility uses a language feature called classes. The advantage of being able to define your own types is that you can encapsulate data in objects of your chosen type, and use the type to manage the lifetime of that data. You can also define the actions that can be performed on that data. In other words, you are able to define custom types that have state and behavior, which is the basis of object-orientated programming.

## Writing classes

When you use built-in types, the data is directly available to whatever code has access to that data. C++ provides a mechanism (const) to prevent write access, but any code can use const_cast to cast away const-ness. Your data could be complex, such as a pointer to a file mapped into memory with the intention that your code will change a few bytes and then write the file back to disk. Such raw pointers are dangerous because other code with access to the pointer could change part of the buffer that should not be changed. What is needed is a mechanism to encapsulate the data into a type that knows what bytes to change, and only allow that type to access the data. This is the basic idea behind classes.

# Reviewing structures

We have already seen one mechanism in C++ to encapsulate data: struct. A structure allows you to declare data members that are built-in types, pointers, or references. When you create a variable from that struct, you are creating an **instance** of the structure, also known as an **object**. You can create variables that are references to this object or pointers that point to the object. You can even pass the object by value to a function where the compiler will make a copy of the object (it will call the *copy constructor* for the struct). We have seen that with a struct any code that has access to an instance (even through a pointer or reference) can access the members of the object (although this can be changed). Used like this, a struct can be thought of as **aggregate** types containing the state.

The members of an instance of a struct can be initialized by accessing them directly with the dot operator or using the -> operator through a pointer to the object. We have also seen that you can initialize an instance of a struct with an initializer list (in braces). This is quite restrictive because the initializer list has to match the data members in the struct. In Chapter 2, *Working with Memory, Arrays, and Pointers*, you saw that you can have a pointer as a member of a struct, but you have to explicitly take appropriate action to release the memory pointed to by the pointer; if you don't, then this could result in a memory leak.

A struct is one of the class types that you can use in C++; the other two are union and class. Custom types defined as struct or class can have behaviors as well as state, and C++ allows you to define some special functions to control how instances are created and destroyed, copied, and converted. Furthermore, you can define operators on a struct or class type so that you can use the operators on instances in a similar way to using the operators on built-in types. There is a difference between struct and class which we will address later, but in general the rest of the chapter will be about classes and when a class is mentioned you can usually assume the same applies to a struct as well.

# Defining classes

A class is defined in a statement, and it will define its members in a block with multiple statements enclosed by braces { }. As it's a statement, you have to place a semicolon after the last brace. A class can be defined in a header file (as are many of the **C++ Standard Library** classes), but you have to take steps to ensure that such files are included only once in a source file. There are, however, some rules about specific items in a class that must be defined in a source file, which will be covered later.

If you peruse the C++ Standard Library, you will see that classes contain member functions and, in an attempt to put all the code for a class into a single header file, this makes the code difficult to read and difficult to understand. This may be justifiable for a library file maintained by a legion of expert C++ programmers, but for your own projects readability should be a key design goal. For this reason, a C++ class can be declared in a C++ header file, including its member functions, and the actual implementation of the functions can be placed in a source file. This makes the header files easier to maintain and more reusable.

# Defining class behavior

A class can define functions that can only be called through an instance of the class; such a function is often called a **method**. An object will have state; this is provided by the data members defined by the class and initialized when the object is created. The methods on an object define the behavior of the object, usually acting upon the state of the object. When you design a class, you should think of the methods in this way: they describe the object doing something.

```
class cartesian_vector
{
public:
    double x;
    double y;
    // other methods
    double get_magnitude() { return std::sqrt((x * x) + (y * y)); }
};
```

This class has two data members, x and y, which represent the direction of a two-dimensional vector resolved in the Cartesian x and y directions. The `public` keyword means that any members defined after this specifier are accessible by code defined outside of the class. By default, all the members of a class are `private` unless you indicate otherwise. `private` means that the member can only be accessed by other members of the class.

This is the difference between a `struct` and a `class`: by default, members of a `struct` are `public` and by default, members of a `class` are `private`.

This class has a method called `get_magnituide` that will return the length of the Cartesian vector. This function acts upon the two data members of the class and returns a value. This is a type of **accessor** method; it gives access to the state of the object. Such a method is typical on a `class`, but there is no requirement that methods return values. Like functions, a method can also take parameters. The `get_magnituide` method can be called like this:

```
cartesian_vector vec { 3.0, 4.0 };
double len = vec.get_magnitude(); // returns 5.0
```

Here a `cartesian_vector` object is created on the stack and list initializer syntax is used to initialize it to a value representing a vector of $(3, 4)$. The length of this vector is 5, which is the value returned by calling `get_magnitude` on the object.

## Using the this pointer

The methods in a class have a special calling convention, which in Visual C++ is called `__thiscall`. The reason is that every method in a class has a hidden parameter called `this`, which is a pointer of the class type to the current instance:

```
class cartesian_vector
{
public:
    double x;
    double y;
    // other methods
    double get_magnitude()
    {
        return std::sqrt((this->x * this->x) + (this->y * this->y));
    }
};
```

Here, the `get_magnitude` method returns the length of the `cartesian_vector` object. The members of the object are accessed through the `->` operator. As shown previously, the members of the class can be accessed without the `this` pointer, but it does make it explicit that the items are members of the `class`.

You could define a method on the `cartesian_vector` type that allows you to change its state:

```
class cartesian_vector
{
public:
    double x;
    double y;
```

```
        reset(double x, double y) { this->x = x; this->y = y; }
        // other methods
};
```

The parameters of the `reset` method have the same names as the data members of the class; however, since we use the `this` pointer the compiler knows that this is not ambiguous.

You can dereference the `this` pointer with the `*` operator to get access to the object. This is useful when a member function must return a reference to the current object (as some operators will, as we will see later) and you can do this by returning `*this`. A method in a class can also pass the `this` pointer to an external function, which means that it is passing the current object by reference through a typed pointer.

# Using the scope resolution operator

You can define a method inline in the `class` statement, but you can also separate the declaration and implementation, so the method is declared in the `class` statement but it is defined elsewhere. When defining a method out of the `class` statement, you need to provide the method with the name of the type using the scope resolution operator. For example, using the previous `cartesian_vector` example:

```
class cartesian_vector
{
public:
    double x;
    double y;
    // other methods
    double magnitude();
};

double cartesian_vector::magnitude()
{
    return sqrt((this->x * this->x) + (this->y * this->y));
}
```

The method is defined outside the class definition; it is, however, still the class method, so it has a `this` pointer that can be used to access the object's members. Typically, the class will be declared in a header file with prototypes for the methods and the actual methods will be implemented in a separate source file. In this case, using the `this` pointer to access the class members (methods and data members) make it obvious, when you take a cursory look at a source file, that the functions are methods of a class.

# Defining class state

Your class can have built-in types as data members, or custom types. These data members can be declared in the class (and created when an instance of the class is constructed), or they can be pointers to objects created in the free store or references to objects created elsewhere. Bear in mind that if you have a pointer to an item created in the free store, you need to know whose responsibility it is to deallocate the memory that the pointer points to. If you have a reference (or pointer) to an object created on a stack frame somewhere, you need to make sure that the objects of your class do not live longer than that stack frame.

When you declare data members as `public` it means that external code can read and write to the data members. You can decide that you would prefer to only give read-only access, in which case you can make the members `private` and provide read access through accessors:

```
class cartesian_vector
{
    double x;
    double y;
public:
    double get_x() { return this->x; }
    double get_y() { return this->y; }
    // other methods
};
```

When you make the data members `private` it means that you cannot use the initializer list syntax to initialize an object, but we will address this later. You may decide to use an accessor to give write access to a data member and use this to check the value.

```
void cartesian_vector::set_x(double d)
{
    if (d > -100 && d < 100) this->x = d;
}
```

This is for a type where the range of values must be between (but not including) -100 and 100.

# Creating objects

You can create objects on the stack or in the free store. Using the previous example, this is as follows:

```
cartesian_vector vec { 10, 10 };
cartesian_vector *pvec = new cartesian_vector { 5, 5 };
// use pvec
delete pvec
```

This is **direct initialization** of the object and assumes that the data members of `cartesian_vector` are `public`. The `vec` object is created on the stack and initialized with an initializer list. In the second line, an object is created in the free store and initialized with an initializer list. The object on the free store must be freed at some point and this is carried out by deleting the pointer. The `new` operator will allocate enough memory in the free store for the data members of the class and for any of the infrastructure the class needs.

A new feature of C++11 is to allow direct initialization to provide default values in the class:

```
class point
{
public:
    int x = 0;
    int y = 0;
};
```

This means that if you create an instance of `point` without any other initialization values, it will be initialized so that `x` and `y` are both zero. If the data member is a built-in array, then you can provide direct initialization with an initialization list in the class:

```
class car
{
public:
    double tire_pressures[4] { 25.0, 25.0, 25.0, 25.0 };
};
```

The C++ Standard Library containers can be initialized with an initialize list, so, in this class for `tire_pressures`, instead of declaring the type to be `double[4]` we could use `vector<double>` or `array<double, 4>`, and initialize it in the same way.

# Construction of objects

C++ allows you to define special methods to perform the initialization of the object. These are called **constructors**. In C++11, you will get three such functions generated for you by default, but you can provide your own versions if you wish. These three constructors, along with three other related functions, are as follows:

- **Default constructor:** This is called to create an object with the *default* value.
- **Copy constructor:** This is used to create a new object based on the value of an existing object.
- **Move constructor:** This is used to create a new object using the data moved from an existing object.
- **Destructor:** This is called to clean up the resources used by an object.
- **Copy assignment:** This copies the data from one existing object into another existing object.
- **Move assignment:** This moves the data from one existing object into another existing object.

The compiler-created versions of these functions will be implicitly `public`; however, you may decide to prevent copying or assigning by defining your own versions, and making them `private`, or you can delete them using the `=delete` syntax. You can also provide your own constructors that will take any parameters you decide you need to initialize a new object.

A constructor is a member function that has the same name as the type, but does not return a value, so you cannot return a value if the construction fails, which potentially means that the caller will receive a partially constructed object. The only way to handle this situation is to throw an exception (explained in `Chapter 7`, *Diagnostics and Debugging*).

# Defining constructors

The default constructor is used when an object is created without a value and hence the object will have to be initialized with a default value. The `point` declared previously could be implemented like this:

```
class point
{
    double x; double y;
public:
    point() { x = 0; y = 0; }
};
```

This explicitly initializes the items to a value of zero. If you want to create an instance with the default values, you do not include parentheses.

```
point p;    // default constructor called
```

It is important to be aware of this syntax because it is easy to write the following by mistake:

```
point p();    // compiles, but is a function prototype!
```

This will compile because the compiler will think you are providing a function prototype as a forward declaration. However, you'll get an error when you attempt to use the symbol p as a variable. You can also call the default constructor using initialize list syntax with empty braces:

```
point p {};    // calls default constructor
```

Although it does not matter in this case, where the data members are built-in types, initializing data members in the body of the constructor like this involves a call to the assignment operator of the member type. A more efficient way is to use direct initialization with a **member list**.

The following is a constructor that takes two parameters, which illustrates a member list:

```
point(double x, double y) : x(x), y(y) {}
```

The identifiers outside the parentheses are the names of class members, and the items inside the parentheses are expressions used to initialize that member (in this case, a constructor parameter). This example uses x and y for the parameter names. You don't have to do this; this is only given here as an illustration that the compiler will distinguish between the parameters and data members. You can also use braced initializer syntax in the member list of a constructor:

```
point(double x, double y) : x{x}, y{y} {}
```

You call this constructor when you create an object like this:

```
point p(10.0, 10.0);
```

You can also create an array of objects:

```
point arr[4];
```

This creates four `point` objects, which can be accessed by indexing the `arr` array. Note that when you create an array of objects the *default* constructor is called on the items; there is no way to call any other constructor, and so you have to initialize each one separately.

You can also provide default values for constructor parameters. In the following code, the `car` class has values for the four tires (the first two are the front tires) and for the spare tire. There is one constructor that has mandatory values that will be used for the front and back tires, and an optional value for the spare. If a value is not provided for the spare tire pressure, then a default value will be used:

```
class car
{
    array<double, 4> tire_pressures;;
    double spare;
public:
    car(double front, double back, double s = 25.0)
        : tire_pressures{front, front, back, back}, spare{s} {}
};
```

This constructor can be called with either two values or three values:

```
car commuter_car(25, 27);
car sports_car(26, 28, 28);
```

## Delegating constructors

A constructor may call another constructor using the same member list syntax:

```
class car
{
    // data members
public:
    car(double front, double back, double s = 25.0)
        : tire_pressures{front, front, back, back}, spare{s} {}
    car(double all) : car(all, all) {}
};
```

Here, the constructor that takes one value delegates to the constructor that takes three parameters (in this case using the default value for the spare).

## Copy constructor

A copy constructor is used when you pass an object by value (or return by value) or if you explicitly construct an object based on another object. The last two lines of the following both create a `point` object from another `point` object, and in both cases the copy constructor is called:

```
point p1(10, 10);
```

```
point p2(p1);
point p3 = p1;
```

The last line looks like it involves the assignment operator, but it actually calls the copy constructor. The copy constructor could be implemented like this:

```
class point
{
    int x = 0; int y = 0;
public:
    point(const point& rhs) : x(rhs.x), y(rhs.y) {}
};
```

The initialization accesses the `private` data members on another object (`rhs`). This is acceptable because the constructor parameter is the same type as the object being created. The copy operation may not be as simple as this. For example, if the class contains a data member that is a pointer, you will most likely want to copy the data that the pointer points to, and this will involve creating a new memory buffer in the new object.

# Converting between types

You can also perform conversions. In math, you can define a vector that represents direction, so that the line drawn between two points is a vector. In our code we have already defined a `point` class and a `cartesian_vector` class. You could decide to have a constructor that creates a vector between the origin and a point, in which case you are converting a `point` object to a `cartesian_vector` object:

```
class cartesian_vector
{
    double x; double y;
public:
    cartesian_vector(const point& p) : x(p.x), y(p.y) {}
};
```

There is a problem here, which we will address in a moment. The conversions can be called like this:

```
point p(10, 10);
cartesian_vector v1(p);
cartesian_vector v2 { p };
cartesian_vector v3 = p;
```

# Making friends

The problem with the code above is that the `cartesian_vector` class accesses `private` members of the `point` class. Since we have written both classes, we are happy to bend the rules, and so we make the `cartesian_vector` class a `friend` of the `point` class:

```
class cartesian_vector; // forward decalartion

class point
{
    double x; double y;
public:
    point(double x, double y) : x(x), y(y){}
    friend class cartesian_point;
};
```

Since the `cartesian_vector` class is declared after the `point` class, we have to provide a forward declaration that essentially tells the compiler that the name `cartesian_vector` is about to be used and it will be declared elsewhere. The important line starts with `friend`. This indicates that the code for the entire class, `cartesian_vector`, can have access to the private members (data and methods) of the `point` class.

You can also declare `friend` functions. For example, you could declare an operator such that a `point` object can be inserted into the `cout` object, so it can be printed to the console. You cannot change the `ostream` class, but you can define a global method:

```
ostream& operator<<(ostream& stm, const point& pt)
{
    stm << "(" << pt.x << "," << pt.y << ")";
    return stm;
}
```

This function accesses the `private` members of `point` so you have to make the function a `friend` of the `point` class with:

```
friend ostream& operator<<(ostream&, const point&);
```

Such `friend` declarations have to be declared in the `point` class, but it is irrelevant whether it is put in the `public` or `private` section.

# Marking constructors as explicit

In some cases, you do not want to allow the implicit conversion between one type that is passed as a parameter of the constructor of another type. To do this, you need to mark the constructor with the `explicit` specifier. This now means that the only way to call the constructor is using the parentheses syntax: *explicitly* calling the constructor. In the following code, you cannot implicitly convert a `double` to an object of `mytype`:

```
class mytype
{
public:
    explicit mytype(double x);
};
```

Now you have to *explicitly* call the constructor if you want to create an object with a `double` parameter:

```
mytype t1 = 10.0; // will not compile, cannot convert
mytype t2(10.0);  // OK
```

# Destructing objects

When an object is destroyed, a special method called the destructor is called. This method has the name of the class prefixed with a ~ symbol and it does not return a value.

If the object is an automatic variable, on the stack, then it will be destroyed when the variable goes out of scope. When an object is passed by value, a copy is made on the called function's stack and the object will be destroyed when the called function completes. Furthermore, it does not matter how the function completes, whether an explicit call to `return` or reaching the final brace, or if an exception is thrown; in all of these cases, the destructor is called. If there are multiple objects in a function, the destructors are called in the reverse order to the construction of the objects in the same scope. If you create an array of objects, then the default constructor is called for each object in the array on the statement that declares the array, and all the objects will be destroyed--and the destructor on each one is called, when the array goes out of scope.

Here are some examples, for a class `mytype`:

```
void f(mytype t) // copy created
{
    // use t
}   // t destroyed

void g()
{
    mytype t1;
    f(t1);
    if (true)
    {
        mytype t2;
    }   // t2 destroyed

    mytype arr[4];
}   // 4 objects in arr destroyed in reverse order to creation
    // t1 destroyed
```

An interesting action occurs when you return an object. The following annotation is what you would expect:

```
mytype get_object()
{
    mytype t;               // default constructor creates t
    return t;               // copy constructor creates a temporary
}                           // t destroyed

void h()
{
    test tt = get_object(); // copy constructor creates tt
}                           // temporary destroyed, tt destroyed
```

In fact, the process is more streamlined. In a debug build, the compiler will see that the temporary object created on the return of the `get_object` function is the object that will be used as the variable `tt`, and so there is no extra copy on the return value of the `get_object` function. The function actually looks like this:

```
void h()
{
    mytype tt = get_object();
}   // tt destroyed
```

However, the compiler is able to optimize the code further. In a release build (with optimizations enabled), the temporary will not be created and the object `tt` in the calling function will be the actual object `t` created in `get_object`.

An object will be destroyed when you explicitly delete a pointer to an object allocated on the free store. In this case, the call to the destructor is deterministic: it is called when your code calls `delete`. Again, with the same class `mytype`, this is as follows:

```
mytype *get_object()
{
    return new mytype; // default constructor called
}

void f()
{
    mytype *p = get_object();
    // use p
    delete p;          // object destroyed
}
```

There will be times when you want to use the deterministic aspect of deleting an object (with the possible danger of forgetting to call `delete`) and there will be times when you prefer to have the reassurance that an object is to be destroyed at an appropriate time (with the potential that it may be much later in time).

If a data member in a class is a custom type with a destructor, then when the containing object is destroyed the destructors on the contained objects are called too. Nonetheless, note that this is only if the *object* is a class member. If a class member is a pointer to an object in the free store, then you have to explicitly delete the pointer in the containing object's destructor. However, you need to know where the object the pointer points to is because if it is not in the free store, or if the object is used by other objects, calling `delete` will cause problems.

# Assigning objects

The assignment operator is called when an *already created* object is assigned to the value of another one. By default, you will get a copy assignment operator that will copy all the data members. This is not necessarily what you want, particularly if the object has a data member that is a pointer, in which case your intention is more likely to do a deep copy and copy the data pointed to rather than the value of the pointer (in the latter case, *two* objects will point to the same data).

If you define a copy constructor, you will still get the default copy assignment operator; however, it makes sense that if you regard it important to write your own copy constructor, you should also provide a custom copy assignment operator. (Similarly, if you define a copy assignment operator, you will get the default copy constructor unless you define it.)

The copy assignment operator is typically a `public` member of the class and it takes a `const` reference to the object that will be used to provide the values for the assignment. The semantics of the assignment operator are that you can chain them, so, for example, this code calls the assignment operator on two of the objects:

```
buffer a, b, c;                    // default constructors called
// do something with them
a = b = c;                         // make them all the same value
a.operator=(b.operator=(c));       // make them all the same value
```

The last two lines do the same thing, but clearly the first is more readable. To enable these semantics, the assignment operator must return a reference to the object that has been assigned. So, the class `buffer` will have the following method:

```
class buffer
{
    // data members
public:
    buffer(const buffer&);              // copy constructor
    buffer& operator=(const buffer&);   // copy assignment
};
```

Although the copy constructor and copy assignment methods appear to do similar things, there is a key difference. A copy constructor creates a new object that did not exist before the call. The calling code is aware that if the construction fails, then an exception will be raised. With assignment, both objects already exist, so you are copying the value from one object to another. This should be treated as an atomic action and all the copy should be performed; it is not acceptable for the assignment to fail halfway through, resulting in an object that is a bit of both objects. Furthermore, in construction, an object only exists after the construction is successful, so a copy construction cannot happen on an object itself, but it is perfectly legal (if pointless) for code to assign an object to itself. The copy assignment needs to check for this situation and take appropriate action.

There are various strategies to do this, and a common one is called the copy-and-swap idiom because it uses the Standard Library `swap` function that is marked as `noexcept`, and will not throw an exception. The idiom involves creating a temporary copy of the object on the right-hand side of the assignment and then swapping its data members with the data members of the object on the left-hand side.

# Move semantics

C++11 provides move semantics through a move constructor and a move assignment operator, which are called when a temporary object is used either to create another object or to be assigned to an existing object. In both cases, because the temporary object will not live beyond the statement, the contents of the temporary can be moved to the other object, leaving the temporary object in an invalid state. The compiler will create these functions for you through the default action of moving the data from the temporary to the newly created (or the assigned to) object.

You can write your own versions, and to indicate move semantics these have a parameter that is an rvalue reference (`&&`).

If you want the compiler to provide you with a default version of any of these methods, you can provide the prototype in the class declaration suffixed with `=default`. In most cases, this is self-documenting rather than being a requirement, but if you are writing a POD class you must use the default versions of these functions, otherwise `is_pod` will not return `true`.

If you want to use only move and never to use copy (for example, a file handle class), then you can *delete* the copy functions:

```
class mytype
{
    int *p;
public:
    mytype(const mytype&) = delete;          // copy constructor
    mytype& operator= (const mytype&) = delete; // copy assignment
    mytype& (mytype&&);                       // move constructor
    mytype& operator=(mytype&&);              // move assignment
};
```

This class has a pointer data member and allows move semantics, in which case the move constructor will be called with a reference to a temporary object. Since the object is temporary, it will not survive after the move constructor call. This means that the new object can *move* the state of the temporary object into itself:

```
mytype::mytype(mytype&& tmp)
{
    this->p = tmp.p;
    tmp.p = nullptr;
}
```

The move constructor assigns the temporary object's pointer to `nullptr`, so that any destructor defined for the class does not attempt to delete the pointer.

# Declaring static members

You can declare a member of a class--a data member or a method--`static`. This is similar in some ways to how you use the `static` keyword on automatic variables and functions declared at file scope, but there are some important, and different, properties to this keyword when used on a class member.

# Defining static members

When you use `static` on a class member it means that the item is associated with the class and not with a specific instance. In the case, of data members, this means that there is one data item shared by all instances of the class. Likewise, a `static` method is not attached to an object, it is not `__thiscall` and has no `this` pointer.

A `static` method is part of the namespace of a class, so it can create objects for the class and have access to their `private` members. A `static` method has the `__cdecl` calling convention by default, but you can declare it as `__stdcall` if you wish. This means that, you can write a method within the class that can be used to initialize C-like pointers, which are used by many libraries. Note that the `static` function cannot call nonstatic methods on the class because a nonstatic method will need a `this` pointer, but a nonstatic method can call a `static` method.

A nonstatic method is called through an object, either using the dot operator (for a class instance) or the `->` operator for an object pointer. A `static` method does not need an associated object, but it can be called through one. This gives two ways to call a `static` method, through an object or through the `class` name:

```
class mytype
{
public:
    static void f(){}
    void g(){ f(); }
};
```

Here, the class defines a `static` method called `f` and a nonstatic method called `g`. The nonstatic method `g` can call the `static` method, but the `static` method `f` cannot call the nonstatic method. Since the `static` method `f` is `public`, code outside the `class` can call it:

```
mytype c;
c.g();       // call the nonstatic method
c.f();       // can also call the static method thru an object
mytype::f(); // call static method without an object
```

Although the `static` function can be called through an object, you do not have to create any objects at all to call it.

Static data members need a bit more work because when you use `static` it indicates that the data member is not part of an object, and usually data members are allocated when an object is created. You have to define `static` data members outside of the class:

```
class mytype
{
public:
    static int i;
    static void incr() { i++; }
};

// in a source file
int mytype::i = 42;
```

The data member is defined outside of the class at file scope. It is named using the `class` name, but note that it also has to be defined using the type. In this case the data member is initialized with a value; if you do not do this, then on the first use of the variable it will have the default value of the type (in this case, zero). If you choose to declare the class in a header file (which is common), the definition of the `static` data members must be in a source file.

You can also declare a variable in a method that is `static`. In this case, the value is maintained across method calls, in all objects, so it has the same effect as a `static class` member, but you do not have the issue of defining the variable outside of the class.

## Using static and global objects

A `static` variable in a global function will be created at some point before the function is first called. Similarly, a `static` object that is a member of a class will be initialized at some point before it is first accessed.

Static and global objects are constructed before the `main` function is called, and destroyed after the `main` function finishes. The order of this initialization has some issues. The C++ standard says that the initialization of `static` and global objects defined in a source file will occur before any function or object defined in that source file is used, and if there are several global objects in a source file, they will be initialized in the order that they are *defined*. The issue is if you have several source files with `static` objects in each. There is no guarantee on the order in which these objects will be initialized. It becomes a problem if one `static` object depends on another `static` object because you cannot guarantee that the dependent object will be created after the object it depends upon.

# Named constructors

This is one application for `public static` methods. The idea is that since the `static` method is a member of the `class` it means that it has access to the `private` members of an instance of the `class`, so such a method can create an object, perform some additional initialization, and then return the object to the caller. This is a **factory method**. The `point` class used so far has been constructed using Cartesian points, but we could also create a point based on polar co-ordinates, where the `(x, y)` Cartesian co-ordinates can be calculated as:

```
x = r * cos(theta)
y = r * sin(theta)
```

Here `r` is the length of the vector to the point and `theta` is the angle of this vector counter-clockwise to the x axis. The `point` class already has a constructor that takes two `double` values, so we cannot use this to pass polar co-ordinates; instead, we can use a `static` method as a *named constructor*:

```
class point
{
    double x; double y;
public:
    point(double x, double y) : x(x), y(y){}
    static point polar(double r, double th)
    {
        return point(r * cos(th), r * sin(th));
    }
};
```

The method can be called like this:

```
const double pi = 3.141529;
const double root2 = sqrt(2);
point p11 = point::polar(root2, pi/4);
```

The object `p11` is the `point` with the Cartesian co-ordinates of (1,1). In this example the `polar` method calls a `public` constructor, but it has access to private members, so the same method could be written (less efficiently) as:

```
point point::polar(double r, double th)
{
    point pt;
    pt.x = r * cos(th);
    pt.y = r * sin(th);
    return pt;
}
```

# Nested classes

You can define a class within a class. If the nested class is declared as `public`, then you can create objects in the container class and return them to external code. Typically, however, you will want to declare a class that is used by the class and should be `private`. The following declares a `public` nested class:

```
class outer
{
public:
    class inner
    {
    public:
        void f();
    };

    inner g() { return inner(); }
};

void outer::inner::f()
{
    // do something
}
```

Notice how the name of the nested class is prefixed with the name of the containing class.

# Accessing const objects

You have seen many examples so far of using `const`, and perhaps the most frequent is when it is applied to a reference as a function parameter to indicate to the compiler that the function only has read-only access to the object. Such a `const` reference is used so that objects are passed by reference to avoid the overhead of the copying that would occur if the object were passed by value. Methods on a `class` can access the object data members and, potentially, can change them, so if you pass an object through a `const` reference the compiler will only allow the reference to call methods that do not change the object. The `point` class defined earlier had two accessors to access the data in the class:

```
class point
{
    double x; double y;
public:
    double get_x() { return x; }
    double get_y() { return y: }
};
```

If you define a function that takes a `const` reference to this and you attempt to call these accessors, you will get an error from the compiler:

```
void print_point(const point& p)
{
    cout << "(" << p.get_x() << "," << p.get_y() << ")" << endl;
}
```

The error from the compiler is a bit obscure:

**cannot convert 'this' pointer from 'const point' to 'point &'**

This message is the compiler complaining that the object is `const`, it is immutable, and it does not know whether these methods will preserve the state of the object. The solution is simple--add the `const` keyword to methods that do not change the object state, like this:

```
    double get_x() const { return x; }
    double get_y() const { return y: }
```

This effectively means that the `this` pointer is `const`. The `const` keyword is part of the function prototype, so the method can be overloaded on this. You can have one method that is called when it is called on a `const` object and another called on a non-const object. This enables you to implement a copy-on-write pattern where, for example, a `const` method would return read-only access to the data and the non-const method would return a *copy* of the data that is writeable.

Of course, a method marked with `const` must not alter the data members, not even temporarily. So, such a method can only call `const` methods. There may be rare cases when a data member is designed to be changed through a `const` object; in this case the declaration of the member is marked with the `mutable` keyword.

# Using objects with pointers

Objects can be created on the free store and accessed through a typed pointer. This gives more flexibility because it is efficient to pass pointers to functions, and you can explicitly determine the lifetime of the object because an object is created with the call to `new` and destroyed by the call to `delete`.

# Getting pointers to object members

If you need to get access to the address of a class data member through an instance (assuming the data member is `public`), you simply use the `&` operator:

```
struct point { double x; double y; };
point p { 10.0, 10.0 };
int *pp = &p.x;
```

In this case `struct` is used to declare `point` so that the members are `public` by default. The second line uses an initialization list to construct a `point` object with two values, and then the final line gets a pointer to one of the data members. Of course, the pointer cannot be used after the object has been destroyed. Data members are allocated in memory (in this case on the stack), so the address operator merely gets a pointer to that memory.

Function pointers are a different case. There will only be one copy of the method in memory, regardless of how many instances of the `class` are created, but because methods are called using the `__thiscall` calling convention (with a hidden `this` parameter) you have to have a function pointer that can be initialized with a pointer to an object to provide the `this` pointer. Consider this `class`:

```
class cartesian_vector
{
public:
    // other items
    double get_magnitude() const
    {
        return std::sqrt((this->x * this->x) + (this->y * this->y));
    }
};
```

We can define a function pointer to the `get_magnitude` method like this:

```
double (cartesian_vector::*fn)() const = nullptr;
fn = &cartesian_vector::get_magnitude;
```

The first line declares a function pointer. This is similar to the C function pointer declarations except that there is an inclusion of the `class` name in the pointer type. This is needed so that the compiler knows that it has to provide a `this` pointer in any call through this pointer. The second line obtains a pointer to the method. Notice that no object is involved. You are not getting a function pointer to a method on an object; you are getting a pointer to a method on a `class` that must be called through an object. To call the method through this pointer, you need to use the pointer to the member operator `.*` on an object:

```
cartesian_vector vec(1.0, 1.0);
double mag = (vec.*fn)();
```

The first line creates an object and the second line calls the method. The pointer to the member operator says that the function pointer on the *right* is called with the object on the *left*. The address of the object on the left is used for the `this` pointer when the method is called. As this is a method, we need to provide a parameter list, which in this case is empty (if you have parameters, they would be in the pair of parentheses on the right of this statement). If you have an object pointer, then the syntax is similar, but you use the `->*` pointer to the member operator:

```
cartesian_vector *pvec = new cartesian_vector(1.0, 1.0);
double mag = (pvec->*fn)();
delete pvec;
```

# Operator overloading

One of behaviors of a type is the operations you can apply to it. C++ allows you to overload the C++ operators as part of a class so that it's clear that the operator is acting upon the type. This means that for a unary operator the member method should have no parameters and for a binary operator you need only one parameter, since the current object will be on the left of the operator, and hence the method parameter is the item on the right. The following table summarizes how to implement unary and binary operators, and four exceptions:

| Expression | Name | Member method | Non-member function |
|---|---|---|---|
| +a/-a | Prefix unary | operator■() | operator■(a) |
| a■b | Binary | operator■(b) | operator■(a,b) |
| a+/a- | Postfix unary | operator■(0) | operator■(a,0) |
| a=b | Assignment | operator=(b) | |
| a(b) | Function call | operator()(b) | |
| a[b] | Indexing | operator[](b) | |
| a-> | Pointer access | operator->() | |

Here the ■ symbol is used to indicate any of the acceptable unary or binary operators except for the four operators mentioned in the table.

There are no strict rules over what an operator should return, but it helps if an operator on a custom type behaves like operators on a built-in type. There also has to be some consistency. If you implement the + operator to add two objects together, then the same plus action should be used for the += operator. Also, you could argue that the plus action will also determine what the minus action should be like, and hence the – and –= operators. Similarly, if you want to define the < operator, then you should define <=. >, >=, ==, and != too.

The Standard Library's algorithms (for example, `sort`) will only expect the < operator to be defined on a custom type.

The table shows that you can implement almost all the operators as either a member of the custom type class or as a global function (with the exception of the four listed that have to be member methods). In general, it is best to implement the operator as part of the class because it maintains encapsulation: the member function has access to the non-public members of the class.

An example of a unary operator is the unary negative operator. This usually does not alter an object but returns a new object that is the *negative* of the object. For our `point class`, this means making both co-ordinates negative, which is equivalent to a mirror of the Cartesian point in a line $y = -x$:

```
// inline in point
point operator-() const
{
    return point(-this->x, -this->y);
}
```

The operator is declared as `const` because it's clear the operator does not change the object and hence it's safe to be called on a `const` object. The operator can be called like this:

```
point p1(-1,1);
point p2 = -p1; // p2 is (1,-1)
```

To understand why we have implemented the operator like this, review what the unary operator would do when applied to a built-in type. The second statement here, `int i, j=0; i = -j;`, will only alter `i` and will not alter `j`, so the member `operator-` should not affect the value of the object.

The binary negative operator has a different meaning. First, it has two operands, and, second, in this example, the result is a different type to the operands because the result is a vector that indicates a direction by taking one point away from another. Assuming that the `cartesian_vector` is already defined with a constructor that has two parameters, then we can write:

```
cartesian_vector point::operator-(point& rhs) const
{
    return cartesian_vector(this->x - rhs.x, this->y - rhs.y);
}
```

The increment and decrement operators have a special syntax because they are unary operators that can be prefixed or postfixed, and they alter the object they are applied to. The major difference between the two operators is that the postfixed operator returns the value of the object *before* the increment/decrement action, so a temporary has to be created. For this reason, the prefix operator almost always has better performance than the postfix operator. In a class definition, to distinguish between the two, the prefix operator has no parameters and the postfix operator has a dummy parameter (in the preceding table, 0 is given). For a class `mytype`, this is as follows:

```
class mytype
{
public:
```

```
mytype& operator++()
{
    // do actual increment
    return *this;
}
mytype operator++(int)
{
    mytype tmp(*this);
    operator++(); // call the prefix code
    return tmp;
}
};
```

The actual increment code is implemented by the prefix operator, and this logic is used by the postfix operator through an explicit call to the method.

# Defining function classes

A functor is a class that implements the () operator. This means that you can call an object using the same syntax as a function. Consider this:

```
class factor
{
    double f = 1.0;
public:
    factor(double d) : f(d) {}
    double operator()(double x) const { return f * x; }
};
```

This code can be called like this:

```
factor threeTimes(3);       // create the functor object
double ten = 10.0;
double d1 = threeTimes(ten); // calls operator(double)
double d2 = threeTimes(d1);  // calls operator(double)
```

This code shows that the functor object not only provides some behavior (in this case, performing an action on the parameter) but it also can have a state. The preceding two lines are called through the operator() method on an object:

```
double d2 = threeTimes.operator()(d1);
```

Look at the syntax. The functor object is called as if it is a function declared like this:

```
double multiply_by_3(double d)
{
    return 3 * d;
}
```

Imagine that you want to pass a pointer to a function--perhaps you are want the function's behavior to be altered by external code. To be able to use either a functor or a method pointer, you need to overload your function:

```
void print_value(double d, factor& fn);
void print_value(double d, double(*fn)(double));
```

The first takes a reference to a functor object. The second has a C-type function pointer (to which you can pass a pointer to `multiply_by_3`) and is quite unreadable. In both cases the `fn` parameter is called in the same way in the implementation code, but you need to declare two functions because they are different types. Now, consider the magic of function templates:

```
template<typename Fn>
void print_value(double d, Fn& fn)
{
    double ret = fn(d);
    cout << ret << endl;
}
```

This is generic code; the `Fn` type can be a C function pointer or a functor `class`, and the compiler will generate the appropriate code.

This code can be called by either passing a function pointer to a global function, which will have the __cdecl calling convention, or a functor object where the `operator()` operator will be called, which has a __thiscall calling convention.

This is a mere implementation detail, but it does mean that you can write a generic function that can take either a C-like function pointer or a functor object as a parameter. The C++ Standard Library uses this magic, which means that the algorithms it provides can be called either with a *global function* or a *functor*, or a *lambda expression*.

The Standard Library algorithms use three type of functional classes, generators, and unary and binary functions; that is, functions with zero, one or two parameters. In addition, the Standard Library calls a function object (unary or binary) that returns a `bool` **predicate**. The documentation will tell you if a predicate, unary, or binary function is needed. Older versions of the Standard Library needed to know the types of the return value and parameters (if any) of the function object to work, and, for this reason, functor classes had to be based upon the standard classes, `unary_function` and `binary_function`. In C++11, this requirement has been removed, so there is no requirement to use these classes.

In some cases, you will want to use a binary functor when a unary functor is required. For example, the Standard Library defines the `greater` class that, when used as a function object, takes two parameters and a `bool` to determine whether the first parameter is greater than the second one, using the `operator>` defined by the type of both parameters. This will be used for functions that need a binary functor, and hence the function will compare two values; for example:

```
template<typename Fn>
int compare_vals(vector<double> d1, vector<double> d2, Fn compare)
{
    if (d1.size() > d2.size()) return -1; // error
    int c = 0;
    for (size_t i = 0; i < d1.size(); ++i)
    {
        if (compare(d1[i], d2[i])) c++;
    }
    return c;
}
```

This takes two collections and compares corresponding items using the functor passed as the last parameter. It can be called like this:

```
vector<double> d1{ 1.0, 2.0, 3.0, 4.0 };
vector<double> d2{ 1.0, 1.0, 2.0, 5.0 };
int c = compare_vals(d1, d2, greater<double>());
```

The `greater` functor class is defined in the `<functional>` header and compares two numbers using the `operator>` defined for the type. What if you wanted to compare the items in a container with a fixed value; that is, when the `operator()(double, double)` method on the functor is called, one parameter always has a fixed value? One option is to define a stateful functor class (as shown previously) so that the fixed value is a member of the functor object. Another way to do this is to fill another `vector` with the fixed value and continue to compare two `vector`s (this can get quite expensive for large `vector`s).

Another way is to reuse the functor class, but to *bind* a value to one of its parameters. A version of the `compare_vals` function can be written like this, to take just one `vector`:

```
template<typename Fn>
int compare_vals(vector<double> d, Fn compare)
{
    int c = 0;
    for (size_t i = 0; i < d.size(); ++i)
    {
        if (compare(d[i]) c++;
    }
    return c;
}
```

The code is written to call the functor parameter on just one value because it is assumed that the functor object contains the other value to compare. This is carried out by binding the functor class to the parameter:

```
using namespace::std::placeholders;
int c = compare_vals(d1, bind(greater<double>(), _1, 2.0));
```

The `bind` function is variadic. The first parameter is the functor object and it is followed by the parameters that will be passed to the `operator()` method of the functor. The `compare_vals` function is passed a **binder** object that binds the functor to values. In the `compare_vals` function, the call to the functor in `compare(d[i])` is actually a call to the `operator()` method of the binder object, and this method forwards the parameter `d[i]` and the bound value to the `operator()` method of the functor.

In the call to `bind`, if an actual value is provided (here, `2.0`), then that value is passed to the functor at that position in the call to the functor (here, `2,0` is passed to the second parameter). If a symbol preceded by an underscore is used, then it is a **placeholder**. There are 20 such symbols (`_1` to `_20`) defined in the `std::placeholders` namespace. The placeholder means "use the value passed in this position to the binder object `operator()` method call to the functor call `operator()` method indicated by the placeholder." Thus, the placeholder in this call means "pass the first parameter from invoking the binder and pass it to the first parameter of the `greater` functor `operator()`."

The previous code compares each item in the `vector` with `2.0` and will keep a count of those that are greater than `2.0`. You could invoke it this way:

```
int c = compare(d1, bind(greater<double>(), 2.0, _1));
```

The parameter list is swapped, and this means that 2.0 is compared with each item in the vector and the function will keep a count of how many times 2.0 is greater than the item.

The bind function, and placeholders, are new to C++11. In prior versions you could use the bind1st and bind2nd functions to bind a value to either the first or second parameter of the functor.

# Defining conversion operators

We have already seen that a constructor can be used to convert from another type to your custom type if your custom type has a constructor that takes the type you are converting. You can also perform the conversion in the other direction: converting the object into another type. To do this, you provide an operator without a return type with the name of the type to convert to. In this case, you need a space between the operator keyword and the name:

```
class mytype
{
    int i;
public:
    mytype(int i) : i(i) {}
    explicit mytype(string s) : i(s.size()) {}
    operator int () const { return i; }
};
```

This code can convert an int or a string to mytype; in the latter case, only through an explicit mention of the constructor. The last line allows you to convert an object back to an int:

```
string s = "hello";
mytype t = mytype(s); // explicit conversion
int i = t;            // implicit conversion
```

You can make such conversion operators explicit so that they will be called only when an explicit cast is used. In many cases, you will want to leave off this keyword because implicit conversions are useful when you want to wrap a resource in a class and use the destructor to do automatic resource management for you.

Another example of using a conversion operator is returning values from a stateful functor. The idea here is that the operator() will perform some action and the result is maintained by the functor. The issue is how do you obtain this state of the functor, especially when they are often created as temporary objects? A conversion operator can provide this functionality.

For example, when you calculate an average, you do it in two stages: the first stage is to accumulate the values and then the second stage is to calculate the average by dividing it by the number of items. The following functor class does this with the division performed as part of the conversion to a `double`:

```
class averager
{
    double total;
    int count;
public:
    averager() : total(0), count(0) {}
    void operator()(double d) { total += d; count += 1; }
    operator double() const
    {
        return (count != 0) ? (total / count) :
            numeric_limits<double>::signaling_NaN();
    }
};
```

This can be called like this:

```
vector<double> vals { 100.0, 20.0, 30.0 };
double avg = for_each(vals.begin(), vals.end(), averager());
```

The `for_each` function calls the functor for every item in the `vector`, and the `operator()` simply sums the items passed to it and maintains a count. The interesting part is that after the `for_each` function has iterated over all of the items in the `vector` it returns the functor, and so there is an implicit conversion to a `double`, which calls the conversion operator that calculates the average.

# Managing resources

We have already seen one sort of resource that requires careful management: memory. You allocate memory with `new`, and when you have finished with the memory you must deallocate the memory with `delete`. A failure to deallocate the memory will cause a memory leak. Memory is, perhaps, the most fundamental of system resources, but most operating systems have many others: file handles, handles to graphic objects, synchronization objects, threads, and processes. Sometimes possession of such a resource is exclusive and will prevent other code from accessing the resource accessed through the resource. Thus, it is important that such resources are freed at some point, and, usually, that they are freed in a timely manner.

Classes help here with a mechanism called **Resource Acquisition Is Initialization** (RAII) invented by Bjarne Stroustrup, the author of C++. Put simply, the resource is allocated in the constructor of an object and freed in the destructor, so it means that the lifetime of the resource is the lifetime of the object. Typically, such wrapper objects are allocated on the stack, and this means that you are guaranteed that the resource will be freed when the object goes out of scope *regardless of how this happens*.

So, if objects are declared in the code block for a looping statement (`while`, `for`), then at the end of each loop the destructor for each will be called (in reverse order of creation) and the object will be created again when the loop is repeated. This occurs whether the loop is repeated because the end of the code block has been reached or if the loop is repeated through a call to `continue`. Another way to leave a code block is through a call to `break`, a `goto`, or if the code calls `return` to leave the function. If the code raises an exception (see Chapter 7, *Diagnostics and Debugging*), the destructor will be called as the object goes out of scope, so if the code is guarded by a `try` block, the destructor of objects declared in the block will be called before the `catch` clause is called. If there is no guard block, then the destructor will be called before the function stack is destroyed and the exception propagated.

# Writing wrapper classes

There are several issues that you must address when writing a class to wrap a resource. The constructor will be used, either to obtain the resource using some library function (usually accessed through some kind of opaque handle) or will take the resource as a parameter. This resource is stored as a data member so other methods on the class can use it. The resource will be released in the destructor using whatever function your library provides to do this. This is the bare minimum. In addition, you have to think how the object will be used. Often such wrapper classes are most convenient if you can use instances as if they are the resource handle. This means that you maintain the same style of programming to access the resource, but you just don't have to worry too much about releasing the resource.

You should think about whether you want to be able convert between your wrapper class and the resource handle. If you do allow this, it means that you may have to think about cloning the resource, so that you do not have two copies of the handle--one that is managed by the class and the other copy that could be released by external code. You also need to think about whether you want to allow the object to be copied or assigned, and if so, then you will need to appropriately implement the copy constructor, a move constructor, and the copy and move assignment operators.

# Using smart pointers

The C++ Standard Library provides several classes to wrap resources accessed through pointers. To prevent memory leaks, you have to ensure that memory allocated on the free store is freed at some point. The idea of a smart pointer is that you treat an instance as if it is the pointer, so you use the * operator to dereference to get access to the object it points to or use the -> operator to access a member of the wrapped object. The smart pointer class will manage the lifetime of the pointer it wraps and will release the resource appropriately.

The Standard Library has three smart pointer classes: `unique_ptr`, `shared_ptr`, and `weak_ptr`. Each handles how the resource is released in a different way, and how or whether you can copy a pointer.

## Managing exclusive ownership

The `unique_ptr` class is constructed with a pointer to the object it will maintain. This class provides the operator * to give access to the object, dereferencing the wrapped pointer. It also provides the -> operator, so that if the pointer is for a class, you can access the members through the wrapped pointer.

The following allocates an object on the free store and manually maintains its lifetime:

```
void f1()
{
    int* p = new int;
    *p = 42;
    cout << *p << endl;
    delete p;
}
```

In this case, you get a pointer to the memory on the free store allocated for an `int`. To access the memory--either to write to it or read from it--you dereference the pointer with the * operator. When you are finished with the pointer, you must call `delete` to deallocate the memory and return it to the free store. Now consider the same code, but with a smart pointer:

```
void f2()
{
    unique_ptr<int> p(new int);
    *p = 42;
    cout << *p << endl;
    delete p.release();
}
```

The two main differences are that the smart pointer object is constructed explicitly by calling the constructor that takes a pointer of the type that is used as the template parameter. This pattern reinforces the idea that the resource should only be managed by the smart pointer.

The second change is that the memory is deallocated by calling the `release` method on the smart pointer object to take ownership of the wrapped pointer, so that we can delete the pointer explicitly.

Think of the `release` method releasing the pointer from the ownership of the smart pointer. After this call, the smart pointer no longer wraps the resource. The `unique_ptr` class also has a method `get` that will give access to the wrapped pointer, but the smart pointer object will still retain ownership; *do not delete the pointer obtained this way*!

Note that a `unique_ptr` object wraps a pointer, and just the pointer. This means that the object is the same size in memory as the pointer it wraps. So far, the smart pointer has added very little, so let's look at another way to deallocate the resource:

```
void f3()
{
    unique_ptr<int> p(new int);
    *p = 42;
    cout << *p << endl;
    p.reset();
}
```

This is *deterministic* releasing of the resource, and means that the resource is released just when you want it to happen, which is similar to the situation with the pointer. The code here is not releasing the resource itself; it is allowing the smart pointer to do it, using a **deleter**. The default deleter for `unique_ptr` is a functor class called `default_delete`, which calls the `delete` operator on the wrapped pointer. If you intend to use deterministic destruction, `reset` is the preferred method. You can provide your own deleter by passing the type of a custom functor class as the second parameter to the `unique_ptr` template:

```
template<typename T> struct my_deleter
{
    void operator()(T* ptr)
    {
        cout << "deleted the object!" << endl;
        delete ptr;
    }
};
```

In your code, you will specify that you want the custom deleter, like this:

```
unique_ptr<int, my_deleter<int> > p(new int);
```

You may need to carry out an additional clean up before deleting the pointer, or the pointer could be a obtained by a mechanism other than new, so you can use a custom deleter to ensure that the appropriate releasing function is called. Note that the deleter is part of the smart pointer class, so if you have two different smart pointers using two different deleter this way, the smart pointer types are different even if they wrap the same type of resource.

 When you use a custom deleter, the size of a unique_ptr object may be larger than the pointer wrapped. If the deleter is a functor object, each smart pointer object will need memory for this, but if you use a lambda expression, no more extra space will be required.

Of course, you are most likely to allow the smart pointer to manage the resource lifetime for you, and to do this you simply allow the smart pointer object to go out of scope:

```
void f4()
{
    unique_ptr<int> p(new int);
    *p = 42;
    cout << *p << endl;
} // memory is deleted
```

Since the pointer created is a single object, it means that you can call the new operator on an appropriate constructor to pass in initialization parameters. The constructor of unique_ptr is passed a pointer to an already constructed object, and the class manages the lifetime of the object after that. Although a unique_ptr object can be created directly by calling its constructor, you cannot call the copy constructor, so you cannot use initialization syntax during construction. Instead, the Standard Library provides a function called make_unique. This has several overloads, and for this reason it is the preferred way to create smart pointers based on this class:

```
void f5()
{
    unique_ptr<int> p = make_unique<int>();
    *p = 42;
    cout << *p << endl;
} // memory is deleted
```

This code will call the default constructor on the wrapped type (`int`), but you can provide parameters that will be passed to the appropriate constructor of the type. For example, for a `struct` that has a constructor with two parameters, the following may be used:

```
void f6()
{
    unique_ptr<point> p = make_unique<point>(1.0, 1.0);
    p->x = 42;
    cout << p->x << "," << p->y << endl;
} // memory is deleted
```

The `make_unique` function calls the constructor that assigns the members with non-default values. The `->` operator returns a pointer and the compiler will access the object members through this pointer.

There is also a specialization of `unique_ptr` and `make_unique` for arrays. The default deleter for this version of `unique_ptr` will call `delete[]` on the pointer, and thus it will delete every object in the array (and call each object's destructor). The class implements an indexer operator (`[]`) so you can access each item in the array. However, note that there are no range checks, so, like a built-in array variable, you can access beyond the end of the array. There are no dereferencing operators (`*` or `->`), so a `unique_ptr` object based on an array can only be accessed with array syntax.

The `make_unique` function has an overload that allows you to pass the size of the array to create, but you have to initialize each object individually:

```
unique_ptr<point[]> points = make_unique<point[]>(4);
points[1].x = 10.0;
points[1].y = -10.0;
```

This creates an array with four `point` objects initially set to the default value, and the following lines initialize the second point to a value of (`10.0, -10.0`). It is almost always better to use `vector` or `array` than `unique_ptr` to manage arrays of objects.

Earlier versions of the C++ Standard Library had a smart pointer class called `auto_ptr`. This was a first attempt, and worked in most cases, but also had some limitations; for example, `auto_ptr` objects could not be stored in Standard Library containers. C++11 introduces rvalue references and other language features such as move semantics, and, through these, `unique_ptr` objects can be stored in containers. The `auto_ptr` class is still available through the `<new>` header, but only so that older code can still compile.

The important point about the `unique_ptr` class is that it ensures that there is a single copy of the pointer. This is important because the class destructor will release the resource, so if you *could* copy a `unique_ptr` object it would mean more than one destructor will attempt to release the resource. Objects of `unique_ptr` have *exclusive ownership*; an instance always owns what it points to.

You cannot copy assign `unique_ptr` smart pointers (the copy assignment operator and copy constructor are deleted), but you can *move* them by transferring ownership of the resource from the source pointer to the destination pointer. So, a function can return a `unique_ptr` because the ownership is transferred through move semantics to the variable being assigned to the value of the function. If the smart pointer is put into a container, there is another move.

# Sharing ownership

There are occasions when you will need to share a pointer: you may create several objects and pass a pointer to a single object to each of them so they can call this object. Ordinarily, when an object has a pointer to another object, that pointer represents a resource that should be destroyed during the destruction of the containing object. If a pointer is shared, it means that when one of the objects deletes the pointer, the pointers in all of the other objects will be invalid (this is called a **dangling pointer** because it no longer points to an object). You need a mechanism where several objects can hold a pointer that will remain valid until *all* the objects using that pointer have indicated they will no longer need to use it.

C++11 provides this facility with the `shared_ptr` class. This class maintains a **reference count** on the resource, and each copy of the `shared_ptr` for that resource will increment the reference count. When one instance of `shared_ptr` for that resource is destroyed, it will decrement the reference count. The reference count is shared, so it means that a non-zero value signifies that at least one `shared_ptr` exists accessing the resource. When the last `shared_ptr` object decrements the reference count to zero, it is safe to release the resource. This means that the reference count must be managed in an atomic way to handle multithreaded code.

Since the reference count is shared, it means that each `shared_ptr` object holds a pointer to a shared buffer called the **control block**, and this means it holds the raw pointer and a pointer to the control block, and so each `shared_ptr` object will hold more data than a `unique_ptr`. The control block is used for more than just the reference count.

A `shared_ptr` object can be created to use a custom deleter (passed as a constructor parameter), and the deleter is stored in the control block. This is important because it means that the custom deleter is not part of the type of the smart pointer, so several `shared_ptr` objects wrapping the same resource type but using different deleters are still the same type and can be put in a container for that type.

You can create a `shared_ptr` object from another `shared_ptr` object, and this will initialize the new object with the raw pointer and the pointer to the control block, *and* increment the reference count.

```
point* p = new point(1.0, 1.0);
shared_ptr<point> sp1(p); // Important, do not use p after this!
shared_ptr<point> sp2(sp1);
p = nullptr;
sp2->x = 2.0;
sp1->y = 2.0;
sp1.reset(); // get rid of one shared pointer
```

Here, the first shared pointer is created using a raw pointer. This is not the recommended way to use `shared_ptr`. The second shared pointer is created using the first smart pointer, so now there are two shared pointers to the same resource (p is assigned to `nullptr` to prevent its further use). After this, either `sp1` or `sp2` can be used to access the *same* resource. At the end of this code, one shared pointer is reset to `nullptr`; this means that `sp1` no longer has a reference count on the resource, and you cannot use it to access the resource. However, you can still use `sp2` to access the resource until it goes out of scope, or you call `reset`.

In this code, the smart pointers were created from a separate raw pointer. Since the shared pointers now have taken over the lifetime management of the resource it is important to no longer use the raw pointer, and in this case it is assigned to `nullptr`. It is better to avoid the use of raw pointers, and the Standard Library enables this with a function called `make_shared`, which can be used like this:

```
shared_ptr<point> sp1 = make_shared<point>(1.0,1.0);
```

The function will create the specified object using a call to `new`, and since it takes a variable number of parameters, you can use it to call any constructor on the wrapped class.

You can create a `shared_ptr` object from a `unique_ptr` object, which means that the pointer is *moved* to the new object and the reference counting control block created. Since the resource will now be shared, it means that there is no longer exclusive ownership on the resource, so the pointer in the `unique_ptr` object will be made a `nullptr`. This means that you can have a factory function that returns a pointer to an object wrapped in a `unique_ptr` object, and the calling code can determine if it will use a `unique_ptr` object to get exclusive access to the resource or a `shared_ptr` object to share it.

There is little point in using `shared_ptr` for arrays of objects; there are much better ways to store collections of objects (`vector` or `array`). In any case, there is an indexing operator (`[]`) and the default deleter calls `delete`, not `delete[]`.

## Handling dangling pointers

Earlier in this book we made the point that, when you delete a resource, you should set the pointer to `nullptr` and you should check a pointer before using it to see if it is `nullptr`. This is so that you do not call a pointer to memory for an object that has been deleted: a dangling pointer.

There are situations when a dangling pointer can occur by design. For example, a *parent* object may create *child* objects that have a **back pointer** to the parent so that the child has access to the parent. (An example of this is a window that creates child controls; it is often useful for the child controls to have access to the parent window.) The problem with using a shared pointer in this situation is that the parent will have a reference count on each child control and each child control has a reference count on the parent, and this creates a circular dependency.

Another example is if you have a container of observer objects with the intention of being able to inform each of these observer objects when an event occurs by calling a method on each one. Maintaining this list can be complicated, particularly if an observer object can be deleted, and hence you have to provide a means to remove the object from the container (where there will be a `shared_ptr` reference count) before you can completely delete the object. It becomes easier if your code can simply add a pointer to the object to the container in a way that does not maintain a reference count, but allows you to check when the pointer is used if the pointer is dangling or points to an existing object.

Such a pointer is called a **weak pointer** and the C++11 Standard Library provides a class called weak_ptr. You cannot use a weak_ptr object directly and there is no dereference operator. Instead, you create a weak_ptr object from a shared_ptr object and, when you want to access the resource, you create a shared_ptr object from the weak_ptr object. This means that a weak_ptr object has the same raw pointer, and access to the same control block as the shared_ptr object, but it does not take part in reference counting.

Once created, the weak_ptr object will enable you to test whether the wrapper pointer is to an existing resource or to a resource that has been destroyed. There are two ways to do this: either call the member function expired or attempt to create a shared_ptr from the weak_ptr. If you are maintaining a collection of weak_ptr objects, you may decide to periodically iterate through the collection, call expired on each one, and if the method returns true, remove that object from the collection. Since the weak_ptr object has access to the control block created by the original shared_ptr object, it can test to see if the reference count is zero.

The second way to test to see if a weak_ptr object is dangling is to create a shared_ptr object from it. There are two options. You can create the shared_ptr object by passing the weak pointer to its constructor and if the pointer has expired, the constructor will throw a bad_weak_ptr exception. The other way is to call the lock method on the weak pointer and if the weak pointer has expired, then the shared_ptr object will be assigned to nullptr and you can test for this. These three ways are shown here:

```
shared_ptr<point> sp1 = make_shared<point>(1.0,1.0);
weak_ptr<point> wp(sp1);

// code that may call sp1.reset() or may not

if (!wp.expired())  { /* can use the resource */}

shared_ptr<point> sp2 = wp.lock();
if (sp2 != nullptr) { /* can use the resource */}

try
{
    shared_ptr<point> sp3(wp);
    // use the pointer
}
catch(bad_weak_ptr& e)
{
    // dangling weak pointer
}
```

Since a weak pointer does not alter the reference count on a resource it means that you can use it for a back pointer to break the cyclic dependency (although, often it makes sense to use a raw pointer instead because a child object cannot exist without its parent object).

# Templates

Classes can be templated, which means that you can write generic code and the compiler will generate a class with the types that your code uses. The parameters can be types, constant integer values, or variadic versions (zero or more parameters, as provided by the code using the class). For example:

```cpp
template <int N, typename T> class simple_array
{
    T data[N];
public:
    const T* begin() const { return data; }
    const T* end() const { return data + N; }
    int size() const { return N; }

    T& operator[](int idx)
    {
        if (idx < 0 || idx >= N)
            throw range_error("Range 0 to " + to_string(N));
        return data[idx];
    }
};
```

Here is a very simple array class that defines the basic iterator functions and the indexing operator, so that you can call it like this:

```cpp
simple_array<4, int> four;
four[0] = 10; four[1] = 20; four[2] = 30; four[3] = 40;
for(int i : four) cout << i << " "; // 10 20 30 40
cout << endl;
four[4] = -99;                // throws a range_error exception
```

If you choose to define a function out of the `class` declaration, then you need to give the template and its parameters as part of the `class` name:

```
template<int N, typename T>
T& simple_array<N,T>::operator[](int idx)
{
    if (idx < 0 || idx >= N)
        throw range_error("Range 0 to " + to_string(N));
    return data[idx];
}
```

You can also have default values for template parameters:

```
template<int N, typename T=int> class simple_array
{
    // same as before
};
```

If you think you should have a specific implementation for a template parameter, then you can provide the code for that version as a specialization of the template:

```
template<int N> class simple_array<N, char>
{
    char data[N];
public:
    simple_array<N, char>(const char* str)
    {
        strncpy(data, str, N);
    }
    int size() const { return N; }
    char& operator[](int idx)
    {
        if (idx < 0 || idx >= N)
            throw range_error("Range 0 to " + to_string(N));
        return data[idx];
    }
    operator const char*() const { return data; }
};
```

Note that, with a specialization, you do not get any code from the fully templated class; you have to implement all the methods you want to provide, and, as illustrated here, methods that are relevant to the specialization but not available on the fully templated class. This example is a **partial specialization**, meaning that it is specialized on just one parameter (T, the type of the data). This class will be used for declared variables of the type `simple_array<n, char>`, where n is an integer. You are free to have a fully specialized template, which, in this case, will be a specialization for a fixed size and a specified type:

```
template<> class simple_array<256, char>
{
    char data[256];
public:
    // etc
};
```

It is probably not useful in this case, but the idea is that there will be special code for variables that need 256 chars.

# Using classes

The **Resource Acquisition Is Initialization** technique is useful for managing resources provided by other libraries, such as the C Runtime Library or the Windows SDK. It simplifies your code because you do not have to think about where a resource handle will go out of scope and provide clean-up code at every point. If the clean-up code is complicated, it is typical in C code to see it put at the end of a function and every exit point in the function will have a `goto` jump to that code. This results in messy code. In this example, we will wrap the C files functions with a class, so that the lifetime of the file handle is maintained automatically.

The C runtime `_findfirst` and `_findnext` functions allow you to search for a file or directory that matches a pattern (including wildcard symbols). The `_findfirst` function returns an `intptr_t`, which is relevant to just that search and this is passed to the `_findnext` function to get subsequent values. This `intptr_t` is an opaque pointer to resources that the C Runtime maintains for the search, and so when you are finished with the search you must call `_findclose` to clean up any resources associated with it. To prevent memory leaks, it is important to call `_findclose`.

Under the `Beginning_C++` folder, create a folder called `Chapter_06`. In Visual C++, create a new C++ source file, save it to the `Chapter_06` folder, and call it `search.cpp`. The application will use the Standard Library console and strings, and it will use the C Runtime file functions, so add these lines to the top of the file:

```
#include <iostream>
#include <string>
#include <io.h>
using namespace std;
```

The application will be called with a file search pattern and it will use the C functions to search for files, so you will need a `main` function that has parameters. Add the following to the bottom of the file:

```
void usage()
{
    cout << "usage: search pattern" << endl;
    cout << "pattern is the file or folder to search for "
        << "with or without wildcards * and ?" << endl;
}

int main(int argc, char* argv[])
{
    if (argc < 2)
    {
        usage();
        return 1;
    }
}
```

The first thing is to create a wrapper class for the search handle that will manage this resource. Above the usage function, add a class called `search_handle`:

```
class search_handle
{
    intptr_t handle;
public:
    search_handle() : handle(-1) {}
    search_handle(intptr_t p) : handle(p) {}
    void operator=(intptr_t p) { handle = p; }
    void close()
    { if (handle != -1) _findclose(handle); handle = 0; }
    ~search_handle() { close(); }
};
```

This class has a separate function to release the handle. This is so that a user of this class can release the wrapper resource as soon as possible. If the object is used in code that could throw an exception, the `close` method won't be called directly, but the destructor will be called instead. The wrapper object can be created with a `intptr_t` value. If this value is -1, then the handle is invalid, so the close method will only call `_findclose` if the handle does not have this value.

We want objects of this class to have exclusive ownership of the handle, so delete the copy constructor and copy assignment by putting the following in the public part of the class:

```
void operator=(intptr_t p) { handle = p; }
search_handle(search_handle& h) = delete;
void operator=(search_handle& h) = delete;
```

If an object is moved, then any handle in the existing object must be released, so add the following after the lines you just added:

```
search_handle(search_handle&& h)  { close(); handle = h.handle; }
void operator=(search_handle&& h) { close(); handle = h.handle; }
```

The wrapper class will be allocated by a call to `_findfirst` and will be passed to a call to `_findnext`, so the wrapper class needs two operators: one to convert to an `intptr_t`, so objects of this class can be used wherever an `intptr_t` is needed, and the other so that object can be used when a `bool` is needed. Add these to the `public` part of the class:

```
operator bool() const { return (handle != -1); }
operator intptr_t() const { return handle; }
```

The conversion to `bool` allows you to write code like this:

```
search_handle handle = /* initialize it */;
if (!handle) { /* handle is invalid */ }
```

If you have a conversion operator that returns a pointer, then the compiler will call this in preference to the conversion to `bool`.

You should be able to compile this code (remember to use the `/EHsc` switch) to confirm that there are no typos.

Next, write a wrapper class to perform the search. Below the `search_handle` class, add a `file_search` class:

```
class file_search
{
    search_handle handle;
    string search;
public:
    file_search(const char* str) : search(str) {}
    file_search(const string& str) : search(str) {}
};
```

This class is created with the search criteria, and we have the option of passing a C or C++ string. The class has a `search_handle` data member, and, since the default destructor will call the destructor of member objects, we do not need to provide a destructor ourselves. However, we will add a `close` method so that a user can explicitly release resources. Furthermore, so that users of the class can determine the search path, we need an accessor. At the bottom of the class, add the following:

```
const char* path() const { return search.c_str(); }
void close() { handle.close(); }
```

We do not want instances of the `file_search` object to be copied because that would mean two copies of the search handle. You could delete the copy constructor and assignment operator, but there is no need. Try this: in the `main` function, add this test code (it does not matter where):

```
file_search f1("");
file_search f2 = f1;
```

Compile the code. You'll get an error and an explanation:

```
error C2280: 'file_search::file_search(file_search &)':  attempting to
reference a deleted function
note: compiler has generated 'file_search::file_search' here
```

Without a copy constructor, the compiler will generate one (this is the second line). The first line is a bit odd because it is saying that you are trying to call a deleted method that the compiler has generated! In fact, the error is saying that the generated copy constructor is attempting to copy the `handle` data member and the `search_handle` copy constructor that has been deleted. Thus you are protected against copying `file_search` objects without adding any other code. Delete the test lines you just added.

Next add the following lines to the bottom of the `main` function. This will create a `file_search` object and print out information to the console.

```
file_search files(argv[1]);
cout << "searching for " << files.path() << endl;
```

Then you need to add code to perform the search. The pattern used here will be a method that has an out parameter and returns a `bool`. If a call to the method succeeds, then the file found will be returned in the out parameter and the method will return `true`. If the call fails, then the out parameter is left untouched and the method returns `false`. In the `public` section of the `file_search` class, add this function:

```
bool next(string& ret)
{
    _finddata_t find{};
    if (!handle)
    {
        handle = _findfirst(search.c_str(), &find);
        if (!handle) return false;
    }
    else
    {
        if (-1 == _findnext(handle, &find)) return false;
    }

    ret = find.name;
    return true;
}
```

If this is the first call to this method, then `handle` will be invalid and so `_findfirst` is called. This will fill a `_finddata_t` structure with the results of the search and return an `intptr_t` value. The `search_handle` object data member is assigned to this value returned from this function, and if `_findfirst` returns -1, the method returns `false`. If the call is successful, then the out parameter (a reference to a `string`) is initialized using a C string pointer in the `_finddata_t` structure.

If there are more files that match the pattern, then you can call the `next` function repeatedly, and on these subsequent calls the `_findnext` function is called to get the next file. In this case the `search_handle` object is passed to the function and there is an implicit conversion to `intptr_t` through the class's conversion operator. If the `_findnext` function returns -1, it means there are no more files in the search.

At the bottom of the `main` function, add the following lines to perform the search:

```
string file;
while (files.next(file))
{
    cout << file << endl;
}
```

Now you can compile the code and run it with a search criterion. Bear in mind that this is constrained by the facilities of the `_findfirst`/`_findnext` functions, so the searches you can do will be quite simple. Try running this at the command line with a parameter to search for the subfolders in the `Beginning_C++` folder:

**search Beginning_C++Ch\***

This will give a list of the subfolders starting with `Ch`. Since there is no reason for `search_handle` to be a separate class, move the entire class to the `private` section of the `search_handle`, above the declaration of the `handle` data member. Compile and run the code.

# Summary

With classes, C++ provides a powerful and flexible mechanism to encapsulate data and methods to provide behavior that acts on the data. You can template this code so that you can write generic code and get the compiler to generate code for the types that you require. In the example, you have seen how classes are the basis of object orientation. A class encapsulates data, so that the caller only needs to know about the expected behavior (in this example, getting the next result in a search), without needing to know the details of how the class does this.

# 5
# Using the Standard Library Containers

The Standard Library provides several types of containers; each is provided through a templated class so that the behavior of the container can be used for items of any type. There are classes for sequential containers, where the ordering of the items in the container is dependent on the order that the items are inserted into the container. Also there are sorted and unsorted associated containers that associate a value with a key, and subsequently the value is accessed using the key.

Although not containers themselves, in this chapter we will also cover two related classes: pair that links two values together in one object, and tuple, that can hold one or more values in a single object.

## Working with pairs and tuples

In many cases you will want to associate two items together; for example, an associative container allows you to create a type of array where items other than numbers are used as an index. The <utility> header file contains a templated class called pair, which has two data members called first and second.

```
template <typename T1, typename T2>
struct pair
{
    T1 first;
    T2 second;
    // other members
};
```

Since the class is templated, it means that you can associate any items, including pointers or references. Accessing the members is simple since they are public. You can also use the get templated function, so for a pair object p you can call get<0>(p) rather than p.first. The class also has a copy constructor, so that you can create an object from another object, and a move constructor. There is also a function called make_pair that will deduce the types of the members from the parameters:

```
auto name_age = make_pair("Richard", 52);
```

Be wary because the compiler will use the type that it thinks is most appropriate; in this case the pair object created will be pair<const char*, int>, but if you want the first item to be a string, it is simpler to use the constructor. You can compare pair objects; the comparison is performed on the first member and only if they are equal is the second then compared:

```
pair <int, int> a(1, 1);
pair <int, int> a(1, 2);
cout << boolalpha;
cout << a << " < " << b << " " << (a < b) << endl;
```

The parameters can be references:

```
int i1 = 0, i2 = 0;
pair<int&, int&> p(i1, i2);
++p.first; // changes i1
```

The make_pair function will deduce the types from the parameters. The compiler cannot tell the difference between a variable and a reference to a variable. In C++11 you can use the ref function (in <functional>) to specify that the pair will be for references:

```
auto p2 = make_pair(ref(i1), ref(i2));
++p2.first; // changes i1
```

If you want to return two values from a function, you could do it via parameters passed by reference, but the code is less readable because you expect a return value to come through the return of a function rather than through its parameters. The pair class allows you to return two values in one object. One example is the minmax function in <algorithm>. This returns a pair object containing the parameters in order of the smallest first, and there is an overload where you can provide a predicate object if the default operator < should not be used. The following will print {10,20}:

```
auto p = minmax(20,10);
cout << "{" << p.first << "," << p.second << "}" << endl;
```

The `pair` class associates two items. The Standard Library provides the `tuple` class that has a similar functionality, but since the template is variadic it means that you can have any number of parameters of any type. However, the data members are not named as in `pair`, instead you access them via the templated `get` function:

```
tuple<int, int, int> t3 { 1,2,3 };
cout << "{"
    << get<0>(t3) << "," << get<1>(t3) << "," << get<2>(t3)
    << "}" << endl; // {1,2,3}
```

The first line creates a `tuple` that holds three `int` items and it is initialized using an initialize list (you could use constructor syntax). The `tuple` is then printed to the console by accessing each data member in the object using a version of the `get` function where the template parameter indicates the index of the item. Note that the index is a template parameter, so you cannot provide it at runtime using a variable. If this is what you want to do, then it is a clear indication that you need to use a container such as `vector`.

The `get` function returns a reference, so this can be used to change the value of the item. For a `tuple` `t3`, this code changes the first item to `42` and the second to `99`:

```
int& tmp = get<0>(t3);
tmp = 42;
get<1>(t3) = 99;
```

You can also extract all the items with one call, by using the `tie` function:

```
int i1, i2, i3;
tie(i1, i2, i3) = t3;
cout << i1 << "," << i2 << "," << i3 << endl;
```

The `tie` function returns a `tuple` in which each parameter is a reference and initialized to the variables that you pass as parameters. The previous code is easier to understand if you write it like this:

```
tuple<int&, int&, int&> tr3 = tie(i1, i2, i3);
tr3 = t3;
```

A `tuple` object can be created from a `pair` object, and so you can use the `tie` function to extract values from a `pair` object too.

There is a helper function called `make_tuple`, which will deduce the types of the parameters. As with the `make_pair` function, you have to be wary of the deductions, so a floating-point number will be deduced to be a `double` and an integer will be an `int`. If you want the parameters to be references to specific variables, you can use the `ref` function or the `cref` function for a `const` reference.

You can compare `tuple` objects as long as there are equal numbers of items and equivalent types. The compiler will refuse to compile comparisons of `tuple` objects that have different numbers of items or if the types of the items of one `tuple` objects cannot be converted to the types of the other `tuple` object.

# Containers

The Standard Library containers allow you to group together zero or more items of the same type and access them serially through iterators. Every such object has a `begin` method that returns an iterator object to the first item and an `end` function that returns an iterator object for the item after the last item in the container. The iterator objects support pointer-like arithmetic, so that `end()` – `begin()` will give the number of items in the container. All container types will implement the `empty` method to indicate if there are no items in the container, and (except for `forward_list`) the `size` method is the number of items in the container. You are tempted to iterate through a container as if it is an array:

```
vector<int> primes{1, 3, 5, 7, 11, 13};
for (size_t idx = 0; idx < primes.size(); ++idx)
{
    cout << primes[idx] << " ";
}
cout << endl;
```

The problem is that not all containers allow random access, and if you decide it is more efficient to use another container, you'll have to change how the container is accessed. This code also does not work well if you want to write generic code using templates. The previous code is better written using iterators:

```
template<typename container> void print(container& items)
{
    for (container::iterator it = items.begin();
    it != items.end(); ++it)
    {
        cout << *it << " ";
    }
    cout << endl;
}
```

All of the containers have a `typedef` member called `iterator` that gives the type of the iterator returned from the `begin` method. Iterator objects behave like pointers, so you can obtain the item an iterator refers to using the dereference operator and move to the next item using the increment operator.

For all containers except for `vector`, there is a guarantee that an iterator will remain valid even if other elements are deleted. If you insert items, then only `lists`, `forward_lists`, and associated container guarantee that the iterators remain valid. Iterators will be covered in more depth later.

All containers have to have an exception safe (nothrow) method called `swap`, and (with two exceptions) they must have *transactional* semantics; that is, an operation must succeed or fail. If the operation fails, the container is in the same state as before the operation is called. For every container, this rule is relaxed when it comes to multi-element inserts. If you insert many items at a time using an iterator range, for example, and the insert fails for one of the items in the range, then the method will not be able to undo the previous inserts.

It is important to point out that objects are copied into containers, so the type of the objects that you put into a container must have a copy and copy assignment operator. Also, be aware that if you put a derived class object into a container that requires a base class object, then the copying will slice the object, meaning that anything to do with the derived class is removed (data members and virtual method pointers).

# Sequence containers

Sequence containers store a series of items and the order that they are stored in, and, when you access them with an iterator, the items are retrieved in the order in which they were put into the container. After creating a container, you can change the sort order with library functions.

# List

As the name suggests, a `list` object is implemented by a doubly linked list in which each item has a link to the next item and the previous one. This means that it is quick to insert items (as the example in Chapter 2, *Working with Memory, Arrays, and Pointers*, showed with a singly linked list), but since, in a linked list, an item only has access to the items in front and behind it, there is no random access with the `[]` indexoperator.

The class allows you to provide values through the constructor, or you can use member methods. For example, the `assign` method allows you fill the container in one action using an initializer list, or, with iterators, to a range in another container. You can also insert a single item using the `push_back` or `push_front` method:

```
list<int> primes{ 3,5,7 };
primes.push_back(11);
primes.push_back(13);
primes.push_front(2);
primes.push_front(1);
```

The first line creates a `list` object that contains 3, 5, and 7, and then pushes 11 and 13 to the end (in that order), so that the `list` contains {3,5,7,11,13}. The code then pushes the numbers 2 and 1 to the front, so that the final `list` is {1,2,3,5,7,11,13}. In spite of the names, the `pop_front` and `pop_back` methods just remove the item at the front or back of the list, but will not return the item. If you want to get the item that has been removed, you must *first* access the item through the `front` or `back` method:

```
int last = primes.back();  // get the last item
primes.pop_back();         // remove it
```

The `clear` method will remove all items in the `list` and the `erase` method will delete items. There are two versions: one with an iterator that identifies a single item and another that has two iterators that indicate a range. A range is indicated by providing the first item in the range and the item *after* the range.

```
auto start = primes.begin(); // 1
start++;                     // 2
auto last = start;           // 2
last++;                      // 3
last++;                      // 5
primes.erase(start, last);   // remove 2 and 3
```

This is a general principle with iterators and the Standard Library containers; a range is indicated by iterators by the first item and the item *after* the last item. The `remove` method will remove all items with a specified value:

```
list<int> planck{ 6,6,2,6,0,7,0,0,4,0 };
planck.remove(6);            // {2,0,7,0,0,4,0}
```

There is also a method `remove_if` that takes a predicate and will only remove an item if the predicate returns `true`. Similarly, you can insert items into a list with an iterator, and the item is inserted before the specified item:

```
list<int> planck{ 6,6,2,6,0,7,0,0,4,0 };
auto it = planck.begin();
++it;
++it;
planck.insert(it, -1); // {6,6,-1,2,6,0,7,0,0,4,0}
```

You can also indicate that the item should be inserted more than once at that position (and if so, how many copies) and you can provide several items to be inserted at one point. Of course, if the iterator you pass is obtained by calling the `begin` method, then the item is inserted at the beginning of the `list`. The same can be achieved by calling the `push_front` method. Similarly, if the iterator is obtained by calling the `end` method, then the item is inserted at the end of the `list`, which is the same as calling `push_back`.

When you call the `insert` method, you provide an object that will either be copied into the `list` or moved into the `list` (through rvalue semantics). The class also provides several **emplace** methods (`emplace`, `emplace_front`, and `emplace_back`) that will construct a new object based on the data you provide, and insert that object in the `list`. For example, if you have a `point` class that can be created from two `double` values, you can either `insert` a constructed `point` object or `emplace` a `point` object by providing two `double` values:

```
struct point
{
    double x = 0, y = 0;
    point(double _x, double _y) : x(_x), y(_y) {}
};

list<point> points;
point p(1.0, 1.0);
points.push_back(p);
points.emplace_back(2.0, 2.0);
```

Once you have created a `list`, you can manipulate it with member functions. The `swap` method takes a suitable `list` object as a parameter, it moves the items from the parameter into the current object, and moves the items in the current `list` to the parameter. Since the `list` object is implemented using linked lists, this operation is quick.

```
list<int> num1 { 2,7,1,8,2,8 }; // digits of Euler's number
list<int> num2 { 3,1,4,5,6,8 }; // digits of pi
num1.swap(num2);
```

After this, code num1 will contain {3,1,4,5,6,8} and num2 will contain {2,7,1,8,2,8}, as the following illustrates:

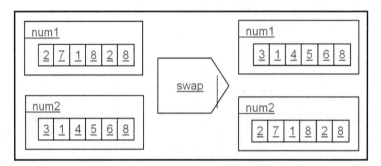

A list will hold the items in the order that they were inserted into the container; however, you can sort them by calling the sort method that will, by default, order items in ascending order using the < operator for the items in the list container. You can also pass a function object for a comparison operation. Once sorted, you can reverse the order of items by calling the reverse method. Two sorted lists can be merged, which involves taking the items from the argument list and inserting them into the calling list, in order:

```
list<int> num1 { 2,7,1,8,2,8 }; // digits of Euler's number
list<int> num2 { 3,1,4,5,6,8 }; // digits of pi
num1.sort();                     // {1,2,2,7,8,8}
num2.sort();                     // {1,3,4,5,6,8}
num1.merge(num2);                // {1,1,2,2,3,4,5,6,7,8,8,8}
```

Merging two lists may result in duplicates, and these can be removed by calling the unique method:

```
num1.unique(); // {1,2,3,4,5,6,7,8}
```

# Forward list

As the name suggests, the forward_list class is like the list class, but it only allows items to insert and remove items from the front of the list. It also means that the iterators used with the class can only be incremented; the compiler will refuse to allow you to decrement such an iterator. The class has a subset of the methods of list, so it has the push_front, pop_front, and emplace_front methods, but not the corresponding _back methods. There are some other methods that it implements, and, because the list items can only be accessed in a forward direction, it means that insertions will occur after an existing item, and hence the class implements insert_after and emplace_after.

Similarly, you can remove items at the beginning of the list (`pop_front`) or after a specified item (`erase_after`), or tell the class to iterate in a forward direction through the list and remove items with a specific value (`remove` and `remove_if`):

```
forward_list<int> euler { 2,7,1,8,2,8 };
euler.push_front(-1);        // { -1,2,7,1,8,2,8 }
auto it = euler.begin();     // iterator points to -1
euler.insert_after(it, -2);  // { -1,-2,2,7,1,8,2,8 }
euler.pop_front();           // { -2,2,7,1,8,2,8 }
euler.remove_if([](int i){return i < 0;});
                             // { 2,7,1,8,2,8 }
```

In the preceding code, `euler` is initialized with the digits of Euler's number and a value of -1 is pushed to the front. Next, an iterator is obtained that points to the first value in the container; that is, to the position of the value of -1. A value of -2 is inserted after the position of the iterator; that is, -2 is inserted after the value of -1. The last two lines show how to remove items; `pop_front` removes the item at the front of the container and `remove_if` will remove items that satisfy the predicate (in this case when the item is less than zero).

# Vector

The `vector` class has the behavior of a dynamic array; that is, there is indexed random access to items and the container will grow as more items are inserted into it. You can create a `vector` object with an initialization list, and with a specified number of copies of an item. You can also base a vector on values in another container by passing iterators that indicate the range of items in that container. You can create a vector with a pre-determined size by providing a capacity as the constructor parameter, and the specified number of default items will be created in the container. If, at a later stage, you need to specify the container size, you can call the `reserve` method to specify the minimum size or the `resize` method, which may mean deleting excess items or creating new items depending on whether the existing `vector` object is bigger or smaller than the requested size.

When you insert items into a `vector` container and there is not enough memory allocated, then the container will allocate enough memory. This will involve allocating new memory, copying the existing items into the new memory, creating the new item, and, finally, destroying the old copy of the items and deallocating the old memory. Clearly, if you know the number of items and you know that the `vector` container will not be able to contain them without a new allocation, you should indicate how much space you need by calling the `reserve` method.

Inserting items other than the constructor is straightforward. You can use `push_back` to insert an item at the end (which is a fast action, assuming no allocation is needed) and there is also `pop_back` to remove the last item. You can also use the `assign` method to clear the entire container and insert the specified items (either a multiple of the same item, an initializer list of items, or items in another container specified with iterators). As with `list` objects, you can clear the entire `vector`, erase items at a position, or insert items at a specified position. However, there is no equivalent of the `remove` method to remove items with a specific value.

The main reason to use the `vector` class is to get random access using either the `at` method or the `[]` indexing operator:

```
vector<int> distrib(10); // ten intervals
for (int count = 0; count < 1000; ++count)
{
    int val = rand() % 10;
    ++distrib[val];
}
for (int i : distrib) cout << i << endl;
```

The first line creates a `vector` with ten items, and then in the loop the C runtime function `rand` is called a thousand times each time to get a pseudo random number between 0 and 32767. The modulus operator is used to get, in approximate terms, a random number between 0 and 9. This random number is then used as an index for the `distrib` object to select a specified item, which is then incremented. Finally, the distribution is printed out and, as you would expect, this gives a value of roughly 100 in each item.

This code relies on the fact that the `[]` operator returns a reference to the item, which is why the item can be incremented in this manner. The `[]` operator can be used to read and write to an item in the container. The container gives iterator access through the `begin` and `end` methods, and (since they are needed by the container adapters) the `front` and `back` methods.

A `vector` object can hold any type that has a copy constructor and assignment operator, which means all the built-in types. As it stands, a `vector` of `bool` items would be a waste of memory because a Boolean value can be stored as a single bit and the compiler will treat a `bool` as an integer (32 bits). The Standard Library has a specialization of the `vector` class for `bool` that stores items more efficiently. However, although the class at first sight looks like a good idea, the problem is that, since the container holds Boolean values as bits, this means that the `[]` operator doesn't return a reference to a `bool` (instead it returns an object that behaves like one).

If you want to hold Boolean values and manipulate them then, as long as you know at compile time how many items there are, the `bitset` class is probably a better choice.

# Deque

The name `deque` means *double-ended queue*, which means that it can grow from both ends, and, although you can insert items in the middle, it is more expensive. As a queue, it means that the items are ordered, but, because the items can be put into the queue from either end, the order is not necessarily the same order in which you put items into the container.

The interface of `deque` is similar to a `vector`, so you have iterator access as well as random access using the `at` function and the `[]` operator. As with a `vector`, you can access items from the end of a `deque` container using the `push_back`, `pop_back`, and `back` methods, but, unlike a `vector`, you can also access the front of a `deque` container using the `push_front`, `pop_front`, and `front` methods. Although the `deque` class has methods to allow you to insert and erase items within the container, and to `resize`, these are expensive operations, and if you need to use them then you should reconsider using this container type. Furthermore, the `deque` class does not have methods to pre-allocate memory, so, potentially, when you add an item to this container, it could cause a memory allocation.

# Associative containers

With a C-like `array` or a `vector`, each item is associated with its numeric index. Earlier this was exploited in one of the examples in the section on `vector` in which the index provided the decile of the distribution and, conveniently, the distribution was split in a way that the ten deciles of data are numbered.

An associative container allows you to provide indexes that are not numeric; these are the keys, and you can associate values with them. As you insert key-value pairs into the container, they will be ordered so that the container can subsequently efficiently access the value by its key. Typically, this order should not matter to you since you will not use the container to access items sequentially, and instead you will access values by their keys. A typical implementation will use a binary tree or a hash table, which means that it is a quick operation to find an item according to its key.

For ordered containers, such as map, there will be comparisons carried out between the key and the existing keys in the container using < (the less predicate). The default predicate means that the keys are compared, and if this is, say, a smart pointer, then it will be the smart pointer objects that will be compared and used for the ordering, not the object that they wrap. In this case, you will want to write your own predicate to perform the appropriate comparison and pass it as a template parameter.

This means it is typically expensive to insert or erase items, and the key is treated as immutable, so you cannot alter it for an item. For all associative containers, there are no remove methods, but there are erase methods. However, for those containers that keep items sorted, erasing an item could affect performance.

There are several types of associative containers, and the main difference is how they handle duplicate keys and the level of ordering that occurs. The map class has key-value pairs sorted by unique keys, so duplicate keys are not allowed. If you want to allow duplicate keys, then you can use the multimap class. The set class is essentially a map where the key is the same as the value, which, again, does not allow duplicates. The multiset class does allow duplicates.

It may seem odd to have an associative class where the key is the same as the value, but the reason for including the class in this section is because, like the map class, the set class has a similar interface to find a value. Also similar to the map class, the set class is fast at finding an item.

## Maps and multimaps

A map container stores two different items, a key and a value, and it maintains the items in an sort order according to the key. A sorted map means that it is quick to locate an item. The class has the same interface as other containers to add items: you can put them into the container via the constructor, or you can use member methods insert and emplace. You also have access to items via iterators. Of course, an iterator gives access to a single value, so with a map this will be to a pair object that has both the key and the value:

```
map<string, int> people;
people.emplace("Washington", 1789);
people.emplace("Adams", 1797);
people.emplace("Jefferson", 1801);
people.emplace("Madison", 1809);
people.emplace("Monroe", 1817);

auto it = people.begin();
pair<string, int> first_item = *it;
cout << first_item.first << " " << first_item.second << endl;
```

The calls to `emplace` puts items into the `map` where the key is a `string` (the name of a president) and the value is an `int` (the year the president started their term of office). The code then obtains an iterator to the first item in the container, and the item is accessed by dereferencing the iterator to give a `pair` object. Since the items are stored in the `map` in a sorted order, the first item will be set to `"Adams"`. You can also insert items as `pair` objects, either as objects or through iterators to `pair` objects in another container using the `insert` method.

Most of the `emplace` and `insert` methods will return a `pair` object of the following form, where the `iterator` type is relevant to the `map`:

```
pair<iterator, bool>
```

You use this object to test for two things. First, the `bool` indicates if the insertion was successful (it will fail if an item with the same key is already in the container). Secondly, the `iterator` part of the `pair` either indicates the position of the new item or it indicates the position of the existing item that will not be replaced (and will cause the insertion to fail).

The *failure* depends on *equivalence* rather than *equality*. If there is an item with a key that is equivalent to the item you are trying to insert, then the insertion will fail. The definition of equivalence depends on the comparator predicate being used with the `map` object. So, if the `map` uses a predicate `comp`, then equivalence between the two items, a and b, is determined by testing `!comp(a,b) && !comp(b,a)`. This is not the same as testing for `(a==b)`.

Assuming the previous `map` object, you can do this:

```
auto result = people.emplace("Adams", 1825);
if (!result.second)
    cout << (*result.first).first << " already in map" << endl;
```

The second item in the `result` variable is tested to see if the insertion was successful, and if not, then the first item is an iterator to a `pair<string,int>`, which is the existing item, and the code dereferences the iterator to get the `pair` object and then prints out the first item, which is the key (in this case, the name of the person).

If you know where in the `map` the item should go, then you can call `emplace_hint`:

```
auto result = people.emplace("Monroe", 1817);
people.emplace_hint(result.first, "Polk", 1845);
```

Here we know that `Polk` comes after `Monroe` so we can pass the iterator to `Monroe` as the hint. The class gives access to items via iterators, so you can use ranged `for` (which is based on iterator access):

```
for (pair<string, int> p : people)
{
    cout << p.first << " " << p.second << endl;
}
```

In addition, there is access to individual items using the `at` method and the `[]` operator. In both cases the class will search for an item with the provided key and if the item is found, a reference to the item's value is returned. The `at` method and the `[]` operator behave differently in a situation where there is no item with the specified key. If the key does not exist, the `at` method will throw an exception; if the `[]` operator cannot find the specified key, it will create a new item using the key and calling the default constructor of the value type. The `[]` operator will return a reference to the value if the key exists, so you can write code like this:

```
people["Adams"] = 1825;
people["Jackson"] = 1829;
```

The second line behaves as you expect: there will be no item with a key of `Jackson`, so the `map` will create an item with that key, initialize it by calling the default constructor of the value type (`int`, so the value is initialized to zero), and then it returns a reference to this value, which is assigned a value of `1829`. The first line, however, will look up `Adams`, see that there is an item, and return a reference to its value, which is then assigned a value of `1825`. There is no indication that the value of an item has been changed as opposed to a new item being inserted. You may want this behavior in some circumstances, but it is not the intention in this code, where, clearly, an associative container that allows duplicate keys (such as `multimap`) is needed. Furthermore, in both of these cases, there is a search for the key, a reference is returned, and then an assignment is performed. Be aware that, although it is valid to insert items this way, it is more efficient to emplace a new key-value pair in the container because you do not have this extra assignment.

Once you have filled the `map` you can search for a value using the following:

- The `at` method, which is passed a key and returns a reference to the value for that key
- The `[]` operator, which when passed a key returns a reference to the value for that key

- The `find` function, which will use the predicate specified in the template (unlike the global `find` function, mentioned later) and it will give you an iterator to the entire item as a `pair` object
- The `begin` method will give you an iterator to the first item and the `end` method will give you an iterator *after* the last item
- The `lower_bound` method returns an iterator to the item that has a key *equalto or greater* than the key that you pass as a parameter
- The `upper_bound` method returns an iterator of the first item in the map that has a key *greater* than the key provided
- The `equal_range` method returns both the lower and upper bounds values in a `pair` object

# Sets and multisets

Sets behave as if they are maps, but the key is the same as the value; for example, the following:

```
set<string> people{
    "Washington","Adams", "Jefferson","Madison","Monroe",
    "Adams", "Van Buren","Harrison","Tyler","Polk"};
for (string s : people) cout << s << endl;
```

This will print out *nine* people in alphabetical order because there are two items called `Adams`, and the `set` class will reject duplicates. As the items are inserted into the set it will be ordered, and in this case the order is determined by the lexicon ordering of comparing two `string` objects. If you want to allow duplicates, so that ten people will be placed in the container, then you should use `multiset` instead.

As with a `map`, you cannot change the key of an item in the container because the key is used to determine the ordering. For a `set`, the key is the same as the value, so this means that you cannot change the item at all. If the intention is to perform lookups, then it may be better to use a sorted `vector` instead. A `set` will have more memory allocation overhead than a `vector`. Potentially, a lookup on a `set` container will be quicker than on a `vector` container if the search is sequential, but if you use a call to `binary_search` (explained in the *Sorting items* section, later) it could be faster than the associative container.

The interface to the `set` class is a restricted version of the `map` class, so you can `insert` and `emplace` items in the container, assign it to values in another container, and you have iterator access (`begin` and `end` methods).

Since there is no distinct key, it means that the `find` method looks for a value, not a key (and similarly with the bounds methods; for example, `equal_range`). There is no `at` method, nor an `[]` operator.

## Unordered containers

The `map` and `set` classes allow you to find objects quickly, and this is facilitated by these classes holding the items in a sorted order. If you iterate through the items (from `begin` to `end`), then you will get those items in the sorted order. If you want a selection of objects within a range of the key values, you can make calls to the `lower_bound` and `upper_bound` methods, to get iterators to the appropriate ranges of keys. This are two important features of these associative containers: lookup and sorting. In some cases the actual order of the values is not important, and the behavior you want is efficient lookup. In this case, you can use the `unordered_` versions of the `map` and `set` classes. Since the order is unimportant, these are implemented using a hash table.

## Special purpose containers

The containers described so far are flexible and can be used for all kinds of purposes. The Standard Library provides classes that have specific purposes, but, because they are implemented by wrapping other classes, they are called **container adapters**. For example, a `deque` object can be used as a **first-in first-out** (**FIFO**) queue, by pushing objects to the back of the `deque` (with `push_back`) and then accessing objects from the front of the queue using the `front` method (and removing them with `pop_front`). The Standard Library implements a container adapter called `queue` that has this FIFO behavior, and it is based on the `deque` class.

```
queue<int> primes;
primes.push(1);
primes.push(2);
primes.push(3);
primes.push(5);
primes.push(7);
primes.push(11);
while (primes.size() > 0)
{
    cout << primes.front() << ",";
    primes.pop();
}
cout << endl; // prints 1,2,3,5,7,11
```

You `push` items into the queue and remove them with `pop`, and the next item is accessed using the `front` method. The Standard Library containers that can be wrapped by this adapter must implement the `push_back`, `pop_front`, and `front` methods. That is, items are put into the container at one end and accessed (and removed) from the other end.

A **last-in first-out** (**LIFO**) container will put in items and access (and remove) items from the same end. Again, a `deque` object can be used to implement this behavior by pushing items using `push_back`, accessing the items using `front`, and removing them with the `pop_back` method. The Standard Library provides an adapter class called `stack` to provide this behavior. This has a method called `push` to push items into the container, a method called `pop` to remove items, but, oddly, you access the next item using the `top` method, even though it is implemented using the `back` method of the wrapped container.

The adapter class `priority_queue`, in spite of the name, is used like the `stack` container; that is, items are accessed using the `top` method. The container ensures that when an item is pushed in, the top of the queue will always be the item with the highest priority. A predicate (the default is `<`) is used to order the items in the queue. For example, we could have an aggregate type that has the name of a task and the priority in which you must complete the task compared to other tasks:

```
struct task
{
string name;
int priority;
task(const string& n, int p) : name(n), priority(p) {}
bool operator <(const task& rhs) const {
    return this->priority < rhs.priority;
    }
};
```

The aggregate type is straightforward; it has two data members that are initialized by the constructor. So that tasks can be ordered, we need to be able to compare two task objects. One option (given earlier) is to define a separate predicate class. In this example, we use the default predicate, which the documentation says will be `less<task>`, and this compares items based on the `<` operator. So that we can use the default predicate, we define the `<` operator for the `task` class. Now we can add tasks to a `priority_queue` container:

```
priority_queue<task> to_do;
to_do.push(task("tidy desk", 1));
to_do.push(task("check in code", 10));
to_do.push(task("write spec", 8));
to_do.push(task("strategy meeting", 8));

while (to_do.size() > 0)
```

```
        {
            cout << to_do.top().name << " " << to_do.top().priority << endl;
            to_do.pop();
        }
```

The result of this code is:

```
        check in code 10
    write spec 8
    strategy meeting 8
    tidy desk 1
```

The queue has ordered the tasks according to the `priority` data item, and the combination of `top` and `pop` method calls reads the items in priority order and removes them from the queue. Items with the same priority are placed in the queue in the order in which they were pushed in.

# Using iterators

So far, in this chapter we have indicated that containers give access to items through iterators. The implication is that iterators are simply pointers, and this is deliberate because iterators behave *like* pointers. However, they are usually objects of iterator classes (see the `<iterator>` header). All iterators have the following behaviors:

| Operator | Behaviors |
|---|---|
| * | Gives access to the element at the current position |
| ++ | Moves forward to the next element (usually you will use the prefix operator)(this is only if the iterator allows forward movement) |
| -- | Moves backward to the previous element (usually you will use the prefix operator)(this is only if the iterator allows backward movement) |
| == and != | Compares if two iterators are in the same position |
| = | Assigns an iterator |

Unlike a C++ pointer, which assumes that data is contiguous in memory, iterators can be used for more complex data structures, such as linked lists, where the items may not be contiguous. The operators ++ and -- work as expected, regardless of the underlying storage mechanism.

The `<iterator>` header declares the `next` global function that will increment an iterator and the `advance` function that will change an iterator by a specified number of positions (forward or backward depending on whether the parameter is negative and the direction allowed by the iterator). There is also a `prev` function to decrement an iterator by one or more positions. The `distance` function can be used to determine how many items are between two iterators.

All containers have a `begin` method, which returns the iterator for the first item, and an `end` method, which returns an iterator *after* the last item. This means that you can iterate through all items in the container by calling `begin` and then incrementing the iterator until it has the value returned from `end`. The `*` operator on an iterator gives access to the element in the container, and if the iterator is read-write (as it will be if returned from the begin method) it means the item can be changed. Containers also have the `cbegin` and `cend` methods that will return a constant iterator that gives just read-only access to elements:

```
vector<int> primes { 1,2,3,5,7,11,13 };
const auto it = primes.begin(); // const has no effect
*it = 42;
auto cit = primes.cbegin();
*cit = 1;                       // will not compile
```

Here `const` has no effect because the variable is `auto` and the type is deduced from the item used to initialize the variable. The `cbegin` method is defined to return a `const` iterator, so you cannot alter the item it refers to.

The `begin` and `cbegin` methods return **forward iterators** so that the `++` operator moves the iterator forward. Containers may also support **reverse iterators**, where `rbegin` is the last item in the container (that is, the item *before* the position returned by `end`) and `rend` is the position *before* the first item. (There are also `crbegin` and `crend`, which return `const` iterators.) It is important to realize that the `++` operator for a reverse iterator moves *backwards*, as in the following example:

```
vector<int> primes { 1,2,3,5,7,11,13 };
auto it = primes.rbegin();
while (it != primes.rend())
{
    cout << *it++ << " ";
}
cout << endl; // prints 13,11,7,5,4,3,2,1
```

The `++` operator increments the iterator according to the type of the iterator that it is applied to. It is important to note that the `!=` operator is used here to determine if the looping should end because the `!=` operator will be defined on all iterators.

The iterator type here is ignored by using the `auto` keyword. In fact, all containers will have `typedef` for all the iterator types they use, so in the previous case we can use the following:

```
vector<int> primes { 1,2,3,5,7,11,13 };
vector<int>::iterator it = primes.begin();
```

Containers that allow forward iteration will have a `typedef` for `iterator` and `const_iterator`, and containers that allow reverse iteration will have a `typedef` for `reverse_iterator` and `const_reverse_iterator`. To be complete, containers will also have `typedef` for `pointer` and `const_pointer` for the methods that return pointers to the elements, and `reference` and `const_reference` for methods that return references to elements. These type definitions enable you to write generic code where you do not know the types in a container, but the code will still be able to declare variables of the right type.

Although they look like they are pointers, iterators are often implemented by classes. These types may only allow iteration in one direction: a forward iterator will only have the ++ operator, a reverse iterator will have the – operator, or the type may allow iteration in both directions (bidirectional iterators) and so they implement both the ++ and –– operators. For example, the iterators on the `list`, `set`, `multiset`, `map`, and `multimap` classes are bidirectional. The `vector`, `deque`, `array`, and `string` class have iterators that allow random access, so these iterator types have the same behavior as bidirectional iterators, but also have pointers like arithmetic, so they can be changed by more than one item position at a time.

## Input and output iterators

As the name suggests, an input iterator will only move forward and will have read access, and an output iterator will only move forward but will have write access. These iterators do not have random access and they do not allow backward movement. For example, an output stream may be used with an output iterator: you assign the dereferenced iterator with a data item in order to write that data item to the stream. Similarly, an input stream could have an input iterator and you dereference the iterator to get access to the next item in the stream. This behavior means that for an output iterator the only valid use of the dereference operator (\*) is on the left-hand side of an assignment. It makes no sense to check the value of an iterator with !=, and you cannot check if assigning a value through the output iterator is successful.

For example, the `transform` function takes three iterators and a function. The first two iterators are input iterators and indicate a range of items to be transformed by the function. The result will be put in a range of items (the same size as the range of the input iterator), the first of which is indicated by the third iterator, which is an output iterator. One way to do this is as follows:

```
vector<int> data { 1,2,3,4,5 };
vector<int> results;
results.resize(data.size());
transform(
    data.begin(), data.end(),
    results.begin(),
    [](int x){ return x*x; } );
```

Here the `begin` and `end` methods return iterators on the `data` container that are safe to be used as input iterators. The `begin` method on the `results` container can only be used as an output iterator as long as the container has enough allocated items, and this is the case in this code because they have been allocated with `resize`. The function will then transform each input item by passing it to the lambda function given in the last parameter (which simply returns the square of the value). It is important to reassess what is happening here; the third parameter of the `transform` function is an output iterator, which means that you should expect the function to write values through this iterator.

This code works, but it requires the extra step to allocate the space, and you have the extra allocations of default objects in the container just so that you can overwrite them. It is also important to mention that the output iterator does not have to be to another container. It can be to the same container as long as it refers to a range that can be written to:

```
vector<int> vec{ 1,2,3,4,5 };
vec.resize(vec.size() * 2);
transform(vec.begin(), vec.begin() + 5,
    vec.begin() + 5, [](int i) { return i*i; });
```

The `vec` container is resized so that there is space for the results. The range of values to transform are from the beginning item to the fifth item (`vec.begin() + 5` is the next item), and the place to write the transformed value is the sixth to tenth items. If you print out the vector you will get `{1,2,3,4,5,1,4,9,16,25}`.

Another type of output iterator is the inserter. The `back_inserter` is used on containers with `push_back`, and `front_inserter` is used on containers with `push_front`. As the name suggests, an inserter calls the `insert` method on the container. For example, you can use a `back_inserter` like this:

```
vector<int> data { 1,2,3,4,5 };
vector<int> results;
transform(
    data.begin(), data.end(),
    back_inserter(results),
    [](int x){ return x*x; } ); // 1,4,9,16,25
```

The results of the transformation are inserted into the `results` container with the temporary object created from the `back_inserter` class. Using a `back_inserter` object ensures that when the `transform` function writes through the iterator the item is *inserted* into the wrapped container using `push_back`. Note that the results container should be different to the source container.

If you want the values in reverse order, then if the container supports `push_front` (for example, `deque`), then you can use a `front_inserter`. The `vector` class does not have a `push_front` method, but it does have reverse iterators, so you can use them instead:

```
vector<int> data { 1,2,3,4,5 };
vector<int> results;
transform(
    data.rbegin(), data.rend(),
    back_inserter(results),
    [](int x){ return x*x; } ); // 25,16,9,4,1
```

All you need to do to reverse the order of the results is to change `begin` to `rbegin` and `end` to `rend`.

## Stream iterators

These are adapter classes in `<iterators>` that can be used to read items from an input stream or write items to an output stream. For example, so far, we have used iterators via ranged `for` loops to print out the contents of a container:

```
vector<int> data { 1,2,3,4,5 };
for (int i : data) cout << i << " ";
cout << endl;
```

Instead, you can create an output stream iterator based on `cout`, so that the `int` values will be written to the `cout` stream through this iterator using the stream operator `<<`. To print out a container of `int` values, you simply copy the container to the output iterator:

```
vector<int> data { 1,2,3,4,5 };
ostream_iterator<int> my_out(cout, " ");
copy(data.cbegin(), data.cend(), my_out);
cout << endl;
```

The first parameter of the `ostream_iterator` class is the output stream it will adapt, and the optional second parameter is a delimiter string used between each item. The `copy` function (in `<algorithm>`) will copy the items in the range indicated by the input iterators, passed as the first two parameters, to the output iterator, passed as the last parameter.

Similarly, there is an `istream_iterator` class that will wrap an input stream object and provide an input iterator. This class will use the stream `>>` operator to extract objects of the specified type, which can be read through the stream iterator. However, reading data from a stream is more complicated than writing to one, since there must be detection of when there is no more data in the input stream for the iterator to read (an end of file situation).

The `istream_iterator` class has two constructors. One constructor has a single parameter that is the input stream to read, and the other constructor, the default constructor, has no parameters and is used to create an **end of stream iterator**. The end of stream iterator is used to indicate that there is no more data in the stream:

```
vector<int> data;
copy(
    istream_iterator<int>(cin), istream_iterator<int>(),
    back_inserter(data));

ostream_iterator<int> my_out(cout, " ");
copy(data.cbegin(), data.cend(), my_out);
cout << endl;
```

The first call to `copy` provides two input iterators, as the first parameters, and an output iterator. The function copies data from the first iterator to the output iterator in the last parameter. Since the last parameter is created from `back_inserter`, this means that the items are inserted into the `vector` object. The input iterators are based on an input stream (`cin`) and thus the `copy` function will read `int` values from the console (each one separated by white space) until no more are available (for example, if you press *CTRL + Z* to end the stream or you type a non-numeric item). Since you can initialize a container with a range of values given by iterators, you can use `istream_iterator` as constructor parameters:

```
vector<int> data {
    istream_iterator<int>(cin), istream_iterator<int>() };
```

Here the constructor is called using the initializer list syntax; if you use parentheses, the compiler will interpret this as the declaration of a function!

As noted earlier, the `istream_iterator` will use the stream's >> operator to read objects of the specified type from the stream and this operator uses whitespace to delimit the items (and hence it just ignores all whitespace). If you read in a container of `string` objects, then each word you type on the console will be an item in the container. A `string` is a container of characters, and it can be also initialized using iterators, so you could try to input data into a `string` from the console using an `istream_iterator`:

```
string data {
        istream_iterator<char>(cin), istream_iterator<char>() };
```

In this case the stream is `cin`, but it could easily be an `ifstream` object to a file. The problem is that the `cin` object will strip out the white space, so the `string` object will contain everything that you type except for white space, so there will be no spaces and no newlines.

This problem is caused by the `istream_iterator` using the stream's >> operator, and can only be avoided by using another class, `istreambuf_iterator`:

```
string data {
    istreambuf_iterator<char>(cin), istreambuf_iterator<char>() };
```

This class reads each character from the stream and copies each one into the container without the processing of >>.

# Using iterators with the C Standard Library

The C Standard Library will often require pointers to data. For example, when a C function requires a string, it will need a `const char*` pointer to the character array containing the string. The C++ Standard Library has been designed to allow you to use its classes with the C Standard Library; indeed, the C Standard Library is part of the C++ Standard Library. In the case of `string` objects, the solution is simple: when you need a `const char*` pointer, you simply call the `c_str` method on a `string` object.

The containers that store data in contiguous memory (`array`, `string`, or `data`) have a method called `data` that gives access to the container's data as a C array. Further, these containers have `[]` operator access to their data, so you can also treat the address of the first item as being `&container[0]` (where `container` is the container object), just as you do with C arrays. However, if the container is empty, this address will be invalid, so before using it you should call the `empty` method. The number of items in these containers is returned from the `size` method, so for any C function that takes a pointer to the start of a C array and its size, you can call it with `&container[0]` and the value from the `size` method.

You may be tempted to get the beginning of the container that has contiguous memory by calling its `begin` function, but this will return an iterator (usually an object). So, to get a C pointer to the first item, you should call `&*begin`; that is, dereference the iterator returned from the `begin` function to get the first item and then use the address operator to get its address. To be frank, `&container[0]` is simpler and more readable.

If the container does not store its data in contiguous memory (for example, `deque` and `list`), then you can obtain a C pointer by simply copying the data into a temporary vector.

```
list<int> data;
// do some calculations and fill the list
vector<int> temp(data.begin(), data.end());
size_t size = temp.size(); // can pass size to a C function
int *p = &temp[0];         // can pass p to a C function
```

In this case, we have chosen to use a `list` and the routine will manipulate the `data` object. Later in the routine, these values will be passed to a C function so the `list` is used to initialize a `vector` object, and these values are obtained from the `vector`.

# Algorithms

The Standard Library has an extensive collection of generic functions in the `<algorithm>` header file. By generic we mean that they access data via iterators without knowing what the iterators refer to and so it means that you can write generic code to work for any appropriate container. However, if you know the container type and that container has a member method to perform the same action, you should use the member.

# Iteration of items

Many of the routines in `<algorithm>` will take ranges and iterate over those ranges performing some action. As the name suggests, the `fill` function will fill a container with a value. The function takes two iterators to specify the range and a value that will be placed into each position of the container:

```
vector<int> vec;
vec.resize(5);
fill(vec.begin(), vec.end(), 42);
```

Since the `fill` function will be called for a range, it means that you have to pass iterators to a container that already has values, and this is the reason why this code calls the `resize` method. This code will put the value of 42 into each of the items of the container, so when it has completed the `vector` contains {42,42,42,42,42}. There is another version of this function called `fill_n` that specifies the range by a single iterator to the start of the range and a count of the items in the range.

The `generate` function is similar, but, rather than a single value, it has a function, which can be a function, a function object, or a lambda expression. The function is called to provide each item in the container, so it has no parameters and returns an object of the type accessed by the iterator:

```
vector<int> vec(5);
generate(vec.begin(), vec.end(),
    []() {static int i; return ++i; });
```

Again, you have to make sure that the `generate` function is passed a range that already exists, and this code does this by passing the initial size as a constructor parameter. In this example, the lambda expression has a `static` variable, which is incremented with each call, so this means that after the `generate` function has completed the `vector` contains `{1,2,3,4,5}`. There is another version of this function called `generate_n` that specifies the range by a single iterator to the start of the range and a count of the items in the range.

The `for_each` function will iterate over a range provided by two iterators and, for each item in the range, call a specified function. This function must have a single parameter that is the same type as the items in the container:

```
vector<int> vec { 1,4,9,16,25 };
for_each(vec.begin(), vec.end(),
    [](int i) { cout << i << " "; });
cout << endl;
```

The `for_each` function iterates over all the items specified by the iterators (in this case the entire range), dereferences the iterator, and passes the item to the function, The effect of this code is to print the contents of the container. The function can take the item by value (as in this case) or by reference. If you pass the item by reference, then the function can change the item:

```
vector<int> vec { 1,2,3,4,5 };
for_each(vec.begin(), vec.end(),
    [](int& i) { i *= i; });
```

After calling this code, the items in the `vector` will be replaced with the squares of those items. If you use a functor or a lambda expression, you can pass a container to capture the result of the function; for example:

```
vector<int> vec { 1,2,3,4,5 };
vector<int> results;
for_each(vec.begin(), vec.end(),
    [&results](int i) { results.push_back(i*i); });
```

Here, a container is declared to accept the results of each call to the lambda expression, and the variable is passed by reference to the expression by capturing it.

 Recall from `Chapter 3`, *Using Functions*, that the square brackets contain the names of the captured variables declared outside the expression. Once captured, it means that the expression is able to access the object.

In this example the result of each iteration (`i*i`) is pushed into the captured collection so that the results are stored for later.

The `transform` function has two forms; they both provide a function (a pointer, functor, or a lambda expression) and they both have an input range of items in a container passed via iterators. In this respect, they are similar to `for_each`. The `transform` function also allows you to pass an iterator to a container that is used to store the results of the function. The function must have a single parameter that is the same type as the type (or a reference) of the type referred to the input iterators and it must return the type accessed by the output iterator.

The other version of `transform` uses a function to combine the values in two ranges, so this means that the function must have two parameters (which will be the corresponding items in the two iterators) and return the type of the output iterator. You only need to give the full range of items in one of the input ranges because it is assumed that the other range is at least as large, and hence you only have to provide the beginning iterator of the second range:

```
vector<int> vec1 { 1,2,3,4,5 };
vector<int> vec2 { 5,4,3,2,1 };
vector<int> results;
transform(vec1.begin(), vec1.end(), vec2.begin(),
    back_inserter(results), [](int i, int j) { return i*j; });
```

# Getting information

Once you have values in a container, you can call functions to get information about those items. The `count` function is used to count the number items with a specified value in a range:

```
vector<int> planck{ 6,6,2,6,0,7,0,0,4,0 };
auto number = count(planck.begin(), planck.end(), 6);
```

This code will return a value of 3 because there are three copies of 6 in the container. The return type of the function is the type specified in the `difference_type` typedef of the container, and in this case it will be `int`. The `count_if` function works in a similar way, but you pass a predicate that takes a single parameter (the current item in the container) and returns a `bool` specifying if this is the value that is being counted.

The `count` functions count the number of occurrences of a specific value. If you want to aggregate all the values, then you can use the `accumulate` function in `<numeric>`. This will iterate over the range, access each item and keep a running sum of all the items. The sum will be carried out using the + operator of the type, but there is also a version that takes a binary function (two parameters of the container type and returns the same type) that specifies what happens when you add two such types together.

The `all_of`, `any_of`, and `none_of` functions are passed a predicate with a single argument of the same type of the container; there are also given iterators indicating a range over which they iterate, testing each item with the predicate. The `all_of` function will return `true` only if the predicate is `true` for all items, the `any_of` function returns `true` if predicate is `true` for at least one of the items, and the `none_of` function will return `true` only if the predicate is `false` for all items.

# Comparing containers

If you have two containers of data, there are various ways that you can compare them. For every container type, there are <, <=, ==, !=, >, and >= operators defined. The == and != operators compare the containers, both in terms of how many items they have and the values of those items. So, if the items have different numbers of items, different values, or both, then they are not equal. The other comparisons prefer values over the number of items:

```
vector<int> v1 { 1,2,3,4 };
vector<int> v2 { 1,2 };
vector<int> v3 { 5,6,7 };
cout << boolalpha;
cout << (v1 > v2) << endl; // true
cout << (v1 > v3) << endl; // false
```

In the first comparison, the two vectors have similar items, but v2 has fewer, so v1 is "greater than" v2. In the second case, v3 has larger values than v1, but fewer of them, so v3 is *greater than* v1.

You can also compare ranges with the `equal` function. This is passed two ranges (which are assumed to be the same size, so only an iterator to the start of the second range is needed), and it compares corresponding items in both ranges using the == operator for the type accessed by the iterator, or a user-supplied predicate. Only if all such comparisons are `true` will the function return `true`. Similarly, the `mismatch` function compares corresponding items in two ranges. However, this function returns a `pair` object with iterators in each of the two ranges for the first item that is not the same. You can also provide a comparison function. The `is_permutation` is similar in that it compares the values in two ranges, but it returns `true` if the two ranges have the same values but not necessarily in the same order.

# Changing Items

The **reverse** function acts on a range in a container and reverses the order of the items; this means that the iterators must be writeable. The copy and copy_n functions copy every item from one range to another in a forward direction; for copy, the input range is given by two input iterators, and for copy_n, the range is an input iterator and a count of items. The copy_backward function will copy the items, starting at the end of the range, so that the output range will have the items in the same order as the original. This means that the output iterator will indicate the *end* of the range to copy to. You can also copy items only if they satisfy some condition specified by a predicate.

- The reverse_copy function will create a copy in the reverse order to the input range; in effect, the function iterates backward through the original and copies items to the output range forward.

- In spite of the name, the move and move_backward functions are semantically equivalent to the copy and copy_backward functions. Thus, in the following, the original container will have the same values after the operation:

```
vector<int> planck{ 6,6,2,6,0,7,0,0,4,0 };
vector<int> result(4);            // we want 4 items
auto it1 = planck.begin();        // get the first position
it1 += 2;                         // move forward 2 places
auto it2 = it1 + 4;               // move 4 items
move(it1, it2, result.begin());   // {2,6,0,7}
```

- This code will copy four items from the first container to the second container, starting at the item in the third position.

- The remove_copy and remove_copy_if functions iterate through the source range and copy items other than those with the specified value.

```
vector<int> planck{ 6,6,2,6,0,7,0,0,4,0 };
vector<int> result;
remove_copy(planck.begin(), planck.end(),
    back_inserter(result), 6);
```

- Here, the planck object is left the same as before and the result object will contain {2,0,7,0,0,4,0}. The remove_copy_if function behaves similarly, but is given a predicate rather than an actual value.

- The `remove` and `remove_if` functions don't quite do what their names suggest. These functions act on a single range and iterate looking for a specific value (`remove`), or pass each item to a predicate that will indicate if the item should be removed (`remove_if`). When an item is removed, the items later in the container are shifted forward, but the container remains the same size, which means that the items at the end remain as they were. The reason the `remove` functions behave like this is because they only know about reading and writing items through iterators (which is generic for all containers). To erase an item, the function will need to have access to the `erase` method of the container, and the `remove` functions only have access to iterators.

- If you want to remove the items at the end, then you must resize the container accordingly. Typically, this means calling a suitable `erase` method on the container, and this is made possible because the `remove` method returns an iterator to the new end position:

```
vector<int> planck { 6,6,2,6,0,7,0,0,4,0 };
auto new_end = remove(planck.begin(), planck.end(), 6);
                                        // {2,0,7,0,0,4,0,0,4,0}
planck.erase(new_end, planck.end()); // {2,0,7,0,0,4,0}
```

- The `replace` and `replace_if` functions iterate through a single range, and if the value is a specified value (`replace`) or returns `true` from a predicate (`replace_if`), then the item is replaced with a specified new value. There are also two functions, `replace_copy` and `replace_copy_if`, that leave the original alone and make the change to another range (similar to `remove_copy` and `remove_copy_if` functions).

- The `rotate` functions treat the range as if the end is joined to the beginning, and so you can shift items forward so that when an item falls off the end it gets put in the first position. If you want to move every item forward four places, you can do this:

```
vector<int> planck{ 6,6,2,6,0,7,0,0,4,0 };
auto it = planck.begin();
it += 4;
rotate(planck.begin(), it, planck.end());
```

- The result of this rotation is {0,7,0,0,4,0,6,6,2,6}. The `rotate_copy` function does the same thing, but, rather than affecting the original container, it copies the items into another container.

- The `unique` function acts on a range and "removes" (in the manner explained previously) the items that are duplicates of adjacent items, and you can provide a predicate for the function to call to test if two items are the same. This function only checks adjacent items, so a duplicate later in the container will remain. If you want to remove all duplicates, then you should sort the container first, so that similar items are adjacent.

- The `unique_copy` function will copy items from one range to another only if they are unique, so one way to remove duplicates is to use this function on a temporary container and then assign the original to the temporary:

```
vector<int> planck{ 6,6,2,6,0,7,0,0,4,0 };
vector<int> temp;
unique_copy(planck.begin(), planck.end(), back_inserter(temp));
planck.assign(temp.begin(), temp.end());
```

- After this code, the `planck` container will have {6,2,6,0,7,0,4,0}.

- Finally, the `iter_swap` will swap the items indicated by two iterators, and the `swap_ranges` function swaps the items in one range to the other range (the second range is indicated by one iterator and it is assumed to refer to a range of the same size as the first).

# Finding Items

The Standard Library has a wide range of functions to search for items:

- The `min_element` function will return an iterator to the smallest item in a range and the `max_element` function will return an iterator to the maximum item. These functions are passed iterators for the range of items to check and a predicator that returns a `bool` from the comparison of two items. If you don't provide a predicator, the < operator for the type will be used.

```
vector<int> planck{ 6,6,2,6,0,7,0,0,4,0 };
auto imin = min_element(planck.begin(), planck.end());
auto imax = max_element(planck.begin(), planck.end());
cout << "values between " << *imin << " and "<< *imax << endl;
```

- The `imin` and `imax` values are iterators, which is why they are dereferenced to get the value. If you want to get the minimum element and the maximum element in one go, you can call the `minmax_element`, which will return a `pair` object with iterators to these items. As the name suggests, the `adjacent_find` function will return the position of the first two items that have the same value (and you can provide a predicate to determine what *same value* means). This allows you to search for duplicates and get the position of those duplicates.

```
vector<int> vec{0,1,2,3,4,4,5,6,7,7,7,8,9};
vector<int>::iterator it = vec.begin();

do
{
    it = adjacent_find(it, vec.end());
    if (it != vec.end())
    {
        cout << "duplicate " << *it << endl;
        ++it;
    }
} while (it != vec.end());
```

- This code has a sequence of numbers in which there are some numbers duplicated that are next to each other. In this case there are *three* adjacent duplicates: 4 followed by 4, and the sequence 7, 7, 7 is 7 followed by 7, and 7 followed by 7. The `do` loop calls `adjacent_find` repeatedly until it returns the `end` iterator, indicating that it has searched all items. When a duplicate pair is found, the code prints out the value and then increments the start position for the next search.
- The `find` function searches a container for a single value, and returns an iterator to that item or the `end` iterator if the value cannot be found. The `find_if` function is passed a predicate and it returns an iterator to the first item it finds that satisfies the predicate; similarly, the `find_if_not` function finds the first item that does not satisfy the predicate.
- There are several functions that are given two ranges, one is the range to search and the other has the values to look for. The different functions will either look for one of the items in the search criteria or it will look for all of them. These functions use the `==` operator for the type that the container holds or a predicate.

- The `find_first_of` function returns the position of the first item that it finds in the search list. The `search` function looks for a specific sequence, and it returns the *first* position of the whole sequence, whereas the `find_end` function returns the *last* position of the entire search sequence. Finally, the `search_n` function looks for a sequence that is a value repeated a number of times (the value and the repeat are given) in a specified container's range.

# Sorting items

The sequence containers can be sorted, and once you have done this you can use methods to search for items, to merge containers, or to get the difference between the containers. The `sort` function will order the items in a range according to the < operator or a predicate that you provide. If there are items that are equal in the range, then the order of these items after the sort is not guaranteed; if this order is important, you should call the `stable_sort` function instead. If you want to preserve the input range and copy the sorted items into another range, you use the confusingly named `partial_sort_copy` function. This is not a partial sort. This function is passed iterators to the input range and iterators for the output range, so you have to ensure that output range has a suitable capacity.

You can check if a range is sorted by calling the `is_sorted` function, and this will iterate through all items and return `false` if it finds an item that is not in sorted order, in which case you can locate the first item that is out of sort order by calling the `is_sorted_until` function.

As the name suggests, the `partial_sort` function does not place every item in its exact order relative to every other item. Instead, it will create two groups, or partitions, where the first partition will have the smallest items (not necessarily in any order) and the other partition will have the biggest items. You are guaranteed that the smallest items are in the first partition. To call this function you pass three iterators, two of which are the range to sort, and the third is a position somewhere between the other two that indicates the boundary before which are the smallest values.

```
vector<int> vec{45,23,67,6,29,44,90,3,64,18};
auto middle = vec.begin() + 5;
partial_sort(vec.begin(), middle, vec.end());
cout << "smallest items" << endl;
for_each(vec.begin(), middle, [](int i) {cout << i << " "; });
cout << endl; // 3 6 18 23 29
cout << "biggest items" << endl;
for_each(middle, vec.end(), [](int i) {cout << i << " "; });
cout << endl; // 67 90 45 64 44
```

In this example there is a vector of ten items, so we define the `middle` iterator as five items from the beginning (this is just a choice, it could be some other value depending on how many items you want to obtain). In this example, you can see that the five smallest items have been sorted to the first half and the last half have the biggest items.

The oddly named `nth_element` function acts like `partial_sort`. You provide an iterator to the *nth* element and the function ensures that first *n* items in the range are the smallest. The `nth_element` function is faster than `partial_sort`, and, although you are guaranteed that the items before the *nth* element are less than or equal to the *nth* element, there are no other guarantees of the sort order within the partitions.

The `partial_sort` and `nth_element` functions are versions of partitioned sort functions. The `partition` function is a more generic version. You pass this function a range and a predicate that determines in which of the two partitions an item will be placed. The items that meet the predicate will be put in the first partition of the range, and the other items will be placed in the range following the first partition. The first item of the second partition is called the partition point and it is returned from the `partition` function, but you can calculate it later by passing iterators to the partitioned range and the predicate to the `partition_point` function. The `partition_copy` function will also partition values, but it will leave the original range untouched and put the values in a range that has been already allocated. These partition functions do not guarantee the order of equivalent items, and if this order is important then you should call the `stable_partitian` function. Finally, you can determine if a container is partitioned by calling the `is_partitioned` function.

The `shuffle` function will rearrange the items in a container into a random order. This function needs a uniform random number generator from the `<random>` library. For example, the following will fill a container with ten integers and then place them in a random order:

```
vector<int> vec;
for (int i = 0; i < 10; ++i) vec.push_back(i);
random_device rd;
shuffle(vec.begin(), vec.end(), rd);
```

A heap is a partially sorted sequence in which the first item is always the largest, and items are added and removed from the heap in logarithmic time. Heaps are based upon sequence containers and, oddly, rather than the Standard Library providing an adapter class, you have to use function calls on an existing container. To create a heap from an existing container, you pass the range iterators to the `make_heap` function, which will order the container as a heap. You can then add new items to the container using its `push_back` method, but each time you do this you have to call `push_heap` to re-order the heap.

Similarly, to get an item from the heap you call the `front` method on the container and then remove the item by calling the `pop_heap` function, which ensures that the heap is kept ordered. You can test to see if a container is arranged as a heap by calling `is_heap`, and if the container is not entirely arranged as a heap you can get an iterator to the first item that does not satisfy the heap criteria by calling `is_heap_until`. Finally, you can sort a heap into a sorted sequence with `sort_heap`.

Once you have sorted a container, there are functions that you can call to get information about the sequence. The `lower_bound` and `upper_bound` methods have already been described for containers, and the functions behave in the same way: `lower_bound` returns the position of the first element that has a value greater than or equal to the value provided and `upper_bound` returns the position of the next item that is greater than the value provided. The `includes` function tests to see if one sorted range contains the items in a second sorted range.

The functions beginning with `set_` will combine two sorted sequences into a third, container. The `set_difference` function will copy the items that are in the first sequence but not in the second sequence. This is not a symmetric action because it does not include the items that are in the second sequence but not in the first. If you want a symmetric difference, then you should call the `set_symmetric_difference` function. The `set_intersection` will copy the items that are in both sequences. The `set_union` function will combine the two sequences. There is another function that will combine two sequences, which is the `merge` function. The difference between these two functions is that with the `set_union` function, if an item is in both of the sequences, there will only be one copy put in the results container, whereas with `merge` there will be two copies in the results container.

If a range is sorted, then you can call the `equal_range` function to obtain the range of elements that are equivalent to a value passed to the function or a predicate. This function returns a pair of iterators that represent the range of values in the container.

The final method that needs a sorted container is `binary_search`. This function is used to test if a value is in the container. The function is passed iterators indicating the range to test and a value, and it will return `true` if there is an item in the range equal to that value (you can provide a predicate to perform this equality test).

# Using the numeric libraries

The Standard Library has several libraries of classes to perform numeric manipulations. In this section we will cover two: compile-time arithmetic, using <ratio>, and complex numbers, using <complex>.

# Compile time arithmetic

Fractions are a problem because there are some for which there are not enough significant figures to accurately represent them, resulting in losing accuracy when you use them in further arithmetic. Furthermore, computers are binary and merely converting decimal fractional parts to binary will lose accuracy. The <ratio> library provides classes that allow you to represent fractional numbers as objects that are ratios of integers, and perform fraction calculations as ratios. Only once you have performed all the fractional arithmetic will you convert the number to decimal, and this means that the potential loss of accuracy is minimized. The calculations performed by the classes in the <ratio> library are carried out at *compile time* so the compiler will catch errors such as divide by zero and overflows.

Using the library is simple; you use the ratio class, and provide the numerator and denominator as template parameters. The numerator and denominator will be stored factorized, and you can access these values through the num and den members of the object:

```
ratio<15, 20> ratio;
cout << ratio.num << "/" << ratio.den << endl;
```

This will print out 3/4.

Fractional arithmetic is carried out using templates (these are, in fact, specializations of the ratio template). At first sight it may appear a little odd, but you soon get used to it!

```
ratio_add<ratio<27, 11>, ratio<5, 17>> ratio;
cout << ratio.num << "/" << ratio.den << endl;
```

This will print out 514/187 (you may want to get some paper and do the fractional calculations to confirm this). The data members are actually static members, so it makes little sense to create variables. Furthermore, because arithmetic is carried out using *types* rather than *variables*, it is best to access the members through those types:

```
typedef ratio_add<ratio<27, 11>, ratio<5, 17>> sum;
cout << sum::num << "/" << sum::den << endl;
```

You can now use the sum type as a parameter to any of the other operations that you can perform. The four binary arithmetic operations are carried out with `ratio_add`, `ratio_subtract`, `ratio_multiply`, and `ratio_divide`. Comparisons are carried out through `ratio_equal`, `ratio_not_equal`, `ratio_greater`, `ratio_greater_equal`, `ratio_less`, and `ratio_less_equal`.

```
bool result = ratio_greater<sum, ratio<25, 19> >::value;
cout << boolalpha << result << endl;
```

This operation tests to see if the calculation performed before (514/187) is greater than the fraction 25/19 (it is). The compiler will pick up divide-by-zero errors and overflows, so the following will not compile:

```
typedef ratio<1, 0> invalid;
cout << invalid::num << "/" << invalid::den << endl;
```

However, it is important to point out that the compiler will issue the error on the second line, when the denominator is accessed. There are also typedefs of ratio for the SI prefixes. This means that you can perform your calculations in nanometers, and when you need to present the data in meters you can use the `nano` type to obtain the ratio:

```
double radius_nm = 10.0;
double volume_nm = pow(radius_nm, 3) * 3.1415 * 4.0 / 3.0;
cout << "for " << radius_nm << "nm "
    "the volume is " << volume_nm << "nm3" << endl;
double factor = ((double)nano::num / nano::den);
double vol_factor = pow(factor, 3);
cout << "for " << radius_nm * factor << "m "
    "the volume is " << volume_nm * vol_factor << "m3" << endl;
```

Here, we are doing calculations on a sphere in **nanometers** (**nm**). The sphere has a radius of 10 nm, so the first calculation gives the volume as 4188.67 nm3. The second calculation converts nanometers into meters; the factor is determined from the `nano` ratio (note that for volumes the factor is cubed). You could define a class to do such conversions:

```
template<typename units>
class dist_units
{
    double data;
    public:
        dist_units(double d) : data(d) {}

    template <class other>
    dist_units(const dist_units<other>& len) : data(len.value() *
      ratio_divide<units, other>::type::den /
      ratio_divide<units, other>::type::num) {}
```

```
        double value() const { return data; }
    };
```

The class is defined for a particular type of unit, which will be expressed through an instantiation of the `ratio` template. The class has a constructor to initialize it for values in those units and a constructor to convert from other units, and that simply divides the current units by the units of the other type. This class can be used like this:

```
dist_units<kilo> earth_diameter_km(12742);
cout << earth_diameter_km.value() << "km" << endl;
dist_units<ratio<1>> in_meters(earth_diameter_km);
cout << in_meters.value()<< "m" << endl;
dist_units<ratio<1609344, 1000>> in_miles(earth_diameter_km);
cout << in_miles.value()<< "miles" << endl;
```

The first variable is based on `kilo` and hence the units are kilometers. To convert this to meters, the second variable type is based on `ratio<1>`, which is the same as `ratio<1,1>`. The result is that the values in the `earth_diameter_km` are multiplied by 1000 when placed in `in_meters`. The conversion to miles is a bit more involved. There are 1609.344 m in a mile. The ratio used for the `in_miles` variable is 1609344/1000 or 1609.344. We are initializing the variable with the `earth_diameter_km`, so isn't that value too big by a factor of 1000? No, the reason is that the type of `earth_diameter_km` is `dist_units<kilo>`, so the conversion between km and miles will include that factor of 1000.

# Complex numbers

Complex numbers are not just of mathematical interest, they are also vital in engineering and science, so a `complex` type is an important part of any type library. A complex number is made of two parts--the real and imaginary parts. As the name suggests, an imaginary number is not real, and cannot be treated as real.

In mathematics, complex numbers are usually represented as coordinates in two-dimensional space. If a real number can be thought of as being one of an infinite number of points on the x-axis, an imaginary number can be thought of being one of an infinite number of points on the y-axis. The only intersection between these two is the origin and since zero is zero, is nothing, it can be a zero real number or a zero imaginary number. A complex number has both real and imaginary parts, and hence this can be visualized as a Cartesian point. Indeed, another way of visualizing a complex number is as a polar number where the point is represented as a vector of a specified length at a specified angle to the position on the x-axis (the positive real number axis).

The `complex` class is based on a floating point type, and there are specializations for `float`, `double`, and `long double`. The class is simple; it has a constructor with two parameters for the real and imaginary parts of the number, and it defines operators (member methods and global functions) for assignment, comparisons, +, −, /, and *, acting on the real and imaginary parts.

An operation like + is simple for a complex number: you just add the real parts together and the imaginary parts together, and these two sums are the real and imaginary parts of the result. However, multiplication and division are a bit more, umm, complex. In multiplication, you get a quadratic: the aggregation of the two real parts multiplied, the two imaginary parts multiplied, the two values of the real part of the first multiplied with the imaginary part of the second, and the imaginary part of the first multiplied with the real part of the second. The complication is that two imaginary numbers multiplied is equivalent to the multiplication of two equivalent real numbers multiplied by -1. Furthermore, multiplying a real and an imaginary number results in an imaginary number that is equivalent in size to the multiplication of two equivalent real numbers.

There are also functions to perform trigonometric operations on complex numbers: `sin`, `cos`, `tan`, `sinh`, `cosh`, and `tanh`; and basic math operations such as `log`, `exp`, `log10`, `pow`, and `sqrt`. You can also call functions to create complex numbers and get information about them. So, the `polar` function will take two floating-point numbers representing the polar coordinates of the length of the vector and the angle. If you have a `complex` number object you can get the polar coordinates by calling `abs` (to get the length) and `arg` (to get the angle).

```
complex<double> a(1.0, 1.0);
complex<double> b(-0.5, 0.5);
complex<double> c = a + b;
cout << a << " + " << b << " = " << c << endl;
complex<double> d = polar(1.41421, -3.14152 / 4);
cout << d << endl;
```

The first point to make is that there is an `ostream` insertion operator defined for `complex` numbers so you can insert them into the `cout` stream object. The output from this code is as follows:

```
(1,1) + (-0.5,0.5) = (0.5,1.5)
(1.00002,-0.999979)
```

The second line shows the limitations of using just five decimal places for the square root of 2 and -1/4 pi, this number is, in fact, the complex number `(1, -1)`.

# Using the Standard Library

In this example, we will develop a simple parser for **Comma Separated Value (CSV)** files. The rules we will follow are as follows:

- Each record will occupy one line, and newline indicates a new record
- Fields in the record are separated by commas, unless they are within a quoted string
- Strings can be quoted using single (') or double quotes ("), in which case they can contain commas as part of the string
- Quotes immediately repeated ('' or "") is a literal, and a part of the string rather than a delimiter of a string
- If a string is quoted, then spaces outside of the string are ignored

This is a very basic implementation, and omits the usual requirement that quoted strings can contain newlines.

In this example, much of the manipulation will be using `string` objects as containers of individual characters.

Start by creating a folder for the chapter called `Chapter_08` in the folder for this book. In that folder, create a file called `csv_parser.cpp`. Since the application will use console output and file input, add the following lines at the top of the file:

```
#include <iostream>
#include <fstream>

using namespace std;
```

The application will also take a command line parameter that is the CSV file to parse, so add the following code at the bottom of the file:

```
void usage()
{
    cout << "usage: csv_parser file" << endl;
    cout << "where file is the path to a csv file" << endl;
}

int main(int argc, const char* argv[])
{
    if (argc <= 1)
    {
        usage();
        return 1;
    }
    return 0;
}
```

The application will read a file line by line into a `vector` of `string` objects, so add `<vector>` to the list of include files. To make the coding easier, define the following above the `usage` function:

```
using namespace std;
using vec_str = vector<string>;
```

The `main` function will read the file in line by line and the simplest way to do this is to use the `getline` function, so add the `<string>` header file to the include file list. Add the following lines to the end of the `main` function:

```
ifstream stm;
stm.open(argv[1], ios_base::in);
if (!stm.is_open())
{
    usage();
    cout << "cannot open " << argv[1] << endl;
    return 1;
}

vec_str lines;
for (string line; getline(stm, line); )
{
    if (line.empty()) continue;
    lines.push_back(move(line));
}
stm.close();
```

The first few lines open the file using an `ifstream` class. If the file cannot be found, then the operation to open the file fails and this is tested by calling `is_open`. Next, a `vector` of `string` objects is declared and filled with lines read from the file. The `getline` function has two parameters: the first is the open file stream object and the second is a string to contain the character data. This function returns the stream object, which has a `bool` conversion operator, and hence the `for` statement will loop until this stream object indicates that it can read no more data. When the stream gets to the end of the file, an internal end-of-file flag is set and this causes the `bool` conversion operator to return a value of `false`.

If the `getline` function reads a blank line, then the `string` will not be able to be parsed, so there is a test for this, and such blank lines are not stored. Each legitimate line is pushed into the `vector`, but, since this `string` variable will not be used after this operation, we can use move semantics and so this is made explicit by calling the `move` function.

This code will now compile and run (although it will produce no output). You can use it on any CSV file that meets the criteria given previously, but as a test file we have used the following file:

```
George Washington,1789,1797
"John Adams, Federalist",1797,1801
"Thomas Jefferson, Democratic Republican",1801,1809
"James Madison, Democratic Republican",1809,1817
"James Monroe, Democratic Republican",1817,1825
"John Quincy Adams, Democratic Republican",1825,1829
"Andrew Jackson, Democratic",1829,1837
"Martin Van Buren, Democratic",1837,1841
"William Henry Harrison, Whig",1841,1841
"John Tyler, Whig",1841,1841
John Tyler,1841,1845
```

These are US presidents up to 1845; the first string is the name of the president and their affiliation, but when the president has no affiliation then it is missed out (Washington and Tyler). The names are then followed by the start and end years of their terms of office.

Next, we want to parse the data in the vector and split the items into individual fields according to the rules given previously (fields separated by commas, but quotation marks are respected). To do this, we will represent each line as a `list` of fields, with each field being a `string`. Add an include for `<list>` near the top of the file. At the top of the file, where the `using` declarations are made, add the following:

```
using namespace std;
using vec_str = vector<string>;
using list_str = list<string>;using vec_list = vector<list_str>;
```

Now, at the bottom of the `main` function, add:

```
vec_list parsed;
for (string& line : lines)
{
    parsed.push_back(parse_line(line));
}
```

The first line creates the `vector` of `list` objects, and the `for` loop iterates through each line calling a function called `parse_line` that parses a string and returns a `list` of `string` objects. The return value of the function will be a temporary object and hence an rvalue, so this means that the version of `push_back` with move semantics will be called.

Above the usage function, add the start of the `parse_line` function:

```
list_str parse_line(const string& line)
{
    list_str data;
    string::const_iterator it = line.begin();

    return data;
}
```

The function will treat the string as a container of characters and hence it will iterate through the line parameter with a `const_iterator`. The parsing will be carried out in a do loop, so add the following:

```
list_str data;
string::const_iterator it = line.begin();
string item;
bool bQuote = false;
bool bDQuote = false;
do{
    ++it;
} while (it != line.end());
data.push_back(move(item));
return data;
```

The Boolean variables will be explained in a moment. The do loop increments the iterator, and when it reaches the end value, the loop finishes. The `item` variable will hold the parsed data (at this point it is empty) and the last line will put the value into the `list`; this is so that any unsaved data is stored in the `list` before the function finishes. Since the item variable is about to be destroyed, the call to `move` ensures that its contents are moved into the `list` rather than copied. Without this call, the string copy constructor will be called when putting the item into the `list`.

Next, you need to do the parsing of the data. To do this, add a switch to test for the three cases: a comma (to indicate the end of a field), and a quote or a double quote to indicate a quoted string. The idea is to read each field and build its value up character by character, using the item variable.

```
do
{
    switch (*it)    {
        case ''':
        break;
        case '"':
        break;
        case ',':
        break;
        default:
        item.push_back(*it);
    };
    ++it;
} while (it != line.end());
```

The default action is simple: it copies the character into the temporary string. If the character is a single quote, we have two options. Either the quote is within a string that is double-quoted, in which case we want the quote to be stored in item, or the quote is a delimiter, in which case we store whether it is the opening or closing quote by setting the bQuote value. For the case of a single quote, add the following:

```
case ''':
if (bDQuote) item.push_back(*it);
else    {
    bQuote = !bQuote;
    if (bQuote) item.clear();
}
break;
```

This is simple enough. If this is in a double-quoted string (bDQuote is set), then we store the quote. If not, then we flip the bQuote bool so that if this is the first quote, we register that the string is quoted, otherwise we register that it is the end of a string. If we are at the start of a quoted string, we clear the item variable to ignore any spaces between the previous comma (if there is one) and the quote. However, this code does not take into account the use of two quote marks next to each other, which means that the quote is a literal and part of the string. Change the code to add a check for this situation:

```
if (bDQuote) item.push_back(*it);
else
{
    if ((it + 1) != line.end() && *(it + 1) == ''')    {
```

```
            item.push_back(*it);
            ++it;
    }
    else
    {
        bQuote = !bQuote;
        if (bQuote) item.clear();
    }
}
```

The `if` statement checks to make sure that if we increment the iterator, we are not at the end of the line (short-circuiting will kick in here in this case and the rest of the expression will not be evaluated). We can test the next item, and we then peek at the next item to see if it is a single quote; if it is, then we add it to the `item` variable and increment the iterator so that both quotes are consumed in the loop.

The code for the double quote is similar, but switches over the Boolean variables and tests for double quotes:

```
case '"':
if (bQuote) item.push_back(*it);
else    {
    if ((it + 1) != line.end() && *(it + 1) == '"') {
        item.push_back(*it);
        ++it;
    }
    else {
        bDQuote = !bDQuote;
        if (bDQuote) item.clear();
    }
}
break;
```

Finally, we need code to test for a comma. Again, we have two situations: either this is a comma in a quoted string, in which case we need to store the character, or it's the end of a field, in which case we need to finish the parsing for this field. The code is quite simple:

```
case ',':
if (bQuote || bDQuote)    item.push_back(*it);
else                      data.push_back(move(item));
break;
```

The `if` statement tests to see if we are in a quoted string (in which case either `bQuote` or `bDQuote` will be true), and if so, the character is stored. If this is the end of the field, we push the `string` into the `list`, but we use `move` so that the variable data is moved across and the `string` object left in an uninitialized state.

This code will compile and run. However, there is still no output, so before we redress that, review the code that you have written. At the end of the `main` function you will have a `vector` in which each item has a `list` object representing each row in the CSV file, and each item in the `list` is a field. You have now parsed the file and can use this data accordingly. So that you can see that the data has been parsed, add the following lines to the bottom of the `main` function:

```
int count = 0;
for (list_str row : parsed)
{
    cout << ++count << "> ";
    for (string field : row)
    {
        cout << field << " ";
    }
    cout << endl;
}
```

You can now compile the code (use the `/EHsc` switch) and run the application passing the name of a CSV file.

# Summary

In this chapter, you have seen some of the main classes in the C++ Standard Library, and investigated in depth the container and iterator classes. One such container is the `string` class; this is such an important class that will be covered in more depth in the next chapter.

# 6
# Using Strings

At some point your application will need to communicate with people, and that means using text; such as outputting text, taking in data as text, and then converting that data to appropriate types. The C++ Standard Library has a rich collection of classes to manipulate strings, convert between strings and numbers, and to obtain string values localized for specified languages and cultures.

## Using the string class as a container

C++ strings are based on the `basic_string` template class. This class is a container, so it uses iterator access and methods to obtain information, and has template parameters that contain information about the character type it holds. There are different `typedef` for specific character types:

```
typedef basic_string<char,
    char_traits<char>, allocator<char> > string;
typedef basic_string<wchar_t,
    char_traits<wchar_t>, allocator<wchar_t> > wstring;
typedef basic_string<char16_t,
    char_traits<char16_t>, allocator<char16_t> > u16string;
typedef basic_string<char32_t,
    char_traits<char32_t>, allocator<char32_t> > u32string;
```

The `string` class is based on `char`, `wstring` is based on `wchar_t` wide characters, and the `16string` and `u32string` classes are based upon 16-bit and 32-bit characters, respectively. For the rest of the chapter, we will concentrate on just the `string` class, but it equally applies to the other classes.

Comparing, copying, and accessing characters in a string will require a different code for the different-sized characters, while the traits template parameter provides the implementations. For string, this is the char_traits class. When this class, for example, copies characters, it will delegate this action to the char_traits class and its copy method. The traits classes are also used by stream classes, so they also define an end of file value that is appropriate to the file stream.

A string is essentially an array of zero or more characters that allocates memory when it is needed and deallocates it when a string object is destroyed. In some respects, it is very similar to a vector<char> object. As a container, the string class gives iterator access through the begin and end methods:

```
string s = "hellon";
copy(s.begin(), s.end(), ostream_iterator<char>(cout));
```

Here, the begin and end methods are called to get iterators from the items in the string, which are passed to the copy function from <algorithm> to copy each character to the console via the ostream_iterator temporary object. In this respect, the string object is similar to a vector, so we use the previously defined s object:

```
vector<char> v(s.begin(), s.end());
copy(v.begin(), v.end(), ostream_iterator<char>(cout));
```

This fills the vector object using the range of characters provided using the begin and end methods on the string object and then prints those characters to the console using the copy function in exactly the same way as we used previously.

# Getting information about a string

The max_size method will give the maximum size of the string of the specified character type on your computer architecture and this can be surprisingly large. For example, on a 64-bit Windows computer with 2 GB of memory, max_size for a string object will return 4 billion characters, and for a wstring object the method will return 2 billion characters. This is clearly more than the memory in the machine! The other size methods return more meaningful values. The length method returns the same value as the size method, that is, how many items (characters) there are in the string. The capacity method indicates how much memory is already allocated for the string in terms of the number of characters.

You can compare a `string` with another by calling its `compare` method. This returns an `int` and not a `bool` (but note that an `int` can be converted silently to a `bool`), where a return value of 0 means that the two strings are the same. If they are not the same, this method returns a negative value if the parameter string is greater that the operand string, or a positive value if the parameter is less than the operand string. In this respect *greater* and *less than* will test the ordering of the strings alphabetically. In addition, there are global operators defined for <, <=, ==, >=, and > to compare string objects.

A `string` object can be used like a C string through the `c_str` method. The pointer returned is `const`; you should be aware that the pointer may be invalidated if the `string` object is changed, so you should not store this pointer. You should not use `&str[0]` to get a C string pointer for the C++ string `str` because the internal buffer used by the string classes is not guaranteed to be `NUL` terminated. The `c_str` method is provided to return a pointer that *can* be used as a C string, and hence `NUL` terminated.

If you want to copy data from the C++ string to a C buffer you can call the `copy` method. You pass the destination pointer and the number of characters to copy as parameters (and optionally an offset) and the method will attempt to copy, at most, the specified number of characters to the destination buffer: *but without a null termination character*. This method assumes that the destination buffer is big enough to hold the copied characters (and you should take steps to ensure this). If you want to pass the size of the buffer so that the method performs this check for you, call the `_Copy_s` method instead.

# Altering strings

The string classes have standard container access methods, so you can access individual characters through a reference (read and write access) with the `at` method and `[]` operator. You can replace the entire string using the `assign` method, or swap the contents of two string objects with the `swap` method. Further, you can insert characters in specified places with the `insert` method, remove specified characters with the `erase` method, and remove all characters with the `clear` method. The class also allows you to push characters to the end of the string (and remove the last character) with the `push_back` and `pop_back` methods:

```
string str = "hello";
cout << str << "n"; // hello
str.push_back('!');
cout << str << "n"; // hello!
str.erase(0, 1);
cout << str << "n"; // ello!
```

You can add one or more characters to the end of a string using the `append` method or the `+=` operator:

```
string str = "hello";
cout << str << "n";   // hello
str.append(4, '!');
cout << str << "n";   // hello!!!!
str += " there";
cout << str << "n";   // hello!!!! there
```

The `<string>` library also defines a global + operator that will concatenate two strings in a third string.

If you want to change characters in a string you can access the character through an index with the `[]` operator, using the reference to overwrite the character. You can also use the `replace` method to replace one or more characters at a specified position with characters from a C string or from a C++ string, or some other container accessed through iterators:

```
string str = "hello";
cout << str << "n";     // hello
str.replace(1, 1, "a");
cout << str << "n";     // hallo
```

Finally, you can extract part of a string as a new string. The `substr` method takes an offset and an optional count. If the count of characters is omitted, then the substring will be from the specified position until the end of the string. This means that you can copy a left-hand part of a string by passing an offset of 0 and a count that is less than the size of the string, or you can copy a right-hand part of the string by passing just the index of the first character.

```
string str = "one two three";
string str1 = str.substr(0, 3);
cout << str1 << "n";          // one
string str2 = str.substr(8);
cout << str2 << "n";          // three
```

In this code, the first example copies the first three characters into a new string. In the second example, the copying starts at the eighth character and continues to the end.

# Searching strings

The find method is passed using either a character, a C string, or a C++ string, and you can provide an initial search position to start the search. The find method returns the position (rather than an iterator) to where the search text was located, or a value of npos if the text cannot be found. The offset parameter, and a successful return value from the find method, enables you to parse a string repeatedly to find specific items. The find method searches for the specified text in the forward direction, and there is also an rfind method that performs the search in the reverse direction.

Note that rfind is not the complete opposite of the find method. The find method moves the search point forward in the string and at each point compares the search string with the characters from the search point forwards (so the first search text character, then the second, and so on). The rfind method moves the search point *backwards,* but the comparisons are still made *forwards.* So, assuming the rfind method is not given an offset, the first comparison will be made at an offset from the end of the string the size of the search text. Then, the comparison is made by comparing the first character in the search text with the character at the search point in the searched string, and if this succeeds, the second character in the search text is compared with the character after the search point. So, the comparisons are made in a direction opposite to the direction of the movement of the search point.

This becomes important because if you want to parse a string using the return value from the find method as an offset, after each search you should move the search offset *forwards,* and for rfind you should move it *backwards.*

For example, to search for all the positions of the in the following string, you can call:

```
string str = "012the678the234the890";
string::size_type pos = 0;
while(true)
{
    pos++;
    pos = str.find("the",pos);
    if (pos == string::npos) break;
    cout << pos << " " << str.substr(pos) << "n";
}
// 3 the678the234the890
// 9 the234the890
// 15 the890
```

This will find the search text at the character positions of 3, 9, and 15. To search the string backwards, you could call:

```
string str = "012the678the234the890";
string::size_type pos = string::npos;
while(true)
{
    pos--;
    pos = str.rfind("the",pos);
    if (pos == string::npos) break;
    cout << pos << " " << str.substr(pos) << "n";
}
// 15 the890
// 9 the234the890
// 3 the678the234the890
```

The highlighted code shows the changes that should be made, showing you that you need to search from the end and use the `rfind` method. When you have a successful result you need to decrement the position before the next search. Like the `find` method, the `rfind` method returns `npos` if it cannot find the search text.

There are four methods that allow you to search for one of several individual characters. For example:

```
string str = "012the678the234the890";
string::size_type pos = str.find_first_of("eh");
if (pos != string::npos)
{
    cout << "found " << str[pos] << " at position ";
    cout << pos << " " << str.substr(pos) << "n";
}
// found h at position 4 he678the234the890
```

The search string is eh and the `find_first_of` will return when it finds either the character e or h in the string. In this example, the character h is found first at position 4. You can provide an offset parameter to start the search, so you can use the return value from `find_first_of` to parse through a string. The `find_last_of` method is similar, but it searches the string in the reverse direction for one of the characters in the search text.

There are also two search methods that will look for a character *other than* the characters provided in the search text: `find_first_not_of` and `find_last_not_of`. For example:

```
string str = "012the678the234the890";
string::size_type pos = str.find_first_not_of("0123456789");
cout << "found " << str[pos] << " at position ";
cout << pos << " " << str.substr(pos) << "n";
// found t at position 3 the678the234the890
```

This code looks for a character other than a digit and so it finds the t at position 3 (the fourth character).

There is no library function to trim whitespace from a `string`, but you can trim spaces on the left and right of strings by using the find functions to find non-whitespace and then use this as an appropriate index for the `substr` method.

```
string str = "  hello  ";
cout << "|" << str << "|n"; // |  hello  |
string str1 = str.substr(str.find_first_not_of(" trn"));
cout << "|" << str1 << "|n"; // |hello  |
string str2 = str.substr(0, str.find_last_not_of(" trn") + 1);
cout << "|" << str2 << "|n"; // |  hello|
```

In the preceding code, two new strings are created: one left-trims spaces, and the other right-trims spaces. The first forward searches for the first character that is not whitespace and uses this as the start index of the substring (no count is provided because all of the remaining string is copied). In the second case the string is reverse searched for a character that is not whitespace, but the location returned will be the last character of `hello`; since we need the substring from the first character, we increment this index to get the count of characters to copy.

# Internationalization

The `<locale>` header contains the classes for localizing how time, dates, and currency are formatted, and also to provide localized rules for string comparisons and ordering.

The C Runtime Library also has global functions to carry out localization. However, it is important in the following discussion that we distinguish between C functions and the C locale. The C locale is the default locale, including the rules for localization, used in C and C++ programs and it can be replaced with a locale for a country or culture. The C Runtime Library provides functions to change the locale, as does the C++ Standard Library.

Since the C++ Standard Library provides classes for localization, this means that you can create more than one object representing a locale. A locale object can be created in a function and can only be used there, or it can be applied globally to a thread and used only by code running on that thread. This is in contrast to the C localization functions, where changing the locale is global, so all code (and all threads of execution) will be affected.

Instances of the `locale` class are either created through the class constructor or through static members of the class. The C++ stream classes will use a locale (as explained later), and if you want to change the locale you call the `imbue` method on the stream object. In some cases, you will want to access one of these rules directly, and you have access to them through the locale object.

# Using facets

Internationalization rules are known as **facets**. A locale object is a container of facets, and you can test if the locale has a specific facet using the `has_facet` function; if it does, you can get a `const` reference to the facet by calling the `use_facet` function. There are six types of facets summarized by seven categories of class in the following table. A facet class is a subclass of the `locale::facet` nested class.

| Facet type | Description |
| --- | --- |
| `codecvt, ctype` | Converts between one encoding scheme to another and is used to classify characters and convert them to upper or lowercase |
| `collate` | Controls the ordering and grouping of characters in a string, including comparing and hashing of strings |
| `messages` | Retrieves localized messages from a catalog |
| `money` | Converts numbers representing currency to and from strings |
| `num` | Converts numbers to and from strings |
| `time` | Converts times and dates in numeric form to and from strings |

The facet classes are used to convert the data to strings and so they all have a template parameter for the character type used. The `money`, `num`, and `time` facets are represented by three classes each. A class with the `_get` suffix that handles parsing strings, while a class with the `_put` suffix handles formatting as strings. For the `money` and `num` facets there is a class with the `punct` suffix that contains the rules and symbols for punctuation.

Since the _get facets are used to convert sequences of characters into numeric types, the classes have a template parameter that you can use to indicate the input iterator type that the get methods will use to represent a range of characters. Similarly, the _put facet classes have a template parameter that you can use to provide the output iterator type the put methods will write the converted string to. There are default types provided for both iterators types.

The messages facet is used for compatibility with POSIX code. The class is intended to allow you to provide localized strings for your application. The idea is that the strings in your user interface are indexed and at runtime you access the localized string using the index through the messages facet. However, Windows applications typically use message resource files compiled using the **Message Compiler**. It is perhaps for this reason that the messages facet provided as part of the Standard Library does not do anything, but the infrastructure is there, and you can derive your own messages facet class.

The has_facet and use_facet functions are templated for the specific type of facet that you want. All facet classes are subclasses of the locale::facet class, but through this template parameter the compiler will instantiate a function that returns the specific type you request. So, for example, if you want to format time and date strings for the French locale, you can call this code:

```
locale loc("french");
const time_put<char>& fac = use_facet<time_put<char>>(loc);
```

Here, the french string identifies the locale, and this is the language string used by the C Runtime Library setlocale function. The second line obtains the facet for converting numeric times into strings, and hence the function template parameter is time_put<char>. This class has a method called put that you can call to perform the conversion:

```
time_t t = time(nullptr);
tm *td = gmtime(&t);
ostreambuf_iterator<char> it(cout);
fac.put(it, cout, ' ', td, 'x', '#');
cout << "n";
```

The time function (via <ctime>) returns an integer with the current time and date, and this is converted to a tm structure using the gmtime function. The tm structure contains individual members for the year, month, day, hours, minutes, and seconds. The gmtime function returns the address to a structure that is statically allocated in the function, so you do not have to delete the memory it occupies.

The facet will format the data in the `tm` structure as a string through the output iterator passed as the first parameter. In this case, the output stream iterator is constructed from the `cout` object and so the facet will write the format stream to the console (the second parameter is not used, but because it is a reference you have to pass something, so the `cout` object is used there too). The third parameter is the separator character (again, this is not used). The fifth and (optional) sixth parameters indicate the formatting that you require. These are the same formatting characters as used in the C Runtime Library function `strftime`, as two single characters rather than the format string used by the C function. In this example, x is used to get the date and # is used as a modifier to get the long version of the string.

The  code will give the following output:

```
samedi 28 janvier 2017
```

Notice that the words are not capitalized and there is no punctuation, also notice the order: weekday name, day number, month, then year.

If the `locale` object constructor parameter is changed to `german` then the output will be:

```
Samstag, 28. January 2017
```

The items are in the same order as in French, but the words are capitalized and punctuation is used. If you use `turkish` then the result is:

```
28 Ocak 2017 Cumartesi
```

In this case, the day of the week is at the end of the string.

Two countries divided by a common language will give two different strings, and the following are the results for `american` and `english-uk`:

```
Saturday, January 28, 2017
28 January 2017
```

Time is used as the example here because there is no stream, an insertion operator is used for the `tm` structure, and it is an unusual case. For other types, there are insertion operators that put them into a stream, and so the stream can use a locale to internationalize how it shows the type. For example, you can insert a `double` into the `cout` object and the value will be printed to the console. The default locale, American English, uses the period to separate whole numbers from the fractional part, but in other cultures a comma is used.

The `imbue` function will change the localization until the method is called subsequently:

```
cout.imbue(locale("american"));
cout << 1.1 << "n";
cout.imbue(locale("french"));
cout << 1.1 << "n";
cout.imbue(locale::classic());
```

Here, the stream object is localized to US English and then the floating-point number `1.1` is printed on the console. Next, the localization is changed to French, and this time the console will show `1,1`. In French, the decimal point is the comma. The last line resets the stream object by passing the locale returned from the `static classic` method. This returns the so-called **C locale**, which is the default in C and C++ and is American English.

The `static` method `global` can be used to set the locale that will be used as the default by each stream object. When an object is created from a stream class it calls the `locale::global` method to get the default locale. The stream clones this object so that it has its own copy independent of any local subsequently set by calling the `global` method. Note that the `cin` and `cout` stream objects are created before the `main` function is called, and these objects will use the default C locale until you imbue another locale. However, it is important to point out that, once a stream has been created, the `global` method has no effect on the stream, and `imbue` is the only way to change the locale used by the stream.

The `global` method will also call the C `setlocale` function to change the locale used by the C Runtime Library functions. This is important because some of the C++ functions (for example `to_string`, `stod`, as explained in the following text) will use the C Runtime Library functions to convert values. However, the C Runtime Library knows nothing about the C++ Standard Library, so calling the C `setlocale` function to change the default locale will not affect subsequently created stream objects.

It is worth pointing out that the `basic_string` class compares strings using the character traits class indicated by a template parameter. The `string` class uses the `char_traits` class and its version of the `compare` method does a straight comparison of the corresponding characters in the two strings. This comparison does not take into account cultural rules for comparing characters. If you want to do a comparison that uses cultural rules, you can do this through the `collate` facet:

```
int compare(
    const string& lhs, const string& rhs, const locale& loc)
{
    const collate<char>& fac = use_facet<collate<char>>(loc);
    return fac.compare(
        &lhs[0], &lhs[0] + lhs.size(), &rhs[0], &rhs[0] + rhs.size());
}
```

# Strings and numbers

The Standard Library contains various functions and classes to convert between C++ strings and numeric values.

## Converting strings to numbers

The C++ standard library contains functions with names like `stod` and `stoi` that convert a C++ `string` object to a numeric value (`stod` converts to a `double` and `stoi` converts to an `integer`). For example:

```
double d = stod("10.5");
d *= 4;
cout << d << "n"; // 42
```

This will initialize the floating-point variable `d` with a value of `10.5`, which is then used in a calculation and the result is printed on the console. The input string may have characters that cannot be converted. If this is the case then the parsing of the string ends at that point. You can provide a pointer to a `size_t` variable, which will be initialized to the location of the first character that cannot be converted:

```
string str = "49.5 red balloons";
size_t idx = 0;
double d = stod(str, &idx);
d *= 2;
string rest = str.substr(idx);
cout << d << rest << "n"; // 99 red balloons
```

In the preceding code, the `idx` variable will be initialized with a value of `4`, indicating that the space between the `5` and `r` is the first character that cannot be converted to a `double`.

## Converting numbers to strings

The `<string>` library provides various overloads of the `to_string` function to convert integer types and floating point types into a `string` object. This function does not allow you to provide any formatting details, so for an integer you cannot indicate the radix of the string representation (for example, hex), and for floating point conversions, you have no control over options like the number of significant figures. The `to_string` function is a simple function with limited facilities. A better option is to use the stream classes, as explained in the following section.

# Using stream classes

You can print floating point numbers and integers to the console using the `cout` object (an instance of the `ostream` class) or to files with an instance of `ofstream`. Both of these classes will convert numbers to strings using member methods and manipulators to affect the formatting of the output string. Similarly, the `cin` object (an instance of the `istream` class) and the `ifstream` class can read data from formatted streams.

Manipulators are functions that take a reference to a stream object and return that reference. The Standard Library has various global insertion operators whose parameters are a reference to a stream object and a function pointer. The appropriate insertion operator will call the function pointer with the stream object as its parameter. This means that the manipulator will have access to, and can manipulate, the stream it is inserted into. For input streams, there are also extraction operators that have a function parameter which will call the function with the stream object.

The architecture of C++ streams means that there is a buffer between the stream interface that you call in your code and the low-level infrastructure that obtains the data. The C++ Standard Library provides stream classes that have string objects as the buffer. For an output stream, you access the string after items have been inserted in the stream, which means that the string will contain those items formatted according to those insertion operators. Similarly, you can provide a string with formatted data as the buffer for an input stream, and when you use extraction operators to extract the data from the stream you are actually parsing the string and converting parts of the string to numbers.

In addition, stream classes have a `locale` object and stream objects will call the conversion facet of this locale to convert character sequences from one encoding to another.

# Outputting floating point numbers

The `<ios>` library has manipulators that alter how streams handle numbers. By default, the output stream will print floating-point numbers in a decimal format for numbers in the range `0.001` to `100000,` and for numbers outside this range it will use a scientific format with a mantissa and exponent. This mixed format is the default behavior of the `defaultfloat` manipulator. If you always want to use scientific notation, then you should insert the `scientific` manipulator into the output stream.

If you want to display floating point numbers using just the decimal format (that is the whole number on the left side of a decimal point and the factional part on the right side), then modify the output stream with the `fixed` manipulator. The number of decimal places can be altered by calling the `precision` method:

```
double d = 123456789.987654321;
cout << d << "n";
cout << fixed;
cout << d << "n";
cout.precision(9);
cout << d << "n";
cout << scientific;
cout << d << "n";
```

The output from the preceding code is:

```
1.23457e+08
123456789.987654
123456789.987654328
1.234567900e+08
```

The first line shows that scientific notation is used for large numbers. The second line shows the default behavior of `fixed`, which is to give the decimal number to 6 decimal places. This is changed in the code by calling the `precision` method to give 9 decimal places (the same effect can be achieved by inserting the `setprecision` manipulator in the `<iomanip>` library in the stream). Finally, the format is switched over to the scientific format with 9 decimal places to the mantissa from calling the `precision` method. The default is that the exponent is identified by the lowercase e. If you prefer, you can make this uppercase using the `uppercase` manipulator (and lowercase with `nouppercase`). Notice that the way that fractional parts are stored means that in fixed formats with 9 decimal places we see that the ninth digit is 8 rather than 1 as expected.

You can also specify whether a + symbol is shown for a positive number; the `showpos` manipulator will show the symbol, but the default `noshowpos` manipulator will not show the symbol. The `showpoint` manipulator will ensure that the decimal point is shown even if the floating-point number is a whole number. The default is `noshowpoint`, which means that, if there is no fractional part, no decimal point is displayed.

The `setw` manipulator (defined in the `<iomanip>` header) can be used with both integer and floating point numbers. In effect, this manipulator defines the minimum width of the space that the next (and only the next) item placed in the stream will occupy when printed on the console:

```
double d = 12.345678;
cout << fixed;
cout << setfill('#');
cout << setw(15) << d << "n";
```

To illustrate the effect of the `setw` manipulator, this code calls `setfill` manipulator, which indicates that instead of spaces a hash symbol (#) should be printed. The rest of the code says that the number should be printed using the fixed format (to 6 decimal places by default) in a space 15 characters wide. The result is:

**######12.345678**

If the number is negative (or `showpos` is used), then by default the sign will be with the number; if the `internal` manipulator (defined in `<ios>`) is used, then the sign will be left-justified in the space set for the number:

```
double d = 12.345678;
cout << fixed;
cout << showpos << internal;
cout << setfill('#');
cout << setw(15) << d << "n";
```

The result of the preceding code is as follows:

**+#####12.345678**

Notice that the + sign to the right of the spaces is indicated by the pound symbol.

The `setw` manipulator is typically used to allow you to output tables of data in formatted columns:

```
vector<pair<string, double>> table
{ { "one",0 },{ "two",0 },{ "three",0 },{ "four",0 } };

double d = 0.1;
for (pair<string,double>& p : table)
{
    p.second = d / 17.0;
    d += 0.1;
}

cout << fixed << setprecision(6);
```

```
for (pair<string, double> p : table)
{
    cout << setw(6)  << p.first << setw(10) << p.second << "n";
}
```

This fills a `vector` of pairs with a string and a number. The `vector` is initialized with the string values and a zero, then the floating-point number is altered in the `for` loop (the actual calculation is irrelevant here; the point is to create some numbers with multiple decimal places). The data is printed out in two columns with the numbers printed with 6 decimal places. This means that, including the leading zero and decimal point, each number will take up 8 spaces. The text column is specified as being 6 characters wide and the number column is specified as 10 characters wide. By default, when you specify a column width, the output will be right justified, meaning that each number is preceded by two spaces and the text is padded according to the length of the string. The output looks like this:

```
one    0.005882
two    0.011765
three   0.017647
four   0.023529
```

If you want the items in a column to be left justified, then you can use the `left` manipulator. This will affect all columns until the `right` manipulator is used to change the justification to right:

```
cout << fixed << setprecision(6) << left;
```

The output from this will be:

```
one    0.005882
two    0.011765
three 0.017647
four   0.023529
```

If you want different justification for the two columns, then you need to set the justification before printing a value. For example, to left justify the text and right justify the numbers, use this:

```
for (pair<string, double> p : table)
{
    cout << setw(6) << left << p.first
         << setw(10) << right << p.second << "n";
}
```

The result of the preceding code is as follows:

```
one     0.005882
two     0.011765
three   0.017647
four    0.023529
```

# Outputting integers

Integers can also be printed in columns using the `setw` and `setfill` methods. You can insert manipulators to print integers in base 8 (`oct`), base 10 (`dec`), and base 16 (`hex`). (You can also use the `setbase` manipulator and pass the base you want to use, but the only values allowed are 8, 10, and 16.) The number can be printed with the base indicated (prefixed with `0` for octal or `0x` for hex) or without using the `showbase` and `noshowbase` manipulators. If you use `hex`, then the digits above `9` are the letters `a` to `f`, and by default these are lowercase. If you prefer these to be uppercase, then you can use the `uppercase` manipulator (and lowercase with `nouppercase`).

# Outputting time and money

The `put_time` function in `<iomanip>` is passed a `tm` structure initialized with a time and date and a format string. The function returns an instance of the `_Timeobj` class. As the name suggests, you are not really expected to create variables of this class; instead, the function should be used to insert a time/date with a specific format into a stream. There is an insertion operator that will print a `_Timeobj` object. The function is used like this:

```
time_t t = time(nullptr);
tm *pt = localtime(&t);
cout << put_time(pt, "time = %X date = %x") << "n";
```

The output from this is:

```
time = 20:08:04 date = 01/02/17
```

The function will use the locale in the stream, so if you imbue a locale into the stream and then call `put_time`, the time/date will be formatted using the format string and the time/date localization rules for the locale. The format string uses format tokens for `strftime`:

```
time_t t = time(nullptr);
tm *pt = localtime(&t);
cout << put_time(pt, "month = %B day = %A") << "n";
cout.imbue(locale("french"));
cout << put_time(pt, "month = %B day = %A") << "n";
```

The output of the preceding code is:

```
month = March day = Thursday
month = mars day = jeudi
```

Similarly, the `put_money` function returns a `_Monobj` object. Again, this is simply a container for the parameters that you pass to this function and you are not expected to use instances of this class. Instead, you are expected to insert this function into an output stream. The actual work occurs in the insertion operator that obtains the money facet on the current locale, which uses this to format the number to the appropriate number of decimal places and determine the decimal point character; if a thousands separator is used, what character to use, before it is inserted it in the appropriate place.

```
Cout << showbase;
cout.imbue(locale("German"));
cout << "German" << "n";
cout << put_money(109900, false) << "n";
cout << put_money("1099", true) << "n";
cout.imbue(locale("American"));
cout << "American" << "n";
cout << put_money(109900, false) << "n";
cout << put_money("1099", true) << "n";
```

The output of the preceding code is:

```
German
1.099,00 euros
EUR10,99
American
$1,099.00
USD10.99
```

You provide the number in either a `double` or a string as Euro cents or cents and the `put_money` function formats the number in Euros or dollars using the appropriate decimal point (, for German, . for American) and the appropriate thousands separator (. for German, , for American). Inserting the `showbase` manipulator into the output stream means that the `put_money` function will show the currency symbol, otherwise just the formatted number will be shown. The second parameter to the `put_money` function specifies whether the currency character (`false`) or the international symbol (`true`) is used.

# Converting numbers to strings using streams

Stream buffer classes are responsible for obtaining characters and writing characters from the appropriate source (file, console, and so on) and are derived from the abstract class `basic_streambuf` from `<streambuf>`. This base class defines two virtual methods, `overflow` and `underflow`, which are overridden by the derived classes to write and read characters (respectively) to and from the device associated with the derived class. The stream buffer class does the basic action of getting or putting items into a stream, and since the buffer handles characters, the class is templated with parameters for the character type and character traits.

As the name suggests, if you use a `basic_stringbuf` the stream buffer will be a string, so the source for read characters and the destination for written characters is that string. If you use this class to provide the buffer for a stream object, it means that you can use the insertion or extraction operators written for streams to write or read formatted data into or out of a string. The `basic_stringbuf` buffer is extendable, so as you insert items in the stream, the buffer will extend appropriately. There are `typedef`, where the buffer is a `string` (`stringbuf`) or a `wstring` (`wstringbuf`).

For example, imagine you have a class that you have defined and you have also defined an insertion operator so that you can use this with the `cout` object to print the value to the console:

```
struct point
{
    double x = 0.0, y = 0.0;
    point(){}
    point(double _x, double _y) : x(_x), y(_y) {}
};
```

```
ostream& operator<<(ostream& out, const point& p)
{
    out << "(" << p.x << "," << p.y << ")";
    return out;
}
```

Using this with the `cout` object is simple--consider the following piece of code:

```
point p(10.0, -5.0);
cout << p << "n";          // (10,-5)
```

You can use the `stringbuf` to direct the formatted output to a string rather than the console:

```
stringbuf buffer;
ostream out(&buffer);
out << p;
string str = buffer.str(); // contains (10,-5)
```

Since the stream object handles the formatting it means that you can insert any data type for which there is an insertion operator, and you can use any of the `ostream` formatting methods and any of the manipulators. The formatted output from all of these methods and manipulators will be inserted into the string object in the buffer.

Another option is to use the `basic_ostringstream` class in `<sstream>`. This class is templated on the character type of the strings used as the buffer (so the `string` version is `ostringstream`). It is derived from the `ostream` class, so you can use instances wherever you would use an `ostream` object. The formatted results can be accessed through the `str` method:

```
ostringstream os;
os << hex;
os << 42;
cout << "The value is: " << os.str() << "n";
```

This code obtains the value of 42 in hexadecimal (2a); this is achieved by inserting the `hex` manipulator in the stream and then inserting the integer. The formatted string is obtained by calling the `str` method.

# Reading numbers from strings using streams

The `cin` object, an instance of the `istream` class (in the `<istream>` library), can input characters from the console and convert them to the numeric form you specify. The `ifstream` class (in the `<ifstream>` library) will also allow you to input characters from a file and convert them to numeric form. As with outputting streams, you can use the stream classes with a string buffer so that you can convert from a string object to a numeric value.

The `basic_istringstream` class (in the `<sstream>` library) is derived from the `basic_istream` class, so you can create stream objects and extract items (numbers and strings) from these objects. The class provides this stream interface on a string object (the `typedefs` keyword `istringstream` is based on a `string` and `wistringstream` is based on a `wstring`). When you construct objects of this class you initialize the object with a `string` containing a number and then you use the `>>` operator to extract objects for the fundamental built-in types, just as you would extract those items from the console using `cin`.

It is important to reiterate that the extraction operators treat whitespaces as the separators between items in a stream, and hence they will ignore all leading whitespaces, read the non-whitespaces characters up to the next whitespaces and attempt to convert this substring into the appropriate type as follows:

```
istringstream ss("-1.0e-6");
double d;
ss >> d;
```

This will initialize the `d` variable with the value of $-1e-6$. As with `cin`, you have to know the format of the item in the stream; so if, instead of extracting a `double` from the string in the preceding example, you try to extract an integer, the object will stop extracting characters when it comes to the decimal point. If some of the string is not converted, you can extract the rest into a string object:

```
istringstream ss("-1.0e-6");
int i;
ss >> i;
string str;
ss >> str;
cout << "extracted " << i << " remainder " << str << "n";
```

This will print the following at the console:

```
extracted -1 remainder .0e-6
```

If you have more than one number in the string you can extract these with several calls to the >> operator. The stream also supports some manipulators. For example, if the number in the string is in hex format you can inform the stream that this is the case using the hex manipulator as follows:

```
istringstream ss("0xff");
int i;
ss >> hex;
ss >> i;
```

This says that the number in the string is in hexadecimal format and the variable i will be initialized with a value of 255. If the string contains non-numeric values, then the stream object will still try to convert the string to the appropriate format. In the following snippet you can test if such an extraction fails by calling the fail function:

```
istringstream ss("Paul was born in 1942");
int year;
ss >> year;
if (ss.fail()) cout << "failed to read number" << "n";
```

If you know that the string contains text, you can extract it into string objects, but bear in mind that whitespace characters are treated as delimiters:

```
istringstream ss("Paul was born in 1942");
string str;
ss >> str >> str >> str >> str;
int year;
ss >> year;
```

Here, there are four words before the number, so the code reads a string four times. If you don't know where in the string the number is but you know there is a number in the string, you can move the internal buffer pointer until it points to a digit:

```
istringstream ss("Paul was born in 1942");
string str;
while (ss.eof() && !(isdigit(ss.peek()))) ss.get();
int year;
ss >> year;
if (!ss.fail()) cout << "the year was " << year << "n";
```

The peek method returns the character at the current position, but does not move the buffer pointer. This code checks to see if this character is a digit, and if not, the internal buffer pointer is moved by calling the get method. (This code tests the eof method to ensure that there is no attempt to read a character after the end of the buffer.) If you know where the number starts then you can call the seekg method to move the internal buffer pointer to a specified position.

The `<istream>` library has a manipulator called `ws` that removes whitespace from a stream. Recall earlier that we said that there is no function to remove whitespace from a string. This is true because the `ws` manipulator removes whitespace from a *stream* and not from a *string*, but since you can use a string as the buffer for a stream it means that you can use this function to remove white space from a string indirectly:

```
string str = "  hello  ";
cout << "|" << str1 << "|n"; // |  hello  |
istringstream ss(str);
ss >> ws;
string str1;
ss >> str1;
ut << "|" << str1 << "|n";   // |hello|
```

The `ws` function essentially iterates through the items in the input stream and returns when a character is not whitespace. If the stream is a file or the console stream then the `ws` function will read in the characters from those streams; in this case, the buffer is provided by an already-allocated string and so it skips over the whitespaces at the beginning of the string. Note that stream classes treat subsequent whitespaces as being separators between values in the stream, so in this example the stream will read in characters from the buffer until there is a whitespace, and will essentially *left-and right-trim* the string. However, this is not necessarily what you want. If you have a string with several words padded by whitespace, this code will only provide the first word.

The `get_money` and `get_time` manipulators in the `<iomanip>` library allow you to extract money and time from strings using the money and time facets for a locale:

```
tm indpday = {};
string str = "4/7/17";
istringstream ss(str);
ss.imbue(locale("french"));
ss >> get_time(&indpday, "%x");
if (!ss.fail())
{
    cout.imbue(locale("american"));
    cout << put_time(&indpday, "%x") << "n";
}
```

In the preceding code, the stream is first initialized with a date in the French format (day/month/year) and the date is extracted with `get_time` using the locale's standard date representation. The date is parsed into a `tm` structure, which is then printed out in standard date representation for the American locale using `put_time`. The results is:

**7/4/2017**

# Using regular expressions

Regular expressions are patterns of text that can be used by a regular expression parser to search a string for text that matches the pattern, and if required, replace the matched items with other text.

# Defining regular expressions

A **regular expression** (**regex**) is made up of characters that define a pattern. The expression contains special symbols that are meaningful to the parser, and if you want to use those symbols in the search pattern in the expression then you can escape them with a backslash (\). Your code will typically pass the expression as a `string` object to an instance of the `regex` class as a constructor parameter. This object is then passed to functions in `<regex>` that will use the expression to parse text for sequences that match the pattern.

The following table summarizes *some* of the patterns that you can match with the `regex` class.

| Pattern | Explanation | Example |
|---------|-------------|---------|
| literals | Matches the exact characters | `li` matches `flip lip plier` |
| [group] | Matches a single character in a group | `[at]` matches c**a**t, ca**t**, **t**op, pe**a**r |
| [^group] | Matches a single character not in the group | `[^at]` matches **c**at, **top**, to**p**, **p**e**ar**, pear |
| [first-last] | Matches any character in the range `first` to `last` | `[0-9]` matches digits **1**02, 1**0**2, 10**2** |
| {n} | The element is matched exactly n times | **91{2} matches 911** |
| {n,} | The element is matched n or more times | `wel{1,}` matches `well` and **welcome** |
| {n,m} | The element is matched between n and m times | `9{2,4}` matches `99, 999, 9999, 99999` but not 9 |
| . | Wildcard, any character except n | `a.e` matches `ate` and `are` |
| * | The element is matched zero or more times | `d*.d` matches `.1, 0.1, 10.1` but not 10 |
| + | The element is matched one or more times | `d*.d` matches `0.1, 10.1` but not 10 or .1 |
| ? | The element is matched zero or one time | `tr?ap` matches `trap` and `tap` |
| \| | Matches any one of the elements separated by the \| | `th(e\|is\|at)` matches `the`, `this`, `that` |
| [[:class:]] | Matches the character class | `[[:upper:]]` matches uppercase characters: **I** am **R**ichard |
| n | Matches a newline | |
| s | Matches any single whitespace | |

| d | Matches any single digit | d is [0-9] |
|---|---|---|
| w | Matches a character that can be in a word (upper case and lower case characters) | |
| b | Matches at a boundary between alphanumeric characters and non-alphanumeric characters | d{2}b matches 999 and 9999  bd{2} matches 999 and 9999 |
| $ | End of the line | s$ matches a single white space at the end of a line |
| ^ | Start of line | ^d matches if a line starts with a digit |

You can use regular expressions to define a pattern to be matched--the Visual C++ editor allows you to do this in the search dialog (which is a good test bed to develop your expressions).

It is much easier to define a pattern to match rather than a pattern *not* to match. For example, the expression w+b<w+> will match the string "vector<int>", because this has one or more word characters followed by a non-word character (<), followed by one or more word characters followed by >. This pattern will not match the string "#include <regex>" because there is a space after the include and the b indicates that there is a boundary between alphanumeric characters and non-alphanumeric characters.

The th(e|is|at) example in the table shows that you can use parentheses to group patterns when you want to provide alternatives. However, parentheses have another use-- they allow you to capture groups. So, if you want to perform a replace action, you can search for a pattern as a group and then refer to that group as a named subgroup later (for example, search for (Joe) so that you can replace Joe with Tom). You can also refer to a sub-expression specified by parentheses in the expression (called back references):

```
([A-Za-z]+) +1
```

This expression says: *search for words with one or more characters in the ranges a to z and A to Z; the word is called 1 so find where it appears twice with a space between them.*

# Standard Library classes

To perform matching or replacement you have to create a regular expression object. This is an object of the class basic_regex that has template parameters for the character type and a regular expression traits class. There are two typedefs for this class: regex for char and wregex for wide chars, which have traits described by the regex_traits and wregex_traits classes.

The traits class determines how the regex class parses the expression. For example, recall from previous text that you can use w for a word, d for a digit, and s for whitespace. The [[::]] syntax allows you to use a more descriptive name for the character class: alnum, digit, lower, and so on. And since these are text sequences that depend upon a character set, the traits class will have the appropriate code to test whether the expression uses a supported character class.

The appropriate regex class will parse the expression to enable functions in the <regex> library to use the expression to identify patterns in some text:

```
regex rx("([A-Za-z]+) +1");
```

This searches for repeated words using a back reference. Note that the regular expression uses 1 for the back reference, but in a string the backslash has to be escaped (\). If you use character classes such as s and d then you will need to do a lot of escaping. Instead, you can use raw strings (R" () "), but bear in mind that the first set of parentheses inside the quote marks is part of the syntax for raw strings and does not form a regex group:

```
regex rx(R"(([A-Za-z]+) +1)");
```

It is entirely up to you as to which is the more readable; both introduce extra characters within the double quotes, which has the potential to confuse a quick glance-over what the regular expression matches.

Bear in mind that the regular expression is essentially a program in itself, so the regex parser will determine whether that expression is valid, and if it isn't the object, the constructor, will throw an exception of type regex_error. Exception handling is explained in the next chapter, but it is important to point out that if the exception is not caught it will result in the application aborting at runtime. The exception's what method will return a basic description of the error, and the code method will return one of the constants in the error_type enumeration in the regex_constants namespace. There is no indication of where in the expression the error occurs. You should thoroughly test your expression in an external tool (for example Visual C++ search).

The constructor can be called with a string (C or C++) or a pair of iterators to a range of characters in a string (or other container), or you can pass an initialization list where each item in the list is a character. There are various flavors of the language of regex; the default for the basic_regex class is **ECMAScript**. If you want a different language (basic POSIX, extended POSIX, awk, grep, or egrep), you can pass one of the constants defined in the syntax_option_type enumeration in the regex_constants namespace (copies are also available as constants defined in the basic_regex class) as a constructor parameter.

You can only specify one language flavor, but you can combine this with some of the other syntax_option_type constants: icase specifies case insensitivity, collate uses the locale in matches, nosubs means you do not want to capture groups, and optimize optimizes matching.

The class uses the method getloc to obtain the locale used by the parser and imbue to reset the locale. If you imbue a locale, then you will not be able to use the regex object to do any matching until you reset it with the assign method. This means there are two ways to use a regex object. If you want to use the current locale then pass the regular expression to the constructor: if you want to use a different locale create an empty regex object with the default constructor, then call imbue with the locale and pass the regular expression using the assign method. Once a regular expression has been parsed you can call the mark_count method to get the number of capture groups in the expression (assuming you did not use nosubs).

# Matching expressions

Once you have constructed a regex object you can pass it to the methods in the <regex> library to search for the pattern in a string. The regex_match function is passed in a string (C or C++) or iterators to a range of characters in a container and a constructed regex object. In its simplest form, the function will return true only if there is an exact match, that is, the expression exactly matches the search string:

```
regex rx("[at]"); // search for either a or t
cout << boolalpha;
cout << regex_match("a", rx) << "\n";  // true
cout << regex_match("a", rx) << "\n";  // true
cout << regex_match("at", rx) << "\n"; // false
```

In the previous code, the search expression is for a single character in the range given (a or t), so the first two calls to regex_match return true because the searched string is one character. The last call returns false because the match is not the same as the searched string. If you remove the [] in the regular expression, then just the third call returns true because you are looking for the exact string at. If the regular expression is [at]+ so that you are looking for one or more of the characters a and t, then all three calls return true. You can alter how the match is determined by passing one or more of the constants in the match_flag_type enumeration.

If you pass a reference to a `match_results` object to this function, then after the search the object will contain information about the position and the string that matches. The `match_results` object is a container of `sub_match` objects. If the function succeeds it means that the entire search string matches the expression, and in this case the first `sub_match` item returned will be the entire search string. If the expression has subgroups (patterns identified with parentheses) then these sub groups will be additional `sub_match` objects in the `match_results` object.

```cpp
string str("trumpet");
regex rx("(trump)(.*)");
match_results<string::const_iterator> sm;
if (regex_match(str, sm, rx))
{
    cout << "the matches were: ";
    for (unsigned i = 0; i < sm.size(); ++i)
    {
        cout << "[" << sm[i] << "," << sm.position(i) << "] ";
    }
    cout << "n";
} // the matches were: [trumpet,0] [trump,0] [et,5]
```

Here, the expression is the literal `trump` followed by any number of characters. The entire string matches this expression and there are two sub groups: the literal string `trump` and whatever is left over after the `trump` is removed.

Both the `match_results` class and the `sub_match` class are templated on the type of iterator that is used to indicate the matched item. There are `typedef` call's `cmatch` and `wcmatch` where the template parameter is `const char*` and `const wchar_t*`, respectively, and `smatch` and `wsmatch` where the parameter is the iterator used in `string` and `wstring` objects, respectively (similarly, there are submatch classes: `csub_match`, `wcsub_match`, `ssub_match`, and `wssub_match`).

The `regex_match` function can be quite restrictive because it looks for an exact match between the pattern and the searched string. The `regex_search` function is more flexible because it returns `true` if there is a substring within the search string that matches the expression. Note that even if there are multiple matches in the search string, the `regex_search` function will only find the first. If you want to parse through the string you will have to call the function multiple times until it indicates that there are no more matches. This is where the overload with iterator access to the search string becomes useful:

```cpp
regex rx("bd{2}b");
smatch mr;
string str = "1 4 10 42 100 999";
string::const_iterator cit = str.begin();
```

```
while (regex_search(cit, str.cend(), mr, rx))
{
    cout << mr[0] << "n";
    cit += mr.position() + mr.length();
}
```

Here, the expression will match a 2 digit number (d{2}) that is surrounded by whitespace (the two b patterns mean a boundary before and after). The loop starts with an iterator pointing to the start of the string, and when a match is found this iterator is incremented to that position and then incremented by the length of the match. The regex_iterator object, explained further, wraps this behavior.

The match_results class gives iterator access to the contained sub_match objects so you can use ranged for. Initially, it appears that the container works in an odd way because it knows the position in the searched string of the sub_match object (through the position method, which takes the index of the sub match object), but the sub_match object appears to only know the string it refers to. However, on closer inspection of the sub_match class, it shows that it derives from pair, where both parameters are string iterators. This means that a sub_match object has iterators specifying the range in the original string of the sub string. The match_result object knows the start of the original string and can use the sub_match.first iterator to determine the character position of the start of the substring.

The match_result object has a [] operator (and the str method) that returns the substring of the specified group; this will be a string constructed using the iterators to the range of characters in the original string. The prefix method returns the string that precedes the match and the suffix method returns the string that follows the match. So, in the previous code, the first match will be 10, the prefix will be 1 4, and the suffix will be 42 100 999. In contrast, if you access the sub_match object itself, it only knows its length and the string, which is obtained by calling the str method.

The match_result object can also return the results through the format method. This takes a format string where the matched groups are identified through numbered placeholders identified by the $ symbol ($1, $2, and so on). The output can either be to a stream or returned from the method as a string:

```
string str("trumpet");
regex rx("(trump)(.*)");
match_results<string::const_iterator> sm;
if (regex_match(str, sm, rx))
{
    string fmt = "Results: [$1] [$2]";
    cout << sm.format(fmt) << "n";
} // Results: [trump] [et]
```

With `regex_match` or `regex_search`, you can use parentheses to identify subgroups. If the pattern matches then you can obtain these subgroups using an appropriate `match_results` object passed by reference to the function. As shown earlier, the `match_results` object is a container for `sub_match` objects. Sub matches can be compared with the <, !=, ==, <=, >, and >= operators, which compare items that the iterators point to (that is, the sub strings). Further, `sub_match` objects can be inserted into a stream.

# Using iterators

The library also provides an iterator class for regular expressions, which provides a different way to parse strings. Since the class will involve comparisons of strings it is templated with the element type and traits. The class will need to iterate through strings, so the first template parameter is the string iterator type and the element and traits types can be deduced from that. The `regex_iterator` class is a forward iterator so it has a ++ operator and it provides a * operator that gives access to a `match_result` object. In the previous code, you saw that a `match_result` object is passed to the `regex_match` and `regex_search` functions, which use it to contain their results. This raises the question of what code fills the `match_result` object accessed through the `regex_iterator`. The answer lies in the iterator's ++ operator:

```
string str = "the cat sat on the mat in the bathroom";
regex rx("(b(.at)([^ ]*)");
regex_iterator<string::iterator> next(str.begin(), str.end(), rx);
regex_iterator<string::iterator> end;

for (; next != end; ++next)
{
    cout << next->position() << " " << next->str() << ", ";
}
cout << "n";
// 4 cat, 8 sat, 19 mat, 30 bathroom
```

In this code, a string is searched for words where the second and third letters are `at`. The `b` says that the pattern must be at the start of a word (the . means that the word can start with any letter). There is a capture group around these three characters and a second capture group for one or more characters other than spaces.

The iterator object `next` is constructed with iterators to the string to search and the `regex` object. The `++` operator essentially calls the `regex_search` function while maintaining the position of the place to perform the next search. If the search fails to find the pattern then the operator returns the **end of sequence** iterator, which is the iterator that is created by the default constructor (the `end` object in this code). This code prints out the full match because we use the default parameter for the `str` method (0). If you want the actual substring matched, use `str(1)` and the result will be:

```
4 cat, 8 sat, 19 mat, 30 bat
```

Since the `*` (and the `->`) operator gives access to a `match_result` object, you can also access the `prefix` method to get the string that precedes the match and the `suffix` method will return the string that follows the match.

The `regex_iterator` class allows you to iterate over the matched substrings, whereas the `regex_token_iterator` goes one step further in that it also gives you access to all submatches. In use, this class is the same as `regex_iterator`, except in construction. The `regex_token_iterator` constructor has a parameter to indicate which submatch you wish to access through the `*` operator. A value of `-1` means you want the prefix, a value of `0` means you want the whole match, and a value of `1` or above means you want the numbered sub match. If you wish, you can pass an `int vector` or C array with the submatch types that you want:

```cpp
using iter = regex_token_iterator<string::iterator>;
string str = "the cat sat on the mat in the bathroom";
regex rx("b(.at)([^ ]*)");
iter next, end;

// get the text between the matches
next = iter(str.begin(), str.end(), rx, -1);
for (; next != end; ++next) cout << next->str() << ", ";
cout << "n";
// the ,  ,  on the ,  in the ,

// get the complete match
next = iter(str.begin(), str.end(), rx, 0);
for (; next != end; ++next) cout << next->str() << ", ";
cout << "n";
// cat, sat, mat, bathroom,

// get the sub match 1
next = iter(str.begin(), str.end(), rx, 1);
for (; next != end; ++next) cout << next->str() << ", ";
cout << "n";
// cat, sat, mat, bat,
```

```
// get the sub match 2
next = iter(str.begin(), str.end(), rx, 2);
for (; next != end; ++next) cout << next->str() << ", ";
cout << "n";
// , , , hroom,
```

# Replacing strings

The `regex_replace` method is similar to the other methods in that it takes a string (a C string or C++ `string` object, or iterators to a range of characters), a `regex` object, and optional flags. In addition, the function has a format string and returns a `string`. The format string is essentially passed to the `format` method of each `results_match` object from the result of the matches to the regular expression. This formatted string is then used as the replacement for the corresponding matched substring. If there are no matches, then a copy of the searched string is returned.

```
string str = "use the list<int> class in the example";
regex rx("b(list)(<w*> )");
string result = regex_replace(str, rx, "vector$2");
cout << result << "n"; // use the vector<int> class in the example
```

In the preceding code, we say that the entire matched string (which should be `list<` followed by some text followed by > and a space) should be replaced with `vector`, followed by the second sub match (< followed by some text followed by > and a space). The result is that `list<int>` will be replaced with `vector<int>`.

# Using strings

The example will read in emails as a text file and processed. An email in Internet message format will be in two parts: the header and message body. This is simple processing, so no attempt is carried out to process MIME email body formatting (although this code can be used as a starting point for that). The email body will start after the first blank line, and Internet standards say that lines should be no longer than 78 characters. If they are longer they must not be longer than 998 characters. This means that newlines (carriage return, linefeed pairs) are used to maintain this rule, and that an end of paragraph is indicated by a blank line.

Headers are more complicated. In their simplest form, a header is on a single line and is in the form `name:value`. The header name is separated from the header value by a colon. A header may be split over more than one line using a format called folded white space, where the newline splitting a header is placed before whitespace (space, tab, and so on). This means that a line that starts with whitespace is the continuation of the header on the previous line. Headers often contain `name=value` pairs separated by semicolons, so it is useful to be able separate these subitems. Sometimes these subitems do not have a value, that is, there will be a subitem terminated by a semicolon.

The example will take an email as a series of strings and using these rules will create an object with a collection of headers and a string containing the body.

# Creating the project

Create a folder for the project and create a C++ file called `email_parser.cpp`. Since this application will read files and process strings, add includes for the appropriate libraries and add code to take the name of a file from the command-line:

```cpp
#include <iostream>
#include <fstream>
#include <string>

using namespace std;

void usage()
{
    cout << "usage: email_parser file" << "n";
    cout << "where file is the path to a file" << "n";
}

int main(int argc, char *argv[])
{
    if (argc <= 1)
    {
        usage();
        return 1;
    }

    ifstream stm;
    stm.open(argv[1], ios_base::in);
    if (!stm.is_open())
    {
        usage();
        cout << "cannot open " << argv[1] << "n";
```

```
                return 1;
        }

        return 0;
    }
```

A header will have a name and a body. The body could be a single string, or one or more subitems. Create a class to represent the body of a header, and for the time being, treat this as a single line. Add the following class above the usage function:

```
class header_body
{
    string body;
public:
    header_body() = default;
    header_body(const string& b) : body(b) {}
    string get_body() const { return body; }
};
```

This simply wraps the class around a string; later on we will add code to separate out the subitems in the body data member. Now create a class to represent the email. Add the following code after the header_body class:

```
class email
{
    using iter = vector<pair<string, header_body>>::iterator;
    vector<pair<string, header_body>> headers;
    string body;

public:
    email() : body("") {}

    // accessors
    string get_body() const { return body; }
    string get_headers() const;
    iter begin() { return headers.begin(); }
    iter end() { return headers.end(); }

    // two stage construction
    void parse(istream& fin);
private:
    void process_headers(const vector<string>& lines);
};
```

The headers data member holds the headers as name/value pairs. The items are stored in a vector rather than a map because as an email is passed from mail server to mail server, headers may be added by each server that already exist in the email, so headers are duplicated. We could use a multimap, but then we will lose the ordering of the headers, since a multimap will store the items in an order that aids searching for items.

A vector keeps the items in the order that they are inserted in the container, and since we will parse the e-mail serially, this means that the headers data member will have the header items in the same order as in the e-mail. Add an appropriate include so that you can use the vector class.

There are accessors for the body and the headers as a single string. In addition, there are accessors that return iterators from the headers data member, so that external code can iterate through the headers data member (a complete implementation of this class would have accessors that allow you to search for a header by name, but for the purpose of this example, only iteration is permitted).

The class supports two-stage construction, where most of the work is carried out by passing an input stream to the parse method. The parse method reads in the email as a series of lines in a vector object and it calls a private function, process_headers, to interpret these lines as headers.

The get_headers method is simple: it just iterates through the headers and puts one header on each line in the format name: value. Add the inline function:

```
string get_headers() const
{
    string all = "";
    for (auto a : headers)
    {
        all += a.first + ": " + a.second.get_body();
        all += "n";
    }
    return all;
}
```

Next, you need to read in the email from a file and extract the body and the headers. The `main` function already has the code to open a file, so create an `email` object and pass the `ifstream` object for the file to the `parse` method. Now print out the parsed email using the accessors. Add the following to the end of the `main` function:

```
email eml;
eml.parse(stm);
cout << eml.get_headers();
cout << "n";
cout << eml.get_body() << "n";

return 0;
}
```

After the `email` class declaration, add the definition for the `parse` function:

```
void email::parse(istream& fin)
{
    string line;
    vector<string> headerLines;
    while (getline(fin, line))
    {
        if (line.empty())
        {
            // end of headers
            break;
        }
        headerLines.push_back(line);
    }

    process_headers(headerLines);

    while (getline(fin, line))
    {
        if (line.empty()) body.append("n");
        else body.append(line);
    }
}
```

This method is simple: it repeatedly calls the `getline` function in the `<string>` library to read a `string` until a newline is detected. In the first half of the method, the strings are stored in a `vector` and then passed to the `process_headers` method. If the string read in is empty, it means a blank line has been read--in which case, all of the headers have been read. In the second half of the method, the body of the e-mail is read in.

The `getline` function will have stripped the newlines used to format the email to 78-character line lengths, so the loop merely appends the lines as one string. If a blank line is read in, it indicates the end of a paragraph, and so a newline is added to the body string.

After the `parse` method, add the `process_headers` method:

```
void email::process_headers(const vector<string>& lines)
{
    string header = "";
    string body = "";
    for (string line : lines)
    {
        if (isspace(line[0])) body.append(line);
        else
        {
            if (!header.empty())
            {
                headers.push_back(make_pair(header, body));
                header.clear();
                body.clear();
            }

            size_t pos = line.find(':');
            header = line.substr(0, pos);
            pos++;
            while (isspace(line[pos])) pos++;
            body = line.substr(pos);
        }
    }

    if (!header.empty())
    {
        headers.push_back(make_pair(header, body));
    }
}
```

This code iterates through each line in the collection, and when it has a complete header it splits the string into the name/body pair on the colon. Within the loop, the first line tests to see if the first character is whitespace; if not, then the `header` variable is checked to see if it has a value; and if so, the name/body pair are stored in the class `headers` data member before clearing the `header` and `body` variables.

The following code acts upon the line read from the collection. This code assumes that this is the start of the header line, so the string is searched for the colon and split at this point. the name of the header is before the colon and the body of the header (trimmed of leading whitespace) is after the colon. Since we do not know if the header body will be folded onto the next line, the name/body is not stored; instead, the `while` loop is allowed to repeat another time so that the first character of the next line can be tested to see if it is whitespace, and if so, it is appended to the body. This action of holding the name/body pair until the next iteration of the `while` loop means that the last line will not be stored in the loop, and hence there is a test at the end of the method to see if the `header` variable is empty, and if not, the name/body pair is stored.

You can now compile the code (remember to use the `/EHsc` switch) to test that there are no typos. To test the code, you should save an email from your email client as a file and then run the `email_parser` application with the path to this file. The following is one of the example email messages given in the Internet Message Format RFC 5322, which you can put into a text file to test the code:

```
   Received: from x.y.test
   by example.net
   via TCP
   with ESMTP
   id ABC12345
   for <mary@example.net>;   21 Nov 1997 10:05:43 -0600
 Received: from node.example by x.y.test; 21 Nov 1997 10:01:22 -0600
 From: John Doe <jdoe@node.example>
 To: Mary Smith <mary@example.net>
 Subject: Saying Hello
 Date: Fri, 21 Nov 1997 09:55:06 -0600
 Message-ID: <1234@local.node.example>

 This is a message just to say hello.
 So, "Hello".
```

You can test the application with an email message to show that the parsing has taken into account header formatting, including folding whitespace.

# Processing header subitems

The next action is to process the header bodies into subitems. To do this, add the following highlighted declaration to the `public` section of the `header_body` class:

```
public:
    header_body() = default;
    header_body(const string& b) : body(b) {}
```

```
        string get_body() const { return body; }
        vector<pair<string, string>> subitems();
};
```

Each subitem will be a name/value pair, and since the order of a subitem may be important, the subitems are stored in a `vector`. Change the `main` function, remove the call to `get_headers`, and instead print out each header individually:

```
email eml;
eml.parse(stm);
for (auto header : eml) {
    cout << header.first << " : ";
    vector<pair<string, string>> subItems = header.second.subitems();
    if (subItems.size() == 0)    {
        cout << header.second.get_body() << "n";
    }   else    {
        cout << "n";
        for (auto sub : subItems) {
            cout << "    " << sub.first;
            if (!sub.second.empty())
            cout << " = " << sub.second;
            cout << "n";
        }
    }
}
cout << "n";
cout << eml.get_body() << endl;
```

Since the `email` class implements the `begin` and `end` methods, it means that the ranged `for` loop will call these methods to get access to the iterators on the `email::headers` data member. Each iterator will give access to a `pair<string, header_body>` object, so in this code we first print out the header name and then access the subitems on the `header_body` object. If there are no subitems, there will still be some text for the header, but it won't be split into subitems, so we call the `get_body` method to get the string to print. If there are subitems then these are printed out. Some items will have a body and some will not. If the item has a body then the subitem is printed in the form `name = value`.

The final action is to parse the header bodies to split them into subitems. Below the `header_body` class, add the definition of the method to this:

```
vector<pair<string, string>> header_body::subitems()
{
    vector<pair<string, string>> subitems;
    if (body.find(';') == body.npos) return subitems;

    return subitems;
```

```
}
```

Since subitems are separated using semicolons there is a simple test to look for a semicolon on the body string. If there is no semicolon, then an empty `vector` is returned.

Now the code must repeatedly parse through the string, extracting subitems. There are several cases that need to be addressed. Most subitems will be in the form `name=value;`, so this subitem must be extracted and split at the equals character and the semicolon discarded.

Some subitems do not have a value and are in the form `name;` in which case, the semicolon is discarded and an item is stored with an empty string for the subitem value. Finally, the last item in a header may not be terminated with a semicolon, so this must be taken into account.

Add the following `while` loop:

```
vector<pair<string, string>> subitems;
if (body.find(';') == body.npos) return subitems;
size_t start = 0;
size_t end = start;
while (end != body.npos){}
```

As the name suggests, the `start` variable is the start index of a subitem and `end` is the end index of a subitem. The first action is to ignore any whitespace, so within the `while` loop add:

```
while (start != body.length() && isspace(body[start]))
{
    start++;
}
if (start == body.length()) break;
```

This simply increments the `start` index while it refers to a whitespace character and as long as it has not reached the end of the string. If the end of the string is reached, it means there are no more characters and so the loop is finished.

Next, add the following to search for the = and ; characters and handle one of the search situations:

```
string name = "";
string value = "";
size_t eq = body.find('=', start);
end = body.find(';', start);

if (eq == body.npos)
```

```
    {
        if (end == body.npos) name = body.substr(start);
        else name = body.substr(start, end - start);
    }
    else
    {
    }
    subitems.push_back(make_pair(name, value));
    start = end + 1;
```

The `find` method will return the `npos` value if the searched item cannot be found. The first call looks for the = character and the second call looks for a semicolon. If no = can be found then the item has no value, just a name. If the semicolon cannot be found, then it means that the `name` is the entire string from the `start` index until the end of the string. If there is a semicolon, then the `name` is from the `start` index until the index indicated by `end` (and hence the number of characters to copy is `end-start`). If an = character is found then the string needs to be split at this point, and that code will be shown in a moment. Once the `name` and `value` variables have been given values, these are inserted into the `subitems` data member and the `start` index is moved to the character after the `end` index. If the `end` index is `npos` then the value of the `start` index will be invalid, but this does not matter because the `while` loop will test the value of the `end` index and will break the loop if the index is `npos`.

Finally, you need to add the code for when there is an = character in the subitem. Add the following highlighted text:

```
if (eq == body.npos)
{
    if (end == body.npos) name = body.substr(start);
    else name = body.substr(start, end - start);
}
else
{
    if (end == body.npos)
    {
        name = body.substr(start, eq - start);
        value = body.substr(eq + 1);
    }   else   {
        if (eq < end) {
            name = body.substr(start, eq - start);
            value = body.substr(eq + 1, end - eq - 1);
        } else {
            name = body.substr(start, end - start);
        }
    }
}
```

The first line tests to see if the search for a semicolon failed. In this case, the name is from the `start` index until the character before the equals character, and the value is the text following the equals sign until the end of the string.

If there are valid indices for the equals and semicolon characters then there is one more situation to check for. It is possible that the location of the equals character could be after the semicolon, in which case it means that this subitem does not have a value, and the equals character will be for a subsequent subitem.

At this point you can compile the code and test it with a file containing an email. The output from the program should be the email split into headers and a body, and each header split into subitems, which may be a simple string or a `name=value` pair.

# Summary

In this chapter, you have seen the various C++ standard library classes that support strings. You have seen how to read strings from streams, how to write strings to streams, how to convert between numbers and strings, and how to manipulate strings using regular expressions. When you write code, you will inevitably spend time running your code to check if it works according to your specifications. This will involve providing code that checks the results of your algorithms, code that logs intermediate code to a debugging device, and, of course, running the code under a debugger. The next chapter is all about debugging code!

# 7
# Diagnostics and Debugging

Software is complex; however, well you design your code, at some point you'll have to debug it, whether during the normal testing phases of developing your code, or when a bug report has been issued. It's prudent to design your code to make testing and debugging as straightforward as possible. This means adding tracing and reporting code, determining invariants and pre- and post-conditions, so that you have a starting point to test your code, and writing functions with understandable and meaningful error codes.

## Preparing your code

The C++ and C Standard Libraries have a wide range of functions that allow you to apply tracing and reporting functions so that you can test if code is handling data in expected ways. Much of these facilities use conditional compilation so that the reporting only occurs in debug builds, but if you provide the traces with meaningful messages they will form part of the documentation of your code. Before you can report on the behavior of your code, you first have to know what to expect from it.

## Invariants and conditions

Class invariants are conditions, the object state, that you know remain true. During a method call the object state will change, possibly to something that invalidates the object, but once a public method has completed, the object state must be left in a consistent state. There is no guarantee what order the user will call methods on a class, or even if they call methods at all, so an object must be usable whatever methods the user calls. The invariant aspects of an object applies on a method calls level: between method calls the object must be consistent and usable.

For example, imagine you have a class that represents a date: it holds a day number between 1 and 31, a month number between 1 and 12, and a year number. The class invariant is that, whatever you do to objects of the date class, it will always hold a valid date. This means that users can safely use objects of your date class. It also means that other methods on the class (say, a method to determine how many days between two dates, operator-) can assume that the values in the date objects are valid, so those methods do not have to check the validity of the data they act upon.

However, a valid date is more than the ranges 1 to 31 for days and 1 to 12 for months, because not every month has 31 days. So, if you have a valid date, say 5 April 1997, and you call a set_day method to set the day number to 31, the class invariant condition has been violated since 31 April is not a valid date. If you want to change the values in a date object, the only safe way to do this is to change all the values: the day, month, and year--at the same time, because this is the only way to maintain the class invariance.

One approach is to define a private method in debug builds that tests the invariant conditions for the class and ensures with asserts (see later) that the invariants are maintained. You can call such a method before a publicly-accessible method leaves to ensure that the object remains in a consistent state. Methods should also have defined pre- and post-conditions. Pre-conditions are conditions that you mandate are true before the method is called, and post-conditions are conditions that you guarantee are true after the method has completed. For the methods on a class, the class invariants are pre-conditions (because the state of the object should be consistent before the method is called) and the invariants are also a post-condition (because after the method has finished the object state should be consistent).

There are also pre-conditions that are the responsibility of the caller of a method. The pre-condition is a documented responsibility that the caller ensures. For example, the date class will have a pre-condition that day numbers are between 1 and 31. This simplifies the class code because methods that take a day number can assume that values passed are never out of range (although, because some months have fewer than 31 days, values may still not be valid). Again, in debug builds you can use asserts to check that such pre-conditions are true, and the tests in the assert will be compiled away in the release build. At the end of a method there will be post-conditions, that is, the class invariants will be maintained (and the state of the object will be valid), and the return value will be valid.

# Conditional compilation

As explained in Chapter 1, *Starting with C++*, when your C++ program is compiled there is a pre-compilation step that collates all the file included in a C++ source file into a single file, which is then compiled. The pre-processor also expands macros and, depending on the value of symbols, includes some code and exclude others code.

In its simplest form, conditional compilation brackets code with #ifdef and #endif (and optionally using #else), so that the code between these directives is only compiled if the specified symbol has been defined.

```
#ifdef TEST
    cout << "TEST defined" << endl;
#else
    cout << "TEST not defined" << endl;
#endif
```

You are guaranteed that only one of these lines will be compiled, and you are guaranteed that at least one of them will be compiled. If the symbol TEST is defined then the first line will be compiled and, as far as the compiler is concerned, the second line does not exist. If the symbol TEST is not defined, then the second line will be compiled. If you want to type these lines in the opposite order, you can use the #ifndef directive. The text provided through the conditional compilation can be C++ code, or it can be defined using other symbols in the current translation unit with #define or undefined existing symbols with #undef.

The #ifdef directive simply determines if the symbol exists: it does not test its value. The #if directive allows you to test an expression. You can set a symbol to have a value and compile specific code depending on the value. The expression must be integral, so a single #if block can test for several values using #if and multiple #elif directives and (at most) one #else:

```
#if TEST < 0
    cout << "negative" << endl;
#elif TEST > 0
    cout << "positive" << endl;
#else
    cout << "zero or undefined" << endl;
#endif
```

If the symbol is not defined then the `#if` directive treats the symbol as having a value of 0; if you want to distinguish between these cases you can use the `defined` operator to test if a symbol is defined. At most, only one of the sections in the `#if`/`#endif` block will be compiled, and if a value is not matched then no code will be compiled. The expression can be a macro, in which case the macro will be expanded before the condition is tested.

There are three ways to define a symbol. The first way is out of your control: the compiler will define some symbols (typically with the __ or _ prefix) that give you information about the compiler and the compilation process. Some of these symbols will be described in a later section. The other two ways are entirely under your control--you can define symbols in a source file (or header file) using `#define` or you can define them on the command line using the `/D` switch:

```
cl /EHsc prog.cpp /DTEST=1
```

This will compile the source code with the symbol TEST set to a value of 1.

You will typically use conditional compilation to provide code that should not be used in production code, for example, extra tracing code to use in debug mode or when you are testing code. For example, imagine you have library code to return data from a database, but you suspect that the SQL statement in the library function is faulty and returning too many values. Here, you may decide to test, add code to log the number of values returned:

```
vector<int> data = get_data();
#if TRACE_LEVEL > 0
cout << "number of data items returned: " << data.size() << endl;
#endif
```

Trace messages like this pollute your user interface and you will want to avoid them in production code. However, in debugging they can be invaluable in determining where problems are occurring.

Any code that you call in debug mode, conditional code should be `const` methods (here `vector::size`), that is, they should not affect the state of any objects or the application data. You must ensure that the logic of your code is *exactly* the same in debug mode as in release mode.

# Using pragmas

Pragmas are compiler-specific and often are concerned with the technical details about the code sections in the object files. There are a couple of Visual C++ pragmas that are useful in debugging code.

In general, you will want your code to compile with as few warnings as possible. The default warning for the Visual C++ compiler is /W1, which means that only the most severe warnings are listed. Increasing the value to 2, 3, or the highest value of 4 progressively increases the number of warnings that are given during a compilation. Using /Wall will give level-4 warnings and warnings that have been disabled by default. This last option, even for the simplest code, will produce a screen full of warnings. When you have hundreds of warnings useful error messages will be hidden between the reams of unimportant warnings. Since the C++ Standard Library is complex and uses some code that is decades old, there are some constructs that the compiler will warn you about. To prevent these warnings polluting the output from your builds, specific warnings in selective files have been disabled.

If you are supporting older library code, you may find that the code compiles with warnings. You may be tempted to reduce the warning levels using the compiler /W switch, but that will suppress all warnings higher than the ones you enable, and it applies equally to your code as to the library code that you may be including into your project. The warning pragma gives you a lot more flexibility. There are two ways to call this--you can reset the warning level to override the compiler /W switch and you can change the warning level of a particular warning or disable the warning reporting altogether.

For example, at the top of the <iostream> header is the line:

```
#pragma warning(push,3)
```

This says store the current warning level and, for the rest of this file (or until it is changed), make the warning level 3. At the bottom of the file is the line:

```
#pragma warning(pop)
```

This restores the warning level to that stored earlier.

You can also change how one or more warnings are reported. For example, at the top of <istream> is:

```
#pragma warning(disable: 4189)
```

The first part of this `pragma` is the specifier `disable`, which indicates that reporting of a warning type (in this case, 4189) is disabled. If you choose, you can change the warning level of a warning by using the warning level (1, 2, 3, or 4) as the specifier. One use for this is to lower the warning level just for a piece of code that you are working on and then return it to its default level after the code. For example:

```
#pragma warning(2: 4333)
unsigned shift8(unsigned char c)
{
    return c >> 8;
}
#pragma warning(default: 4333)
```

This function shifts a char right by 8 bits, which will generate the level-1 warning 4333 (*right shift by too large amount, data loss*). This is a problem and needs to be fixed, but for the time being, you want to compile the code without warnings from this code and so the warning level is changed to level 2. Using the default warning level (/W1) the warning will not be shown. However, if you compile with a more sensitive warning level (for example, /W2) then this warning will be reported. This change in the warning level is only temporary because the last line resets the warning level back to its default (which is 1). In this case, the warning level is increased, meaning that you will only see it with a more sensitive warning level on the compiler. You can also reduce the warning level, which means that the warning is more likely to be reported. You can even change a warning level to `error` so the code will not compile while warnings of this type exist in the code.

# Adding informational messages

As you test and debug code you will inevitably come across places where you can see a potential problem but it has low priority compared to what you are working on. It is important to make a note of the issue so that you can address the problem at a later stage. In Visual C++, there are two ways to do this in a benign way and two ways that will generate an error.

The first way is to add a `TODO:` comment, shown as follows:

```
// TODO: potential data loss, review use of shift8 function
unsigned shift8(unsigned char c)
{
    return c >> 8;
}
```

The Visual Studio editor has a tool window called the **Task List**. This lists the comments in the project that start with one of the predetermined tasks (the defaults are TODO, HACK, and UNDONE).

If the Task List window is not visible, enable it via the **View** menu. The default setting in Visual Studio 2015 is to enable tasks in C++. This is not the case for earlier versions, but it can be enabled through the **Tools** menu, **Options** dialog and then **Text Editor, C/C++, Formatting, View** by setting **Enumerate Comment Tasks** to **Yes**. The list of task labels can be found on the **Options** dialog under the **Environment, Task List** item.

The **Task List** lists the tasks with the file and line number, and you can open the file and locate the comment by double-clicking on an entry.

The second way to identify code that needs attention is the message pragma. As the name suggests, this simply allows you to place an informational message in your code. When the compiler comes across this pragma it simply puts the message on the output stream. Consider the following code:

```
#pragma message("review use of shift8 function")
unsigned shift8(unsigned char c)
{
    return c >> 8;
}
```

If the test.cpp file is compiled with this code and /W1 (the default) warning level, the output will be something like this:

```
    Microsoft (R) C/C++ Optimizing Compiler Version 19.00.24215.1 for x86
Copyright (C) Microsoft Corporation.  All rights reserved.

test.cpp
review the use of shift8 function
test.cpp(8): warning C4333: '>>': right shift by too large amount, data
loss
```

As you can see, the string is printed just as the compiler sees it, and there is no indication of the file or line number in contrast to the warning message. There are ways to address this using compiler symbols.

If the condition is important, you'll want to issue an error and one way to do this is with the `#error` directive. When the compiler reaches this directive, it will issue an error. This is a serious action, so you will only use it when there is another option. You'll most likely want to use it with a conditional compilation. A typical use is for code that can only be compiled with a C++ compiler:

```
#ifndef __cplusplus
#error C++ compiler required.
#endif
```

If you compile a file with this code using the `/Tc` switch to compile code as C then the `__cplusplus` preprocessor symbol will not be defined and an error will be generated.

C++11 adds a new directive called `static_assert`. This is called like a function (and *calls* are terminated with a semicolon), but it is not a function because it is only used at compile time. Further, the directive can be used in places where function calls are not used. The directive has two parameters: an expression and a string literal. If the expression is `false` then the string literal will be outputted at compile time with the source file and line number and an error will be generated. At the simplest level, you could use this to issue a message:

```
#ifndef __cplusplus
static_assert(false, "Compile with /TP");
#endif
#include <iostream> // needs the C++ compiler
```

Since the first parameter is `false`, the directive will issue the error message during compilation. The same thing could be achieved with the `#error` directive. The `<type_traits>` library has various predicates for testing the properties of types. For example, the `is_class` template class has a simple template parameter that is a type, and if the type is a `class` then the `static` member `value` is set to `true`. If you have a templated function that should only be instantiated for classes, you could add this `static_assert`:

```
#include <type_traits>

template <class T>
void func(T& value)
{
    static_assert(std::is_class<T>::value, "T must be a class");
    // other code
}
```

At compile time, the compiler will attempt to instantiate the function and instantiate `is_class` on that type using `value` to determine if the compilation should continue. For example, the following code:

```
func(string("hello"));
func("hello");
```

The first line will compile correctly because the compiler will instantiate a function, `func<string>`, and the parameter is a `class`. However, the second line will not compile because the function instantiated is `func<const char*>` and `const char*` is not a `class`. The output is:

```
Microsoft (R) C/C++ Optimizing Compiler Version 19.00.24215.1 for x86
Copyright (C) Microsoft Corporation.  All rights reserved.

test.cpp
test.cpp(25): error C2338: T must be a class
test.cpp(39): note: see reference to function template instantiation

'void func<const char*>(T)' being compiled
with
[
    T=const char *
]
```

The `static_assert` is on *line 25*, and hence this generates the error that `T must be a class`. *Line 39* is the first call to `func<const char*>` and gives context to the error.

# Compiler switches for debugging

To allow you to single-step through a program with a debugger, you have to provide information to allow the debugger to associate machine code with source code. At the very least, this means switching off all optimizations, since in an attempt to optimize code the C++ compiler will rearrange code. Optimizations are switched off by default (so the using the `/Od` switch is redundant), but clearly, to be able to debug a process and single-step through C++ code you need to remove all the `/O` optimization switches.

Since the C++ Standard Library uses the C Runtime, you will need to compile your code to use the latter's debug builds. The switch you use depends on whether you are building a process or **Dynamic Link Library (DLL)**, and whether you will statically link the C runtime or access it through a DLL. If you are compiling a process, you use /MDd to get the debug version of the C runtime in a DLL, and if you use /MTd you will get the debug version of the static linked C runtime. If you are writing a dynamic linked library, you have to use /LDd in addition to one of the C runtime switches (/MTd is the default). These switches will define a pre-processor symbol called _DEBUG.

A debugger will need to know debugger symbolic information--the names and types of variables and the names of functions and line numbers associated with code. The accepted way to do this is through a file called a **program database**, with an extension of pdb. You use one of the /Z switches to generate a pdb file: the /Zi or /ZI switch will create two files, one with a name starting with VC (for example VC140.pdb) that contains the debugging information for all of the obj files, and a file with the name of the project that contains debugging for the process. If you compile without linking (/c) then only the first file is created. The Visual C++ project wizard will use /Od /MDd /ZI by default for debug builds. The /ZI switch means that a program database is created in a format that allows the Visual C++ debugger to perform Edit and Continue, that is, you can change some code and continue to single-step through the code without recompiling. When you compile for a release build, the wizard will use the /O2 /MD /Zi switches, which means that the code is optimized for speed but a program database (without Edit and Continue support) will still be created. The code does not need the program database to run (in fact, you should not distribute it with your code), but it is useful if you have a crash report and need to run the release build code under the debugger.

These /Z compiler switches assume the linker is run with the /debug switch (and if the compiler invokes the linker it will pass this switch). The linker will create the project program database from the debug information in the VC program database file.

This raises the question of why a release build file will need a program database. If you run a program under the debugger and look at the call stack, you will often see a long list of stack frames in operating system files. These usually have fairly meaningless names made up of the DLL name and some numbers and characters. It is possible to install the symbols (the pdb files) for Windows or, if they are not installed, instruct the Visual C++ debugger to download the symbols for a library being used from a computer on the network called a **symbol server**. These symbols are not the source code for the library, but they do give you the names of the functions and the types of the parameters, which gives you additional information about the state of the call stack at the point where you are single stepping.

# Pre-processor symbols

To get access to the tracing, asserts, and reporting facilities in your code, you have to enable the debugging runtime library, and this is done by using the /MDd, /MTd, or /LDd compiler switches, which will define the _DEBUG pre-processor symbol. The _DEBUG pre-processor symbol enables a lot of facilities, and conversely, not defining this symbol will help in optimizing your code.

```
#ifdef _DEBUG
    cout << "debug build" << endl;
#else
    cout << "release built" << endl;
#endif
```

The C++ compiler will also provide information through some standard pre-processor symbols. Most of these are useful only for library writers, but there are some that you may want to use.

The ANSI standard says that the __cplusplus symbol should be defined when the compiler is compiling code as C++ (rather than C), and it also specifies that the __FILE__ symbol should contain the name of the file and that __LINE__ symbol will have the line number at the point where you access it. The __func__ symbol will have the current function name. This means that you can create tracing code like the following:

```
#ifdef _DEBUG
#define TRACE cout << __func__ << " (" << __LINE__ << ")" << endl;
#else
#define TRACE
#endif
```

If this code is compiled for debugging (for example, /MTd) then the cout line will be put inline whenever TRACE is used; if the code is not compiled for debugging then TRACE will do nothing. The __func__ symbol is simply the function name, it is not qualified, so if you use it in a class method it will provide no information about the class.

Visual C++ also defines Microsoft-specific symbols. The __FUNCSIG__ symbol gives the complete signature including the class name (and any namespace names), the return type, and parameters. If you just want the fully qualified name, then you can use the __FUNCTION__ symbol. A symbol that you will see frequently in the Windows header files is _MSC_VER. This has a number that is the version of the current C++ compiler, and it is used with a conditional compilation so that newer language features are only compiled with a compiler that supports them.

The Visual C++ project pages define *build macros* with names like $(ProjectDir) and $(Configuration). These are used only by the MSBuild tool so they are not automatically available in a source file during compilation, however, if you set a pre-processor symbol to the value of a build macro, the value will be available through that symbol at compile time. The system environment variables are also available as build macros, so it is possible to use them to influence the build. For example, on Windows the system environment variable USERNAME has the name of the current logged on user so you could use it to set a symbol and then access that at compile time.

In the Visual C++ project pages, you can add a **Preprocessor Definition** on the **C/C++** preprocessor project page called:

```
DEVELOPER="$(USERNAME)"
```

Then, in your code, you could add a line using this symbol:

```
cout << "Compiled by " << DEVELOPER << endl;
```

If you are using a make file, or just invoking cl from the command line, you can add a switch to define the symbol like this:

```
/DDEVELOPER="$(USERNAME)"
```

Escaping the double quotes here is important because without them the quotes are eaten by the compiler.

Earlier, you saw how the #pragma message and #error directives can be used to put messages into the output stream of the compiler. When you compile code in Visual Studio the compiler and linker outputs will appear in the output window. If the message is in the form:

```
path_to_source_file(line) message
```

where path_to_source_file is the full path to the file, line is the line number where the message appears. Then, when you double click on this line in the output window, the file will be loaded (if not already) and the insertion point placed on the line.

The __FILE__ and __LINE__ symbols provide you with the information that you need to make #pragma message and #error directives more useful. Outputting __FILE__ is simple because it is a string and C++ will concatenate string literals:

```
#define AT_FILE(msg) __FILE__ " " msg

#pragma message(AT_FILE("this is a message"))
```

The macro is called as part of the pragma to format the message correctly; however, you cannot call the pragma from a macro because the # has a special purpose (that will be of use in a moment). The result of this code will be something like:

```
c:\Beginning_C++Chapter_10test.cpp this is a message
```

Outputting __LINE__ via a macro requires a bit more work because it holds a number. This issue is a common one in C, so there is a standard solution using two macros and the stringing operator, #.

```
#define STRING2(x)  #x
#define STRING(x)  STRING2(x)
#define AT_FILE(msg)  __FILE__  "(" STRING(__LINE__) ") " msg
```

The STRING macro is used to expand the __LINE__ symbol to a number and the STRING2 macro to stringify the number. The AT_FILE macro formats the entire string in the correct format.

# Producing diagnostic messages

The effective use of diagnostic messages is a broad topic, so this section will just give you the basics. When you design your code, you should make it easy to write diagnostic messages, for example, providing mechanisms to dump the contents of an object and providing access to the code that tests for class invariants and pre- and post-conditions. You should also analyze the code to make sure that appropriate messages are logged. For example, issuing a diagnostic message in a loop will often fill up your log files, making it difficult to read the other messages in the log file. However, the fact that something is consistently failing in a loop may in itself be an important diagnostic, as may be the number of attempts to carry out a failing act, so you may want to record that.

Using cout for diagnostic messages has the advantage of integrating these messages with your user output, so that you can see the final effects of the intermediate results. The disadvantage is that the diagnostic messages are integrated with the user output, and since there are usually a large number of diagnostic messages, these will completely swamp the user output of your program.

C++ has two stream objects that you can use instead of `cout`. The `clog` and `cerr` stream objects will write character data to the standard error stream (the C stream pointer `stderr`), which will usually show on the console as if you are using `cout` (which outputs to the standard output stream, the C stream pointer `stdout`), but you can redirect it elsewhere. The difference between `clog` and `cerr` is that `clog` uses buffered output, which is potentially better-performing than the unbuffered `cerr`. However, there is the danger that the data may be lost if the application stops unexpectedly without flushing the buffer.

Since the `clog` and `cerr` stream objects are available in release builds as well as debug builds, you should use them only for messages that you are happy that your end user will see. This makes them inappropriate for trace messages (which will be covered shortly). Instead, you should use them for diagnostic messages that the user will be in a position to address (perhaps a file cannot be found or the process does not have the security access to perform an action).

```
ofstream file;
if (!file.open(argv[1], ios::out))
{
    clog << "cannot open " << argv[1] << endl;
    return 1;
}
```

This code opens a file in two steps (rather than using the constructor) and the `open` method will return `false` if the file cannot be opened. The code checks to see if opening the file was successful, and if it fails, it will tell the user via the `clog` object and then return from whatever function contains the code, as the `file` object is now invalid and cannot be used. The `clog` object is buffered but in this case we want to inform the user immediately, and this is performed by the `endl` manipulator, which inserts a newline in the stream and then flushes the stream.

By default, the `clog` and `cerr` stream objects will output to the standard error stream and this means that for a console application you can separate out the output stream and error stream by redirecting the streams. On the command-line, the standard streams can be redirected by using a value of 0 for `stdin`, 1 for `stdout`, and 2 for `stderr` and the redirection operator >. For example, an application `app.exe` could have this code in the `main` function:

```
clog << "clog" << endl;
cerr << "cerrn";
cout << "cout" << endl;
```

The `cerr` object is not buffered so whether you use n or `endl` for a newline is irrelevant. When you run this on the command line, you'll see something like this:

```
C:\Beginning_C++\Chapter_10>app
clog
cerr
cout
```

To redirect a stream to a file, redirect the stream handle (1 for `stdout`, 2 for `stderr`) to the file; the console will open the file and write the stream to the file:

```
C:\Beginning_C++\Chapter_10>app 2>log.txt
cout

C:\Beginning_C++\Chapter_10>type log.txt
clog
cerr
```

As the last chapter showed, C++ stream objects are layered so that calls to insert data into a stream will write the data to the underlying stream object, depending on the type of stream, with or without buffering. This stream buffer object is obtained, and replaced, using the `rdbuf` method. If you want the `clog` object redirected to a file by the application, you can write code like the following:

```
extern void run_code();

int main()
{
    ofstream log_file;
    if (log_file.open("log.txt")) clog.rdbuf(log_file.rdbuf());

    run_code();

    clog.flush();
    log_file.close();
    clog.rdbuf(nullptr);
    return 0;
}
```

In this code the application code will be in the `run_code` function, and the rest of the code sets up the `clog` object to redirect to files.

Note that the file is explicitly closed when the `run_code` function returns (the application has finished); this is not entirely necessarily because the `ofstream` destructor will close the file, and in this case this will happen when the `main` function returns. The last line is important. The standard stream objects are created before the `main` function is called, and they will be destroyed sometime after the `main` function returns, that is, well after the file objects have been destroyed. To prevent the `clog` object accessing the destroyed file object, the `rdbuf` method is called passing `nullptr` to indicate that there is no buffer.

# Trace messages with the C runtime

Often you will want to test your code by running the application in real time and output the *trace messages* to test that your algorithms work. Sometimes you will want to test the order that functions are called (for example, that correct branching occurs in a `switch` statement or in an `if` statement), and in other cases you'll want to test intermediate values to see that the input data is correct and the calculations on that data are correct.

Trace messages can produce a lot of data, so it is unwise to send these to the console. It is extremely important that trace messages are only produced in debug builds. If you leave trace messages in product code, it could seriously impact the performance of your application (as will be explained later). Further, trace messages are unlikely to be localized, nor will they be checked to see if they contain information that could be used to reverse-engineer your algorithms. One final issue with trace messages in release builds is that your client will think that you are providing them with code that has not been completely tested. It is important, then, that trace messages are only generated in debug builds, when the `_DEBUG` symbol is defined.

The C Runtime provides a series of macros with names starting with `_RPT` that can be used to trace messages when `_DEBUG` is defined. There are `char` and wide char versions of these macros, and there are versions that will report just the trace messages and others that will report the message and the location (source file and line number) of the message. Ultimately these macros will call a function called `_CrtDbgReport` that will generate the message with the settings that have been determined elsewhere.

The `_RPTn` macros (where n is 0, 1, 2, 3, 4, or 5) will take a format string and 0 to 5 parameters that will be put into the string before being reported. The first parameter of the macros indicates the type of message to report: `_CRT_WARN`, `_CRT_ERROR`, or `_CRT_ASSERT`. The last two of these categories are the same and refer to asserts, which will be covered in a later section. The second parameter of the report macros is a format string, which will then be followed by the required number of parameters. The `_RPTFn` macros are the same format but will report the source file and line number as well as the formatted message.

The default action is that _CRT_WARN messages will produce no output and the _CRT_ERROR and _CRT_ASSERT messages will generate a popup window to allow you to abort or debug the application. You can change the response to any of these message categories by calling the _CrtSetReportMode function and providing the category and a value indicating the action to take. If you use _CRTDBG_MODE_DEBUG then the message will be written to the debugger output window. If you use _CRTDBG_MODE_FILE then the message will be written to a file that you can open and pass the handle to the _CrtSetReportFile function. (You can also use _CRTDBG_FILE_STDERR or _CRTDBG_FILE_STDOUT as the file handle to send the message to the standard output or the error output.) If you use _CRTDBG_MODE_WNDW as the report mode then the message will be displayed using the **Abort/Retry/Ignore** dialog box. Since this will pause the current thread of execution, it should only be used for assert messages (the default action):

```
include <crtdbg.h>

extern void run_code();

int main()
{
    _CrtSetReportMode(_CRT_WARN, _CRTDBG_MODE_DEBUG);
    _RPTF0(_CRT_WARN, "Application startedn");

    run_code();

    _RPTF0(_CRT_WARN, "Application endedn");
    return 0;
}
```

If you do not provide the n in the messages then the next message will be appended to the end of your message, and in most cases this is not what you want (although you could justify this for a series of calls to the _RPTn macros, where the last one is terminated with n).

The Visual Studio output window is shown when you compile a project (to show it at debug time select the **Output** option in the **View** menu), and at the top is a combo box labelled **Show output from**, which will be usually set to **Build**. If you set this to **Debug** then you will see the debugging messages generated during a debugging session. These will include messages about loading debugging symbols and messages redirected from the _RPTn macros to the output window.

If you prefer the messages to be directed to a file then you need to open the file with the Win32 CreateFile function and use the handle from that function in a call to the _CrtSetReportFile function. To do this, you will need to include the Windows header files:

```
#define WIN32_LEAN_AND_MEAN
#include <Windows.h>
#include <crtdbg.h>
```

The WIN32_LEAN_AND_MEAN macro will reduce the size of the Windows files included.

```
HANDLE file =
    CreateFileA("log.txt", GENERIC_WRITE, 0, 0, CREATE_ALWAYS, 0, 0);
_CrtSetReportMode(_CRT_WARN, _CRTDBG_MODE_FILE);
_CrtSetReportFile(_CRT_WARN, file);
_RPTF0(_CRT_WARN, "Application startedn");

run_code();

_RPTF0(_CRT_WARN, "Application endedn");
CloseHandle(file);
```

This code will direct the warning messages to the text file log.txt which will be created new every time the application is run.

## Tracing messages with Windows

The OutputDebugString function is used to send messages to a debugger. The function does this through a *shared memory section* called DBWIN_BUFFER. Shared memory means that any process can access this memory, and so Windows provides two *event objects* called DBWIN_BUFFER_READY and DBWIN_DATA_READY that control read and write access to this memory. These event objects are shared between processes and can be in a signalled or unsignalled state. A debugger will indicate that it is no longer using the shared memory by signalling the DBWIN_BUFFER_READY event, at which point the OutputDebugString function can write the data to the shared memory. The debugger will wait on the DBWIN_DATA_READY event, which will be signalled by the OutputDebugString function when it has finished writing to the memory and it is safe to read the buffer. The data written to the memory section will be the process ID of the process that called the OutputDebugString function, followed by a string of up to 4 KB of data.

The problem is that when you call the `OutputDebugString` function it will wait on the `DBWIN_BUFFER_READY` event, which means that when you use this function you are coupling the performance of your application to the performance of another process, which is usually a debugger (but may not be). It is very easy to write a process to access the `DBWIN_BUFFER` shared memory section and get access to the associated event objects, so it may be possible that your production code will run on a machine where someone has such an application running. For this reason, it is vitally important that you use conditional compilation so that the `OutputDebugString` function is only used in debug builds--code that will never be released to your customers:

```
extern void run_code();

int main()
{
    #ifdef _DEBUG
        OutputDebugStringA("Application startedn");
    #endif

    run_code();

    #ifdef _DEBUG
        OutputDebugStringA("Application endedn");
    #endif
    return 0;
}
```

You will need to include the `windows.h` header file to compile this code. As for the `_RPT` example, you will have to run this code under a debugger to see the output, or have an application like **DebugView** (available from Microsoft's Technet website) running.

Windows provides the `DBWinMutex` mutex object to act as an overall *key* to accessing this shared memory and event objects. As the name suggests, when you have a handle to a mutex you will have mutually exclusive access to the resource. The problem is that processes do not have to have a handle to this mutex to use these resources and consequently you have no guarantee that, if your application thinks it has exclusive access that it will really have exclusive access.

# Using asserts

An assert checks that a condition is true. The assertion means just that: the program should not continue if the condition is not true. Clearly asserts should not be called in release code and hence conditional compilation must be used. Asserts should be used to check for conditions that should never happen: never events. Since the conditions do not happen there should be no need for asserts in release builds.

The C Runtime provides the `assert` macro that is available through the `<cassert>` header file. The macro, and any functions called in the expression passed as its only parameter, will be called unless the NDEBUG symbol is defined. That is, you do not have to define the _DEBUG symbol to use asserts and you should have taken extra action to explicitly prevent `assert` from being called.

It is worth re-iterating this. The `assert` macro is defined even if _DEBUG is not defined, so an assert could be called in release code. To prevent this from happening you must define the NDEBUG symbol in a release build. Conversely, you can define the NDEBUG symbol in a debug build so that you can use tracing but do not have to use asserting.

Typically, you will use asserts in debug builds to check that pre- and post-conditions are met in a function and that class invariant conditions are fulfilled. For example, you may have a binary buffer that has a special value at the tenth byte position and so have written a function to extract that byte:

```
const int MAGIC=9;

char get_data(char *p, size_t size)
{
    assert((p != nullptr));
    assert((size >= MAGIC));
    return p[MAGIC];
}
```

Here, the calls to `assert` are used to check that the pointer is not `nullptr` and that the buffer is big enough. If these asserts are true, then it means that it is safe to access the tenth byte through the pointer.

Although it is not strictly necessary in this code, the assertion expressions are given in parentheses. It is good to get into the habit of doing this because `assert` is a macro and so a comma in the expression will be treated as a macro parameter separator; the parentheses protected against this.

Since the `assert` macro will be defined in release builds by default, you will have to disable them by defining `NDEBUG` on the compiler command line, in your make file, or you may want to use conditional compilation explicitly:

```
#ifndef _DEBUG
#define NDEBUG
#endif
```

If an assert is called and it fails, then an assert message is printed at the console along with source file and line number information and then the process is terminated with a call to `abort`. If the process is built with release build standard libraries then the process `abort` is straightforward, however, if the debug builds are used then the user will see the standard **Abort/Retry/Ignore** message box where the **Abort** and **Ignore** options abort the process. The **Retry** option will use **Just-in-Time** (**JIT**) debugging to attach the registered debugger to the process.

In contrast, the `_ASSERT` and `_ASSERTE` macros are only defined when `_DEBUG` is defined, so these macros will not be available in release builds. Both macros take an expression and generate an assert message when the expression is `false`. The message for the `_ASSERT` macro will include the source file and line number and a message stating that the assertion failed. The message for the `_ASSERTE` macro is similar but includes the expression that failed.

```
_CrtSetReportMode(_CRT_ASSERT, _CRTDBG_MODE_FILE);
_CrtSetReportFile(_CRT_ASSERT, _CRTDBG_FILE_STDOUT);

int i = 99;
_ASSERTE((i > 100));
```

This code sets the reporting mode so that the failed assert will be a message printed on the console (rather than the default, which is the **Abort/Retry/Ignore** dialog). Since the variable is clearly less than 100, the assert will fail and so the process will terminate and the following message will be printed on the console:

```
test.cpp(23) : Assertion failed: (i > 100)
```

The **Abort/Retry/Ignore** dialog gives the person, testing the application, the option of attaching the debugger to the process. If you decide that the failure of the assertion is heinous you can force the debugger to attach to the process by calling `_CrtDbgBreak`.

```
int i = 99;
if (i <= 100) _CrtDbgBreak();
```

You do not need to use conditional compilation because in release builds the _CrtDbgBreak function is a no-operation. In a debug build, this code will trigger JIT debugging, which gives you the option to close the application or launch the debugger, and if you choose the latter, the registered JIT debugger will be started.

# Application termination

The main function is the entry point for your application. However, this isn't called directly by the operating system because C++ will perform initialization before main is called. This includes constructing the Standard Library global objects (cin, cout, cerr, clog, and the wide character versions) and there is a whole host of initialization that is performed for the C Runtime Library that underpins C++ libraries. Further, there are the global and static objects that your code creates. When the main function returns, the destructors of global and static objects will have to be called and a clean-up performed on the C runtime.

There are several ways to stop a process deliberately. The simplest is to return from the main function, but this assumes that there is a simple route back to the main function from the point that your code wants to finish the process. Of course, process termination must be ordered and you should avoid writing code where it is normal to stop the process anywhere in the code. However, if you have a situation where data is corrupted and unrecoverable and any other action could damage more data, you may have no option other than to terminate the application.

The <cstdlib> header file provides access to the header files to the functions that allow you to terminate and to handle the termination of an application. When a C++ program closes down normally, the C++ infrastructure will call the destructors of the objects created in the main function (in the reverse order to their construction) and the destructors of static objects (which may have been created in functions other than the main function). The atexit function allows you to register functions (that have no parameters and no return value) that will be called after the main function completes and static object destructors have been called. You can register more than one function by calling this function several times, and at termination the functions will be called in reverse order to their registering. After the functions registered with the atexit function have been called, the destructors of any global objects will be called.

There is also a Microsoft function called _onexit that also allows you to register functions to be called during normal termination.

The exit and _exit functions perform a normal exit of a process, that is, they clean up the C runtime and flush any open files before shutting down the process. The exit function does additional work by calling any registered termination functions; the _exit function does not call these termination functions and so is a quick exit. These functions will not call the destructors of temporary or automatic objects, so if you use stack objects to manage resources, you will have to explicitly call the destructor code before calling exit. However, the destructors of static and global objects will be called.

The quick_exit function causes normal shutdown, but it does not call any destructors nor flush any streams, so there is no resource clean up. The functions registered with atexit are not called, but you can register that termination functions are called by registering them with the at_quick_exit function. After calling these termination functions, the quick_exit function calls the _Exit function that shuts down the process.

You can also call the terminate function to close down a process with no clean up. This process will call a function that has been registered with the set_terminate function and then calls the abort function. If an exception occurs in the program and is not caught--and hence propagates to the main function - the C++ infrastructure will call the terminate function. The abort function is the most severe of mechanisms that terminate a process. This function will exit the process without calling the destructors of objects or performing any other clean up. The function raises the SIGABORT signal and so it is possible to register a function with the signal function, which will be called before the process terminates.

# Error values

Some functions are designed to perform an action and return a value based on that action, for example, sqrt will return the square root of a number. Other functions perform more complex operations and use the return value to indicate whether the function was successful. There is no common convention about such error values, so if a function returns a simple integer there is no guarantee that the values one library uses have the same meaning as values returned from functions in another library. This means that you have to examine carefully the documentation for any library code that you use.

Windows does provide common error values, which can be found in the winerror.h header file, and the functions in the Windows **Software Development Kit (SDK)** only return values in this file. If you write library code that will be used exclusively in Windows applications, consider using the error values in this file because you can use the Win32 FormatMessage function to obtain a description of the error, as explained in the next section.

The C Runtime Library provides a global variable called errno (in fact it is a macro that you can treat as a variable). C functions will return a value to indicate that they have failed and you access the errno value to determine what the error was. The <errno.h> header file defines the standard POSIX error values. The errno variable does not indicate success, it only indicates errors, so you should only access it when a function has indicated that there is an error. The strerror function will return a C string with a description of the error value that you pass as a parameter; these messages are localized according to the current C locale set through a call to the setlocale function.

# Obtaining message descriptions

To obtain the description at runtime for a Win32 error code you use the Win32 FormatMessage function. This will get the description for a system message or for a custom message (described in the next section). If you want to use a custom message you have to load the executable (or DLL) that has the message resource bound to it and pass the HMODULE handle to the FormatMessage function. If you want to get the description of a system message you do not need to load a module because Windows will do this for you. For example, if you call the Win32 CreateFile function to open a file and the file cannot be found, the function will return a value of INVALID_HANDLE_VALUE, indicating that there is an error. To get details of the error you call the GetLastError function (which returns a 32-bit unsigned value sometimes called DWORD or HRESULT). You can then pass the error value to FormatMessage:

```
HANDLE file = CreateFileA(
    "does_not_exist", GENERIC_READ, 0, 0, OPEN_EXISTING, 0, 0);
if (INVALID_HANDLE_VALUE == file)
{
    DWORD err = GetLastError();
    char *str;
    DWORD ret = FormatMessageA(
        FORMAT_MESSAGE_FROM_SYSTEM|FORMAT_MESSAGE_ALLOCATE_BUFFER,
        0, err, LANG_USER_DEFAULT, reinterpret_cast<LPSTR>(&str),
        0, 0);
    cout << "Error: "<< str << endl;
    LocalFree(str);
}
else
{
    CloseHandle(file);
}
```

This code tries to open a file that does not exist and obtains the error value associated with the failure (this will be a value of ERROR_FILE_NOT_FOUND). The code then calls the FormatMessage function to get the string describing the error. The first parameter of the function is a flag that indicates how the function should work; in this case, the FORMAT_MESSAGE_FROM_SYSTEM flag says that the error is a system error and the FORMAT_MESSAGE_ALLOCATE_BUFFER flag says that the function should allocate a buffer large enough to hold the string using the Win32 LocalAlloc function.

 If the error is a custom value that you have defined then you should use the FORMAT_MESSAGE_FROM_HMODULE flag, open the file with LoadLibrary and use the resulting HMODULE as the parameter passed in through the second parameter.

The third parameter is the error message number (from GetLastError) and the fourth is a LANGID that indicates the language ID to use (in this case LANG_USER_DEFAULT to get the language ID for the current logged on user). The FormatMessage function will generate a formatted for the error value, and this string may have replacement parameters. The formatted string is returned in a buffer and you have two options: you can allocate a character buffer and pass the pointer in as the fifth and the length as the sixth parameter, or you can request the function to allocate a buffer using the LocalAlloc function as in this example. To get access to a function allocated buffer you pass the *address* of a pointer variable via the fifth parameter.

Note that the fifth parameter is used to either take a pointer to a user allocated buffer, or returns the address of system allocated buffer, and this is why in this case the pointer to pointer has to be cast.

Some format strings may have parameters, and if so, the values are passed in through an array in the seventh parameter (in this case, no array is passed). The result of the preceding code is the string:

```
Error: The system cannot find the file specified.
```

Using the message compiler, resource files, and the FormatMessage, you can provide a mechanism to return error values from your functions and then convert these to localized strings according to the current locale.

# Using the Message Compiler

The previous example showed that you can obtain localized strings for Win32 errors, but that you can also create your own errors and provide localized strings that are bound as resources to your process or library. If you intend to report errors to the end user, you have to make sure that the descriptions are localized. Windows provides a tool called the Message Compiler (mc.exe) that will take a text file with entries for messages in various languages and compile them into binary resources that can be bound to a module.

For example:

```
LanguageNames = (British = 0x0409:MSG00409)
LanguageNames = (French  = 0x040c:MSG0040C)

MessageId       = 1
SymbolicName    = IDS_GREETING
Language        = English
Hello
.

Language        = British
Good day
.

Language        = French
Salut
.
```

This defines three localized strings for the same message. The messages here are simple strings, but you can define format messages with placeholders that can be provided at runtime. The *neutral* language is US English, and in addition we define strings for British English, and French. The names used for the languages are defined in the LanguageNames lines at the top of the file. These entries have the name that will be used later in the file, the code page for the language, and the name of the binary resource that will contain the message resource.

The MessageId is the identifier that will be used by the FormatMessage function, and the SymbolicName is a pre-processor symbol that will be defined in a header file, so that you can use this message in your C++ code rather than the number. This file is compiled by passing it to the command line utility mc.exe, which will create five files: a header file with the definition of the symbol, three binary sources (MSG00001.bin, which is created by default for the neutral language, and MSG00409.bin and MSG0040C.bin, which are created because of the LanguageNames lines), and a resource compiler file.

For this example, the resource compiler file (with extension .rc) will contain:

```
LANGUAGE 0xc,0x1
1 11 "MSG0040C.bin"
LANGUAGE 0x9,0x1
1 11 "MSG00001.bin"
LANGUAGE 0x9,0x1
1 11 "MSG00409.bin"
```

This is a standard resource file that can be compiled by the Windows SDK resource compiler (rc.exe), which will compile the message resources into a .res file that can be bound to an executable or DLL. A process or DLL that has a resource of type 11 bound to it can be used by the FormatMessage function as a source of descriptive error strings.

Typically, you will not use a message ID of 1 because it is unlikely to be unique and you are likely to want to take advantage of the *facility code* and *severity code* (for details of facility code, look in the winerror.h header file). Further, to indicate that the message is not Windows you can set the customer bit of the error code using the /c switch when you run mc.exe. This will mean that your error code will not be a simple value like 1, but this should not matter because your code will use the symbol defined in the header file.

# C++ exceptions

As the name suggests, exceptions are for exceptional conditions. They are not normal conditions. They are not conditions that you want to occur but they are conditions that may happen. Any exceptional condition will often mean that your data will be in an inconsistent state, so using exceptions means that you need to think in transactional terms, that is, an operation either succeeds, or the state of an object should remain the same as it was before the operation was attempted. When an exception occurs in a code block, everything that happened in the code block will be invalid. If the code block is part of a wider code block (say, a function that is a series of function calls by another function) then the work in that other code block will be invalid. This means that the exception may propagate out to other code blocks further up the call stack, invalidating the objects that depend on the operation being successful. At some point, the exceptional condition will be recoverable, so you will want to prevent the exception going further.

# Exception specifications

Exception specifications are deprecated in C++11 but you may see them in earlier code. A specification is through the `throw` expression applied to a function declaration giving the exceptions that can be thrown from the function. The `throw` specification can be an ellipsis, which means that the function can throw exceptions but the type is not specified. If the specification is empty then it means the function won't throw exceptions, and this is the same as using the `noexcept` specifier in C++11.

The `noexcept` specifier tells the compiler that exception handling is not required, so if an exception does occur in the function the exception will not be bubbled out of the function and the `terminate` function will be called immediately. In this situation, there is no guarantee that the destructors of the automatic objects are called.

# C++ exception syntax

In C++, an exceptional situation is generated by throwing an exception object. That exception object can be anything you like: an object, a pointer, or a built-in type, but because exceptions may be handled by code written by other people it is best to standardize the objects that are used to represent exceptions. For this, the Standard Library provides the `exception` class, which can be used as a base class.

```
double reciprocal(double d)
{
    if (d == 0)
    {
        // throw 0;
        // throw "divide by zero";
        // throw new exception("divide by zero");
        throw exception("divide by zero");
    }
    return 1.0 / d;
}
```

This code tests the parameter and if it is zero then it throws an exception. Four examples are given and all are valid C++, but only the last version is acceptable because it uses a Standard Library class (or one derived from the Standard Library classes) and it follows the convention that exceptions are thrown by value.

When an exception is thrown, the exception handling infrastructure takes over. Execution will stop in the current code block and the exception will be propagated up the call stack. As the exception propagates through a code block, all the automatic objects will be destroyed, but objects created on the heap in the code black will not be destroyed. This is a process called **stack unwinding,** whereby each stack frame is cleaned up as much as possible before the exception moves to the stack frame above it in the call stack. If the exception is not caught, it will propagate up to the `main` function, at which point the `terminate` function will be called to handle the exception (and hence it will terminate the process).

You can protect code to handle propagated exceptions. Code is protected with a `try` block and it is caught with an associated `catch` block:

```
try
{
    string s("this is an object");
    vector<int> v = { 1, 0, -1};
    reciprocal(v[0]);
    reciprocal(v[1]);
    reciprocal(v[2]);
}
catch(exception& e)
{
    cout << e.what() << endl;
}
```

Unlike other code blocks in C++, braces are mandatory even if the `try` and `catch` blocks contain single lines of code. In the preceding code the second call to the `reciprocal` function will throw an exception. The exception will halt the execution of any more code in the block, so the third call to the `reciprocal` function will not occur. Instead, the exception propagates out of the code block. The `try` block is the scope of the objects defined between the braces, and this means that the destructors of these objects will be called (`s` and `v`). Control is then passed to the associated `catch` blocks, and in this case, there is just one handler. The `catch` block is a separate block to the `try` block, so you cannot access any variables defined in the `try` block. This makes sense because when an exception is generated the entire code block is *tainted* so you cannot trust any object created in that block. This code uses the accepted convention, that is, exceptions are caught by reference, so that the actual exception object, and not a copy, is caught.

The convention is: throw my value, catch-by-reference.

The Standard Library provides a function called `uncaught_exception`, which returns `true` if an exception has been thrown but not yet handled. It may seem odd to be able to test for this since no code other than the exception infrastructure will be called when an exception has occurred (for example the `catch` handlers) and you should put exception code there. However, there *is* other code that is called when an exception is thrown: the destructors of automatic objects that are destroyed during the stack clear up. The `uncaught_exception` function should be used in a destructor to determine if the object is being destroyed due to an exception rather than normal object destruction due to an object going out of scope or being deleted. For example:

```
class test
{
    string str;
public:
    test() : str("") {}
    test(const string& s) : str(s) {}
    ~test()
    {
        cout << boolalpha << str << " uncaught exception = "
            << uncaught_exception() << endl;
    }
};
```

This simple object indicates if it is being destroyed because of exception stack unwinding. It can be tested like this:

```
void f(bool b)
{
    test t("auto f");
    cout << (b ? "f throwing exception" : "f running fine")
        << endl;
    if (b) throw exception("f failed");
}

int main()
{
    test t1("auto main");
    try
    {
        test t2("in try in main");
        f(false);
        f(true);
        cout << "this will never be printed";
    }
    catch (exception& e)
    {
```

```
        cout << e.what() << endl;
    }
    return 0;
}
```

The f function will throw an exception only if it is called with a `true` value. The `main` function calls f twice, once with a value of `false` (so the exception is not thrown in f) and a second time with `true`. The output is:

```
f running fine
auto f uncaught exception = false
f throwing exception
auto f uncaught exception = true
in try in main uncaught exception = true
f failed
auto main uncaught exception = false
```

The first-time f is called, the `test` object is destroyed normally, so `uncaught_exception` will return `false`. The second-time f is called the `test` object in the function is being destroyed before the exception has been caught, so `uncaught_exception` will return `true`. Since an exception is thrown, the execution leaves the `try` block and so the `test` object in the `try` block is destroyed and `uncaught_exception` will return `true`. Finally, when the exception has been handled and control returns to code after the `catch` block, the `test` object created on the stack in the `main` function will be destroyed when the `main` function returns and so `uncaught_exception` will return `false`.

# Standard exception classes

The `exception` class is a simple container for a C string: the string is passed as a constructor parameter and is available through the `what` accessor. The Standard Library declares the exception class in the `<exception>` library, and you are encouraged to derive your own exception classes from this. The Standard Library provides the following derived classes; most are defined in `<stdexcept>`.

| Class | Thrown |
|---|---|
| bad_alloc | When the `new` operator has been unable to allocate memory (in `<new>`) |
| bad_array_new_length | When the `new` operator has been asked to create an array with an invalid length (in `<new>`) |
| bad_cast | When `dynamic_cast` to a reference type fails (in `<typeinfo>`) |
| bad_exception | An unexpected condition has occurred (in `<exception>`) |
| bad_function_call | Invoked an empty `function` object (in `<functional>`) |

| bad_typeid | When the argument of typeid is null (in <typeinfo>) |
|---|---|
| bad_weak_ptr | When accessing a weak pointer, which refers to an already destroyed object (in <memory>) |
| domain_error | When an attempt is made to perform an operation outside the domain on which the operation is defined |
| invalid_argument | When an invalid value has been used for a parameter |
| length_error | When an attempt has been made to exceed the length defined for an object |
| logic_error | When there is a logic error, for example, class invariants or pre-conditions |
| out_of_range | When an attempt has been made to access elements outside of the range defined for the object |
| overflow_error | When a calculation results in a value bigger than the destination type |
| range_error | When a calculation results in a value outside the range for the type |
| runtime_error | When an error occurs outside the scope of the code |
| system_error | Base class to wrap operating system errors (in <system_error>) |
| underflow_error | When a calculation results in an underflow |

All the classes, mentioned in the preceding table, have a constructor that takes a const char* or a const string& parameter, in contrast to the exception class that takes a C string (hence the base class is constructed using the c_str method if the description is passed through a string object). There are no wide character versions, so if you want to construct an exception description from a wide character string you have to convert it. Also, note that the standard exception classes only have one constructor parameter, and this is available through the inherited what accessor.

There is no absolute rule about the data that an exception can hold. You can derive a class from exception and construct it with whatever values you want to make available to the exception handler.

# Catching exceptions by type

There can be more than one `catch` block with each `try` block, which means that you can tailor the exception handling according to the exception type. The types of the parameters in the `catch` clauses will be tested against the type of the exception in the order that they are declared. The exception will be handled by the first handler that matches the exception type, or is a base class. This highlights the convention to catch the exception object via a reference. If you catch as a base class object a copy will be made, slicing the derived class object. In many cases code, will throw objects of a type derived from the `exception` class so it means that a catch handler for `exception` will catch all exceptions.

Since code can throw any object, it is possible that an exception will propagate out of the handler. C++ allows you to catch everything by using an ellipses in the `catch` clause. Clearly, you should order the `catch` handlers from the most derived to the least derived and (if you use it) with the ellipses handler at the end:

```
try
{
    call_code();
}
catch(invalid_argument& iva)
{
    cout << "invalid argument: " << e.what() << endl;
}
catch(exception& exc)
{
    cout << typeid(exc).name() << ": " << e.what() << endl;
}
catch(...)
{
    cout << "some other C++ exception" << endl;
}
```

If the guarded code does not throw an exception, then the `catch` blocks are not executed.

When your handler examines the exception, it may decide that it does not want to suppress the exception; this is called rethrowing the exception. To do this, you can use the `throw` statement without an operand (this is only allowed in a `catch` handler), which will rethrow the actual exception object that was caught, and not a copy.

Exceptions are thread-based and so it is difficult to propagate an exception to another thread. The `exception_ptr` class (in `<exception>`) provides shared ownership semantics for an exception object of any type. You can get a shared copy of an exception object by calling the `make_exception_ptr` object, or you can even get a shared copy of the exception being handled in a `catch` block using `current_exception`. Both functions return an `exception_ptr` object. An `exception_ptr` object can hold an exception of any kind, not just those derived from the `exception` class, so getting information from the wrapped exception is specific to the exception type. The `exception_ptr` object knows nothing about these details, so instead you can pass it to `rethrow_exception` in the context where you want to use the shared exception (another thread) and then catch the appropriate exception object. In the following code, there are two threads running. The `first_thread` function runs on one thread and the `second_thread` function on the other:

```cpp
exception_ptr eptr = nullptr;

void first_thread()
{
    try
    {
        call_code();
    }
    catch (...)
    {
        eptr = current_exception();
    }
    // some signalling mechanism ...
}

void second_thread()
{
    // other code

    // ... some signalling mechanism
    if (eptr != nullptr)
    {
        try
        {
            rethrow_exception(eptr);
        }
        catch(my_exception& e)
```

```
        {
            // process this exception
        }
        eptr = nullptr;
    }
    // other code
}
```

The preceding code looks like it is using `exception_ptr` as a pointer. In fact, `eptr` is created as a global object and the assignment to `nullptr` uses the copy constructor to create an empty object (where the wrapped exception is `nullptr`). Similarly, the comparison with `nullptr` actually tests the wrapped exception.

This book is not about C++ threading, so we won't go into the details of the signalling between two threads. This code shows that a shared copy of an exception, *any exception*, can be stored in one context and then rethrown and processed in another context.

# Function try blocks

You may decide that you want to protect an entire function with a `try` block, in which case you could write code like this:

```
void test(double d)
{
    try
    {
        cout << setw(10) << d << setw(10) << reciprocal(d) << endl;
    }

    catch (exception& e)
    {
        cout << "error: " << e.what() << endl;
    }
}
```

This uses the `reciprocal` function, as defined earlier, that will throw an `exception` if the parameter is zero. An alternative syntax for this is:

```
void test(double d)
try
{
    cout << setw(10) << d << setw(10) << reciprocal(d) << endl;
}
catch (exception& e)
{
    cout << "error: " << e.what() << endl;
}
```

This looks rather odd because the function prototype is followed immediately by the `try... catch` block and there is no outer set of braces. The function body is the code in the `try` block; when this code completes the function returns. If the function returns a value, it must do it in the `try` block. In most cases, you will find that this syntax makes your code less readable, but there is one situation where it may be useful--for initializer lists in constructors.

```
class inverse
{
    double recip;
public:
    inverse() = delete;
    inverse(double d) recip(reciprocal(d)) {}
    double get_recip() const { return recip; }
};
```

In this code, we wrap a `double` value that is simply the reciprocal of the parameter passed to the constructor. The data member is initialized by calling the `reciprocal` function in the initializer list. Since this is outside of the constructor body, an exception that occurs here will be passed straight to the code that calls the constructor. If you want to do some additional processing, then you could call the reciprocal function inside the constructor body:

```
inverse::inverse(double d)
{
    try { recip = reciprocal(d); }
    catch(exception& e) { cout << "invalid value " << d << endl; }
}
```

It is important to note that the exception will be automatically rethrown because any exception in a constructor means that the object is invalid. However, this does allow you to do some additional processing, if necessary. This solution will not work for exceptions thrown in a base object constructor because, although you can call a base constructor in the derived constructor body, the compiler will call the default constructor automatically. If you want the compiler to call a constructor other than the default constructor you have to call it in the initializer list. An alternative syntax to providing exception code in the `inverse` constructor is to use function `try` blocks:

```
inverse::inverse(double d)
try
    : recip (reciprocal(d)) {}
catch(exception& e) { cout << "invalid value " << d << endl; }
```

This looks a little cluttered, but the constructor body is still after the initializer list giving an initial value to the `recip` data member. Any exception from the call to `reciprocal` will be caught and automatically rethrown after processing. The initializer list can contain calls to the base class and any of the data members and all will be protected with the `try` block.

# System errors

The `<system_error>` library defines a series of classes to encapsulate system errors. The `error_category` class provides a mechanism to convert numeric error values into localized descriptive strings. Two objects are available through the `generic_category` and `system_category` functions in `<system_error>`, and `<ios>` has a function called `isostream_category`; all of these functions return an `error_category` object. The `error_category` class has a method called `message` that returns a string description of the error number you pass as the parameter. The object returned from the `generic_category` function will return the descriptive string for a POSIX error, so you can use it to get a description for an `errno` value. The object returned from the `system_category` function will return an error description via the Win32 `FormatMessage` function using `FORMAT_MESSAGE_FROM_SYSTEM` for the flags parameter, and hence this can be used to get the descriptive message for a Windows error message in a `string` object.

Note that `message` has no extra parameters to pass in values for a Win32 error message that takes parameters. Consequently, in those situations you will get back a message that has formatting placeholders.

In spite of the name, the `isostream_category` object essentially returns the same descriptions as the `generic_category` object.

The `system_error` exception is a class that reports one of the values described by one of the `error_category` objects. For example, this is the example used earlier for `FormatMessage` but re-written using `system_error`:

```
HANDLE file = CreateFileA(
    "does_not_exist", GENERIC_READ, 0, 0, OPEN_EXISTING, 0, 0);
if (INVALID_HANDLE_VALUE == file)
{
    throw system_error(GetLastError(), system_category());
}
else
{
    CloseHandle(file);
}
```

The `system_error` constructor used here has the error value as the first parameter (a `ulong` returned from the Win32 function `GetLastError`) and a `system_category` object used to convert the error value to a descriptive string when the `system_error::what` method is called.

# Nested exceptions

A `catch` block may rethrow the current exception by calling `throw` without any operand, and there will be stack unwinding until the next `try` block is reached in the call stack. You can also rethrow the current exception *nested inside* another exception. This is achieved by calling the `throw_with_nested` function (in `<exception>`) and passing the new exception. The function calls `current_exception` and wraps the exception object in a nested exception along with the parameter, which is then thrown. A `try` block further up the call stack can catch this exception, but it can only access the outer exception; it has no direct access to the inner exception. Instead, the inner exception can be thrown with a call to `rethrow_if_nested`. For example, here is another version of code to open a file:

```
void open(const char *filename)
{
    try
    {
        ifstream file(filename);
        file.exceptions(ios_base::failbit);
        // code if the file exists
    }
    catch (exception& e)
```

```
    {
        throw_with_nested(
            system_error(ENOENT, system_category(), filename));
    }
}
```

The code opens a file, and if the file does not exist then a state bit is set (you can test the bits later with a call to the `rdstat` method). The next line indicates the values of the state bits that should be handled by the class throwing an exception, and in this case the `ios_base::failbit` is provided. If the constructor failed to open the file then this bit will be set, so the `exceptions` method will respond by throwing an exception. In this example, the exception is caught and wrapped into a nested exception. The outer exception is a `system_error` exception, which is initialized with an error value of ENOENT (which means that the file does not exist) and an `error_category` object to interpret it, passing the name of the file as additional information.

This function can be called like this:

```
try
{
    open("does_not_exist");
}
catch (exception& e)
{
    cout << e.what() << endl;
}
```

The exception caught here can be accessed, but it just gives information about the outer object:

**does_not_exist: The system cannot find the file specified.**

This message is constructed by the `system_error` object using the additional information passed to its constructor and the description from the category object. To get the inner object in a nested exception you have to tell the system to throw the inner exception with a call to `rethrow_if_nested`. So, instead of printing out the outer exception, you call a function like this:

```
void print_exception(exception& outer)
{
    cout << outer.what() << endl;
    try { rethrow_if_nested(outer); }
    catch (exception& inner) { print_exception(inner); }
}
```

This prints the description for the outer exception and then calls `rethrow_if_nested`, which will only throw the exception if it is nested. If so, it throws the inner exception, which is then caught and recursively calls the `print_exception` function. The result is:

```
does_not_exist: The system cannot find the file specified.
ios_base::failbit set: iostream stream error
```

The last line is the inner exception which was thrown when the `ifstream::exception` method was called.

# Structured Exception Handling

Native exceptions in Windows are **Structured Exceptions Handling** (**SEH**) and Visual C++ has a language extension to allow you to catch these exceptions. It is important to understand that they are not the same as C++ exceptions, which are considered by the compiler to be *synchronous*, that is, the compiler knows if a method may (or specifically, will not) throw a C++ exception, and it uses this information when analysing code. C++ exceptions are also caught by type. SEH is not a C++ concept, so the compiler treats structured exceptions as being *asynchronous*, meaning it treats any code within an SEH protected block as potentially raising a structured exception, and hence the compiler cannot perform optimizations. SEH exceptions are also caught by exception code.

The language extensions for SEH are extensions to Microsoft C/C++, that is, they can be used in C as well as C++ so the handling infrastructure does not know about object destructors. Additionally, when you catch an SEH exception, no assumptions are made about the state of the stack or any other part of your process.

Although most Windows functions will catch the SEH exceptions generated by the kernel in an appropriate way, some purposely allow them to propagate (for example, the **Remote Procedure Calls** (**RPC**) functions, or those used for memory management). With some Windows functions you can explicitly request that errors are handled with SEH exceptions. For example, the `HeapCreate` set of functions will allow a Windows application to create a private heap, and you can pass the `HEAP_GENERATE_EXCEPTIONS` flag to indicate that errors in creating the heap, and allocating, or reallocating memory in a private heap, will generate an SEH exception. This is because the developer calling these functions may regard the failure to be so serious that it is not recoverable, and hence the process should terminate. Since an SEH is such a serious situation, you should review carefully whether it is appropriate (which is not entirely impossible) to do much more than report details of the exception and terminate the process.

SEH exceptions are essentially low-level operating system exceptions, but it is important to be familiar with the syntax because it looks similar to C++ exceptions. For example:

```
char* pPageBuffer;
unsigned long curPages = 0;
const unsigned long PAGESIZE = 4096;
const unsigned long PAGECOUNT = 10;

int main()
{
    void* pReserved = VirtualAlloc(
    nullptr, PAGECOUNT * PAGESIZE, MEM_RESERVE, PAGE_NOACCESS);
    if (nullptr == pReserved)
    {
        cout << "allocation failed" << endl;
        return 1;
    }

    char *pBuffer = static_cast<char*>(pReserved);
    pPageBuffer = pBuffer;

    for (int i = 0; i < PAGECOUNT * PAGESIZE; ++i)
    {
        __try {
            pBuffer[i] = 'X';
        }
        __except (exception_filter(GetExceptionCode())) {
            cout << "Exiting process.n";
            ExitProcess(GetLastError());
        }
    }
    VirtualFree(pReserved, 0, MEM_RELEASE);
    return 0;
}
```

The SEH exception code is highlighted here. This code uses the Windows `VirtualAlloc` function to reserve a number of pages of memory. Reserving does not allocate the memory, that action has to be carried out in a separate operation called **committing the memory**. Windows will reserve (and commit) memory in blocks called **pages** and on most systems a page is 4096 bytes, as assumed here. The call to the `VirtualAlloc` function indicates that it should reserve ten pages of 4096 bytes, which will be committed (and used) later.

The first parameter to `VirtualAlloc` indicates the location of the memory, but since we are reserving memory, this is unimportant so `nullptr` is passed. If the reserving succeeds, then a pointer is returned to the memory. The `for` loop simply writes data to the memory one byte at a time. The highlighted code protects this memory access with structured exception handling. The protected block starts with the `__try` keyword. When an SEH is raised, execution passes to the `__except` block. This is very different to the `catch` block in C++ exceptions. Firstly, `__except` exception handler receives one of three values to indicate how it should behave. Only if this is `EXCEPTION_EXECUTE_HANDLER` will the code in the handler block be run (in this code, to shut down the process abruptly). If the value is `EXCEPTION_CONTINUE_SEARCH` then the exception is not recognized and the search will continue up the stack, *but without C++ stack unwinding*. The surprising value is `EXCEPTION_CONTINUE_EXECUTION`, because this dismisses the exception and execution in the `__try` block will continue. *You cannot do this with C++ exceptions*. Typically, SEH code will use an exception filter function to determine what action is required of the `__except` handler. In this code, this filter is called `exception_filter`, which is passed the exception code obtained by calling the Windows function `GetExceptionCode`. This syntax is important because this function can only be called in the `__except` context.

The first time the loop runs no memory will have been committed and so the code that writes to the memory will raise an exception: a page fault. Execution will pass to the exception handler and through to `exception_filter`:

```
int exception_filter(unsigned int code)
{
    if (code != EXCEPTION_ACCESS_VIOLATION)
    {
        cout << "Exception code = " << code << endl;
        return EXCEPTION_EXECUTE_HANDLER;
    }

    if (curPage >= PAGECOUNT)
    {
        cout << "Exception: out of pages.n";
        return EXCEPTION_EXECUTE_HANDLER;
    }

    if (VirtualAlloc(static_cast<void*>(pPageBuffer), PAGESIZE,
     MEM_COMMIT, PAGE_READWRITE) == nullptr)
    {
        cout << "VirtualAlloc failed.n";
        return EXCEPTION_EXECUTE_HANDLER;
    }

    curPage++;
```

```
            pPageBuffer += PAGESIZE;
            return EXCEPTION_CONTINUE_EXECUTION;
    }
```

It is important in SEH code to only handle exceptions that you know about, and only consume the exception if you know that the condition has been completely addressed. If you access Windows memory that has not been committed, the operating system generates an exception called a page fault. In this code, the exception code is tested to see if it is a page fault, and if not, the filter returns telling the exception handler to run the code in the exception handler block that terminates the process. If the exception is a page fault then we can commit the next page. First, there is a test to see if the page number is within the range that we will use (if not, then close down the process). Then, the next page is committed with another call to `VirtualAlloc` to identify the page to commit and the number of bytes in that page. If the function succeeds, it will return a pointer to the committed page or a null value. Only if committing the page has succeeded will the filter return a value of `EXCEPTION_CONTINUE_EXECUTION`, indicating that the exception has been handled and execution can continue at the point the exception was raised. This code is a standard way to use `VirtualAlloc` because it means that memory pages are only committed when, and if, they are needed.

SEH also has the concept of termination handlers. When execution leaves the __try block of code through a call to `return`, or by completing all of the code in the block, or by calling the Microsoft extension __leave instruction, or has raised an SEH, then the termination handler block of code marked with __finally is called. Since the termination handler is always called, regardless of how the __try block is exited, it is possible to use this as a way to release resources. However, because SEH does not do C++ stack unwinding (nor call destructors), this means that you cannot use this code in a function that has C++ objects. In fact, the compiler will refuse to compile a function that has SEH and created C++ objects, either on the function stack or allocated on the heap. (You can, however, use global objects or objects allocated in calling functions and passed in as parameters.) The __try/__finally construct looks useful, but is constrained by the requirement that you cannot use it with code that creates C++ objects.

# Compiler exception switches

At this point, it is worth explaining why you have compiled your code with the /EHsc switch. The simple answer is, if you do not use this switch the compiler will issue a warning from the Standard Library code, and as the Standard Library uses exceptions you must use the /EHsc switch. The warning tells you to do this, so that is what you do.

The long answer is that the /EH switch has three arguments that you can use to influence how exceptions are handled. Using the s argument tells the compiler to provide the infrastructure for synchronous exceptions, that is, C++ exceptions that may be thrown in a try block and handled in a catch block, and that have stack unwinding that calls the destructors of automatic C++ objects. The c argument indicates that extern C functions (that is, all the Windows SDK functions) never throw C++ exceptions (and hence the compiler can do an additional level of optimization). Hence, you can compile Standard Library code with either /EHs or /EHsc, but the latter will generate more optimized code. There is an additional argument, where /EHa indicates that the code will catch *both* synchronous and asynchronous exceptions (SEH) with try/catch blocks.

# Mixing C++ and SEH exception handling

The RaiseException Windows function will throw an SEH exception. The first parameter is the exception code and the second indicates if the process can continue after this exception is handled (0 means it can). The third and fourth parameters give additional information about the exception. The fourth parameter is a pointer to an array with these additional parameters and the number of parameters is given in the third parameter.

With /EHa, you can write code like this:

```
try
{
    RaiseException(1, 0, 0, nullptr);
}
// legal code, but don't do it
catch(...)
{
    cout << "SEH or C++ exception caught" << endl;
}
```

The problem with this code is that it handles all SEH exceptions. This is quite dangerous because some SEH exceptions may indicate that the process state is corrupted, so it is dangerous for the process to continue. The C Runtime Library provides a function called _set_se_translator that provides a mechanism to indicate which SEH exceptions are handled by try. This function is passed a pointer by a function that you write with this prototype:

```
void func(unsigned int, EXCEPTION_POINTERS*);
```

The first parameter is the exception code (which will be returned from the
GetExceptionCode function) and the second parameter is the return from the
GetExceptionInformation function and has any additional parameters associated with
the exception (for example, those passed through the third and fourth parameters in
RaiseException). You can use these values to throw a C++ exception in place of the SEH.
If you provide this function:

```
void seh_to_cpp(unsigned int code, EXCEPTION_POINTERS*)
{
    if (code == 1) throw exception("my error");
}
```

You can now register the function before handling an SEH exception:

```
_set_se_translator(seh_to_cpp);
try
{
    RaiseException(1, 0, 0, nullptr);
}
catch(exception& e)
{
    cout << e.what() << endl;
}
```

In this code, the RaiseException function is raising a custom SEH with a value of 1. This
translation is perhaps not the most useful, but it illustrates the point. The winnt.h header
file defines the exception code for the standard SEH exceptions that can be raised in
Windows code. A more useful translation function would be:

```
double reciprocal(double d)
{
    return 1.0 / d;
}

void seh_to_cpp(unsigned int code, EXCEPTION_POINTERS*)
{
    if (STATUS_FLOAT_DIVIDE_BY_ZERO == code ||
        STATUS_INTEGER_DIVIDE_BY_ZERO == code)
    {
        throw invalid_argument("divide by zero");
    }
}
```

This allows you to call the reciprocal function as following:

```
_set_se_translator(seh_to_cpp);
try
{
    reciprocal(0.0);
}
catch(invalid_argument& e)
{
    cout << e.what() << endl;
}
```

# Writing exception-safe classes

In general, when you write classes, you should ensure that you protect the users of your classes from exceptions. Exceptions are not an error propagation mechanism. If a method on your class fails but is recoverable (the object state is left consistent) then you should use the return value (most likely an error code) to indicate this. Exceptions are for exceptional situations, those that have invalidated data and where, at the point where the exception is raised, the situation is unrecoverable.

When an exception occurs in your code, you have three options. Firstly, you can allow the exception to propagate up the call stack and put the responsibility of handling the exception on the calling code. This means that you call code without guarding by try blocks, even though the code is documented as being able to throw exceptions. In this situation, you must be reassured that the exception makes sense to the calling code. For example, if your class is documented as a network class and uses a temporary file to buffer some data received from the network, if the file access code throws an exception, the exception object will not make sense to code that calls your code, because that client code thinks that your class is about accessing network data, not file data. If, however, the network code throws an error, it may make sense to allow those exceptions to propagate to calling code, especially if they refer to errors that require external action (say, a network cable is unplugged or there is a security issue).

In this case, you can apply your second option, which is to protect code that can throw exceptions with a try block, catch known exceptions, and throw a more appropriate exception, perhaps nesting the original exception so that the calling code can do more detailed analysis. If the exception is one that makes sense to your calling code, you may allow it to propagate out, but catching the original exception allows you to take additional action before you rethrow it.

Using the buffered network data example, you could decide that since there is an error in the file buffering, it means that you cannot read any more network data, so your exception handling code should shut down the network access in a graceful way. The error occurred in the file code, not the network code, so an abrupt shutdown of the network is not justified, and it makes more sense to allow the current network action to complete (but ignore the data), so that no errors are propagated back to the network code.

The final option is to protect all code with a `try` block, and catch and consume exceptions, so that calling code completes without throwing an exception. There are two main situations where this is appropriate. Firstly, the error may be recoverable, and so in the `catch` clause you can take steps to address the issue. In the buffered network data example, when opening a temporary file, if you get an error that a file with the requested name already exists, you can simply use another name and try again. The user of your code does not need to know that this problem occurred (although, it may make sense to trace this error so that you can investigate the issue in the testing phase of your code). If the error is not recoverable, it may make more sense to invalidate the state of your object and return an error code.

Your code should utilize the behavior of the C++ exception infrastructure, which guarantees that automatic objects are destroyed. Therefore, when you use memory or other appropriate resources, you should wrap them in smart pointers whenever possible so that if an exception is thrown then the resource is released by the smart pointer destructor. Classes that use Resource Acquisition Is Initialization (RAII) are `vector`, `string`, `fstream`, and the `make_shared` function, so if the object construction (or the function call) is successful, it means that the resource has been acquired, and you can use the resource through these objects. These classes are also **Resource Release Destruction** (RRD), which means that the resource is released when the object is destroyed. The smart pointer classes, `unique_ptr` and `shared_ptr`, are not RAII because they simply wrap the resource and the allocation of resources is carried out separately by other code. However, these classes are RRD, so you can be assured that if an exception is thrown the resource is released.

Exception handling can offer three levels of exception safety. At the safest level of the scale is the *no-fail* method and function. This is the code that does not throw exceptions and does not allow exceptions to propagate. Such code will guarantee that class invariants are maintained and that the object state will be consistent. No-fail code is not achieved by simply catching all exceptions and consuming them, instead, you have to protect all code and catch, and handle, all exceptions to ensure that the object is left in a consistent state.

All built-in C++ types are no-fail. You also have a guarantee that all Standard Library types have no-fail destructors, but since containers will call the contained object destructors when instances are destroyed, this means that you have to ensure that the types you write to put in containers also have a no-fail destructor.

Writing no-fail types can involve quite detailed code, so another option is the *strong guarantee*. Such code will throw exceptions, but they ensure that no memory is leaked and that when an exception is thrown the object will be in the same state as when the method was called. This is essentially a transactional operation: either the object is modified or it is left unmodified, as if no attempt was made to perform the operation. In most cases methods, this will offer a *basic guarantee* of exception safety. In this case, there is a guarantee that whatever happens no memory is leaked, but when an exception is thrown, the object may be left in an inconsistent state, so the calling code should handle the exception by discarding the object.

Documentation is important. If the object methods are marked with `throw` or `noexcept` then you know it is no-fail. You should only assume the strong guarantee if the documentation says so. Otherwise, you can assume that objects will have the basic guarantee of exception safety, and if an exception is thrown the object is invalid.

# Summary

When you write your C++ code you should always have one eye looking towards the testing and debugging of your code. The ideal way to prevent the need to debug code is to write robust, well-designed code. Ideals are difficult to achieve, so it is better to write code that is easy for you to diagnose issues and easy to debug with. The C Runtime and the C++ Standard Library provides a wide range of facilities to enable you to trace and report issues, and through error code handling and exceptions you have a rich collection of tools to report and handle the failure of functions.

After reading this book you should be aware that the C++ language and Standard Library provide a rich, flexible, and powerful way to write code. What's more, once you know how to use the language and its libraries, C++ is a pleasure to use.

# 8
# Learning Modern Core Language Features

The recipes included in this chapter are as follows:

- Using auto whenever possible
- Creating type aliases and alias templates
- Understanding uniform initialization
- Understanding the various forms of non-static member initialization
- Controlling and querying object alignment
- Using scoped enumerations
- Using override and final for virtual methods
- Using range-based for loops to iterate on a range
- Enabling range-based for loops for custom types
- Using explicit constructors and conversion operators to avoid implicit conversion
- Using unnamed namespaces instead of static globals
- Using inline namespaces for symbol versioning
- Using structured bindings to handle multi-return values

# Using auto whenever possible

Automatic type deduction is one of the most important and widely used features in modern C++. The new C++ standards have made it possible to use `auto` as a placeholder for types in various contexts and let the compiler deduce the actual type. In C++11, `auto` can be used for declaring local variables and for the return type of a function with a trailing return type. In C++14, `auto` can be used for the return type of a function without specifying a trailing type and for parameter declarations in lambda expressions. Future standard versions are likely to expand the use of `auto` to even more cases. The use of `auto` in these contexts has several important benefits. Developers should be aware of them, and prefer `auto` whenever possible. An actual term was coined for this by Andrei Alexandrescu and promoted by Herb Sutter--*almost always auto (AAA)*.

# How to do it...

Consider using `auto` as a placeholder for the actual type in the following situations:

- To declare local variables with the form `auto name = expression` when you do not want to commit to a specific type:

```
auto i = 42;          // int
auto d = 42.5;        // double
auto s = "text";      // char const *
auto v = { 1, 2, 3 }; // std::initializer_list<int>
```

- To declare local variables with the `auto name = type-id { expression }` form when you need to commit to a specific type:

```
auto b  = new char[10]{ 0 };              // char*
auto s1 = std::string {"text"};           // std::string
auto v1 = std::vector<int> { 1, 2, 3 };   // std::vector<int>
auto p  = std::make_shared<int>(42);      // std::shared_ptr<int>
```

- To declare named lambda functions, with the form `auto name = lambda-expression`, unless the lambda needs to be passed or return to a function:

```
auto upper = [](char const c) {return toupper(c); };
```

- To declare lambda parameters and return values:

```
auto add = [](auto const a, auto const b) {return a + b;};
```

- To declare function return type when you don't want to commit to a specific type:

```
template <typename F, typename T>
auto apply(F&& f, T value)
{
  return f(value);
}
```

# How it works...

The `auto` specifier is basically a placeholder for an actual type. When using `auto`, the compiler deduces the actual type from the following instances:

- From the type of the expression used to initialize a variable, when `auto` is used to declare variables.
- From the trailing return type or the type of the return expression of a function, when `auto` is used as a placeholder for the return type of a function.

In some cases, it is necessary to commit to a specific type. For instance, in the preceding example, the compiler deduces the type of s to be `char const *`. If the intention was to have a `std::string`, then the type must be specified explicitly. Similarly, the type of v was deduced as `std::initializer_list<int>`. However, the intention could be to have a `std::vector<int>`. In such cases, the type must be specified explicitly on the right side of the assignment.

There are some important benefits of using the auto specifier instead of actual types; the following is a list of, perhaps, the most important ones:

- It is not possible to leave a variable uninitialized. This is a common mistake that developers do when declaring variables specifying the actual type, but it is not possible with `auto` that requires an initialization of the variable in order to deduce the type.
- Using `auto` ensures that you always use the correct type and that implicit conversion will not occur. Consider the following example where we retrieve the size of a vector to a local variable. In the first case, the type of the variable is `int`, though the `size()` method returns `size_t`. That means an implicit conversion from `size_t` to `int` will occur. However, using `auto` for the type will deduce the correct type, that is, `size_t`:

```
auto v = std::vector<int>{ 1, 2, 3 };
int size1 = v.size();
```

```
            // implicit conversion, possible loss of data
            auto size2 = v.size();
            auto size3 = int{ v.size() };   // ill-formed (warning in gcc/clang,
  error in VC++)
```

- Using `auto` promotes good object-oriented practices, such as preferring interfaces over implementations. The lesser the number of types specified the more generic the code is and more open to future changes, which is a fundamental principle of object-oriented programming.
- It means less typing and less concern for actual types that we don't care about anyways. It is very often that even though we explicitly specify the type, we don't actually care about it. A very common case is with iterators, but one can think of many more. When you want to iterate over a range, you don't care about the actual type of the iterator. You are only interested in the iterator itself; so, using `auto` saves time used for typing possibly long names and helps you focus on actual code and not type names. In the following example, in the first `for` loop, we explicitly use the type of the iterator. It is a lot of text to type, the long statements can actually make the code less readable, and you also need to know the type name that you actually don't care about. The second loop with the `auto` specifier looks simpler and saves you from typing and caring about actual types.

```
std::map<int, std::string> m;
for (std::map<int,std::string>::const_iterator it = m.cbegin();
   it != m.cend(); ++it)
{ /*...*/ }

for (auto it = m.cbegin(); it != m.cend(); ++it)
{ /*...*/ }
```

- Declaring variables with `auto` provides a consistent coding style with the type always in the right-hand side. If you allocate objects dynamically, you need to write the type both on the left and right side of the assignment, for example, `int* p = new int(42)`. With `auto`, the type is specified only once on the right side.

However, there are some gotchas when using `auto`:

- The `auto` specifier is only a placeholder for the type, not for the `const/volatile` and references specifiers. If you need a `const/volatile` and/or reference type, then you need to specify them explicitly. In the following example, `foo.get()` returns a reference to `int`; when variable x is initialized from the return value, the type deduced by the compiler is `int`, and not `int&`. Therefore, any change to x will not propagate to `foo.x_`. In order to do so, one should use `auto&`:

```cpp
class foo {
   int x_;
public:
   foo(int const x = 0) :x_{ x } {}
   int& get() { return x_; }
};

foo f(42);
auto x = f.get();
x = 100;
std::cout << f.get() << std::endl; // prints 42
```

- It is not possible to use `auto` for types that are not moveable:

```cpp
auto ai = std::atomic<int>(42); // error
```

- It is not possible to use auto for multi-word types, such as `long long`, `long double`, or `struct foo`. However, in the first case, the possible workarounds are to use literals or type aliases; as for the second, using `struct/class` in that form is only supported in C++ for C compatibility and should be avoided anyways:

```cpp
auto l1 = long long{ 42 }; // error
auto l2 = llong{ 42 };     // OK
auto l3 = 42LL;            // OK
```

- If you use the `auto` specifier but still need to know the type, you can do so in any IDE by putting the cursor over a variable, for instance. If you leave the IDE, however, that is not possible anymore, and the only way to know the actual type is to deduce it yourself from the initialization expression, which could probably mean searching through the code for function return types.

The `auto` can be used to specify the return type from a function. In C++11, this requires a trailing return type in the function declaration. In C++14, this has been relaxed, and the type of the return value is deduced by the compiler from the `return` expression. If there are multiple return values they should have the same type:

```cpp
// C++11
auto func1(int const i) -> int
{ return 2*i; }

// C++14
auto func2(int const i)
{ return 2*i; }
```

As mentioned earlier, `auto` does not retain `const`/`volatile` and reference qualifiers. This leads to problems with `auto` as a placeholder for the return type from a function. To explain this, let us consider the preceding example with `foo.get()`. This time we have a wrapper function called `proxy_get()` that takes a reference to a `foo`, calls `get()`, and returns the value returned by `get()`, which is an `int&`. However, the compiler will deduce the return type of `proxy_get()` as being `int`, not `int&`. Trying to assign that value to an `int&` fails with an error:

```
class foo
{
   int x_;
public:
   foo(int const x = 0) :x_{ x } {}
   int& get() { return x_; }
};

auto proxy_get(foo& f) { return f.get(); }

auto f = foo{ 42 };
auto& x = proxy_get(f); // cannot convert from 'int' to 'int &'
```

To fix this, we need to actually return `auto&`. However, this is a problem with templates and perfect forwarding the return type without knowing whether that is a value or a reference. The solution to this problem in C++14 is `decltype(auto)` that will correctly deduce the type:

```
decltype(auto) proxy_get(foo& f) { return f.get(); }
auto f = foo{ 42 };
decltype(auto) x = proxy_get(f);
```

The last important case where `auto` can be used is with lambdas. As of C++14, both lambda return type and lambda parameter types can be `auto`. Such a lambda is called a *generic lambda* because the closure type defined by the lambda has a templated call operator. The following shows a generic lambda that takes two `auto` parameters and returns the result of applying `operator+` on the actual types:

```
auto ladd = [] (auto const a, auto const b) { return a + b; };
struct
{
   template<typename T, typename U>
   auto operator () (T const a, U const b) const { return a+b; }
} L;
```

This lambda can be used to add anything for which the `operator+` is defined. In the following example, we use the lambda to add two integers and to concatenate to `std::string` objects (using the C++14 user-defined literal `operator ""s`):

```
auto i = ladd(40, 2);              // 42
auto s = ladd("forty"s, "two"s);   // "fortytwo"s
```

## See also

- *Creating type aliases and alias templates*
- *Understanding uniform initialization*

# Creating type aliases and alias templates

In C++, it is possible to create synonyms that can be used instead of a type name. This is achieved by creating a `typedef` declaration. This is useful in several cases, such as creating shorter or more meaningful names for a type or names for function pointers. However, `typedef` declarations cannot be used with templates to create `template type aliases`. An `std::vector<T>`, for instance, is not a type (`std::vector<int>` is a type), but a sort of family of all types that can be created when the type placeholder `T` is replaced with an actual type.

In C++11, a type alias is a name for another already declared type, and an alias template is a name for another already declared template. Both of these types of aliases are introduced with a new `using` syntax.

## How to do it...

- Create type aliases with the form `using identifier = type-id` as in the following examples:

```
using byte    = unsigned char;
using pbyte   = unsigned char *;
using array_t = int[10];
using fn      = void(byte, double);

void func(byte b, double d) { /*...*/ }

byte b {42};
```

```
pbyte pb = new byte[10] {0};
array_t a{0,1,2,3,4,5,6,7,8,9};
fn* f = func;
```

- Create alias templates with the form `template<template-params-list>` `identifier = type-id` as in the following examples:

```
template <class T>
class custom_allocator { /* ... */};

template <typename T>
using vec_t = std::vector<T, custom_allocator<T>>;

vec_t<int>           vi;
vec_t<std::string>   vs;
```

For consistency and readability, you should do the following:

- Not mix `typedef` and `using` declarations for creating aliases.
- Use the `using` syntax to create names of function pointer types.

# How it works...

A `typedef` declaration introduces a synonym (or an alias in other words) for a type. It does not introduce another type (like a `class`, `struct`, `union`, or `enum` declaration). Type names introduced with a `typedef` declaration follow the same hiding rules as identifier names. They can also be redeclared, but only to refer to the same type (therefore, you can have valid multiple `typedef` declarations that introduce the same type name synonym in a translation unit as long as it is a synonym for the same type). The following are typical examples of `typedef` declarations:

```
typedef unsigned char     byte;
typedef unsigned char * pbyte;
typedef int               array_t[10];
typedef void(*fn)(byte, double);

template<typename T>
class foo {
  typedef T value_type;
};

typedef std::vector<int> vint_t;
```

A type alias declaration is equivalent to a `typedef` declaration. It can appear in a block scope, class scope, or namespace scope. According to C++11 paragraph 7.1.3.2:

> *A typedef-name can also be introduced by an alias-declaration. The identifier following the using keyword becomes a typedef-name and the optional attribute-specifier-seq following the identifier appertains to that typedef-name. It has the same semantics as if it were introduced by the typedef specifier. In particular, it does not define a new type and it shall not appear in the type-id.*

An alias-declaration is, however, more readable and more clear about the actual type that is aliased when it comes to creating aliases for array types and function pointer types. In the examples from the *How to do it...* section, it is easily understandable that `array_t` is a name for the type array of 10 integers, and `fn` is a name for a function type that takes two parameters of type `byte` and `double` and returns `void`. That is also consistent with the syntax for declaring `std::function` objects (for example, `std::function<void(byte, double)> f`).

The driving purpose of the new syntax is to define alias templates. These are templates which, when specialized, are equivalent to the result of substituting the template arguments of the alias template for the template parameters in the `type-id`.

It is important to take note of the following things:

- Alias templates cannot be partially or explicitly specialized.
- Alias templates are never deduced by template argument deduction when deducing a template parameter.
- The type produced when specializing an alias template is not allowed to directly or indirectly make use of its own type.

# Understanding uniform initialization

Brace-initialization is a uniform method for initializing data in C++11. For this reason, it is also called *uniform initialization*. It is arguably one of the most important features from C++11 that developers should understand and use. It removes previous distinctions between initializing fundamental types, aggregate and non-aggregate types, and arrays and standard containers.

# Getting ready

For continuing with this recipe, you need to be familiar with direct initialization that initializes an object from an explicit set of constructor arguments and copy initialization that initializes an object from another object. The following is a simple example of both types of initialization, but for further details, you should see additional resources:

```
std::string s1("test");   // direct initialization
std::string s2 = "test";  // copy initialization
```

# How to do it...

To uniformly initialize objects regardless of their type, use the brace-initialization form { } that can be used for both direct initialization and copy initialization. When used with brace initialization, these are called direct list and copy list initialization.

```
T object {other};    // direct list initialization
T object = {other};  // copy list initialization
```

Examples of uniform initialization are as follows:

- Standard containers:

```
std::vector<int> v { 1, 2, 3 };
std::map<int, std::string> m { {1, "one"}, { 2, "two" }};
```

- Dynamically allocated arrays:

```
int* arr2 = new int[3]{ 1, 2, 3 };
```

- Arrays:

```
int arr1[3] { 1, 2, 3 };
```

- Built-in types:

```
int i { 42 };
double d { 1.2 };
```

- User-defined types:

```
class foo
{
  int a_;
  double b_;
public:
```

```
        foo():a_(0), b_(0) {}
        foo(int a, double b = 0.0):a_(a), b_(b) {}
    };

    foo f1{};
    foo f2{ 42, 1.2 };
    foo f3{ 42 };
```

- User-defined POD types:

```
    struct bar { int a_; double b_;};
    bar b{ 42, 1.2 };
```

# How it works...

Before C++11 objects required different types of initialization based on their type:

- Fundamental types could be initialized using assignment:

```
    int a = 42;
    double b = 1.2;
```

- Class objects could also be initialized using assignment from a single value if they had a conversion constructor (prior to C++11, a constructor with a single parameter was called a *conversion constructor*):

```
    class foo
    {
       int a_;
    public:
       foo(int a):a_(a) {}
    };
    foo f1 = 42;
```

- Non-aggregate classes could be initialized with parentheses (the functional form) when arguments were provided and only without any parentheses when default initialization was performed (call to the default constructor). In the next example, foo is the structure defined in the *How to do it...* section:

```
    foo f1;              // default initialization
    foo f2(42, 1.2);
    foo f3(42);
    foo f4();            // function declaration
```

- Aggregate and POD types could be initialized with brace-initialization. In the next example, `bar` is the structure defined in the *How to do it...* section:

```
bar b = {42, 1.2};
int a[] = {1, 2, 3, 4, 5};
```

Apart from the different methods of initializing the data, there are also some limitations. For instance, the only way to initialize a standard container was to first declare an object and then insert elements into it; vector was an exception because it is possible to assign values from an array that can be prior initialized using aggregate initialization. On the other hand, however, dynamically allocated aggregates could not be initialized directly.

All the examples in the *How to do it...* section use direct initialization, but copy initialization is also possible with brace-initialization. The two forms, direct and copy initialization, may be equivalent in most cases, but copy initialization is less permissive because it does not consider explicit constructors in its implicit conversion sequence that must produce an object directly from the initializer, whereas direct initialization expects an implicit conversion from the initializer to an argument of the constructor. Dynamically allocated arrays can only be initialized using direct initialization.

Of the classes shown in the preceding examples, `foo` is the one class that has both a default constructor and a constructor with parameters. To use the default constructor to perform default initialization, we need to use empty braces, that is, `{ }`. To use the constructor with parameters, we need to provide the values for all the arguments in braces `{ }`. Unlike non-aggregate types where default initialization means invoking the default constructor, for aggregate types, default initialization means initializing with zeros.

Initialization of standard containers, such as the vector and the map also shown above, is possible because all standard containers have an additional constructor in C++11 that takes an argument of type `std::initializer_list<T>`. This is basically a lightweight proxy over an array of elements of type `T const`. These constructors then initialize the internal data from the values in the initializer list.

The way the initialization using `std::initializer_list` works is the following:

- The compiler resolves the types of elements in the initialization list (all elements must have the same type).
- The compiler creates an array with the elements in the initializer list.
- The compiler creates an `std::initializer_list<T>` object to wrap the previously created array.
- The `std::initializer_list<T>` object is passed as an argument to the constructor.

An initializer list always takes precedence over other constructors where brace-initialization is used. If such a constructor exists for a class, it will be called when brace-initialization is performed:

```
class foo
{
   int a_;
   int b_;
public:
   foo()  :a_(0),  b_(0)  {}

   foo(int  a,  int  b  =  0)  :a_(a),  b_(b)  {}
   foo(std::initializer_list<int>  l)  {}
};

foo f{ 1,  2 };  // calls constructor with initializer_list<int>
```

The precedence rule applies to any function, not just constructors. In the following example, two overloads of the same function exist. Calling the function with an initializer list resolves to a call to the overload with an std::initializer_list:

```
void func(int const a,  int const b,  int const c)
{
   std::cout << a << b << c << std::endl;
}

void func(std::initializer_list<int> const l)
{
   for  (auto const & e  :  l)
      std::cout << e << std::endl;
}

func({ 1,2,3 });  // calls second overload
```

This, however, has the potential of leading to bugs. Let's take, for example, the vector type. Among the constructors of the vector, there is one that has a single argument representing the initial number of elements to be allocated and another one that has an std::initializer_list as an argument. If the intention is to create a vector with a preallocated size, using the brace-initialization will not work, as the constructor with the std::initializer_list will be the best overload to be called:

```
std::vector<int> v {5};
```

The preceding code does not create a vector with five elements, but a vector with one element with a value 5. To be able to actually create a vector with five elements, initialization with the parentheses form must be used:

```
std::vector<int> v (5);
```

Another thing to note is that brace-initialization does not allow narrowing conversion. According to the C++ standard (refer to paragraph 8.5.4 of the standard), a narrowing conversion is an implicit conversion:

> *- From a floating-point type to an integer type*
> *- From long double to double or float, or from double to float, except where the source is a constant expression and the actual value after conversion is within the range of values that can be represented (even if it cannot be represented exactly)*
> *- From an integer type or unscoped enumeration type to a floating-point type, except where the source is a constant expression and the actual value after conversion will fit into the target type and will produce the original value when converted to its original type*
> *- From an integer type or unscoped enumeration type to an integer type that cannot represent all the values of the original type, except where the source is a constant expression and the actual value after conversion will fit into the target type and will produce the original value when converted to its original type.*

The following declarations trigger compiler errors because they require a narrowing conversion:

```
int i{ 1.2 };              // error

double d = 47 / 13;
float f1{ d };             // error
float f2{47/13};           // OK
```

To fix the error, an explicit conversion must be done:

```
int i{ static_cast<int>(1.2) };

double d = 47 / 13;
float f1{ static_cast<float>(d) };
```

A brace-initialization list is not an expression and does not have a type. Therefore, `decltype` cannot be used on a brace-init list, and template type deduction cannot deduce the type that matches a brace-init list.

# There's more

The following sample shows several examples of direct-list-initialization and copy-list-initialization. In C++11, the deduced type of all these expressions is `std::initializer_list<int>`.

```
auto a = {42};   // std::initializer_list<int>
auto b {42};     // std::initializer_list<int>
auto c = {4, 2}; // std::initializer_list<int>
auto d {4, 2};   // std::initializer_list<int>
```

C++17 has changed the rules for list initialization, differentiating between the direct- and copy-list-initialization. The new rules for type deduction are as follows:

- for copy list initialization auto deduction will deduce a `std::initializer_list<T>` if all elements in the list have the same type, or be ill-formed.
- for direct list initialization auto deduction will deduce a `T` if the list has a single element, or be ill-formed if there is more than one element.

Base on the new rules, the previous examples would change as follows: a and c are deduced as `std::initializer_list<int>`; b is deduced as an `int`; d, which uses direct initialization and has more than one value in the brace-init-list, triggers a compiler error.

```
auto a = {42};   // std::initializer_list<int>
auto b {42};     // int
auto c = {4, 2}; // std::initializer_list<int>
auto d {4, 2};   // error, too many
```

# See also

- *Using auto whenever possible*
- *Understanding the various forms of non-static member initialization*

# Understanding the various forms of non-static member initialization

Constructors are a place where non-static class member initialization is done. Many developers prefer assignments in the constructor body. Aside from the several exceptional cases when that is actually necessary, initialization of non-static members should be done in the constructor's initializer list or, as of C++11, using default member initialization when they are declared in the class. Prior to C++11, constants and non-constant non-static data members of a class had to be initialized in the constructor. Initialization on declaration in a class was only possible for static constants. As we will see further, this limitation was removed in C++11 that allows initialization of non-statics in the class declaration. This initialization is called *default member initialization* and is explained in the next sections.

This recipe will explore the ways the non-static member initialization should be done.

## How to do it...

To initialize non-static members of a class you should:

- Use default member initialization for providing default values for members of classes with multiple constructors that would use a common initializer for those members (see [3] and [4] in the following code).
- Use default member initialization for constants, both static and non-static (see [1] and [2] in the following code).
- Use the constructor initializer list to initialize members that don't have default values, but depend on constructor parameters (see [5] and [6] in the following code).
- Use assignment in constructors when the other options are not possible (examples include initializing data members with pointer this, checking constructor parameter values, and throwing exceptions prior to initializing members with those values or self-references of two non-static data members).

The following example shows these forms of initialization:

```
struct Control
{
  const int DefaultHeigh = 14;                   // [1]
  const int DefaultWidth = 80;                   // [2]

  TextVAligment valign = TextVAligment::Middle;  // [3]
  TextHAligment halign = TextHAligment::Left;    // [4]
```

```
    std::string text;

    Control(std::string const & t) : text(t)          // [5]
    {}

    Control(std::string const & t,
        TextVerticalAligment const va,
        TextHorizontalAligment const ha):
    text(t), valign(va), halign(ha)                    // [6]
    {}
};
```

# How it works...

Non-static data members are supposed to be initialized in the constructor's initializer list as shown in the following example:

```
struct Point
{
  double X, Y;
  Point(double const x = 0.0, double const y = 0.0) : X(x), Y(y)   {}
};
```

Many developers, however, do not use the initializer list, but prefer assignments in the constructor's body, or even mix assignments and the initializer list. That could be for several reasons--for larger classes with many members, the constructor assignments may look easier to read than long initializer lists, perhaps split on many lines, or it could be because they are familiar with other programming languages that don't have an initializer list or because, unfortunately, for various reasons they don't even know about it.

 It is important to note that the order in which non-static data members are initialized is the order in which they were declared in the class definition, and not the order of their initialization in a constructor initializer list. On the other hand, the order in which non-static data members are destroyed is the reversed order of construction.

Using assignments in the constructor is not efficient, as this can create temporary objects that are later discarded. If not initialized in the initializer list, non-static members are initialized via their default constructor and then, when assigned a value in the constructor's body, the assignment operator is invoked. This can lead to inefficient work if the default constructor allocates a resource (such as memory or a file) and that has to be deallocated and reallocated in the assignment operator:

```
struct foo
{
  foo()
  { std::cout << "default constructor" << std::endl; }
  foo(std::string const & text)
  { std::cout << "constructor '" << text << "'" << std::endl; }
  foo(foo const & other)
  { std::cout << "copy constructor" << std::endl; }
  foo(foo&& other)
  { std::cout << "move constructor" << std::endl; };
  foo& operator=(foo const & other)
  { std::cout << "assignment" << std::endl; return *this; }
  foo& operator=(foo&& other)
  { std::cout << "move assignment" << std::endl; return *this;}
  ~foo()
  { std::cout << "destructor" << std::endl; }
};

struct bar
{
  foo f;

  bar(foo const & value)
  {
    f = value;
  }
};

foo f;
bar b(f);
```

The preceding code produces the following output showing how data member `f` is first default initialized and then assigned a new value:

```
default constructor
default constructor
assignment
destructor
destructor
```

Changing the initialization from the assignment in the constructor body to the initializer list replaces the calls to the default constructor plus assignment operator with a call to the copy constructor:

```
bar(foo const & value) : f(value) { }
```

Adding the preceding line of code produces the following output:

```
default constructor
copy constructor
destructor
destructor
```

For those reasons, at least for other types than the built-in types (such as `bool`, `char`, `int`, `float`, `double` or pointers), you should prefer the constructor initializer list. However, to be consistent with your initialization style, you should always prefer the constructor initializer list when that is possible. There are several situations when using the initializer list is not possible; these include the following cases (but the list could be expanded with other cases):

- If a member has to be initialized with a pointer or reference to the object that contains it, using the `this` pointer in the initialization list may trigger a warning with some compilers that it is used before the object is constructed.
- If you have two data members that must contain references to each other.
- If you want to test an input parameter and throw an exception before initializing a non-static data member with the value of the parameter.

Starting with C++11, non-static data members can be initialized when declared in the class. This is called *default member initialization* because it is supposed to represent initialization with default values. Default member initialization is intended for constants and for members that are not initialized based on constructor parameters (in other words members whose value does not depend on the way the object is constructed):

```cpp
enum class TextFlow { LeftToRight, RightToLeft };

struct Control
{
   const int DefaultHeight = 20;
   const int DefaultWidth = 100;

   TextFlow textFlow = TextFlow::LeftToRight;
   std::string text;

   Control(std::string t) : text(t)
   {}
};
```

In the preceding example, `DefaultHeight` and `DefaultWidth` are both constants; therefore, the values do not depend on the way the object is constructed, so they are initialized when declared. The `textFlow` object is a non-constant non-static data member whose value also does not depend on the way the object is initialized (it could be changed via another member function), therefore, it is also initialized using default member initialization when it is declared. `text`, on the other hand, is also a non-constant non-static data member, but its initial value depends on the way the object is constructed and therefore it is initialized in the constructor's initializer list using a value passed as an argument to the constructor.

If a data member is initialized both with the default member initialization and constructor initializer list, the latter takes precedence and the default value is discarded. To exemplify this, let's again consider the `foo` class earlier and the following `bar` class that uses it:

```cpp
struct bar
{
   foo f{"default value"};

   bar() : f{"constructor initializer"}
   {
   }
};

bar b;
```

The output differs, in this case, as follows, because the value from the default initializer list is discarded, and the object is not initialized twice:

```
constructor
constructor initializer
destructor
```

Using the appropriate initialization method for each member leads not only to more efficient code but also to better organized and more readable code.

# Controlling and querying object alignment

C++11 provides standardized methods for specifying and querying the alignment requirements of a type (something that was previously possible only through compiler-specific methods). Controlling the alignment is important in order to boost performance on different processors and enable the use of some instructions that only work with data on particular alignments. For example, Intel SSE and Intel SSE2 require 16 bytes alignment of data, whereas for Intel Advanced Vector Extensions (or Intel AVX), it is highly recommended to use 32 bytes alignment. This recipe explores the `alignas` specifier for controlling the alignment requirements and the `alignof` operator that retrieves the alignment requirements of a type.

## Getting ready

You should be familiar with what data alignment is and the way the compiler performs default data alignment. However, basic information about the latter is provided in the *How it works...* section.

## How to do it...

- To control the alignment of a type (both at the class level or data member level) or an object, use the `alignas` specifier:

```
struct alignas(4) foo
{
  char a;
  char b;
```

```
};
struct bar
{
  alignas(2) char a;
  alignas(8) int  b;
};
alignas(8)   int a;
alignas(256) long b[4];
```

- To query the alignment of a type, use the `alignof` operator:

```
auto align = alignof(foo);
```

# How it works...

Processors do not access memory one byte at a time, but in larger chunks of powers of twos (2, 4, 8, 16, 32, and so on). Owing to this, it is important that compilers align data in memory so that it can be easily accessed by the processor. Should this data be misaligned, the compiler has to do extra work for accessing data; it has to read multiple chunks of data, shift, and discard unnecessary bytes and combine the rest together.

C++ compilers align variables based on the size of their data type: 1 byte for `bool` and `char`, 2 bytes for `short`, 4 bytes for `int`, `long` and `float`, 8 bytes for `double` and `long long`, and so on. When it comes to structures or unions, the alignment must match the size of the largest member in order to avoid performance issues. To exemplify, let's consider the following data structures:

```
struct foo1     // size = 1, alignment = 1
{
  char a;
};

struct foo2     // size = 2, alignment = 1
{
  char a;
  char b;
};

struct foo3     // size = 8, alignment = 4
{
  char a;
  int  b;
};
```

`foo1` and `foo2` have different sizes, but the alignment is the same--that is, 1--because all data members are of type `char`, which has a size of 1. In structure `foo3`, the second member is an integer, whose size is 4. As a result, the alignment of members of this structure is done at addresses that are multiples of 4. To achieve that, the compiler introduces padding bytes. The structure `foo3` is actually transformed into the following:

```
struct foo3_
{
  char a;          // 1 byte
  char _pad0[3]; // 3 bytes padding to put b on a 4-byte boundary
  int  b;          // 4 bytes
};
```

Similarly, the following structure has a size of 32 bytes and an alignment of 8; that is because the largest member is a `double` whose size is 8. This structure, however, requires padding in several places to make sure that all members can be accessed at addresses that are multiples of 8:

```
struct foo4
{
  int a;
  char b;
  float c;
  double d;
  bool e;
};
```

The equivalent structure created by the compiler is as follows:

```
struct foo4_
{
  int a;            // 4 bytes
  char b;           // 1 byte
  char _pad0[3]; // 3 bytes padding to put c on a 8-byte boundary
  float c;          // 4 bytes
  char _pad1[4]; // 4 bytes padding to put d on a 8-byte boundary
  double d;         // 8 bytes
  bool e;           // 1 byte
  char _pad2[7]; // 7 bytes padding to make sizeof struct multiple of 8
};
```

In C++11, specifying the alignment of an object or type is done using the `alignas` specifier. This can take either an expression (an integral constant expression that evaluates to 0 or a valid value for an alignment), a type-id, or a parameter pack. The `alignas` specifier can be applied to the declaration of a variable or a class data member that does not represent a bit field, or to the declaration of a class, union, or enumeration. The type or object on which an `alignas` specification is applied will have the alignment requirement equal to the largest, greater than zero, expression of all `alignas` specifications used in the declaration.

There are several restrictions when using the `alignas` specifier:

- The only valid alignments are the powers of two ( 1, 2, 4, 8, 16, 32, and so on). Any other values are illegal, and the program is considered ill-formed; that doesn't necessarily have to produce an error, as the compiler may choose to ignore the specification.
- An alignment of 0 is always ignored.
- If the largest `alignas` on a declaration is smaller than the natural alignment without any `alignas` specifier, then the program is also considered ill-formed.

In the following example, the `alignas` specifier is applied on a class declaration. The natural alignment without the `alignas` specifier would have been 1, but with `alignas(4)` it becomes 4:

```
struct alignas(4) foo
{
   char a;
   char b;
};
```

In other words, the compiler transforms the preceding class into the following:

```
struct foo
{
   char a;
   char b;
   char _pad0[2];
};
```

The `alignas` specifier can be applied both on the class declaration and the member data declarations. In this case, the strictest (that is, largest) value wins. In the following example, member a has a natural size of 1 and requires an alignment of 2; member b has a natural size of 4 and requires an alignment of 8, therefore, the strictest alignment would be 8. The alignment requirement of the entire class is 4, which is weaker (that is, smaller) than the strictest required alignment and therefore it will be ignored, though the compiler will produce a warning:

```
struct alignas(4)  foo
{
   alignas(2)  char a;
   alignas(8)  int   b;
};
```

The result is a structure that looks like this:

```
struct foo
{
   char a;
   char _pad0[7];
   int b;
   char _pad1[4];
};
```

The `alignas` specifier can also be applied on variables. In the next example, variable a, that is an integer, is required to be placed in memory at a multiple of 8. The next variable, the array of 4 a, that is an integer, is required to be placed in memory at a multiple of 8. The next variable, the array of 4 `longs`, is required to be placed in memory at a multiple of 256. As a result, the compiler will introduce up to 244 bytes of padding between the two variables (depending on where in memory, at an address multiple of 8, the variable a is located):

```
alignas(8)    int a;
alignas(256)  long b[4];

printf("%pn", &a); // eg. 0000006C0D9EF908
printf("%pn", &b); // eg. 0000006C0D9EFA00
```

Looking at the addresses, we can see that the address of a is indeed a multiple of 8, and the address of b is a multiple of 256 (hexadecimal 100).

To query the alignment of a type, we use the `alignof` operator. Unlike `sizeof`, this operator can only be applied to type-ids, and not on variables or class data members. The types on which it can be applied can be complete types, an array type, or a reference type. For arrays, the value returned is the alignment of the element type; for references, the value returned is the alignment of the referenced type. Here are several examples:

| Expression | Evaluation |
|---|---|
| `alignof(char)` | 1, because the natural alignment of `char` is 1 |
| `alignof(int)` | 4, because the natural alignment of `int` is 4 |
| `alignof(int*)` | 4 on 32-bit, 8 on 64-bit, the alignment for pointers |
| `alignof(int[4])` | 4, because the natural alignment of the element type is 4 |
| `alignof(foo&)` | 8, because the specified alignment for class `foo` that is the referred type (as shown in the last example) was 8 |

# Using scoped enumerations

Enumeration is a basic type in C++ that defines a collection of values, always of an integral underlying type. Their named values, that are constant, are called enumerators. Enumerations declared with keyword `enum` are called *unscoped enumerations* and enumerations declared with `enum class` or `enum struct` are called *scoped enumerations*. The latter ones were introduced in C++11 and are intended to solve several problems of the unscoped enumerations.

## How to do it...

- Prefer to use scoped enumerations instead of unscoped ones.
- In order to use scoped enumerations, you should declare enumerations using `enum class` or `enum struct`:

```
enum class Status { Unknown, Created, Connected };
Status s = Status::Created;
```

 The `enum class` and `enum struct` declarations are equivalent, and throughout this recipe and the rest of the book, we will use `enum class`.

# How it works...

Unscoped enumerations have several issues that are creating problems for developers:

- They export their enumerators to the surrounding scope (for which reason, they are called unscoped enumerations), and that has the following two drawbacks: it can lead to name clashes if two enumerations in the same namespace have enumerators with the same name, and it's not possible to use an enumerator using its fully qualified name:

    ```
    enum Status {Unknown, Created, Connected};
    enum Codes {OK, Failure, Unknown};    // error
    auto status = Status::Created;        // error
    ```

- Prior to C++ 11, they could not specify the underlying type that is required to be an integral type. This type must not be larger than `int`, unless the enumerator value cannot fit a signed or unsigned integer. Owing to this, forward declaration of enumerations was not possible. The reason was that the size of the enumeration was not known since the underlying type was not known until values of the enumerators were defined so that the compiler could pick the appropriate integer type. This has been fixed in C++11.

- Values of enumerators implicitly convert to `int`. That means you can intentionally or accidentally mix enumerations that have a certain meaning and integers (that may not even be related to the meaning of the enumeration) and the compiler will not be able to warn you:

    ```
    enum Codes { OK, Failure };
    void include_offset(int pixels) {/*...*/}
    include_offset(Failure);
    ```

The scoped enumerations are basically strongly typed enumerations that behave differently than the unscoped enumerations:

- They do not export their enumerators to the surrounding scope. The two enumerations shown earlier would change to the following, no longer generating a name collision and being possible to fully qualify the names of the enumerators:

    ```
    enum class Status { Unknown, Created, Connected };
    enum class Codes { OK, Failure, Unknown }; // OK
    Codes code = Codes::Unknown;               // OK
    ```

- You can specify the underlying type. The same rules for underlying types of unscoped enumerations apply to scoped enumerations too, except that the user can specify explicitly the underlying type. This also solves the problem with forward declarations since the underlying type can be known before the definition is available:

```
enum class Codes : unsigned int;

void print_code(Codes const code) {}

enum class Codes : unsigned int
{
    OK = 0,
    Failure = 1,
    Unknown = 0xFFFF0000U
};
```

- Values of scoped enumerations no longer convert implicitly to `int`. Assigning the value of an `enum class` to an integer variable would trigger a compiler error unless an explicit cast is specified:

```
Codes c1 = Codes::OK;                      // OK
int c2 = Codes::Failure;                   // error
int c3 = static_cast<int>(Codes::Failure); // OK
```

# Using override and final for virtual methods

Unlike other similar programming languages, C++ does not have a specific syntax for declaring interfaces (that are basically classes with pure virtual methods only) and also has some deficiencies related to how virtual methods are declared. In C++, the virtual methods are introduced with the `virtual` keyword. However, the keyword `virtual` is optional for declaring overrides in derived classes that can lead to confusion when dealing with large classes or hierarchies. You may need to navigate throughout the hierarchy up to the base to figure out whether a function is virtual or not. On the other hand, sometimes, it is useful to make sure that a virtual function or even a derived class can no longer be overridden or derived further. In this recipe, we will see how to use C++11 special identifiers `override` and `final` to declare virtual functions or classes.

# Getting ready

You should be familiar with inheritance and polymorphism in C++ and concepts, such as abstract classes, pure specifiers, virtual, and overridden methods.

# How to do it...

To ensure correct declaration of virtual methods both in base and derived classes, but also increase readability, do the following:

- Always use the `virtual` keyword when declaring virtual functions in derived classes that are supposed to override virtual functions from a base class, and
- Always use the `override` special identifier after the declarator part of a virtual function declaration or definition.

```
class Base
{
  virtual void foo() = 0;
  virtual void bar() {}
  virtual void foobar() = 0;
};

void Base::foobar() {}

class Derived1 : public Base
{
  virtual void foo() override = 0;
  virtual void bar() override {}
  virtual void foobar() override {}
};

class Derived2 : public Derived1
{
  virtual void foo() override {}
};
```

 The declarator is the part of the type of a function that excludes the return type.

To ensure that functions cannot be overridden further or classes cannot be derived any more, use the `final` special identifier:

- After the declarator part of a virtual function declaration or definition to prevent further overrides in a derived class:

```
class Derived2 : public Derived1
{
  virtual void foo() final {}
};
```

- After the name of a class in the declaration of the class to prevent further derivations of the class:

```
class Derived4 final : public Derived1
{
  virtual void foo() override {}
};
```

# How it works...

The way `override` works is very simple; in a virtual function declaration or definition, it ensures that the function is actually overriding a base class function, otherwise, the compiler will trigger an error.

It should be noted that both `override` and `final` keywords are special identifiers having a meaning only in a member function declaration or definition. They are not reserved keywords and can still be used elsewhere in a program as user-defined identifiers.

Using the `override` special identifier helps the compiler to detect situations when a virtual method does not override another one like shown in the following example:

```
class Base
{
public:
  virtual void foo() {}
  virtual void bar() {}
};

class Derived1 : public Base
{
public:
  void foo() override {}
  // for readability use the virtual keyword
```

```
    virtual void bar(char const c) override {}
    // error, no Base::bar(char const)
};
```

The other special identifier, `final`, is used in a member function declaration or definition to indicate that the function is virtual and cannot be overridden in a derived class. If a derived class attempts to override the virtual function, the compiler triggers an error:

```
class Derived2 : public Derived1
{
  virtual void foo() final {}
};

class Derived3 : public Derived2
{
  virtual void foo() override {} // error
};
```

The `final` specifier can also be used in a class declaration to indicate that it cannot be derived:

```
class Derived4 final : public Derived1
{
  virtual void foo() override {}
};

class Derived5 : public Derived4 // error
{
};
```

Since both `override` and `final` have this special meaning when used in the defined context and are not in fact reserved keywords, you can still use them anywhere elsewhere in the C++ code. This ensured that existing code written before C++11 did not break because of the use of these names for identifiers:

```
class foo
{
  int final = 0;
  void override() {}
};
```

# Using range-based for loops to iterate on a range

Many programming languages support a variant of a `for` loop called `for each`, that is, repeating a group of statements over the elements of a collection. C++ did not have core language support for this until C++11. The closest feature was the general purpose algorithm from the standard library called `std::for_each`, that applies a function to all the elements in a range. C++11 brought language support for `for each` that is actually called *range-based for loops*. The new C++17 standard provides several improvements to the original language feature.

## Getting ready

In C++11, a range-based for loop has the following general syntax:

```
for ( range_declaration : range_expression ) loop_statement
```

To exemplify the various ways of using a range-based for loops, we will use the following functions that return sequences of elements:

```cpp
std::vector<int> getRates()
{
   return std::vector<int> {1, 1, 2, 3, 5, 8, 13};
}

std::multimap<int, bool> getRates2()
{
   return std::multimap<int, bool> {
      { 1, true },
      { 1, true },
      { 2, false },
      { 3, true },
      { 5, true },
      { 8, false },
      { 13, true }
   };
}
```

# How to do it...

Range-based for loops can be used in various ways:

- By committing to a specific type for the elements of the sequence:

```
auto rates = getRates();
for (int rate : rates)
   std::cout << rate << std::endl;
for (int& rate : rates)
   rate *= 2;
```

- By not specifying a type and letting the compiler deduce it:

```
for (auto&& rate : getRates())
   std::cout << rate << std::endl;

for (auto & rate : rates)
   rate *= 2;

for (auto const & rate : rates)
   std::cout << rate << std::endl;
```

- By using structured bindings and decomposition declaration in C++17:

```
for (auto&& [rate, flag] : getRates2())
   std::cout << rate << std::endl;
```

# How it works...

The expression for the range-based for loops shown earlier in the *How to do it...* section is basically syntactic sugar as the compiler transforms it into something else. Before C++17, the code generated by the compiler used to be the following:

```
{
  auto && __range = range_expression;
  for (auto __begin = begin_expr, __end = end_expr;
  __begin != __end; ++__begin) {
    range_declaration = *__begin;
    loop_statement
  }
}
```

What `begin_expr` and `end_expr` are in this code depends on the type of the range:

- For C-like arrays: `__range` and `__range + __bound` (where `__bound` is the number of elements in the array)
- For a class type with `begin` and `end` members (regardless of their type and accessibility): `__range.begin()` and `__range.end()`.
- For others it is `begin(__range)` and `end(__range)` that are determined via argument-dependent lookup.

It is important to note that if a class contains any members (function, data member, or enumerators) called `begin` or `end`, regardless of their type and accessibility, they will be picked for `begin_expr` and `end_expr`. Therefore, such a class type cannot be used in range-based for loops.

In C++17, the code generated by the compiler is slightly different:

```
{
  auto && __range = range_expression;
  auto __begin = begin_expr;
  auto __end = end_expr;
  for (; __begin != __end; ++__begin) {
    range_declaration = *__begin;
    loop_statement
  }
}
```

The new standard has removed the constraint that the begin expression and end expression must have the same type. The end expression does not need to be an actual iterator, but it has to be able to be compared for inequality with an iterator. A benefit of this is that the range can be delimited by a predicate.

# See also

- *Enabling range-based for loops for custom types*

# Enabling range-based for loops for custom types

As we have seen in the preceding recipe, the range-based for loops, known as `for each` in other programming languages, allows you to iterate over the elements of a range, providing a simplified syntax over the standard `for` loops and making the code more readable in many situations. However, range-based for loops do not work out of the box with any type representing a range, but require the presence of a `begin()` and `end()` function (for non-array types) either as a member or free function. In this recipe, we will see how to enable a custom type to be used in range-based for loops.

# Getting ready

It is recommended that you read the recipe *Using range-based for loops to iterate on a range* before continuing with this one if you need to understand how range-based for loops work and what is the code the compiler generates for such a loop.

To show how we can enable range-based for loops for custom types representing sequences, we will use the following implementation of a simple array:

```cpp
template <typename T, size_t const Size>
class dummy_array
{
  T data[Size] = {};

public:
  T const & GetAt(size_t const index) const
  {
    if (index < Size) return data[index];
    throw std::out_of_range("index out of range");
  }

  void SetAt(size_t const index, T const & value)
  {
    if (index < Size) data[index] = value;
    else throw std::out_of_range("index out of range");
  }

  size_t GetSize() const { return Size; }
};
```

The purpose of this recipe is to enable writing code like the following:

```
dummy_array<int, 3> arr;
arr.SetAt(0, 1);
arr.SetAt(1, 2);
arr.SetAt(2, 3);

for(auto&& e : arr)
{
   std::cout << e << std::endl;
}
```

# How to do it...

To enable a custom type to be used in range-based `for` loops, you need to do the following:

- Create mutable and constant iterators for the type that must implement the following operators:
  - `operator++` for incrementing the iterator.
  - `operator*` for dereferencing the iterator and accessing the actual element pointed by the iterator.
  - `operator!=` for comparing with another iterator for inequality.

- Provide free `begin()` and `end()` functions for the type.

Given the earlier example of a simple range, we need to provide the following:

1. The following minimal implementation of an iterator class:

```
template <typename T, typename C, size_t const Size>
class dummy_array_iterator_type
{
public:
  dummy_array_iterator_type(C& collection,
                            size_t const index) :
    index(index), collection(collection)
    { }

  bool operator!= (dummy_array_iterator_type const & other) const
  {
     return index != other.index;
  }

  T const & operator* () const
  {
```

```
      return collection.GetAt(index);
    }

    dummy_array_iterator_type const & operator++ ()
    {
      ++index;
      return *this;
    }

  private:
    size_t    index;
    C&        collection;
};
```

2. Alias templates for mutable and constant iterators:

```
template <typename T, size_t const Size>
using dummy_array_iterator =
    dummy_array_iterator_type<
      T, dummy_array<T, Size>, Size>;

template <typename T, size_t const Size>
using dummy_array_const_iterator =
    dummy_array_iterator_type<
      T, dummy_array<T, Size> const, Size>;
```

3. Free `begin()` and `end()` functions that return the corresponding begin and end iterators, with overloads for both alias templates:

```
template <typename T, size_t const Size>
inline dummy_array_iterator<T, Size> begin(
  dummy_array<T, Size>& collection)
{
  return dummy_array_iterator<T, Size>(collection, 0);
}

template <typename T, size_t const Size>
inline dummy_array_iterator<T, Size> end(
  dummy_array<T, Size>& collection)
{
  return dummy_array_iterator<T, Size>(
    collection, collection.GetSize());
}

template <typename T, size_t const Size>
inline dummy_array_const_iterator<T, Size> begin(
  dummy_array<T, Size> const & collection)
{
```

```
      return dummy_array_const_iterator<T, Size>(
        collection, 0);
  }

  template <typename T, size_t const Size>
  inline dummy_array_const_iterator<T, Size> end(
    dummy_array<T, Size> const & collection)
  {
    return dummy_array_const_iterator<T, Size>(
      collection, collection.GetSize());
  }
```

# How it works...

Having this implementation available, the range-based for loop shown earlier compiles and executes as expected. When performing argument-dependent lookup, the compiler will identify the two begin() and end() functions that we wrote (that take a reference to a dummy_array) and therefore the code it generates becomes valid.

In the preceding example, we have defined one iterator class template and two alias templates, called dummy_array_iterator and dummy_array_const_iterator. The begin() and end() functions both have two overloads for these two types of iterators. This is necessary so that the container we have considered could be used in range-based for loops with both constant and non-constant instances:

```
template <typename T, const size_t Size>
void print_dummy_array(dummy_array<T, Size> const & arr)
{
  for (auto && e : arr)
  {
    std::cout << e << std::endl;
  }
}
```

A possible alternative to enable range-based for loops for the simple range class we considered for this recipe is to provide member begin() and end() functions. In general, that could make sense only if you own and can modify the source code. On the other hand, the solution shown in this recipe works in all cases and should be preferred to other alternatives.

# See also

- *Creating type aliases and alias templates*

# Using explicit constructors and conversion operators to avoid implicit conversion

Before C++11, a constructor with a single parameter was considered a converting constructor. With C++11, every constructor without the `explicit` specifier is considered a converting constructor. Such a constructor defines an implicit conversion from the type or types of its arguments to the type of the class. Classes can also define converting operators that convert the type of the class to another specified type. All these are useful in some cases, but can create problems in other cases. In this recipe, we will see how to use explicit constructors and conversion operators.

# Getting ready

For this recipe, you need to be familiar with converting constructors and converting operators. In this recipe, you will learn how to write explicit constructors and conversion operators to avoid implicit conversions to and from a type. The use of explicit constructors and conversion operators (called *user-defined conversion functions*) enables the compiler to yield errors--that in some cases are coding errors--and allow developers to spot those errors quickly and fix them.

# How to do it...

To declare explicit constructors and conversion operators (regardless of whether they are functions or function templates), use the `explicit` specifier in the declaration.

The following example shows both an explicit constructor and a converting operator:

```
struct handle_t
{
  explicit handle_t(int const h) : handle(h) {}

  explicit operator bool() const { return handle != 0; };
private:
  int handle;
};
```

# How it works...

To understand why explicit constructors are necessary and how they work, we will first look at converting constructors. The following class has three constructors: a default constructor (without parameters), a constructor that takes an `int`, and a constructor that takes two parameters, an `int` and a `double`. They don't do anything, except printing a message. As of C++11, these are all considered converting constructors. The class also has a conversion operator that converts the type to a `bool`:

```
struct foo
{
  foo()
  { std::cout << "foo" << std::endl; }
  foo(int const a)
  { std::cout << "foo(a)" << std::endl; }
  foo(int const a, double const b)
  { std::cout << "foo(a, b)" << std::endl; }

  operator bool() const { return true; }
};
```

Based on this, the following definitions of objects are possible (note that the comments represent the console output):

```
foo f1;                // foo
foo f2 {};             // foo

foo f3(1);             // foo(a)
foo f4 = 1;            // foo(a)
foo f5 { 1 };          // foo(a)
foo f6 = { 1 };        // foo(a)

foo f7(1, 2.0);        // foo(a, b)
foo f8 { 1, 2.0 };     // foo(a, b)
foo f9 = { 1, 2.0 };   // foo(a, b)
```

`f1` and `f2` invoke the default constructor. `f3`, `f4`, `f5`, and `f6` invoke the constructor that takes an `int`. Note that all the definitions of these objects are equivalent, even if they look different (`f3` is initialized using the functional form, `f4` and `f6` are copy-initialized, and `f5` is directly initialized using brace-init-list). Similarly, `f7`, `f8`, and `f9` invoke the constructor with two parameters.

It may be important to note that if `foo` defines a constructor that takes an `std::initializer_list`, then all the initializations using `{}` would resolve to that constructor:

```
foo(std::initializer_list<int> l)
{ std::cout << "foo(l)" << std::endl; }
```

In this case, `f5` and `f6` will print `foo(l)`, while `f8` and `f9` will generate compiler errors because all elements of the initializer list should be integers.

These may all look right, but the implicit conversion constructors enable scenarios where the implicit conversion may not be what we wanted:

```
void bar(foo const f)
{
}

bar({});               // foo()
bar(1);                // foo(a)
bar({ 1, 2.0 });       // foo(a, b)
```

The conversion operator to `bool` in the example above also enables us to use `foo` objects where boolean values are expected:

```
bool flag = f1;
if(f2) {}
std::cout << f3 + f4 << std::endl;
if(f5 == f6) {}
```

The first two are examples where `foo` is expected to be used as boolean but the last two with addition and test for equality are probably incorrect, as we most likely expect to add `foo` objects and test `foo` objects for equality, not the booleans they implicitly convert to.

Perhaps a more realistic example to understand where problems could arise would be to consider a string buffer implementation. This would be a class that contains an internal buffer of characters. The class may provide several conversion constructors: a default constructor, a constructor that takes a `size_t` parameter representing the size of the buffer to preallocate, and a constructor that takes a pointer to `char` that should be used to allocate and initialize the internal buffer. Succinctly, such a string buffer could look like this:

```
class string_buffer
{
public:
  string_buffer() {}

  string_buffer(size_t const size) {}

  string_buffer(char const * const ptr) {}

  size_t size() const { return ...; }
  operator bool() const { return ...; }
  operator char * const () const { return ...; }
};
```

Based on this definition, we could construct the following objects:

```
std::shared_ptr<char> str;
string_buffer sb1;                // empty buffer
string_buffer sb2(20);            // buffer of 20 characters
string_buffer sb3(str.get());
// buffer initialized from input parameter
```

sb1 is created using the default constructor and thus has an empty buffer; sb2 is initialized using the constructor with a single parameter and the value of the parameter represents the size in characters of the internal buffer; sb3 is initialized with an existing buffer and that is used to define the size of the internal buffer and to copy its value into the internal buffer. However, the same definition also enables the following object definitions:

```
enum ItemSizes {DefaultHeight, Large, MaxSize};

string_buffer b4 = 'a';
string_buffer b5 = MaxSize;
```

In this case, b4 is initialized with a char. Since an implicit conversion to size_t exists, the constructor with a single parameter will be called. The intention here is not necessarily clear; perhaps it should have been "a" instead of 'a', in which case the third constructor would have been called. However, b5 is most likely an error, because MaxSize is an enumerator representing an ItemSizes and should have nothing to do with a string buffer size. These erroneous situations are not flagged by the compiler in any way.

Using the explicit specifier in the declaration of a constructor, that constructor becomes an explicit constructor and no longer allows implicit constructions of objects of a class type. To exemplify this, we will slightly change the string_buffer class earlier to declare all constructors explicit:

```
class string_buffer
{
public:
  explicit string_buffer() {}

  explicit string_buffer(size_t const size) {}

  explicit string_buffer(char const * const ptr) {}

  explicit operator bool() const { return ...; }
  explicit operator char * const () const { return ...; }
};
```

The change is minimal, but the definitions of b4 and b5 in the earlier example no longer work, and are incorrect, since the implicit conversion from char or int to size_t are no longer available during overload resolution to figure out what constructor should be called. The result is compiler errors for both b4 and b5. Note that b1, b2, and b3 are still valid definitions even if the constructors are explicit.

The only way to fix the problem, in this case, is to provide an explicit cast from char or int to string_buffer:

```
string_buffer b4 = string_buffer('a');
string_buffer b5 = static_cast<string_buffer>(MaxSize);
string_buffer b6 = string_buffer{ "a" };
```

With explicit constructors, the compiler is able to immediately flag erroneous situations and developers can react accordingly, either fixing the initialization with a correct value or providing an explicit cast.

> This is only the case when initialization is done with copy initialization and not when using the functional or universal initialization.

The following definitions are still possible (and wrong) with explicit constructors:

```
string_buffer b7{ 'a' };
string_buffer b8('a');
```

Similar to constructors, conversion operators can be declared explicit (as shown earlier). In this case, the implicit conversions from the object type to the type specified by the conversion operator are no longer possible and require an explicit cast. Considering b1 and b2, the string_buffer objects defined earlier, the following are no longer possible with explicit conversion operator bool:

```
std::cout << b1 + b2 << std::endl;
if(b1 == b2) {}
```

Instead, they require explicit conversion to bool:

```
std::cout << static_cast<bool>(b1) + static_cast<bool>(b2);
if(static_cast<bool>(b1) == static_cast<bool>(b2)) {}
```

# See also

- *Understanding uniform initialization*

# Using unnamed namespaces instead of static globals

The larger a program the greater the chances are you could run into name collisions with file locals when your program is linked. Functions or variables that are declared in a source file and are supposed to be local to the translation unit may collide with other similar functions or variables declared in another translation unit. That is because all symbols that are not declared static have external linkage and their names must be unique throughout the program. The typical C solution for this problem is to declare those symbols static, changing their linkage from external to internal and therefore making them local to a translation unit. In this recipe, we will look at the C++ solution for this problem.

## Getting ready

In this recipe, we will discuss concepts such as global functions, static functions, and variables, namespaces, and translation units. Apart from these, it is required that you understand the difference between internal and external linkage; that is key for this recipe.

## How to do it...

When you are in a situation where you need to declare global symbols as statics to avoid linkage problems, prefer to use unnamed namespaces:

1. Declare a namespace without a name in your source file.
2. Put the definition of the global function or variable in the unnamed namespace without making them `static`.

The following example shows two functions called `print()` in two different translation units; each of them is defined in an unnamed namespace:

```cpp
// file1.cpp
namespace
{
  void print(std::string message)
  {
    std::cout << "[file1] " << message << std::endl;
  }
}

void file1_run()
```

```
{
  print ("run");
}

// file2.cpp
namespace
{
  void print (std::string message)
  {
    std::cout << "[file2] " << message << std::endl;
  }
}

void file2_run ()
{
  print ("run");
}
```

# How it works...

When a function is declared in a translation unit, it has external linkage. That means two functions with the same name from two different translation units would generate a linkage error because it is not possible to have two symbols with the same name. The way this problem is solved in C, and by some in C++ also, is to declare the function or variable static and change its linkage from external to internal. In this case, its name is no longer exported outside the translation unit, and the linkage problem is avoided.

The proper solution in C++ is to use unnamed namespaces. When you define a namespace like the ones shown above, the compiler transforms it to the following:

```
// file1.cpp
namespace _unique_name_ {}
using namespace _unique_name_;
namespace _unique_name_
{
  void print (std::string message)
  {
    std::cout << "[file1] " << message << std::endl;
  }
}

void file1_run ()
{
  print ("run");
}
```

First of all, it declares a namespace with a unique name (what the name is and how it generates that name is a compiler implementation detail and should not be a concern). At this point, the namespace is empty, and the purpose of this line is to basically establish the namespace. Second, a using directive brings everything from the _unique_name_ namespace into the current namespace. Third, the namespace, with the compiler-generated name, is defined as it was in the original source code (when it had no name).

By defining the translation unit local print() functions in an unnamed namespace, they have local visibility only, yet their external linkage no longer produces linkage errors since they now have external unique names.

Unnamed namespaces are also working in a perhaps more obscure situation involving templates. Prior to C++11 template non-type arguments could not be names with internal linkage so using static variables was not possible. On the other hand, symbols in an unnamed namespace have external linkage and could be used as template arguments. Although this linkage restriction for template non-type arguments was lifted in C++11, it is still present in the latest version of the VC++ compiler. This problem is shown in the following example where declaring t1 produces a compiler error, because the non-type argument expression has internal linkage, but t2 is correct because Size2 has external linkage. (Note that compiling the code below with Clang and gcc do not produce any error.)

```
template <int const& Size>
class test {};

static int Size1 = 10;

namespace
{
    int Size2 = 10;
}

test<Size1> t1;
test<Size2> t2;
```

# See also

- *Using inline namespaces for symbol versioning*

# Using inline namespaces for symbol versioning

The C++11 standard has introduced a new type of namespace called *inline namespaces* that are basically a mechanism that makes declarations from a nested namespace look and act like they were part of the surrounding namespace. Inline namespaces are declared using the `inline` keyword in the namespace declaration (unnamed namespaces can also be inlined). This is a helpful feature for library versioning, and in this recipe, we will see how inline namespaces can be used for versioning symbols. From this recipe, you will learn how to version your source code using inline namespaces and conditional compilation.

## Getting ready

In this recipe, we will discuss namespaces and nested namespaces, templates and template specializations, and conditional compilation using preprocessor macros. Familiarity with these concepts is required in order to proceed with the recipe.

## How to do it...

To provide multiple versions of a library and let the user decide what version to use, do the following:

- Define the content of the library inside a namespace.
- Define each version of the library or parts of it inside an inner inline namespace.
- Use preprocessor macros and `#if` directives to enable a particular version of the library.

The following example shows a library that has two versions that clients can use:

```
namespace modernlib
{
  #ifndef LIB_VERSION_2
  inline namespace version_1
  {
    template<typename T>
    int test(T value) { return 1; }
  }
  #endif

  #ifdef LIB_VERSION_2
```

```
  inline namespace version_2
  {
    template<typename T>
    int test(T value) { return 2; }
  }
  #endif
}
```

# How it works...

A member of an inline namespace is treated as if it was a member of the surrounding namespace. Such a member can be partially specialized, explicitly instantiated, or explicitly specialized. This is a transitive property, which means that if a namespace A contains an inline namespace B that contains an inline namespace C, then the members of C appear as they were members of both B and A and the members of B appear as they were members of A.

To better understand why inline namespaces are helpful, let's consider the case of developing a library that evolves over time from a first version to a second version (and further on). This library defines all its types and functions under a namespace called modernlib. In the first version, this library could look like this:

```
namespace modernlib
{
  template<typename T>
  int test(T value) { return 1; }
}
```

A client of the library can make the following call and get back the value 1:

```
auto x = modernlib::test(42);
```

However, the client might decide to specialize the template function test() as the following:

```
struct foo { int a; };

namespace modernlib
{
  template<>
  int test(foo value) { return value.a; }
}

auto y = modernlib::test(foo{ 42 });
```

In this case, the value of y is no longer 1, but 42 because the user-specialized function gets called.

Everything is working correctly so far, but as a library developer you decide to create a second version of the library, yet still ship both the first and the second version and let the user control what to use with a macro. In this second version, you provide a new implementation of the test () function that no longer returns 1, but 2. To be able to provide both the first and second implementations, you put them in nested namespaces called version_1 and version_2 and conditionally compile the library using preprocessor macros:

```
namespace modernlib
{
  namespace version_1
  {
    template<typename T>
    int test(T value) { return 1; }
  }

  #ifndef LIB_VERSION_2
  using namespace version_1;
  #endif

  namespace version_2
  {
    template<typename T>
    int test(T value) { return 2; }
  }

  #ifdef LIB_VERSION_2
  using namespace version_2;
  #endif
}
```

Suddenly, the client code will break, regardless of whether it uses the first or second version of the library. That is because the test function is now inside a nested namespace, and the specialization for foo is done in the modernlib namespace, when it should actually be done in modernlib::version_1 or modernlib::version_2. This is because the specialization of a template is required to be done in the same namespace where the template was declared. In this case, the client needs to change the code like this:

```
#define LIB_VERSION_2

#include "modernlib.h"

struct foo { int a; };
```

```
namespace modernlib
{
  namespace version_2
  {
    template<>
    int test(foo value) { return value.a; }
  }
}
```

This is a problem because the library leaks implementation details, and the client needs to be aware of those in order do the template specialization. These internal details are hidden with inline namespaces in the manner shown in the *How to do it...* section of this recipe. With that definition of the modernlib library, the client code with the specialization of the test() function in the modernlib namespace is no longer broken, because either version_1::test() or version_2::test() (depending on what version the client is actually using) acts as being part of the enclosing modernlib namespace when template specialization is done. The details of the implementation are now hidden to the client that only sees the surrounding namespace modernlib.

However, you should keep in mind that:

- The namespace std is reserved for the standard and should never be inlined.
- A namespace should not be defined inline if it was not inline in its first definition.

# See also

- *Using unnamed namespaces instead of static globals*

# Using structured bindings to handle multi-return values

Returning multiple values from a function is something very common, yet there is no first-class solution in C++ to enable it directly. Developers have to choose between returning multiple values through reference parameters to a function, defining a structure to contain the multiple values or returning a `std::pair` or `std::tuple`. The first two use named variables that have the advantage that they clearly indicate the meaning of the return value, but have the disadvantage that they have to be explicitly defined. `std::pair` has its members called `first` and `second`, and `std::tuple` has unnamed members that can only be retrieved with a function call, but can be copied to named variables using `std::tie()`. None of these solutions is ideal.

C++17 extends the semantic use of `std::tie()` into a first-class core language feature that enables unpacking the values of a tuple to named variables. This feature is called *structured bindings*.

## Getting ready

For this recipe, you should be familiar with the standard utility types `std::pair` and `std::tuple` and the utility function `std::tie()`.

## How to do it...

To return multiple values from a function using a compiler that supports C++17 you should do the following:

1. Use an `std::tuple` for the return type.

   ```
   std::tuple<int, std::string, double> find()
   {
      return std::make_tuple(1, "marius", 1234.5);
   }
   ```

2. Use structured bindings to unpack the values of the tuple into named objects.

   ```
   auto [id, name, score] = find();
   ```

3. Use decomposition declaration to bind the returned values to variables inside an `if` statement or `switch` statement.

```
if (auto [id, name, score] = find(); score > 1000)
{
    std::cout << name << std::endl;
}
```

# How it works...

Structured bindings are a language feature that works just like `std::tie()`, except that we don't have to define named variables for each value that needs to be unpacked explicitly with `std::tie()`. With structured bindings, we define all named variables in a single definition using the `auto` specifier so that the compiler can infer the correct type for each variable.

To exemplify this, let's consider the case of inserting items in a `std::map`. The insert method returns a `std::pair` containing an iterator to the inserted element or the element that prevented the insertion, and a boolean indicating whether the insertion was successful or not. The following code is very explicit and the use of `second` or `first->second` makes the code harder to read because you need to constantly figure out what they represent:

```
std::map<int, std::string> m;

auto result = m.insert({ 1, "one" });
std::cout << "inserted = " << result.second << std::endl
          << "value = " << result.first->second << std::endl;
```

The preceding code can be made more readable with the use of `std::tie`, that unpacks tuples into individual objects (and works with `std::pair` because `std::tuple` has a converting assignment from `std::pair`):

```
std::map<int, std::string> m;
std::map<int, std::string>::iterator it;
bool inserted;

std::tie(it, inserted) = m.insert({ 1, "one" });
std::cout << "inserted = " << inserted << std::endl
          << "value = " << it->second << std::endl;

std::tie(it, inserted) = m.insert({ 1, "two" });
std::cout << "inserted = " << inserted << std::endl
          << "value = " << it->second << std::endl;
```

The code is not necessarily simpler because it requires defining in advance the objects that the pair is unpacked to. Similarly, the more elements the tuple has the more objects you need to define, but using named objects makes the code easier to read.

C++17 structured bindings elevate the unpacking of tuple elements into named objects to the rank of a language feature; it does not require the use of std::tie(), and objects are initialized when declared:

```
std::map<int, std::string> m;
{
  auto[it, inserted] = m.insert({ 1, "one" });
  std::cout << "inserted = " << inserted << std::endl
          << "value = " << it->second << std::endl;
}


{
  auto[it, inserted] = m.insert({ 1, "two" });
  std::cout << "inserted = " << inserted << std::endl
          << "value = " << it->second << std::endl;
}
```

The use of multiple blocks in the above example is necessary because variables cannot be redeclared in the same block, and structured bindings imply a declaration using the auto specifier. Therefore, if you need to make multiple calls like in the example above and use structured bindings you must either use different variable names or multiple blocks as shown above. An alternative to that is to avoid structured bindings and use std::tie(), because it can be called multiple times with the same variables, therefore you only need to declare them once.

In C++17, it is also possible to declare variables in if and switch statements with the form if(init; condition) and switch(init; condition). This could be combined with structured bindings to produce simpler code. In the following example, we attempt to insert a new value into a map. The result of the call is unpacked into two variables, it and inserted, defined in the scope of the if statement in the initialization part. The condition of the if statement is evaluated from the value of the inserted object:

```
if(auto [it, inserted] = m.insert({ 1, "two" }); inserted)
{ std::cout << it->second << std::endl; }
```

# Working with Numbers and Strings

9

The recipes included in this chapter are as follows:

- Converting between numeric and string types
- Limits and other properties of numeric types
- Generating pseudo-random numbers
- Initializing all bits of internal state of a pseudo-random number generator
- Using raw string literals to avoid escaping characters
- Creating cooked user-defined literals
- Creating raw user-defined literals
- Creating a library of string helpers
- Verifying the format of a string using regular expressions
- Parsing the content of a string using regular expressions
- Replacing the content of a string using regular expressions
- Using string_view instead of constant string references

# Converting between numeric and string types

Converting between number and string types is a ubiquitous operation. Prior to C++11, there was little support for converting numbers to strings and back, and developers had to resort mostly to type-unsafe functions and usually wrote their own utility functions in order to avoid writing the same code over and over again. With C++11, the standard library provides utility functions for converting between numbers and strings. In this recipe, you will learn how to convert between numbers and strings and the other way around using modern C++ standard functions.

## Getting ready

All the utility functions mentioned in this recipe are available in the `<string>` header.

## How to do it...

Use the following standard conversion functions when you need to convert between numbers and strings:

- To convert from an integer or floating point type to a string type, use `std::to_string()` or `std::to_wstring()` as shown in the following code snippet:

```
auto si = std::to_string(42);      // si="42"
auto sl = std::to_string(421);     // sl="42"
auto su = std::to_string(42u);     // su="42"
auto sd = std::to_wstring(42.0);   // sd=L"42.000000"
auto sld = std::to_wstring(42.0l); // sld=L"42.000000"
```

- To convert from a string type to an integer type, use `std::stoi()`, `std::stol()`, `std::stoll()`, `std::stoul()`, or `std::stoull()`; refer to the following code snippet:

```
auto i1 = std::stoi("42");             // i1 = 42
auto i2 = std::stoi("101010", nullptr, 2); // i2 = 42
auto i3 = std::stoi("052", nullptr, 8);   // i3 = 42
auto i4 = std::stoi("0x2A", nullptr, 16); // i4 = 42
```

- To convert from a string type to a floating point type, use `std::stof()`, `std::stod()`, or `std::stold()`, as shown in the following code snippet:

```
// d1 = 123.45000000000000
auto d1 = std::stod("123.45");
// d2 = 123.45000000000000
auto d2 = std::stod("1.2345e+2");
// d3 = 123.44999980926514
auto d3 = std::stod("0xF.6E6666p3");
```

# How it works...

To convert between an integral or floating point type to a string type, you can use either the `std::to_string()` or `std::to_wstring()` function. These functions are available in the `<string>` header and have overloads for signed and unsigned integer and real types. They produce the same result as `std::sprintf()` and `std::swprintf()` would produce when called with the appropriate format specifier for each type. The following code snippet list all the overloads of these two functions.

```
std::string to_string(int value);
std::string to_string(long value);
std::string to_string(long long value);
std::string to_string(unsigned value);
std::string to_string(unsigned long value);
std::string to_string(unsigned long long value);
std::string to_string(float value);
std::string to_string(double value);
std::string to_string(long double value);
std::wstring to_wstring(int value);
std::wstring to_wstring(long value);
std::wstring to_wstring(long long value);
std::wstring to_wstring(unsigned value);
std::wstring to_wstring(unsigned long value);
std::wstring to_wstring(unsigned long long value);
std::wstring to_wstring(float value);
std::wstring to_wstring(double value);
std::wstring to_wstring(long double value);
```

When it comes to the opposite conversion, there is an entire set of functions that have the name with the format **ston (string to number)**, where **n** stands for **i** (`integer`), **l** (`long`), **ll** (`long long`), **ul** (`unsigned long`), or **ull** (`unsigned long long`). The following listing shows all these functions, each of them with two overloads, one that takes an `std::string` and one that takes an `std::wstring` as the first parameter:

```
int stoi(const std::string& str, std::size_t* pos = 0,
         int base = 10);
int stoi(const std::wstring& str, std::size_t* pos = 0,
         int base = 10);
long stol(const std::string& str, std::size_t* pos = 0,
         int base = 10);
long stol(const std::wstring& str, std::size_t* pos = 0,
         int base = 10);
long long stoll(const std::string& str, std::size_t* pos = 0,
              int base = 10);
long long stoll(const std::wstring& str, std::size_t* pos = 0,
              int base = 10);
unsigned long stoul(const std::string& str, std::size_t* pos = 0,
              int base = 10);
unsigned long stoul(const std::wstring& str, std::size_t* pos = 0,
              int base = 10);
unsigned long long stoull(const std::string& str,
                     std::size_t* pos = 0, int base = 10);
unsigned long long stoull(const std::wstring& str,
                     std::size_t* pos = 0, int base = 10);
float       stof(const std::string& str, std::size_t* pos = 0);
float       stof(const std::wstring& str, std::size_t* pos = 0);
double      stod(const std::string& str, std::size_t* pos = 0);
double      stod(const std::wstring& str, std::size_t* pos = 0);
long double stold(const std::string& str, std::size_t* pos = 0);
long double stold(const std::wstring& str, std::size_t* pos = 0);
```

The way the string to integral type functions work is by discarding all white spaces before a non-whitespace character, then taking as many characters as possible to form a signed or unsigned number (depending on the case), and then converting that to the requested integral type (`stoi()` will return an `integer`, `stoul()` will return an `unsigned long`, and so on). In all the following examples, the result is integer 42, except for the last example where the result is -42:

```
auto i1 = std::stoi("42");          // i1 = 42
auto i2 = std::stoi("   42");       // i2 = 42
auto i3 = std::stoi("   42fortytwo");  // i3 = 42
auto i4 = std::stoi("+42");         // i4 = 42
auto i5 = std::stoi("-42");         // i5 = -42
```

A valid integral number may consist of the following parts:

- A sign, plus (+) or minus (–) (optional).
- Prefix 0 to indicate an octal base (optional).
- Prefix 0x or 0X to indicate a hexadecimal base (optional).
- A sequence of digits.

The optional prefix 0 (for octal) is applied only when the specified base is 8 or 0. Similarly, the optional prefix 0x or 0X (for hexadecimal) is applied only when the specified base is 16 or 0.

The functions that convert a string to an integer have three parameters:

- The input string.
- A pointer that when not null will receive the number of characters that were processed and that can include any leading white spaces that were discarded, the sign, and the base prefix, so it should not be confused with the number of digits the integral value has.
- A number indicating the base; by default, this is 10.

The valid digits in the input string depend on the base. For base 2, the only valid digits are 0 and 1; for base 5, they are 01234. For base 11, the valid digits are 0-9 and characters A and a. This continues until we reach base 36 that has valid characters 0-9, A-Z, and a-z.

The following are more examples of strings with numbers in various bases converted to decimal integers. Again, in all cases, the result is either 42 or –42:

```
auto i6 = std::stoi("052", nullptr, 8);
auto i7 = std::stoi("052", nullptr, 0);
auto i8 = std::stoi("0x2A", nullptr, 16);
auto i9 = std::stoi("0x2A", nullptr, 0);
auto i10 = std::stoi("101010", nullptr, 2);
auto i11 = std::stoi("22", nullptr, 20);
auto i12 = std::stoi("-22", nullptr, 20);

auto pos = size_t{ 0 };
auto i13 = std::stoi("42", &pos);        // pos = 2
auto i14 = std::stoi("-42", &pos);       // pos = 3
auto i15 = std::stoi("  +42dec", &pos);// pos = 5
```

An important thing to note is that these conversion functions throw if the conversion fails. There are two exceptions that can be thrown:

- `std::invalid_argument`: If the conversion cannot be performed:

```
try
{
    auto i16 = std::stoi("");
}
catch (std::exception const & e)
{
    // prints "invalid stoi argument"
    std::cout << e.what() << std::endl;
}
```

- `std::out_of_range`: If the converted value is outside the range of the result type (or if the underlying function sets `errno` to `ERANGE`):

```
try
{
    // OK
    auto i17 = std::stoll("12345678901234");
    // throws std::out_of_range
    auto i18 = std::stoi("12345678901234");
}
catch (std::exception const & e)
{
    // prints "stoi argument out of range"
    std::cout << e.what() << std::endl;
}
```

The other set of functions that convert a string to a floating point type is very similar, except that they don't have a parameter for the numeric base. A valid floating point value can have different representations in the input string:

- Decimal floating point expression (optional sign, sequence of decimal digits with optional point, optional e or E followed by exponent with optional sign).
- Binary floating point expression (optional sign, 0x or 0X prefix, sequence of hexadecimal digits with optional point, optional p or P followed by exponent with optional sign).
- Infinity expression (optional sign followed by case insensitive INF or INFINITY).
- A non-number expression (optional sign followed by case insensitive NAN and possibly other alphanumeric characters).

The following are various examples of converting strings to doubles:

```
auto d1 = std::stod("123.45");          // d1 =   123.45000000000000
auto d2 = std::stod("+123.45");         // d2 =   123.45000000000000
auto d3 = std::stod("-123.45");         // d3 =  -123.45000000000000
auto d4 = std::stod("  123.45");        // d4 =   123.45000000000000
auto d5 = std::stod("  -123.45abc");    // d5 =  -123.45000000000000
auto d6 = std::stod("1.2345e+2");       // d6 =   123.45000000000000
auto d7 = std::stod("0xF.6E6666p3");    // d7 =   123.44999980926514

auto d8 = std::stod("INF");             // d8 = inf
auto d9 = std::stod("-infinity");       // d9 = -inf
auto d10 = std::stod("NAN");            // d10 = nan
auto d11 = std::stod("-nanabc");        // d11 = -nan
```

The floating-point base 2 scientific notation, seen earlier in the form 0xF.6E6666p3, is not the topic of this recipe. However, for a clear understanding, a short description is provided; although, it is recommended that you see additional references for details. A floating-point constant in the base 2 scientific notation is composed of several parts:

- The hexadecimal prefix 0x.
- An integer part, in this example was F, which in decimal is 15.
- A fractional part, which in this example was 6E6666, or 011011100110011001100110 in binary. To convert that to decimal, we need to add inverse powers of two: 1/4 + 1/8 + 1/32 + 1/64 + 1/128 + ....
- A suffix, representing a power of 2; in this example, p3 means 2 at the power of 3.

The value of the decimal equivalent is determined by multiplying the significant (composed of the integer and fractional parts) and the base at the power of exponent. For the given hexadecimal base 2 floating point literal, the significant is 15.4312499... (note that digits after the seventh one are not shown), the base is 2, and the exponent is 3. Therefore, the result is 15.4212499... * 8, which is 123.44999980926514.

# See also

- *Limits and other properties of numeric types*

# Limits and other properties of numeric types

Sometimes, it is necessary to know and use the minimum and maximum values representable with a numeric type, such as `char`, `int`, or `double`. Many developers are using standard C macros for this, such as CHAR_MIN/CHAR_MAX, INT_MIN/INT_MAX, or DBL_MIN/DBL_MAX. C++ provides a class template called `numeric_limits` with specializations for every numeric type that enables you to query the minimum and maximum value of a type, but is not limited to that and offers additional constants for type properties querying, such as whether a type is signed or not, how many bits it needs for representing its values, for floating point types whether it can represent infinity, and many others. Prior to C++11, the use of `numeric_limits<T>` was limited because it could not be used in places where constants were needed (examples can include the size of arrays and switch cases). Due to that, developers preferred to use the C macros throughout their code. In C++11, that is no longer the case, as all the static members of `numeric_limits<T>` are now `constexpr`, which means they can be used everywhere a constant expression is expected.

# Getting ready

The `numeric_limits<T>` class template is available in the namespace `std` in the `<limits>` header.

# How to do it...

Use `std::numeric_limits<T>` to query various properties of a numeric type `T`:

- Use `min()` and `max()` static methods to get the smallest and largest finite numbers of a type:

```
template<typename T, typename I>
T minimum(I const start, I const end)
{
  T minval = std::numeric_limits<T>::max();
  for (auto i = start; i < end; ++i)
  {
    if (*i < minval)
      minval = *i;
  }
  return minval;
}
```

```
int range[std::numeric_limits<char>::max() + 1] = { 0 };

switch(get_value())
{
  case std::numeric_limits<int>::min():
  break;
}
```

- Use other static methods and static constants to retrieve other properties of a numeric type:

```
auto n = 42;
std::bitset<std::numeric_limits<decltype(n)>::digits>
  bits { static_cast<unsigned long long>(n) };
```

 In C++11, there is no limitation to where `std::numeric_limits<T>` can be used; therefore, preferably use it over C macros in your modern C++ code.

# How it works...

The `std::numeric_limits<T>` is a class template that enables developers to query property of numeric types. Actual values are available through specializations, and the standard library provides specializations for all the built-in numeric types (`char`, `short`, `int`, `long`, `float`, `double`, and so on). In addition, third parties may provide additional implementation for other types. An example could be a numeric library that implements a `bigint` integer type and a `decimal` type and provides specializations of `numeric_limits` for these types (such as `numeric_limits<bigint>` and `numeric_limits<decimal>`).

The following specializations of numeric types are available in the `<limits>` header. Note that specializations for `char16_t` and `char32_t` are new in C++11; the others were available previously. Apart from the specializations listed ahead, the library also includes specializations for every `cv-qualified` version of these numeric types, and they are identical to the unqualified specialization. For example, consider type `int`; there are four actual specializations (and they are identical): `numeric_limits<int>`, `numeric_limits<const int>`, `numeric_limits<volatile int>`, and `numeric_limits<const volatile int>`:

```
template<> class numeric_limits<bool>;
template<> class numeric_limits<char>;
template<> class numeric_limits<signed char>;
template<> class numeric_limits<unsigned char>;
```

```
template<> class numeric_limits<wchar_t>;
template<> class numeric_limits<char16_t>;
template<> class numeric_limits<char32_t>;
template<> class numeric_limits<short>;
template<> class numeric_limits<unsigned short>;
template<> class numeric_limits<int>;
template<> class numeric_limits<unsigned int>;
template<> class numeric_limits<long>;
template<> class numeric_limits<unsigned long>;
template<> class numeric_limits<long long>;
template<> class numeric_limits<unsigned long long>;
template<> class numeric_limits<float>;
template<> class numeric_limits<double>;
template<> class numeric_limits<long double>;
```

As mentioned earlier, in C++11, all static members of `numeric_limits` are `constexpr`, which means they can be used in all places where constant expressions are needed. These have several major advantages over C++ macros:

- They are easier to remember, as the only thing you need to know is the name of the type that you should know anyway, and not countless names of macros.
- They support types that are not available in C, such as `char16_t` and `char32_t`.
- They are the only possible solution for templates where you don't know the type.
- Minimum and maximum are only two of the various properties of types it provides; therefore, its actual use is beyond the numeric limits. As a side note, for this reason, the class should have been perhaps called `numeric_properties`, instead of `numeric_limits`.

The following function template `print_type_properties()` prints the minimum and maximum finite values of the type as well as other information:

```
template <typename T>
void print_type_properties()
{
  std::cout
    << "min="
    << std::numeric_limits<T>::min()        << std::endl
    << "max="
    << std::numeric_limits<T>::max()        << std::endl
    << "bits="
    << std::numeric_limits<T>::digits       << std::endl
    << "decdigits="
    << std::numeric_limits<T>::digits10     << std::endl
    << "integral="
    << std::numeric_limits<T>::is_integer   << std::endl
    << "signed="
```

```
    << std::numeric_limits<T>::is_signed     << std::endl
    << "exact="
    << std::numeric_limits<T>::is_exact      << std::endl
    << "infinity="
    << std::numeric_limits<T>::has_infinity << std::endl;
}
```

If we call the `print_type_properties()` function for unsigned `short`, `int`, and `double`, it will have the following output:

| unsigned short | int | double |
|---|---|---|
| min=0 | min=-2147483648 | min=2.22507e-308 |
| max=65535 | max=2147483647 | max=1.79769e+308 |
| bits=16 | bits=31 | bits=53 |
| decdigits=4 | decdigits=9 | decdigits=15 |
| integral=1 | integral=1 | integral=0 |
| signed=0 | signed=1 | signed=1 |
| exact=1 | exact=1 | exact=0 |
| infinity=0 | infinity=0 | infinity=1 |

The one thing to take note of is the difference between the `digits` and `digits10` constants:

- `digits` represent the number of bits (excluding the sign bit if present) and padding bits (if any) for integral types and the number of bits of the mantissa for floating point types.
- `digits10` is the number of decimal digits that can be represented by a type without a change. To understand this better, let's consider the case of unsigned `short`. This is a 16-bit integral type. It can represent numbers between 0 and 65536. It can represent numbers up to five decimal digits, 10,000 to 65,536, but it cannot represent all five decimal digit numbers, as numbers from 65,537 to 99,999 require more bits. Therefore, the largest numbers that it can represent without requiring more bits have four decimal digits (numbers from 1,000 to 9,999). This is the value indicated by `digits10`. For integral types, it has a direct relationship to constant `digits`; for an integral type `T`, the value of `digits10` is `std::numeric_limits<T>::digits * std::log10(2)`.

# Generating pseudo-random numbers

Generating random numbers is necessary for a large variety of applications, from games to cryptography, from sampling to forecasting. However, the term *random numbers* is not actually correct, as the generation of numbers through mathematical formulas is deterministic and does not produce true random numbers, but numbers that look random and are called *pseudo-random*. True randomness can only be achieved through hardware devices, based on physical processes, and even that can be challenged, as one may consider even the universe to be actually deterministic. Modern C++ provides support for generating pseudo-random numbers through a pseudo-random number library containing number generators and distributions. Theoretically, it can also produce true random numbers, but in practice, those could actually be only pseudo-random.

## Getting ready

In this recipe, we discuss the standard support for generating pseudo-random numbers. Understanding the difference between random and pseudo-random numbers is the key. On the other hand, being familiar with various statistical distributions is a plus. It is mandatory, though, that you know what a uniform distribution is because all engines in the library produce numbers that are uniformly distributed.

## How to do it...

To generate pseudo-random numbers in your application, you should perform the following steps:

1. Include the header <random>:

   ```
   #include <random>
   ```

2. Use an `std::random_device` generator for seeding a pseudo-random engine:

   ```
   std::random_device rd{};
   ```

3. Use one of the available engines for generating numbers and initialize it with a random seed:

   ```
   auto mtgen = std::mt19937{ rd() };
   ```

4. Use one of the available distributions for converting the output of the engine to one of the desired statistical distributions:

```
auto ud = std::uniform_int_distribution<>{ 1, 6 };
```

5. Generate the pseudo-random numbers:

```
for(auto i = 0; i < 20; ++i)
    auto number = ud(mtgen);
```

# How it works...

The pseudo-random number library contains two types of components:

- *Engines*, which are generators of random numbers; these could produce either pseudo-random numbers with a uniform distribution or, if available, actual random numbers.
- *Distributions* that convert the output of an engine into a statistical distribution.

All engines (except for `random_device`) produce integer numbers in a uniform distribution, and all engines implement the following methods:

- `min()`: This is a static method that returns the minimum value that can be produced by the generator.
- `max()`: This is a static method that returns the maximum value that can be produced by the generator.
- `seed()`: This initializes the algorithm with a start value (except for `random_device`, which cannot be seeded).
- `operator()`: This generates a new number uniformly distributed between `min()` and `max()`.
- `discard()`: This generates and discards a given number of pseudo-random numbers.

The following engines are available:

- `linear_congruential_engine`: This is a linear congruential generator that produces numbers using the following formula:

$$x(i) = (A * x(i-1) + C) \bmod M$$

- `mersenne_twister_engine`: This is a Mersenne twister generator that keeps a value on $W * (N-1) * R$ bits; each time a number needs to be generated, it extracts $W$ bits. When all bits have been used, it twists the large value by shifting and mixing the bits so that it has a new set of bits to extract from.
- `subtract_with_carry_engine`: This is a generator that implements a *subtract with carry* algorithm based on the following formula:

$$x(i) = (x(i - R) - x(i - S) - cy(i - 1)) \mod M$$

In the preceding formula, *cy* is defined as:

$$cy(i) = x(i - S) - x(i - R) - cy(i - 1) < 0 \; ? \; 1 : 0$$

In addition, the library provides engine adapters that are also engines wrapping another engine and producing numbers based on the output of the base engine. Engine adapters implement the same methods mentioned earlier for the base engines. The following engine adapters are available:

- `discard_block_engine`: A generator that from every block of P numbers generated by the base engine keeps only R numbers, discarding the rest.
- `independent_bits_engine`: A generator that produces numbers with a different number of bits than the base engine.
- `shuffle_order_engine`: A generator that keeps a shuffled table of K numbers produced by the base engine and returns numbers from this table, replacing them with numbers generated by the base engine.

All these engines and engine adaptors are producing pseudo-random numbers. The library, however, provides another engine called `random_device` that is supposed to produce non-deterministic numbers, but this is not an actual constraint as physical sources of random entropy might not be available. Therefore, implementations of `random_device` could actually be based on a pseudo-random engine. The `random_device` class cannot be seeded like the other engines and has an additional method called `entropy()` that returns the random device entropy, which is 0 for a deterministic generator and nonzero for a non-deterministic generator. However, this is not a reliable method for determining whether the device is actually deterministic or non-deterministic. For instance, both GNU `libstdc++` and LLVM `libc++` implement a non-deterministic device, but return 0 for entropy. On the other hand, VC++ and `boost.random` return 32 and 10, respectively, for entropy.

All these generators produce integers in a uniform distribution. This is, however, only one of the many possible statistical distributions that random numbers are needed in most applications. To be able to produce numbers (either integer or real) in other distributions, the library provides several classes that are called *distributions* and are converting the output of an engine according to the statistical distribution it implements. The following distributions are available:

| Type | Class name | Numbers | Statistical distribution |
|------|------------|---------|--------------------------|
| Uniform | `uniform_int_distribution` | integer | Uniform |
| | `uniform_real_distribution` | real | Uniform |
| Bernoulli | `bernoulli_distribution` | boolean | Bernoulli |
| | `binomial_distribution` | integer | binomial |
| | `negative_binomial_distribution` | integer | negative binomial |
| | `geometric_distribution` | integer | geometric |
| Poisson | `poisson_distribution` | integer | poisson |
| | `exponential_distribution` | real | exponential |
| | `gamma_distribution` | real | gamma |
| | `weibull_distribution` | real | Weibull |
| | `extreme_value_distribution` | real | extreme value |
| Normal | `normal_distribution` | real | standard normal (Gaussian) |
| | `lognormal_distribution` | real | lognormal |
| | `chi_squared_distribution` | real | chi-squared |
| | `cauchy_distribution` | real | Cauchy |
| | `fisher_f_distribution` | real | Fisher's F-distribution |
| | `student_t_distribution` | real | Student's t-distribution |
| Sampling | `discrete_distribution` | integer | discrete |
| | `piecewise_constant_distribution` | real | values distributed on constant subintervals |
| | `piecewise_linear_distribution` | real | values distributed on defined subintervals |

Each of the engines provided by the library has advantages and disadvantages. The linear congruential engine has a small internal state, but it is not very fast. On the other hand, the subtract with carry engine is very fast, but requires more memory for its internal state. The Mersenne twister is the slowest of them and the one that has the largest internal state, but when initialized appropriately can produce the longest non-repeating sequence of numbers. In the following examples, we will use `std::mt19937`, a 32-bit Mersenne twister with 19,937 bits of internal state.

The simplest way to generate random numbers looks like this:

```
auto mtgen = std::mt19937 {};
for (auto i = 0; i < 10; ++i)
  std::cout << mtgen() << std::endl;
```

In this example, `mtgen` is an `std::mt19937` Mersenne twister. To generate numbers, you only need to use the call operator that advances the internal state and returns the next pseudo-random number. However, this code is flawed, as the engine is not seeded. As a result, it always produces the same sequence of numbers, which is probably not what you want in most cases.

There are different approaches for initializing the engine. One approach, common with the C rand library, is to use the current time. In modern C++, it should look like this:

```
auto seed = std::chrono::high_resolution_clock::now()
               .time_since_epoch()
               .count();
auto mtgen = std::mt19937{ static_cast<unsigned int>(seed) };
```

In this example, `seed` is a number representing the number of ticks since the clock's epoch until the present moment. This number is then used to seed the engine. The problem with this approach is that the value of that `seed` is actually deterministic, and in some classes of applications it could be prone to attacks. A more reliable approach is to seed the generator with actual random numbers. The `std::random_device` class is an engine that is supposed to return true random numbers, though implementations could actually be based on a pseudo-random generator:

```
std::random_device rd;
auto mtgen = std::mt19937 {rd()};
```

Numbers produced by all engines follow a uniform distribution. To convert the result to another statistical distribution, we have to use a distribution class. To show how generated numbers are distributed according to the selected distribution, we will use the following function. This function generates a specified number of pseudo-random numbers and counts their repetition in a map. The values from the map are then used to produce a bar-like diagram showing how often each number occurred:

```
void generate_and_print(
  std::function<int(void)> gen,
  int const iterations = 10000)
{
  // map to store the numbers and their repetition
  auto data = std::map<int, int>{};

  // generate random numbers
  for (auto n = 0; n < iterations; ++n)
    ++data[gen()];

  // find the element with the most repetitions
  auto max = std::max_element(
             std::begin(data), std::end(data),
             [](auto kvp1, auto kvp2) {
    return kvp1.second < kvp2.second; });

  // print the bars
  for (auto i = max->second / 200; i > 0; --i)
  {
    for (auto kvp : data)
    {
      std::cout
        << std::fixed << std::setprecision(1) << std::setw(3)
        << (kvp.second / 200 >= i ? (char)219 : ' ');
    }

    std::cout << std::endl;
  }

  // print the numbers
  for (auto kvp : data)
  {
    std::cout
      << std::fixed << std::setprecision(1) << std::setw(3)
      << kvp.first;
  }

  std::cout << std::endl;
}
```

The following code generates random numbers using the `std::mt19937` engine with a uniform distribution in the range `[1, 6]`; that is basically what you get when you throw a dice:

```
std::random_device rd{};
auto mtgen = std::mt19937{ rd() };
auto ud = std::uniform_int_distribution<>{ 1, 6 };
generate_and_print([&mtgen, &ud]() {return ud(mtgen); });
```

The output of the program looks like this:

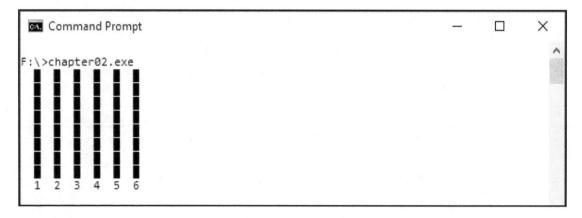

In the next and final example, we change the distribution to a normal distribution with the mean 5 and the standard deviation 2. This distribution produces real numbers; therefore, in order to use the previous `generate_and_print()` function, the numbers must be rounded to integers:

```
std::random_device rd{};
auto mtgen = std::mt19937{ rd() };
auto nd = std::normal_distribution<>{ 5, 2 };

generate_and_print(
  [&mtgen, &nd]() {
    return static_cast<int>(std::round(nd(mtgen))); });
```

The following will be the output of the earlier code:

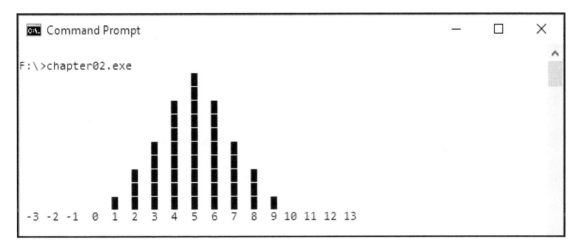

## See also

- *Initializing all bits of internal state of a pseudo-random number generator*

# Initializing all bits of internal state of a pseudo-random number generator

In the previous recipe, we have looked at the pseudo-random number library with its components and how it can be used to produce numbers in different statistical distributions. One important factor that was overlooked in that recipe is the proper initialization of the pseudo-random number generators. In this recipe, you will learn how to initialize a generator in order to produce the best sequence of pseudo-random numbers.

## Getting ready

You should read the previous recipe, *Generating pseudo-random numbers*, to get an overview of what the pseudo-random number library offers.

# How to do it...

To properly initialize a pseudo-random number generator to produce the best sequence of pseudo-random numbers, perform the following steps:

1. Use an `std::random_device` to produce random numbers to be used as seeding values:

   ```
   std::random_device rd;
   ```

2. Generate random data for all internal bits of the engine:

   ```
   std::array<int, std::mt19937::state_size> seed_data {};
   std::generate(std::begin(seed_data), std::end(seed_data),
               std::ref(rd));
   ```

3. Create an `std::seed_seq` object from the previously generated pseudo-random data:

   ```
   std::seed_seq seq(std::begin(seed_data), std::end(seed_data));
   ```

4. Create an engine object and initialize all the bits representing the internal state of the engine; for example, a `mt19937` has 19,937 bits of internal states:

   ```
   auto eng = std::mt19937{ seq };
   ```

5. Use the appropriate distribution based on the requirements of the application:

   ```
   auto dist = std::uniform_real_distribution<>{ 0, 1 };
   ```

# How it works...

In all examples shown in the previous recipe, we used an `std::mt19937` engine to produce pseudo-random numbers. Though the Mersenne twister is slower than the other engines, it can produce the longest sequences of non-repeating numbers and with the best spectral characteristics. However, initializing the engine in the manner shown in the previous recipe will not have this effect. With a careful analysis (that is beyond the purpose of this recipe or this book), it can be shown that the engine has a bias toward producing some values repeatedly and omitting others, thus generating numbers not in a uniform distribution, but rather in a binomial or Poisson distribution. The problem is that the internal state of `mt19937` has 624 32-bit integers, and in the examples from the previous recipe we have only initialized one of them.

When working with the pseudo-random number library, remember the following rule of thumb (shown in the information box):

 In order to produce the best results, engines must have all their internal state properly initialized before generating numbers.

The pseudo-random number library provides a class for this particular purpose, called `std::seed_seq`. This is a generator that can be seeded with any number of 32-bit integers and produces a requested number of integers evenly distributed in the 32-bit space.

In the preceding code from the *How to do it...* section, we defined an array called `seed_data` with a number of 32-bit integers equal to the internal state of the `mt19937` generator; that is 624 integers. Then, we initialized the array with random numbers produced by an `std::random_device`. The array was later used to seed an `std::seed_seq`, which in turn was used to seed the `mt19937` generator.

# Creating cooked user-defined literals

Literals are constants of built-in types (numerical, boolean, character, character string, and pointer) that cannot be altered in a program. The language defines a series of prefixes and suffixes to specify literals (and the prefix/suffix is actually part of the literal). C++11 allows creating user-defined literals by defining functions called *literal operators* that introduce suffixes for specifying literals. These work only with numerical character and character string types. This opens the possibility of defining both standard literals in future versions and allows developers to create their own literals. In this recipe, we will see how we can create our own cooked literals.

# Getting ready

User-defined literals can have two forms: *raw* and *cooked*. Raw literals are not processed by the compiler, whereas cooked literals are values processed by the compiler (examples can include handling escape sequences in a character string or identifying numerical values such as integer 2898 from literal 0xBAD). Raw literals are only available for integral and floating-point types, whereas cooked literals are also available for character and character string literals.

# How to do it...

To create cooked user-defined literals, you should follow these steps:

1. Define your literals in a separate namespace to avoid name clashes.
2. Always prefix the user-defined suffix with an underscore (_).
3. Define a literal operator of the following form for cooked literals:

```
T operator "" _suffix(unsigned long long int);
T operator "" _suffix(long double);
T operator "" _suffix(char);
T operator "" _suffix(wchar_t);
T operator "" _suffix(char16_t);
T operator "" _suffix(char32_t);
T operator "" _suffix(char const *, std::size_t);
T operator "" _suffix(wchar_t const *, std::size_t);
T operator "" _suffix(char16_t const *, std::size_t);
T operator "" _suffix(char32_t const *, std::size_t);
```

The following example creates a user-defined literal for specifying kilobytes:

```
namespace compunits
{
  constexpr size_t operator "" _KB(unsigned long long const size)
  {
    return static_cast<size_t>(size * 1024);
  }
}

auto size{ 4_KB };           // size_t size = 4096;

using byte = unsigned char;
auto buffer = std::array<byte, 1_KB>{};
```

# How it works...

When the compiler encounters a user-defined literal with a user-defined suffix s (it always has a leading underscore for third-party suffixes, as the suffixes without a leading underscore are reserved for the standard library) it does an unqualified name lookup in order to identify a function with the name operator "operator "" s. If it finds one, then it calls it according to the type of the literal and the type of the literal operator. Otherwise, the compiler will yield and error.

In the example from the *How to do it...* section, the literal operator is called `operator ""` `_KB` and has an argument of type `unsigned long long int`. This is the only integral type possible for literal operators for handling integral types. Similarly, for floating-point user-defined literals, the parameter type must be `long double` since for numeric types the literal operators must be able to handle the largest possible values. This literal operator returns a `constexpr` value so that it can be used where compile time values are expected, such as specifying the size of an array as shown in the above example.

When the compiler identifies a user-defined literal and has to call the appropriate user-defined literal operator, it will pick the overload from the overload set according to the following rules:

- **For integral literals**: It calls in the following order: the operator that takes an `unsigned long long`, the raw literal operator that takes a `const char*`, or the literal operator template.
- **For floating-point literals**: It calls in the following order: the operator that takes a `long double`, the raw literal operator that takes a `const char*`, or the literal operator template.
- **For character literals**: It calls the appropriate operator depending on the character type (`char`, `wchar_t`, `char16_t`, and `char32_t`).
- **For string literals**: It calls the appropriate operator, depending on the string type that takes a pointer to the string of characters and the size.

In the following example, we define a system of units and quantities. We want to operate with kilograms, pieces, liters, and other types of units. This could be useful in a system that can process orders and you need to specify the amount and unit for each article. The following are defined in the namespace `units`:

- A scoped enumeration for the possible types of units (kilogram, meter, liter, and pieces):

  ```
  enum class unit { kilogram, liter, meter, piece, };
  ```

- A class template to specify quantities of a particular unit (such as 3.5 kilograms or 42 pieces):

  ```
  template <unit U>
  class quantity
  {
    const double amount;
    public:
      constexpr explicit quantity(double const a) :
        amount(a) {}
  ```

```
      explicit operator double() const { return amount; }
};
```

- The `operator+` and `operator-` functions for the `quantity` class template in order to be able to add and subtract quantities:

```
template <unit U>
constexpr quantity<U> operator+(quantity<U> const &q1,
                                quantity<U> const &q2)
{
  return quantity<U>(static_cast<double>(q1) +
                     static_cast<double>(q2));
}

template <unit U>
constexpr quantity<U> operator-(quantity<U> const &q1,
                                quantity<U> const &q2)
{
  return quantity<U>(static_cast<double>(q1) -
                     static_cast<double>(q2));
}
```

- Literal operators to create `quantity` literals, defined in an inner namespace called `unit_literals`. The purpose of this is to avoid possible name clashes with literals from other namespaces. If such collisions do happen, developers could select the ones that they should use using the appropriate namespace in the scope where the literals need to be defined:

```
namespace unit_literals
{
  constexpr quantity<unit::kilogram> operator "" _kg(
      long double const amount)
  {
    return quantity<unit::kilogram>
      { static_cast<double>(amount) };
  }

  constexpr quantity<unit::kilogram> operator "" _kg(
      unsigned long long const amount)
  {
    return quantity<unit::kilogram>
      { static_cast<double>(amount) };
  }

  constexpr quantity<unit::liter> operator "" _l(
      long double const amount)
  {
```

```
        return quantity<unit::liter>
          { static_cast<double>(amount) };
    }

    constexpr quantity<unit::meter> operator "" _m(
        long double const amount)
    {
      return quantity<unit::meter>
        { static_cast<double>(amount) };
    }

    constexpr quantity<unit::piece> operator "" _pcs(
        unsigned long long const amount)
    {
      return quantity<unit::piece>
        { static_cast<double>(amount) };
    }
  }
```

By looking carefully, you can note that the literal operators defined earlier are not the same:

- _kg is defined for both integral and floating point literals; that enables us to create both integral and floating point values such as 1_kg and 1.0_kg.
- _l and _m are defined only for floating point literals; that means we can only define quantity literals for these units with floating points, such as 4.5_l and 10.0_m.
- _pcs is only defined for integral literals; that means we can only define quantities of an integer number of pieces, such as 42_pcs.

Having these literal operators available, we can operate with various quantities. The following examples show both valid and invalid operations:

```
using namespace units;
using namespace unit_literals;

auto q1{ 1_kg };      // OK
auto q2{ 4.5_kg };    // OK
auto q3{ q1 + q2 };   // OK
auto q4{ q2 - q1 };   // OK

// error, cannot add meters and pieces
auto q5{ 1.0_m + 1_pcs };
// error, cannot have an integer number of liters
auto q6{ 1_l };
// error, can only have an integer number of pieces
auto q7{ 2.0_pcs}
```

q1 is a quantity of 1 kg; that is an integer value. Since an overloaded `operator ""` `_kg(unsigned long long const)` exists, the literal can be correctly created from the integer 1. Similarly, q2 is a quantity of 4.5 kilograms; that is a real value. Since an `overload operator "" _kg(long double)` exists, the literal can be created from the double floating point value 4.5.

On the other hand, q6 is a quantity of 1 liter. Since there is no overloaded `operator ""` `_l(unsigned long long)`, the literal cannot be created. It would require an overload that takes a `unsigned long long`, but such an overload does not exist. Similarly, q7 is a quantity of 2.0 pieces, but piece literals can only be created from integer values and, therefore, this generates another compiler error.

# There's more...

Though user-defined literals are available from C++11, standard literal operators have been available only from C++14. The following is a list of these standard literal operators:

- `operator""s` for defining `std::basic_string` literals:

```
using namespace std::string_literals;

auto s1{  "text"s }; // std::string
auto s2{ L"text"s }; // std::wstring
auto s3{ u"text"s }; // std::u16string
auto s4{ U"text"s }; // std::u32string
```

- `operator""h`, `operator""min`, `operator""s`, `operator""ms`, `operator""us`, and `operator""ns` for creating a `std::chrono::duration` value:

```
using namespace std::literals::chrono_literals;

// std::chrono::duration<long long>
auto timer {2h + 42min + 15s};
```

- `operator""if`, `operator""i`, and `operator""il` for creating a `std::complex` value:

```
using namespace std::literals::complex_literals;

auto c{ 12.0 + 4.5i }; // std::complex<double>
```

# See also

- *Using raw string literals to avoid escaping characters*
- *Creating raw user-defined literals*

# Creating raw user-defined literals

In the previous recipe, we have looked at the way C++11 allows library implementers and developers to create user-defined literals and the user-defined literals available in the C++14 standard. However, user-defined literals have two forms, a cooked form, where the literal value is processed by the compiler before being supplied to the literal operator, and a raw form, in which the literal is not parsed by the compiler. The latter is only available for integral and floating-point types. In this recipe, we will look at creating raw user-defined literals.

## Getting ready

Before continuing with this recipe, it is strongly recommended that you go through the previous one, *Creating cooked user-defined literals*, as general details about user-defined literals will not be reiterated here.

To exemplify the way raw user-defined literals can be created, we will define binary literals. These binary literals can be of 8-bit, 16-bit, and 32-bit (unsigned) types. These types will be called `byte8`, `byte16`, and `byte32`, and the literals we create will be called `_b8`, `_b16`, and `_b32`.

## How to do it...

To create raw user-defined literals, you should follow these steps:

1. Define your literals in a separate namespace to avoid name clashes.
2. Always prefix the used-defined suffix with an underscore (_).
3. Define a literal operator or literal operator template of the following form:

   ```
   T operator "" _suffix(const char*);

   template<char...> T operator "" _suffix();
   ```

The following sample shows a possible implementation of 8-bit, 16-bit, and 32-bit binary literals:

```cpp
namespace binary
{
  using byte8  = unsigned char;
  using byte16 = unsigned short;
  using byte32 = unsigned int;

  namespace binary_literals
  {
    namespace binary_literals_internals
    {
      template <typename CharT, char... bits>
      struct binary_struct;

      template <typename CharT, char... bits>
      struct binary_struct<CharT, '0', bits...>
      {
        static constexpr CharT value{
          binary_struct<CharT, bits...>::value };
      };

      template <typename CharT, char... bits>
      struct binary_struct<CharT, '1', bits...>
      {
        static constexpr CharT value{
          static_cast<CharT>(1 << sizeof...(bits)) |
          binary_struct<CharT, bits...>::value };
      };

      template <typename CharT>
      struct binary_struct<CharT>
      {
        static constexpr CharT value{ 0 };
      };
    }

    template<char... bits>
    constexpr byte8 operator""_b8()
    {
      static_assert(
        sizeof...(bits) <= 8,
        "binary literal b8 must be up to 8 digits long");

      return binary_literals_internals::
               binary_struct<byte8, bits...>::value;
    }
```

```
template<char... bits>
constexpr byte16 operator""_b16()
{
  static_assert(
      sizeof...(bits) <= 16,
      "binary literal b16 must be up to 16 digits long");

  return binary_literals_internals::
          binary_struct<byte16, bits...>::value;
}

template<char... bits>
constexpr byte32 operator""_b32()
{
  static_assert(
      sizeof...(bits) <= 32,
      "binary literal b32 must be up to 32 digits long");

  return binary_literals_internals::
          binary_struct<byte32, bits...>::value;
}

  }
}
```

# How it works...

The implementation in the previous section enables us to define binary literals of the form 1010_b8 (a byte8 value of decimal 10) or 000010101100_b16 (a byte16 value of decimal 2130496). However, we want to make sure that we do not exceed the number of digits for each type. In other words, values such as 111100001_b8 should be illegal and the compiler should yield an error.

First of all, we define everything inside a namespace called binary and start with introducing several type aliases (byte8, byte16, and byte32).

The literal operator templates are defined in a nested namespace called binary_literal_internals. This is a good practice in order to avoid name collision with other literal operators from other namespaces. Should something like that happen, you can choose to use the appropriate namespace in the right scope (such as one namespace in a function or block and another namespace in another function or block).

The three literal operator templates are very similar. The only things that are different are their names (_b8, _16, and _b32), return type (byte8, byte16, and byte32), and the condition in the static assert that checks the number of digits.

We will explore the details of variadic template and template recursion in a later recipe; however, for a better understanding, this is how this particular implementation works: bits is a template parameter pack, that is not a single value, but all the values the template could be instantiated with. For example, if we consider the literal 1010_b8, then the literal operator template would be instantiated as operator"" _b8<'1', '0', '1', '0'>(). Before proceeding with computing the binary value, we check the number of digits in the literal. For _b8, this must not exceed eight (including any trailing zeros). Similarly, it should be up to 16 digits for _b16 and 32 for _b32. For this, we use the sizeof... operator that returns the number of elements in a parameter pack (in this case, bits).

If the number of digits is correct, we can proceed to expand the parameter pack and recursively compute the decimal value represented by the binary literal. This is done with the help of an additional class template and its specializations. These templates are defined in yet another nested namespace, called binary_literals_internals. This is also a good practice because it hides (without proper qualification) the implementation details from the client (unless an explicit using namespace directive makes them available to the current namespace).

 Even though this looks like recursion, it is not a true runtime recursion, because after the compiler expands and generates the code from templates, what we end up with is basically calls to overloaded functions with a different number of parameters. This is later explained in the recipe *Writing a function template with a variable number of arguments*.

The binary_struct class template has a template type CharT for the return type of the function (we need this because our literal operator templates should return either byte8, byte16, or byte32) and a parameter pack:

```
template <typename CharT, char... bits>
struct binary_struct;
```

Several specializations of this class template are available with parameter pack decomposition. When the first digit of the pack is '0', the computed value remains the same, and we continue expanding the rest of the pack. If the first digit of the pack is '1', then the new value is 1 shifted to the left with the number of digits in the remainder of the pack bit, or the value of the rest of the pack:

```
template <typename CharT, char... bits>
struct binary_struct<CharT, '0', bits...>
{
  static constexpr CharT value{
    binary_struct<CharT, bits...>::value };
};

template <typename CharT, char... bits>
struct binary_struct<CharT, '1', bits...>
{
  static constexpr CharT value{
    static_cast<CharT>(1 << sizeof...(bits)) |
    binary_struct<CharT, bits...>::value };
};
```

The last specialization covers the case when the pack is empty; in this case we return 0:

```
template <typename CharT>
struct binary_struct<CharT>
{
  static constexpr CharT value{ 0 };
};
```

After defining these helper classes, we could implement the `byte8`, `byte16`, and `byte32` binary literals as intended. Note that we need to bring the content of the namespace `binary_literals` in the current namespace in order to use the literal operator templates:

```
using namespace binary;
using namespace binary_literals;
auto b1 = 1010_b8;
auto b2 = 101010101010_b16;
auto b3 = 10101010101010101010101010_b32;
```

The following definitions trigger compiler errors because the condition in `static_assert` is not met:

```
// binary literal b8 must be up to 8 digits long
auto b4 = 0011111111_b8;
// binary literal b16 must be up to 16 digits long
auto b5 = 001111111111111111_b16;
// binary literal b32 must be up to 32 digits long
auto b6 = 0011111111111111111111111111111111_b32;
```

## See also

- *Using raw string literals to avoid escaping characters*
- *Creating cooked user-defined literals*
- *Writing a function template with variable number of arguments* recipe of `Chapter 10`, *Exploring Functions*
- *Creating type aliases and alias templates* recipe of `Chapter 8`, *Learning Modern Core Language Features*

# Using raw string literals to avoid escaping characters

Strings may contain special characters, such as non-printable characters (newline, horizontal and vertical tab, and so on), string and character delimiters (double and single quotes) or arbitrary octal, hexadecimal, or Unicode values. These special characters are introduced with an escape sequence that starts with a backslash, followed by either the character (examples include ' and "), its designated letter (examples include n for a new line, t for a horizontal tab), or its value (examples include octal 050, hexadecimal XF7, or Unicode U16F0). As a result, the backslash character itself has to be escaped with another backslash character. This leads to more complicated literal strings that can be hard to read.

To avoid escaping characters, C++11 introduced raw string literals that do not process escape sequences. In this recipe, you will learn how to use the various forms of raw string literals.

# Getting ready

In this recipe, and throughout the rest of the book, I will use the s suffix to define basic_string literals. This has been covered in the recipe *Creating cooked user-defined literals*.

# How to do it...

To avoid escaping characters, define the string literals with the following:

1. R"( literal )" as the default form:

```
auto filename {R"(C:\Users\Marius\Documents\)"s};
auto pattern {R"((\w+)=(\d+)$)"s};

auto sqlselect {
  R"(SELECT *
  FROM Books
  WHERE Publisher='Paktpub'
  ORDER BY PubDate DESC)"s};
```

2. R"delimiter( literal )delimiter" where delimiter is any character sequence not present in the actual string when the sequence ) " should actually be part of the string. Here is an example with ! ! as delimited:

```
auto text{ R"!!(This text contains both "( and )".)!!"s };
std::cout << text << std::endl;
```

# How it works...

When string literals are used, escapes are not processed, and the actual content of the string is written between the delimiter (in other words, what you see is what you get). The following example shows what appears as the same raw literal string; however, the second one still contains escaped characters. Since these are not processed in the case of string literals, they will be printed as they are in the output:

```
auto filename1 {R"(C:\Users\Marius\Documents\)"s};
auto filename2 {R"(C:\\Users\\Marius\\Documents\\)"s};

// prints C:\Users\Marius\Documents\
std::cout << filename1 << std::endl;

// prints C:\\Users\\Marius\\Documents\\
```

```
        std::cout << filename2 << std::endl;
```

In case the text has to contain the ) " sequence, then a different delimiter must be used, in the R"delimiter( literal )delimiter" form. According to the standard, the possible characters in a delimiter can be as follows:

> *any member of the basic source character set except: space, the left parenthesis (the right parenthesis ), the backslash \, and the control characters representing horizontal tab, vertical tab, form feed, and newline.*

Raw string literals can be prefixed by one of L, u8, u, and U to indicate a wide, UTF-8, UTF-16, or UTF-32 string literal. The following are examples of such string literals. Note that the presence of string literal operator ""s at the end of the string makes the compiler deduce the type as various string classes and not character arrays:

```
auto t1{ LR"(text)"  };   // const wchar_t*
auto t2{ u8R"(text)" };   // const char*
auto t3{ uR"(text)"  };   // const char16_t*
auto t4{ UR"(text)"  };   // const char32_t*

auto t5{ LR"(text)"s  };  // wstring
auto t6{ u8R"(text)"s };  // string
auto t7{ uR"(text)"s  };  // u16string
auto t8{ UR"(text)"s  };  // u32string
```

## See also

- *Creating cooked user-defined literals*

# Creating a library of string helpers

The string types from the standard library are a general purpose implementation that lacks many helpful methods, such as changing the case, trimming, splitting, and others that may address different developer needs. Third-party libraries that provide rich sets of string functionalities exist. However, in this recipe, we will look at implementing several simple, yet helpful, methods you may often need in practice. The purpose is rather to see how string methods and standard general algorithms can be used for manipulating strings, but also to have a reference to reusable code that can be used in your applications.

In this recipe, we will implement a small library of string utilities that will provide functions for the following:

- Changing a string to lowercase or uppercase.
- Reversing a string.
- Trimming white spaces from the beginning and/or the end of the string.
- Trimming a specific set of characters from the beginning and/or the end of the string.
- Removing occurrences of a character anywhere in the string.
- Tokenizing a string using a specific delimiter.

# Getting ready

The string library we will be implementing should work with all the standard string types, `std::string`, `std::wstring`, `std::u16string`, and `std::u32string`. To avoid specifying long names such as `std::basic_string<CharT, std::char_traits<CharT>, std::allocator<CharT>>`, we will use the following alias templates for strings and string streams:

```
template <typename CharT>
using tstring =
    std::basic_string<CharT, std::char_traits<CharT>,
                      std::allocator<CharT>>;

template <typename CharT>
using tstringstream =
    std::basic_stringstream<CharT, std::char_traits<CharT>,
                            std::allocator<CharT>>;
```

To implement these string helper functions, we need to include the header `<string>` for strings and `<algorithm>` for the general standard algorithms we will use.

In all the examples in this recipe, we will use the standard user-defined literal operators for strings from C++14, for which we need to explicitly use the `std::string_literals` namespace.

# How to do it...

1. To convert a string to lowercase or uppercase, apply the `tolower()` or `toupper()` functions on the characters of a string using the general purpose algorithm `std::transform()`:

```
template<typename CharT>
inline tstring<CharT> to_upper(tstring<CharT> text)
{
  std::transform(std::begin(text), std::end(text),
                 std::begin(text), toupper);
  return text;
}

template<typename CharT>
inline tstring<CharT> to_lower(tstring<CharT> text)
{
  std::transform(std::begin(text), std::end(text),
                 std::begin(text), tolower);
  return text;
}
```

2. To reverse a string, use the general purpose algorithm `std::reverse()`:

```
template<typename CharT>
inline tstring<CharT> reverse(tstring<CharT> text)
{
  std::reverse(std::begin(text), std::end(text));
  return text;
}
```

3. To trim a string, at the beginning, end, or both, use `std::basic_string`'s methods `find_first_not_of()` and `find_last_not_of()`:

```
template<typename CharT>
inline tstring<CharT> trim(tstring<CharT> const & text)
{
  auto first{ text.find_first_not_of(' ') };
  auto last{ text.find_last_not_of(' ') };
  return text.substr(first, (last - first + 1));
}

template<typename CharT>
inline tstring<CharT> trimleft(tstring<CharT> const & text)
{
  auto first{ text.find_first_not_of(' ') };
  return text.substr(first, text.size() - first);
```

```
}

template<typename CharT>
inline tstring<CharT> trimright(tstring<CharT> const & text)
{
  auto last{ text.find_last_not_of(' ') };
  return text.substr(0, last + 1);
}
```

4. To trim characters in a given set from a string, use overloads of
   `std::basic_string`'s methods `find_first_not_of()` and
   `find_last_not_of()`, that take a string parameter that defines the set of
   characters to look for:

```
template<typename CharT>
inline tstring<CharT> trim(tstring<CharT> const & text,
                           tstring<CharT> const & chars)
{
  auto first{ text.find_first_not_of(chars) };
  auto last{ text.find_last_not_of(chars) };
  return text.substr(first, (last - first + 1));
}

template<typename CharT>
inline tstring<CharT> trimleft(tstring<CharT> const & text,
                               tstring<CharT> const & chars)
{
  auto first{ text.find_first_not_of(chars) };
  return text.substr(first, text.size() - first);
}

template<typename CharT>
inline tstring<CharT> trimright(tstring<CharT> const &text,
                                tstring<CharT> const &chars)
{
  auto last{ text.find_last_not_of(chars) };
  return text.substr(0, last + 1);
}
```

5. To remove characters from a string, use `std::remove_if()` and
   `std::basic_string::erase()`:

```
template<typename CharT>
inline tstring<CharT> remove(tstring<CharT> text,
                             CharT const ch)
{
  auto start = std::remove_if(
```

```
                  std::begin(text), std::end(text),
                  [=](CharT const c) {return c ==  ch; });
    text.erase(start, std::end(text));
    return text;
}
```

6. To split a string based on a specified delimiter, use `std::getline()` to read from an `std::basic_stringstream` initialized with the content of the string. The tokens extracted from the stream are pushed into a vector of strings:

```
template<typename CharT>
inline std::vector<tstring<CharT>> split
   (tstring<CharT> text, CharT const delimiter)
{
   auto sstr = tstringstream<CharT>{ text };
   auto tokens = std::vector<tstring<CharT>>{};
   auto token = tstring<CharT>{};
   while (std::getline(sstr, token, delimiter))
   {
      if (!token.empty()) tokens.push_back(token);
   }
   return tokens;
}
```

# How it works...

For implementing the utility functions from the library, we have two options:

- Functions would modify a string passed by a reference.
- Functions would not alter the original string but return a new string.

The second option has the advantage that it preserves the original string, which may be helpful in many cases. Otherwise, in those cases, you would first have to make a copy of the string and alter the copy. The implementation provided in this recipe takes the second approach.

The first functions we implemented in the *How to do it...* section were `to_upper()` and `to_lower()`. These functions change the content of a string either to uppercase or lowercase. The simplest way to implement this is using the `std::transform()` standard algorithm. This is a general purpose algorithm that applies a function to every element of a range (defined by a begin and end iterator) and stores the result in another range for which only the begin iterator needs to be specified. The output range can be the same as the input range, which is exactly what we did to transform the string. The applied function is `toupper()` or `tolower()`:

```
auto ut{ string_library::to_upper("this is not UPPERCASE"s) };
// ut = "THIS IS NOT UPPERCASE"

auto lt{ string_library::to_lower("THIS IS NOT lowercase"s) };
// lt = "this is not lowercase"
```

The next function we considered was `reverse()`, that, as the name implies, reverses the content of a string. For this, we used the `std::reverse()` standard algorithm. This general purpose algorithm reverses the elements of a range defined by a begin and end iterator:

```
auto rt{string_library::reverse("cookbook"s)}; // rt = "koobkooc"
```

When it comes to trimming, a string can be trimmed at the beginning, end, or both sides. Because of that, we implemented three different functions: `trim()` for trimming at both ends, `trimleft()` for trimming at the beginning of a string, and `trimright()` for trimming at the end of a string. The first version of the functions trims only spaces. In order to find the right part to trim, we use the `find_first_not_of()` and `find_last_not_of()` methods of `std::basic_string`. These return the first and last characters in the string that are not the specified character. Subsequently, a call to the `substr()` method of `std::basic_string` returns a new string. The `substr()` method takes an index in the string and a number of elements to copy to the new string:

```
auto text1{"   this is an example   "s};
// t1 = "this is an example"
auto t1{ string_library::trim(text1) };
// t2 = "this is an example   "
auto t2{ string_library::trimleft(text1) };
// t3 = "   this is an example"
auto t3{ string_library::trimright(text1) };
```

It could be sometimes useful to trim other characters and then spaces from a string. In order to do that, we provided overloads for the trimming functions that specify a set of characters to be removed. That set is also specified as a string. The implementation is very similar to the previous one because both `find_first_not_of()` and `find_last_not_of()` have overloads that take a string containing the characters to be excluded from the search:

```
auto chars1{" !%\n\r"s};
auto text3{"!!  this % needs a lot\rof trimming  !\n"s};
auto t7{ string_library::trim(text3, chars1) };
// t7 = "this % needs a lot\rof trimming"
auto t8{ string_library::trimleft(text3, chars1) };
// t8 = "this % needs a lot\rof trimming  !\n"
auto t9{ string_library::trimright(text3, chars1) };
// t9 = "!!  this % needs a lot\rof trimming"
```

If removing characters from any part of the string is necessary, the trimming methods are not helpful because they only treat a contiguous sequence of characters at the start and end of a string. For that, however, we implemented a simple `remove()` method. This uses the `std:remove_if()` standard algorithm. Both `std::remove()` and `std::remove_if()` work in a way that may not be very intuitive at first. They remove elements that satisfy the criteria from a range defined by a first and last iterator by rearranging the content of the range (using move assignment). The elements that need to be removed are placed at the end of the range, and the function returns an iterator to the first element in the range that represents the removed elements. This iterator basically defines the new end of the range that was modified. If no element was removed, the returned iterator is the end iterator of the original range. The value of this returned iterator is then used to call the `std::basic_string::erase()` method that actually erases the content of the string defined by two iterators. The two iterators in our case are the iterator returned by `std::remove_if()` and the end of the string:

```
auto text4{"must remove all * from text**"s};
auto t10{ string_library::remove(text4, '*') };
// t10 = "must remove all  from text"
auto t11{ string_library::remove(text4, '!') };
// t11 = "must remove all * from text**"
```

The last method we implemented splits the content of a string based on a specified delimiter. There are various ways to implement this. In this implementation, we used `std::getline()`. This function reads characters from an input stream until a specified delimiter is found and places the characters in a string. Before starting to read from the input buffer, it calls `erase()` on the output string to clear its content. Calling this method in a loop produces tokens that are placed in a vector. In our implementation, empty tokens were skipped from the result set:

```
auto text5{"this text will be split    "s};
auto tokens1{ string_library::split(text5, ' ') };
// tokens1 = {"this", "text", "will", "be", "split"}
auto tokens2{ string_library::split(""s, ' ') };
// tokens2 = {}
```

## See also

- *Creating cooked user-defined literals*
- *Creating type aliases and alias templates* recipe of `Chapter 8`, *Learning Modern Core Language Features*

# Verifying the format of a string using regular expressions

Regular expressions are a language intended for performing pattern matching and replacements in texts. C++11 provides support for regular expressions within the standard library through a set of classes, algorithms, and iterators available in the header `<regex>`. In this recipe, we will see how regular expressions can be used to verify that a string matches a pattern (examples can include verifying an e-mail or IP address formats).

## Getting ready

Throughout this recipe, we will explain whenever necessary the details of the regular expressions that we use. However, you should have at least some basic knowledge of regular expressions in order to use the C++ standard library for regular expressions. A description of regular expressions syntax and standards is beyond the purpose of this book; if you are not familiar with regular expressions, it is recommended that you read more about them before continuing with the recipes that focus on regular expressions.

# How to do it...

In order to verify that a string matches a regular expression, perform the following steps:

1.  Include headers `<regex>` and `<string>` and the namespace `std::string_literals` for C++14 standard user-defined literals for strings:

    ```
    #include <regex>
    #include <string>
    using namespace std::string_literals;
    ```

2.  Use raw string literals to specify the regular expression to avoid escaping backslashes (that can occur frequently). The following regular expression validates most e-mails formats:

    ```
    auto pattern {R"(^[A-Z0-9._%+-]+@[A-Z0-9.-]+\.[A-Z]{2,}$)"s};
    ```

3.  Create an `std::regex`/`std::wregex` object (depending on the character set that is used) to encapsulate the regular expression:

    ```
    auto rx = std::regex{pattern};
    ```

4.  To ignore casing or specify other parsing options, use an overloaded constructor that has an extra parameter for regular expression flags:

    ```
    auto rx = std::regex{pattern, std::regex_constants::icase};
    ```

5.  Use `std::regex_match()` to match the regular expression to an entire string:

    ```
    auto valid = std::regex_match("marius@domain.com"s, rx);
    ```

# How it works...

Considering the problem of verifying the format of e-mail addresses, even though this may look like a trivial problem, in practice it is hard to find a simple regular expression that covers all the possible cases for valid e-mail formats. In this recipe, we will not try to find that ultimate regular expression, but rather to apply a regular expression that is good enough for most cases. The regular expression we will use for this purpose is this:

```
^[A-Z0-9._%+-]+@[A-Z0-9.-]+\.[A-Z]{2,}$
```

The following table explains the structure of the regular expression:

| Part | Description |
|---|---|
| ^ | Start of string |
| [A-Z0-9._%+-]+ | At least one character in the range A-Z, 0-9, or one of -, %, + or - that represents the local part of the email address |
| @ | Character @ |
| [A-Z0-9.-]+ | At least one character in the range A-Z, 0-9, or one of -, %, + or - that represents the hostname of the domain part |
| \. | A dot that separates the domain hostname and label |
| [A-Z]{2,} | The DNS label of a domain that can have between 2 and 63 characters |
| $ | End of the string |

Bear in mind that in practice a domain name is composed of a hostname followed by a dot-separated list of DNS labels. Examples include `localhost`, `gmail.com`, or `yahoo.co.uk`. This regular expression we are using does not match domains without DNS labels, such as localhost (an e-mail, such as `root@localhost` is a valid e-mail). The domain name can also be an IP address specified in brackets, such as `[192.168.100.11]` (as in `john.doe@[192.168.100.11]`). E-mail addresses containing such domains will not match the regular expression defined above. Even though these rather rare formats will not be matched, the regular expression can cover most of the e-mail formats.

The regular expression in the example in this chapter is provided for didactical purposes only, and it is not intended for being used as it is in production code. As explained earlier, this sample does not cover all possible e-mail formats.

We began by including the necessary headers, `<regex>` for regular expressions and `<string>` for strings. The `is_valid_email()` function shown in the following (that basically contains the samples from the *How to do it...* section) takes a string representing an e-mail address and returns a boolean indicating whether the e-mail has a valid format or not. We first construct an `std::regex` object to encapsulate the regular expression indicated with the raw string literal. Using raw string literals is helpful because it avoids escaping backslashes that are used for escape characters in regular expressions too. The function then calls `std::regex_match()`, passing the input text and the regular expression:

```
bool is_valid_email_format(std::string const & email)
{
    auto pattern {R"(^[A-Z0-9._%+-]+@[A-Z0-9.-]+\.[A-Z]{2,}$)"s};

    auto rx = std::regex{pattern};

    return std::regex_match(email, rx);
}
```

The `std::regex_match()` method tries to match the regular expression against the entire string. If successful it returns `true`, otherwise `false`:

```
auto ltest = [](std::string const & email)
{
    std::cout << std::setw(30) << std::left
              << email << " : "
              << (is_valid_email_format(email) ?
                  "valid format" : "invalid format")
              << std::endl;
};

ltest("JOHN.DOE@DOMAIN.COM"s);           // valid format
ltest("JOHNDOE@DOMAIL.CO.UK"s);          // valid format
ltest("JOHNDOE@DOMAIL.INFO"s);           // valid format
ltest("J.O.H.N_D.O.E@DOMAIN.INFO"s);     // valid format
ltest("ROOT@LOCALHOST"s);                // invalid format
ltest("john.doe@domain.com"s);           // invalid format
```

In this simple test, the only e-mails that do not match the regular expression are `ROOT@LOCALHOST` and `john.doe@domain.com`. The first contains a domain name without a dot-prefixed DNS label and that case is not covered in the regular expression. The second contains only lowercase letters, and in the regular expression, the valid set of characters for both the local part and the domain name was uppercase letters, A to Z.

Instead of complicating the regular expression with additional valid characters (such as [A-Za-z0-9._%+-]), we can specify that the match can ignore the case. This can be done with an additional parameter to the constructor of the std::basic_regex class. The available constants for this purpose are defined in the regex_constants namespace. The following slight change to the is_valid_email_format() will make it ignore the case and allow e-mails with both lowercase and uppercase letters to correctly match the regular expression:

```
bool is_valid_email_format(std::string const & email)
{
  auto rx = std::regex{
    R"(^[A-Z0-9._%+-]+@[A-Z0-9.-]+\.[A-Z]{2,}$)"s,
    std::regex_constants::icase};

  return std::regex_match(email, rx);
}
```

This is_valid_email_format() function is pretty simple, and if the regular expression was provided as a parameter along with the text to match, it could be used for matching anything. However, it would be nice to be able to handle with a single function not only multi-byte strings (std::string) but also wide strings (std::wstring). This can be achieved by creating a function template where the character type is provided as a template parameter:

```
template <typename CharT>
using tstring = std::basic_string<CharT, std::char_traits<CharT>,
                                  std::allocator<CharT>>;

template <typename CharT>
bool is_valid_format(tstring<CharT> const & pattern,
                     tstring<CharT> const & text)
{
  auto rx = std::basic_regex<CharT>{
    pattern, std::regex_constants::icase };

  return std::regex_match(text, rx);
}
```

We start by creating an alias template for `std::basic_string` in order to simplify its use. The new `is_valid_format()` function is a function template very similar to our implementation of `is_valid_email()`. However, we now use `std::basic_regex<CharT>` instead of the typedef `std::regex`, which is `std::basic_regex<char>`, and the pattern is provided as the first argument. We now implement a new function called `is_valid_email_format_w()` for wide strings that relies on this function template. The function template, however, can be reused for implementing other validations, such as if a license plate has a particular format:

```
bool is_valid_email_format_w(std::wstring const & text)
{
  return is_valid_format(
    LR"(^[A-Z0-9._%+-]+@[A-Z0-9.-]+\.[A-Z]{2,}$)"s,
    text);
}

auto ltest2 = [](auto const & email)
{
  std::wcout << std::setw(30) << std::left
    << email << L" : "
    << (is_valid_email_format_w(email) ? L"valid" : L"invalid")
    << std::endl;
};

ltest2(L"JOHN.DOE@DOMAIN.COM"s);        // valid
ltest2(L"JOHNDOE@DOMAIL.CO.UK"s);       // valid
ltest2(L"JOHNDOE@DOMAIL.INFO"s);        // valid
ltest2(L"J.O.H.N_D.O.E@DOMAIN.INFO"s);  // valid
ltest2(L"ROOT@LOCALHOST"s);             // invalid
ltest2(L"john.doe@domain.com"s);        // valid
```

Of all the examples shown above, the only one that does not match is ROOT@LOCAHOST, as already expected.

The `std::regex_match()` method has, in fact, several overloads, and some of them have a parameter that is a reference to an `std::match_results` object to store the result of the match. If there is no match, then `std::match_results` is empty and its size is 0. Otherwise, if there is a match, the `std::match_results` object is not empty and its size is 1 plus the number of matched subexpressions.

The following version of the function uses the mentioned overloads and returns the matched subexpressions in an `std::smatch` object. Note that the regular expression is changed, as three caption groups are defined-- one for the local part, one for the hostname part of the domain, and one for the DNS label. If the match is successful, then the `std::smatch` object will contain four submatch objects: the first to match the entire string, the second for the first capture group (the local part), the third for the second capture group (the hostname), and the fourth for the third and last capture group (the DNS label). The result is returned in a tuple, where the first item actually indicates success or failure:

```
std::tuple<bool, std::string, std::string, std::string>
is_valid_email_format_with_result(std::string const & email)
{
  auto rx = std::regex{
    R"(^([A-Z0-9._%+-]+)@([A-Z0-9.-]+)\.([A-Z]{2,})$)"s,
    std::regex_constants::icase };
  auto result = std::smatch{};
  auto success = std::regex_match(email, result, rx);

  return std::make_tuple(
    success,
    success ? result[1].str() : ""s,
    success ? result[2].str() : ""s,
    success ? result[3].str() : ""s);
}
```

Following the preceding code, we use C++17 structured bindings to unpack the content of the tuple into named variables:

```
auto ltest3 = [](std::string const & email)
{
  auto [valid, localpart, hostname, dnslabel] =
    is_valid_email_format_with_result(email);

  std::cout << std::setw(30) << std::left
    << email << " : "
    << std::setw(10) << (valid ? "valid" : "invalid")
    << "local=" << localpart
    << ";domain=" << hostname
    << ";dns=" << dnslabel
    << std::endl;
```

```
    };

    ltest3("JOHN.DOE@DOMAIN.COM"s);
    ltest3("JOHNDOE@DOMAIL.CO.UK"s);
    ltest3("JOHNDOE@DOMAIL.INFO"s);
    ltest3("J.O.H.N_D.O.E@DOMAIN.INFO"s);
    ltest3("ROOT@LOCALHOST"s);
    ltest3("john.doe@domain.com"s);
```

The output of the program will be as follows:

```
    JOHN.DOE@DOMAIN.COM                 : valid
        local=JOHN.DOE;domain=DOMAIN;dns=COM
    JOHNDOE@DOMAIL.CO.UK                 : valid
        local=JOHNDOE;domain=DOMAIL.CO;dns=UK
    JOHNDOE@DOMAIL.INFO                  : valid
        local=JOHNDOE;domain=DOMAIL;dns=INFO
    J.O.H.N_D.O.E@DOMAIN.INFO            : valid
        local=J.O.H.N_D.O.E;domain=DOMAIN;dns=INFO
    ROOT@LOCALHOST                       : invalid
        local=;domain=;dns=
    john.doe@domain.com                  : valid
        local=john.doe;domain=domain;dns=com
```

# There's more...

There are multiple versions of regular expressions, and the C++ standard library supports six of them: ECMAScript, basic POSIX, extended POSIX, awk, grep, and egrep (grep with option -E). The default grammar used is ECMAScript, and in order to use another, you explicitly have to specify the grammar when defining the regular expression. In addition to specifying the grammar, you can also specify parsing options, such as matching by ignoring the case.

The standard library provides more classes and algorithms than what we have seen so far. The main classes available in the library are the following (all of them are class templates and, for convenience, typedefs are provided for different character types):

- The class template std::basic_regex defines the regular expression object:

```
    typedef basic_regex<char>    regex;
    typedef basic_regex<wchar_t> wregex;
```

- The class template `std::sub_match` represents a sequence of characters that matches a capture group; this class is actually derived from `std::pair`, and its `first` and `second` members represent iterators to the first and the one-past-end characters in the match sequence; if there is no match sequence, the two iterators are equal:

```
typedef sub_match<const char *>            csub_match;
typedef sub_match<const wchar_t *>         wcsub_match;
typedef sub_match<string::const_iterator>  ssub_match;
typedef sub_match<wstring::const_iterator> wssub_match;
```

- The class template `std::match_results` is a collection of matches; the first element is always a full match in the target, and the other elements are matches of subexpressions:

```
typedef match_results<const char *>            cmatch;
typedef match_results<const wchar_t *>         wcmatch;
typedef match_results<string::const_iterator>  smatch;
typedef match_results<wstring::const_iterator> wsmatch;
```

The algorithms available in the regular expressions standard library are the following:

- `std::regex_match()`: This tries to match a regular expression (represented by a `std::basic_regex` instance) to an entire string.
- `std::regex_search()`: This tries to match a regular expression (represented by a `std::basic_regex` instance) to a part of a string (including the entire string).
- `std::regex_replace()`: This replaces matches from a regular expression according to a specified format.

The iterators available in the regular expressions standard library are the following:

- `std::regex_interator`: A constant forward iterator used to iterate through the occurrences of a pattern in a string. It has a pointer to an `std::basic_regex` that must live until the iterator is destroyed. Upon creation and when incremented, the iterator calls `std::regex_search()` and stores a copy of the `std::match_results` object returned by the algorithm.
- `std::regex_token_iterator`: A constant forward iterator used to iterate through the submatches of every match of a regular expression in a string. Internally, it uses an `std::regex_iterator` to step through the submatches. Since it stores a pointer to an `std::basic_regex` instance, the regular expression object must live until the iterator is destroyed.

## See also

- *Parsing the content of a string using regular expressions*
- *Replacing the content of a string using regular expressions*
- *Using structured bindings to handle multi-return values* recipe of Chapter 8, *Learning Modern Core Language Features*

# Parsing the content of a string using regular expressions

In the previous recipe, we have looked at how to use `std::regex_match()` to verify that the content of a string matches a particular format. The library provides another algorithm called `std::regex_search()` that matches a regular expression against any part of a string, and not only the entire string as `regex_match()` does. This function, however, does not allow searching through all the occurrences of a regular expression in an input string. For this purpose, we need to use one of the iterator classes available in the library.

In this recipe, you will learn how to parse the content of a string using regular expressions. For this purpose, we will consider the problem of parsing a text file containing name-value pairs. Each such pair is defined on a different line having the format `name = value`, but lines starting with a # represent comments and must be ignored. The following is an example:

```
#remove # to uncomment the following lines
timeout=120
server = 127.0.0.1
#retrycount=3
```

## Getting ready

For general information about regular expressions support in C++11, refer to the *Verifying the format of a string using regular expressions* recipe. Basic knowledge of regular expressions is required for proceeding with this recipe.

In the following examples, `text` is a variable defined as shown here:

```
auto text {
  R"(
    #remove # to uncomment the following lines
    timeout=120
    server = 127.0.0.1

    #retrycount=3
  )"s};
```

# How to do it...

In order to search for occurrences of a regular expression through a string you should perform the following:

1. Include headers `<regex>` and `<string>` and the namespace
   `std::string_literals` for C++14 standard user-defined literals for strings:

   ```
   #include <regex>
   #include <string>
   using namespace std::string_literals;
   ```

2. Use raw string literals to specify the regular expression to avoid escaping backslashes (that can occur frequently). The following regular expression validates the file format proposed earlier:

   ```
   auto pattern {R"(^(?!#)(\w+)\s*=\s*([\w\d]+[\w\d._,\-:]*)$)"s};
   ```

3. Create an `std::regex`/`std::wregex` object (depending on the character set that is used) to encapsulate the regular expression:

   ```
   auto rx = std::regex{pattern};
   ```

4. To search for the first occurrence of a regular expression in a given text, use the general purpose algorithm `std::regex_search()` (example 1):

   ```
   auto match = std::smatch{};
   if (std::regex_search(text, match, rx))
   {
     std::cout << match[1] << '=' << match[2] << std::endl;
   }
   ```

5. To find all the occurrences of a regular expression in a given text, use the iterator `std::regex_iterator` (example 2):

```
auto end = std::sregex_iterator{};
for (auto it=std::sregex_iterator{ std::begin(text),
                                    std::end(text), rx };
     it != end; ++it)
{
  std::cout << ''' << (*it)[1] << "'='"
             << (*it)[2] << ''' << std::endl;
}
```

6. To iterate through all the subexpressions of a match, use the iterator `std::regex_token_iterator` (example 3):

```
auto end = std::sregex_token_iterator{};
for (auto it = std::sregex_token_iterator{
                  std::begin(text),    std::end(text), rx };
     it != end; ++it)
{
  std::cout << *it << std::endl;
}
```

# How it works...

A simple regular expression that can parse the input file shown earlier may look like this:

```
^(?!#)(\w+)\s*=\s*([\w\d]+[\w\d._,\-:]*)$
```

This regular expression is supposed to ignore all lines that start with a #; for those that do not start with #, match a name followed by the equal sign and then a value that can be composed of alphanumeric characters and several other characters (underscore, dot, comma, and so on). The exact meaning of this regular expression is explained as follows:

| Part | Description |
|------|-------------|
| ^ | Start of line |
| (?!#) | A negative lookahead that makes sure that it is not possible to match the # character |
| (\w)+ | A capturing group representing an identifier of at least a one word character |
| \s* | Any white spaces |
| = | Equal sign |
| \s* | Any white spaces |

| | |
|---|---|
| `([\w\d]+[\w\d._,\-:]*)` | A capturing group representing a value that starts with an alphanumeric character, but can also contain a dot, comma, backslash, hyphen, colon, or an underscore. |
| `$` | End of line |

We can use `std::regex_search()` to search for a match anywhere in the input text. This algorithm has several overloads, but in general they work in the same way. You must specify the range of characters to work through, an output `std::match_results` object that will contain the result of the match, and a `std::basic_regex` object representing the regular expression and matching flags (that define the way the search is done). The function returns `true` if a match was found or `false` otherwise.

In the first example from the previous section (see the 4th list item), `match` is an instance of `std::smatch` that is a `typedef` of `std::match_results` with `string::const_iterator` as the template type. If a match was found, this object will contain the matching information in a sequence of values for all matched subexpressions. The submatch at index 0 is always the entire match. The submatch at index 1 is the first subexpression that was matched, the submatch at index 2 is the second subexpression that was matched, and so on. Since we have two capturing groups (that are subexpressions) in our regular expression, the `std::match_results` will have three submatches in case of success. The identifier representing the name is at index 1, and the value after the equal sign is at index 2. Therefore, this code only prints the following:

```
timeout=120
```

The `std::regex_search()` algorithm is not able to iterate through all the possible matches in a text. To do that, we need to use an iterator. `std::regex_iterator` is intended for this purpose. It allows not only iterating through all the matches, but also accessing all the submatches of a match. The iterator actually calls `std::regex_search()` upon construction and on each increment, and it remembers the result `std::match_results` from the call. The default constructor creates an iterator that represents the end of the sequence and can be used to test when the loop through the matches should stop.

In the second example from the previous section (see the 5th list item), we first create an end of sequence iterator, and then we start iterating through all the possible matches. When constructed, it will call `std::regex_match()`, and if a match is found, we can access its results through the current iterator. This will continue until no match is found (end of the sequence). This code will print the following output:

```
'timeout'='120'
'server'='127.0.0.1'
```

An alternative to `std::regex_iterator` is `std::regex_token_iterator`. This works similar to the way `std::regex_iterator` works and, in fact, it contains such an iterator internally, except that it enables us to access a particular subexpression from a match. This is shown in the third example in the *How to do it...* section (the the 6th list item). We start by creating an end-of-sequence iterator and then loop through the matches until the end-of-sequence is reached. In the constructor we used, we did not specify the index of the subexpression to access through the iterator; therefore, the default value of 0 is used. That means this program will print the entire matches:

```
timeout=120
server = 127.0.0.1
```

If we wanted to access only the first subexpression (that means the names in our case), all we had to do was specify the index of the subexpression in the constructor of the token iterator. This time, the output that we get is only the names:

```
auto end = std::sregex_token_iterator{};
for (auto it = std::sregex_token_iterator{ std::begin(text),
              std::end(text), rx, 1 };
     it != end; ++it)
{
  std::cout << *it << std::endl;
}
```

An interesting thing about the token iterator is that it can return the unmatched parts of the string if the index of the subexpressions is `-1`, in which case it returns an `std::match_results` object that corresponds to the sequence of characters between the last match and the end of the sequence:

```
auto end = std::sregex_token_iterator{};
for (auto it = std::sregex_token_iterator{ std::begin(text),
              std::end(text), rx, -1 };
     it != end; ++it)
{
  std::cout << *it << std::endl;
}
```

This program will output the following (note that the empty lines are actually part of the output):

```
#remove # to uncomment the following lines


#retrycount=3
```

# See also

- *Verifying the format of a string using regular expressions*
- *Replacing the content of a string using regular expressions*

# Replacing the content of a string using regular expressions

In the last two recipes, we have looked at how to match a regular expression on a string or a part of a string and iterate through matches and submatches. The regular expression library also supports text replacement based on regular expressions. In this recipe, we will see how to use `std::regex_replace()` to perform such text transformations.

# Getting ready

For general information about regular expressions support in C++11, refer to the *Verifying the format of a string using regular expressions* recipe.

# How to do it...

In order to perform text transformations using regular expressions, you should perform the following:

1. Include the `<regex>` and `<string>` and the namespace `std::string_literals` for C++14 standard user defined literals for strings:

```
#include <regex>
#include <string>
using namespace std::string_literals;
```

2. Use the `std::regex_replace()` algorithm with a replacement string as the third argument. Consider this example: replace all words composed of exactly three characters that are either a, b, or c with three hyphens:

```
auto text{"abc aa bca ca bbbb"s};
auto rx = std::regex{ R"(\b[a|b|c]{3}\b)"s };
auto newtext = std::regex_replace(text, rx, "---"s);
```

3. Use the `std::regex_replace()` algorithm with match identifiers prefixed with a $ for the third argument. For example, replace names in the "lastname, firstname" with names in the format "firstname lastname", as follows:

```
auto text{ "bancila, marius"s };
auto rx = std::regex{ R"((\w+),\s*(\w+))"s };
auto newtext = std::regex_replace(text, rx, "$2 $1"s);
```

# How it works...

The `std::regex_replace()` algorithm has several overloads with different types of parameters, but the meaning of the parameters is as follows:

- The input string on which the replacement is performed.
- An `std::basic_regex` object that encapsulates the regular expression used to identify the parts of the strings to be replaced.
- The string format used for replacement.
- Optional matching flags.

The return value is, depending on the overload used, either a string or a copy of the output iterator provided as an argument. The string format used for replacement can either be a simple string or a match identifier indicated with a $ prefix:

- `$&` indicates the entire match.
- `$1`, `$2`, `$3`, and so on, indicate the first, second, third submatch, and so on.
- `` $` `` indicates the part of the string before the first match.
- `$'` indicates the part of the string after the last match.

In the first example shown in the *How to do it...* section, the initial text contains two words made of exactly three a, b, or c characters, abc and bca. The regular expression indicates an expression of exactly three characters between word boundaries. That means a subtext, such as bbbb, will not match the expression. The result of the replacement is that the string text will be --- aa --- ca bbbb.

Additional flags for the match can be specified to the `std::regex_replace()` algorithm. By default, the matching flag is `std::regex_constants::match_default` that basically specifies ECMAScript as the grammar used for constructing the regular expression. If we want, for instance, to replace only the first occurrence, then we can specify `std::regex_constants::format_first_only`. In the next example, the result is `--- aa bca ca bbbb` as the replacement stops after the first match is found:

```
auto text{ "abc aa bca ca bbbb"s };
auto rx = std::regex{ R"(\b[a|b|c]{3}\b)"s };
auto newtext = std::regex_replace(text, rx, "---"s,
              std::regex_constants::format_first_only);
```

The replacement string, however, can contain special indicators for the whole match, a particular submatch, or the parts that were not matched, as explained earlier. In the second example shown in the *How to do it...* section, the regular expression identifies a word of at least one character, followed by a coma and possible white spaces and then another word of at least one character. The first word is supposed to be the last name and the second word is supposed to be the first name. The replacement string has the `$2 $1` format. This is an instruction to replace the matched expression (in this example, the entire original string) with another string formed of the second submatch followed by space and then the first submatch.

In this case, the entire string was a match. In the next example, there will be multiple matches inside the string, and they will all be replaced with the indicated string. In this example, we are replacing the indefinite article *a* when preceding a word that starts with a vowel (this, of course, does not cover words that start with a vowel sound) with the indefinite article *an*:

```
auto text{"this is a example with a error"s};
auto rx = std::regex{R"(\ba ((a|e|i|u|o)\w+))"s};
auto newtext = std::regex_replace(text, rx, "an $1");
```

The regular expression identifies the letter *a* as a single word (`\b` indicates a word boundary, so `\ba` means a word with a single letter *a*) followed by a space and a word of at least two characters starting with a vowel. When such a match is identified, it is replaced with a string formed of the fixed string *an* followed by a space and the first subexpression of the match, which is the word itself. In this example, the `newtext` string will be *this is an example with an error*.

Apart from the identifiers of the subexpressions ($1, $2, and so on), there are other identifiers for the entire match ($&), the part of the string before the first match ($`) and the part of the string after the last match ($'). In the last example, we change the format of a date from dd.mm.yyyy to yyyy.mm.dd, but also show the matched parts:

```
auto text{"today is 1.06.2016!!"s};
auto rx =
    std::regex{R"((\d{1,2})(\.|-|/)(\d{1,2})(\.|-|/)(\d{4}))"s};
// today is 2016.06.1!!
auto newtext1 = std::regex_replace(text, rx, R"($5$4$3$2$1)");
// today is [today is ][1.06.2016][!!]!!
auto newtext2 = std::regex_replace(text, rx, R"([$`][$&][$'])");
```

The regular expression matches a one- or two-digit number followed by a dot, hyphen, or slash; followed by another one- or two-digit number; then a dot, hyphen, or slash; and last a four-digit number.

For newtext1, the replacement string is $5$4$3$2$1; that means year, followed by the second separator, then month, the first separator, and finally day. Therefore, for the input string *"today is 1.06.2016!"*, the result is *"today is 2016.06.1!!"*.

For newtext2, the replacement string is [$`][$&][$']; that means the part before the first match, followed by the entire match, and finally the part after the last match are in square brackets. However, the result is not *"[!!][1.06.2016][today is ]"* as you perhaps might expect at a first glance, but *"today is [today is ][1.06.2016][!!]!!"*. The reason is that what is replaced is the matched expression, and, in this case, that is only the date (*"1.06.2016"*). This substring is replaced with another string formed of the all parts of the initial string.

# See also

- *Verifying the format of a string using regular expressions*
- *Parsing the content of a string using regular expressions*

# Using string_view instead of constant string references

When working with strings, temporary objects are created all the time, even if you might not be really aware of it. Many times the temporary objects are irrelevant and only serve the purpose of copying data from one place to another (for example, from a function to its caller). This represents a performance issue because they require memory allocation and data copying, which is desirable to be avoided. For this purpose, the C++17 standard provides a new string class template called `std::basic_string_view` that represents a non-owning constant reference to a string (that is, a sequence of characters). In this recipe, you will learn when and how you should use this class.

## Getting ready

The `string_view` class is available in the namespace `std` in the `string_view` header.

## How to do it...

You should use `std::string_view` to pass a parameter to a function (or return a value from a function), instead of `std::string const &` unless your code needs to call other functions that take `std::string` parameters (in which case, conversions would be necessary):

```
std::string_view get_filename(std::string_view str)
{
  auto const pos1 {str.find_last_of('')};
  auto const pos2 {str.find_last_of('.')};
  return str.substr(pos1 + 1, pos2 - pos1 - 1);
}

char const file1[] {R"(c:\test\example1.doc)"};
auto name1 = get_filename(file1);

std::string file2 {R"(c:\test\example2)"};
auto name2 = get_filename(file2);

auto name3 = get_filename(std::string_view{file1, 16});
```

# How it works...

Before we look at how the new string type works, let's consider the following example of a function that is supposed to extract the name of a file without its extension. This is basically how you would write the function from the previous section before C++17.

 Note that in this example the file separator is \ (backslash) as in Windows. For Linux-based systems, it has to be changed to / (slash).

```cpp
std::string get_filename(std::string const & str)
{
  auto const pos1 {str.find_last_of('')};
  auto const pos2 {str.find_last_of('.')};
  return str.substr(pos1 + 1, pos2 - pos1 - 1);
}

auto name1 = get_filename(R"(c:\test\example1.doc)"); // example1
auto name2 = get_filename(R"(c:\test\example2)");      // example2
if(get_filename(R"(c:\test\_sample_.tmp)").front() == '_') {}
```

This is a relatively simple function. It takes a constant reference to an `std::string` and identifies a substring bounded by the last file separator and the last dot that basically represents a filename without an extension (and without folder names).

The problem with this code, however, is that it creates one, two, or, possibly, even more temporaries, depending on the compiler optimizations. The function parameter is a constant `std::string` reference, but the function is called with a string literal, which means `std::string` needs to be constructed from the literal. These temporaries need to allocate and copy data, which is both time- and resource-consuming. In the last example, all we want to do is check whether the first character of the filename is an underscore, but we create at least two temporary string objects for that purpose.

The `std::basic_string_view` class template is intended to solve this problem. This class template is very similar to `std::basic_string`, the two having almost the same interface. The reasons for this is that the `std::basic_string_view` is intended to be used instead of a constant reference to an `std::basic_string` without further code changes.

Just like with `std::basic_string`, there are specializations for all types of standard characters:

```
typedef basic_string_view<char>     string_view;
typedef basic_string_view<wchar_t>  wstring_view;
typedef basic_string_view<char16_t> u16string_view;
typedef basic_string_view<char32_t> u32string_view;
```

The `std::basic_string_view` class template defines a reference to a constant contiguous sequence of characters. As the name implies, it represents a view and cannot be used to modify the reference sequence of characters. An `std::basic_string_view` object has a relatively small size because all that it needs is a pointer to the first character in the sequence and the length. It can be constructed not only from an `std::basic_string` object but also from a pointer and a length or from a null-terminated sequence of characters (in which case, it will require an initial traversing of the string in order to find the length). Therefore, the `std::basic_string_view` class template can also be used as a common interface for multiple types of strings (as long as data only needs to be read). On the other hand, converting from an `std::basic_string_view` to an `std::basic_string` is easy because the former has both a `to_string()` and a converting `operator` `std::basic_string` to create a new `std::basic_string` object.

Passing `std::basic_string_view` to functions and returning `std::basic_string_view` still creates temporaries of this type, but these are small size objects on the stack (a pointer and a size could be 16 bytes for 64-bit platforms); therefore, they should incur fewer performance costs than allocating heap space and copying data.

> Notice that all major compilers provide an implementation of std::basic_string that includes a small string optimization. Although the implementation details are different, they typically rely on having a statically allocated buffer of a number of characters (16 for VC++ and gcc 5 or newer) that does not involve heap operations, which are only required when the size of the string exceeds that number of characters.

In addition to the methods that are identical to those available in `std::basic_string`, the `std::basic_string_view` has two more:

- `remove_prefix()`: Shrinks the view by incrementing the start with *N* characters and decrementing the length with *N* characters.
- `remove_suffix()`: Shrinks the view by decrementing the length with *N* characters.

The two member functions are used in the following example to trim an std::string_view from spaces, both at the beginning and the end. The implementation of the function first looks for the first element that is not a space and then for the last element that is not a space. Then, it removes from the end everything after the last non-space character, and from the beginning everything until the first non-space character. The function returns the new view trimmed at both ends:

```cpp
std::string_view trim_view(std::string_view str)
{
    auto const pos1{ str.find_first_not_of(" ") };
    auto const pos2{ str.find_last_not_of(" ") };
    str.remove_suffix(str.length() - pos2 - 1);
    str.remove_prefix(pos1);

    return str;
}

auto sv1{ trim_view("sample") };
auto sv2{ trim_view("  sample") };
auto sv3{ trim_view("sample  ") };
auto sv4{ trim_view("  sample  ") };

auto s1{ sv1.to_string() };
auto s2{ sv2.to_string() };
auto s3{ sv3.to_string() };
auto s4{ sv4.to_string() };
```

 When using an std::basic_string_view, you must be aware of two things: you cannot change the underlying data referred by a view and you must manage the lifetime of the data, as the view is a non-owning reference.

# See also

- *Creating a library of string helpers*

# 10
# Exploring Functions

The recipes included in this chapter are as follows:

- Defaulted and deleted functions
- Using lambdas with standard algorithms
- Using generic lambdas
- Writing a recursive lambda
- Writing a function template with a variable number of arguments
- Using fold expressions to simplify variadic function templates
- Implementing higher-order functions map and fold
- Composing functions into a higher-order function
- Uniformly invoking anything callable

## Defaulted and deleted functions

In C++, classes have special members (constructors, destructors, and operators) that may be either implemented by default by the compiler or supplied by the developer. However, the rules for what can be default implemented are a bit complicated and can lead to problems. On the other hand, developers sometimes want to prevent objects from being copied, moved, or constructed in a particular way. That is possible by implementing different tricks using these special members. The C++11 standard has simplified many of these by allowing functions to be deleted or defaulted in the manner we will see in the next section.

## Getting started

For this recipe, you need to know what special member functions are and what copyable and moveable means.

# How to do it...

Use the following syntax to specify how functions should be handled:

- To default a function, use =default instead of the function body. Only special class member functions that have defaults can be defaulted:

```
struct foo
{
    foo() = default;
};
```

- To delete a function, use =delete instead of the function body. Any function, including non-member functions, can be deleted:

```
struct foo
{
    foo(foo const &) = delete;
};

void func(int) = delete;
```

Use defaulted and deleted functions to achieve various design goals, such as the following examples:

- To implement a class that is not copyable, and implicitly not movable, declare the copy operations as deleted:

```
class foo_not_copyable
{
public:
    foo_not_copyable() = default;

    foo_not_copyable(foo_not_copyable const &) = delete;
    foo_not_copyable& operator=(foo_not_copyable const&) = delete;
};
```

- To implement a class that is not copyable, but is movable, declare the copy operations as deleted and explicitly implement the move operations (and provide any additional constructors that are needed):

```
class data_wrapper
{
    Data* data;
public:
    data_wrapper(Data* d = nullptr) : data(d) {}
    ~data_wrapper() { delete data; }
```

```
data_wrapper(data_wrapper const&) = delete;
data_wrapper& operator=(data_wrapper const &) = delete;

data_wrapper(data_wrapper&& o) :data(std::move(o.data))
{
  o.data = nullptr;
}

data_wrapper& operator=(data_wrapper&& o)
{
  if (this != &o)
  {
    delete data;
    data = std::move(o.data);
    o.data = nullptr;
  }

  return *this;
}
};
```

- To ensure a function is called only with objects of a specific type, and perhaps prevent type promotion, provide deleted overloads for the function (the following example with free functions can also be applied to any class member functions):

```
template <typename T>
void run(T val) = delete;

void run(long val) {} // can only be called with long integers
```

# How it works...

A class has several special members that can be implemented, by default, by the compiler. These are the default constructor, copy constructor, move constructor, copy assignment, move assignment, and destructor. If you don't implement them, then the compiler does it so that instances of a class can be created, moved, copied, and destructed. However, if you explicitly provide one or more of these special methods, then the compiler will not generate the others according to the following rules:

- If a user-defined constructor exists, the default constructor is not generated by default.
- If a user-defined virtual destructor exists, the default constructor is not generated by default.

- If a user-defined move constructor or move assignment operator exists, then the copy constructor and copy assignment operator are not generated by default.
- If a user-defined copy constructor, move constructor, copy assignment operator, move assignment operator, or destructor exists, then the move constructor and move assignment operator are not generated by default.
- If a user-defined copy constructor or destructor exists, then the copy assignment operator is generated by default.
- If a user-defined copy assignment operator or destructor exists, then the copy constructor is generated by default.

 Note that the last two rules in the preceding list are deprecated rules and may no longer be supported by your compiler.

Sometimes, developers need to provide empty implementations of these special members or hide them in order to prevent the instances of the class from being constructed in a specific manner. A typical example is a class that is not supposed to be copyable. The classical pattern for this is to provide a default constructor and hide the copy constructor and copy assignment operators. While this works, the explicitly defined default constructor ensures the class is no longer considered trivial and, therefore, a POD type. The modern alternative to this is using a deleted function as shown in the preceding section.

When the compiler encounters =default in the definition of a function, it will provide the default implementation. The rules for special member functions mentioned earlier still apply. Functions can be declared =default outside the body of a class if and only if they are inlined:

```
class foo
{
public:
  foo() = default;

  inline foo& operator=(foo const &);
};

inline foo& foo::operator=(foo const &) = default;
```

When the compiler encounters the `=delete` in the definition of a function, it will prevent the calling of the function. However, the function is still considered during overload resolution, and only if the deleted function is the best match, the compiler generates an error. For example, by giving the previously defined overloads for the `run()` function, only calls with long integers are possible. Calls with arguments of any other type, including `int`, for which an automatic type promotion to `long` exists, will determine a deleted overload to be considered the best match and therefore the compiler will generate an error:

```
run(42);  // error, matches a deleted overload
run(42L); // OK, long integer arguments are allowed
```

Note that previously declared functions cannot be deleted, as the `=delete` definition must be the first declaration in a translation unit:

```
void forward_declared_function();
// ...
void forward_declared_function() = delete; // error
```

 The rule of thumb (also known as *The Rule of Five*) for class special member functions is that, if you explicitly define any copy constructor, move constructor, copy assignment operator, move assignment operator, or destructor, then you must either explicitly define or default all of them.

# Using lambdas with standard algorithms

One of the most important modern features of C++ is lambda expressions, also referred to as lambda functions or simply lambdas. Lambda expressions enable us to define anonymous function objects that can capture variables in the scope and be invoked or passed as arguments to functions. Lambdas are useful for many purposes, and in this recipe, we will see how to use them with standard algorithms.

# Getting ready

In this recipe, we discuss standard algorithms that take an argument that is a function or predicate applied to the elements it iterates through. You need to know what unary and binary functions are and what predicates and comparison functions are. You also need to be familiar with function objects because lambda expressions are syntactic sugar for function objects.

# How to do it...

You should prefer to use lambda expressions to pass callbacks to standard algorithms instead of functions or function objects:

- Define anonymous lambda expressions in the place of the call if you only need to use the lambda in a single place:

```
auto numbers =
    std::vector<int>{ 0, 2, -3, 5, -1, 6, 8, -4, 9 };
auto positives = std::count_if(
    std::begin(numbers), std::end(numbers),
    [](int const n) {return n > 0; });
```

- Define a named lambda, that is, one assigned to a variable (usually with the `auto` specifier for the type), if you need to call the lambda in multiple places:

```
auto ispositive = [](int const n) {return n > 0; };
auto positives = std::count_if(
    std::begin(numbers), std::end(numbers), ispositive);
```

- Use generic lambda expressions if you need lambdas that only differ in their argument types (available since C++14):

```
auto positives = std::count_if(
    std::begin(numbers), std::end(numbers),
    [](auto const n) {return n > 0; });
```

# How it works...

The non-generic lambda expression shown on the second bullet earlier takes a constant integer and returns `true` if it is greater than 0, or `false` otherwise. The compiler defines an unnamed function object with the call operator having the signature of the lambda expression:

```
struct __lambda_name__
{
  bool operator()(int const n) const { return n > 0; }
};
```

The way the unnamed function object is defined by the compiler depends on the way we define the lambda expression that can capture variables, use the `mutable` specifier or exception specifications, or have a trailing return type. The __lambda_name__ function object shown earlier is actually a simplification of what the compiler generates because it also defines a default copy and move constructor, a default destructor, and a deleted assignment operator.

> It must be well understood that the lambda expression is actually a class. In order to call it, the compiler needs to instantiate an object of the class. The object instantiated from a lambda expression is called a *lambda closure*.

In the next example, we want to count the number of elements in a range that are greater than or equal to 5 and less than or equal to 10. The lambda expression, in this case, will look like this:

```
auto numbers = std::vector<int>{ 0, 2, -3, 5, -1, 6, 8, -4, 9 };
auto start{ 5 };
auto end{ 10 };
auto inrange = std::count_if(
        std::begin(numbers), std::end(numbers),
        [start, end](int const n) {
            return start <= n && n <= end; });
```

This lambda captures two variables, `start` and `end`, by copy (that is, value). The resulting unnamed function object created by the compiler looks very much like the one we defined earlier. With the default and deleted special members mentioned earlier, the class looks like this:

```
class __lambda_name_2__
{
  int start_;
  int end_;
public:
  explicit __lambda_name_2__(int const start, int const end) :
    start_(start), end_(end)
  {}

  __lambda_name_2__(const __lambda_name_2__&) = default;
  __lambda_name_2__(__lambda_name_2__&&) = default;
  __lambda_name_2__& operator=(const __lambda_name_2__&)
      = delete;
  ~__lambda_name_2__() = default;

  bool operator() (int const n) const
  {
```

```
        return start_ <= n && n <= end_;
    }
};
```

The lambda expression can capture variables by copy (or value) or by reference, and different combinations of the two are possible. However, it is not possible to capture a variable multiple times, and it is only possible to have & or = at the beginning of the capture list.

 A lambda can only capture variables from an enclosing function scope. It cannot capture variables with static storage duration (that is, variables declared in a namespace scope or with the `static` or `external` specifier).

The following table shows various combinations for lambda captures semantics.

| Lambda | Description |
|---|---|
| `[] () {}` | Does not capture anything |
| `[&] () {}` | Captures everything by reference |
| `[=] () {}` | Captures everything by copy |
| `[&x] () {}` | Capture only x by reference |
| `[x] () {}` | Capture only x by copy |
| `[&x...] () {}` | Capture pack extension x by reference |
| `[x...] () {}` | Capture pack extension x by copy |
| `[&, x] () {}` | Captures everything by reference except for x that is captured by copy |
| `[=, &x] () {}` | Captures everything by copy except for x that is captured by reference |
| `[&, this] () {}` | Captures everything by reference except for pointer `this` that is captured by copy (`this` is always captured by copy) |
| `[x, x] () {}` | Error, x is captured twice |
| `[&, &x] () {}` | Error, everything is captured by reference, cannot specify again to capture x by reference |
| `[=, =x] () {}` | Error, everything is captured by copy, cannot specify again to capture x by copy |
| `[&this] () {}` | Error, pointer `this` is always captured by copy |
| `[&, =] () {}` | Error, cannot capture everything both by copy and by reference |

The general form of a lambda expression, as of C++17, looks like this:

```
[capture-list] (params) mutable constexpr exception attr -> ret
{ body }
```

All parts shown in this syntax are actually optional except for the capture list, that can, however, be empty, and the body, that can also be empty. The parameter list can actually be omitted if no parameters are needed. The return type does not need to be specified, as the compiler can infer it from the type of the returned expression. The `mutable` specifier (that tells the compiler the lambda can actually modify variables captured by copy), the `constexpr` specifier (that tells the compiler to generate a `constexpr` call operator), and the exception specifiers and attributes are all optional.

 The simplest possible lambda expression is `[]{}`, though it is often written as `[](){}`.

# There's more...

There are cases where lambda expressions only differ in the type of their arguments. In this case, the lambdas can be written in a generic way, just like templates, but using the `auto` specifier for the type parameters (no template syntax is involved). This is addressed in the next recipe, mentioned in the *See also* section.

# See also

- *Using generic lambdas*
- *Writing a recursive lambda*

# Using generic lambdas

In the preceding recipe, we saw how to write lambda expressions and use them with standard algorithms. In C++, lambdas are basically syntactic sugar for unnamed function objects, which are classes that implement the call operator. However, just like any other function, this can be implemented generically with templates. C++14 takes advantage of this and introduces generic lambdas that do not need to specify actual types for their parameters and use the `auto` specifier instead. Though not referred with this name, generic lambdas are basically lambda templates. They are useful in cases where we want to use the same lambda but with different types of parameter.

# Getting started

It is recommended that you read the preceding recipe, *Using lambdas with standard algorithms*, before you continue with this one.

# How to do it...

Write generic lambdas:

- By using the `auto` specifier instead of actual types for lambda expression parameters.
- When you need to use multiple lambdas that only differ by their parameter types.

The following example shows a generic lambda used with the `std::accumulate()` algorithm first with a vector of integers and then with a vector of strings.

```
auto numbers =
  std::vector<int>{0, 2, -3, 5, -1, 6, 8, -4, 9};
auto texts =
  std::vector<std::string>{"hello"s, " "s, "world"s, "!"s};

auto lsum = [](auto const s, auto const n) {return s + n;};

auto sum = std::accumulate(
  std::begin(numbers), std::end(numbers), 0, lsum);
  // sum = 22

auto text = std::accumulate(
  std::begin(texts), std::end(texts), ""s, lsum);
  // sum = "hello world!"s
```

# How it works...

In the example from the previous section, we have defined a named lambda expression, that is, a lambda expression that has its closure assigned to a variable. This variable is then passed as an argument to the `std::accumulate()` function. This general algorithm takes the begin and the end iterators that define a range, an initial value to accumulate over, and a function that is supposed to accumulate each value in the range to the total. This function takes a first parameter representing the currently accumulated value and a second parameter representing the current value to accumulate to the total, and it returns the new accumulated value.

Note that I did not use the term `add` because this can be used for other things than just adding. It can also be used for calculating a product, concatenating, or other operations that aggregate values together.

The two calls to `std::accumulate()` in this example are almost the same, only the types of the arguments are different:

- In the first call, we pass iterators to a range of integers (from a `vector<int>`), 0 for the initial sum and a lambda that adds two integers and returns their sum. This produces a sum of all integers in the range; for this example, it is 22.
- In the second call, we pass iterators to a range of strings (from a `vector<string>`), an empty string for the initial value, and a lambda that concatenates two strings by adding them together and returning the result. This produces a string that contains all the strings in the range put together one after an other; for this example, the result is *"hello world!"*.

Though generic lambdas can be defined anonymously in the place where they are called, it does not really make sense because the very purpose of a generic lambda (that is basically, as mentioned earlier, a lambda expression template) is to be reused, as shown in the example from the *How to do it...* section.

When defining this lambda expression used with multiple calls to `std::accumulate()`, instead of specifying concrete types for the lambda parameters (such as `int` or `std::string`) we used the `auto` specifier and let the compiler deduce the type. When encountering a lambda expression that has the `auto` specifier for a parameter type, the compiler generates an unnamed function object that has a call operator template. For the generic lambda expression in this example, the function object would look like this:

```
struct __lambda_name__
{
  template<typename T1, typename T2>
  auto operator()(T1 const s, T2 const n) const { return s + n; }

  __lambda_name__(const __lambda_name__&) = default;
  __lambda_name__(__lambda_name__&&) = default;
  __lambda_name__& operator=(const __lambda_name__&) = delete;
  ~__lambda_name__() = default;
};
```

The call operator is a template with a type parameter for each parameter in the lambda that was specified with `auto`. The return type of the call operator is also `auto`, which means the compiler will deduce it from the type of the returned value. This operator template will be instantiated with the actual types the compiler will identify in the context where the generic lambda is used.

## See also

- *Using lambdas with standard algorithms*
- *Using auto whenever possible* recipe of `Chapter 8`, *Learning Modern Core Language Features*

# Writing a recursive lambda

Lambdas are basically unnamed function objects, which means that it should be possible to call them recursively. Indeed, they can be called recursively; however, the mechanism for doing it is not obvious, as it requires assigning the lambda to a function wrapper and capturing the wrapper by reference. Though it can be argued that a recursive lambda does not really make sense and a function is probably a better design choice, in this recipe we will look at how to write a recursive lambda.

## Getting ready

To demonstrate how to write a recursive lambda, we will consider the well-known example of the Fibonacci function. This is usually implemented recursively in C++, as follows:

```
constexpr int fib(int const n)
{
   return n <= 2 ? 1 : fib(n - 1) + fib(n - 2);
}
```

# How to do it...

In order to write a recursive lambda function, you must perform the following:

- Define the lambda in a function scope.
- Assign the lambda to an std::function wrapper.
- Capture the std::function object by reference in the lambda in order to call it recursively.

The following are examples of recursive lambdas:

- A recursive Fibonacci lambda expression in the scope of a function that is invoked from the scope where it is defined:

```
void sample()
{
  std::function<int(int const)> lfib =
    [&lfib](int const n)
    {
      return n <= 2 ? 1 : lfib(n - 1) + lfib(n - 2);
    };

  auto f10 = lfib(10);
}
```

- A recursive Fibonacci lambda expression returned by a function, that can be invoked from any scope:

```
std::function<int(int const)> fib_create()
{
  std::function<int(int const)> f = [](int const n)
  {
    std::function<int(int const)> lfib = [&lfib](int n)
    {
      return n <= 2 ? 1 : lfib(n - 1) + lfib(n - 2);
    };
    return lfib(n);
  };
  return f;
}

void sample()
{
  auto lfib = fib_create();
  auto f10 = lfib(10);
}
```

# How it works...

The first thing you need to consider when writing a recursive lambda is that a lambda expression is a function object and, in order to call it recursively from the lambda's body, the lambda must capture its closure (that is, the instantiation of the lambda). In other words, the lambda must capture itself and this has several implications:

- First of all, the lambda must have a name; an unnamed lambda cannot be captured in order to be called again.
- Secondly, the lambda can only be defined in a function scope. The reason for this is that a lambda can only capture variables from a function scope; it cannot capture any variable that has a static storage duration. Objects defined in a namespace scope or with the static or external specifiers have static storage duration. If the lambda was defined in a namespace scope, its closure would have static storage duration and therefore the lambda would not capture it.
- The third implication is that the type of the lambda closure cannot remain unspecified, that is, be declared with the auto specifier. It is not possible for a variable declared with the auto type specifier to appear in its own initializer because the type of the variable is not known when the initializer is being processed. Therefore, you must specify the type of the lambda closure. The way we can do this is using the general purpose function wrapper `std::function`.
- Last, but not least, the lambda closure must be captured by reference. If we capture by copy (or value), then a copy of the function wrapper is made, but the wrapper is uninitialized when the capturing is done. We end up with an object that we are not able to call. Even though the compiler will not complain about capturing by value, when the closure is invoked, an `std::bad_function_call` is thrown.

In the first example from the *How to do it...* section, the recursive lambda is defined inside another function called `sample()`. The signature and the body of the lambda expression are the same as those of the regular recursive function `fib()` defined in the introductory section. The lambda closure is assigned to a function wrapper called `lfib` that is then captured by reference by the lambda and called recursively from its body. Since the closure is captured by reference, it will be initialized at the time it has to be called from the lambda's body.

In the second example, we have defined a function that returns the closure of a lambda expression that, in turn, defines and invokes a recursive lambda with the argument it was, in turn, invoked with. This is a pattern that must be implemented when a recursive lambda needs to be returned from a function. This is necessary because the lambda closure must still be available at the time the recursive lambda is called. If it is destroyed before that, we are left with a dangling reference and calling it will cause the program to terminate abnormally. This erroneous situation is exemplified in the following sample:

```cpp
// this implementation of fib_create is faulty
std::function<int(int const)> fib_create()
{
   std::function<int(int const)> lfib = [&lfib](int const n)
   {
      return n <= 2 ? 1 : lfib(n - 1) + lfib(n - 2);
   };

   return lfib;
}

void sample()
{
   auto lfib = fib_create();
   auto f10 = lfib(10);        // crash
}
```

The solution for this is to create two nested lambda expressions as shown in the *How to do it...* section. The `fib_create()` method returns a function wrapper that when invoked creates the recursive lambda that captures itself. This is slightly and subtly, yet fundamentally, different from the implementation shown in the preceding sample. The outer `f` lambda does not capture anything, especially by reference; therefore, we don't have the issue with dangling references. However, when invoked, it creates a closure of the nested lambda, the actual lambda we are interested in calling and returns the result of applying that recursive `lfib` lambda to its parameter.

# Writing a function template with a variable number of arguments

It is sometimes useful to write functions with a variable number of arguments or classes with a variable number of members. Typical examples include functions such as `printf` that take a format and a variable number of arguments, or classes such as `tuple`. Before C++11, the former was possible only with the use of variadic macros (that enable writing only type-unsafe functions) and the latter was not possible at all. C++11 introduced variadic templates, which are templates with a variable number of arguments that make it possible to write both type-safe function templates with a variable number of arguments and also class templates with a variable number of members. In this recipe, we will look at writing function templates.

## Getting ready

Functions with a variable number of arguments are called *variadic functions*. Function templates with a variable number of arguments are called *variadic function templates*. Knowledge of C++ variadic macros (`va_start`, `va_end`, `va_arg` and `va_copy`, `va_list`) is not necessary for learning how to write variadic function templates, but it represents a good starting point.

We have already used variadic templates in our previous recipes, but this one will provide detailed explanations.

## How to do it...

In order to write variadic function templates, you must perform the following steps:

1. Define an overload with a fixed number of arguments to end compile-time recursion if the semantics of the variadic function template require it (refer to [1] in the following code).
2. Define a template parameter pack to introduce a template parameter that can hold any number of arguments, including zero; these arguments can be either types, non-types, or templates (refer to [2]).
3. Define a function parameter pack to hold any number of function arguments, including zero; the size of the template parameter pack and the corresponding function parameter pack is the same and can be determined with the `sizeof...` operator (refer to [3]).

4. Expand the parameter pack in order to replace it with the actual arguments being supplied (refer to `[4]`).

The following example that illustrates all the preceding points, is a variadic function template that adds a variable number of arguments using `operator+`:

```
template <typename T>                  // [1] overload with fixed
T add(T value)                         //     number of arguments
{
  return value;
}

template <typename T, typename... Ts> // [2] typename... Ts
T add(T head, Ts... rest)              // [3] Ts... rest
{
  return head + add(rest...);          // [4] rest...
}
```

# How it works...

At a first look, the preceding implementation looks like recursion, because function `add()` calls itself, and in a way it is, but it is a compile-time recursion that does not incur any sort of runtime recursion and overhead. The compiler actually generates several functions with a different number of arguments, based on the variadic function template usage, so it is only function overloading that is involved and not any sort of recursion. However, implementation is done as if parameters would be processed in a recursive manner with an end condition.

In the preceding code we can identify the following key parts:

- `Typename... Ts` is a template parameter pack that indicates a variable number of template type arguments.
- `Ts... rest` is a function parameter pack that indicates a variable number of function arguments.
- `Rest...` is an expansion of the function parameter pack.

 The position of the ellipsis is not syntactically relevant. `typename... Ts,` `typename ... Ts,` and `typename ...Ts` are all equivalent.

In the `add(T head, Ts... rest)` parameter, `head` is the first element of the list of arguments, and `...rest` is a pack with the rest of the parameters in the list (this can be zero or more). In the body of the function, `rest...` is an expansion of the function parameter pack. This means the compiler replaces the parameter pack with its elements in their order. In the `add()` function, we basically add the first argument to the sum of the remaining arguments, which gives the impression of a recursive processing. This recursion ends when there is a single argument left, in which case the first `add()` overload (with a single argument) is called and returns the value of its argument.

This implementation of the function template `add()` enables us to write code, as shown here:

```
auto s1 = add(1, 2, 3, 4, 5);
// s1 = 15
auto s2 = add("hello"s, " "s, "world"s, "!"s);
// s2 = "hello world!"
```

When the compiler encounters `add(1, 2, 3, 4, 5)`, it generates the following functions (`arg1`, `arg2`, and so on, are not the actual names the compiler generates) that show this is actually only calls to overloaded functions and not recursion:

```
int add(int head, int arg1, int arg2, int arg3, int arg4)
{return head + add(arg1, arg2, arg3, arg4);}
int add(int head, int arg1, int arg2, int arg3)
{return head + add(arg1, arg2, arg3);}
int add(int head, int arg1, int arg2)
{return head + add(arg1, arg2);}
int add(int head, int arg1)
{return head + add(arg1);}
int add(int value)
{return value;}
```

 With GCC and Clang, you can use the __PRETTY_FUNCTION__ macro to print the name and the signature of the function.

By adding a `std::cout << __PRETTY_FUNCTION__ << std::endl` at the beginning of the two functions we wrote, we get the following when running the code:

```
T add(T, Ts ...) [with T = int; Ts = {int, int, int, int}]
T add(T, Ts ...) [with T = int; Ts = {int, int, int}]
T add(T, Ts ...) [with T = int; Ts = {int, int}]
T add(T, Ts ...) [with T = int; Ts = {int}]
T add(T) [with T = int]
```

Since this is a function template, it can be used with any type that supports `operator+`. The other example, `add("hello"s, " "s, "world"s, "!"s)`, produces the *"hello world!"* string. However, the `std::basic_string` type has different overloads for `operator+`, including one that can concatenate a string to a character, so we should be able to also write the following:

```
auto s3 = add("hello"s, ' ', "world"s, '!');
// s3 = "hello world!"
```

However, that will generate compiler errors as follows (note that I actually replaced `std::basic_string<char, std::char_traits<char>, std::allocator<char> >` with string *"hello world"* for simplicity):

```
In instantiation of 'T add(T, Ts ...) [with T = char; Ts = {string,
char}]':
16:29:   required from 'T add(T, Ts ...) [with T = string; Ts = {char,
string, char}]'
22:46:   required from here
16:29: error: cannot convert 'string' to 'char' in return
 In function 'T add(T, Ts ...) [with T = char; Ts = {string, char}]':
17:1: warning: control reaches end of non-void function [-Wreturn-type]
```

What happens is that the compiler generates the code shown next where the return type is the same as the type of the first argument. However, the first argument is either a `std::string` or a `char` (again, `std::basic_string<char, std::char_traits<char>, std::allocator<char> >` was replaced with `string` for simplicity). In cases where `char` is the type of the first argument, the type of the return value `head+add(...)` that is an `std::string` does not match the function return type and does not have an implicit conversion to it:

```
string add(string head, char arg1, string arg2, char arg3)
{return head + add(arg1, arg2, arg3);}
char add(char head, string arg1, char arg2)
{return head + add(arg1, arg2);}
string add(string head, char arg1)
{return head + add(arg1);}
char add(char value)
{return value;}
```

We can fix this by modifying the variadic function template to have `auto` for the return type instead of `T`. In this case, the return type is always inferred from the return expression, and in our example, it will be `std::string` in all cases:

```
template <typename T, typename... Ts>
auto add(T head, Ts... rest)
{
   return head + add(rest...);
}
```

It should be further added that a parameter pack can appear in a brace-initialization and its size can be determined using the `sizeof...` operator. Also, variadic function templates do not necessarily imply compile-time recursion as we have shown in this recipe. All these are shown in the following example where we define a function that creates a tuple with an even number of members. We first use `sizeof...(a)` to make sure that we have an even number of arguments and assert by generating a compiler error otherwise. The `sizeof...` operator can be used with both template parameter packs and function parameter packs. `sizeof...(a)` and `sizeof...(T)` would produce the same value. Then, we create and return a tuple. The template parameter pack `T` is expanded (with `T...`) into the type arguments of the `std::tuple` class template, and the function parameter pack `a` is expanded (with `a...`) into the values for the tuple members using brace initialization:

```
template<typename... T>
auto make_even_tuple(T... a)
{
   static_assert(sizeof...(a) % 2 == 0,
               "expected an even number of arguments");
   std::tuple<T...> t { a... };

   return t;
}

auto t1 = make_even_tuple(1, 2, 3, 4); // OK

// error: expected an even number of arguments
auto t2 = make_even_tuple(1, 2, 3);
```

# See also

- *Using fold expressions to simplify variadic function templates*
- *Creating raw user-defined literals* recipe of `Chapter 9`, *Working with Numbers and Strings*

# Using fold expressions to simplify variadic function templates

In this chapter, we are discussing folding several times; this is an operation that applies a binary function to a range of values to produce a single value. We have seen this when we discussed variadic function templates and will see it again with higher-order functions. It turns out there is a significant number of cases where the expansion of a parameter pack in variadic function templates is basically a folding operation. To simplify writing such variadic function templates C++17 introduced fold expressions that fold an expansion of a parameter pack over a binary operator. In this recipe, we will see how to use fold expressions to simplify writing variadic function templates.

## Getting ready

The examples in this recipe are based on the variadic function template `add()` that we wrote in the previous recipe, *Writing a function template with a variable number of arguments*. That implementation is a left-folding operation. For simplicity, we present the function again:

```
template <typename T>
T add(T value)
{
   return value;
}

template <typename T, typename... Ts>
T add(T head, Ts... rest)
{
   return head + add(rest...);
}
```

# How to do it...

To fold a parameter pack over a binary operator, use one of the following forms:

- Left folding with a unary form (`... op pack`):

```
template <typename... Ts>
auto add(Ts... args)
{
   return (... + args);
}
```

- Left folding with a binary form (`init op ... op pack`):

```
template <typename... Ts>
auto add_to_one(Ts... args)
{
   return (1 + ... + args);
}
```

- Right folding with a unary form (`pack op ...`):

```
template <typename... Ts>
auto add(Ts... args)
{
   return (args + ...);
}
```

- Right folding with a binary form (`pack op ... op init`):

```
template <typename... Ts>
auto add_to_one(Ts... args)
{
   return (args + ... + 1);
}
```

 The parentheses shown above are part of the fold expression and cannot be omitted.

# How it works...

When the compiler encounters a fold expression, it expands it in one of the following expressions:

| Expression | Expansion |
|---|---|
| `(... op pack)` | ((pack$1 op pack$2) op ...) op pack$n |
| `(init op ... op pack)` | (((init op pack$1) op pack$2) op ...) op pack$n |
| `(pack op ...)` | pack$1 op (... op (pack$n-1 op pack$n)) |
| `(pack op ... op init)` | pack$1 op (... op (pack$n-1 op (pack$n op init))) |

When the binary form is used, the operator on both the left-hand and right-hand side of the ellipses must be the same, and the initialization value must not contain an unexpanded parameter pack.

The following binary operators are supported with fold expressions:

| + | - | * | / | % | ^ | & | \| | = | < | > | << |
|---|---|---|---|---|---|---|---|---|---|---|---|
| >> | += | -= | *= | /= | %= | ^= | &= | \|= | <<= | >>= | == |
| != | <= | >= | && | \|\| | , | .* | ->*. | | | | |

When using the unary form, only operators such as *, +, &, |, &&, ||, and , (comma) are allowed with an empty parameter pack. In this case, the value of the empty pack is as follows:

| + | 0 |
|---|---|
| * | 1 |
| & | -1 |
| \| | 0 |
| && | `true` |
| \|\| | `false` |
| , | `void()` |

Now that we have the function templates implemented earlier (let's consider the left-folding version), we can write the following code:

```
auto sum = add(1, 2, 3, 4, 5);          // sum = 15
auto sum1 = add_to_one(1, 2, 3, 4, 5); // sum = 16
```

Considering the `add(1, 2, 3, 4, 5)` call, it would produce the following function:

```
int add(int arg1, int arg2, int arg3, int arg4, int arg5)
{
   return ((((arg1 + arg2) + arg3) + arg4) + arg5);
}
```

Due to the aggressive ways modern compilers do optimizations, this function can be inlined and eventually end up with an expression such as `auto sum = 1 + 2 + 3 + 4 + 5`.

# There's more...

Fold expressions work with all overloads for the supported binary operators, but do not work with arbitrary binary functions. It is possible to implement a workaround for that by providing a wrapper type to hold a value and an overloaded operator for that wrapper type:

```
template <typename T>
struct wrapper
{
   T const & value;
};

template <typename T>
constexpr auto operator<(wrapper<T> const & lhs,
                         wrapper<T> const & rhs)
{
   return wrapper<T> {
      lhs.value < rhs.value ? lhs.value : rhs.value};
}

template <typename... Ts>
constexpr auto min(Ts&&... args)
{
   return (wrapper<Ts>{args} < ...).value;
}
```

In the preceding code, `wrapper` is a simple class template that holds a constant reference to a value of type `T`. An overloaded `operator<` is provided for this class template; this overload does not return a Boolean to indicate that the first argument is less than the second, but actually an instance of the `wrapper` class type to hold the minimum value of the two arguments. The variadic function template `min()` uses this overloaded `operator<` to fold the pack of arguments expanded to instances of the wrapper class template:

```
auto m = min(1, 2, 3, 4, 5); // m = 1
```

## See also

- *Implementing higher-order functions map and fold*

# Implementing higher-order functions map and fold

Throughout the preceding recipes in this book, we have used the general purpose algorithms `std::transform()` and `std::accumulate()` in several examples, such as implementing string utilities to create uppercase or lowercase copies of a string or summing the values of a range. These are basically implementations of higher-order functions, `map` and `fold`. A higher-order function is a function that takes one or more other functions as arguments and applies them to a range (a list, vector, map, tree, and so on), producing either a new range or a value. In this recipe, we will see how to implement `map` and `fold` functions to work with C++ standard containers.

## Getting ready

*Map* is a higher-order function that applies a function to the elements of a range and returns a new range in the same order.

*Fold* is a higher-order function that applies a combining function to the elements of the range producing a single result. Since the order of the processing can be important, there are usually two versions of this function--`foldleft`, that processes elements from left to right, and `foldright` that combines the elements from right to left.

Most descriptions of the function map indicate that it is applied to a `list`, but this is a general term that can indicate different sequential types, such as list, vector, and array, and also dictionaries (that is, maps), queues, and so on. For this reason, I prefer to use the term range when describing these higher-order functions.

# How to do it...

To implement the `map` function you should:

- Use `std::transform` on containers that support iterating and assignment to the elements, such as `std::vector` or `std::list`:

```
template <typename F, typename R>
R mapf(F&& f, R r)
{
  std::transform(
    std::begin(r), std::end(r), std::begin(r),
    std::forward<F>(f));
  return r;
}
```

- Use other means such as explicit iteration and insertion for containers that do not support assignment to the elements, such as `std::map`:

```
template<typename F, typename T, typename U>
std::map<T, U> mapf(F&& f, std::map<T, U> const & m)
{
  std::map<T, U> r;
  for (auto const kvp : m)
    r.insert(f(kvp));
  return r;
}

template<typename F, typename T>
std::queue<T> mapf(F&& f, std::queue<T> q)
{
  std::queue<T> r;
  while (!q.empty())
  {
    r.push(f(q.front()));
    q.pop();
  }
  return r;
}
```

To implement the `fold` function you should:

- Use `std::accumulate()` on containers that support iterating:

```
template <typename F, typename R, typename T>
constexpr T foldl(F&& f, R&& r, T i)
{
  return std::accumulate(
    std::begin(r), std::end(r),
    std::move(i),
    std::forward<F>(f));
}

template <typename F, typename R, typename T>
constexpr T foldr(F&& f, R&& r, T i)
{
  return std::accumulate(
    std::rbegin(r), std::rend(r),
    std::move(i),
    std::forward<F>(f));
}
```

- Use other means to explicitly process containers that do not support iterating, such as `std::queue`:

```
template <typename F, typename T>
constexpr T foldl(F&& f, std::queue<T> q, T i)
{
  while (!q.empty())
  {
    i = f(i, q.front());
    q.pop();
  }
  return i;
}
```

# How it works...

In the preceding examples, we have implemented the map in a functional way, without side-effects. That means it preserves the original range and returns a new one. The arguments of the function are the function to apply and the range. In order to avoid confusion with the `std::map` container, we have called this function `mapf`. There are several overloads for `mapf` as shown earlier:

- The first overload is for containers that support iterating and assignment to its elements; this includes `std::vector`, `std::list`, and `std::array`, but also C-like arrays. The function takes an `rvalue` reference to a function and a range for which `std::begin()` and `std::end()` are defined. The range is passed by value so that modifying the local copy does not affect the original range. The range is transformed by applying the given function to each element using the standard algorithm `std::transform()`; the transformed range is then returned.

- The second overload is specialized for `std::map` that does not support direct assignment to its elements (`std::pair<T, U>`). Therefore, this overload creates a new map, then iterates through its elements using a range-based for loop, and inserts into the new map the result of applying the input function to each element of the original map.

- The third overload is specialized for `std::queue`, which is a container that does not support iterating. It can be argued that a queue is not a typical structure to map over, but for the sake of demonstrating different possible implementations, we are considering it. In order to iterate over the elements of a queue, the queue must be altered--you need to pop elements from the front until the list is empty. This is what the third overload does--it processes each element of the input queue (passed by value) and pushes the result of applying the given function to the front element of the remaining queue.

Now that we have these overloads implemented, we can apply them to a lot of containers, as shown in the following examples (notice that the map and fold functions used here are implemented in a namespace called funclib in the code accompanying the book and therefore shown with the fully qualified name):

- Retain absolute values from a vector. In this example, the vector contains both negative and positive values. After applying the mapping, the result is a new vector with only positive values.

```
auto vnums =
   std::vector<int>{0, 2, -3, 5, -1, 6, 8, -4, 9};
auto r = funclib::mapf([](int const i) {
   return std::abs(i); }, vnums);
// r = {0, 2, 3, 5, 1, 6, 8, 4, 9}
```

- Square the numerical values of a list. In this example, the list contains integral values. After applying the mapping, the result is a list containing the squares of the initial values.

```
auto lnums = std::list<int>{1, 2, 3, 4, 5};
auto l = funclib::mapf([](int const i) {
   return i*i; }, lnums);
// l = {1, 4, 9, 16, 25}
```

- Rounded amounts of floating point. For this example, we need to use `std::round()`; however, this has overloads for all floating point types, which makes it impossible for the compiler to pick the right one. As a result, we either have to write a lambda that takes an argument of a specific floating point type and returns the value of `std::round()` applied to that value or create a function object template that wraps `std::round()` and enables its call operator only for floating point types. This technique is used in the following example:

```
template<class T = double>
struct fround
{
   typename std::enable_if<
      std::is_floating_point<T>::value, T>::type
   operator()(const T& value) const
   {
      return std::round(value);
   }
};

auto amounts =
   std::array<double, 5> {10.42, 2.50, 100.0, 23.75, 12.99};
auto a = funclib::mapf(fround<>(), amounts);
// a = {10.0, 3.0, 100.0, 24.0, 13.0}
```

- Uppercase the string keys of a map of words (where the key is the word and the value is the number of appearances in the text). Note that creating an uppercase copy of a string is itself a mapping operation. Therefore, in this example, we use `mapf` to apply `toupper()` to the elements of the string representing the key in order to produce an uppercase copy:

```
auto words = std::map<std::string, int>{
  {"one", 1}, {"two", 2}, {"three", 3}
};
auto m = funclib::mapf(
  [](std::pair<std::string, int> const kvp) {
    return std::make_pair(
      funclib::mapf(toupper, kvp.first),
      kvp.second);
  },
  words);
// m = {{"ONE", 1}, {"TWO", 2}, {"THREE", 3}}
```

- Normalize values from a queue of priorities--initially, the values are from 1 to 100, but we want to normalize them into two values, 1=high and 2=normal. All initial priorities that have a value up to 30 become a high priority, the others get a normal priority:

```
auto priorities = std::queue<int>();
priorities.push(10);
priorities.push(20);
priorities.push(30);
priorities.push(40);
priorities.push(50);
auto p = funclib::mapf(
  [](int const i) { return i > 30 ? 2 : 1; },
  priorities);
// p = {1, 1, 1, 2, 2}
```

To implement `fold`, we actually have to consider the two possible types of folding, that is, from left to right and from right to left. Therefore, we have provided two functions called `foldl` (for left folding) and `foldr` (for right folding). The implementations shown in the previous section are very similar--they both take a function, a range, and an initial value and call `std::algorithm()` to fold the values of the range into a single value. However, `foldl` uses direct iterators, whereas `foldr` uses reverse iterators to traverse and process the range. The second overload is a specialization for type `std::queue`, which does not have iterators.

Based on these implementations for folding, we can do the following examples:

- Adding the values of a vector of integers. In this case, both left and right folding will produce the same result. In the following examples, we pass either a lambda that takes a sum and a number and returns a new sum or the function object `std::plus<>` from the standard library that applies `operator+` to two operands of the same type (basically similar to the closure of the lambda):

```
auto vnums =
    std::vector<int>{0, 2, -3, 5, -1, 6, 8, -4, 9};

auto s1 = funclib::foldl(
    [](const int s, const int n) {return s + n; },
    vnums, 0);                    // s1 = 22

auto s2 = funclib::foldl(
    std::plus<>(), vnums, 0); // s2 = 22

auto s3 = funclib::foldr(
    [](const int s, const int n) {return s + n; },
    vnums, 0);                    // s3 = 22

auto s4 = funclib::foldr(
    std::plus<>(), vnums, 0); // s4 = 22
```

- Concatenating strings from a vector into a single string:

```
auto texts =
    std::vector<std::string>{"hello"s, " "s, "world"s, "!"s};

auto txt1 = funclib::foldl(
    [](std::string const & s, std::string const & n) {
    return s + n;},
    texts, ""s);     // txt1 = "hello world!"

auto txt2 = funclib::foldr(
    [](std::string const & s, std::string const & n) {
    return s + n; },
    texts, ""s);     // txt2 = "!world hello"
```

- Concatenating an array of characters into a string:

```
char chars[] = {'c','i','v','i','c'};

auto str1 = funclib::foldl(std::plus<>(), chars, ""s);
// str1 = "civic"

auto str2 = funclib::foldr(std::plus<>(), chars, ""s);
// str2 = "civic"
```

- Counting the number of words from a text based on their already computed appearances available in a map<string, int>:

```
auto words = std::map<std::string, int>{
    {"one", 1}, {"two", 2}, {"three", 3} };

auto count = funclib::foldl(
    [](int const s, std::pair<std::string, int> const kvp) {
        return s + kvp.second; },
    words, 0); // count = 6
```

# There's more...

These functions can be pipelined, that is, they can call one function with the result of another. The following example maps a range of integers into a range of positive integers by applying the std::abs() function to its elements. The result is then mapped into another range of squares. These are then summed together by applying a left fold on the range:

```
auto vnums = std::vector<int>{ 0, 2, -3, 5, -1, 6, 8, -4, 9 };

auto s = funclib::foldl(
  std::plus<>(),
  funclib::mapf(
    [](int const i) {return i*i; },
    funclib::mapf(
      [](int const i) {return std::abs(i); },
      vnums)),
  0); // s = 236
```

As an exercise, we could implement the fold function as a variadic function template, in the manner seen in a previous recipe. The function that performs the actual folding is provided as an argument:

```
template <typename F, typename T1, typename T2>
auto foldl(F&&f, T1 arg1, T2 arg2)
{
   return f(arg1, arg2);
}

template <typename F, typename T, typename... Ts>
auto foldl(F&& f, T head, Ts... rest)
{
   return f(head, foldl(std::forward<F>(f), rest...));
}
```

When we compare this with the `add()` function template that we wrote in the recipe *Writing a function template with a variable number of arguments*, we can notice several differences:

- The first argument is a function, which is perfectly forwarded when calling `foldl` recursively.
- The end case is a function that requires two arguments because the function we use for folding is a binary one (taking two arguments).
- The return type of the two functions we wrote is declared as `auto` because it must match the return type of the supplied binary function `f` that is not known until we call `foldl`:

```
auto s1 = foldl(std::plus<>(), 1, 2, 3, 4, 5);
// s1 = 15
auto s2 = foldl(std::plus<>(), "hello"s, ' ', "world"s, '!');
// s2 = "hello world!"
auto s3 = foldl(std::plus<>(), 1); // error, too few arguments
```

# See also

- *Creating a library of string helpers* recipe of `Chapter 9`, *Working with Numbers and Strings*
- *Writing a function template with a variable number of arguments*
- *Composing functions into a higher-order function*

# Composing functions into a higher-order function

In the previous recipe, we implemented two higher-order functions, map and fold, and saw various examples of using them. At the end of the recipe, we saw how they can be pipelined to produce a final value after several transformations of the original data. Pipelining is a form of composition, which means creating one new function from two or more given functions. In the mentioned example, we didn't actually compose functions; we only called a function with the result produced by another, but in this recipe, we will see how to actually compose functions together into a new function. For simplicity, we will only consider unary functions (functions that take only one argument).

## Getting ready

Before you go forward, it is recommended that you read the previous recipe, *Implementing higher-order functions map and fold*. It is not mandatory for understanding this recipe, but we will refer to the map and fold functions implemented here.

## How to do it...

To compose unary functions into a higher-order function, you should:

- For composing two functions, provide a function that takes two functions, f and g, as arguments and returns a new function (a lambda) that returns f(g(x)) where x is the argument of the composed function:

```
template <typename F, typename G>
auto compose(F&& f, G&& g)
{
  return [=](auto x) { return f(g(x)); };
```

```
}

auto v = compose(
    [](int const n) {return std::to_string(n); },
    [](int const n) {return n * n; })(-3); // v = "9"
```

- For composing a variable number of functions, provide a variadic template overload of the function described previously:

```
template <typename F, typename... R>
auto compose(F&& f, R&&... r)
{
    return [=](auto x) { return f(compose(r...)(x)); };
}

auto n = compose(
    [](int const n) {return std::to_string(n); },
    [](int const n) {return n * n; },
    [](int const n) {return n + n; },
    [](int const n) {return std::abs(n); })(-3); // n = "36"
```

# How it works...

Composing two unary functions into a new one is relatively trivial. Create a template function that we called `compose()` in the earlier examples, with two arguments--f and g-- that represent functions, and return a function that takes one argument x and returns `f(g(x))`. It is important though that the type of the value returned by the g function is the same as the type of the argument of the f function. The returned value of the compose function is a closure, that is, an instantiation of a lambda.

In practice, it is useful to be able to combine more than just two functions together. This can be achieved by writing a variadic template version of the `compose()` function. Variadic templates are explained in more detail in the *Writing a function template with a variable number of arguments* recipe. Variadic templates imply compile-time recursion by expanding the parameter pack. This implementation is very similar to the first version of `compose()`, except as follows:

- It takes a variable number of functions as arguments.
- The returned closure calls `compose()` recursively with the expanded parameter pack; recursion ends when only two functions are left, in which case, the previously implemented overload is called.

Even if the code looks like recursion is happening, this is not true recursion. It could be called compile-time recursion, but with every expansion, we get a call to another method with the same name but a different number of arguments, which does not represent recursion.

Now that we have these variadic template overloads implemented, we can rewrite the last example from the previous recipe, *Implementing higher-order functions map and fold*. Having an initial vector of integers, we map it to a new vector with only positive values by applying std::abs() on each element. The result is then mapped to a new vector by doubling the value of each element. Finally, the values in the resulting vector are folded together by adding them to the initial value 0:

```
auto s = compose(
  [](std::vector<int> const & v) {
    return foldl(std::plus<>(), v, 0); },
  [](std::vector<int> const & v) {
    return mapf([](int const i) {return i + i; }, v); },
  [](std::vector<int> const & v) {
    return mapf([](int const i) {return std::abs(i); }, v); })(vnums);
```

# There's more...

Composition is usually represented by a dot (.) or asterisk (*), such as f . g or f * g. We can actually do something similar in C++ by overloading operator* (it would make little sense to try to overload operator dot). Similar to the compose() function, operator* should work with any number of arguments; therefore, we will have two overloads, just like in the case of compose():

- The first overload takes two arguments and calls compose() to return a new function.
- The second overload is a variadic template function that again calls operator* by expanding the parameter pack:

```
template <typename F, typename G>
auto operator*(F&& f, G&& g)
{
    return compose(std::forward<F>(f), std::forward<G>(g));
}

template <typename F, typename... R>
auto operator*(F&& f, R&&... r)
{
    return operator*(std::forward<F>(f), r...);
```

```
    }
```

We can now simplify the actual composition of functions by applying `operator*` instead
of the more verbose call to compose:

```
auto n =
  ([] (int const n) {return std::to_string(n); } *
   [] (int const n) {return n * n; } *
   [] (int const n) {return n + n; } *
   [] (int const n) {return std::abs(n); }) (-3); // n = "36"

auto c =
  [] (std::vector<int> const & v) {
    return foldl(std::plus<>(), v, 0); } *
  [] (std::vector<int> const & v) {
    return mapf([] (int const i) {return i + i; }, v); } *
  [] (std::vector<int> const & v) {
    return mapf([] (int const i) {return std::abs(i); }, v); };

auto s = c(vnums); // s = 76
```

## See also

- *Writing a function template with a variable number of arguments*

# Uniformly invoking anything callable

Developers, and especially those who implement libraries, sometimes need to invoke a
callable object in a uniform manner. This can be a function, a pointer to a function, a pointer
to a member function, or a function object. Examples of such cases include `std::bind`,
`std::function`, `std::mem_fn`, and `std::thread::thread`. C++17 defines a standard
function called `std::invoke()` that can invoke any callable object with the provided
arguments. This is not intended to replace direct calls to functions or function objects, but it
is useful in template metaprogramming for implementing various library functions.

# Getting ready

For this recipe, you should be familiar with how to define and use function pointers.

To exemplify how `std::invoke()` can be used in different contexts, we will use the following function and class:

```
int add(int const a, int const b)
{
  return a + b;
}

struct foo
{
  int x = 0;

  void increment_by(int const n) { x += n; }
};
```

# How to do it...

The `std::invoke()` function is a variadic function template that takes the callable object as the first argument and a variable list of arguments that are passed to the call. `std::invoke()` can be used to call the following:

- Free functions:

  ```
  auto a1 = std::invoke(add, 1, 2);    // a1 = 3
  ```

- Free functions through pointer to function:

  ```
  auto a2 = std::invoke(&add, 1, 2);   // a2 = 3
  int(*fadd)(int const, int const) = &add;
  auto a3 = std::invoke(fadd, 1, 2);   // a3 = 3
  ```

- Member functions through pointer to member function:

  ```
  foo f;
  std::invoke(&foo::increment_by, f, 10);
  ```

- Data members:

  ```
  foo f;
  auto x1 = std::invoke(&foo::x, f);   // x1 = 0
  ```

- Function objects:

```
foo f;
auto x3 = std::invoke(std::plus<>(),
    std::invoke(&foo::x, f), 3); // x3 = 3
```

- Lambda expressions:

```
auto l = [](auto a, auto b) {return a + b; };
auto a = std::invoke(l, 1, 2); // a = 3
```

In practice, `std:invoke()` should be used in template meta-programming for invoking a function with an arbitrary number of arguments. To exemplify such a case, we present a possible implementation for our `std::apply()` function, and also a part of the standard library as of C++17 that calls a function by unpacking the members of a tuple into the arguments of the function:

```
namespace details
{
  template <class F, class T, std::size_t... I>
  auto apply(F&& f, T&& t, std::index_sequence<I...>)
  {
    return std::invoke(
      std::forward<F>(f),
      std::get<I>(std::forward<T>(t))...);
  }
}

template <class F, class T>
auto apply(F&& f, T&& t)
{
  return details::apply(
    std::forward<F>(f),
    std::forward<T>(t),
    std::make_index_sequence<
      std::tuple_size<std::decay_t<T>>::value> {});
}
```

# How it works...

Before we see how `std::invoke()` works, let's have a short look at how different callable objects can be invoked. Given a function, obviously, the ubiquitous way of invoking it is directly passing it the necessary parameters. However, we can also invoke the function using function pointers. The trouble with function pointers is that defining the type of the pointer can be cumbersome. Using `auto` can simplify things (as shown in the following code), but in practice, you usually need to define the type of the pointer to function first and then define an object and initialize it with the correct function address. Here are several examples:

```
// direct call
auto a1 = add(1, 2);     // a1 = 3

// call through function pointer
int(*fadd)(int const, int const) = &add;
auto a2 = fadd(1, 2);    // a2 = 3

auto fadd2 = &add;
auto a3 = fadd2(1, 2);   // a3 = 3
```

Calling through a function pointer becomes more cumbersome when you need to invoke a class function through an object that is an instance of the class. The syntax for defining the pointer to a member function and invoking it is not simple:

```
foo f;
f.increment_by(3);
auto x1 = f.x;     // x1 = 3

void(foo::*finc)(int const) = &foo::increment_by;
(f.*finc)(3);
auto x2 = f.x;     // x2 = 6

auto finc2 = &foo::increment_by;
(f.*finc2)(3);
auto x3 = f.x;     // x3 = 9
```

Regardless of how cumbersome this kind of call may look, the actual problem is writing library components (functions or classes) that are able to call any of these types of callable objects, in a uniform manner. This is what benefits in practice from a standard function, such as `std::invoke()`.

The implementation details of `std::invoke()` are complex, but the way it works can be explained in simple terms. Supposing the call has the form `invoke(f, arg1, arg2, ..., argN)`, then consider the following:

- If `f` is a pointer to a member function of a `T` class, then the call is equivalent with either:
  - `(arg1.*f)(arg2, ..., argN)`, if `arg1` is an instance of `T`
  - `(arg1.get().*f)(arg2, ..., argN)`, if `arg1` is a specialization of `reference_wrapper`
  - `((*arg1).*f)(arg2, ..., argN)`, if it is otherwise
- If `f` is a pointer to a data member of a `T` class and there is a single argument, in other words, the call has the form `invoke(f, arg1)`, then the call is equivalent to either:
  - `arg1.*f` if `arg1` is an instance class `T`
  - `arg1.get().*f` if `arg1` is a specialization of `reference_wrapper`
  - `(*arg1).*f`, if it is otherwise
- If `f` is a function object, then the call is equivalent to `f(arg1, arg2, ..., argN)`

# See also

- *Writing a function template with a variable number of arguments*

# 11
# Standard Library Containers, Algorithms, and Iterators

We will cover the following recipes in this chapter:

- Using vector as a default container
- Using bitset for fixed-size sequences of bits
- Using vector<bool> for variable-size sequences of bits
- Finding elements in a range
- Sorting a range
- Initializing a range
- Using set operations on a range
- Using iterators to insert new elements in a container
- Writing your own random access iterator
- Container access with non-member functions

# Using vector as a default container

The standard library provides various types of containers that store collections of objects; the library includes sequence containers (such as `vector`, `array`, or `list`), ordered and unordered associative containers (such as `set` and `map`), and container adapters that do not store data but provide an adapted interface towards a sequence container (such as `stack` and `queue`). All of them are implemented as class templates, which means they can be used with any type (providing it meets the container requirements). Though you should always use the container that is the most appropriate for a particular problem (which not only provides good performance in terms of speed of inserts, deletes, access to elements, and memory usage but also makes the code easy to read and maintain), the default choice should be `vector`. In this recipe, we will see why `vector` should be the preferred choice for a container and what are the most common operations with `vector`.

# Getting ready

The reader is expected to be familiar with C-like arrays, both statically and dynamically allocated.

The class template `vector` is available in the `std` namespace in the `<vector>` header.

# How to do it...

To initialize a `std::vector` class template, you can use any of the following methods, but you are not restricted to only these:

- Initialize from an initialization list:

```
std::vector<int> v1 { 1, 2, 3, 4, 5 };
```

- Initialize from a C-like array:

```
int arr[] = { 1, 2, 3, 4, 5 };
std::vector<int> v2(arr, arr + 5); // { 1, 2, 3, 4, 5 }
```

- Initialize from another container:

```
std::list<int> l{ 1, 2, 3, 4, 5 };
std::vector<int> v3(l.begin(), l.end()); //{ 1, 2, 3, 4, 5 }
```

- Initialize from a count and a value:

```
std::vector<int> v4(5, 1); // {1, 1, 1, 1, 1}
```

To modify the content of `std::vector`, use any of the following methods, but you are not restricted to only these:

- Add an element at the end of the vector with `push_back()`:

```
std::vector<int> v1{ 1, 2, 3, 4, 5 };
v1.push_back(6); // v1 = { 1, 2, 3, 4, 5, 6 }
```

- Remove an element from the end of the vector with `pop_back()`:

```
v1.pop_back();
```

- Insert anywhere in the vector with `insert()`:

```
int arr[] = { 1, 2, 3, 4, 5 };
std::vector<int> v2;
v2.insert(v2.begin(), arr, arr + 5); // v2 = { 1, 2, 3, 4, 5 }
```

- Add an element by creating it at the end of the vector with `emplace_back()`:

```
struct foo
{
  int a;
  double b;
  std::string c;

  foo(int a, double b, std::string const & c) :
    a(a), b(b), c(c) {}
};

std::vector<foo> v3;
v3.emplace_back(1, 1.0, "one"s);
// v3 = { foo{1, 1.0, "one"} }
```

- Insert an element by creating it anywhere in the vector with `emplace()`:

```
v3.emplace(v3.begin(), 2, 2.0, "two"s);
// v3 = { foo{2, 2.0, "two"}, foo{1, 1.0, "one"} }
```

To modify the whole content of the vector, use any of the following methods, but you are not restricted to only these:

- Assign from another vector with `operator=`; this replaces the content of the container:

```
std::vector<int> v1{ 1, 2, 3, 4, 5 };
std::vector<int> v2{ 10, 20, 30 };
v2 = v1; // v1 = { 1, 2, 3, 4, 5 }
```

- Assign from another sequence defined by a begin and end iterator with the `assign()` method; this replaces the content of the container:

```
int arr[] = { 1, 2, 3, 4, 5 };
std::vector<int> v3;
v3.assign(arr, arr + 5); // v3 = { 1, 2, 3, 4, 5 }
```

- Swap the content of two vectors with the `swap()` method:

```
std::vector<int> v4{ 1, 2, 3, 4, 5 };
std::vector<int> v5{ 10, 20, 30 };
v4.swap(v5); // v4 = { 10, 20, 30 }, v5 = { 1, 2, 3, 4, 5 }
```

- Remove all the elements with the `clear()` method:

```
std::vector<int> v6{ 1, 2, 3, 4, 5 };
v6.clear(); // v6 = { }
```

- Remove one or more elements with the `erase()` method (which requires either an iterator or a pair of iterators that define the range of elements from the vector to be removed):

```
std::vector<int> v7{ 1, 2, 3, 4, 5 };
v7.erase(v7.begin() + 2, v7.begin() + 4); // v7 = { 1, 2, 5 }
```

To get the address of the first element in a vector, usually to pass the content of a vector to a C-like API, use any of the following methods:

- Use the `data()` method, which returns a pointer to the first element, providing direct access to the underlying contiguous sequence of memory where the vector elements are stored; this is only available since C++11:

```
void process(int const * const arr, int const size)
{ /* do something */ }

std::vector<int> v{ 1, 2, 3, 4, 5 };
process(v.data(), static_cast<int>(v.size()));
```

- Get the address of the first element:

```
process(&v[0], static_cast<int>(v.size()));
```

- Get the address of the element referred by the `front()` method:

```
process(&v.front(), static_cast<int>(v.size()));
```

- Get the address of the element pointed by the iterator returned from `begin()`:

```
process(&*v.begin(), static_cast<int>(v.size()));
```

# How it works...

The `std::vector` class is designed to be the C++ container most similar to and inter-operable with C-like arrays. A vector is a variable-sized sequence of elements, guaranteed to be stored contiguously in memory, which makes the content of a vector easily passable to a C-like function that takes a pointer to an element of an array and, usually, a size. There are many benefits of using a vector instead of C-like arrays and these benefits include:

- No direct memory management is required from the developer, as the container does this internally, allocating memory, reallocating, and releasing.

 Note that a vector is intended for storing object instances. If you need to store pointers, do not store raw pointers but smart pointers. Otherwise, you need to handle the lifetime management of the pointed objects.

- The possibility of modifying the size of the vector.

- Simple assignment or concatenation of two vectors.
- Direct comparison of two vectors.

The `vector` class is a very efficient container, with all implementations providing a lot of optimizations that most developers are not capable of doing with C-like arrays. Random access to its elements and insertion and removal at the end of a vector is a constant *O(1)* operation (provided that reallocation is not necessary), while insertion and removal anywhere else is a linear *O(n)* operation.

Compared to other standard containers, the vector has various benefits:

- It is compatible with C-like arrays and C-like APIs; the content of other containers (except for `std::array`) needs to be copied to a vector before being passed to a C-like API expecting an array.
- It has the fastest access to elements of all containers.
- It has no per-element memory overhead for storing elements, as elements are stored in a contiguous space, like a C array (and unlike other containers such as `list` that requires additional pointers to other elements, or associative containers that require hash values).

`std::vector` is very similar in semantics to C-like arrays but has a variable size. The size of a vector can increase and decrease. There are two properties that define the size of a vector:

- *Capacity* is the number of elements the vector can accommodate without performing additional memory allocations; this is indicated by the `capacity()` method.
- *Size* is the actual number of elements in the vector; this is indicated by the `size()` method.

Size is always smaller or equal to capacity. When size is equal to capacity and a new element needs to be added, the capacity needs to be modified so that the vector has space for more elements. In this case, the vector allocates a new chunk of memory and moves the previous content to the new location and then frees the previously allocated memory. Though this sounds time-consuming (and it is), implementations increase the capacity exponentially, by doubling it each time it needs to be changed. As a result, on average, each element of the vector only needs to be moved once (that is because all the elements of the vector are moved during an increase of capacity, but then an equal number of elements can be added without incurring more moves, given that insertions are performed at the end of the vector).

If you know beforehand how many elements will be inserted in the vector, you can first call the `reserve()` method to increase the capacity to at least the specified amount (this method does nothing if the specified size is smaller than the current capacity) and only then insert the elements.

On the other hand, if you need to free additional reserved memory, you can use the `shrink_to_fit()` method to request this, but it is an implementation decision whether to free any memory or not. An alternative to this non-binding method, available since C++11, is to do a swap with a temporary, empty vector:

```
std::vector<int> v{ 1, 2, 3, 4, 5 };
std::vector<int>().swap(v); // v.size = 0, v.capacity = 0
```

Calling the `clear()` method only removes all the elements from the vector but does not free any memory.

It should be noted that the vector implements operations specific to other types of containers:

- `stack`: With `push_back()` and `emplace_back()` to add at the end and `pop_back()` to remove from the end. Keep in mind that `pop_back()` does not return the last element that has been removed. You need to access that explicitly, if that is necessary, for instance, using the `back()` method before removing the element.
- `list`: With `insert()` and `emplace()` to add elements in the middle of the sequence and `erase()` to remove elements from anywhere in the sequence.

# There's more...

The rule of thumb for C++ containers is: use `std::vector` as the default container unless you have good reasons to use another one.

# See also

- *Using bitset for fixed-size sequences of bits*
- *Using vector<bool> for variable-size sequences of bits*

# Using bitset for fixed-size sequences of bits

It is not uncommon for developers to operate with bit flags; this can be either because they work with operating system APIs, usually written in C, that take various types of arguments (such as options or styles) in the form of bit flags, or because they work with libraries that do similar things, or simply because some types of problems are naturally solved with bit flags. One can think of alternatives to working with bits and bit operations, such as defining arrays having one element for every option/flag, or defining a structure with members and functions to model the bit flags, but these are often more complicated, and in case you need to pass a numerical value representing bit flags to a function you still need to convert the array or the structure to a sequence of bits. For this reason, the C++ standard provides a container called `std::bitset` for fixed-size sequences of bits.

## Getting ready

For this recipe, you must be familiar with bitwise operations (and, or, xor, not, and shifting).

The `bitset` class is available in the `std` namespace in the `<bitset>` header. A bitset represents a fixed-size sequence of bits, with the size defined at compile time. For convenience, in this recipe, all examples will be with bitsets of 8 bits.

## How to do it...

To construct an `std::bitset` object, use one of the available constructors:

- An empty bitset with all bits set to 0:

    ```
    std::bitset<8> b1; // [0,0,0,0,0,0,0,0]
    ```

- A bitset from a numerical value:

    ```
    std::bitset<8> b2{ 10 }; // [0,0,0,0,1,0,1,0]
    ```

- A bitset from a string of '0' and '1':

    ```
    std::bitset<8> b3{ "1010"s }; // [0,0,0,0,1,0,1,0]
    ```

- A bitset from a string containing any two characters representing `'0'` and `'1'`; in this case, we must specify which character represents a 0 and which character represents a 1:

```
std::bitset<8> b4
   { "ooooxoxo"s, 0, std::string::npos, 'o', 'x' };
   // [0,0,0,0,1,0,1,0]
```

To test individual bits in the set or the entire set for specific values, use any of the available methods:

- `count()` to get the number of bits set to 1:

```
std::bitset<8> bs{ 10 };
std::cout << "has " << bs.count() << " 1s" << std::endl;
```

- `any()` to check whether there is at least one bit set to 1:

```
if (bs.any()) std::cout << "has some 1s" << std::endl;
```

- `all()` to check whether all the bits are set to 1:

```
if (bs.all()) std::cout << "has only 1s" << std::endl;
```

- `none()` to check whether all the bits are set to 0:

```
if (bs.none()) std::cout << "has no 1s" << std::endl;
```

- `test()` to check the value of an individual bit:

```
if (!bs.test(0)) std::cout << "even" << std::endl;
```

- `operator[]` to access and test individual bits:

```
if(!bs[0]) std::cout << "even" << std::endl;
```

To modify the content of a bitset, use any of the following methods:

- Member operators |=, &=, ^= , and ~ to perform binary or, and, xor, and not operations, or non-member operators |, &, and ^:

```
std::bitset<8> b1{ 42 }; // [0,0,1,0,1,0,1,0]
std::bitset<8> b2{ 11 }; // [0,0,0,0,1,0,1,1]
auto b3 = b1 | b2;       // [0,0,1,0,1,0,1,1]
auto b4 = b1 & b2;       // [0,0,0,0,1,0,1,0]
auto b5 = b1 ^ b2;       // [1,1,0,1,1,1,1,0]
auto b6 = ~b1;           // [1,1,0,1,0,1,0,1]
```

- Member operators <<=, <<, >>=, >> to perform shifting operations:

```
auto b7 = b1 << 2;       // [1,0,1,0,1,0,0,0]
auto b8 = b1 >> 2;       // [0,0,0,0,1,0,1,0]
```

- flip() to toggle the entire set or an individual bit from 0 to 1 or from 1 to 0:

```
b1.flip();               // [1,1,0,1,0,1,0,1]
b1.flip(0);              // [1,1,0,1,0,1,0,0]
```

- set() to change the entire set or an individual bit to true or the specified value:

```
b1.set(0, true);         // [1,1,0,1,0,1,0,1]
b1.set(0, false);        // [1,1,0,1,0,1,0,0]
```

- reset() to change the entire set or an individual bit to false:

```
b1.reset(2);             // [1,1,0,1,0,0,0,0]
```

To convert a bitset to a numerical or string value, use the following methods:

- to_ulong() and to_ullong() to convert to unsigned long or unsigned long long:

```
std::bitset<8> bs{ 42 };
auto n1 = bs.to_ulong();  // n1 = 42UL
auto n2 = bs.to_ullong(); // n2 = 42ULL
```

- to_string() to convert to std::basic_string; by default the result is a string containing '0' and '1', but you can specify a different character for these two values:

```
auto s1 = bs.to_string();        // s1 = "00101010"
auto s2 = bs.to_string('o', 'x'); // s2 = "ooxoxoxo"
```

# How it works...

If you've ever worked with C or C-like APIs, chances are you either wrote or at least have seen code that manipulates bits to define styles, options, or other kinds of values. This usually involves operations, such as:

- Defining the bit flags; these can be enumerations, static constants in a class, or macros introduced with `#define` in the C style. Usually, there is a flag representing no value (style, option, and so on). Since these are supposed to be bit flags, their values are powers of 2.
- Adding and removing flags from the set (that is, a numerical value). Adding a bit flag is done with the bit-or operator (`value |= FLAG`) and removing a bit flag is done with the bit-and operator, with the negated flag (`value &= ~FLAG`).
- Testing whether a flag is added to the set (`value & FLAG == FLAG`).
- Calling functions with the flags as an argument.

The following shows a simple example of flags defining the border style of a control that can have a border on the left, right, top, or bottom side, or any combination of these, including no border:

```
#define BORDER_NONE    0x00
#define BORDER_LEFT    0x01
#define BORDER_TOP     0x02
#define BORDER_RIGHT   0x04
#define BORDER_BOTTOM 0x08

void apply_style(unsigned int const style)
{
  if (style & BORDER_BOTTOM) { /* do something */ }
}

// initialize with no flags
unsigned int style = BORDER_NONE;
// set a flag
style = BORDER_BOTTOM;
// add more flags
style |= BORDER_LEFT | BORDER_RIGHT | BORDER_TOP;
// remove some flags
style &= ~BORDER_LEFT;
style &= ~BORDER_RIGHT;
// test if a flag is set
if ((style & BORDER_BOTTOM) == BORDER_BOTTOM) {}
// pass the flags as argument to a function
apply_style(style);
```

The standard `std::bitset` class is intended as a C++ alternative to this C-like working style with sets of bits. It enables us to write more robust and safer code because it abstracts the bit operations with member functions, though we still need to identify what each bit in the set is representing:

- Adding and removing flags is done with the `set()` and `reset()` methods, which set the value of a bit indicated by its position to 1 or 0 (or `true` and `false`); alternatively, we can use the index operator for the same purpose.
- Testing if a bit is set is done with the `test()` method.
- Conversion from an integer or a string is done through the constructor, and conversion to an integer or string is done with member functions so that the values from bitsets can be used where integers are expected (such as arguments to functions).

In addition to these mentioned operations, the `bitset` class has additional methods for performing bitwise operations on bits, shifting, testing, and others that have been shown in the previous section.

Conceptually, `std::bitset` is a representation of a numerical value that enables you to access and modify individual bits. Internally, however, a bitset has an array of integer values on which it performs bit operations. The size of a bitset is not limited to the size of a numerical type; it can be anything, except that it is a compile-time constant.

The example with the control border styles from the previous section can be written using `std::bitset` in the following manner:

```
struct border_flags
{
  static const int left = 0;
  static const int top = 1;
  static const int right = 2;
  static const int bottom = 3;
};

// initialize with no flags
std::bitset<4> style;
// set a flag
style.set(border_flags::bottom);
// set more flags
style
  .set(border_flags::left)
  .set(border_flags::top)
  .set(border_flags::right);
// remove some flags
```

```
style[border_flags::left] = 0;
style.reset(border_flags::right);
// test if a flag is set
if (style.test(border_flags::bottom)) {}
// pass the flags as argument to a function
apply_style(style.to_ulong());
```

# There's more...

The bitset can be created from an integer and can convert its value to an integer using the `to_ulong()` or `to_ullong()` methods. However, if the size of the bitset is larger than the size of these numerical types and any of the bits beyond the size of the requested numerical type is set to 1, then these methods throw an `std::overflow_error` exception because the value cannot be represented on `unsigned long` or `unsigned long long`. In order to extract all the bits, we need to do the following operations, as shown in the next code:

- Clear the bits beyond the size of `unsigned long` or `unsigned long long`.
- Convert the value to `unsigned long` or `unsigned long long`.
- Shift the bitset with the number of bits in `unsigned long` or `unsigned long long`.
- Do this until all the bits are retrieved.

```
template <size_t N>
std::vector<unsigned long> bitset_to_vectorulong(std::bitset<N> bs)
{
   auto result = std::vector<unsigned long> {};
   auto const size = 8 * sizeof(unsigned long);
   auto const mask = std::bitset<N>{ static_cast<unsigned long>(-1) };

   auto totalbits = 0;
   while (totalbits < N)
   {
      auto value = (bs & mask).to_ulong();
      result.push_back(value);
      bs >>= size;
      totalbits += size;
   }

   return result;
}

std::bitset<128> bs =
        (std::bitset<128>(0xFEDC) << 96) |
        (std::bitset<128>(0xBA98) << 64) |
```

```
        (std::bitset<128>(0x7654) << 32) |
        std::bitset<128>(0x3210);

std::cout << bs << std::endl;

auto result = bitset_to_vectorulong(bs);
for (auto const v : result)
   std::cout << std::hex << v << std::endl;
```

For cases where the size of the `bitset` cannot be known at compile time, the alternative is `std::vector<bool>`, which we will cover in the next recipe.

## See also

- *Using vector<bool> for variable-size sequences of bits*

# Using vector<bool> for variable-size sequences of bits

In the previous recipe, we looked at using `std::bitset` for fixed-size sequences of bits. Sometimes, however, an `std::bitset` is not a good choice because you do not know the number of bits at compile time, and just defining a set of a large enough number of bits is not a good idea because you can get into a situation when the number is not actually large enough. The standard alternative for this is to use the `std::vector<bool>` container that is a specialization of `std::vector` with space and speed optimizations, as implementations do not actually store Boolean values, but individual bits for each element.

 For this reason, however, `std::vector<bool>` does not meet the requirements of a standard container or sequential container, nor does `std::vector<bool>::iterator` meet the requirements of a forward iterator. As a result, this specialization cannot be used in generic code where a vector is expected. On the other hand, being a vector, it has a different interface from that of `std::bitset` and cannot be viewed as a binary representation of a number. There are no direct ways to construct `std::vector<bool>` from a number or string nor to convert to a number or string.

# Getting ready...

This recipe assumes you are familiar with both `std::vector` and `std::bitset`. If you didn't read the previous recipes, *Using vector as a default container* and *Using bitset for fixed-size sequences of bits*, you should do that before continuing.

The `vector<bool>` class is available in the `std` namespace in the `<vector>` header.

# How to do it...

To manipulate an `std::vector<bool>`, use the same methods you would use for an `std::vector<T>`, as shown in the following examples:

- Creating an empty vector:

      std::vector<bool> bv; // []

- Adding bits to the vector:

      bv.push_back(true);  // [1]
      bv.push_back(true);  // [1, 1]
      bv.push_back(false); // [1, 1, 0]
      bv.push_back(false); // [1, 1, 0, 0]
      bv.push_back(true);  // [1, 1, 0, 0, 1]

- Setting the values of individual bits:

      bv[3] = true;        // [1, 1, 0, 1, 1]

- Using generic algorithms:

      auto count_of_ones = std::count(bv.cbegin(), bv.cend(), true);

- Removing bits from the vector:

      bv.erase(bv.begin() + 2); // [1, 1, 1, 1]

# How it works...

`std::vector<bool>` is not a standard vector because it is designed to provide space optimization by storing a single bit for each element instead of a Boolean value. Therefore, its elements are not stored in a contiguous sequence and cannot be substituted for an array of Booleans. Due to this:

- The index operator cannot return a reference to a specific element because elements are not stored individually:

  ```
  std::vector<bool> bv;
  bv.resize(10);
  auto& bit = bv[0];        // error
  ```

- Dereferencing an iterator cannot produce a reference to `bool` for the same reason as mentioned earlier:

  ```
  auto& bit = *bv.begin(); // error
  ```

- There is no guarantee that individual bits can be manipulated independently at the same time from different threads.
- The vector cannot be used with algorithms that require forward iterators, such as `std::search()`.
- The vector cannot be used in some generic code where `std::vector<T>` is expected if such code requires any of the operations mentioned in this list.

 An alternative to `std::vector<bool>` is `std::dequeu<bool>`, which is a standard container (a double-ended queue) that meets all container and iterator requirements and can be used with all standard algorithms. However, this will not have the space optimization that `std::vector<bool>` is providing.

# There's more...

The `std::vector<bool>` interface is very different from `std::bitset`. If you want to be able to write code in a similar manner, you can create a wrapper on `std::vector<bool>`, which looks like `std::bitset`, where possible. The following implementation provides members similar to what is available in `std::bitset`:

```
class bitvector
{
  std::vector<bool> bv;
```

```
public:
  bitvector(std::vector<bool> const & bv) : bv(bv) {}
  bool operator[](size_t const i) { return bv[i]; }

  inline bool any() const {
    for (auto b : bv) if (b) return true;
      return false;
  }

  inline bool all() const {
    for (auto b : bv) if (!b) return false;
      return true;
  }

  inline bool none() const { return !any(); }

  inline size_t count() const {
    return std::count(bv.cbegin(), bv.cend(), true);
  }

  inline size_t size() const { return bv.size(); }

  inline bitvector & add(bool const value) {
    bv.push_back(value);
    return *this;
  }

  inline bitvector & remove(size_t const index) {
    if (index >= bv.size())
      throw std::out_of_range("Index out of range");
    bv.erase(bv.begin() + index);
    return *this;
  }

  inline bitvector & set(bool const value = true) {
    for (size_t i = 0; i < bv.size(); ++i)
      bv[i] = value;
    return *this;
  }

  inline bitvector& set(size_t const index, bool const value = true) {
    if (index >= bv.size())
      throw std::out_of_range("Index out of range");
    bv[index] = value;
    return *this;
  }

  inline bitvector & reset() {
```

```
                for (size_t i = 0; i < bv.size(); ++i) bv[i] = false;
                return *this;
        }

        inline bitvector & reset(size_t const index) {
            if (index >= bv.size())
                throw std::out_of_range("Index out of range");
            bv[index] = false;
            return *this;
        }

        inline bitvector & flip() {
            bv.flip();
            return *this;
        }

        std::vector<bool>& data() { return bv; }
};
```

This is only a basic implementation, and if you want to use such a wrapper, you should add additional methods, such as bit logic operations, shifting, maybe reading and writing from and to streams, and so on. However, with the preceding code, we can write the following examples:

```
bitvector bv;
bv.add(true).add(true).add(false);  // [1, 1, 0]
bv.add(false);                      // [1, 1, 0, 0]
bv.add(true);                       // [1, 1, 0, 0, 1]

if (bv.any()) std::cout << "has some 1s" << std::endl;
if (bv.all()) std::cout << "has only 1s" << std::endl;
if (bv.none()) std::cout << "has no 1s" << std::endl;
std::cout << "has " << bv.count() << " 1s" << std::endl;

bv.set(2, true);                    // [1, 1, 1, 0, 1]
bv.set();                           // [1, 1, 1, 1, 1]

bv.reset(0);                        // [0, 1, 1, 1, 1]
bv.reset();                         // [0, 0, 0, 0, 0]

bv.flip();                          // [1, 1, 1, 1, 1]
```

# See also

- *Using vector as a default container*
- *Using bitset for fixed-size sequences of bits*

# Finding elements in a range

One of the most common operations we do in any application is searching through data. Therefore, it is not surprising that the standard library provides many generic algorithms for searching through standard containers or anything that can represent a range and is defined by a start and a past-the-end iterator. In this recipe, we will see what these standard algorithms are and how they can be used.

## Getting ready

For all the examples in this recipe, we will use `std::vector`, but all algorithms work with ranges defined by a begin and past-the-end, either input or forward iterators, depending on the algorithm (for more information about the various types of iterators, see the recipe, *Writing your own random access iterator*). All these algorithms are available in the `std` namespace in the `<algorithm>` header.

## How to do it...

The following is a list of algorithms that can be used for finding elements in a range:

- Use `std::find()` to find a value in a range; this algorithm returns an iterator to the first element equal to the value:

  ```
  std::vector<int> v{ 1, 1, 2, 3, 5, 8, 13 };

  auto it = std::find(v.cbegin(), v.cend(), 3);
  if (it != v.cend()) std::cout << *it << std::endl;
  ```

- Use `std::find_if()` to find a value in a range that meets a criterion from a unary predicate; this algorithm returns an iterator to the first element for which the predicate returns `true`:

```
std::vector<int> v{ 1, 1, 2, 3, 5, 8, 13 };

auto it = std::find_if(v.cbegin(), v.cend(),
                       [](int const n) {return n > 10; });
if (it != v.cend()) std::cout << *it << std::endl;
```

- Use `std::find_if_not()` to find a value in a range that does not meet a criterion from a unary predicate; this algorithm returns an iterator to the first element for which the predicate returns `false`:

```
std::vector<int> v{ 1, 1, 2, 3, 5, 8, 13 };

auto it = std::find_if_not(v.cbegin(), v.cend(),
                       [](int const n) {return n % 2 == 1; });
if (it != v.cend()) std::cout << *it << std::endl;
```

- Use `std::find_first_of()` to search for the occurrence of any value from a range in another range; this algorithm returns an iterator to the first element that is found:

```
std::vector<int> v{ 1, 1, 2, 3, 5, 8, 13 };
std::vector<int> p{ 5, 7, 11 };

auto it = std::find_first_of(v.cbegin(), v.cend(),
                             p.cbegin(), p.cend());
if (it != v.cend())
  std::cout << "found " << *it
            << " at index " << std::distance(v.cbegin(), it)
            << std::endl;
```

- Use `std::find_end()` to find the last occurrence of a subrange of elements in a range; this algorithm returns an iterator to the first element of the last subrange in the range:

```
std::vector<int> v1{ 1, 1, 0, 0, 1, 0, 1, 0, 1, 0, 1, 1 };
std::vector<int> v2{ 1, 0, 1 };

auto it = std::find_end(v1.cbegin(), v1.cend(),
                        v2.cbegin(), v2.cend());
if (it != v1.cend())
  std::cout << "found at index "
            << std::distance(v1.cbegin(), it) << std::endl;
```

- Use `std::search()` to search for the first occurrence of a subrange in a range; this algorithm returns an iterator to the first element of the subrange in the range:

```
auto text = "The quick brown fox jumps over the lazy dog"s;
auto word = "over"s;

auto it = std::search(text.cbegin(), text.cend(),
                      word.cbegin(), word.cend());

if (it != text.cend())
  std::cout << "found " << word
            << " at index "
            << std::distance(text.cbegin(), it) << std::endl;
```

- Use `std::search()` with a *searcher,* which is a class that implements a searching algorithm and meets some predefined criteria. This overload of `std::search()` was introduced in C++17, and available standard searchers implement the *Boyer-Moore* and the *Boyer-Moore-Horspool* string searching algorithms:

```
auto text = "The quick brown fox jumps over the lazy dog"s;
auto word = "over"s;

auto it = std::search(
  text.cbegin(), text.cend(),
  std::make_boyer_moore_searcher(word.cbegin(), word.cend()));

if (it != text.cend())
  std::cout << "found " << word
            << " at index "
            << std::distance(text.cbegin(), it) << std::endl;
```

- Use `std::search_n()` to search for *N* consecutive occurrences of a value in a range; this algorithm returns an iterator to the first element of the found sequence in the range:

```
std::vector<int> v{ 1, 1, 0, 0, 1, 0, 1, 0, 1, 0, 1, 1 };

auto it = std::search_n(v.cbegin(), v.cend(), 2, 0);
if (it != v.cend())
  std::cout << "found at index "
            << std::distance(v.cbegin(), it) << std::endl;
```

- Use `std::adjacent_find()` to find two adjacent elements in a range that are equal or satisfy a binary predicate; this algorithm returns an iterator to the first element that is found:

```
std::vector<int> v{ 1, 1, 2, 3, 5, 8, 13 };

auto it = std::adjacent_find(v.cbegin(), v.cend());
if (it != v.cend())
  std::cout << "found at index "
            << std::distance(v.cbegin(), it) << std::endl;

auto it = std::adjacent_find(
  v.cbegin(), v.cend(),
  [](int const a, int const b) {
    return IsPrime(a) && IsPrime(b); });

if (it != v.cend())
  std::cout << "found at index "
            << std::distance(v.cbegin(), it) << std::endl;
```

- Use `std::binary_search()` to find whether an element exists in a sorted range; this algorithm returns a Boolean value to indicate whether the value was found or not:

```
std::vector<int> v{ 1, 1, 2, 3, 5, 8, 13 };

auto success = std::binary_search(v.cbegin(), v.cend(), 8);
if (success) std::cout << "found" << std::endl;
```

- Use `std::lower_bound()` to find the first element in a range not less than a specified value; this algorithm returns an iterator to the element:

```
std::vector<int> v{ 1, 1, 2, 3, 5, 8, 13 };

auto it = std::lower_bound(v.cbegin(), v.cend(), 1);
if (it != v.cend())
  std::cout << "lower bound at "
            << std::distance(v.cbegin(), it) << std::endl;
```

- Use `std::upper_bound()` to find the first element in a range greater than a specified value; this algorithm returns an iterator to the element:

```
std::vector<int> v{ 1, 1, 2, 3, 5, 8, 13 };

auto it = std::upper_bound(v.cbegin(), v.cend(), 1);
if (it != v.cend())
  std::cout << "upper bound at "
```

```
                    << std::distance(v.cbegin(), it) << std::endl;
```

- Use `std::equal_range()` to find a subrange in a range whose values are equal to a specified value. This algorithm returns a pair of iterators defining the first and the one-past-end iterators to the subrange; these two iterators are equivalent to those returned by `std::lower_bound()` and `std::upper_bound()`:

```
std::vector<int> v{ 1, 1, 2, 3, 5, 8, 13 };

auto bounds = std::equal_range(v.cbegin(), v.cend(), 1);
std::cout << "range between indexes "
          << std::distance(v.cbegin(), bounds.first)
          << " and "
          << std::distance(v.cbegin(), bounds.second)
          << std::endl;
```

# How it works...

The way these algorithms work is very similar: they all take as arguments iterators that define the searchable range and additional arguments that depend on each algorithm. Except for `std::search()`, which returns a Boolean, and `std::equal_range()`, which returns a pair of iterators, they all return an iterator to the searched element or to a subrange. These iterators must be compared with the end iterator (that is, the past-last-element) of the range to check whether the search was successful or not. If the search did not find an element or a subrange, then the returned value is the end iterator.

All these algorithms have multiple overloads, but in the *How to do it...* section, we only looked at one particular overload to show how the algorithm can be used. For a complete reference of all overloads, you should see other sources.

In all the preceding examples, we used constant iterators, but all these algorithms work the same with mutable iterators and with reverse iterators. Because they take iterators as input arguments, they can work with standard containers, C-like arrays, or anything that represents a sequence and has iterators available.

A special note on the `std::binary_search()` algorithm is necessary: the iterator parameters that define the range to search in should at least meet the requirements of the forward iterators. Regardless of the type of the supplied iterators, the number of comparisons is always logarithmic on the size of the range. However, the number of iterator increments is different if the iterators are random access, in which case the number of increments is also logarithmic, or are not random access, in which case, it is linear and proportional to the size of the range.

All these algorithms, except for `std::find_if_not()`, were available before C++11. However, some overloads of them have been introduced in the newer standards. An example is `std::search()` that has several overloads introduced in C++17. One of these overloads has the following form:

```
template<class ForwardIterator, class Searcher>
ForwardIterator search(ForwardIterator first, ForwardIterator last,
                       const Searcher& searcher );
```

This overload searches for the occurrence of a pattern defined by a searcher function object for which the standard provides several implementations:

- `default_searcher` basically delegates the searching to the standard `std::search()` algorithm.
- `boyer_moore_searcher` implements the Boyer-Moore algorithm for string searching.
- `boyer_moore_horspool_algorithm` implements the Boyer-Moore-Horspool algorithm for string searching.

## There's more...

Many standard containers have a member function `find()`, for finding elements in the container. When such a method is available and suits your needs, it should be preferred to the general algorithms because these member functions are optimized based on the particularities of each container.

## See also

- *Using vector as a default container*
- *Initializing a range*
- *Using set operations on a range*
- *Sorting a range*

# Sorting a range

In the previous recipe, we looked at the standard general algorithms for searching in a range. Another common operation we often need to do is sorting a range because many routines, including some of the algorithms for searching, require a sorted range. The standard library provides several general algorithms for sorting ranges, and in this recipe, we will see what these algorithms are and how they can be used.

# Getting ready

The sorting general algorithms work with ranges defined by a start and end iterator and, therefore, can sort standard containers, C-like arrays, or anything that represents a sequence and has random iterators available. However, all the examples in this recipe will use `std::vector`.

# How to do it...

The following is a list of standard general algorithms for searching a range:

- Use `std::sort()` for sorting a range:

  ```
  std::vector<int> v{3, 13, 5, 8, 1, 2, 1};

  std::sort(v.begin(), v.end());
  // v = {1, 1, 2, 3, 5, 8, 13}

  std::sort(v.begin(), v.end(), std::greater<>());
  // v = {13, 8, 5, 3, 2, 1 ,1}
  ```

- Use `std::stable_sort()` for sorting a range but keeping the order of the equal elements:

  ```
  struct Task
  {
    int priority;
    std::string name;
  };

  bool operator<(Task const & lhs, Task const & rhs) {
    return lhs.priority < rhs.priority;
  }

  bool operator>(Task const & lhs, Task const & rhs) {
  ```

```
        return lhs.priority > rhs.priority;
    }

    std::vector<Task> v{
        { 10, "Task 1"s }, { 40, "Task 2"s }, { 25, "Task 3"s },
        { 10, "Task 4"s }, { 80, "Task 5"s }, { 10, "Task 6"s },
    };

    std::stable_sort(v.begin(), v.end());
    // {{ 10, "Task 1" },{ 10, "Task 4" },{ 10, "Task 6" },
    //   { 25, "Task 3" },{ 40, "Task 2" },{ 80, "Task 5" }}

    std::stable_sort(v.begin(), v.end(), std::greater<>());
    // {{ 80, "Task 5" },{ 40, "Task 2" },{ 25, "Task 3" },
    //   { 10, "Task 1" },{ 10, "Task 4" },{ 10, "Task 6" }}
```

- Use `std::partial_sort()` for sorting a part of a range (and leaving the rest in an unspecified order):

```
    std::vector<int> v{ 3, 13, 5, 8, 1, 2, 1 };

    std::partial_sort(v.begin(), v.begin() + 4, v.end());
    // v = {1, 1, 2, 3, ?, ?, ?}

    std::partial_sort(v.begin(), v.begin() + 4, v.end(),
                      std::greater<>());
    // v = {13, 8, 5, 3, ?, ?, ?}
```

- Use `std::partial_sort_copy()` for sorting a part of a range by copying the sorted elements to a second range and leaving the original range unchanged:

```
    std::vector<int> v{ 3, 13, 5, 8, 1, 2, 1 };
    std::vector<int> vc(v.size());

    std::partial_sort_copy(v.begin(), v.end(),
                           vc.begin(), vc.end());
    // v = {3, 13, 5, 8, 1, 2, 1}
    // vc = {1, 1, 2, 3, 5, 8, 13}

    std::partial_sort_copy(v.begin(), v.end(),
                           vc.begin(), vc.end(), std::greater<>());
    // vc = {13, 8, 5, 3, 2, 1, 1}
```

- Use `std::nth_element()` for sorting a range so that the *N*th element is the one that would be in that position if the range was completely sorted, and the elements before it are all smaller and the ones after it are all greater, without any guarantee that they are also ordered:

```
std::vector<int> v{ 3, 13, 5, 8, 1, 2, 1 };

std::nth_element(v.begin(), v.begin() + 3, v.end());
// v = {1, 1, 2, 3, 5, 8, 13}

std::nth_element(v.begin(), v.begin() + 3, v.end(),
                 std::greater<>());
// v = {13, 8, 5, 3, 2, 1, 1}
```

- Use `std::is_sorted()` to check whether a range is sorted:

```
std::vector<int> v { 1, 1, 2, 3, 5, 8, 13 };

auto sorted = std::is_sorted(v.cbegin(), v.cend());
sorted = std::is_sorted(v.cbegin(), v.cend(),
                        std::greater<>());
```

- Use `std::is_sorted_until()` to find a sorted subrange from the beginning of a range:

```
std::vector<int> v{ 3, 13, 5, 8, 1, 2, 1 };

auto it = std::is_sorted_until(v.cbegin(), v.cend());
auto length = std::distance(v.cbegin(), it);
```

# How it works...

All the preceding general algorithms take random iterators as arguments to define the range to be sorted and, some of them additionally take an output range. They all have overloads, one that requires a comparison function for sorting the elements, and one that does not and uses `operator<` for comparing the elements.

These algorithms work in the following way:

- `std::sort()` modifies the input range so that its elements are sorted according to the default or the specified comparison function; the actual algorithm for sorting is an implementation detail.

- `std::stable_sort()` is similar to `std::sort()`, but it guarantees to preserve the original order of elements that are equal.
- `std::partial_sort()` takes three iterator arguments indicating the first, middle, and last element in a range, where middle can be any element, not just the one at the natural middle position. The result is a partially sorted range so that that first `middle - first` smallest elements from the original range, that is, [`first, last`), are found in the [`first, middle`) subrange and the rest of the elements are in an unspecified order, in the [`middle, last`) subrange.
- `std::partial_sort_copy()` is not a variant of `std::partial_copy()`, as the name may suggest, but of `std::sort()`. It sorts a range without altering it by copying its elements to an output range. The arguments of the algorithm are the first and last iterators of the input and output ranges. If the output range has a size *M* that is greater than or equal to the size *N* of the input range, the input range is entirely sorted and copied to the output range; the first *N* elements of the output range are overwritten, and the last *M* - *N* elements are left untouched. If the output range is smaller than the input range, then only the first *M* sorted elements from the input range are copied to the output range (which is entirely overwritten in this case).
- `std::nth_element()` is basically an implementation of a selection algorithm, which is an algorithm for finding the Nth smallest element of a range. This algorithm takes three iterator arguments representing the first, Nth, and last element, and partially sorts the range so that after sorting, the Nth element is the one that would be in that position if the range had been entirely sorted. In the modified range, all the *N-1* elements before the *n*th one are smaller than it, and all the elements after the *n*th element are greater than it. However, there is no guarantee on the order of these other elements.
- `std::is_sorted()` checks whether the specified range is sorted according to the specified or default comparison function and returns a Boolean value to indicate that.
- `std::is_sorted_until()` finds a sorted subrange of the specified range, starting from the beginning, using either a provided comparison function or the default `operator<`. The returned value is an iterator representing the upper bound of the sorted subrange, which is also the iterator of the one-past-last sorted element.

# There's more...

Some standard containers, `std::list` and `std::forward_list`, provide a member function, `sort()`, which is optimized for those containers. These member functions should be preferred over the general standard algorithm, `std::sort()`.

# See also

- *Using vector as a default container*
- *Initializing a range*
- *Using set operations on a range*
- *Finding elements in a range*

# Initializing a range

In the previous recipes, we explored the general standard algorithms for searching in a range and sorting a range. The algorithms library provides many other general algorithms and among them are several that are intended for filling a range with values. In this recipe, you will learn what these algorithms are and how they should be used.

# Getting ready

All the examples in this recipe use `std::vector`. However, like all the general algorithms, the ones we will see in this recipe take iterators to define the bounds of a range and can therefore be used with any standard container, C-like arrays, or custom types representing a sequence that have forward iterators defined.

Except for `std::iota()`, which is available in the `<numeric>` header, all the other algorithms are found in the `<algorithm>` header.

# How to do it...

To assign values to a range, use any of the following standard algorithms:

- `std::fill()` to assign a value to all the elements of a range; the range is defined by a first and last forward iterator:

```
std::vector<int> v(5);
std::fill(v.begin(), v.end(), 42);
// v = {42, 42, 42, 42, 42}
```

- `std::fill_n()` to assign values to a number of elements of a range; the range is defined by a first forward iterator and a counter that indicates how many elements should be assigned the specified value:

```
std::vector<int> v(10);
std::fill_n(v.begin(), 5, 42);
// v = {42, 42, 42, 42, 42, 0, 0, 0, 0, 0}
```

- `std::generate()` to assign the value returned by a function to the elements of a range; the range is defined by a first and last forward iterator, and the function is invoked once for each element in the range:

```
std::random_device rd{};
std::mt19937 mt{ rd() };
std::uniform_int_distribution<> ud{1, 10};
std::vector<int> v(5);
std::generate(v.begin(), v.end(),
              [&ud, &mt] {return ud(mt); });
```

- `std::generate_n()` to assign the value returned by a function to a number of elements of a range; the range is defined by a first forward iterator and a counter that indicates how many elements should be assigned the value from the function that is invoked once for each element:

```
std::vector<int> v(5);
auto i = 1;
std::generate_n(v.begin(), v.size(), [&i] { return i*i++; });
// v = {1, 4, 9, 16, 25}
```

- `std::iota()` to assign sequentially increasing values to the elements of a range; the range is defined by a first and last forward iterator, and the values are incremented using the prefix `operator++` from an initial specified value:

```
std::vector<int> v(5);
std::iota(v.begin(), v.end(), 1);
// v = {1, 2, 3, 4, 5}
```

# How it works...

`std::fill()` and `std::fill_n()` work similarly but differ in the way the range is specified: for the former by a first and last iterator, for the latter by a first iterator and a count. The second algorithm returns an iterator, representing either the one-past-last assigned element if the counter is greater than zero, or an iterator to the first element of the range otherwise.

`std::generate()` and `std::generate_n()` are also similar, differing only in the way the range is specified. The first takes two iterators, defining the range's lower and upper bounds, and the second, an iterator to the first element and a count. Like `std::fill_n()`, `std::generate_n()` also returns an iterator, representing either the one-past-last assigned element if the count is greater than zero, or an iterator to the first element of the range, otherwise. These algorithms call a specified function for each element in the range and assign the returned value to the element. The generating function does not take any argument, so the value of the argument cannot be passed to the function as this is intended as a function to initialize the elements of a range. If you need to use the value of the elements to generate new values, you should use `std::transform()`.

`std::iota()` takes its name from the ι (iota) function from the APL programming language, and though it was a part of the initial STL, it was only included in the standard library in C++11. This function takes a first and last iterator to a range and an initial value that is assigned to the first element of the range and then used to generate sequentially increasing values using the prefix `operator++` for the rest of the elements in the range.

# See also

- *Using vector as a default container*
- *Sorting a range*
- *Using set operations on a range*
- *Finding elements in a range*

- *Generating pseudo-random numbers* recipe of `Chapter 9`, *Working with Numbers and Strings*
- *Initializing all bits of internal state of a pseudo-random number generator* recipe of `Chapter 9`, *Working with Numbers and Strings*

# Using set operations on a range

The standard library provides several algorithms for set operations that enable us to do unions, intersections, or differences of sorted ranges. In this recipe, we will see what these algorithms are and how they work.

# Getting ready

The algorithms for set operations work with iterators, which means they can be used for standard containers, C-like arrays, or any custom type representing a sequence that has input iterators available. All the examples in this recipe will use `std::vector`.

For all the examples in the next section, we will use the following ranges:

```
std::vector<int> v1{ 1, 2, 3, 4, 4, 5 };
std::vector<int> v2{ 2, 3, 3, 4, 6, 8 };
std::vector<int> v3;
```

# How to do it...

Use the following general algorithms for set operations:

- `std::set_union()` to compute the union of two ranges into a third range:

```
std::set_union(v1.cbegin(), v1.cend(),
               v2.cbegin(), v2.cend(),
               std::back_inserter(v3));
// v3 = {1, 2, 3, 3, 4, 4, 5, 6, 8}
```

- `std::merge()` to merge the content of two ranges into a third one; this is similar to `std::set_union()` except that it copies the entire content of the input ranges into the output one, not just their union:

```
std::merge(v1.cbegin(), v1.cend(),
           v2.cbegin(), v2.cend(),
```

```
        std::back_inserter(v3));
    // v3 = {1, 2, 2, 3, 3, 3, 4, 4, 4, 5, 6, 8}
```

- `std::set_intersection()` to compute the intersection of the two ranges into a third range:

```
std::set_intersection(v1.cbegin(), v1.cend(),
                      v2.cbegin(), v2.cend(),
                      std::back_inserter(v3));
// v3 = {2, 3, 4}
```

- `std::set_difference()` to compute the difference of two ranges into a third range; the output range will contain elements from the first range, which are not present in the second range:

```
std::set_difference(v1.cbegin(), v1.cend(),
                    v2.cbegin(), v2.cend(),
                    std::back_inserter(v3));
// v3 = {1, 4, 5}
```

- `std::set_symmetric_difference()` to compute a dual difference of the two ranges into a third range; the output range will contain elements that are present in any of the input ranges, but only in one:

```
std::set_symmetric_difference(v1.cbegin(), v1.cend(),
                              v2.cbegin(), v2.cend(),
                              std::back_inserter(v3));
// v3 = {1, 3, 4, 5, 6, 8}
```

- `std::includes()` to check if one range is a subset of another range (that is, all its elements are also present in the other range):

```
std::vector<int> v1{ 1, 2, 3, 4, 4, 5 };
std::vector<int> v2{ 2, 3, 3, 4, 6, 8 };
std::vector<int> v3{ 1, 2, 4 };
std::vector<int> v4{ };

auto i1 = std::includes(v1.cbegin(), v1.cend(),
                        v2.cbegin(), v2.cend()); // i1 = false
auto i2 = std::includes(v1.cbegin(), v1.cend(),
                        v3.cbegin(), v3.cend()); // i2 = true
auto i3 = std::includes(v1.cbegin(), v1.cend(),
                        v4.cbegin(), v4.cend()); // i3 = true
```

# How it works...

All the set operations that produce a new range from two input ranges, in fact, have the same interface and work in a similar way:

- They take two input ranges, each defined by a first and last input iterator.
- They take an output iterator to an output range where elements will be inserted.
- They have an overload that takes an extra argument representing a comparison binary function object that must return `true` if the first argument is less than the second. When a comparison function object is not specified, `operator<` is used.
- They return an iterator past the end of the constructed output range.
- The input ranges must be sorted using either `operator<` or the provided comparison function, depending on the overload that is used.
- The output range must not overlap any of the two input ranges.

We will demonstrate the way they work with additional examples using vectors of a POD type `Task` that we also used in a previous recipe:

```
struct Task
{
   int priority;
   std::string name;
};

bool operator<(Task const & lhs, Task const & rhs) {
   return lhs.priority < rhs.priority;
}

bool operator>(Task const & lhs, Task const & rhs) {
   return lhs.priority > rhs.priority;
}

std::vector<Task> v1{
   { 10, "Task 1.1"s },
   { 20, "Task 1.2"s },
   { 20, "Task 1.3"s },
   { 20, "Task 1.4"s },
   { 30, "Task 1.5"s },
   { 50, "Task 1.6"s },
};

std::vector<Task> v2{
   { 20, "Task 2.1"s },
   { 30, "Task 2.2"s },
   { 30, "Task 2.3"s },
```

```
    { 30, "Task 2.4"s },
    { 40, "Task 2.5"s },
    { 50, "Task 2.6"s },
};
```

The particular way each algorithm produces the output range is described here:

- `std::set_union()` copies all the elements present in one or both of the input ranges to the output range, producing a new sorted range. If an element is found *M* times in the first range and *N* times in the second range, then all the *M* elements from the first range will be copied to the output range in their existing order, and then the *N-M* elements from the second range are copied to the output range if *N* > *M*, or 0 elements otherwise:

```
std::vector<Task> v3;
std::set_union(v1.cbegin(), v1.cend(),
               v2.cbegin(), v2.cend(),
               std::back_inserter(v3));
// v3 = {{10, "Task 1.1"},{20, "Task 1.2"},{20, "Task 1.3"},
//        {20, "Task 1.4"},{30, "Task 1.5"},{30, "Task 2.3"},
//        {30, "Task 2.4"},{40, "Task 2.5"},{50, "Task 1.6"}}
```

- `std::merge()` copies all the elements from both the input ranges into the output range, producing a new range sorted with respect to the comparison function:

```
std::vector<Task> v4;
std::merge(v1.cbegin(), v1.cend(),
           v2.cbegin(), v2.cend(),
           std::back_inserter(v4));
// v4 = {{10, "Task 1.1"},{20, "Task 1.2"},{20, "Task 1.3"},
//        {20, "Task 1.4"},{20, "Task 2.1"},{30, "Task 1.5"},
//        {30, "Task 2.2"},{30, "Task 2.3"},{30, "Task 2.4"},
//        {40, "Task 2.5"},{50, "Task 1.6"},{50, "Task 2.6"}}
```

- `std::set_intersection()` copies all the elements that are found in both the input ranges into the output range, producing a new range sorted with respect to the comparison function:

```
std::vector<Task> v5;
std::set_intersection(v1.cbegin(), v1.cend(),
                      v2.cbegin(), v2.cend(),
                      std::back_inserter(v5));
// v5 = {{20, "Task 1.2"},{30, "Task 1.5"},{50, "Task 1.6"}}
```

- `std::set_difference()` copies to the output range all the elements from the first input range that are not found in the second input range. For equivalent elements that are found in both the ranges, the following rule applies: if an element is found $M$ times in the first range and $N$ times in the second range, and if $M > N$, then it is copied $M$-$N$ times; otherwise it is not copied:

```
std::vector<Task> v6;
std::set_difference(v1.cbegin(), v1.cend(),
                    v2.cbegin(), v2.cend(),
                    std::back_inserter(v6));
// v6 = {{10, "Task 1.1"},{20, "Task 1.3"},{20, "Task 1.4"}}
```

- `std::set_symmetric_difference()` copies to the output range all the elements that are found in either of the two input ranges but not in both of them. If an element is found $M$ times in the first range and $N$ times in the second range, then if $M > N$, the last $M$-$N$ of those elements from the first range are copied into the output rage, else, the last $N$-$M$ of those elements from the second range will be copied into the output range:

```
std::vector<Task> v7;
std::set_symmetric_difference(v1.cbegin(), v1.cend(),
                              v2.cbegin(), v2.cend(),
                              std::back_inserter(v7));
// v7 = {{10, "Task 1.1"},{20, "Task 1.3"},{20, "Task 1.4"}
//       {30, "Task 2.3"},{30, "Task 2.4"},{40, "Task 2.5"}}
```

On the other hand, `std::includes()` does not produce an output range; it only checks whether the second range is included in the first range. It returns a Boolean value that is `true` if the second range is empty or all its elements are included in the first range, or `false` otherwise. It also has two overloads, one of them specifying a comparison binary function object.

# See also

- *Using vector as a default container*
- *Sorting a range*
- *Initializing a range*
- *Using iterators to insert new elements in a container*
- *Finding elements in a range*

# Using iterators to insert new elements in a container

When you're working with containers, it is often useful to insert new elements at the beginning, end, or somewhere in the middle. There are algorithms, such as the ones we saw in the previous recipe, *Using set operations on a range*, that require an iterator to a range to insert into, but if you simply pass an iterator, such as the one returned by begin(), it will not insert but overwrite the elements of the container. Moreover, it's not possible to insert at the end by using the iterator returned by end(). In order to perform such operations, the standard library provides a set of iterators and iterator adapters that enable these scenarios.

## Getting ready

The iterators and adapters discussed in this recipe are available in the std namespace in the <iterator> header. If you include headers such as, <algorithm>, you do not have to explicitly include <iterator>.

## How to do it...

Use the following iterator adapters to insert new elements in a container:

- std::back_inserter() to insert elements at the end, for containers that have a push_back() method:

  ```
  std::vector<int> v{ 1,2,3,4,5 };
  std::fill_n(std::back_inserter(v), 3, 0);
  // v={1,2,3,4,5,0,0,0}
  ```

- std::front_inserter() to insert elements at the beginning, for containers that have a push_front() method:

  ```
  std::list<int> l{ 1,2,3,4,5 };
  std::fill_n(std::front_inserter(l), 3, 0);
  // l={0,0,0,1,2,3,4,5}
  ```

- std::inserter() to insert anywhere in a container, for containers that have an insert() method:

  ```
  std::vector<int> v{ 1,2,3,4,5 };
  std::fill_n(std::inserter(v, v.begin()), 3, 0);
  ```

```
// v={0,0,0,1,2,3,4,5}

std::list<int> l{ 1,2,3,4,5 };
auto it = l.begin();
std::advance(it, 3);
std::fill_n(std::inserter(l, it), 3, 0);
// l={1,2,3,0,0,0,4,5}
```

# How it works...

`std::back_inserter()`, `std::front_inserter()`, and `std::inserter()` are all helper functions that create iterator adapters of types, `std::back_insert_iterator`, `std::front_insert_iterator`, and `std::insert_iterator`. These are all output iterators that append, prepend, or insert into the container for which they were constructed. Incrementing and dereferencing these iterators does not do anything. However, upon assignment, these iterators call the following methods from the container:

- `std::back_insterter_iterator` calls `push_back()`
- `std::front_inserter_iterator` calls `push_front()`
- `std::insert_iterator` calls `insert()`

The following is the over-simplified implementation of `std::back_inserter_iterator`:

```cpp
template<class C>
class back_insert_iterator {
public:
  typedef back_insert_iterator<C> T;
  typedef typename C::value_type V;

  explicit back_insert_iterator( C& c ) :container( &c ) { }

  T& operator=( const V& val ) {
    container->push_back( val );
    return *this;
  }

  T& operator*() { return *this; }

  T& operator++() { return *this; }

  T& operator++( int ) { return *this; }
protected:
  C* container;
};
```

Because of the way the assignment operator works, these iterators can only be used with some standard containers:

- `std::back_insert_iterator` can be used with `std::vector`, `std::list`, `std::deque`, and `std::basic_string`.
- `std::front_insert_iterator` can be used with `std::list`, `std::forward_list`, and `std:deque`.
- `std::insert_iterator` can be used with all the standard containers.

The following example inserts three elements with the value 0 at the beginning of an `std::vector`:

```
std::vector<int> v{ 1,2,3,4,5 };
std::fill_n(std::inserter(v, v.begin()), 3, 0);
// v={0,0,0,1,2,3,4,5}
```

The `std::inserter()` adapter takes two arguments: the container, and the iterator where an element is supposed to be inserted. Upon calling `insert()` on the container, the `std::insert_iterator` increments the iterator, so upon being assigned again, it can insert a new element into the next position. Here is how the assignment operator is implemented for this iterator adapter:

```
T& operator=(const V& v)
{
  iter = container->insert(iter, v);
  ++iter;
  return (*this);
}
```

# There's more...

These iterator adapters are intended to be used with algorithms or functions that insert multiple elements into a range. They can be used, of course, to insert a single element, but that is rather an anti-pattern, since simply calling `push_back()`, `push_front()`, or `insert()` is much simpler and intuitive in this case. The following examples should be avoided:

```
std::vector<int> v{ 1,2,3,4,5 };
*std::back_inserter(v) = 6; // v = {1,2,3,4,5,6}

std::back_insert_iterator<std::vector<int>> it(v);
*it = 7;                    // v = {1,2,3,4,5,6,7}
```

# See also

- *Using set operations on a range*

# Writing your own random access iterator

In Chapter 8, *Learning Modern Core Language Features*, we saw how we can enable range-based for loops for custom types by implementing iterators and free `begin()` and `end()` functions to return iterators to the first and one-past-the-last element of the custom range. You might have noticed that the minimal iterator implementation that we provided in that recipe does not meet the requirements for a standard iterator because it cannot be copy constructible or assigned and cannot be incremented. In this recipe, we will build upon that example and show how to create a random access iterator that meets all requirements.

## Getting ready

For this recipe, you should know the types of iterators the standard defines and how they are different. A good overview of their requirements is available at `http://www.cplusplus.com/reference/iterator/`.

To exemplify how to write a random access iterator, we will consider a variant of the `dummy_array` class used in the *Enabling range-based for loops for custom types* recipe of Chapter 8, *Learning Modern Core Language Features*. This is a very simple array concept, with no practical value, other than serving as a code base for demonstrating iterators:

```
template <typename Type, size_t const SIZE>
class dummy_array
{
  Type data[SIZE] = {};
public:
  Type& operator[](size_t const index)
  {
    if (index < SIZE) return data[index];
    throw std::out_of_range("index out of range");
  }

  Type const & operator[](size_t const index) const
  {
    if (index < SIZE) return data[index];
    throw std::out_of_range("index out of range");
```

```
    }

    size_t size() const { return SIZE; }
};
```

All the code shown in the next section, the iterator classes, `typedefs`, and the `begin()` and `end()` functions, will be a part of this class.

# How to do it...

To provide mutable and constant random access iterators for the `dummy_array` class shown in the previous section, add the following members to the class:

- An iterator class template, which is parameterized with the type of elements and the size of the array. The class must have the following public `typedefs` that define standard synonyms:

```
template <typename T, size_t const Size>
class dummy_array_iterator
{
public:
    typedef dummy_array_iterator              self_type;
    typedef T                                 value_type;
    typedef T&                                reference;
    typedef T*                                pointer;
    typedef std::random_access_iterator_tag iterator_category;
    typedef ptrdiff_t                         difference_type;
};
```

- Private members for the iterator class: a pointer to the array data and a current index into the array:

```
private:
    pointer ptr = nullptr;
    size_t index = 0;
```

- Private method for the iterator class to check whether two iterator instances point to the same array data:

```
private:
    bool compatible(self_type const & other) const
    {
        return ptr == other.ptr;
    }
```

- An explicit constructor for the iterator class:

```
public:
    explicit dummy_array_iterator(pointer ptr,
                                  size_t const index)
        : ptr(ptr), index(index) { }
```

- Iterator class members to meet common requirements for all iterators: copy-constructible, copy-assignable, destructible, prefix, and postfix incrementable. In this implementation, the post increment operator is implemented in terms of the pre-increment operator to avoid code duplication:

```
dummy_array_iterator(dummy_array_iterator const & o)
    = default;
dummy_array_iterator& operator=(dummy_array_iterator const & o)
    = default;
~dummy_array_iterator() = default;

self_type & operator++ ()
{
    if (index >= Size)
        throw std::out_of_range("Iterator cannot be incremented past
                                 the end of range.");
    ++index;
    return *this;
}

self_type operator++ (int)
{
    self_type tmp = *this;
    ++*this;
    return tmp;
}
```

- Iterator class members to meet input iterator requirements: test for equality/inequality, dereferenceable as rvalues:

```
bool operator== (self_type const & other) const
{
    assert(compatible(other));
    return index == other.index;
}

bool operator!= (self_type const & other) const
{
    return !(*this == other);
}
```

```
reference operator* () const
{
  if (ptr == nullptr)
    throw std::bad_function_call();
  return *(ptr + index);
}

reference operator-> () const
{
  if (ptr == nullptr)
    throw std::bad_function_call();
  return *(ptr + index);
}
```

- Iterator class members to meet forward iterator requirements: default constructible:

```
dummy_array_iterator() = default;
```

- Iterator class members to meet bidirectional iterator requirements: decrementable:

```
self_type & operator--()
{
  if (index <= 0)
    throw std::out_of_range("Iterator cannot be decremented
                             past the end of range.");
  --index;
  return *this;
}

self_type operator--(int)
{
  self_type tmp = *this;
  --*this;
  return tmp;
}
```

- Iterator class members to meet random access iterator requirements: arithmetic add and subtract, comparable for inequality with other iterators, compound assignments, and offset dereferenceable:

```
self_type operator+(difference_type offset) const
{
  self_type tmp = *this;
  return tmp += offset;
}
```

```
self_type operator-(difference_type offset) const
{
  self_type tmp = *this;
  return tmp -= offset;
}

difference_type operator-(self_type const & other) const
{
  assert(compatible(other));
  return (index - other.index);
}

bool operator<(self_type const & other) const
{
  assert(compatible(other));
  return index < other.index;
}

bool operator>(self_type const & other) const
{
  return other < *this;
}

bool operator<=(self_type const & other) const
{
  return !(other < *this);
}

bool operator>=(self_type const & other) const
{
  return !(*this < other);
}

self_type & operator+=(difference_type const offset)
{
  if (index + offset < 0 || index + offset > Size)
    throw std::out_of_range("Iterator cannot be incremented
                             past the end of range.");
  index += offset;
  return *this;
}

self_type & operator-=(difference_type const offset)
{
  return *this += -offset;
}

value_type & operator[](difference_type const offset)
```

```
{
  return (*(*this + offset));
}

value_type const & operator[](difference_type const offset) const
{
  return (*(*this + offset));
}
```

- Add `typedefs` to the `dummy_array` class for mutable and constant iterator synonyms:

```
public:
    typedef dummy_array_iterator<Type, SIZE>
            iterator;
    typedef dummy_array_iterator<Type const, SIZE>
            constant_iterator;
```

- Add the public `begin()` and `end()` functions to the `dummy_array` class to return the iterators to the first and one-past-last elements in the array:

```
iterator begin()
{
  return iterator(data, 0);
}

iterator end()
{
  return iterator(data, SIZE);
}

constant_iterator begin() const
{
  return constant_iterator(data, 0);
}

constant_iterator end() const
{
  return constant_iterator(data, SIZE);
}
```

# How it works...

The standard library defines five categories of iterators:

- *Input iterators*: These are the simplest category and guarantee validity only for single-pass sequential algorithms. After being incremented, the previous copies may become invalid.
- *Output iterators*: These are basically input iterators that can be used to write to the pointed element.
- *Forward iterators*: These can read (and write) data to the pointed element. They satisfy the requirements for input iterators and, in addition, must be default constructible and must support multi-pass scenarios without invalidating the previous copies.
- *Bidirectional iterators*: These are forward iterators that, in addition, support decrementing, so they can move in both directions.
- *Random access iterators*: These support access to any element in the container in constant time. They implement all the requirements for bidirectional iterators, and, in addition, support arithmetic operations + and −, compound assignments += and −=, comparisons with other iterators with <, <=, >, >=, and the offset dereference operator.

Forward, bidirectional, and random access iterators that also implement the requirements of output iterators are called *mutable iterators*.

In the previous section, we saw how to implement random access iterators, with a step-by-step walkthrough of the requirements of each category of iterators (as each iterator category includes the requirements of the previous category and adds new requirements). The iterator class template is common for both constant and mutable iterators, and we have defined two synonyms for it called `iterator` and `constant_iterator`.

After implementing the inner iterator class template, we also defined the `begin()` and `end()` member functions that return an iterator to the first and the one-past-last element in the array. These methods have overloads to return mutable or constant iterators, depending on whether the `dummy_array` class instance is mutable or constant.

With this implementation of the `dummy_array` class and its iterators, we can write the following samples. For more examples, check the source code that accompanies this book:

```
dummy_array<int, 3> a;
a[0] = 10;
a[1] = 20;
a[2] = 30;
```

```
std::transform(a.begin(), a.end(), a.begin(),
               [](int const e) {return e * 2; });

for (auto&& e : a) std::cout << e << std::endl;

auto lp = [](dummy_array<int, 3> const & ca)
{
  for (auto const & e : ca)
    std::cout << e << std::endl;
};

lp(a);

dummy_array<std::unique_ptr<Tag>, 3> ta;
ta[0] = std::make_unique<Tag>(1, "Tag 1");
ta[1] = std::make_unique<Tag>(2, "Tag 2");
ta[2] = std::make_unique<Tag>(3, "Tag 3");

for (auto it = ta.begin(); it != ta.end(); ++it)
  std::cout << it->id << " " << it->name << std::endl;
```

# There's more...

Apart from `begin()` and `end()`, a container may have additional methods such as `cbegin()`/`cend()` (for constant iterators), `rbegin()`/`rend()` (for mutable reverse iterators), and `crbegin()`/ `crend()` (for constant reverse iterators). Implementing this is left as an exercise for you.

On the other hand, in modern C++, these functions that return the first and last iterators do not have to be member functions but can be provided as non-member functions. In fact, this is the topic of the next recipe, *Container access with non-member functions*.

# See also

- *Enabling range-based for loops for custom types* recipe of `Chapter 8`, *Learning Modern Core Language Features*
- *Creating type aliases and alias templates* recipe of `Chapter 8`, *Learning Modern Core Language Features*

# Container access with non-member functions

Standard containers provide the `begin()` and `end()` member functions for retrieving iterators to the first and one-past-last element of the container. There are actually four sets of these functions. Apart from `begin()`/`end()`, containers provide `cbegin()`/`cend()` to return constant iterators, `rbegin()`/`rend()` to return mutable reverse iterators, and `crbegin()`/`crend()` to return constant reverse iterators. In C++11/C++14, all these have non-member equivalents that work with standard containers, C-like arrays, and any custom type that specializes them. In C++17, even more non-member functions have been added; `std::data()`--that returns a pointer to the block of memory containing the elements of the container, `std::size()`--that returns the size of a container or array, and `std::empty()`--that returns whether the given container is empty. These non-member functions are intended for generic code but can be used anywhere in your code.

## Getting ready

In this recipe, we will use as an example, the `dummy_array` class and its iterators that we implemented in the previous recipe, *Writing your own random access iterator*. You should read that recipe before continuing with this one.

Non-member `begin()`/`end()` functions and the other variants, as well as non-member `data()`, `size()` and `empty()` are available in the `std` namespace in the `<iterator>` header, which is implicitly included with any of the following headers: `<array>`, `<deque>`, `<forward_list>`, `<list>`, `<map>`, `<regex>`, `<set>`, `<string>`, `<unordered_map>`, `<unordered_set>`, and `<vector>`.

In this recipe, we will refer to the `std::begin()`/`std::end()` functions, but everything discussed also applies to the other functions: `std::cbegin()`/`std::cend()`, `std::rbegin()`/`std::rend()`, and `std::crbegin()`/`std::crend()`.

# How to do it...

Use the non-member `std::begin()`/`std::end()` function and the other variants, as well as `std::data()`, `std::size()` and `std::empty()` with:

- Standard containers:

```
std::vector<int> v1{ 1, 2, 3, 4, 5 };
auto sv1 = std::size(v1);   // sv1 = 5
auto ev1 = std::empty(v1);  // ev1 = false
auto dv1 = std::data(v1);   // dv1 = v1.data()
for (auto i = std::begin(v1); i != std::end(v1); ++i)
  std::cout << *i << std::endl;

std::vector<int> v2;
std::copy(std::cbegin(v1), std::cend(v1),
      std::back_inserter(v2));
```

- (C-like) arrays:

```
int a[5] = { 1, 2, 3, 4, 5 };
auto pos = std::find_if(std::crbegin(a), std::crend(a),
                [](int const n) {return n % 2 == 0; });
auto sa = std::size(a);   // sa = 5
auto ea = std::empty(a);  // ea = false
auto da = std::data(a);   // da = a
```

- Custom types that provide corresponding member functions, `begin()`/`end()`, `data()`, `empty()`, or `size()`:

```
dummy_array<std::string, 5> sa;
dummy_array<int, 5> sb;
sa[0] = "1"s;
sa[1] = "2"s;
sa[2] = "3"s;
sa[3] = "4"s;
sa[4] = "5"s;

std::transform(
  std::begin(sa), std::end(sa),
  std::begin(sb),
  [](std::string const & s) {return std::stoi(s); });
// sb = [1, 2, 3, 4, 5]

auto sa_size = std::size(sa); // sa_size = 5
```

- Generic code where the type of the container is not known:

```
template <typename F, typename C>
void process(F&& f, C const & c)
{
   std::for_each(std::begin(c), std::end(c),
                 std::forward<F>(f));
}

auto l = [](auto const e) {std::cout << e << std::endl; };

process(l, v1); // std::vector<int>
process(l, a);  // int[5]
process(l, sa); // dummy_array<std::string, 5>
```

# How it works...

These non-member functions were introduced in different versions of the standard, but all of them were modified in C++17 to return `constexpr auto`:

- `std::begin()` and `std::end()` in C++11
- `std::cbegin()`/`std::cend()`, `std::rbegin()`/`std::rend()`, and `std::crbegin()`/`std::crend()` in C++14
- `std::data()`, `std::size()`, and `std::empty()` in C++17

The `begin()`/`end()` family of functions have overloads for container classes and arrays, and all they do is the following:

- Return the results of calling the container-corresponding member function for containers.
- Return a pointer to the first or one-past-last element of the array for arrays.

The actual typical implementation for `std::begin()`/`std::end()` is the following:

```
template<class C>
constexpr auto inline begin(C& c) -> decltype(c.begin())
{
   return c.begin();
}
```

```
template<class C>
constexpr auto inline end(C& c) -> decltype(c.end())
{
  return c.end();
}

template<class T, std::size_t N>
constexpr T* inline begin(T (&array)[N])
{
  return array;
}

template<class T, std::size_t N>
constexpr T* inline begin(T (&array)[N])
{
  return array+N;
}
```

Custom specialization can be provided for containers that do not have corresponding `begin()`/`end()` members but can still be iterated. The standard library actually provides such specializations for `std::initializer_list` and `std::valarray`.

 Specializations must be defined in the same namespace where the original class or function template has been defined. Therefore, if you want to specialize any of the `std::begin()`/`std::end()` pairs you must do it in the `std` namespace.

The other non-member functions for container access, that were introduced in C++17, have also several overloads:

- `std::data()` has several overloads; for a class `C` it returns `c.data()`, for arrays it returns the `array`, and for `std::initializer_list<T>` it returns the `il.begin()`.

  ```
  template <class C>
  constexpr auto data(C& c) -> decltype(c.data())
  {
    return c.data();
  }

  template <class C>
  constexpr auto data(const C& c) -> decltype(c.data())
  {
    return c.data();
  }
  ```

```
template <class T, std::size_t N>
constexpr T* data(T (&array)[N]) noexcept
{
  return array;
}

template <class E>
constexpr const E* data(std::initializer_list<E> il) noexcept
{
  return il.begin();
}
```

- `std::size()` has two overloads; for a class `C` it returns `c.size()`, and for arrays it returns the size `N`.

```
template <class C>
constexpr auto size(const C& c) -> decltype(c.size())
{
  return c.size();
}

template <class T, std::size_t N>
constexpr std::size_t size(const T (&array)[N]) noexcept
{
  return N;
}
```

- `std::empty()` has several overloads; for a class `C` it returns `c.empty()`, for arrays it returns `false`, and for `std::initializer_list<T>` it returns `il.size() == 0`.

```
template <class C>
constexpr auto empty(const C& c) -> decltype(c.empty())
{
  return c.empty();
}

template <class T, std::size_t N>
constexpr bool empty(const T (&array)[N]) noexcept
{
  return false;
}
```

```
template <class E>
constexpr bool empty(std::initializer_list<E> il) noexcept
{
  return il.size() == 0;
}
```

# There's more...

These non-member functions are mainly intended for template code where the container is not known and can be a standard container, a C-like array, or a custom type. Using the non-member version of these functions enables us to write simpler and less code that works with all these types of containers.

However, the use of these functions is not and should not be limited to generic code. Though it is rather a matter of personal preference, it can be a good habit to be consistent and use them everywhere in your code. All these methods have lightweight implementations that will most likely be inlined by the compiler, which means that there will be no overhead at all over using the corresponding member functions.

# See also

- *Writing your own random access iterator*

# 12
## Math Problems

## Problems

Here are the problem-solving sections for this chapter.

## 1. Sum of naturals divisible by 3 and 5

Write a program that calculates and prints the sum of all the natural numbers divisible by either 3 or 5, up to a given limit entered by the user.

## 2. Greatest common divisor

Write a program that, given two positive integers, will calculate and print the greatest common divisor of the two.

## 3. Least common multiple

Write a program that will, given two or more positive integers, calculate and print the least common multiple of them all.

# 4. Largest prime smaller than given number

Write a program that computes and prints the largest prime number that is smaller than a number provided by the user, which must be a positive integer.

# 5. Sexy prime pairs

Write a program that prints all the sexy prime pairs up to a limit entered by the user.

# 6. Abundant numbers

Write a program that prints all abundant numbers and their abundance, up to a number entered by the user.

# 7. Amicable numbers

Write a program that prints the list of all pairs of amicable numbers smaller than 1,000,000.

# 8. Armstrong numbers

Write a program that prints all Armstrong numbers with three digits.

# 9. Prime factors of a number

Write a program that prints the prime factors of a number entered by the user.

# 10. Gray code

Write a program that displays the normal binary representations, Gray code representations, and decoded Gray code values for all 5-bit numbers.

# 11. Converting numerical values to Roman

Write a program that, given a number entered by the user, prints its Roman numeral equivalent.

# 12. Largest Collatz sequence

Write a program that determines and prints which number up to 1 million produces the longest Collatz sequence and what its length is.

# 13. Computing the value of Pi

Write a program that computes the value of Pi with a precision of two decimal digits.

# 14. Validating ISBNs

Write a program that validates that 10-digit values entered by the user, as a string, represent valid ISBN-10 numbers.

# Solutions

Here are the solutions for the above problem-solving sections.

# 1. Sum of naturals divisible by 3 and 5

The solution to this problem is to iterate through all numbers from 3 (1 and 2 are not divisible by 3 so it does not make sense to test them) up to the limit entered by the user. Use the modulo operation to check that the rest of the division of a number by 3 and 5 is 0. However, the trick to being able to sum up to a larger limit is to use `long long` and not `int` or `long` for the sum, which would result in an overflow before summing up to 100,000:

```
int main()
{
    unsigned int limit = 0;
    std::cout << "Upper limit:";
    std::cin >> limit;

    unsigned long long sum = 0;
    for (unsigned int i = 3; i < limit; ++i)
    {
        if (i % 3 == 0 || i % 5 == 0)
            sum += i;
    }

    std::cout << "sum=" << sum << std::endl;
}
```

# 2. Greatest common divisor

The greatest common divisor (*gcd* in short) of two or more non-zero integers, also known as the greatest common factor (*gcf*), highest common factor (*hcf*), greatest common measure (*gcm*), or highest common divisor, is the greatest positive integer that divides all of them. There are several ways the gcd could be computed; an efficient method is Euclid's algorithm. For two integers, the algorithm is:

```
gcd(a,0) = a
gcd(a,b) = gcd(b, a mod b)
```

This can be very simply implemented in C++ using a recursive function:

```
unsigned int gcd(unsigned int const a, unsigned int const b)
{
    return b == 0 ? a : gcd(b, a % b);
}
```

A non-recursive implementation of Euclid's algorithm should look like this:

```
unsigned int gcd(unsigned int a, unsigned int b)
{
    while (b != 0) {
        unsigned int r = a % b;
        a = b;
        b = r;
    }
    return a;
}
```

In C++17 there is a `constexpr` function called `gcd()` in the header `<numeric>` that computes the greatest common divisor of two numbers.

# 3. Least common multiple

The **least common multiple** (**lcm**) of two or more non-zero integers, also known as the lowest common multiple, or smallest common multiple, is the smallest positive integer that is divisible by all of them. A possible way to compute the least common multiple is by reducing the problem to computing the greatest common divisor. The following formula is used in this case:

```
lcm(a, b) = abs(a, b) / gcd(a, b)
```

A function to compute the least common multiple may look like this:

```
int lcm(int const a, int const b)
{
    int h = gcd(a, b);
    return h ? (a * (b / h)) : 0;
}
```

To compute the *lcm* for more than two integers, you could use the `std::accumulate` algorithm from the header `<numeric>`:

```cpp
template<class InputIt>
int lcmr(InputIt first, InputIt last)
{
    return std::accumulate(first, last, 1, lcm);
}
```

In C++17 there is a `constexpr` function called `lcm()` in the header `<numeric>` that computes the least common multiple of two numbers.

# 4. Largest prime smaller than given number

A prime number is a number that has only two divisors, 1 and the number itself. To find the largest prime smaller than a given number you should first write a function that determines if a number is prime and then call this function, starting from the given number, towards 1 until the first prime is encountered. There are various algorithms for determining if a number is prime. Common implementations for determining the primality appear as follows:

```cpp
bool is_prime(int const num)
{
    if (num <= 3) { return num > 1; }
    else if (num % 2 == 0 || num % 3 == 0)
    {
        return false;
    }
    else
    {
        for (int i = 5; i * i <= num; i += 6)
        {
            if (num % i == 0 || num % (i + 2) == 0)
            {
                return false;
            }
        }
        return true;
    }
}
```

This function can be used as follows:

```
int main()
{
    int limit = 0;
    std::cout << "Upper limit:";
    std::cin >> limit;

    for (int i = limit; i > 1; i--)
    {
        if (is_prime(i))
        {
            std::cout << "Largest prime:" << i << std::endl;
            return 0;
        }
    }
}
```

# 5. Sexy prime pairs

Sexy prime numbers are prime numbers that differ from each other by six (for example 5 and 11, or 13 and 19). There are also *twin primes*, which differ by two, and *cousin primes*, which differ by four.

In the previous challenge, we implemented a function that determines whether an integer is a prime number. We will reuse that function for this exercise. What you have to do is check that if a number n is prime, the number n+6 is also prime, and in this case print the pair to the console:

```
int main()
{
    int limit = 0;
    std::cout << "Upper limit:";
    std::cin >> limit;

    for (int n = 2; n <= limit; n++)
    {
        if (is_prime(n) && is_prime(n+6))
        {
            std::cout << n << "," << n+6 << std::endl;
        }
    }
}
```

You could take it as a further exercise to compute and displays the sexy prime triples, quadruplets, and quintuplets.

# 6. Abundant numbers

An abundant number, also known as an excessive number, is a number for which the sum of its proper divisors is greater than the number itself. The proper divisors of a number are the positive prime factors of the number, other than the number itself. The amount by which the sum of proper divisors exceeds the number itself is called abundance. For instance, the number 12 has the proper divisors 1, 2, 3, 4, and 6. Their sum is 16, which makes 12 an abundant number. Its abundance is 4 (that is, 16 - 12).

To determine the sum of proper divisors, we try all numbers from 2 to the square root of the number (all prime factors are less than or equal to this value). If the current number, let's call it i, divides the number, then i and num/i are both divisors. However, if they are equal (for example, if i = 3, and n = 9, then i divides 9, but n/i = 3), we add only i because proper divisors must only be added once. Otherwise, we add both i and num/i and continue:

```cpp
int sum_proper_divisors(int const number)
{
    int result = 1;
    for (int i = 2; i <= std::sqrt(number); i++)
    {
        if (number%i == 0)
        {
            result += (i == (number / i)) ? i : (i + number / i);
        }
    }
    return result;
}
```

Printing abundant numbers is as simple as iterating up to the specified limit, computing the sum of proper divisors and comparing it to the number:

```
void print_abundant(int const limit)
{
    for (int number = 10; number <= limit; ++number)
    {
        auto sum = sum_proper_divisors(number);
        if (sum > number)
        {
            std::cout << number << ", abundance="
                      << sum - number << std::endl;
        }
    }
}

int main()
{
    int limit = 0;
    std::cout << "Upper limit:";
    std::cin >> limit;

    print_abundant(limit);
}
```

# 7. Amicable numbers

Two numbers are said to be amicable if the sum of the proper divisors of one number is equal to that of the other number. The proper divisors of a number are the positive prime factors of the number other than the number itself. Amicable numbers should not be confused with *friendly numbers*. For instance, the number 220 has the proper divisors 1, 2, 4, 5, 10, 11, 20, 22, 44, 55, and 110, whose sum is 284. The proper divisors of 284 are 1, 2, 4, 71, and 142; their sum is 220. Therefore, the numbers 220 and 284 are said to be amicable.

The solution to this problem is to iterate through all the numbers up to the given limit. For each number, compute the sum of its proper divisors. Let's call this `sum1`. Repeat the process and compute the sum of the proper divisors of `sum1`. If the result is equal to the original number, then the number and `sum1` are amicable numbers:

```cpp
void print_amicables(int const limit)
{
    for (int number = 4; number < limit; ++number)
    {
        auto sum1 = sum_proper_divisors(number);
        if (sum1 < limit)
        {
            auto sum2 = sum_proper_divisors(sum1);
            if (sum2 == number && number != sum1)
            {
                std::cout << number << "," << sum1 << std::endl;
            }
        }
    }
}
```

In the above sample, `sum_proper_divisors()` is the function seen in the solution to the abundant numbers problem.

The above function prints pairs of numbers twice, such as 220,284 and 284,220. Modify this implementation to only print each pair a single time.

# 8. Armstrong numbers

An Armstrong number (named so after Michael F. Armstrong), also called a narcissistic number, a pluperfect digital invariant, or a plus perfect number, is a number that is equal to the sum of its own digits when they are raised to the power of the number of digits. As an example, the smallest Armstrong number is 153, which is equal to $1^3 + 5^3 + 3^3$.

To determine if a number with three digits is a narcissistic number, you must first determine its digits in order to sum their powers. However, this involves division and modulo operations, which are expensive. A much faster way to compute it is to rely on the fact that a number is a sum of digits multiplied by 10 at the power of their zero-based position. In other words, for numbers up to 1,000, we have $a*10^2 + b*10^2 + c$. Since you are only supposed to determine numbers with three digits, that means a would start from 1. This would be faster than other approaches because multiplications are faster to compute than divisions and modulo operations. An implementation of such a function would look like this:

```
void print_narcissistics()
{
    for (int a = 1; a <= 9; a++)
    {
        for (int b = 0; b <= 9; b++)
        {
            for (int c = 0; c <= 9; c++)
            {
                auto abc = a * 100 + b * 10 + c;
                auto arm = a * a * a + b * b * b + c * c * c;
                if (abc == arm)
                {
                    std::cout << arm << std::endl;
                }
            }
        }
    }
}
```

You could take it as a further exercise to write a function that determines the narcissistic numbers up to a limit, regardless their number of digits. Such a function would be slower because you first have to determine the sequence of digits of the number, store them in a container, and then sum together the digits raised to the appropriate power (the number of the digits).

# 9. Prime factors of a number

The prime factors of a positive integer are the prime numbers that divide that integer exactly. For instance, the prime factors of 8 are 2 x 2 x 2, and the prime factors of 42 are 2 x 3 x 7. To determine the prime factors you should use the following algorithm:

1. While n is divisible by 2, 2 is a prime factor and must be added to the list, while n becomes the result of n/2. After completing this step, n is an odd number.

2. Iterate from 3 to the square root of n. While the current number, let's call it i, divides n, i is a prime factor and must be added to the list, while n becomes the result of n/i. When i no longer divides n, increment i by 2 (to get the next odd number).

3. When n is a prime number greater than 2, the steps above will not result in n becoming 1. Therefore, if at the end of step 2 n is still greater than 2, then n is a prime factor.

```cpp
std::vector<unsigned long long> prime_factors(unsigned long long n)
{
    std::vector<unsigned long long> factors;
    while (n % 2 == 0) {
        factors.push_back(2);
        n = n / 2;
    }
    for (unsigned long long i = 3; i <= std::sqrt(n); i += 2)
    {
        while (n%i == 0) {
            factors.push_back(i);
            n = n / i;
        }
    }

    if (n > 2)
        factors.push_back(n);
    return factors;
}

int main()
{
    unsigned long long number = 0;
    std::cout << "number:";
    std::cin >> number;
```

```
    auto factors = prime_factors(number);
    std::copy(std::begin(factors), std::end(factors),
        std::ostream_iterator<unsigned long long>(std::cout, " "));
}
```

As a further exercise, determine the largest prime factor for the number 600,851,475,143.

# 10. Gray code

Gray code, also known as reflected binary code or simply reflected binary, is a form of binary encoding where two consecutive numbers differ by only one bit. To perform a binary reflected Gray code encoding, we need to use the following formula:

```
if b[i-1] = 1 then g[i] = not b[i]
else g[i] = b[i]
```

This is equivalent to the following:

```
g = b xor (b logically right shifted 1 time)
```

For decoding a binary reflected Gray code, the following formula should be used:

```
b[0] = g[0]
b[i] = g[i] xor b[i-1]
```

These can be written in C++ as follows, for 32-bit unsigned integers:

```
unsigned int gray_encode(unsigned int const num)
{
    return num ^ (num >> 1);
}

unsigned int gray_decode(unsigned int gray)
{
    for (unsigned int bit = 1U << 31; bit > 1; bit >>= 1)
    {
        if (gray & bit) gray ^= bit >> 1;
    }
    return gray;
}
```

To print the all 5-bit integers, their binary representation, the encoded Gray code representation, and the decoded value, we could use the following code:

```
std::string to_binary(unsigned int value, int const digits)
{
    return std::bitset<32>(value).to_string().substr(32-digits, digits);
}

int main()
{
    std::cout << "Number\tBinary\tGray\tDecoded\n";
    std::cout << "------\t------\t----\t-------\n";

    for (unsigned int n = 0; n < 32; ++n)
    {
        auto encg = gray_encode(n);
        auto decg = gray_decode(encg);

        std::cout
            << n << "\t" << to_binary(n, 5) << "\t"
            << to_binary(encg, 5) << "\t" << decg << "\n";
    }
}
```

# 11. Converting numerical values to Roman

Roman numerals, as they are known today, use seven symbols: I = 1, V = 5, X = 10, L = 50, C = 100, D = 500, and M = 1000. The system uses additions and subtractions in composing the numerical symbols. The symbols from 1 to 10 are I, II, III, IV, V, VI, VII, VIII, IX, and X. Romans did not have a symbol for zero and used to write *nulla* to represent it. In this system, the largest symbols are on the left, and the least significant are on the right. As an example, the Roman numeral for 1994 is MCMXCIV. If you are not familiar with the rules for Roman numerals, you should read more on the web.

To determine the Roman numeral of a number, use the following algorithm:

1. Check every Roman base symbol from the highest (M) to the lowest (I)
2. If the current value is greater than the value of the symbol, then concatenate the symbol to the Roman numeral and subtract its value from the current one
3. Repeat until the current value reaches zero

For example, consider 42: the first Roman base symbol smaller than 42 is XL, which is 40. We concatenate it to the numeral, resulting in XL, and subtract from the current number, resulting in 2. The first Roman base symbol smaller than 2 is I, which is 1. We add that to the numeral, resulting in XLI, and subtract 1 from the number, resulting in 1. We add one more I to the numeral, which becomes XLII, and subtract again 1 from the number, reaching 0 and therefore stopping:

```cpp
std::string to_roman(unsigned int value)
{
    std::vector<std::pair<unsigned int, char const*>> roman {
        { 1000, "M" },{ 900, "CM" }, { 500, "D" },{ 400, "CD" },
        { 100, "C" },{ 90, "XC" }, { 50, "L" },{ 40, "XL" },
        { 10, "X" },{ 9, "IX" }, { 5, "V" },{ 4, "IV" }, { 1, "I" }};

    std::string result;
    for (auto const & kvp : roman) {
        while (value >= kvp.first) {
            result += kvp.second;
            value -= kvp.first;
        }
    }
    return result;
}
```

This function can be used as follows:

```cpp
int main()
{
    for(int i = 1; i <= 100; ++i)
    {
        std::cout << i << "\t" << to_roman(i) << std::endl;
    }

    int number = 0;
    std::cout << "number:";
    std::cin >> number;
    std::cout << to_roman(number) << std::endl;
}
```

# 12. Largest Collatz sequence

The Collatz conjecture, also known as the Ulam conjecture, Kakutani's problem, the Thwaites conjecture, Hasse's algorithm, or the Syracuse problem, is an unproven conjecture that states that a sequence defined as explained in the following always reaches 1. The series is defined as follows: start with any positive integer n and obtain each new term from the previous one: if the previous term is even, the next term is half the previous term, or else it is 3 times the previous term plus 1.

The problem you are to solve is to generate the Collatz sequence for all positive integers up to one million, determine which of them is the longest, and print its length and the starting number that produced it. Although we could apply brute force to generate the sequence for each number and count the number of terms until reaching 1, a faster solution would be to save the length of all the sequences that have already been generated. When the current term of a sequence that started from a value n becomes smaller than n, then it is a number whose sequence has already been determined, so we could simply fetch its cached length and add it to the current length to determine the length of the sequence started from n. This approach, however, introduces a limit to the Collatz sequences that could be computed, because at some point the cache will exceed the amount of memory the system can allocate:

```cpp
std::pair<unsigned long long, long> longest_collatz(
    unsigned long long const limit)
{
    long length = 0;
    unsigned long long number = 0;
    std::vector<int> cache(limit + 1, 0);
    for (unsigned long long i = 2; i <= limit; i++)
    {
        auto n = i;
        long steps = 0;
        while (n != 1 && n >= i)
        {
            if ((n % 2) == 0) n = n / 2;
            else n = n * 3 + 1;
            steps++;
        }
        cache[i] = steps + cache[n];

        if (cache[i] > length)
        {
            length = cache[i];
            number = i;
```

```
        }
    }

    return std::make_pair(number, length);
}
```

# 13. Computing the value of Pi

A suitable solution for approximately determining the value of Pi is using a Monte Carlo simulation. This is a method that uses random samples of inputs to explore the behavior of complex processes or systems. The method is used in a large variety of applications and domains, including physics, engineering, computing, finance, business, and others.

To do this we will rely on the following idea: the area of a circle with diameter d is PI * d^2 / 4. The area of a square that has the length of its sides equal to d is d^2. If we divide the two we get PI/4. If we put the circle inside the square and generate random numbers uniformly distributed within the square, then the count of numbers in the circle should be directly proportional to the circle area, and the count of numbers inside the square should be directly proportional to the square's area. That means that dividing the total number of hits in the square and circle should give PI/4. The more points generated, the more accurate the result shall be.

For generating pseudo-random numbers we will use a Mersenne twister and a uniform statistical distribution:

```
template <typename E = std::mt19937,
          typename D = std::uniform_real_distribution<>>
double compute_pi(E& engine, D& dist, int const samples = 1000000)
{
    auto hit = 0;
    for (auto i = 0; i < samples; i++)
    {
        auto x = dist(engine);
        auto y = dist(engine);
        if (y <= std::sqrt(1 - std::pow(x, 2))) hit += 1;
    }
    return 4.0 * hit / samples;
}

int main()
{
    std::random_device rd;
    auto seed_data = std::array<int, std::mt19937::state_size> {};
    std::generate(std::begin(seed_data), std::end(seed_data),
```

```
                            std::ref(rd));
        std::seed_seq seq(std::begin(seed_data), std::end(seed_data));
        auto eng = std::mt19937{ seq };
        auto dist = std::uniform_real_distribution<>{ 0, 1 };

        for (auto j = 0; j < 10; j++)
            std::cout << compute_pi(eng, dist) << std::endl;
    }
```

# 14. Validating ISBNs

The **International Standard Book Number** (**ISBN**) is a unique numeric identifier for books. Currently, a 13-digit format is used. However, for this problem, you are to validate the former format that used 10 digits. The last of the 10 digits is a checksum. This digit is chosen so that the sum of all the ten digits, each multiplied by its (integer) weight, descending from 10 to 1, is a multiple of 11.

The `validate_isbn_10` function, shown as follows, takes an ISBN as a string, and returns `true` if the length of the string is 10, all ten elements are digits, and the sum of all digits multiplied by their weight (or position) is a multiple of 11:

```cpp
bool validate_isbn_10(std::string_view isbn)
{
    auto valid = false;
    if (isbn.size() == 10 &&
        std::count_if(std::begin(isbn), std::end(isbn), isdigit) == 10)
    {
        auto w = 10;
        auto sum = std::accumulate(
            std::begin(isbn), std::end(isbn), 0,
            [&w](int const total, char const c) {
                return total + w-- * (c - '0'); });

        valid = !(sum % 11);
    }
    return valid;
}
```

 You can take it as a further exercise to improve this function to also correctly validate ISBN-10 numbers that include hyphens, such as `3-16-148410-0`. Also, you can write a function that validates ISBN-13 numbers.

# 13
# Language Features

## Problems

Here are the problem-solving sections for this chapter.

## 15. IPv4 data type

Write a class that represents an IPv4 address. Implement the functions required to be able to read and write such addresses from or to the console. The user should be able to input values in dotted form, such as `127.0.0.1` or `168.192.0.100`. This is also the form in which IPv4 addresses should be formatted to an output stream.

## 16. Enumerating IPv4 addresses in a range

Write a program that allows the user to input two IPv4 addresses representing a range and list all the addresses in that range. Extend the structure defined for the previous problem to implement the requested functionality.

## 17. Creating a 2D array with basic operations

Write a class template that represents a two-dimensional array container with methods for element access (`at()` and `data()`), capacity querying, iterators, filling, and swapping. It should be possible to move objects of this type.

# 18. Minimum function with any number of arguments

Write a function template that can take any number of arguments and returns the minimum value of them all, using `operator` < for comparison. Write a variant of this function template that can be parameterized with a binary comparison function to use instead of `operator` <.

# 19. Adding a range of values to a container

Write a general-purpose function that can add any number of elements to the end of a container that has a method `push_back(T&& value)`.

# 20. Container any, all, none

Write a set of general-purpose functions that enable checking whether any, all, or none of the specified arguments are present in a given container. These functions should make it possible to write code as follows:

```cpp
std::vector<int> v{ 1, 2, 3, 4, 5, 6 };
assert(contains_any(v, 0, 3, 30));

std::array<int, 6> a{ { 1, 2, 3, 4, 5, 6 } };
assert(contains_all(a, 1, 3, 5, 6));

std::list<int> l{ 1, 2, 3, 4, 5, 6 };
assert(!contains_none(l, 0, 6));
```

# 21. System handle wrapper

Consider an operating system handle, such as a file handle. Write a wrapper that handles the acquisition and release of the handle, as well as other operations such as verifying the validity of the handle and moving handle ownership from one object to another.

# 22. Literals of various temperature scales

Write a small library that enables expressing temperatures in the three most used scales, Celsius, Fahrenheit, and Kelvin, and converting between them. The library must enable you to write temperature literals in all these scales, such as `36.5_deg` for Celsius, `97.7_f` for Fahrenheit, and `309.65_K` for Kelvin; perform operations with these values; and convert between them.

# Solutions

Here are the solutions for the above problem-solving sections.

# 15. IPv4 data type

The problem requires writing a class to represent an IPv4 address. This is a 32-bit value, usually represented in decimal dotted format, such as `168.192.0.100`; each part of it is an 8-bit value, ranging from 0 to 255. For easy representation and handling, we can use four `unsigned char` to store the address value. Such a value could be constructed either from four `unsigned char` or from an `unsigned long`. In order to be able to read a value directly from the console (or any other input stream) and be able to write the value to the console (or any other output stream), we have to overload `operator>>` and `operator<<`. The following listing shows a minimal implementation that can meet the requested functionality:

```
class ipv4
{
   std::array<unsigned char, 4> data;
public:
   constexpr ipv4() : data{ {0} } {}
   constexpr ipv4(unsigned char const a, unsigned char const b,
                  unsigned char const c, unsigned char const d):
      data{{a,b,c,d}} {}
   explicit constexpr ipv4(unsigned long a) :
      data{ { static_cast<unsigned char>((a >> 24) & 0xFF),
              static_cast<unsigned char>((a >> 16) & 0xFF),
              static_cast<unsigned char>((a >> 8) & 0xFF),
              static_cast<unsigned char>(a & 0xFF) } } {}
   ipv4(ipv4 const & other) noexcept : data(other.data) {}
   ipv4& operator=(ipv4 const & other) noexcept
   {
      data = other.data;
      return *this;
```

```
    }

    std::string to_string() const
    {
        std::stringstream sstr;
        sstr << *this;
        return sstr.str();
    }

    constexpr unsigned long to_ulong() const noexcept
    {
        return (static_cast<unsigned long>(data[0]) << 24) |
               (static_cast<unsigned long>(data[1]) << 16) |
               (static_cast<unsigned long>(data[2]) << 8) |
                static_cast<unsigned long>(data[3]);
    }

    friend std::ostream& operator<<(std::ostream& os, const ipv4& a)
    {
       os << static_cast<int>(a.data[0]) << '.'
          << static_cast<int>(a.data[1]) << '.'
          << static_cast<int>(a.data[2]) << '.'
          << static_cast<int>(a.data[3]);
       return os;
    }

    friend std::istream& operator>>(std::istream& is, ipv4& a)
    {
        char d1, d2, d3;
        int b1, b2, b3, b4;
        is >> b1 >> d1 >> b2 >> d2 >> b3 >> d3 >> b4;
        if (d1 == '.' && d2 == '.' && d3 == '.')
            a = ipv4(b1, b2, b3, b4);
        else
            is.setstate(std::ios_base::failbit);
        return is;
    }
};
```

The `ipv4` class can be used as follows:

```
int main()
{
    ipv4 address(168, 192, 0, 1);
    std::cout << address << std::endl;

    ipv4 ip;
    std::cout << ip << std::endl;
```

```
    std::cin >> ip;
    if(!std::cin.fail())
        std::cout << ip << std::endl;
}
```

# 16. Enumerating IPv4 addresses in a range

To be able to enumerate IPv4 addresses in a given range, it should first be possible to compare IPv4 values. Therefore, we should implement at least operator<, but the following listing contains implementation for all comparison operators: ==, !=, <, >, <=, and >=. Also, in order to increment an IPv4 value, implementations for both the prefix and postfix operator++ are provided. The following code is an extension of the IPv4 class from the previous problem:

```
ipv4& operator++()
{
    *this = ipv4(1 + to_ulong());
    return *this;
}

ipv4& operator++(int)
{
    ipv4 result(*this);
    ++(*this);
    return *this;
}

friend bool operator==(ipv4 const & a1, ipv4 const & a2) noexcept
{
    return a1.data == a2.data;
}

friend bool operator!=(ipv4 const & a1, ipv4 const & a2) noexcept
{
    return !(a1 == a2);
}

friend bool operator<(ipv4 const & a1, ipv4 const & a2) noexcept
{
    return a1.to_ulong() < a2.to_ulong();
}

friend bool operator>(ipv4 const & a1, ipv4 const & a2) noexcept
{
    return a2 < a1;
```

```
    }

    friend bool operator<=(ipv4 const & a1, ipv4 const & a2) noexcept
    {
        return !(a1 > a2);
    }

    friend bool operator>=(ipv4 const & a1, ipv4 const & a2) noexcept
    {
        return !(a1 < a2);
    }
```

With these changes to the `ipv4` class from the previous problem, we can write the following program:

```cpp
int main()
{
    std::cout << "input range: ";
    ipv4 a1, a2;
    std::cin >> a1 >> a2;
    if (a2 > a1)
    {
        for (ipv4 a = a1; a <= a2; a++)
        {
            std::cout << a << std::endl;
        }
    }
    else
    {
        std::cerr << "invalid range!" << std::endl;
    }
}
```

# 17. Creating a 2D array with basic operations

Before looking at how we could define such a structure, let's consider several test cases for it. The following snippet shows all the functionality that was requested:

```cpp
int main()
{
    // element access
    array2d<int, 2, 3> a {1, 2, 3, 4, 5, 6};
    for (size_t i = 0; i < a.size(1); ++i)
        for (size_t j = 0; j < a.size(2); ++j)
            a(i, j) *= 2;
```

```
// iterating
std::copy(std::begin(a), std::end(a),
    std::ostream_iterator<int>(std::cout, " "));

// filling
array2d<int, 2, 3> b;
b.fill(1);

// swapping
a.swap(b);

// moving
array2d<int, 2, 3> c(std::move(b));
}
```

Note that for element access, we are using `operator()`, such as in `a(i,j)`, and not
`operator[]`, such as in `a[i][j]`, because only the former can take multiple arguments
(one for the index on each dimension). The latter can only have a single argument, and in
order to enable expressions like `a[i][j]`, it has to return an intermediate type (one that
basically represents a row) that in turn overloads `operator[]` to return a single element.

There are already standard containers that store either fixed or variable-length sequences of
elements. This two-dimensional array class should be just an adapter for such a container.
In choosing between `std::array` and `std::vector`, we should consider two things:

- The `array2d` class should have move semantics to be able to move objects
- It should be possible to list initialize an object of this type

The `std::array` container is movable only if the elements it holds are move-constructible
and move-assignable. On the other hand, it cannot be constructed from an
`std::initializer_list`. Therefore, the more viable option remains an `std::vector`.

Internally, this adapter container can store its data either in a vector of vectors (each row is
a `vector<T>` with C elements, and the 2D array has R such elements stored in a
`vector<vector<T>>`) or single vector of R×C elements of type T. In the latter case, the
element on row i and column j is found at index `i * C + j`. This approach has a smaller
memory footprint, stores all data in a single contiguous chunk, and is also simpler to
implement. For these reasons, it is the preferred solution.

A possible implementation of the two-dimensional array class with the requested
functionality is shown here:

```
template <class T, size_t R, size_t C>
class array2d
{
```

```
        typedef T                value_type;
        typedef value_type*      iterator;
        typedef value_type const* const_iterator;
        std::vector<T>           arr;
public:
        array2d() : arr(R*C) {}
        explicit array2d(std::initializer_list<T> l):arr(l) {}
        constexpr T* data() noexcept { return arr.data(); }
        constexpr T const * data() const noexcept { return arr.data(); }

        constexpr T& at(size_t const r, size_t const c)
        {
            return arr.at(r*C + c);
        }

        constexpr T const & at(size_t const r, size_t const c) const
        {
            return arr.at(r*C + c);
        }

        constexpr T& operator() (size_t const r, size_t const c)
        {
            return arr[r*C + c];
        }

        constexpr T const & operator() (size_t const r, size_t const c) const
        {
            return arr[r*C + c];
        }

        constexpr bool empty() const noexcept { return R == 0 || C == 0; }

        constexpr size_t size(int const rank) const
        {
            if (rank == 1) return R;
            else if (rank == 2) return C;
            throw std::out_of_range("Rank is out of range!");
        }

        void fill(T const & value)
        {
            std::fill(std::begin(arr), std::end(arr), value);
        }

        void swap(array2d & other) noexcept { arr.swap(other.arr); }

        const_iterator begin() const { return arr.data(); }
        const_iterator end() const   { return arr.data() + arr.size(); }
```

```
    iterator      begin()      { return arr.data(); }
    iterator      end()        { return arr.data() + arr.size(); }
};
```

# 18. Minimum function with any number of arguments

It is possible to write function templates that can take a variable number of arguments using variadic function templates. For this, we need to implement compile-time recursion (which is actually just calls through a set of overloaded functions). The following snippet shows how the requested function could be implemented:

```
template <typename T>
T minimum(T const a, T const b) { return a < b ? a : b; }

template <typename T1, typename... T>
T1 minimum(T1 a, T... args)
{
    return minimum(a, minimum(args...));
}

int main()
{
    auto x = minimum(5, 4, 2, 3);
}
```

In order to be able to use a user-provided binary comparison function, we need to write another function template. The comparison function must be the first argument because it cannot follow the function parameter pack. On the other hand, this cannot be an overload of the previous minimum function, but a function with a different name. The reason is that the compiler would not be able to differentiate between the template parameter lists `<typename T1, typename... T>` and `<class Compare, typename T1, typename... T>`. The changes are minimal and should be easy to follow in this snippet:

```
template <class Compare, typename T>
T minimumc(Compare comp, T const a, T const b)
{ return comp(a, b) ? a : b; }

template <class Compare, typename T1, typename... T>
T1 minimumc(Compare comp, T1 a, T... args)
{
    return minimumc(comp, a, minimumc(comp, args...));
}
```

```
int main()
{
    auto y = minimumc(std::less<>(), 3, 2, 1, 0);
}
```

# 19. Adding a range of values to a container

Writing functions with any number of arguments is possible using variadic function templates. The function should have the container as the first parameter, followed by a variable number of arguments representing the values to be added at the back of the container. However, writing such a function template can be significantly simplified using fold expressions. Such an implementation is shown here:

```
template<typename C, typename... Args>
void push_back(C& c, Args&&... args)
{
    (c.push_back(args), ...);
}
```

Examples of using this function template, with various container types, can be seen in the following listing:

```
int main()
{
    std::vector<int> v;
    push_back(v, 1, 2, 3, 4);
    std::copy(std::begin(v), std::end(v),
              std::ostream_iterator<int>(std::cout, " "));

    std::list<int> l;
    push_back(l, 1, 2, 3, 4);
    std::copy(std::begin(l), std::end(l),
              std::ostream_iterator<int>(std::cout, " "));
}
```

# 20. Container any, all, none

The requirement to be able to check the presence or absence of a variable number of arguments suggests that we should write variadic function templates. However, these functions require a helper function, a general-purpose one that checks whether an element is found in a container or not and returns a `bool` to indicate success or failure. Since all these functions, which we could call `contains_all`, `contains_any`, and `contains_none`, do is apply logical operators on the results returned by the helper function, we would use fold expressions to simplify the code. Short circuit evaluation is enabled after the expansion of the fold expression, which means we are evaluating only the elements that lead to a definitive result. So if we are looking for the presence of all 1, 2, and 3, and 2 is missing, the function will return after looking up value 2 in the container without checking value 3:

```cpp
template<class C, class T>
bool contains(C const & c, T const & value)
{
    return std::end(c) != std::find(std::begin(c), std::end(c), value);
}

template<class C, class... T>
bool contains_any(C const & c, T &&... value)
{
    return (... || contains(c, value));
}

template<class C, class... T>
bool contains_all(C const & c, T &&... value)
{
    return (... && contains(c, value));
}

template<class C, class... T>
bool contains_none(C const & c, T &&... value)
{
    return !contains_any(c, std::forward<T>(value)...);
}
```

# 21. System handle wrapper

System handles are a form of reference to system resources. Because all operating systems were at least initially written in C, creating and releasing the handles is done through dedicated system functions. This increases the risk of leaking resources because of erroneous disposal, such as in the case of an exception. In the following snippet, specific to Windows, you can see a function where a file is opened, read from, and eventually closed. However, this has a couple of problems: in one case, the developer forgot to close the handle before leaving the function; in another case, a function that throws is called before the handle is properly closed, without the exception being caught. However, since the function throws, that cleanup code never executes:

```cpp
void bad_handle_example()
{
    bool condition1 = false;
    bool condition2 = true;
    HANDLE handle = CreateFile(L"sample.txt",
                               GENERIC_READ,
                               FILE_SHARE_READ,
                               nullptr,
                               OPEN_EXISTING,
                               FILE_ATTRIBUTE_NORMAL,
                               nullptr);

    if (handle == INVALID_HANDLE_VALUE)
        return;

    if (condition1)
    {
        CloseHandle(handle);
        return;
    }

    std::vector<char> buffer(1024);
    unsigned long bytesRead = 0;
    ReadFile(handle,
             buffer.data(),
             buffer.size(),
             &bytesRead,
             nullptr);

    if (condition2)
    {
        // oops, forgot to close handle
        return;
    }
```

```
    // throws exception; the next line will not execute
    function_that_throws();

    CloseHandle(handle);
}
```

A C++ wrapper class can ensure proper disposal of the handle when the wrapper object goes out of scope and is destroyed (whether that happens through a normal execution path or as the result of an exception). A proper implementation should account for different types of handles, with a range of values to indicate an invalid handle (such as 0/null or -1). The implementation shown next provides:

- Explicit acquisition and automatic release of the handle when the object is destroyed
- Move semantics to enable transfer of ownership of the handle
- Comparison operators to check whether two objects refer to the same handle
- Additional operations such as swapping and resetting

The implementation shown here is a modified version of the handle class implemented by Kenny Kerr and published in the article *Windows with C++ - C++ and the Windows API*, MSDN Magazine, July 2011, https://msdn.microsoft.com/en-us/magazine/hh288076.aspx. Although the handle traits shown here refer to Windows handles, it should be fairly simple to write traits appropriate for other platforms.

```
template <typename Traits>
class unique_handle
{
    using pointer = typename Traits::pointer;
    pointer m_value;
public:
    unique_handle(unique_handle const &) = delete;
    unique_handle& operator=(unique_handle const &) = delete;

    explicit unique_handle(pointer value = Traits::invalid()) noexcept
        :m_value{ value }
    {}

    unique_handle(unique_handle && other) noexcept
        : m_value{ other.release() }
    {}

    unique_handle& operator=(unique_handle && other) noexcept
    {
        if (this != &other)
```

```
            reset(other.release());
        return *this;
    }

    ~unique_handle() noexcept
    {
        Traits::close(m_value);
    }

    explicit operator bool() const noexcept
    {
        return m_value != Traits::invalid();
    }

    pointer get() const noexcept { return m_value; }

    pointer release() noexcept
    {
        auto value = m_value;
        m_value = Traits::invalid();
        return value;
    }

    bool reset(pointer value = Traits::invalid()) noexcept
    {
        if (m_value != value)
        {
            Traits::close(m_value);
            m_value = value;
        }
        return static_cast<bool>(*this);
    }

    void swap(unique_handle<Traits> & other) noexcept
    {
        std::swap(m_value, other.m_value);
    }
};

template <typename Traits>
void swap(unique_handle<Traits> & left, unique_handle<Traits> & right)
noexcept
{
    left.swap(right);
}

template <typename Traits>
bool operator==(unique_handle<Traits> const & left,
```

```
                        unique_handle<Traits> const & right) noexcept
{
    return left.get() == right.get();
}

template <typename Traits>
bool operator!=(unique_handle<Traits> const & left,
                unique_handle<Traits> const & right) noexcept
{
    return left.get() != right.get();
}

struct null_handle_traits
{
    using pointer = HANDLE;
    static pointer invalid() noexcept { return nullptr; }
    static void close(pointer value) noexcept
    {
        CloseHandle(value);
    }
};

struct invalid_handle_traits
{
    using pointer = HANDLE;
    static pointer invalid() noexcept { return INVALID_HANDLE_VALUE; }
    static void close(pointer value) noexcept
    {
        CloseHandle(value);
    }
};

using null_handle = unique_handle<null_handle_traits>;
using invalid_handle = unique_handle<invalid_handle_traits>;
```

With this handle type defined, we can rewrite the previous example in simpler terms, avoiding all those problems with handles not properly closed because of exceptions occurring that are not properly handled, or simply because developers forget to release resources when no longer needed. This code is both simpler and more robust:

```
void good_handle_example()
{
   bool condition1 = false;
   bool condition2 = true;

   invalid_handle handle{
      CreateFile(L"sample.txt",
               GENERIC_READ,
               FILE_SHARE_READ,
               nullptr,
               OPEN_EXISTING,
               FILE_ATTRIBUTE_NORMAL,
               nullptr) };

   if (!handle) return;

   if (condition1) return;

   std::vector<char> buffer(1024);
   unsigned long bytesRead = 0;
   ReadFile(handle.get(),
           buffer.data(),
           buffer.size(),
           &bytesRead,
           nullptr);

   if (condition2) return;

   function_that_throws();
}
```

# 22. Literals of various temperature scales

To meet this requirement, we need to provide an implementation for several types, operators, and functions:

- An enumeration of supported temperature scales called `scale`.
- A class template to represent a temperature value, parameterized with the scale, called `quantity`.

- Comparison operators ==, !=, <, >, <=, and >= that compare two quantities of the same time.
- Arithmetic operators + and – that add and subtract values of the same quantity type. Additionally, we could implement member operators += and –+.
- A function template to convert temperatures from one scale to another, called `temperature_cast`. This function does not perform the conversion itself but uses type traits to do that.
- Literal operators `""_deg`, `""_f`, and `""_k` for creating user-defined temperature literals.

 For brevity, the following snippet only contains the code that handles Celsius and Fahrenheit temperatures. You should take it as a further exercise to extend the code with support for the Kelvin scale. The code accompanying the book contains the full implementation of all three required scales.

The `are_equal()` function is a utility function used to compare floating-point values:

```
bool are_equal(double const d1, double const d2,
               double const epsilon = 0.001)
{
    return std::fabs(d1 - d2) < epsilon;
}
```

The enumeration of possible temperature scales and the class that represents a temperature value are defined as follows:

```
namespace temperature
{
    enum class scale { celsius, fahrenheit, kelvin };

    template <scale S>
    class quantity
    {
        const double amount;
    public:
        constexpr explicit quantity(double const a) : amount(a) {}
        explicit operator double() const { return amount; }
    };
}
```

The comparison operators for the `quantity<S>` class can be seen here:

```
namespace temperature
{
    template <scale S>
    inline bool operator==(quantity<S> const & lhs, quantity<S> const & rhs)
    {
        return are_equal(static_cast<double>(lhs), static_cast<double>(rhs));
    }

    template <scale S>
    inline bool operator!=(quantity<S> const & lhs, quantity<S> const & rhs)
    {
        return !(lhs == rhs);
    }

    template <scale S>
    inline bool operator< (quantity<S> const & lhs, quantity<S> const & rhs)
    {
        return static_cast<double>(lhs) < static_cast<double>(rhs);
    }

    template <scale S>
    inline bool operator> (quantity<S> const & lhs, quantity<S> const & rhs)
    {
        return rhs < lhs;
    }

    template <scale S>
    inline bool operator<=(quantity<S> const & lhs, quantity<S> const & rhs)
    {
        return !(lhs > rhs);
    }

    template <scale S>
    inline bool operator>=(quantity<S> const & lhs, quantity<S> const & rhs)
    {
        return !(lhs < rhs);
    }

    template <scale S>
    constexpr quantity<S> operator+(quantity<S> const &q1,
                                    quantity<S> const &q2)
    {
        return quantity<S>(static_cast<double>(q1) +
                           static_cast<double>(q2));
    }
```

```
    template <scale S>
    constexpr quantity<S> operator-(quantity<S> const &q1,
                                    quantity<S> const &q2)
    {
        return quantity<S>(static_cast<double>(q1) -
                           static_cast<double>(q2));
    }
}
```

To convert between temperature values of different scales, we will define a function template called `temperature_cast()` that utilizes several type traits to perform the actual conversion. All these are shown here, although not all type traits; the others can be found in the code accompanying the book:

```
namespace temperature
{
    template <scale S, scale R>
    struct conversion_traits
    {
        static double convert(double const value) = delete;
    };

    template <>
    struct conversion_traits<scale::celsius, scale::fahrenheit>
    {
        static double convert(double const value)
        {
            return (value * 9) / 5 + 32;
        }
    };

    template <>
    struct conversion_traits<scale::fahrenheit, scale::celsius>
    {
        static double convert(double const value)
        {
            return (value - 32) * 5 / 9;
        }
    };

    template <scale R, scale S>
    constexpr quantity<R> temperature_cast(quantity<S> const q)
    {
        return quantity<R>(conversion_traits<S, R>::convert(
            static_cast<double>(q)));
    }
}
```

The literal operators for creating temperature values are shown in the following snippet. These operators are defined in a separate namespace, called `temperature_scale_literals`, which is a good practice in order to minimize the risk of name collision with other literal operators:

```cpp
namespace temperature
{
    namespace temperature_scale_literals
    {
        constexpr quantity<scale::celsius> operator "" _deg(
            long double const amount)
        {
            return quantity<scale::celsius> {static_cast<double>(amount)};
        }

        constexpr quantity<scale::fahrenheit> operator "" _f(
            long double const amount)
        {
            return quantity<scale::fahrenheit> {static_cast<double>(amount)};
        }
    }
}
```

The following example shows how to define two temperature values, one in Celsius and one in Fahrenheit, and convert between the two:

```cpp
int main()
{
    using namespace temperature;
    using namespace temperature_scale_literals;

    auto t1{ 36.5_deg };
    auto t2{ 79.0_f };

    auto tf = temperature_cast<scale::fahrenheit>(t1);
    auto tc = temperature_cast<scale::celsius>(tf);
    assert(t1 == tc);
}
```

# Strings and Regular Expressions

## Problems

Here are the problem-solving sections for this chapter.

## 23. Binary to string conversion

Write a function that, given a range of 8-bit integers (such as an array or vector), returns a string that contains a hexadecimal representation of the input data. The function should be able to produce both uppercase and lowercase content. Here are some input and output examples:

Input: `{ 0xBA, 0xAD, 0xF0, 0x0D }`, output: `"BAADF00D"` or `"baadf00d"`
Input: `{ 1,2,3,4,5,6 }`, output: `"010203040506"`

## 24. String to binary conversion

Write a function that, given a string containing hexadecimal digits as the input argument, returns a vector of 8-bit integers that represent the numerical deserialization of the string content. The following are examples:

Input: `"BAADF00D"` or `"baadF00D"`, output: `{0xBA, 0xAD, 0xF0, 0x0D}`
Input `"010203040506"`, output: `{1, 2, 3, 4, 5, 6}`

## 25. Capitalizing an article title

Write a function that transforms an input text into a capitalized version, where every word starts with an uppercase letter and has all the other letters in lowercase. For instance, the text `"the c++ challenger"` should be transformed to `"The C++ Challenger"`.

## 26. Joining strings together separated by a delimiter

Write a function that, given a list of strings and a delimiter, creates a new string by concatenating all the input strings separated with the specified delimiter. The delimiter must not appear after the last string, and when no input string is provided, the function must return an empty string.

Example: input { `"this"`,`"is"`,`"an"`,`"example"` } and delimiter `' '` (space), output: `"this is an example"`.

## 27. Splitting a string into tokens with a list of possible delimiters

Write a function that, given a string and a list of possible delimiter characters, splits the string into tokens separated by any of the delimiters and returns them in an `std::vector`.

Example: input: `"this,is.a sample!!"` with delimiters `",.! "`, output: `{"this",` `"is"`, `"a"`, `"sample"}`.

## 28. Longest palindromic substring

Write a function that, given an input string, locates and returns the longest sequence in the string that is a palindrome. If multiple palindromes of the same length exist, the first one should be returned.

# 29. License plate validation

Considering license plates with the format LLL-LL DDD or LLL-LL DDDD (where L is an uppercase letter from *A* to *Z* and D is a digit), write:

- One function that validates that a license plate number is of the correct format
- One function that, given an input text, extracts and returns all the license plate numbers found in the text

# 30. Extracting URL parts

Write a function that, given a string that represents a URL, parses and extracts the parts of the URL (protocol, domain, port, path, query, and fragment).

# 31. Transforming dates in strings

Write a function that, given a text containing dates in the format dd.mm.yyyy or dd-mm-yyyy, transforms the text so that it contains dates in the format yyyy-mm-dd.

# Solutions

Here are the solutions for the above problem-solving sections.

# 23. Binary to string conversion

In order to write a general-purpose function that can handle various sorts of ranges, such as an std::array, std::vector, a C-like array, or others, we should write a function template. In the following, there are two overloads; one that takes a container as an argument and a flag indicating the casing style, and one that takes a pair of iterators (to mark the first and then one past the end element of the range) and the flag to indicate casing. The content of the range is written to an std::ostringstream object, with the appropriate I/O manipulators, such as width, filling character, or case flag:

```
template <typename Iter>
std::string bytes_to_hexstr(Iter begin, Iter end,
                            bool const uppercase = false)
{
    std::ostringstream oss;
```

```
    if(uppercase) oss.setf(std::ios_base::uppercase);
    for (; begin != end; ++begin)
      oss << std::hex << std::setw(2) << std::setfill('0')
          << static_cast<int>(*begin);
    return oss.str();
}

template <typename C>
std::string bytes_to_hexstr(C const & c, bool const uppercase = false)
{
    return bytes_to_hexstr(std::cbegin(c), std::cend(c), uppercase);
}
```

These functions can be used as follows:

```
int main()
{
    std::vector<unsigned char> v{ 0xBA, 0xAD, 0xF0, 0x0D };
    std::array<unsigned char, 6> a{ {1,2,3,4,5,6} };
    unsigned char buf[5] = {0x11, 0x22, 0x33, 0x44, 0x55};

    assert(bytes_to_hexstr(v, true) == "BAADF00D");
    assert(bytes_to_hexstr(a, true) == "010203040506");
    assert(bytes_to_hexstr(buf, true) == "1122334455");

    assert(bytes_to_hexstr(v) == "baadf00d");
    assert(bytes_to_hexstr(a) == "010203040506");
    assert(bytes_to_hexstr(buf) == "1122334455");
}
```

# 24. String to binary conversion

The operation requested here is the opposite of the one implemented in the previous problem. This time, however, we could write a function and not a function template. The input is an `std::string_view`, which is a lightweight wrapper for a sequence of characters. The output is a vector of 8-bit unsigned integers. The following `hexstr_to_bytes` function transforms every two text characters into an `unsigned char` value ("A0" becomes 0xA0), puts them into an `std::vector`, and returns the vector:

```
unsigned char hexchar_to_int(char const ch)
{
    if (ch >= '0' && ch <= '9') return ch - '0';
    if (ch >= 'A' && ch <= 'F') return ch - 'A' + 10;
    if (ch >= 'a' && ch <= 'f') return ch - 'a' + 10;
```

```
        throw std::invalid_argument("Invalid hexadecimal character");
}

std::vector<unsigned char> hexstr_to_bytes(std::string_view str)
{
    std::vector<unsigned char> result;
    for (size_t i = 0; i < str.size(); i += 2)
    {
        result.push_back(
            (hexchar_to_int(str[i]) << 4) | hexchar_to_int(str[i+1]));
    }
    return result;
}
```

 This function assumes the input string contains an even number of hexadecimal digits. In cases where the input string contains an odd number of hexadecimal digits, the last one is discarded (so that "BAD" becomes {0xBA}). As a further exercise, modify the preceding function so that, instead of discarding the last odd digit, it considers a leading zero so that "BAD" becomes {0x0B, 0xAD}. Also, as yet another exercise, you can write a version of the function that deserializes content that has the hexadecimal digits separated by a delimiter, such as space (for example "BA AD F0 0D").

The next code sample shows how this function can be used:

```
int main()
{
    std::vector<unsigned char> expected{ 0xBA, 0xAD, 0xF0, 0x0D, 0x42 };
    assert(hexstr_to_bytes("BAADF00D42") == expected);
    assert(hexstr_to_bytes("BaaDf00d42") == expected);
}
```

# 25. Capitalizing an article title

The function template `capitalize()`, implemented as follows, works with strings of any type of characters. It does not modify the input string but creates a new string. To do so, it uses an `std::stringstream`. It iterates through all the characters in the input string and sets a flag indicating a new word to `true` every time a space or punctuation is encountered. Input characters are transformed to uppercase when they represent the first character in a word and to lowercase otherwise:

```
template <class Elem>
using tstring = std::basic_string<Elem, std::char_traits<Elem>,
```

```
                                        std::allocator<Elem>>;
template <class Elem>
using tstringstream = std::basic_stringstream<
    Elem, std::char_traits<Elem>, std::allocator<Elem>>;

template <class Elem>
tstring<Elem> capitalize(tstring<Elem> const & text)
{
    tstringstream<Elem> result;
    bool newWord = true;
    for (auto const ch : text)
    {
        newWord = newWord || std::ispunct(ch) || std::isspace(ch);
        if (std::isalpha(ch))
        {
            if (newWord)
            {
                result << static_cast<Elem>(std::toupper(ch));
                newWord = false;
            }
            else
                result << static_cast<Elem>(std::tolower(ch));
        }
        else result << ch;
    }
    return result.str();
}
```

In the following program you can see how this function is used to capitalize texts:

```
int main()
{
    using namespace std::string_literals;
    assert("The C++ Challenger"s ==
            capitalize("the c++ challenger"s));
    assert("This Is An Example, Should Work!"s ==
            capitalize("THIS IS an ExamplE, should wORk!"s));
}
```

# 26. Joining strings together separated by a delimiter

Two overloads called `join_strings()` are listed in the following code. One takes a container of strings and a pointer to a sequence of characters representing a separator, while the other takes two random access iterators, representing the first and one past the last element of a range, and a separator. They both return a new string created by concatenating all the input strings, using an output string stream and the `std::copy` function. This general-purpose function copies all the elements in the specified range to an output range, represented by an output iterator. We are using here an `std::ostream_iterator` that uses `operator<<` to write the assigned value to the specified output stream each time the iterator is assigned a value:

```
template <typename Iter>
std::string join_strings(Iter begin, Iter end,
                         char const * const separator)
{
    std::ostringstream os;
    std::copy(begin, end-1,
            std::ostream_iterator<std::string>(os, separator));
    os << *(end-1);
    return os.str();
}

template <typename C>
std::string join_strings(C const & c, char const * const separator)
{
    if (c.size() == 0) return std::string{};
    return join_strings(std::begin(c), std::end(c), separator);
}

int main()
{
    using namespace std::string_literals;
    std::vector<std::string> v1{ "this","is","an","example" };
    std::vector<std::string> v2{ "example" };
    std::vector<std::string> v3{ };

    assert(join_strings(v1, " ") == "this is an example"s);
    assert(join_strings(v2, " ") == "example"s);
    assert(join_strings(v3, " ") == ""s);
}
```

As a further exercise, you should modify the overload that takes iterators as arguments so that it works with other types of iterators, such as bidirectional iterators, thereby enabling the use of this function with lists or other containers.

# 27. Splitting a string into tokens with a list of possible delimiters

Two different versions of a splitting function are listed as follows:

- The first one uses a single character as the delimiter. To split the input string it uses a string stream initialized with the content of the input string, using std::getline() to read chunks from it until the next delimiter or an end-of-line character is encountered.

- The second one uses a list of possible character delimiters, specified in an std::string. It uses std:string::find_first_of() to locate the first position of any of the delimiter characters, starting from a given position. It does so in a loop until the entire input string is being processed. The extracted substrings are added to the result vector:

```
template <class Elem>
using tstring = std::basic_string<Elem, std::char_traits<Elem>,
                                  std::allocator<Elem>>;

template <class Elem>
using tstringstream = std::basic_stringstream<
    Elem, std::char_traits<Elem>, std::allocator<Elem>>;
template<typename Elem>
inline std::vector<tstring<Elem>> split(tstring<Elem> text,
                                        Elem const delimiter)
{
    auto sstr = tstringstream<Elem>{ text };
    auto tokens = std::vector<tstring<Elem>>{};
    auto token = tstring<Elem>{};
    while (std::getline(sstr, token, delimiter))
    {
        if (!token.empty()) tokens.push_back(token);
    }
    return tokens;
}

template<typename Elem>
inline std::vector<tstring<Elem>> split(tstring<Elem> text,
```

```
                                        tstring<Elem> const & delimiters)
{
    auto tokens = std::vector<tstring<Elem>>{};
    size_t pos, prev_pos = 0;
    while ((pos = text.find_first_of(delimiters, prev_pos)) !=
    std::string::npos)
    {
        if (pos > prev_pos)
        tokens.push_back(text.substr(prev_pos, pos - prev_pos));
        prev_pos = pos + 1;
    }
    if (prev_pos < text.length())
    tokens.push_back(text.substr(prev_pos, std::string::npos));
    return tokens;
}
```

The following sample code shows two examples of how different strings can be split using either one delimiter character or multiple delimiters:

```
int main()
{
    using namespace std::string_literals;
    std::vector<std::string> expected{"this", "is", "a", "sample"};
    assert(expected == split("this is a sample"s, ' '));
    assert(expected == split("this,is a.sample!!"s, ",.! "s));
}
```

# 28. Longest palindromic substring

The simplest solution to this problem is to try a brute-force approach, checking if each substring is a palindrome. However, this means we need to check C(N, 2) substrings (where N is the number of characters in the string), and the time complexity would be $O(N^3)$. The complexity could be reduced to $O(N^2)$ by storing results of sub problems. To do so we need a table of Boolean values, of size $N \times N$, where the element at [i, j] indicates whether the substring from position i to j is a palindrome. We start by initializing all elements [i, i] with true (one-character palindromes) and all the elements [i, i+i] with true for all consecutive two identical characters (for two-character palindromes). We then go on to inspect substrings greater than two characters, setting the element at [i, j] to true if the element at [i+i, j-1] is true and the characters on the positions i and j in the string are also equal. Along the way, we retain the start position and length of the longest palindromic substring in order to extract it after finishing computing the table.

In code, this solution appears as follows:

```cpp
std::string longest_palindrome(std::string_view str)
{
    size_t const len = str.size();
    size_t longestBegin = 0;
    size_t maxLen = 1;
    std::vector<bool> table(len * len, false);
    for (size_t i = 0; i < len; i++)
        table[i*len + i] = true;

    for (size_t i = 0; i < len - 1; i++)
    {
        if (str[i] == str[i + 1])
        {
            table[i*len + i + 1] = true;
            if (maxLen < 2)
            {
                longestBegin = i;
                maxLen = 2;
            }
        }
    }

    for (size_t k = 3; k <= len; k++)
    {
        for (size_t i = 0; i < len - k + 1; i++)
        {
            size_t j = i + k - 1;
            if (str[i] == str[j] && table[(i + 1)*len + j - 1])
            {
                table[i*len +j] = true;
                if (maxLen < k)
                {
                    longestBegin = i;
                    maxLen = k;
                }
            }
        }
    }
    return std::string(str.substr(longestBegin, maxLen));
}
```

Here are some test cases for the `longest_palindrome()` function:

```cpp
int main()
{
    using namespace std::string_literals;
```

```
    assert(longest_palindrome("sahararahnide") == "hararah");
    assert(longest_palindrome("level") == "level");
    assert(longest_palindrome("s") == "s");
}
```

# 29. License plate validation

The simplest way to solve this problem is by using regular expressions. The regular expression that meets the described format is "`[A-Z]{3}-[A-Z]{2} \d{3,4}`".

The first function only has to validate that an input string contains only text that matches this regular expression. For that, we can use `std::regex_match()`, as follows:

```
bool validate_license_plate_format(std::string_view str)
{
    std::regex rx(R"([A-Z]{3}-[A-Z]{2} \d{3,4})");
    return std::regex_match(str.data(), rx);
}

int main()
{
    assert(validate_license_plate_format("ABC-DE 123"));
    assert(validate_license_plate_format("ABC-DE 1234"));
    assert(!validate_license_plate_format("ABC-DE 12345"));
    assert(!validate_license_plate_format("abc-de 1234"));
}
```

The second function is slightly different. Instead of matching the input string, it must identify all occurrences of the regular expression within the string. The regular expression would therefore change to "`([A-Z]{3}-[A-Z]{2} \d{3,4})*`". To iterate through all matches we have to use `std::sregex_iterator`, which is as follows:

```
std::vector<std::string> extract_license_plate_numbers(
                        std::string const & str)
{
    std::regex rx(R"(([A-Z]{3}-[A-Z]{2} \d{3,4})*)");
    std::smatch match;
    std::vector<std::string> results;

    for(auto i = std::sregex_iterator(std::cbegin(str), std::cend(str), rx);
        i != std::sregex_iterator(); ++i)
    {
        if((*i)[1].matched)
        results.push_back(i->str());
    }
    return results;
```

```
}

int main()
{
    std::vector<std::string> expected {
        "AAA-AA 123", "ABC-DE 1234", "XYZ-WW 0001"};
    std::string text("AAA-AA 123qwe-ty 1234 ABC-DE 123456..XYZ-WW 0001");
    assert(expected == extract_license_plate_numbers(text));
}
```

# 30. Extracting URL parts

This problem is also suited to being solved using regular expressions. Finding a regular expression that could match any URL is, however, a difficult task. The purpose of this exercise is to help you practice your skills with the regex library, and not to find the ultimate regular expression for this particular purpose. Therefore, the regular expression used here is provided only for didactic purposes.

 You can try regular expressions using online testers and debuggers, such as `https://regex101.com/`. This can be useful in order to work out your regular expressions and try them against various datasets.

For this task we will consider that a URL has the following parts: `protocol` and `domain` are mandatory, and `port`, `path`, `query`, and `fragment` are all optional. The following structure is used to return results from parsing an URL (alternatively, you could return a tuple and use structured binding to bind variables to the various sub parts of the tuple):

```
struct uri_parts
{
    std::string                 protocol;
    std::string                 domain;
    std::optional<int>          port;
    std::optional<std::string>  path;
    std::optional<std::string>  query;
    std::optional<std::string>  fragment;
};
```

A function that can parse a URL and extract and return its parts could have the following implementation. Note that the return type is an `std::optional<uri_parts>` because the function might fail in matching the input string to the regular expression; in this case, the return value is `std::nullopt`:

```
std::optional<uri_parts> parse_uri(std::string uri)
```

```
{
    std::regex rx(R"(^(\w+):\/\/([\w.-
]+)(:(\d+))?([\w\/\.]+)?(\?([\w=&]*)(#?(\w+))?)?$)");
    auto matches = std::smatch{};
    if (std::regex_match(uri, matches, rx))
    {
        if (matches[1].matched && matches[2].matched)
        {
            uri_parts parts;
            parts.protocol = matches[1].str();
            parts.domain = matches[2].str();
            if (matches[4].matched)
                parts.port = std::stoi(matches[4]);
            if (matches[5].matched)
                parts.path = matches[5];
            if (matches[7].matched)
                parts.query = matches[7];
            if (matches[9].matched)
                parts.fragment = matches[9];
            return parts;
        }
    }
    return {};
}
```

The following program tests the parse_uri() function with two URLs that contain different parts:

```
int main()
{
    auto p1 = parse_uri("https://packt.com");
    assert(p1.has_value());
    assert(p1->protocol == "https");
    assert(p1->domain == "packt.com");
    assert(!p1->port.has_value());
    assert(!p1->path.has_value());
    assert(!p1->query.has_value());
    assert(!p1->fragment.has_value());

    auto p2 = parse_uri("https://bbc.com:80/en/index.html?lite=true#ui");
    assert(p2.has_value());
    assert(p2->protocol == "https");
    assert(p2->domain == "bbc.com");
    assert(p2->port == 80);
    assert(p2->path.value() == "/en/index.html");
    assert(p2->query.value() == "lite=true");
    assert(p2->fragment.value() == "ui");
}
```

# 31. Transforming dates in strings

Text transformation can be performed with regular expressions using `std::regex_replace()`. A regular expression that can match dates with the specified formats is `(\d{1,2})(\.|-|/)(\d{1,2})(\.|-|/)(\d{4})`. This regex defines five capture groups; the 1st is for the day, the 2nd is for the separator (. or –), the 3rd is for the month, the 4th is again for the separator (. or –), and the 5th is for the year.

Since we want to transform dates from the format `dd.mm.yyyy` or `dd-mm-yyyy` to `yyyy-mm-dd`, the regex replacement format string for `std::regex_replace()` should be `"($5-$3-$1)"`:

```
std::string transform_date(std::string_view text)
{
    auto rx = std::regex{ R"((\d{1,2})(\.|-|/)(\d{1,2})(\.|-|/)(\d{4}))" };
    return std::regex_replace(text.data(), rx, R"($5-$3-$1)");
}

int main()
{
    using namespace std::string_literals;
    assert(transform_date("today is 01.12.2017!"s) ==
           "today is 2017-12-01!"s);
}
```

# 15
# Streams and Filesystems

## Problems

Here are the problem-solving sections for this chapter.

## 32. Pascal's triangle

Write a function that prints up to 10 rows of Pascal's triangle to the console.

## 33. Tabular printing of a list of processes

Suppose you have a snapshot of the list of all processes in a system. The information for each process includes name, identifier, status (which can be either *running* or *suspended*), account name (under which the process runs), memory size in bytes, and platform (which can be either 32-bit or 64-bit). Your task is to write a function that takes such a list of processes and prints them to the console alphabetically, in tabular format. All columns must be left-aligned, except for the memory column which must be right-aligned. The value of the memory size must be displayed in KB. The following is an example of the output of this function:

```
chrome.exe      1044    Running    marius.bancila     25180   32-bit
chrome.exe      10100   Running    marius.bancila    227756   32-bit
cmd.exe         512     Running    SYSTEM                48   64-bit
explorer.exe    7108    Running    marius.bancila     29529   64-bit
skype.exe       22456   Suspended  marius.bancila       656   64-bit
```

# 34. Removing empty lines from a text file

Write a program that, given the path to a text file, modifies the file by removing all empty lines. Lines containing only whitespaces are considered empty.

# 35. Computing the size of a directory

Write a function that computes the size of a directory, in bytes, recursively. It should be possible to indicate whether symbolic links should be followed or not.

# 36. Deleting files older than a given date

Write a function that, given the path to a directory and a duration, deletes all the entries (files or subdirectories) older than the specified duration, in a recursive manner. The duration can represent anything, such as days, hours, minutes, seconds, and so on, or a combination of that, such as one hour and twenty minutes. If the specified directory is itself older than the given duration, it should be deleted entirely.

# 37. Finding files in a directory that match a regular expression

Write a function that, given the path to a directory and a regular expression, returns a list of all the directory entries whose names match the regular expression.

# 38. Temporary log files

Create a logging class that writes text messages to a discardable text file. The text file should have a unique name and must be located in a temporary directory. Unless specified otherwise, this log file should be deleted when the instance of the class is destroyed. However, it should be possible to retain the log file by moving it to a permanent location.

# Solutions

Here are the solutions for the above problem-solving sections.

## 32. Pascal's triangle

Pascal's triangle is a construction representing binomial coefficients. The triangle starts with a row that has a single value of 1. Elements of each row are constructed by summing the numbers above, to the left and right, and treating blank entries as 0. Here is an example of the triangle with five rows:

```
            1
          1   1
        1   2   1
      1   3   3   1
    1   4   6   4   1
```

To print the triangle, we must:

- Shift the output position to the right with an appropriate number of spaces, so that the top is projected on the middle of the triangle's base.
- Compute each value by summing the above left and right values. A simpler formula is that for a row $i$ and column $j$, each new value $x$ is equal to the previous value of $x$ multiplied by $(i - j) / (j + 1)$, where $x$ starts at 1.

The following is a possible implementation of a function that prints the triangle:

```cpp
unsigned int number_of_digits(unsigned int const i)
{
    return i > 0 ? (int)log10((double)i) + 1 : 1;
}

void print_pascal_triangle(int const n)
{
    for (int i = 0; i < n; i++)
    {
        auto x = 1;
        std::cout << std::string((n - i - 1)*(n / 2), ' ');
        for (int j = 0; j <= i; j++)
        {
            auto y = x;
            x = x * (i - j) / (j + 1);
            auto maxlen = number_of_digits(x) - 1;
            std::cout << y << std::string(n - 1 - maxlen - n%2, ' ');
```

```
    }
        std::cout << std::endl;
    }
}
```

The following program asks the user to enter the number of levels and prints the triangle to the console:

```
int main()
{
    int n = 0;
    std::cout << "Levels (up to 10): ";
    std::cin >> n;
    if (n > 10)
        std::cout << "Value too large" << std::endl;
    else
        print_pascal_triangle(n);
}
```

# 33. Tabular printing of a list of processes

To solve this problem, we will consider the following class representing information about a process:

```
enum class procstatus {suspended, running};
enum class platforms {p32bit, p64bit};

struct procinfo
{
    int         id;
    std::string name;
    procstatus  status;
    std::string account;
    size_t      memory;
    platforms   platform;
};
```

In order to print the status and platform as text and not as numerical values, we need conversion functions from the enumerations to std::string:

```
std::string status_to_string(procstatus const status)
{
    if (status == procstatus::suspended) return "suspended";
    else return "running";
}
```

```
std::string platform_to_string(platforms const platform)
{
    if (platform == platforms::p32bit) return "32-bit";
    else return "64-bit";
}
```

The processes are required to be sorted alphabetically by process name. Therefore, the first step would be to sort the input range of processes. For the printing itself, we should use the I/O manipulators:

```
void print_processes(std::vector<procinfo> processes)
{
    std::sort(
        std::begin(processes), std::end(processes),
        [](procinfo const & p1, procinfo const & p2) {
            return p1.name < p2.name; });

    for (auto const & pi : processes)
    {
        std::cout << std::left << std::setw(25) << std::setfill(' ')
                  << pi.name;
        std::cout << std::left << std::setw(8) << std::setfill(' ')
                  << pi.id;
        std::cout << std::left << std::setw(12) << std::setfill(' ')
                  << status_to_string(pi.status);
        std::cout << std::left << std::setw(15) << std::setfill(' ')
                  << pi.account;
        std::cout << std::right << std::setw(10) << std::setfill(' ')
                  << (int)(pi.memory/1024);
        std::cout << std::left << ' ' << platform_to_string(pi.platform);
        std::cout << std::endl;
    }
}
```

The following program defines a list of processes (you can actually retrieve the list of running processes using operating system-specific APIs) and prints it to the console in the requested format:

```
int main()
{
    using namespace std::string_literals;

    std::vector<procinfo> processes
    {
        {512, "cmd.exe"s, procstatus::running, "SYSTEM"s,
            148293, platforms::p64bit },
        {1044, "chrome.exe"s, procstatus::running, "marius.bancila"s,
            25180454, platforms::p32bit},
```

```
        {7108, "explorer.exe"s, procstatus::running, "marius.bancila"s,
            2952943, platforms::p64bit },
        {10100, "chrome.exe"s, procstatus::running, "marius.bancila"s,
            227756123, platforms::p32bit},
        {22456, "skype.exe"s, procstatus::suspended, "marius.bancila"s,
            16870123, platforms::p64bit },
    };

    print_processes(processes);
}
```

# 34. Removing empty lines from a text file

A possible approach to solving this task is to do the following:

1. Create a temporary file to contain only the text you want to retain from the original file
2. Read line by line from the input file and copy to the temporary file all lines that are not empty
3. Delete the original file after finishing processing it
4. Move the temporary file to the path of the original file

An alternative is to move the temporary file and overwrite the original one. The following implementation follows the steps listed. The temporary file is created in the temporary directory returned by `filesystem::temp_directory_path()`:

```
namespace fs = std::experimental::filesystem;

void remove_empty_lines(fs::path filepath)
{
    std::ifstream filein(filepath.native(), std::ios::in);
    if (!filein.is_open())
        throw std::runtime_error("cannot open input file");
    auto temppath = fs::temp_directory_path() / "temp.txt";
    std::ofstream fileout(temppath.native(),
    std::ios::out | std::ios::trunc);
    if (!fileout.is_open())
        throw std::runtime_error("cannot create temporary file");

    std::string line;
    while (std::getline(filein, line))
    {
        if (line.length() > 0 &&
        line.find_first_not_of(' ') != line.npos)
        {
```

```
                    fileout << line << '\n';
            }
        }
        filein.close();
        fileout.close();

        fs::remove(filepath);
        fs::rename(temppath, filepath);
    }
```

# 35. Computing the size of a directory

To compute the size of a directory, we have to iterate through all the files and sum the size of individual files.

`filesystem::recursive_directory_iterator` is an iterator from the `filesystem` library that allows iterating all the entries of a directory in a recursive manner. It has various constructors, some of them taking a value of the type `filesystem::directory_options` that indicates whether symbolic links should be followed or not. The general purpose `std::accumulate()` algorithm can be used to sum together the file sizes. Since the total size of a directory could exceed 2 GB, you should not use `int` or `long`, but `unsigned long long` for the sum type. The following function shows a possible implementation for the required task:

```
    namespace fs = std::experimental::filesystem;

    std::uintmax_t get_directory_size(fs::path const & dir,
                                      bool const follow_symlinks = false)
    {
        auto iterator = fs::recursive_directory_iterator(
            dir,
            follow_symlinks ? fs::directory_options::follow_directory_symlink :
                              fs::directory_options::none);

        return std::accumulate(
            fs::begin(iterator), fs::end(iterator),
            0ull,
            [](std::uintmax_t const total,
                fs::directory_entry const & entry) {
                    return total + (fs::is_regular_file(entry) ?
                            fs::file_size(entry.path()) : 0);
            });
    }

    int main()
```

```
{
    std::string path;
    std::cout << "Path: ";
    std::cin >> path;
    std::cout << "Size: " << get_directory_size(path) << std::endl;
}
```

# 36. Deleting files older than a given date

To perform filesystem operations, you should be using the `filesystem` library. For working with time and duration, you should be using the `chrono` library. A function that implements the requested functionality has to do the following:

1. Check whether the entry indicated by the target path exists and is older than the given duration, and if so, delete it
2. If it is not older and it's a directory, iterate through all its entries and call the function recursively:

```
namespace fs = std::experimental::filesystem;
namespace ch = std::chrono;

template <typename Duration>
bool is_older_than(fs::path const & path, Duration const duration)
{
    auto ftimeduration = fs::last_write_time(path).time_since_epoch();
    auto nowduration = (ch::system_clock::now() - duration)
                        .time_since_epoch();
    return ch::duration_cast<Duration>(nowduration - ftimeduration)
                        .count() > 0;
}

template <typename Duration>
void remove_files_older_than(fs::path const & path,
                             Duration const duration)
{
    try
    {
        if (fs::exists(path))
        {
            if (is_older_than(path, duration))
            {
                fs::remove(path);
            }
            else if(fs::is_directory(path))
            {
```

```
            for (auto const & entry : fs::directory_iterator(path))
            {
                remove_files_older_than(entry.path(), duration);
            }
        }
    }
}
catch (std::exception const & ex)
{
    std::cerr << ex.what() << std::endl;
}
}
```

An alternative to using `directory_iterator` and recursively calling
`remove_files_older_than()` would be to use `recursive_directory_iterator` and
simply delete the entry if older than the given duration. However, this approach would
employ undefined behavior, because if a file or a directory is deleted or added to the
directory tree after the recursive directory iterator has been created, it is not specified
whether the change would be observed through the iterator. Therefore, this method should
be avoided.

The `is_older_than()` function template determines the time that has passed since the
system's clock epoch for the current moment and the last file writing operation and checks
whether the difference of the two is greater than the specified duration.

The `remove_files_older_than()` function can be used as follows:

```
int main()
{
    using namespace std::chrono_literals;

#ifdef _WIN32
    auto path = R"(..\Test\)";
#else
    auto path = R"(../Test/)";
#endif

    remove_files_older_than(path, 1h + 20min);
}
```

# 37. Finding files in a directory that match a regular expression

Implementing the specified functionality should be straightforward: iterate recursively through all the entries of the specified directory and retain all the entries that are regular files and whose name matches the regular expression. To do that, you should use the following:

- `filesystem::recursive_directory_iterator` to iterate through directory entries
- `regex` and `regex_match()` to check whether the filename matches the regular expression
- `copy_if()` and `back_inserter` to copy, at the end of a `vector`, the directory entries that match a specific criteria.

Such a function may look like this:

```cpp
namespace fs = std::experimental::filesystem;

std::vector<fs::directory_entry> find_files(
    fs::path const & path,
    std::string_view regex)
{
    std::vector<fs::directory_entry> result;
    std::regex rx(regex.data());

    std::copy_if(
        fs::recursive_directory_iterator(path),
        fs::recursive_directory_iterator(),
        std::back_inserter(result),
        [&rx](fs::directory_entry const & entry) {
            return fs::is_regular_file(entry.path()) &&
                    std::regex_match(entry.path().filename().string(), rx);
        });

    return result;
}
```

With this available, we can write the following code:

```
int main()
{
    auto dir = fs::temp_directory_path();
    auto pattern = R"(wct[0-9a-zA-Z]{3}\.tmp)";
    auto result = find_files(dir, pattern);

    for (auto const & entry : result)
    {
        std::cout << entry.path().string() << std::endl;
    }
}
```

# 38. Temporary log files

The logging class that you have to implement for this task should:

- Have a constructor that creates a text file in a temporary directory and opens it for writing
- During destruction, if the file still exists, close and delete it
- Have a method that closes the file and moves it to a permanent path
- Overloads operator<< to write a text message to the output file

In order to create unique names for the file, you could use a UUID (also known as GUID). The C++ standard does not support any functionality related to that, but there are third-party libraries, such as boost::uuid, *CrossGuid*, or stduuid, which is actually a library that I created. For this implementation, I will use the last one. You can find it at https://github.com/mariusbancila/stduuid:

```
namespace fs = std::experimental::filesystem;

class logger
{
    fs::path logpath;
    std::ofstream logfile;
public:
    logger()
    {
        auto name = uuids::to_string(uuids::uuid_random_generator{}());
        logpath = fs::temp_directory_path() / (name + ".tmp");
        logfile.open(logpath.c_str(), std::ios::out|std::ios::trunc);
    }
```

```cpp
    ~logger() noexcept
    {
        try {
            if(logfile.is_open()) logfile.close();
            if (!logpath.empty()) fs::remove(logpath);
        }
        catch (...) {}
    }

    void persist(fs::path const & path)
    {
        logfile.close();
        fs::rename(logpath, path);
        logpath.clear();
    }

    logger& operator<<(std::string_view message)
    {
        logfile << message.data() << '\n';
        return *this;
    }
};
```

An example of using this class is as follows:

```cpp
int main()
{
    logger log;
    try
    {
        log << "this is a line" << "and this is another one";
        throw std::runtime_error("error");
    }
    catch (...)
    {
        log.persist(R"(lastlog.txt)");
    }
}
```

# 16
# Date and Time

## Problems

Here are the problem-solving sections for this chapter.

## 39. Measuring function execution time

Write a function that can measure the execution time of a function (with any number of arguments) in any required duration (such as seconds, milliseconds, microseconds, and so on).

## 40. Number of days between two dates

Write a function that, given two dates, returns the number of days between the two dates. The function should work regardless of the order of the input dates.

## 41. Day of the week

Write a function that, given a date, determines the day of the week. This function should return a value between 1 (for Monday) and 7 (for Sunday).

## 42. Day and week of the year

Write a function that, given a date, returns the day of the year (from 1 to 365 or 366 for leap years) and another function that, for the same input, returns the calendar week of the year.

# 43. Meeting time for multiple time zones

Write a function that, given a list of meeting participants and their time zones, displays the local meeting time for each participant.

# 44. Monthly calendar

Write a function that, given a year and month, prints to the console the month calendar. The expected output format is as follows (the example is for December 2017):

```
Mon  Tue  Wed  Thu  Fri  Sat  Sun
                         1    2    3
  4    5    6    7    8    9   10
 11   12   13   14   15   16   17
 18   19   20   21   22   23   24
 25   26   27   28   29   30   31
```

# Solutions

Here are the solutions for the above problem-solving sections.

# 39. Measuring function execution time

To measure the execution time of a function, you should retrieve the current time before the function execution, execute the function, then retrieve the current time again and determine how much time passed between the two time points. For convenience, this can all be put in a `variadic` function template that takes as arguments the function to execute and its arguments, and:

- Uses `std::high_resolution_clock` by default to determine the current time.
- Uses `std::invoke()` to execute the function to measure, with its specified arguments.
- Returns a duration and not a number of ticks for a particular duration. This is important so that you don't lose resolution. It enables you to add execution time duration of various resolutions, such as seconds and milliseconds, which would not be possible by returning a tick count:

```
template <typename Time = std::chrono::microseconds,
          typename Clock = std::chrono::high_resolution_clock>
struct perf_timer
```

```
    {
        template <typename F, typename... Args>
        static Time duration(F&& f, Args... args)
        {
            auto start = Clock::now();
            std::invoke(std::forward<F>(f), std::forward<Args>(args)...);
            auto end = Clock::now();

            return std::chrono::duration_cast<Time>(end - start);
        }
    };
```

This function template can be used as follows:

```
    void f()
    {
        // simulate work
        std::this_thread::sleep_for(2s);
    }

    void g(int const a, int const b)
    {
        // simulate work
        std::this_thread::sleep_for(1s);
    }

    int main()
    {
        auto t1 = perf_timer<std::chrono::microseconds>::duration(f);
        auto t2 = perf_timer<std::chrono::milliseconds>::duration(g, 1, 2);

        auto total = std::chrono::duration<double, std::nano>(t1 + t2).count();
    }
```

# 40. Number of days between two dates

As of C++17, the chrono standard library does not have support for working with dates, weeks, calendars, time zones, and other useful related features. This will change in C++20, as time zones and calendar support have been added to the standard at the Jacksonville meeting, in March 2018. The new additions are based on an open source library called date, built on top of chrono, developed by Howard Hinnant and available on GitHub at https://github.com/HowardHinnant/date. We will use this library to solve several of the problems in this chapter. Although in this implementation the namespace is date, in C++20 it will be part of std::chrono. However, you should be able to simply replace the namespace without any further code changes.

To solve this task, you could use the `date::sys_days` class, available in the `date.h` header. It represents a count of days since the `std::system_clock` epoch. This is a `time_point` with a resolution of a day and is implicitly convertible to `std::system_clock::time_point`. Basically, you have to construct two objects of this type and subtract them. The result is exactly the number of days between the two dates. The following is a simple implementation of such a function:

```
inline int number_of_days(
    int const y1, unsigned int const m1, unsigned int const d1,
    int const y2, unsigned int const m2, unsigned int const d2)
{
    using namespace date;

    return (sys_days{ year{ y1 } / month{ m1 } / day{ d1 } } -
            sys_days{ year{ y2 } / month{ m2 } / day{ d2 } }).count();
}

inline int number_of_days(date::sys_days const & first,
                          date::sys_days const & last)
{
    return (last - first).count();
}
```

Here are a couple of examples of how these overloaded functions could be used:

```
int main()
{
    auto diff1 = number_of_days(2016, 9, 23, 2017, 5, 15);

    using namespace date::literals;
    auto diff2 = number_of_days(2016_y/sep/23, 15_d/may/2017);
}
```

# 41. Day of the week

Solving this problem is again relatively straightforward if you use the `date` library. However, this time, you have to use the following types:

- `date::year_month_day`, a structure that represents a day with fields for year, month (1 to 12), and day (1 to 31).

- `date::iso_week::year_weeknum_weekday`, from the `iso_week.h` header, is a structure that has fields for year, number of weeks in a year, and number of days in a week (1 to 7). This class is implicitly convertible to and from `date::sys_days`, which makes it explicitly convertible to any other calendar system that is implicitly convertible to and from `date::sys_days`, such as `date::year_month_day`.

With that being said, the problem resolves to creating a `year_month_day` object to represent the desired date and then a `year_weeknum_weekday` object from it, and retrieving the day of the week with `weekday()`:

```
unsigned int week_day(int const y, unsigned int const m,
                      unsigned int const d)
{
   using namespace date;

   if(m < 1 || m > 12 || d < 1 || d > 31) return 0;

   auto const dt = date::year_month_day{year{ y }, month{ m }, day{ d }};
   auto const tiso = iso_week::year_weeknum_weekday{ dt };

   return (unsigned int)tiso.weekday();
}

int main()
{
   auto wday = week_day(2018, 5, 9);
}
```

# 42. Day and week of the year

The solution to this two-part problem should be straightforward from the previous two:

- To compute the day of the year, you subtract two `date::sys_days` objects, one representing the given day and the other January 0 of the same year. Alternatively, you could start from January 1 and add 1 to the result.
- To determine the week number of the year, construct a `year_weeknum_weekday` object, like in the previous problem, and retrieve the `weeknum()` value:

```
int day_of_year(int const y, unsigned int const m,
                unsigned int const d)
{
   using namespace date;
```

```
        if(m < 1 || m > 12 || d < 1 || d > 31) return 0;

        return (sys_days{ year{ y } / month{ m } / day{ d } } -
               sys_days{ year{ y } / jan / 0 }).count();
    }

    unsigned int calendar_week(int const y, unsigned int const m,
                               unsigned int const d)
    {
        using namespace date;

        if(m < 1 || m > 12 || d < 1 || d > 31) return 0;

        auto const dt = date::year_month_day{year{ y }, month{ m }, day{ d }};
        auto const tiso = iso_week::year_weeknum_weekday{ dt };

        return (unsigned int)tiso.weeknum();
    }
```

These functions can be used as follows:

```
    int main()
    {
        int y = 0;
        unsigned int m = 0, d = 0;
        std::cout << "Year:"; std::cin >> y;
        std::cout << "Month:"; std::cin >> m;
        std::cout << "Day:"; std::cin >> d;

        std::cout << "Calendar week:" << calendar_week(y, m, d) << std::endl;
        std::cout << "Day of year:" << day_of_year(y, m, d) << std::endl;
    }
```

# 43. Meeting time for multiple time zones

To work with time zones, you must use the `tz.h` header of the `date` library. However, this needs the *IANA Time Zone Database* to be downloaded and uncompressed on your machine.

This is how to prepare the time zone database for the date library:

- Download the latest version of the database from `https://www.iana.org/time-zones`. Currently, the latest version is called `tzdata2017c.tar.gz`.

- Uncompress this to any location on your machine, in a subdirectory called `tzdata`. Let's suppose the parent directory is `c:\work\challenges\libs\date` (on a Windows machine); this will have a subdirectory called `tzdata`.

- For Windows, you need to download a file called `windowsZones.xml`, containing mappings of Windows time zones to IANA time zones. This is available at `https://unicode.org/repos/cldr/trunk/common/supplemental/windowsZones.xml`. The file must be stored in the same `tzdata` subdirectory created earlier.

- In your project settings, define a preprocessor macro called `INSTALL` that indicates the parent directory for the `tzdata` subdirectory. For the example given here, you should have `INSTALL=c:\\work\\challenges\\libs\\date`. (Note that the double backslash is necessary because the macro is used to create a file path using stringification and concatenation, and would otherwise result in an incorrect path.)

To solve this problem, we will consider a user structure with minimal information, such as name and time zone. The time zone is created using the `date::locate_zone()` function:

```
struct user
{
    std::string Name;
    date::time_zone const * Zone;

    explicit user(std::string_view name, std::string_view zone)
        : Name{name.data()}, Zone(date::locate_zone(zone.data()))
    {}
};
```

A function that displays a list of users and their local time for the start of a meeting should transform the given time from a reference zone to the time in their own zone. To do that, we can use a conversion constructor of the `date::zoned_time` class:

```
template <class Duration, class TimeZonePtr>
void print_meeting_times(
    date::zoned_time<Duration, TimeZonePtr> const & time,
    std::vector<user> const & users)
{
    std::cout
        << std::left << std::setw(15) << std::setfill(' ')
        << "Local time: "
        << time << std::endl;

    for (auto const & user : users)
```

```
    {
        std::cout
            << std::left << std::setw(15) << std::setfill(' ')
            << user.Name
            << date::zoned_time<Duration, TimeZonePtr>(user.Zone, time)
            << std::endl;
    }
}
```

This function can be used as follows, where the given time (hour and minute) is represented in the current time zone:

```
int main()
{
    std::vector<user> users{
        user{ "Ildiko", "Europe/Budapest" },
        user{ "Jens", "Europe/Berlin" },
        user{ "Jane", "America/New_York" }
    };

    unsigned int h, m;
    std::cout << "Hour:"; std::cin >> h;
    std::cout << "Minutes:"; std::cin >> m;

    date::year_month_day today =
        date::floor<date::days>(ch::system_clock::now());

    auto localtime = date::zoned_time<std::chrono::minutes>(
        date::current_zone(),
        static_cast<date::local_days>(today)+ch::hours{h}+ch::minutes{m});

    print_meeting_times(localtime, users);
}
```

# 44. Monthly calendar

Solving this task is actually partially based on the previous tasks. In order to print the days of the month as indicated in the problem, you should know:

- What weekday is the first day of the month. This can be determined using the `week_day()` function created for a previous problem.
- The number of days in the month. This can be determined using the `date::year_month_day_last` structure and retrieving the value of `day()`.

With this information determined first, you should:

- Print empty values for the first week before the first weekday
- Print the day number with the proper formatting from 1 to the last day of the month
- Break on a new line after every seven days (counting from day 1 of the first week, even though that could belong to the previous month)

The implementation of all this is shown here:

```
unsigned int week_day(int const y, unsigned int const m,
                      unsigned int const d)
{
    using namespace date;

    if (m < 1 || m > 12 || d < 1 || d > 31) return 0;

    auto const dt = date::year_month_day{year{ y }, month{ m }, day{ d }};
    auto const tiso = iso_week::year_weeknum_weekday{ dt };

    return (unsigned int)tiso.weekday();
}

void print_month_calendar(int const y, unsigned int m)
{
    using namespace date;
    std::cout << "Mon Tue Wed Thu Fri Sat Sun" << std::endl;

    auto first_day_weekday = week_day(y, m, 1);
    auto last_day = (unsigned int)year_month_day_last(
        year{ y }, month_day_last{ month{ m } }).day();

    unsigned int index = 1;
    for (unsigned int day = 1; day < first_day_weekday; ++day, ++index)
    {
        std::cout << "    ";
    }

    for (unsigned int day = 1; day <= last_day; ++day)
    {
        std::cout << std::right << std::setfill(' ') << std::setw(3)
                  << day << ' ';
        if (index++ % 7 == 0) std::cout << std::endl;
    }

    std::cout << std::endl;
}
```

```
int main()
{
    print_month_calendar(2017, 12);
}
```

# Algorithms and Data Structures **17**

## Problems

Here are the problem-solving sections for this chapter.

## 45. Priority queue

Write a data structure that represents a priority queue that provides constant time lookup for the largest element, but has logarithmic time complexity for adding and removing elements. A queue inserts new elements at the end and removes elements from the top. By default, the queue should use `operator<` to compare elements, but it should be possible for the user to provide a comparison function object that returns `true` if the first argument is less than the second. The implementation must provide at least the following operations:

- `push()` to add a new element
- `pop()` to remove the top element
- `top()` to provide access to the top element
- `size()` to indicate the number of elements in the queue
- `empty()` to indicate whether the queue is empty

## 46. Circular buffer

Create a data structure that represents a circular buffer of a fixed size. A circular buffer overwrites existing elements when the buffer is being filled beyond its fixed size. The class you must write should:

- Prohibit default construction
- Support the creation of objects with a specified size

- Allow checking of the buffer capacity and status (`empty()`, `full()`, `size()`, `capacity()`)
- Add a new element, an operation that could potentially overwrite the oldest element in the buffer
- Remove the oldest element from the buffer
- Support iteration through its elements

# 47. Double buffer

Write a class that represents a buffer that could be written and read at the same time without the two operations colliding. A read operation must provide access to the old data while a write operation is in progress. Newly written data must be available for reading upon completion of the write operation.

# 48. The most frequent element in a range

Write a function that, given a range, returns the most frequent element and the number of times it appears in the range. If more than one element appears the same maximum number of times then the function should return all the elements. For instance, for the range `{1,1,3,5,8,13,3,5,8,8,5}`, it should return `{5, 3}` and `{8, 3}`.

# 49. Text histogram

Write a program that, given a text, determines and prints a histogram with the frequency of each letter of the alphabet. The frequency is the percentage of the number of appearances of each letter from the total count of letters. The program should count only the appearances of letters and ignore digits, signs, and other possible characters. The frequency must be determined based on the count of letters and not the text size.

# 50. Filtering a list of phone numbers

Write a function that, given a list of phone numbers, returns only the numbers that are from a specified country. The country is indicated by its phone country code, such as 44 for Great Britain. Phone numbers may start with the country code, a + followed by the country code, or have no country code. The ones from this last category must be ignored.

# 51. Transforming a list of phone numbers

Write a function that, given a list of phone numbers, transforms them so they all start with a specified phone country code, preceded by the + sign. Any whitespaces from a phone number should also be removed. The following is a list of input and output examples:

```
07555 123456      => +447555123456
07555123456       => +447555123456
+44 7555 123456   => +447555123456
44 7555 123456    => +447555123456
7555 123456       => +447555123456
```

# 52. Generating all the permutations of a string

Write a function that, prints on the console all the possible permutations of a given string. You should provide two versions of this function: one that uses recursion, and one that does not.

# 53. Average rating of movies

Write a program that calculates and prints the average rating of a list of movies. Each movie has a list of ratings from 1 to 10 (where 1 is the lowest and 10 is the highest rating). In order to compute the rating, you must remove 5% of the highest and lowest ratings before computing their average. The result must be displayed with a single decimal point.

# 54. Pairwise algorithm

Write a general-purpose function that, given a range, returns a new range with pairs of consecutive elements from the input range. Should the input range have an odd number of elements, the last one must be ignored. For example, if the input range was {1, 1, 3, 5, 8, 13, 21}, the result must be { {1, 1}, {3, 5}, {8, 13}}.

## 55. Zip algorithm

Write a function that, given two ranges, returns a new range with pairs of elements from the two ranges. Should the two ranges have different sizes, the result must contain as many elements as the smallest of the input ranges. For example, if the input ranges were `{ 1, 2, 3, 4, 5, 6, 7, 8, 9, 10 }` and `{ 1, 1, 3, 5, 8, 13, 21 }`, the result should be `{{1,1}, {2,1}, {3,3}, {4,5}, {5,8}, {6,13}, {7,21}}`.

## 56. Select algorithm

Write a function that, given a range of values and a projection function, transforms each value into a new one and returns a new range with the selected values. For instance, if you have a type book that has an `id`, `title`, and `author`, and have a range of such book values, it should be possible for the function to select only the title of the books. Here is an example of how the function should be used:

```cpp
struct book
{
    int         id;
    std::string title;
    std::string author;
};

std::vector<book> books{
    {101, "The C++ Programming Language", "Bjarne Stroustrup"},
    {203, "Effective Modern C++", "Scott Meyers"},
    {404, "The Modern C++ Programming Cookbook", "Marius Bancila"}};

auto titles = select(books, [](book const & b) {return b.title; });
```

## 57. Sort algorithm

Write a function that, given a pair of random-access iterators to define its lower and upper bounds, sorts the elements of the range using the quicksort algorithm. There should be two overloads of the sort function: one that uses `operator<` to compare the elements of the range and put them in ascending order, and one that uses a user-defined binary comparison function for comparing the elements.

# 58. The shortest path between nodes

Write a program that, given a network of nodes and the distances between them, computes and displays the shortest distance from a specified node to all the others, as well as the path between the start and end node. As input, consider the following undirected graph:

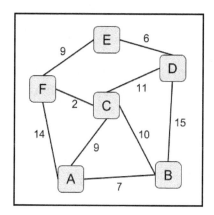

The program output for this graph should be the following:

```
A -> A : 0      A
A -> B : 7      A -> B
A -> C : 9      A -> C
A -> D : 20     A -> C -> D
A -> E : 20     A -> C -> F -> E
A -> F : 11     A -> C -> F
```

# 59. The Weasel program

Write a program that implements Richard Dawkins' weasel computer simulation, described in Dawkins' words as follows (*The Blind Watchmaker*, chapter 3):

> *We again use our computer monkey, but with a crucial difference in its program. It again begins by choosing a random sequence of 28 letters, just as before ... it duplicates it repeatedly, but with a certain chance of random error – 'mutation' – in the copying. The computer examines the mutant nonsense phrases, the 'progeny' of the original phrase, and chooses the one which, however slightly, most resembles the target phrase, METHINKS IT IS LIKE A WEASEL.*

# 60. The Game of Life

Write a program that implements the *Game of Life* cellular automaton proposed by *John Horton Conway*. The universe of this game is a grid of square cells that could have one of two states: dead or alive. Every cell interacts with its adjacent neighbors, with the following transactions occurring on every step:

- Any live cell with fewer than two live neighbors dies, as if caused by under-population
- Any live cell with two or three live neighbors lives on to the next generation
- Any live cell with more than three live neighbors dies, as if by overpopulation
- Any dead cell with exactly three live neighbors becomes a live cell, as if by reproduction

The status of the game on each iteration should be displayed on the console, and for convenience, you should pick a reasonable size, such as 20 rows x 50 columns.

# Solutions

Here are the solutions for the above problem-solving sections.

# 45. Priority queue

A priority queue is an abstract data type whose elements have a priority attached to them. Instead of working as a first-in-first-out container, a priority queue makes elements available in the order of their priority. This data structure is used in algorithms such as Dijkstra's shortest path, Prim's algorithm, heap sort, the A* search algorithm, in Huffman codes used for data compression, and others.

A very simple approach to implement a priority queue would be to use an `std::vector` as the underlying container of elements and always maintain it sorted. That means the maximum and minimum elements are always at the two ends. However, this approach does not provide the most efficient operations.

The most suitable data structure that can be used to implement a priority queue is a heap. This is a tree-based data structure that satisfies the following property: if $P$ is a parent node of $C$, then the key (the value) of $P$ is either greater than or equal to (in a max heap) or less than or equal to (in a min heap) the key of $C$.

The standard library provides several operations for working with heaps:

- `std::make_heap()`: This creates a max heap for the given range, using either `operator<` or a user-provided comparison function to order the elements
- `std::push_heap()`: This inserts a new element at the end of the max heap
- `std::pop_heap()`: This removes the first element of the heap (by swapping the values in the first and last position and making the sub-range `[first, last-1)` a max heap)

A priority queue implementation, that uses `std::vector` to hold data and the standard functions for heaps, can look as follows:

```
template <class T,
    class Compare = std::less<typename std::vector<T>::value_type>>
class priority_queue
{
    typedef typename std::vector<T>::value_type value_type;
    typedef typename std::vector<T>::size_type size_type;
    typedef typename std::vector<T>::reference reference;
    typedef typename std::vector<T>::const_reference const_reference;
public:
    bool empty() const noexcept { return data.empty(); }
    size_type size() const noexcept { return data.size(); }

    void push(value_type const & value)
    {
        data.push_back(value);
        std::push_heap(std::begin(data), std::end(data), comparer);
    }

    void pop()
    {
        std::pop_heap(std::begin(data), std::end(data), comparer);
        data.pop_back();
    }

    const_reference top() const { return data.front(); }
    void swap(priority_queue& other) noexcept
    {
        swap(data, other.data);
        swap(comparer, other.comparer);
    }
private:
    std::vector<T> data;
    Compare comparer;
};
```

```
template<class T, class Compare>
void swap(priority_queue<T, Compare>& lhs,
          priority_queue<T, Compare>& rhs)
noexcept(noexcept(lhs.swap(rhs)))
{
    lhs.swap(rhs);
}
```

This class can be used as follows:

```
int main()
{
    priority_queue<int> q;
    for (int i : {1, 5, 3, 1, 13, 21, 8})
    {
        q.push(i);
    }

    assert(!q.empty());
    assert(q.size() == 7);

    while (!q.empty())
    {
        std::cout << q.top() << ' ';
        q.pop();
    }
}
```

# 46. Circular buffer

A circular buffer is a fixed-size container that behaves as if its two ends were connected to form a virtual circular memory layout. Its main benefit is that you don't need a large amount of memory to retain data, as older entries are overwritten by newer ones. Circular buffers are used in I/O buffering, bounded logging (when you only want to retain the last messages), buffers for asynchronous processing, and others.

We can differentiate between two situations:

1. The number of elements added to the buffer has not reached its capacity (its user-defined fixed size). In this case, it behaves likes a regular container, such as a vector.

2. The number of elements added to the buffer has reached and exceeded its capacity. In this case, the buffer's memory is reused and older elements are being overwritten.

We could represent such a structure using:

- A regular container with a pre-allocated number of elements
- A head pointer to indicate the position of the last inserted element
- A size counter to indicate the number of elements in the container, which cannot exceed its capacity (since elements are being overwritten in this case)

The two main operations with a circular buffer are:

- Adding a new element to the buffer. We always insert at the next position of the head pointer (or index). This is the `push()` method shown below.
- Removing an existing element from the buffer. We always remove the oldest element. That element is at position `head - size` (this must account for the circular nature of the index). This is the `pop()` method shown below.

The implementation of such a data structure is shown here:

```
template <class T>
class circular_buffer
{
    typedef circular_buffer_iterator<T> const_iterator;

    circular_buffer() = delete;
public:
    explicit circular_buffer(size_t const size) :data_(size)
    {}

    bool clear() noexcept { head_ = -1; size_ = 0; }
    bool empty() const noexcept { return size_ == 0; }
    bool full() const noexcept { return size_ == data_.size(); }
    size_t capacity() const noexcept { return data_.size(); }
    size_t size() const noexcept { return size_; }

    void push(T const item)
    {
        head_ = next_pos();
        data_[head_] = item;
        if (size_ < data_.size()) size_++;
    }

    T pop()
    {
```

```
        if (empty()) throw std::runtime_error("empty buffer");
        auto pos = first_pos();
        size_--;
        return data_[pos];
    }

    const_iterator begin() const
    {
        return const_iterator(*this, first_pos(), empty());
    }

    const_iterator end() const
    {
        return const_iterator(*this, next_pos(), true);
    }

private:
    std::vector<T> data_;
    size_t head_ = -1;
    size_t size_ = 0;

    size_t next_pos() const noexcept
    { return size_ == 0 ? 0 : (head_ + 1) % data_.size(); }
    size_t first_pos() const noexcept
    { return size_ == 0 ? 0 : (head_ + data_.size() - size_ + 1) %
                                data_.size(); }

    friend class circular_buffer_iterator<T>;
};
```

Because of the circular nature of the indexes mapped on a contiguous memory layout, the iterator type for this class cannot be a pointer type. The iterators must be able to point elements by applying modulo operations on the index. Here is a possible implementation for such an iterator:

```
template <class T>
class circular_buffer_iterator
{
    typedef circular_buffer_iterator           self_type;
    typedef T                                  value_type;
    typedef T&                                 reference;
    typedef T const&                           const_reference;
    typedef T*                                 pointer;
    typedef std::random_access_iterator_tag    iterator_category;
    typedef ptrdiff_t                          difference_type;
public:
    circular_buffer_iterator(circular_buffer<T> const & buf,
                             size_t const pos, bool const last) :
```

```
        buffer_(buf), index_(pos), last_(last)
        {}

        self_type & operator++ ()
        {
            if (last_)
                throw std::out_of_range("Iterator cannot be incremented past the
end of range.");
            index_ = (index_ + 1) % buffer_.data_.size();
            last_ = index_ == buffer_.next_pos();
            return *this;
        }

        self_type operator++ (int)
        {
            self_type tmp = *this;
            ++*this;
            return tmp;
        }

        bool operator== (self_type const & other) const
        {
            assert(compatible(other));
            return index_ == other.index_ && last_ == other.last_;
        }

        bool operator!= (self_type const & other) const
        {
            return !(*this == other);
        }

        const_reference operator* () const
        {
            return buffer_.data_[index_];
        }

        const_reference operator-> () const
        {
            return buffer_.data_[index_];
        }
    private:
        bool compatible(self_type const & other) const
        {
            return &buffer_ == &other.buffer_;
        }

        circular_buffer<T> const & buffer_;
        size_t index_;
```

```
    bool last_;
};
```

With all these implemented, we could write code such as the following. Notice that in the comments, the first range shows the actual content of the internal vector, and the second range shows the logical content as exposed with iterator access:

```
int main()
{
    circular_buffer<int> cbuf(5);  // {0, 0, 0, 0, 0} -> {}

    cbuf.push(1);                  // {1, 0, 0, 0, 0} -> {1}
    cbuf.push(2);                  // {1, 2, 0, 0, 0} -> {1, 2}
    cbuf.push(3);                  // {1, 2, 3, 0, 0} -> {1, 2, 3}

    auto item = cbuf.pop();        // {1, 2, 3, 0, 0} -> {2, 3}
    cbuf.push(4);                  // {1, 2, 3, 4, 0} -> {2, 3, 4}
    cbuf.push(5);                  // {1, 2, 3, 4, 5} -> {2, 3, 4, 5}
    cbuf.push(6);                  // {6, 2, 3, 4, 5} -> {2, 3, 4, 5, 6}

    cbuf.push(7);                  // {6, 7, 3, 4, 5} -> {3, 4, 5, 6, 7}
    cbuf.push(8);                  // {6, 7, 8, 4, 5} -> {4, 5, 6, 7, 8}

    item = cbuf.pop();             // {6, 7, 8, 4, 5} -> {5, 6, 7, 8}
    item = cbuf.pop();             // {6, 7, 8, 4, 5} -> {6, 7, 8}
    item = cbuf.pop();             // {6, 7, 8, 4, 5} -> {7, 8}

    item = cbuf.pop();             // {6, 7, 8, 4, 5} -> {8}
    item = cbuf.pop();             // {6, 7, 8, 4, 5} -> {}

    cbuf.push(9);                  // {6, 7, 8, 9, 5} -> {9}
}
```

# 47. Double buffer

The problem described here is a typical double buffering situation. Double buffering is the most common case of multiple buffering, which is a technique that allows a reader to see a complete version of the data and not a partially updated version produced by a writer. This is a common technique – especially in computer graphics – for avoiding flickering.

In order to implement the requested functionality, the buffer class that we should write must have two internal buffers: one that contains temporary data being written, and another one that contains completed (or committed) data. Upon the completion of a write operation, the content of the temporary buffer is written in the primary buffer. For the internal buffers, the implementation below uses `std::vector`. When the write operation completes, instead of copying data from one buffer to the other, we just swap the content of the two, which is a much faster operation. Access to the completed data is provided with either the `read()` function, which copies the content of the read buffer into a designated output, or with direct element access (overloaded `operator[]`). Access to the read buffer is synchronized with an `std::mutex` to make it safe to read from one thread while another is writing to the buffer:

```
template <typename T>
class double_buffer
{
    typedef T           value_type;
    typedef T&          reference;
    typedef T const &   const_reference;
    typedef T*          pointer;
public:
    explicit double_buffer(size_t const size) :
        rdbuf(size), wrbuf(size)
    {}

    size_t size() const noexcept { return rdbuf.size(); }

    void write(T const * const ptr, size_t const size)
    {
        std::unique_lock<std::mutex> lock(mt);
        auto length = std::min(size, wrbuf.size());
        std::copy(ptr, ptr + length, std::begin(wrbuf));
        wrbuf.swap(rdbuf);
    }

    template <class Output>
    void read(Output it) const
    {
        std::unique_lock<std::mutex> lock(mt);
        std::copy(std::cbegin(rdbuf), std::cend(rdbuf), it);
    }
    pointer data() const
    {
        std::unique_lock<std::mutex> lock(mt);
        return rdbuf.data();
    }
```

```
        reference operator[](size_t const pos)
        {
            std::unique_lock<std::mutex> lock(mt);
            return rdbuf[pos];
        }
        const_reference operator[](size_t const pos) const
        {
            std::unique_lock<std::mutex> lock(mt);
            return rdbuf[pos];
        }

        void swap(double_buffer other)
        {
            std::swap(rdbuf, other.rdbuf);
            std::swap(wrbuf, other.wrbuf);
        }

    private:
        std::vector<T>      rdbuf;
        std::vector<T>      wrbuf;
        mutable std::mutex mt;
    };
```

The following is an example of how this double buffer class can be used for both writing and reading by two different entities:

```
template <typename T>
void print_buffer(double_buffer<T> const & buf)
{
    buf.read(std::ostream_iterator<T>(std::cout, " "));
    std::cout << std::endl;
}

int main()
{
    double_buffer<int> buf(10);

    std::thread t([&buf]() {
        for (int i = 1; i < 1000; i += 10)
        {
            int data[] = { i, i + 1, i + 2, i + 3, i + 4,
                           i + 5, i + 6,i + 7,i + 8,i + 9 };
            buf.write(data, 10);

            using namespace std::chrono_literals;
            std::this_thread::sleep_for(100ms);
        }
    });
```

```
auto start = std::chrono::system_clock::now();
do
{
    print_buffer(buf);

    using namespace std::chrono_literals;
    std::this_thread::sleep_for(150ms);
} while (std::chrono::duration_cast<std::chrono::seconds>(
        std::chrono::system_clock::now() - start).count() < 12);

    t.join();
}
```

# 48. The most frequent element in a range

In order to determine and return the most frequent element in a range you should do the following:

- Count the appearances of each element in an `std::map`. The key is the element and the value is its number of appearances.
- Determine the maximum element of the map using `std::max_element()`. The result is a map element, that is, a pair containing the element and its number of appearances.

- Copy all map elements that have the value (appearance count) equal to the maximum element's value and return that as the final result.

An implementation of the steps described previously is shown in the following listing:

```
template <typename T>
std::vector<std::pair<T, size_t>> find_most_frequent(
    std::vector<T> const & range)
{
    std::map<T, size_t> counts;
    for (auto const & e : range) counts[e]++;

    auto maxelem = std::max_element(
        std::cbegin(counts), std::cend(counts),
        [](auto const & e1, auto const & e2) {
            return e1.second < e2.second;
    });

    std::vector<std::pair<T, size_t>> result;

    std::copy_if(
```

```
        std::begin(counts), std::end(counts),
        std::back_inserter(result),
        [maxelem](auto const & kvp) {
            return kvp.second == maxelem->second;
    });

    return result;
}
```

The `find_most_frequent()` function can be used as follows:

```
int main()
{
    auto range = std::vector<int>{1,1,3,5,8,13,3,5,8,8,5};
    auto result = find_most_frequent(range);

    for (auto const & e : result)
    {
        std::cout << e.first << " : " << e.second << std::endl;
    }
}
```

# 49. Text histogram

A histogram is a representation of the distribution of numerical data. Widely known histograms are the color and image histograms that are used in photography and image processing. A text histogram, as described here, is a representation of the frequency of letters in a given text. This problem is partially similar to the previous one, except that the range elements are characters now and we must determine the frequency of them all. To solve this problem you should:

- Count the appearances of each letter using a map. The key is the letter and the value is its appearance count.
- When counting, ignore all characters that are not letters. Uppercase and lowercase characters must be treated as identical, as they represent the same letter.

- Use `std::accumulate()` to count the total number of appearances of all the letters in the given text.
- Use `std::for_each()` or a range-based `for` loop to go through all the elements of the map and transform the appearance count into a frequency.

The following is a possible implementation of the problem:

```
std::map<char, double> analyze_text(std::string_view text)
{
    std::map<char, double> frequencies;
    for (char ch = 'a'; ch <= 'z'; ch++)
        frequencies[ch] = 0;

    for (auto ch : text)
    {
        if (isalpha(ch))
            frequencies[tolower(ch)]++;
    }

    auto total = std::accumulate(
        std::cbegin(frequencies), std::cend(frequencies),
        0ull,
        [](auto sum, auto const & kvp) {
            return sum + static_cast<unsigned long long>(kvp.second);
    });

    std::for_each(
        std::begin(frequencies), std::end(frequencies),
        [total](auto & kvp) {
            kvp.second = (100.0 * kvp.second) / total;
    });

    return frequencies;
}
```

The following program prints the frequency of the letters from a text on the console:

```
int main()
{
    auto result = analyze_text(R"(Lorem ipsum dolor sit amet, consectetur
        adipiscing elit, sed do eiusmod tempor incididunt ut labore et
        dolore magna aliqua.)");

    for (auto const & kvp : result)
    {
        std::cout << kvp.first << " : "
                  << std::fixed
```

```
                      << std::setw(5) << std::setfill(' ')
                      << std::setprecision(2) << kvp.second << std::endl;
      }
  }
```

# 50. Filtering a list of phone numbers

The solution to this problem is relatively simple: you have to iterate through all the phone numbers and copy to a separate container (such as an `std::vector`) the phone numbers that start with the country code. If the specified country code is, for instance, 44, then you must check for both 44 and +44. Filtering the input range in this manner is possible using the `std::copy_if()` function. A solution to this problem is shown here:

```
bool starts_with(std::string_view str, std::string_view prefix)
{
    return str.find(prefix) == 0;
}

template <typename InputIt>
std::vector<std::string> filter_numbers(InputIt begin, InputIt end,
                                        std::string const & countryCode)
{
    std::vector<std::string> result;
    std::copy_if(
        begin, end,
        std::back_inserter(result),
        [countryCode](auto const & number) {
            return starts_with(number, countryCode) ||
                   starts_with(number, "+" + countryCode);
    });
    return result;
}

std::vector<std::string> filter_numbers(
    std::vector<std::string> const & numbers,
    std::string const & countryCode)
{
    return filter_numbers(std::cbegin(numbers), std::cend(numbers),
                          countryCode);
}
```

This is how this function can be used:

```
int main()
{
    std::vector<std::string> numbers{
```

```
        "+40744909080",
        "44 7520 112233",
        "+44 7555 123456",
        "40 7200 123456",
        "7555 123456"
    };

    auto result = filter_numbers(numbers, "44");

    for (auto const & number : result)
    {
        std::cout << number << std::endl;
    }
}
```

# 51. Transforming a list of phone numbers

This problem is somewhat similar in some aspects to the previous one. However, instead of selecting phone numbers that start with a specified country code, we must transform each number so that they all start with that country code preceded by a +. There are several cases that must be considered:

- The phone number starts with a 0. That indicates a number without a country code. To modify the number to include the country code we must replace the 0 with the actual country code, preceded by +.
- The phone number starts with the country code. In this case, we just prepend + sign to the beginning.
- The phone number starts with + followed by the country code. In this case, the number is already in the expected format.
- None of these cases applies, therefore the result is obtained by concatenating the country code preceded by + and the phone number.

 For simplicity, we will ignore the possibility that the number is actually prefixed with another country code. You can take it as a further exercise to modify the implementation so that it can handle phone numbers with a different country prefix. These numbers should be removed from the list.

In all of the preceding cases, it is possible that the number could contain spaces. According to the requirements, these must be removed. The std::remove_if() and isspace() functions are used for this purpose.

The following is an implementation of the described solution:

```cpp
bool starts_with(std::string_view str, std::string_view prefix)
{
    return str.find(prefix) == 0;
}


void normalize_phone_numbers(std::vector<std::string>& numbers,
                             std::string const & countryCode)
{
    std::transform(
        std::cbegin(numbers), std::cend(numbers),
        std::begin(numbers),
        [countryCode](std::string const & number) {
            std::string result;
            if (number.size() > 0)
            {
                if (number[0] == '0')
                    result = "+" + countryCode +
                                number.substr(1);
                else if (starts_with(number, countryCode))
                    result = "+" + number;
                else if (starts_with(number, "+" + countryCode))
                    result = number;
                else
                    result = "+" + countryCode + number;
            }

            result.erase(
                std::remove_if(std::begin(result), std::end(result),
                    [](const char ch) {return isspace(ch); }),
                std::end(result));
            return result;
        });
}
```

The following program normalizes a given list of phone numbers according to the requirement and prints them on the console:

```cpp
int main()
{
    std::vector<std::string> numbers{
        "07555 123456",
        "07555123456",
        "+44 7555 123456",
        "44 7555 123456",
        "7555 123456"
    };
```

```
    normalize_phone_numbers(numbers, "44");

    for (auto const & number : numbers)
    {
        std::cout << number << std::endl;
    }
}
```

# 52. Generating all the permutations of a string

You can solve this problem by taking advantage of some general-purpose algorithms from the standard library. The simplest of the two required versions is the non-recursive one, at least when you use `std::next_permutation()`. This function transforms the input range (that is required to be sorted) into the next permutation from the set of all possible permutations, ordered lexicographically with `operator<` or the specified comparison function object. If such a permutation exists then it returns `true`, otherwise, it transforms the range into the first permutation and returns `false`. Therefore, a non-recursive implementation based on `std::next_permuation()` looks like this:

```
void print_permutations(std::string str)
{
    std::sort(std::begin(str), std::end(str));

    do
    {
        std::cout << str << std::endl;
    } while (std::next_permutation(std::begin(str), std::end(str)));
}
```

The recursive alternative is a little bit more complex. One way to implement it is to have an input and output string; initially, the input string is the string for which we want to generate permutations and the output string is empty. We take one character at a time from the input string and put it in the output string. When the input string becomes empty, the output string represents the next permutation. The recursive algorithm for doing this is the following:

- If the input string is empty, then print the output string and return

- Otherwise iterate through all the characters in the input string, and for each element:
  - Call the method recursively by removing the first character from the input string and concatenating it at the end of the output string
  - Rotate the input string so that the first character becomes the last, the second becomes the first, and so on

This algorithm is visually explained in the following diagram:

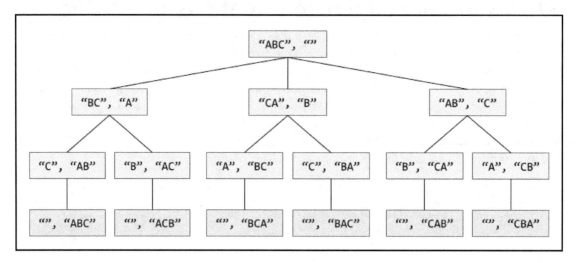

For rotating the input string, we could use the standard library function `std::rotate()`, which performs a left rotation on a range of elements. An implementation of the described recursive algorithm looks like this:

```cpp
void next_permutation(std::string str, std::string perm)
{
    if (str.empty()) std::cout << perm << std::endl;
    else
    {
        for (size_t i = 0; i < str.size(); ++i)
        {
            next_permutation(str.substr(1), perm + str[0]);

            std::rotate(std::begin(str), std::begin(str) + 1, std::end(str));
        }
    }
}

void print_permutations_recursive(std::string str)
```

```
{
    next_permutation(str, "");
}
```

This is how both of these implementations can be used:

```
int main()
{
    std::cout << "non-recursive version" << std::endl;
    print_permutations("main");

    std::cout << "recursive version" << std::endl;
    print_permutations_recursive("main");
}
```

# 53. Average rating of movies

The problem requires the computing of a movie rating using a truncated mean. This is a statistical measure of a central tendency where the mean is calculated after discarding parts of a probability distribution or sample at the high and low ends. Typically, this is done by removing an equal amount of points at the two ends. For this problem, you are required to remove 5% of both the highest and lowest user ratings.

A function that calculates a truncated mean for a given range should do the following:

- Sort the range so that elements are ordered (either ascending or descending)
- Remove the required percentage of elements at both ends
- Count the sum of all remaining elements
- Compute the average by dividing the sum to the remaining count of elements

The truncated_mean() function shown here implements the described algorithm:

```
double truncated_mean(std::vector<int> values, double const percentage)
{
    std::sort(std::begin(values), std::end(values));
    auto remove_count = static_cast<size_t>(
                            values.size() * percentage + 0.5);

    values.erase(std::begin(values), std::begin(values) + remove_count);
    values.erase(std::end(values) - remove_count, std::end(values));

    auto total = std::accumulate(
        std::cbegin(values), std::cend(values),
        0ull,
        [](auto const sum, auto const e) {
```

```
        return sum + e; });
    return static_cast<double>(total) / values.size();
}
```

A program that uses this function in order to calculate and print movie average ratings may look like the following:

```
struct movie
{
    int             id;
    std::string     title;
    std::vector<int> ratings;
};

void print_movie_ratings(std::vector<movie> const & movies)
{
    for (auto const & m : movies)
    {
        std::cout << m.title << " : "
                  << std::fixed << std::setprecision(1)
                  << truncated_mean(m.ratings, 0.05) << std::endl;
    }
}

int main()
{
    std::vector<movie> movies
    {
        { 101, "The Matrix", {10, 9, 10, 9, 9, 8, 7, 10, 5, 9, 9, 8} },
        { 102, "Gladiator", {10, 5, 7, 8, 9, 8, 9, 10, 10, 5, 9, 8, 10} },
        { 103, "Interstellar", {10, 10, 10, 9, 3, 8, 8, 9, 6, 4, 7, 10} }
    };

    print_movie_ratings(movies);
}
```

# 54. Pairwise algorithm

The pairwise function proposed for this problem must pair adjacent elements of an input range and produce std::pair elements that are added to an output range. The following code listing provides two implementations:

- A general function template that takes iterators as arguments: a begin and end iterator define the input range, and an output iterator defines the position in the output range where the results are to be inserted

- An overload that takes an `std::vector<T>` as the input argument and returns an `std::vector<std::pair<T, T>>` as the result; this one simply calls the first overload:

```
template <typename Input, typename Output>
void pairwise(Input begin, Input end, Output result)
{
   auto it = begin;
   while (it != end)
   {
      auto v1 = *it++; if (it == end) break;
      auto v2 = *it++;
      result++ = std::make_pair(v1, v2);
   }
}
template <typename T>
std::vector<std::pair<T, T>> pairwise(std::vector<T> const & range)
{
   std::vector<std::pair<T, T>> result;
   pairwise(std::begin(range), std::end(range),
            std::back_inserter(result));
   return result;
}
```

The following program pairs the elements of a vector of integers and prints the pairs on the console:

```
int main()
{
   std::vector<int> v{ 1, 1, 3, 5, 8, 13, 21 };
   auto result = pairwise(v);

   for (auto const & p : result)
   {
      std::cout << '{' << p.first << ',' << p.second << '}' << std::endl;
   }
}
```

# 55. Zip algorithm

This problem is relatively similar to the previous one, although there are two input ranges instead of just one. The result is again a range of `std::pair`. However, the two input ranges may hold elements of different types. Again, the implementation shown here contains two overloads:

- A general-purpose function with iterators as arguments. A begin and end iterator for each input range define its bounds, and an output iterator defines the position in the output range where the result must be written.
- A function that takes two `std::vector` arguments, one that holds elements of type `T` and one that holds elements of type `U` and returns an `std::vector<std::pair<T, U>>`. This overload simply calls the previous one:

```
template <typename Input1, typename Input2, typename Output>
void zip(Input1 begin1, Input1 end1,
         Input2 begin2, Input1 end2,
         Output result)
{
    auto it1 = begin1;
    auto it2 = begin2;
    while (it1 != end1 && it2 != end2)
    {
        result++ = std::make_pair(*it1++, *it2++);
    }
}

template <typename T, typename U>
std::vector<std::pair<T, U>> zip(
    std::vector<T> const & range1,
    std::vector<U> const & range2)
{
    std::vector<std::pair<T, U>> result;

    zip(std::begin(range1), std::end(range1),
        std::begin(range2), std::end(range2),
        std::back_inserter(result));

    return result;
}
```

In the following listing, you can see two vectors of integers zipped together and the result printed on the console:

```
int main()
{
    std::vector<int> v1{ 1, 2, 3, 4, 5, 6, 7, 8, 9, 10 };
    std::vector<int> v2{ 1, 1, 3, 5, 8, 13, 21 };

    auto result = zip(v1, v2);
    for (auto const & p : result)
    {
        std::cout << '{' << p.first << ',' << p.second << '}' << std::endl;
    }
}
```

# 56. Select algorithm

The `select()` function that you have to implement takes an `std::vector<T>` as an input argument and a function of type F and returns a `std::vector<R>` as the result, where R is the result of applying F to T. We could use `std::result_of()` to deduce the return type of an invoke expression at compile time. Internally, the `select()` function should use `std::transform()` to iterate over the elements of the input vector, apply function f to each element, and insert the result in an output vector.

The following listing shows the implementation for this function:

```
template <
    typename T, typename A, typename F,
    typename R = typename std::decay<typename std::result_of<
                    typename std::decay<F>::type&(
                    typename std::vector<T, A>::const_reference)>::type>::type>
std::vector<R> select(std::vector<T, A> const & c, F&& f)
{
    std::vector<R> v;
    std::transform(std::cbegin(c), std::cend(c),
                    std::back_inserter(v),
                    std::forward<F>(f));
    return v;
}
```

This function can be used as follows:

```cpp
int main()
{
    std::vector<book> books{
        {101, "The C++ Programming Language", "Bjarne Stroustrup"},
        {203, "Effective Modern C++", "Scott Meyers"},
        {404, "The Modern C++ Programming Cookbook", "Marius Bancila"}};

    auto titles = select(books, [](book const & b) {return b.title; });
    for (auto const & title : titles)
    {
        std::cout << title << std::endl;
    }
}
```

# 57. Sort algorithm

**Quicksort** is a comparison sorting algorithm for elements of an array for which a total order is defined. When implemented well, it is significantly faster than *merge sort* or *heap sort*.

Although in worst-case scenarios the algorithm makes $O(n^2)$ comparisons (when the range is already sorted), on average the complexity is only $O(n \cdot log(n))$. Quicksort is a divide and conquer algorithm; it partitions (divides) a large range into smaller ones and sorts them recursively. There are several partitioning schemes. In the implementation shown here, we use the original one developed by *Tony Hoare*. The algorithm for this scheme is described in pseudocode as follows:

```
algorithm quicksort(A, lo, hi) is
    if lo < hi then
        p := partition(A, lo, hi)
        quicksort(A, lo, p)
        quicksort(A, p + 1, hi)

algorithm partition(A, lo, hi) is
    pivot := A[lo]
    i := lo - 1
    j := hi + 1
    loop forever
        do
            i := i + 1
        while A[i] < pivot

        do
```

```
        j := j - 1
    while A[j] > pivot

    if i >= j then
        return j

    swap A[i] with A[j]
```

A general-purpose implementation of the algorithm should use iterators and not arrays and indexes. The requirement for the following implementation is that the iterators are random-access (so they could be moved to any element in constant time):

```cpp
template <class RandomIt>
RandomIt partition(RandomIt first, RandomIt last)
{
    auto pivot = *first;
    auto i = first + 1;
    auto j = last - 1;
    while (i <= j)
    {
        while (i <= j && *i <= pivot) i++;
        while (i <= j && *j > pivot) j--;
        if (i < j) std::iter_swap(i, j);
    }

    std::iter_swap(i - 1, first);

    return i - 1;
}

template <class RandomIt>
void quicksort(RandomIt first, RandomIt last)
{
    if (first < last)
    {
        auto p = partition(first, last);
        quicksort(first, p);
        quicksort(p + 1, last);
    }
}
```

The `quicksort()` function, shown as follows, can be used to sort various types of containers:

```cpp
int main()
{
    std::vector<int> v{ 1,5,3,8,6,2,9,7,4 };
    quicksort(std::begin(v), std::end(v));
```

```
std::array<int, 9> a{ 1,2,3,4,5,6,7,8,9 };
quicksort(std::begin(a), std::end(a));

int a[]{ 9,8,7,6,5,4,3,2,1 };
quicksort(std::begin(a), std::end(a));
}
```

The requirement was that the sorting algorithm must allow the specifying of a user-defined comparison function. The only change, in this case, is the partitioning function, where instead of using operator < and > to compare the current element with the pivot, we use the user-defined comparison function:

```
template <class RandomIt, class Compare>
RandomIt partitionc(RandomIt first, RandomIt last, Compare comp)
{
    auto pivot = *first;
    auto i = first + 1;
    auto j = last - 1;
    while (i <= j)
    {
        while (i <= j && comp(*i, pivot)) i++;
        while (i <= j && !comp(*j, pivot)) j--;
        if (i < j) std::iter_swap(i, j);
    }

    std::iter_swap(i - 1, first);

    return i - 1;
}

template <class RandomIt, class Compare>
void quicksort(RandomIt first, RandomIt last, Compare comp)
{
    if (first < last)
    {
        auto p = partitionc(first, last, comp);
        quicksort(first, p, comp);
        quicksort(p + 1, last, comp);
    }
}
```

With this overload we could sort a range in descending order, as shown in the following example:

```
int main()
{
    std::vector<int> v{ 1,5,3,8,6,2,9,7,4 };
    quicksort(std::begin(v), std::end(v), std::greater<>());
```

```
}
```

It is possible to implement an iterative version of the quicksort algorithm also. The performance of the iterative version is the same as for the recursive version $(O(n \cdot log(n))$ for most cases, but degrading to $O(n^2)$ in the worst case when the range is already sorted). Converting from the recursive version of the algorithm to an iterative one is relatively simple; it is done by using a stack to emulate the recursive calls and to store the bounds of the partitions. The following is an iterative implementation of the version that uses `operator<` to compare elements:

```cpp
template <class RandomIt>
void quicksorti(RandomIt first, RandomIt last)
{
    std::stack<std::pair<RandomIt, RandomIt>> st;
    st.push(std::make_pair(first, last));
    while (!st.empty())
    {
        auto iters = st.top();
        st.pop();

        if (iters.second - iters.first < 2) continue;

        auto p = partition(iters.first, iters.second);

        st.push(std::make_pair(iters.first, p));
        st.push(std::make_pair(p+1, iters.second));
    }
}
```

This iterative implementation can be used just like its recursive counterpart:

```cpp
int main()
{
    std::vector<int> v{ 1,5,3,8,6,2,9,7,4 };
    quicksorti(std::begin(v), std::end(v));
}
```

# 58. The shortest path between nodes

To solve the proposed problem you must use the Dijkstra algorithm for finding the shortest path in a graph. Although the original algorithm finds the shortest path between two given nodes, the requirement here is to find the shortest path between one specified node and all the others in the graph, which is another version of the algorithm.

An efficient way to implement the algorithm is using a priority queue. The pseudocode for the algorithm (see `https://en.wikipedia.org/wiki/Dijkstra%27s_algorithm`) is the following:

```
function Dijkstra(Graph, source):
    dist[source] ← 0                        // Initialization

    create vertex set Q
    for each vertex v in Graph:
        if v ≠ source
            dist[v] ← INFINITY              // Unknown distance from source to v
            prev[v] ← UNDEFINED             // Predecessor of v

        Q.add_with_priority(v, dist[v])

    while Q is not empty:                    // The main loop
        u ← Q.extract_min()                  // Remove and return best vertex
        for each neighbor v of u:            // only v that is still in Q
            alt ← dist[u] + length(u, v)
            if alt < dist[v]
                dist[v] ← alt
                prev[v] ← u
                Q.decrease_priority(v, alt)

    return dist[], prev[]
```

To represent the graph we could use the following data structure, which can be used for both directional or unidirectional graphs. The class provides support for adding new vertices and edges, and can return the list of vertices and the neighbors of a specified vertex (that is, both the nodes and the distance to them):

```
template <typename Vertex = int, typename Weight = double>
class graph
{
public:
    typedef Vertex                        vertex_type;
    typedef Weight                        weight_type;
    typedef std::pair<Vertex, Weight>     neighbor_type;
    typedef std::vector<neighbor_type>    neighbor_list_type;
public:
    void add_edge(Vertex const source, Vertex const target,
                  Weight const weight, bool const bidirectional = true)
    {
        adjacency_list[source].push_back(std::make_pair(target, weight));
        adjacency_list[target].push_back(std::make_pair(source, weight));
    }
```

```
size_t vertex_count() const { return adjacency_list.size(); }
std::vector<Vertex> verteces() const
{
    std::vector<Vertex> keys;
    for (auto const & kvp : adjacency_list)
        keys.push_back(kvp.first);
    return keys;
}

neighbor_list_type const & neighbors(Vertex const & v) const
{
    auto pos = adjacency_list.find(v);
    if (pos == adjacency_list.end())
        throw std::runtime_error("vertex not found");
    return pos->second;
}

constexpr static Weight Infinity =
        std::numeric_limits<Weight>::infinity();
private:
    std::map<vertex_type, neighbor_list_type> adjacency_list;
};
```

The implementation of the shortest path algorithm as described in the preceding pseudocode could look like the following. An `std::set` (that is, a self-balancing binary search tree) is used instead of the priority queue. `std::set` has the same $O(log(n))$ complexity for adding and removing the top element as a binary heap (used for a priority queue). On the other hand, `std::set` also allows finding and removing any other element in $O(log(n))$, which is helpful in order to implement the decrease-key step in logarithmic time by removing and inserting again:

```
template <typename Vertex, typename Weight>
void shortest_path(
    graph<Vertex, Weight> const & g,
    Vertex const source,
    std::map<Vertex, Weight>& min_distance,
    std::map<Vertex, Vertex>& previous)
{
    auto const n = g.vertex_count();
    auto const verteces = g.verteces();

    min_distance.clear();
    for (auto const & v : verteces)
        min_distance[v] = graph<Vertex, Weight>::Infinity;
    min_distance[source] = 0;
```

```
        previous.clear();

        std::set<std::pair<Weight, Vertex> > vertex_queue;
        vertex_queue.insert(std::make_pair(min_distance[source], source));

        while (!vertex_queue.empty())
        {
            auto dist = vertex_queue.begin()->first;
            auto u = vertex_queue.begin()->second;

            vertex_queue.erase(std::begin(vertex_queue));

            auto const & neighbors = g.neighbors(u);
            for (auto const & neighbor : neighbors)
            {
                auto v = neighbor.first;
                auto w = neighbor.second;
                auto dist_via_u = dist + w;
                if (dist_via_u < min_distance[v])
                {
                    vertex_queue.erase(std::make_pair(min_distance[v], v));

                    min_distance[v] = dist_via_u;
                    previous[v] = u;
                    vertex_queue.insert(std::make_pair(min_distance[v], v));
                }
            }
        }
    }
```

The following helper functions print the results in the specified format:

```
template <typename Vertex>
void build_path(
    std::map<Vertex, Vertex> const & prev, Vertex const v,
    std::vector<Vertex> & result)
{
    result.push_back(v);

    auto pos = prev.find(v);
    if (pos == std::end(prev)) return;

    build_path(prev, pos->second, result);
}

template <typename Vertex>
std::vector<Vertex> build_path(std::map<Vertex, Vertex> const & prev,
                                Vertex const v)
```

```
{
    std::vector<Vertex> result;
    build_path(prev, v, result);
    std::reverse(std::begin(result), std::end(result));
    return result;
}

template <typename Vertex>
void print_path(std::vector<Vertex> const & path)
{
    for (size_t i = 0; i < path.size(); ++i)
    {
        std::cout << path[i];
        if (i < path.size() - 1) std::cout << " -> ";
    }
}
```

The following program solves the given task:

```
int main()
{
    graph<char, double> g;
    g.add_edge('A', 'B', 7);
    g.add_edge('A', 'C', 9);
    g.add_edge('A', 'F', 14);
    g.add_edge('B', 'C', 10);
    g.add_edge('B', 'D', 15);
    g.add_edge('C', 'D', 11);
    g.add_edge('C', 'F', 2);
    g.add_edge('D', 'E', 6);
    g.add_edge('E', 'F', 9);

    char source = 'A';
    std::map<char, double> min_distance;
    std::map<char, char> previous;
    shortest_path(g, source, min_distance, previous);

    for (auto const & kvp : min_distance)
    {
        std::cout << source << " -> " << kvp.first << " : "
                  << kvp.second << '\t';

        print_path(build_path(previous, kvp.first));

        std::cout << std::endl;
    }
}
```

# 59. The Weasel program

The Weasel program is a thought experiment proposed by Richard Dawkins, intended to demonstrate how the accumulated small improvements (mutations that bring a benefit to the individual so that it is chosen by natural selection) produce fast results as opposed to the mainstream misinterpretation that evolution happens in big leaps. The algorithm for the Weasel simulation, as described on Wikipedia (see `https://en.wikipedia.org/wiki/Weasel_program`), is as follows:

1. Start with a random string of 28 characters.
2. Make 100 copies of this string, with a 5% chance per character of that character being replaced with a random character.
3. Compare each new string with the target METHINKS IT IS LIKE A WEASEL, and give each a score (the number of letters in the string that are correct and in the correct position).
4. If any of the new strings has a perfect score (28), then stop.
5. Otherwise, take the highest-scoring string and go to step 2.

A possible implementation is as follows. The `make_random()` function creates a random starting sequence of the same length as the target; the `fitness()` function computes the score of each mutated string (that is, resemblance with the target); the `mutate()` function produces a new string from a parent with a given chance for each character to mutate:

```cpp
class weasel
{
    std::string target;
    std::uniform_int_distribution<> chardist;
    std::uniform_real_distribution<> ratedist;
    std::mt19937 mt;
    std::string const allowed_chars = "ABCDEFGHIJKLMNOPQRSTUVWXYZ ";
public:
    weasel(std::string_view t) :
        target(t), chardist(0, 26), ratedist(0, 100)
    {
        std::random_device rd;
        auto seed_data = std::array<int, std::mt19937::state_size> {};
        std::generate(std::begin(seed_data), std::end(seed_data),
            std::ref(rd));
        std::seed_seq seq(std::begin(seed_data), std::end(seed_data));
        mt.seed(seq);
    }
    void run(int const copies)
    {
        auto parent = make_random();
```

```
    int step = 1;
    std::cout << std::left << std::setw(5) << std::setfill(' ')
          << step << parent << std::endl;

    do
    {
        std::vector<std::string> children;
        std::generate_n(std::back_inserter(children), copies,
            [parent, this]() {return mutate(parent, 5); });

        parent = *std::max_element(
            std::begin(children), std::end(children),
            [this](std::string_view c1, std::string_view c2) {
                return fitness(c1) < fitness(c2); });

        std::cout << std::setw(5) << std::setfill(' ') << step
              << parent << std::endl;

        step++;
    } while (parent != target);
}
private:
    weasel() = delete;

    double fitness(std::string_view candidate) const
    {
        int score = 0;
        for (size_t i = 0; i < candidate.size(); ++i)
        {
            if (candidate[i] == target[i])
                score++;
        }
        return score;
    }

    std::string mutate(std::string_view parent, double const rate)
    {
        std::stringstream sstr;
        for (auto const c : parent)
        {
            auto nc = ratedist(mt) > rate ? c : allowed_chars[chardist(mt)];
            sstr << nc;
        }
        return sstr.str();
    }

    std::string make_random()
    {
```

```
        std::stringstream sstr;
        for (size_t i = 0; i < target.size(); ++i)
        {
            sstr << allowed_chars[chardist(mt)];
        }
        return sstr.str();
    }
};
```

This is how the class can be used:

```
int main()
{
    weasel w("METHINKS IT IS LIKE A WEASEL");
    w.run(100);
}
```

# 60. The Game of Life

The class `universe` presented below implements the game as described. There are several functions of interest:

- `initialize()` generates a starting layout; although the code accompanying the book contains more options, only two are listed here: random, which generates a random layout, and `ten_cell_row`, which represents a line of 10 cells in the middle of the grid.
- `reset()` sets all the cells as dead.
- `count_neighbors()` returns the number of alive neighbors. It uses a helper variadic function template `count_alive()`. Although this could be implemented with fold expressions, this is not yet supported in Visual C++ and therefore I have opted not to use it here.
- `next_generation()` produces a new state of the game based on the transition rules.
- `display()` shows the game status on the console; this uses a system call to erase the console, although you could use other means to do so, such as specific operating system APIs.

- `run()` initializes the starting layout and then produces a new generation at a user-specified interval, for a user-specified number of iterations, or indefinitely (if the number of iterations was set to 0).

```cpp
class universe
{
private:
   universe() = delete;
public:
   enum class seed
   {
      random, ten_cell_row
   };
public:
   universe(size_t const width, size_t const height):
      rows(height), columns(width),grid(width * height), dist(0, 4)
   {
      std::random_device rd;
      auto seed_data = std::array<int, std::mt19937::state_size> {};
      std::generate(std::begin(seed_data), std::end(seed_data),
      std::ref(rd));
      std::seed_seq seq(std::begin(seed_data), std::end(seed_data));
      mt.seed(seq);
   }

   void run(seed const s, int const generations,
            std::chrono::milliseconds const ms =
               std::chrono::milliseconds(100))
   {
      reset();
      initialize(s);
      display();

      int i = 0;
      do
      {
         next_generation();
         display();

         using namespace std::chrono_literals;
         std::this_thread::sleep_for(ms);
      } while (i++ < generations || generations == 0);
   }

private:
   void next_generation()
   {
      std::vector<unsigned char> newgrid(grid.size());
```

```
        for (size_t r = 0; r < rows; ++r)
        {
            for (size_t c = 0; c < columns; ++c)
            {
                auto count = count_neighbors(r, c);

                if (cell(c, r) == alive)
                {
                    newgrid[r * columns + c] =
                        (count == 2 || count == 3) ? alive : dead;
                }
                else
                {
                    newgrid[r * columns + c] = (count == 3) ? alive : dead;
                }
            }
        }

        grid.swap(newgrid);
    }

    void reset_display()
    {
#ifdef WIN32
        system("cls");
#endif
    }

    void display()
    {
        reset_display();

        for (size_t r = 0; r < rows; ++r)
        {
            for (size_t c = 0; c < columns; ++c)
            {
                std::cout << (cell(c, r) ? '*' : ' ');
            }
            std::cout << std::endl;
        }
    }

    void initialize(seed const s)
    {
        if (s == seed::ten_cell_row)
        {
            for (size_t c = columns / 2 - 5; c < columns / 2 + 5; c++)
                cell(c, rows / 2) = alive;
```

```
      }
      else
      {
         for (size_t r = 0; r < rows; ++r)
         {
            for (size_t c = 0; c < columns; ++c)
            {
               cell(c, r) = dist(mt) == 0 ? alive : dead;
            }
         }
      }
   }

   void reset()
   {
      for (size_t r = 0; r < rows; ++r)
      {
         for (size_t c = 0; c < columns; ++c)
         {
            cell(c, r) = dead;
         }
      }
   }

   int count_alive() { return 0; }

   template<typename T1, typename... T>
   auto count_alive(T1 s, T... ts) { return s + count_alive(ts...); }

   int count_neighbors(size_t const row, size_t const col)
   {
      if (row == 0 && col == 0)
         return count_alive(cell(1, 0), cell(1,1), cell(0, 1));
      if (row == 0 && col == columns - 1)
         return count_alive(cell(columns - 2, 0), cell(columns - 2, 1),
                            cell(columns - 1, 1));
      if (row == rows - 1 && col == 0)
         return count_alive(cell(0, rows - 2), cell(1, rows - 2),
                            cell(1, rows - 1));
      if (row == rows - 1 && col == columns - 1)
         return count_alive(cell(columns - 1, rows - 2),
                            cell(columns - 2, rows - 2),
                            cell(columns - 2, rows - 1));
      if (row == 0 && col > 0 && col < columns - 1)
         return count_alive(cell(col - 1, 0), cell(col - 1, 1),
                            cell(col, 1), cell(col + 1, 1),
                            cell(col + 1, 0));
      if (row == rows - 1 && col > 0 && col < columns - 1)
```

```
            return count_alive(cell(col - 1, row), cell(col - 1, row - 1),
                               cell(col, row - 1), cell(col + 1, row - 1),
                               cell(col + 1, row));
        if (col == 0 && row > 0 && row < rows - 1)
            return count_alive(cell(0, row - 1), cell(1, row - 1),
                               cell(1, row), cell(1, row + 1),
                               cell(0, row + 1));
        if (col == columns - 1 && row > 0 && row < rows - 1)
            return count_alive(cell(col, row - 1), cell(col - 1, row - 1),
                               cell(col - 1, row), cell(col - 1, row + 1),
                               cell(col, row + 1));

        return count_alive(cell(col - 1, row - 1), cell(col, row - 1),
                           cell(col + 1, row - 1), cell(col + 1, row),
                           cell(col + 1, row + 1), cell(col, row + 1),
                           cell(col - 1, row + 1), cell(col - 1, row));
    }

    unsigned char& cell(size_t const col, size_t const row)
    {
        return grid[row * columns + col];
    }

private:
    size_t rows;
    size_t columns;

    std::vector<unsigned char> grid;
    const unsigned char alive = 1;
    const unsigned char dead = 0;

    std::uniform_int_distribution<> dist;
    std::mt19937 mt;
};
```

This is how the game can be run for 100 iterations starting from a random state:

```
int main()
{
    using namespace std::chrono_literals;
    universe u(50, 20);
    u.run(universe::seed::random, 100, 100ms);
}
```

Here is an example of the program output (the screenshot represents a single iteration in the Game of Life's universe):

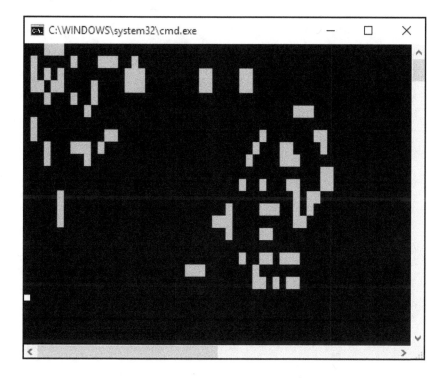

# Other Books You May Enjoy

If you enjoyed this book, you may be interested in these other books by Packt:

**C++ Reactive Programming**
Praseed Pai and Peter Abraham

ISBN: 978-1-78862-977-5

- Understand language-level concurrency in C++
- Explore advanced C++ programming for the FRP
- Uncover the RxCpp library and its programming model
- Mix the FP and OOP constructs in C++ 17 to write well-structured programs
- Master reactive microservices in C++
- Create custom operators for RxCpp
- Learn advanced stream processing and error handling

**C++17 By Example**
Stefan Björnander

ISBN: 978-1-78839-181-8

- Create object-oriented hierarchies and how to compile, link, and execute a simple program
- Implement classes with linked lists, templates, inheritance, operator overloading, and exception handling
- Efficient file handling and pointer structures
- Dynamic allocation and deallocation along with marshmallowing
- Qt features, including menus, toolbars, caret handling, and more
- Implement a Domain Specific Language in C++

# Leave a Review - Let Other Readers Know What You Think

Please share your thoughts on this book with others by leaving a review on the site that you bought it from. If you purchased the book from Amazon, please leave us an honest review on this book's Amazon page. This is vital so that other potential readers can see and use your unbiased opinion to make purchasing decisions, we can understand what our customers think about our products, and our authors can see your feedback on the title that they have worked with Packt to create. It will only take a few minutes of your time, but is valuable to other potential customers, our authors, and Packt. Thank you!

# Index

www.ingramcontent.com/pod-product-compliance
Lightning Source LLC
LaVergne TN
LVHW081505050326
832903LV00025B/1391